2490

0195 Purchase

1515

THE PSYCHOANALYTIC STUDY OF SOCIETY

Volume 18

Alan Dundes

THE PSYCHOANALYTIC STUDY
OF SOCIETY

Volume 18

Essays in Honor of Alan Dundes

Edited by

L. Bryce Boyer
Ruth M. Boyer
Stephen M. Sonnenberg

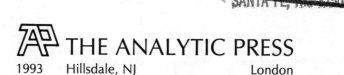 THE ANALYTIC PRESS

1993   Hillsdale, NJ   London

The Analytic Press
365 Broadway
Hillsdale, NJ 07642

ISBN 0-88163-161-2
ISSN 0079-7294

Printed in the United States of America
1 2 3 4 5 6 7 8 9 10

The Editors and Editorial Board

acknowledge with thanks

the generous support of

Boyer House Foundation

and

Dr. and Mrs. L. Bryce Boyer

Professor and Mrs. A. L. Epstein

Professor and Mrs. Norman N. Holland

Dr. and Mrs. Eric R. Marcus

Professor and Mrs. John Morton

Dr. and Mrs. Gilbert J. Rose

Dr. and Mrs. Stephen M. Sonnenberg

Professor and Mrs. Howard F. Stein

Editors

A. L. Epstein, LL.B., Ph.D., Falmer, Brighton, England
Aaron H. Esman, M.D., New York, NY
Avner Falk, Ph.D., Jerusalem, Israel
Stuart Feder, M.D., New York, NY
Edward F. Foulks, M.D., Ph.D., New Orleans, LA
Daniel M. A. Freeman, M.D., Piscataway, NJ
Norman N. Holland, Ph.D., Gainesville, FL
Benjamin Kilborne, Ph.D., Los Angeles, CA
Waud Kracke, Ph.D., Chicago, IL
Paul M. Lerner, Ed.D., ABPP, Asheville, NC
Eric R. Marcus, M.D., New York, NY
W. W. Meissner, S.J., M.D., Cambridge, MA
Daniel Merkur, Ph.D., Toronto, Ontario, Canada
John Morton, Ph.D., Bundoora, Victoria, Australia
Robert A. Paul, Ph.D., Atlanta, GA
Fitz John Porter Poole, Ph.D., La Jolla, CA
Gilbert J. Rose, M.D., Rowayton, CT
Richard Sennett, Ph.D., New York, NY
Bennett Simon, M.D., Cambridge, MA
Howard F. Stein, Ph.D., Oklahoma City, OK
H. U. E. Thoden van Velsen, Ph.D., Amsterdam, Netherlands
Donald F. Tuzin, Ph.D., La Jolla, CA
Piers Vitebsky, Ph.D., Cambridge, England
Vamık D. Volkan, M.D., Charlottesville, VA
Aaron Wildavsky, Ph.D., Berkeley, CA

Contributors

L. Bryce Boyer, M.D. (coeditor), Director, Boyer Research Institute, Berkeley, CA; Codirector, Center for the Advanced Study of the Psychoses, San Francisco; Training and Supervising Analyst, Psychoanalytic Institute of Northern California and San Francisco Institute for Psychoanalytic Psychotherapy and Psychoanalysis.

Ruth M. Boyer, Ph.D. (coeditor), Professor Emerita, Humanities and Sciences, California College of Arts and Crafts, Oakland.

Stanley Brandes, Ph.D., Professor and Chair, Department of Anthropology, University of California, Berkeley.

Michael P. Carroll, Ph.D., Professor, Department of Sociology, University of Western Ontario.

Wendy Doniger, Mircea Eliade Professor, History of Religions, University of Chicago.

Saul Dubow, Ph.D., Lecturer in History, School of African and Asian Studies, University of Sussex, England.

Alan Dundes, Ph.D., Professor of Anthropology and Folklore, University of California, Berkeley.

Avner Falk, Ph.D., Independent Scholar and Psychotherapist in private practice, Jerusalem, Israel.

Elizabeth Fuller, Ph.D., Assistant Professor, Department of Philosophy, Ohio University, Athens.

Lawrence M. Ginsburg, J.D., Attorney at Law, Syracuse, NY.

Tor-Björn Hägglund, M.D., Emeritus Professor of Psychotherapy, Oulu University, Finland, and Training and Supervising Analyst, Finnish Psychoanalytic Society.

Moshe Hazani, Ph.D., Lecturer, Department of Criminology, Bar-Ilan University, Israel, and Fellow, Jerusalem Center for Public Affairs, Jerusalem, Israel.

Bengt Holbek, Ph.D., Professor, Department of Folklore, University of Copenhagen, Denmark (deceased).

W. W. Meissner, S.J., M.D., University Professor of Psychoanalysis, Boston College, and Training and Supervising Analyst, Boston Psychoanalytic Institute.

Dan Merkur, Ph.D., Lecturer, Department of Religion, University of Toronto, Canada.

John Morton, Ph.D., Lecturer, Social Anthropology, La Trobe University, Melbourne, Australia.

M. Omidsalar, Ph.D., Professor, Middle Eastern Studies Program, Indiana University, Bloomington.

Emanuel Rice, M.D., Clinical Professor of Psychiatry, Mt. Sinai School of Medicine, The City University of New York.

Robert A. Segal, Ph.D., Professor of Religious Studies, Louisiana State University, Baton Rouge.

Stephen M. Sonnenberg, M.D. (coeditor), Clinical Professor of Psychiatry and Behavioral Sciences, George Washington University School of Medicine and Health Sciences, Washington, DC; Adjunct Clinical Professor of Psychiatry, Cornell University Medical College, New York City.

Marcelo M. Suárez-Orozco, Ph.D., Assistant Professor, Department of Anthropology, University of California, La Jolla.

Contents

CONTENTS

xiii

Preface

L. BRYCE BOYER,[1] RUTH M. BOYER,[2] AND STEPHEN M. SONNENBERG

As this volume goes to press, the editors have learned of the passing of the great Danish folklorist Bengt Holbek, a contributor to this book. We are certain that our sadness reflects the feeling of loss of the world's social scientists.

Géza Róheim introduced *Psychoanalysis and the Social Sciences* in 1947, and between then and 1958, edited five volumes. Following his death, Werner Muensterberger, administrator of Róheim's papers and unpublished manuscripts, continued the series, using the name *The Psychoanalytic Study of Society.* He was Senior Coeditor of ten volumes between 1960 and 1984 and was assisted successively by Sidney Axelrad, Aaron H. Esman, L. Bryce Boyer, and Simon A. Grolnick. Muensterberger then retired his editorship to devote more time to his own writing and to complete the translation and editing of Róheim's remaining manuscripts. Boyer and Grolnick edited Volumes 11 through 15 between 1985 and 1990 and after Grolnick's untimely demise, Ruth M. Boyer coedited Volume 16 in 1991. With Volume 17 (1992), Stephen M. Sonnenberg became Associate Editor, and with this volume has assumed the responsibilities of Coeditor.

Beginning with the coeditorship of Boyer and Grolnick, each

---

[1]Boyer has contributed frequently to the *Study* (L. B. Boyer, 1962, 1964, 1975, 1988, 1989, 1990; L. B. Boyer and R. M. Boyer, 1967, 1972, 1976, 1990, 1991; Boyer, DeVos, and R. M. Boyer, 1985; Boyer and Grolnick, 1988; R. M. Boyer and L. B. Boyer, 1981; R. M. Boyer, C. W. Dithrich, H. Harned, A. E. Hippler, J. S. Stone, A. Walt, and L. B. Boyer, 1990; Hippler, Boyer, and Boyer, 1975, 1976).

[2]R. M. Boyer has contributed frequently to the *Study* (L. B. Boyer and R. M. Boyer, 1967, 1972, 1976, 1991; Boyer, De Vos, and Boyer, 1985; R. M. Boyer and L. B. Boyer, 1981; R. M. Boyer, C. W. Dithrich, H. Harned, A. E. Hippler, J. S. Stone, A. Walt, and L. B. Boyer, 1990).

volume of the *Study* has honored living individuals who have been
particularly influential in the cross-disciplinary use of psychoanalysis,
Werner Muensterberger, George Devereux,[3] Weston La Barre, Paul
Parin, and Melford E. Spiro. An exception was made in one instance,
Volume 16, which honored A. Irving Hallowell after his demise. Volume
17 honored George and Louise Spindler.

Volume 18 honors Alan Dundes, surely the world's foremost
psychoanalytically oriented folklorist.

Most of the contributions to this volume were written by other
renowned folklorists and Alan's former students, although a few essays
were written by other admirers, not necessarily folklorists. To attempt
adequate recapitulations of their contributions to this volume and their
relationships to Dundes' multifaceted activities and thinking would be
presumptuous and impossible. The editors have sought to resolve the
dilemma by offering some brief résumés and quotations.

Chapter 1
Michael P. Carroll.[4] "Alan Dundes: An Introduction."

Carroll begins by expressing his appreciation of Dundes' scholarship: it
is exciting, imaginative, playful, and wide-ranging. He notes that Dundes
the folklorist has been responsible for building up the Berkeley Folklore
Archives over the past 25 years; Dundes likes to be a part of the folklore
transmission process, and this enjoyment rubs off on his students.
Dundes has two core messages: to folklorists it is that folklore is the
result of the psychological processes described by Freud; to psychoanalysts, it is that folklore exists in multiple versions.

Dundes believes folklore represents the gratification of unconscious
wishes that are often disguised by projection, or what he calls projective
inversion. An unconscious wish commonly expressed by folklore is the
desire for the male to be able to bear children. Dundes also shows how
the study of folklore allows us to understand a culture and validates the
symbolic equivalents psychoanalysts use in their interpretations.

Carroll concludes with the view that Dundes is a vibrant contributor
to folklore and psychoanalytic scholarship, from whom we can expect
much more in the future.

---

[3]Devereux died while the volume honoring him was in the press.
[4]Carroll has contributed to the *Study* previously (Carroll, 1988).

Chapter 2
*Alan Dundes.[5] "Gallus as Phallus: A Psychoanalytic Cross-Cultural
Consideration of the Cockfight as Fowl Play."*

This contribution is a model for investigation and reporting by anthropologists and folklorists, as well as psychoanalysts doing research on any cultural activity. Its very title suggests the erudition, provocative insight, and double entendre humor so frequently characteristic of the author's style. Based on a comprehensive list of references, Dundes illustrates the almost unbelievable lack of analytical, psychological insight to be found in ethnographical literature on the subject. Heretofore, scholars have chosen to ignore the obvious and overt symbolism in cockfighting and even ignored cross-cultural factors.

Dundes reviews the antiquity, history, diffusion, and popularity of the cockfight, which is, indeed, a prime example of folklore. He cites the telling conscious and unconscious linguistic implications of the sport, describes specific local techniques and their elaborations, and lists objections of those offended by "cruelty" to animals as well as those defending the fights.

Dundes suggests that the cockfight should be seen as "the exemplar of a more comprehensive paradigm involving the male gladiatorial combat." He analyzes the sport in terms of three categories of male competition: 1) human male versus human male; 2) human male versus male animal (as in a bullfight); 3) male animal versus male animal. The latter contest occurs in the cockfight. In all three categories the underlying theme is the same—phallic combat. Among other implications: cockfighting is but thinly veiled homoerotic masturbation; it is associated with gambling, which has a somewhat similar symbology; oedipal implications may be present in the breeding of the roosters.

All in all, the cockfight is far more than a reflection of status hierarchy and prestige, as some anthropologists and folklorists claim. If, indeed, the fighting is a form of "mutual masturbation or phallic brag duel" as the article suggests, it is not surprising that females are typically unwelcome at the duels.

In his brilliant "Gallus as Phallus," in the "Fowl Play" of the cockfight, Alan Dundes exhibits both intellect and style. He challenges the symbolically blind.

---

[5]Dundes has contributed to the *Study* previously (Dundes, 1981a,b).

Chapter 3
Michael P. Carroll. "Folklore and Psychoanalysis:
Another Look at 'The Boyfriend's Death.'"

Carroll writes of the meaning of The Boyfriend's Death (TBD) legend, showing how it can be understood in terms of the work of Alan Dundes. In particular, he notes that it represents a wish-fulfillment, which can be understood if phonetic associations and reversals are taken into account in understanding the story. The explanations of collectors and informants are also essential to an understanding. In sum, the myth involves a teen couple driving to a secluded area and parking. Then the boy can't start the car; he goes for help and the girl waits, hearing sounds against the outside of the car. In the morning a policeman arrives and tells the girl to come with him and not look back. She does look back and sees the boyfriend dead, usually hanging from a tree above the car. The body was brushing against the roof, making the sounds heard in the night.

Carroll shows that the myth represents the teenage girl's fear of pregnancy if she goes parking and "necking," that the boyfriend's death represents the reversal of the fear of pregnancy, and that the involvement of his neck is the reversal of her fear of "necking."

Chapter 4
Wendy Doniger. "When a Lingam Is Just a Good Cigar:
Psychoanalysis and Hindu Sexual Fantasies."

There is blatant sexuality in Hindu myths; fantasies that depth psychologists speculate might exist in children are recorded in the literature of the Hindus. These begin with infantile sexuality. There are stories that describe intermediate-state beings visualizing their future conception, and of sexual fantasies within the womb in which the fetus prevents a rival's phallus from intruding.

Infantile sexuality involves stories of incest, castration, chastity, and guilt. Oedipal themes are clear, especially in the myths of Krishna and his son, Pradyumna, both of whom achieve oedipal satisfaction. Krishna and his father Indra also engage in notorious battle, and Indra's son Kutsa sleeps with his mother and ties down Indra's testicles. Doniger demonstrates in detail, then, that there is in Hindu mythology clear confirmation of Freud's ideas about infantile sexuality.

Then she raises a very important question about the nature of symbols. She notes that in the process of symbolization found in Hindu mythology the question arises: What is the latent content? Myths are found to be related to dreams but are not personal experiences designed to be forgotten, as are dreams. They are structured to be remembered, to be a part of culture. Thus, in such culturally and psychologically based stories, it would be important if the manifest and latent content were identical, that is, as we usually think of them. Doniger decides that there is disguised and latent content—death and unhappy endings may be what is disguised.

Chapter 5
M. Omidsalar. "Of the Usurper's Ears, the Demon's Toes,
and the Ayatollah's Fingers."

Omidsalar notes Dundes' two steps in the proper analysis of folk narrative: first, it must be identified; second, it must be interpreted.

The narrative on which he focuses has two versions. Americans assert that the Ayatollah is an impostor because the true Ayatollah has four fingers, while the leader in Iran has five. The anti-Ayatollah Iranian version states that the true Ayatollah has six fingers, so the Iranian ruler with five is an impostor.

Omidsalar traces the history of the impostor in Iran, noting that 500 years before Christ there was a story of an impostor with a bodily defect. The details involve the ruler Darius: the impostor he killed to ascend to the throne had no ears. Similarly, there is a legend involving King Solomon and a demon: the demon tries to impersonate Solomon and take his place, but his true identity is discovered because he has no toes.

Omidsalar notes that the American version of the rumor/folk narrative allows the Americans to castrate the Ayatollah (he had four fingers), and to view him as either dead or kidnapped, the latter version being more gratifying because it is similar to what was done to American hostages under the Ayatollah's rule.

The anti-Ayatollah Iranian form of the rumor assigns to the true Ayatollah special greatness: he is superphallic (six fingers) and is therefore holy; he may be dead and is therefore a revered martyr; if alive, he is in hiding and then like a sacred living saint. These anti-Ayatollah Iranians who circulate this rumor are Shi'ites, who have great reverence for their religious institutions and beliefs. So, by believing the visible Iranian ruler is not the true Ayatollah they can revere the "missing" person, and oppose the man in power because he is an impostor. In both the American and the Iranian cases frustrated aggressions and tabooed wishes are gratified, and cultural values and beliefs are reaffirmed.

Dundes believes that cultural and unconscious meanings can be understood through interpretation of folk narrative; Omidsalar hopes to pay homage to his mentor, Dundes, by applying his method, and in this study he succeeds admirably.

Chapter 6
Stanley H. Brandes. "Spatial Symbolism in Southern Spain."

Brandes, writing on his observations in a southern Spanish town between 1975 and 1980, notes that in the experience of the nuclear family a spatial metaphor — size, height, higher position — becomes available for symbolization of power, superiority, maturation, competence, advantage and, very often, manliness. He notes that he first became aware of this when Alan Dundes pointed out that in an annual parade Brandes observed in an Andalusian town, Monteros, the large and small figures known as Giants and Big-Heads reminded him (Dundes) of parents and children.

Brandes observes that the universal experience of being small in the family and observing the powerful adults provides a motivator for cognitive and motor skill development. Through provision of metaphor it also affects the residents of Monteros in many ways — in the conduct of the annual parade, in the way communion is given and taken, in religious processional behavior (women crawl on hands and knees, men do not), in male and female roles during the olive harvest (and in general), and in children's games. In a very elaborate section on children's games, Brandes shows how young boys master the feminine components of their personalities, and grow into the manly superior position of their culture, by playing games in which the object is to move into a higher, superior (masculine) position and tolerate, when necessary, being in an inferior (feminine) position.

Brandes' analysis "reinforces the convictions and opinions of those who believe that symbols are not arbitrary, who conceive of the world in terms of common human experiences, and who recognize that . . . in each (culture's) set of symbols, fundamental, common experience is represented."

Chapter 7
Ruth M. Boyer. " 'Sweet Dreams, My Daughters':
An Alaskan Eskimo Bedtime Story."

Ruth Boyer presents a bedtime story told in 1973 by a master narrator living in the Alaskan Yukon Delta. Not only does the tale (given in only slightly abbreviated form) reflect typical Eskimo village life in that area (and some individual family history as well), it also poignantly and terrifyingly depicts one significant means of educating youngsters, thus contributing to the overall development of their personalities.

Among the more important points stressed in the discussion are the ambivalent nature of most interpersonal relationships. Teasing, discipline, expectations, the value of supernatural intervention are topics touched upon, all factors conducive to the development of the "burnt child reaction" among the Inuit.

Chapter 8
Lawrence M. Ginsburg, "A Phantom Fairy Tale,
Among Others, Along Sigmund Freud's Intellectual Itinerary."

Sigmund Freud respected fairy tales as a genre for portraying the fantasy realms of a culture. The timeless struggles they memorialize often paralleled the unconscious human concerns of his own patients. He recognized that fairy tales cast a mysterious spell whose remarkable power is retained long beyond the first two decades of life. At 21 years of age, Freud had in his personal library a copy of *The Dream Ladder: A Fairy Tale,* which was first published in 1832. Despite the ostensible simplicity of the theme that the title suggests, the modern reader is presented with a number of prepsychoanalytic narratives and poetic paradigms about the dream process itself. It merits further study in addition to other fairy tales whose analyses still resonate in 20th-century schools of psychological thought.

Chapter 9
Saul Dubow. "Black Hamlet: A Case of Psychic Vivisection?"

In this essay Dubow describes Wulf Sachs, a Russian-born, German-trained psychoanalyst who had contact with, but was not analyzed by, Freud. Sachs migrated to South Africa, where he fathered psychoanalysis in that country. In 1933, he met the black man John Chavafambira whom he befriended and "psychoanalyzed" with the goal of understanding psychoanalytically the structure of a native African's mind. Although he consciously believed blacks were psychologically the same as whites, he was initially condescending toward Chawafambira.

There are two versions of Sachs' "psychoanalysis" of John, the first described in *Black Hamlet* and the second in *Black Anger.* The first account emphasizes much less the psychosocial forces of oppression, but instead describes John's emergence as a leader who wishes to work with European South Africans, and the diminution of his passivity. The second account pictures John as appreciating the violent forces of oppression under which he has lived, and his realistic standing as a leader in opposition to the white oppressors. Dubow indicates that the two versions of Sachs' experiences with John reveal the analyst's increase in political sensitivity, growth, and awareness.

Concentrating on the complex relationship between Sachs and John, Dubow argues that *Black Hamlet* describes, in novelistic form, the story of John's awakening *through* Sachs. He suggests that Sachs inscribes himself in the figure of John and that the story can be read as a parable or an allegory.

Whereas from a contemporary perspective Sachs' work neither represents good analytic nor anthropological fieldwork, his experience is historically important, illuminating the development of psychoanalytic anthropology and, as Dubow's study indicates, the influence of the informant on the observer, as well as the effects of countertransference on the understanding of field data.

Chapter 10
Marcelo Suárez-Orozco. "A Study of Argentine Soccer:
The Dynamics of Its Fans and Their Folklore."

Suárez-Orozco, a soccer fan from Argentina, examines the songs of male Argentinean soccer fans. He notes that the fans are characterized by the *macho* ethic and that the unconscious homosexual aspects of *machismo* have not been understood sufficiently. The author holds that the fan's assertion that he will sadistically tear the opposing player's anus and rape him there represents his wish to be forcibly penetrated anally. In the songs, men call their opponents passive homosexuals; the ball is equated with the phallus, which the player seeks to get past the defender of the goal-anus. Suárez-Orozco demonstrates how Dundes' concept of projective inversion is present in the construction of the folkloristic soccer songs. The author stresses that in Argentina the anal penetrator is not considered a homosexual; thus the soccer songs protect the singer-fan from experiencing his own homosexual desires.

Chapter 11
Bengt Holbek. "Interpretation by Allomotifs."

Holbek, relying on Dundes' theory of allomotifs, has written *Interpretation of Fairy Tales*. His basic idea is that folktales are utterances in a highly specialized language, using a traditional form, in which the storyteller responds to human stress and conflict experienced within the context of his peasant community. The tale is an ever-changing story employing symbols that continue to represent the essential problems of that society or community. The problems transcend time, because for the greater part they are developmental and inhere in all generations. Yet, at times, the problems may represent aspects of a community that changes, such as in levels of poverty.

This idea is illustrated by analysis of versions of the fairy tale "The Forgotten Fiancée," recorded between 1865 and 1905. He describes one version in seven parts: 1) a man and his wife are challenged by a troll and agree to give him their unborn son in exchange for their freedom; 2) the son is given to the troll and the troll gives him three impossible tasks, which he performs with the help of a girl who first exacts from him a promise of fidelity; 3) the troll is angry and they flee; the girl performs various feats to enable them to escape; 4) the boy returns home and his mother causes him to forget the girl; 5) the girl follows the boy secretly and prepares to win him back; 6) the girl helps the boy get to his wedding; 7) at the wedding she reminds him of his vow to her and he marries her instead of his bride-to-be.

Holbek shows how this story in its many versions reflects poverty in peasant communities and shows how children have to leave home and work before they are truly able, how they need courage and have to learn patience, how peasants always view others as a foreign out-group, how in their flight the youths represent the ways younger generations assert independence and parents give it grudgingly, how flight represents emotional distancing, how transformations have sexual meanings, how children struggle against the wishes of the parents to determine their marriage partners, how first love is strong and may persevere, how the scorned woman fights for her love and will not settle for the role of mistress, and how she succeeds in making the boy remember.

Holbek's essay is persuasive and is a fine illustration of his method and Dundes' contribution. Holbek notes that the storyteller makes his substitutions consciously and that we as interpreters can move from "clear text" to symbolic expression and back again, as Dundes suggested.

Chapter 12
Tor-Björn Hägglund. "The Forging of the Sampo and Its Capture:
The Oedipus Complex of Adolescence in Finnish Folklore."

Hägglund continues here his discussion of the Oedipus theme in Finnish folklore, noting that the major theme running through the Finnish national epic, the *Kalevala,* is that of the Sampo. The Sampo is a word symbolizing an object longed for by the heroes of the *Kalevala,* who believe it to be a source of happiness. It is fashioned from the bones of a lamb, the point of a swan's feather, the milk of a farrow cow, a grain of barley, the scraps from a distaff, and other objects. Hägglund finds the fashioning and capture of the Sampo to be a metaphorical representation of the adolescent's struggle to free his own sexual body from the rule and dominion of the mother. The several heroes of the *Kalevala* seek to do this in varying ways corresponding to variations in the adolescent's efforts to resolve his oedipal conflicts.

Hägglund notes that the epic was fashioned while the Finnish people suffered from a smallness complex with regard to Sweden and Russia and sought to establish their national independence. Thus, the Finns related in an oedipal fashion to mighty neighbors, and the *Kalevala* metaphorically represents that relationship.

Hägglund stresses an important and frequently overlooked oedipal theme: that the child cannot comprehend the mystery of his mother's inner space, her ability to bear children, and her inner sexuality that binds his father to her. In the story of the Sampo that mystery, too, is dealt with metaphorically.

Chapter 13
Elizabeth F. Fuller. "Pierced by Murugan's Lance:
The Symbolism of Vow Fulfillment."

In this essay Fuller describes the Thaipusam Festival, honoring the god Murugan, son of Siva and Parvati, as celebrated by the Tamils of Penang, Malaysia.

After an initial procession, Murugan is carried to a temple; then an all-night procession follows. There is widespread participation rather than priestly devotion. The many devotees engage in austerity, including chastity and fasting, expecting a favor from the god. They enter a trance during which their flesh is pierced by hooks representing Murugan's invisible lance. The devotees neither feel pain nor do they bleed. Later they awaken and experience amnesia, sometimes with elation. They believe themselves to be possessed. They are unable to explain the symbolism of their acts. Yet these vow fulfillments do explain conflicts over sexuality and aggression, rebellion and submission, and paradoxes of gender identification.

Murugan, by asceticism, forces Siva to recognize his power. Fuller

stresses that this is a theme in many Indian tales. The devotee of
Murugan has also seen a demonic inner self, aggressive and sexual,
transformed in Murugan's loyal servant. In one story, Murugan so
transformed demons who opposed him. Murugan removes himself from
the oedipal situation by becoming an ascetic, and his devotees share this
solution, although they acknowledge as well as abstain from acting on
their sexual desire. Female devotees see their malevolence transformed
into benevolence, renouncing violence and becoming virtuous; they are
assured that they will become ideal mothers. Male devotees identify with
women and thereby avoid the possibility of harmful relations with them;
they relate to Murugan as women. Female devotees, possessed by
Murugan, experience themselves as male. In each instance, the trans-
sexual identification removes the devotee from the danger inherent in
sexuality.

Ideas of caste, power, the inner world, sexuality, the psychological
relations between men and women, and those between humans and gods
are present in the worship of Murugan. We observe culture providing a
framework for "psychologically structured" conflict solutions, in which
each individual uses culture to manage his or her unique, culturally
shaped needs. As Fuller says, "Successful fulfillment of a vow raises a
devotee's status in the eyes of self and society."

Chapter 14
Avner Falk.[6] "The Problem of Mourning in Jewish History."

The ethnic groups known successively as Hebrews, Israelites, and Jews
have suffered terrible losses and group-narcissistic injuries throughout
their history. They lost their kingdom of Israel to the Assyrians in
722–721 B.C.E. They lost their kingdom of Judah along with their
sovereignty, their language, their Holy City of Jerusalem, and the
Temple of Yawvew to the Babylonians in 587–586 B.C.E. They lost their
Second Temple along with their Holy City to the Romans in 70 C.E. Half
a million Jews were slaughtered by the Romans during the tragic
Bar-Kochba revolt of 132–135 C.E. For eighteen centuries thereafter, with
few exceptions, the Jews lived as a hated, despised, persecuted minority
everywhere.

For many centuries the Jews lived in a kind of ahistoric time bubble.
They lived more in fantasy than in reality, more in the past than in the

---

[6]Falk has contributed previously to the *Study* (Falk, 1989, 1992).

present. They developed the Myth of Jewish Election, the myth of Jerusalem as the center of the world, and the myth of the ten lost tribes living in a faraway land beyond the Raging River (*Sambation* symbolizing the rage of the Jews at their own fate). The psychological function of these myths was to deny the unbearable Jewish reality. For 1,500 years, from Flavius Josephus in the first century to Bonaiuto (Azariah) de'Rossi in the 16th, there was no scientific chronological Jewish historiography. On the other hand, there was a vast body of fantastic, mystical, and Messianic Jewish literature. The medieval Jews gave the nations and countries with which they came in contact obscure, anachronistic biblical names which had nothing to do with these people and places. Thus, Rome was called *Edom,* Byzantium *Yavan,* Germany *Ashkenaz,* France *Tsarephath,* Spain *Sepharad,* and Turkey *Togarman.* This was a striking refusal to live in harsh reality and an escape into a glorified past.

The target of unconscious projections and externalizations everywhere, the Jews suffered from the external hatred of their host enemies, from ritual murder and host desecration libels, executions, persecutions, discrimination, massacres by the Crusaders in 1096, expulsion from several countries, and murder at the hands of Ukrainian Cossacks in 1648-1649. They were persecuted all over Europe. The Jewish self suffered severe damage. Finally, six million Jewish men, women, and children were slaughtered by the Nazis in the unprecedented Holocaust of the Second World War.

These losses were impossible to mourn properly. The psychological reactions included denial, viewing the present in terms of the past, and longing for Messianic redemption. Political Zionism sought to turn back the wheel of history, to restore the losses rather than to mourn them, and to mend the damaged Jewish self. It denied the demographic Arab reality of Palestine, proclaiming "a land without a people for a people without a land." The tragic Arab–Israeli conflict is one result. The "Land of Israel" is imagined by Zionist Jews as high above all other countries. Hence the Zionist terms *aliyah* (ascent) for immigration into Israel and *yeridah* (descent) for emigration from it. These terms are sheer psychogeographical fantasy. The other notions Israeli Jews swear by, such as the Jewish People, the Nation of Israel, the Land of Israel, the Chosen People, the Holy Land, the Holy City, the Diaspora, the Exile, are all anachronistic myths based on *denial* of the harsh reality of a small Jewish nation living in a sea of hostile Arabs. Like other nationalisms, Israeli nationalism is a defensive group narcissism.

Chapter 15
John Morton.[7] "Sensible Beasts: Psychoanalysis, Structuralism, and the Analysis of Myth."

Morton's scholarly article assumes sophistication concerning the ideas of Freud, Lévi-Strauss, Róheim, and others about myths and mythology. He explores Lévi-Strauss' ideas with regard to Myth, Self, Other, etc., indicating their deficiencies and their actual revelation of the author's personal problems. "It is not for nothing that Lévi-Strauss denies his own pain in objective distance, so transforming his sense of marginality into a 'prestigious immunity' (Diamond, 1981), and it would appear that he is quite unable to embrace his own image in his myth. It is particularly interesting that while Lévi-Strauss repeatedly engages Freud and the myth of Oedipus (Lévi-Strauss, 1969, 1972, 1977, 1988), he never tackles the problem presented by Narcissus. Narcissus, of course, solved his difficulty by killing himself; Lévi-Strauss appears to prefer the murder of myth at the same time he claims for himself a mythic intelligence imaged in a primary narcissistic play of mirrors (1966).

Chapter 16
Dan Merkur.[8] "Mythology into Metapsychology. Freud's Misappropriation of Romanticism."

Freud suggests that metaphysics (myths) are projections onto the environment of divisions of the psychic apparatus. Interpretation allows reversal—metaphysics can be reversed to structure or metapsychology. The classic example was Freud's treatment of the Oedipus legend, which he used (reversed) to construct a picture of complex unconscious psychic structures.

According to Merkur, German Romantic myths were the basis of Freud's metapsychology, German Romanticism was mystical, and Freud was imbued with this tradition. His controversial thesis continues as follows: In Freud's work there are residues of Romanticism and its traditions—he reasons by analogy, he tolerates the irrational, he focuses on the individual. His focus on Oedipus is in the Romantic tradition; his view of Oedipus as a hero who opposes fate is a Romantic view. But

---

[7] Morton has contributed previously to the *Study* (1989).
[8] Merkur has contributed previously to the *Study* (1988a,b, 1989).

Merkur also finds Freud to be a lapsed, apostate, anti-Romantic. For that reason he travels a reverse path, moving from Romantic myth to metapsychology.

The Romantics saw, in a mystical way, the Unconscious as the locus of "contact of the individual with the universal powers of nature." Thus, Freud demythologized the Unconscious, in effect secularized mysticism, moved from the Romantic myth to metapsychology. Freud's dualism is in the Romantic tradition (Nietzsche was also a dualist). Freud's conflict model represents scientific secularization of Romanticism's bipolar metaphysics, of its mythology. The concepts of trance and reverie within the Romantic tradition give rise to Freud's Systems Ucs. and Pcpt-Cs. Freud was familiar with mysticism and can be considered to have been a Jewish mystic.

Chapter 17
Emanuel Rice. "Freud, Goethe, and Origen:
The Duality and Slaying of Moses."

The intent of this study is to further explore the possibility that Freud's major work, *Moses and Monotheism,* written in the last years of his life, contains many autobiographical elements that are projected onto Moses. This quest in the realm of culture and society may, among other factors, have been a displacement from an inquiry into the very origins of the religious, cultural, and societal roots of his own family. Freud's postulate of the existence of two major figures named *Moses,* though with significant differences, is shared by the German poet Goethe and the early Christian father Origen. Freud's overwhelming use of a paternal perspective of intergenerational conflict may have masked his own unresolved conflicts toward his mother, thus leading to a relative neglect of maternal influence in decisive preoedipal experiences in his theoretical formulations.

Similarities between the prophetic strivings of Moses and those of the psychoanalytic endeavor of Freud are discussed.

Chapter 18
Robert A. Segal. "Fairy Tales Sí, Myths No:
Bruno Bettelheim's Antithesis."

Segal notes Alan Dundes' documentation of Bettelheim's failure to consider past Freudians in his study of fairy tales and his equally surprising failure to consider contemporary Freudians in his discussion of myths. In praising fairy tales and damning myths, Bettelheim at once characterizes fairy tales in the way that contemporary Freudians characterize myths and characterizes myths in the way that early Freudians characterized fairy tales.

Chapter 19
W. W. Meissner.[9] "Christian Messianism."

Meissner shows that Christian Messianism preserved a historical and doctrinal continuity with some Jewish traditions and that some psychological forces and dynamics are at work in variant forms in both traditions. Early Christian Messianism is an expression of early church development and as such was a vehicle for expressing the dynamics of the paranoid process.

Meissner makes his case using scripture, particularly the Gospels of Matthew, Mark, Luke, and John, as well as secondary sources. To Christians Jesus gathered into his own person and amalgamated into a new synthesis the many strands of prior Jewish Messianic traditions. He was prophet, savior, royal king-Messiah of the time of David, Son of Man, Son of God, and Words of God. He also avoided publicizing his Messianic role during his public ministry. He was a humble and suffering Messiah and not the triumphant, victorious king of prior Jewish expectation. His Messianic mission, therefore, was spiritual and divine. He was the Christ, the Greek word for Messiah.

Meissner notes the characteristics of the cult, including the early Christian cult. There is an in-group–out-group tension, an alloplastic, revolutionary, conversionist interaction with the out-group; the cult is individually responsive and introversionist, promising salvation; there is an adventist orientation focusing on the end of time and beyond; there is a mysterious focus and an elite capable of knowing these mysteries; there are a charismatic leader and authority figures; there is a spiritualized kingdom.

Meissner reviews paranoid dynamics. There is an in-group–out-group dynamic in the paranoid process, which characterized the early Christian church, with its different views of the Messiah and of religious life, when contrasted with the Jewish view. Christians, again in keeping with

---

[9]Meissner has been a frequent contributor to the *Study* (Meissner, 1984, 1988a,b, 1989, 1990, 1991, 1992).

paranoid dynamics, saw themselves as persecuted victims living under the
threat of death, and martyrdom was elevated to an ideal. Projections
abounded and paranoid dynamics were savagely unleashed in an actual-
ized form. These dynamics were a reinforcing system—paranoia fed on
paranoia.

The Christian ethic was caught in internal conflict over aggression,
and paranoia reinforced a sense of victimization, persecution, and the
glory of martyrdom as a member of the in-group. The outward
expression of aggression was prevented; instead, aggression was turned
against the self. The paranoid process leads to narcissistic enhancement,
which also occurs in the early Christian faith, due to its Messianism.

Chapter 20
Moshe Hazani. "Sacrificial Immortality: Toward a Theory
of Suicidal Terrorism and Related Phenomena."

Hazani begins by noting that suicidal terrorism is an unexplained
phenomenon, and one of great interest. He believes that the occurrences
of suicidal terrorism are related phenomena and can be explained on the
individual and group level through the ideas of Robert J. Lifton, based
on years of study of immigrant groups in Israel.

He notes that individuals within groups that experience dislocation
develop an impaired sense of immortality. This results in the development within the individual of two hostile inner selves, a victim self and
an aggressor self. Inner torment is created and a societal state in which
there is victimization by all. These individuals may adopt a totalistic
ideology, the functional equivalent of a paranoid system, and project
their inner enemy outward. Their self-destructive wishes are transformed
into an organized state of victimization. Yet in some cases they continue
being haunted and must commit suicide and homicide simultaneously,
destroying the projected enemy and themselves, to achieve an acceptable
psychological solution. Hazani notes that Lifton has described the
sequence of group dislocation, totalism, and victimization, and his own
work adds an understanding of the dimension of simultaneous suicide
and destruction of the victim, as well as an enhanced understanding that
this is possible because the dislocated person is both victim and aggressor, and can project either facet.

To make his point, Hazani writes of the Sephardic Jews he has studied
closely that in each affected member of the community there is a core
inner idea: "I want to hurt/kill myself." Two derivative ideas are "They

want to hurt/kill me," and "I want to hurt/kill them." He notes that Holocaust survivors are also victim-aggressors.

Hazani explains further that desymbolization occurs when there is dislocation, that there then develops a divided self of two hostile selves, and that totalistic ideologies offer a steady anchor that mitigates death anxiety. He also elaborates on how he disagrees with and adds to Lifton's idea that the survivor is always essentially the victim: this elaboration is absolutely necessary if the core idea is "I want to hurt/kill me." He also explains the suicide of the terrorist as a search for immortality and comfort in death.

Chapter 21
Stephen M. Sonnenberg. "Self-analysis, Applied Analysis,
and Analytic Fieldwork: A Discussion of Methodology
in Psychoanalytic Interdisciplinary Research."

Sonnenberg, as a new coeditor of the *Study,* discusses the conduct of applied psychoanalytic and psychoanalytic interdisciplinary research. He notes that much applied analytic investigation benefits when an analyst and an expert from another field work collaboratively: hence the term interdisciplinary research. He indicates that the introspective skills of the psychoanalyst may be the critical contribution to the research team effort, from the psychoanalytic side.

Sonnenberg states that in recent years psychoanalytic writers have elaborated on their use of introspective skills, in examining countertransference in the service of better understanding their analysands. In describing a research project carried out over a period of almost a decade he notes that he began to employ self-analytic skills in order to understand his thoughts and observations as an investigator. As his self-understanding grew he was able to engage his collaborator, a political scientist, in a process that enhanced his colleagues' insight as well, and the result was that the research team was able to focus more effectively on the psychological aspects of their topic, the U.S.-Soviet nuclear relationship.

Sonnenberg writes that his ideas are similar to those of certain psychoanalytic anthropological and sociological fieldworkers, and shows that his method can be understood in light of the intellectual traditions of such fieldwork. He describes the central role in his work of his efforts to understand his emotional involvement with his collaborator, and notes that his colleague can be described as an informant in the field, and his research effort as the study of a culture.

BIBLIOGRAPHY

BOYER, L. B. (1962), Remarks on the personality of shamans, with reference to the Apache of the Mescalero Indian Reservation. *Psychoanal. Study Soc.,* 2:233-254. New York: International Universities Press.
_____ (1964), Psychological problems of a group of Apaches: Alcoholic hallucinations and latent homosexuality among typical men. *Psychoanal. Study Soc.,* 3:203-277. New York: International Universities Press.
_____ (1975), The man who turned into a water monster: A psychoanalytic contribution to folklore. *Psychoanal. Study Soc.,* 6:100-133. New York: International Universities Press.
_____ (1988), Preface. *Psychoanal. Study Soc.,* 13:xiii-xvii. Hillsdale, NJ: The Analytic Press.
_____ (1989), Preface. *Psychoanal. Study Soc.,* 14:xiii-xxi. Hillsdale, NJ: The Analytic Press.
_____ (1990), Preface. *Psychoanal. Study Soc.,* 15:xiii-xxviii. Hillsdale, NJ: The Analytic Press.
_____ (1991a), A tribute to Simon A. Grolnick. *Psychoanal. Study Soc.,* 16:xiii-xiv. Hillsdale, NJ: The Analytic Press.
_____ (1991b), Preface. *Psychoanal. Study Soc.,* 16:xv-xxxiii. Hillsdale, NJ: The Analytic Press.
_____ & BOYER, R. M. (1967), Some influences of acculturation on the personality traits of the old people of the Mescalero and Chiricahua Apaches. *Psychoanal. Study Soc.,* 4:170-184. New York: International Universities Press.
_____ & _____ (1972), Effects of acculturation on the vicissitudes of the aggressive drive among the Apaches of the Mescalero Indian Reservation. *Psychoanal. Study Soc.,* 5:40-82. New York: International Universities Press.
_____ & _____ (1976), Prolonged adolescence and early identification: A cross-cultural study. *Psychoanal. Study Soc.,* 7:95-106. New Haven: Yale University Press.
_____ DE VOS, G. A. & BOYER, R. M. (1985), Crisis and continuity in the personality of an Apache shaman. *Psychoanal. Study Soc.,* 11:63-114. Hillsdale, NJ: The Analytic Press.
_____ & BOYER, R. M. (1992), Preface. *Psychoanal. Study Soc.,* 17:xiii-xxxi. Hillsdale, NJ: The Analytic Press.
BOYER, R. M. & BOYER, L. B. (1981), Apache lore of the bat. *Psychoanal. Study Soc.,* 9:263-300. New York: Psychohistory Press.
_____ DITHRICH, C. W., HARNED, H., HIPPLER, A. E. STONE, J. S., WALT, A. & BOYER, L. B. (1990), An ethnological and Rorschach study of three groups of Australian aborigines: The Yolgnu, the Pitjatjatjara, and the "dark people" of Bourke. *Psychoanal. Study Soc.,* 15:271-310. Hillsdale, NJ: The Analytic Press.
CARROLL, M. P. (1988), The sick old lady who is a man. A contribution to the psychoanalytic study of urban legends. *Psychoanal. Study Soc.,* 13:133-148. Hillsdale, NJ: The Analytic Press.

DIAMOND, S. (1981), *In Search of the Primitive: A Critique of Civilization*. Second edition. New Brunswick: Transaction, p. 305.

DUNDES, A. (1981a), The hero pattern and the life of Jesus. *Psychoanal. Study Soc.*, 9:49–84. New York: The Psychohistory Press.

_____ (1981b), Discussion of "Apache lore of the bat," by R. M. and L. B. Boyer. *Psychoanal. Study Soc.*, 9:301–312. New York: The Psychohistory Press.

FALK, A. (1989), Incest and parricide on the throne of Judah? *Psychoanal. Study Soc.*, 14:149–166. Hillsdale, NJ: The Analytic Press.

_____ (1992), Unconscious aspects of the Arab–Israeli conflict. *Psychoanal. Study Soc.*, 17:213–248. Hillsdale, NJ: The Analytic Press.

HIPPLER, A. E., BOYER, L. B. & BOYER, R. M. (1976), The subarctic Athabascans of Alaska: The ecological grounding of certain cultural personality characteristics. *Psychoanal. Study Soc.*, 7:293–330. New Haven: Yale University Press.

LEVI-STRAUSS, C. (1966), *The Savage Mind*. London: Weidenfeld & Nicolson, p. 263.

_____ (1969), *The Elementary Structures of Kinship*. London: Eyre & Spottiswoode, pp. 490–492.

_____ (1972), *Structural Anthropology*. Harmondsworth, Middlesex: Penguin, pp. 206–231.

_____ (1977), *Structural Anthropology. Volume II*. London: Allen Lane, pp. 21–24.

_____ (1988), *The Jealous Potter*. Chicago: University of Chicago Press, pp. 185–206.

MEISSNER, W. W. (1984), The cult phenomenon: Psychoanalytic perspective. *Psychoanal. Study Soc.*, 10:91–112. Hillsdale, NJ: The Analytic Press.

_____ (1988a), The cult phenomenon and the paranoid process. *Psychoanal. Study Soc.*, 12:69–96. Hillsdale, NJ: The Analytic Press.

_____ (1988b), The origins of christianity. *Psychoanal. Study Soc.*, 13:29–62. Hillsdale, NJ: The Analytic Press.

_____ (1989), Cultic elements in early christianity: Antioch and Jerusalem. *Psychoanal. Study Soc.*, 14:89–118. Hillsdale, NJ: The Analytic Press.

_____ (1990), Jewish messianism and the cultic process. *Psychoanal. Study Soc.*, 15:349–370. Hillsdale, NJ: The Analytic Press.

_____ (1991), Cultic elements in early christianity: Rome, Corinth, and the Johannine community. *Psychoanal. Study Soc.*, 16:265–286. Hillsdale, NJ: The Analytic Press.

_____ (1992), Medieval messianism and sabbatianism. *Psychoanal. Study Soc.*, 17:289–326. Hillsdale, NJ: The Analytic Press.

MERKUR, D. (1988a), Prophetic initiation in Israel and Judah. *Psychoanal. Study Soc.*, 12:37–68. Hillsdale, NJ: The Analytic Press.

_____ (1988b), Adaptive symbolism and the theory of myth: The symbolic understanding of myths in Inuit religion. *Psychoanal. Study Soc.*, 13:63–94. Hillsdale, NJ: The Analytic Press.

_____ (1989), The visionary practices of Jewish apocalyptists. *Psychoanal. Study Soc.*, 14:119–148. Hillsdale, NJ: The Analytic Press.

MORTON, J. (1989), Mama, *Papa,* and the space between: Children, sacred objects, and transitional phenomena in Aboriginal Central Australia. *Psychoanal. Study Soc.*, 14:191–226. Hillsdale, NJ: The Analytic Press.

Publications of Alan Dundes

This bibliography does not include book reviews or reprintings or translations of books and articles.

1960

French Tongue-Twisters. *French Review,* 33:604–605.

1961

Parallel Paths (with M. Schmaier). *Journal of American Folklore,* 74:142–145.
Brown County Superstitions. *Midwest Folklore,* 11:25–56.
Mnemonic Devices. *Midwest Folklore,* 11:139–147.

1962

From Etic to Emic Units in the Structural Study of Folktales. *Journal of American Folklore,* 75:95–105.
The Folklore of Wishing Wells. *American Imago,* 19:27–34.
Trends in Content Analysis: A Review Article. *Midwest Folklore,* 12:31–38.
Some Minor Genres of Obscene Folklore (with R. Georges). *Journal of American Folklore,* 75:221–226.
Mother Goose Vice Verse (with J. Hickerson). *Journal of American Folklore,* 75:249–259.
The Binary Structure of "Unsuccessful Repetition" in Lithuanian Folk Tales. *Western Folklore,* 21:165–174.
On the Psychology of Collecting Folklore. *Tennessee Folklore Society Bulletin,* 28:65–74.
Earth-Diver: Creation of the Mythopoeic Male. *American Anthropologist,* 64:1032–1051.
Re: Joyce—No In at the Womb. *Modern Fiction Studies,* 8:137–147.
Some Examples of Infrequently Reported Autograph Verse. *Southern Folklore Quarterly,* 26:127–130.
Washington Irving's Version of the Seminole Origin of Races. *Ethnohistory,* 9:257–264.
The Father, the Son, and the Holy Grail. *Literature and Psychology,* 12:101–112.
Folklore: A Key to Culture. *Overseas: The Magazine of Educational Exchange,* 2(4):8–14.

1963

Structural Typology of North American Indian Folktales. *Southwestern Journal of Anthropology,* 19:121–130.

The President's Statue and the Promised Land. *Midcontinent American Studies Journal,* 4:52–55.

Toward a Structural Definition of the Riddle (with R. Georges). *Journal of American Folklore,* 76:111–118.

The Elephant Joking Question. *Tennessee Folklore Society Bulletin,* 29:40–42.

Advertising and Folklore. *New York Folklore Quarterly,* 19:143–151.

Rejoinder to Parker's Comments on Dundes' Article. *American Anthropologist,* 65:915–917.

Dundes' Reply to Mann. *American Anthropologist,* 65:919–921.

Comment (on J. Fischer's "The Sociopsychological Analysis of Folktales"). *Current Anthropology,* 4:276–277.

Summoning Deity Through Ritual Fasting. *American Imago,* 20:213–220.

Kansas University Slang: A New Generation (with M. Schonhorn). *American Speech,* 38:163–177.

American Indian Student Slang (with C. F. Porter). *American Speech,* 38:270–277.

Tales of a Tunisian Trickster (with T. Bradai). *Southern Folklore Quarterly,* 27:300–315.

1964

The Morphology of North American Indian Folktales. FF Communications No. 195. Helsinki: Academia Scientiarum Fennica.

Twenty-Three Riddles from Central Burma (with M. T. Sein). *Journal of American Folklore,* 77:69–75.

Robert Lee J. Vance: American Folklore Surveyor of the 1890's. *Western Folklore,* 23:27–34.

A Cheyenne Version of Aarne-Thompson Tale Type 1176. *Western Folklore,* 34:41–42.

Some Yoruba Wellerisms, Dialogue Proverbs, and Tongue-Twisters. *Folklore,* 75:113–120.

Potawatomi Squaw Dice (with C. F. Porter). *Midwest Folklore,* 13:217–227.

The Passing of the President in Oral Tradition (with R. Abrahams). *Tennessee Folklore Society Bulletin,* 30:127–128.

A Choctaw Tongue-Twister and Two Examples of Creek Word Play. *International Journal of American Linguistics,* 30:194–196.

On Game Morphology: A Study of the Structure of Non-Verbal Folklore. *New York Folklore Quarterly,* 20:276–288.

Proverbs and the Ethnography of Speaking Folklore (with E. O. Arewa). *American Anthropologist,* 66(6), Part 2:70–85.

Texture, Text and Context. *Southern Folklore Quarterly,* 28:251–265.

1965

The Study of Folklore (editor). Englewood Cliffs: Prentice-Hall.

Mythology, Primitive. *Encyclopedia Britannica,* 16:1140–1142.

The Study of Folklore in Literature and Culture: Identification and Interpretation. *Journal of American Folklore,* 78:136–142.

On Computers and Folktales. *Western Folklore,* 24:185–189.

African Tales among the North American Indians. *Southern Folklore Quarterly,* 29:207–219.

1966

Introduction. *The Complete Bibliography of Robert H. Lowie*. Berkeley: Robert H. Lowie Museum of Anthropology, pp. 2–5.

Here I Sit—A Study of American Latrinalia. *Papers of the Kroeber Anthropological Society*, 34:91–105.

American Folklore. *The New Book of Knowledge*. New York: Grolier, pp. 309–314.

Proverbs. *The New Book of Knowledge*. New York: Grolier, p. 487.

Reply and Commentary (A Symposium Review of Alan Dundes' *The Study of Folklore*). *Keystone Folklore Quarterly*, 11:138–143.

Metafolklore and Oral Literary Criticism. *The Monist*, 50:505–516.

The American Concept of Folklore. *Journal of the Folklore Institute*, 3:226–249.

1967

Notes. In: Mae Durham, *Tit for Tat and Other Latvian Folk Tales*. New York: Harcourt, Brace, and World, pp. 117–126.

Comment (on B. Sandford's "Cinderella"). *The Psychoanalytic Forum*, 2:139–141.

Christmas as a Reflection of American Culture. *California Monthly*, 78(3):9–14.

Some Minor Genres of American Folklore. *Southern Folklore Quarterly*, 31:20–36.

North American Indian Folklore Studies. *Journal de la Société des Américanistes*, 56:53–79.

1968

Every Man His Way: Readings in Cultural Anthropology (editor). Englewood Cliffs: Prentice-Hall.

The Number Three in American Culture. In: *Every Man His Way*, pp. 401–424.

Guide to Research in Cultural Anthropology (with R. E. Pfeiffer). In: *Every Man His Way*, pp. 537–551.

Oral Literature. In: *Introduction to Cultural Anthropology*, ed. J. Clifton. Boston: Houghton Mifflin, pp. 117–129.

Ways of Studying Folklore. In: *Our Living Traditions: An Introduction to American Folklore*, ed. T. P. Coffin. New York: Basic Books, pp. 37–46.

One Hundred Years of California Traditions. *California Monthly*, 78(5):19–32.

1969

Folklore as a Mirror of Culture. *Elementary English*, 46:471–482.

Thinking Ahead: A Folkloristic Reflection of the Future Orientation in American Worldview. *Anthropological Quarterly*, 42:53–72.

Comment (on H. Jason's "A Multidimensional Approach to Oral Literature"). *Current Anthropology*, 10:421–422.

On Elephantasy and Elephanticide (with R. Abrahams). *The Psychoanalytic Review*, 56:225–241.

The Devolutionary Premise in Folklore Theory. *Journal of the Folklore Institute*, 6:5–19.

Introduction to the Second Edition. Vladimir Propp, *Morphology of the Folktale*. Austin: University of Texas Press, pp. xi–xvii.

1970

Forward. Roger D. Abrahams, *Deep Down in the Jungle*, 2nd ed. Chicago: Aldine, p. vii.

The Strategy of Turkish Boys' Verbal Dueling Rhymes (with J. W. Leach and B. Özkök). *Journal of American Folklore*, 83:325–349.

Myths, Tales, and Games: What Do They Really Mean? *1971 Britannica Yearbook of Science and the Future.* Chicago: Encyclopedia Britannica, pp. 324–337.

1971

The Making and Breaking of Friendship as a Structural Frame in African Folktales. In: *The Structural Analysis of Oral Tradition,* ed. P. Maranda and E. Maranda. Philadelphia: University of Pennsylvania Press, pp. 171–185.

The Sherente Retellings of Genesis. In: *The Structural Analysis of Oral Tradition,* pp. 295–298.

Laughter Behind the Iron Curtain: A Sample of Rumanian Political Jokes. *The Ukrainian Quarterly,* 27:50–59.

Folk Ideas as Units of Worldview. *Journal of American Folklore,* 84:93–103.

A Study of Ethnic Slurs: The Jew and the Polack in the United States. *Journal of American Folklore,* 84:186–203.

On the Psychology of Legend. In: *American Folk Legend: A Symposium.* ed. W. D. Hand. Berkeley and Los Angeles: University of California Press, pp. 21–36.

1972

Folklore. *Lands and Peoples,* 7. New York: Grolier, pp. 45–50.

Comment (on W. T. Jones' "World Views: Their Nature and Their Function"). *Current Anthropology,* 13:92–93.

Seeing Is Believing. *Natural History,* 81(5):8, 10–12, 86–87.

Ghost, Ouija Board, Werewolf. 1972 *World Book Encyclopedia.*

Riddles (with R. Abrahams). In: *Folklore and Folklife: An Introduction.* ed. R. M. Dorson. Chicago: University of Chicago Press, pp. 129–143.

1973

Mother Wit from the Laughing Barrel: Readings in the Interpretation of Afro-American Folklore (editor). Englewood Cliffs: Prentice-Hall.

Amulet, Divination, Evil Eye, Fetish, Gremlin, Magic, Mask, Omen, Sea Serpent, Superstition, Taboo, Vampire, Will-o'-the-Wisp, and Witchcraft. *World Book Encyclopedia.*

1974

Archer Taylor: A Personal Reminiscence. *American Folklore Society Newsletter,* 3(1);3.

Some Characteristic Meters of Hindi Riddle Prosody (with V. P. Vatuk). *Asian Folklore Studies,* 33:85–153.

The Henny-Penny Phenomenon: A Study of Folk Phonological Esthetics in American Speech. *Southern Folklore Quarterly,* 38:1–9.

Response (to Luis Alonso-Schokel's *Narrative Structures in the Book of Judith*), *Protocol of the 11th Colloquy of the Center for Hermeneutical Studies in Hellenistic and Modern Culture* (Berkeley), pp. 27–29.

1975

La Terra in Piazza: An Interpretation of the Palio of Siena (with A. Falassi). Berkeley: University of California Press.

Urban Folklore from the Paperwork Empire (with C. R. Pagter). Austin: American Folklore Society.

Analytic Essays in Folklore. The Hague: Mouton.

Slurs International: Folk Comparisons of Ethnicity and National Character. *Southern Folklore Quarterly,* 39:15–38.

On the Structure of the Proverb. *Proverbium,* 25:961–973.

1976

A Psychoanalytic Study of the Bullroarer. *Man,* 11:220–238.

Happy Birthday, Uncle Sam. *California Monthly,* 86(7):1, 10.

Folklore, Myth. *Encyclopedia of Anthropology,* ed. David E. Hunter and Phillip Whitten. New York: Harper and Row, pp. 173–174, 279–281.

The Crowing Hen and the Easter Bunny: Male Chauvinism in American Folklore. In: *Folklore Today.* Bloomington: Indiana University Press, pp. 123–138.

Structuralism and Folklore. *Studia Fennica,* 20:75–93.

Projection in Folklore: A Plea for Psychoanalytic Semiotics. *Modern Language Notes,* 91:1500–1533.

Getting the Folk and the Lore Together. *Johns Hopkins Magazine,* 27(1):23–31.

African and Afro-American Tales. *Research in African Literatures,* 7:181–199.

Folklore Theses and Dissertations in the United States (compiler). Austin: University of Texas Press.

To Love My Father All: A Psychoanalytic Study of the Folktale Source of *King Lear. Southern Folklore Quarterly,* 40:353–366.

Folkloristic Commentary. A. L. Kroeber, *Yurok Myths.* Berkeley: University of California Press, pp. xxi–xxxviii.

Who Are the Folk? In: *Frontiers of Folklore,* ed. William Bascom. Washington, DC: American Association for the Advancement of Science, pp. 17–35.

Fairy, Folklore. *World Book Encyclopedia.*

The Hero Pattern and the Life of Jesus. Protocol of the 25th Colloquy of the Center for Hermeneutical Studies in Hellenistic and Modern Culture (Berkeley).

Science in Folklore? Folklore in Science? *New Scientist,* 76(1083):774–776.

Jokes and Covert Language Attitudes: The Curious Case of the Wide-Mouth Frog. *Language in Society,* 6:141–147.

1978

Essays in Folkloristics. Meerut, India: Folklore Institute.

Varia Folklorica (editor). The Hague: Mouton Publishers.

Mairymaking in *Ulysses:* A Legendary Source for a Lost Pin. *Cahiers du Centre d'Etudes Irlandaises,* 3:69–73.

A Potawatomi Version of Aarne-Thompson Tale Type 297A, Turtle's War Party. *Norveg,* 21:47–57.

The Gomer: A Figure of American Hospital Folk Speech (with V. George). *Journal of American Folklore,* 91:568–581.

Bar Dice in the San Francisco Bay Area (with C. R. Pagter). *Papers of the Kroeber Anthropological Society,* 51–52:1–18.

Into the Endzone for a Touchdown: A Psychoanalytic Consideration of American Football. *Western Folklore,* 37:75–88.

1979

Heads or Tails: A Psychoanalytic Study of Potlatch. *Journal of Psychological Anthropology,* 2:395–424.

The Dead Baby Joke Cycle. *Western Folklore,* 38:145–157.
Polish Pope Jokes. *Journal of American Folklore,* 92:219–222.
Foreword, L. Bryce Boyer, *Childhood and Folklore.* New York: Library of Psychological
Anthropology, pp. vii–ix.

1980

Interpreting Folklore. Bloomington: Indiana University Press.
Wet and Dry, the Evil Eye: An Essay in Semitic and Indo-European Worldview. In:
Folklore Studies in the Twentieth Century, ed. Venetia J. Newall. Totowa, New Jersey:
Rowman & Littlefield, pp. 37–63.
The Kushmaker. In: *Folklore on Two Continents,* ed. Nikolai Burklakoff and Carl
Lindahl. Bloomington: Trickster Press, pp. 210–216.
Foreword. Mellie Leandicho Lopez, *A Study of Philippine Games.* Quezon City: Univer-
sity of the Philippines Press, pp. xiii–xv.
Folkloristic Commentary. A. L. Kroeber and E. W. Gifford, *Karok Myths.* Berkeley:
University of California Press, pp. xxxiii–xli.

1981

Many Hands Make Light Work or Caught in the Act of Screwing in Light Bulbs. *Western
Folklore,* 40:261–266.
The Evil Eye: A Folklore Casebook (editor). New York: Garland.
The Wisdom of Many: Essays on the Proverb (coeditor with W. Mieder). New York:
Garland.
*The Art of Mixing Metaphors: A Folkloristic Interpretation of the Netherlandish Proverbs
by Pieter Bruegel the Elder* (with Claudia A. Stibbe). Helsinki: Academia Scientiarum
Fennica.
Life Is Like a Chicken Coop Ladder: A Study of German National Character Through
Folklore. *Journal of Psychoanalytic Anthropology,* 4:265–364.
Introduction. *The Seven Visions of Tyl Ulenspiegel.* Deurge, Belgium: MIM Publications,
pp. 1–10.

1982

Cinderella: A Folklore Casebook (editor). New York: Garland.
Misunderstanding Humour: An American Stereotype of the Englishman. *International
Folklore Review,* 2:10–15.
The Symbolic Equivalence of Allomotifs in the Rabbit-Herd (AT 570). *Arv: Scandinavian
Yearbook of Folklore,* 36(1980)[1982]:91–98.
Releasing Caged Birds in Iran. *Midwestern Journal of Language and Folklore,* 8:116–119.
Volkskunde, Völkerkunde and the Study of German National Character. In: *Europäische
Ethnologie,* ed. Heide Nixdorff and Thomas Hauschild. Berlin: Dietrich Reimer Verlag,
pp. 257–265.
Introduction. Richard M. Dorson, *Man and Beast in American Comic Legend.* Blooming-
ton: Indiana University Press, pp. x–xix.
Comment (on Michael Winkelman's "Magic: A Theoretical Reassessment"). *Current
Anthropology,* 23:46–47.
William Russel Bascom (1912–1981) (with D. Crowley). *Journal of American Folklore,*
95:465–467.

1983

Oedipus: A Folklore Casebook (coeditor with L. Edmunds). New York: Garland.
Couvade in Genesis. *Studies in Aggadah and Jewish Folklore,* Folklore Research Center Studies 7. Jerusalem: Magnes Press, pp. 35–53.
Defining Identity Through Folklore. In: *Identity: Personal and Socio-Cultural,* ed. Anita Jacobson-Widding. *Uppsala Studies in Cultural Anthropology 5.* Uppsala, pp. 235–261.
Auschwitz Jokes (with T. Hauschild). *Western Folklore,* 42:249–260.
Office Folklore. In: *Handbook of American Folklore,* ed. Richard M. Dorson. Bloomington: Indiana University Press, pp. 115–120.

1984

Life Is Like a Chicken Coop Ladder: A Portrait of German Culture Through Folklore. New York: Columbia University Press.
On Whether Weather "Proverbs" Are Proverbs. *Proverbium,* 1:39–46.
Sacred Narrative: Readings in the Theory of Myth (editor). Berkeley: University of California Press.
The *Piropo* and the Dual Image of Women in the Spanish-Speaking World (with M. Suárez-Orozco). *Journal of Latin American Lore,* 10:111–133.
The Symbolic Equivalence of Allomotifs: Towards a Method of Analyzing Folktales. *Le Conte, pourquoi? Comment?* Paris, pp. 187–197.

1985

The Psychoanalytic Study of Folklore. *Annals of Scholarship,* 3(3):1–42.
Nationalistic Inferiority Complexes and the Fabrication of Fakelore: A Reconsideration of Ossian, the *Kinder- und Hausmärchen,* the *Kalevala* and Paul Bunyan. *Journal of Folklore Research,* 22:5–18.
The J.A.P. and the J.A.M. in American Jokelore. *Journal of American Folklore,* 98:456–475.
Game of the Name: A Quadriplegic Sick Joke Cycle. *Names,* 33:289–292.
The American Game of "Smear the Queer" and the Homosexual Component of Male Competitive Sport and Warfare. *Journal of Psychoanalytic Anthropology,* 8:115–129.

1986

The Wandering Jew: Essays in the Interpretation of a Christian Legend (coeditor with Galit Hasan-Roken). Bloomington: Indiana University Press.
First Prize: Fifteen Years! An Annotated Collection of Romanian Political Jokes (with C. Banc). Rutherford, New Jersey: Fairleigh Dickinson University Press.
Fairy Tales from a Folkloristic Perspective. In: *Fairy Tales and Society,* ed. Ruth Bottigheimer. Philadelphia: University of Pennsylvania Press, pp. 259–269.
The Flood as Male Myth of Creation. *Journal of Psychoanalytic Anthropology,* 9:359–372.
The Anthropologist and the Comparative Method in Folklore. *Journal of Folklore Research,* 23:125–146.
Pickende Hühner: Thesen zum Weltbild im Spielzeug. *Volkskultur in der Moderne: Probleme und Perspektiven empirischer Kulturforschung.* Reinbek bei Hamburg: Rowohlt Taschenbuch Verlag, pp. 323–331.
Comment (Colloquy on National Character). *Focaal: Tydschrift voor Anthropologie* (April):33–37.

1987

Cracking Jokes: Studies of Sick Humor Cycles and Stereotypes. Berkeley: Ten Speed Press.
Parsing Through Customs: Essays by a Freudian Folklorist. Madison: University of Wisconsin Press.
When You're Up to Your Ass in Alligators: More Urban Folklore from the Paperwork Empire (with C. R. Pagter). Detroit: Wayne State University Press.
The Psychoanalytic Study of the Grimms' Tales with Special Reference to "The Maiden Without Hands" (AT 706). *The Germanic Review,* 62:50–65.
At Ease, Disease – AIDS Jokes as Sick Humor. *American Behavioral Scientist,* 30:72–81.

1988

The Flood Myth (editor). Berkeley: University of California Press.
April Fool and April Fish: Towards a Theory of Ritual Pranks. *Etnofoor,* 1:4–14.
More on Auschwitz Jokes (with U. Linke). *Folklore,* 99:3–10.
Interpreting Little Red Riding Hood Psychoanalytically. In: *The Brothers Grimm and Folktale.* Urbana: University of Illinois Press, pp. 16–51.

1989

Folklore Matters. Knoxville: University of Tennessee Press.
Little Red Riding Hood: A Casebook (editor). Madison: University of Wisconsin Press.
Foreword. Ibrahim Muhawi and Sharif Kanaana, *Speak, Bird, Speak Again: Palestinian Arab Folktales.* Berkeley: University of California Press, pp. ix–xiii.
Arse Longa, Vita Brevis: Jokes about AIDS. *Zyzzyva,* 5(4):33–39.
The Ritual Murder or Blood Libel Legend: A Study of Anti-Semitic Victimization Through Projective Inversion. *Temenos,* 25:7–32.

1990

Essays in Folklore Theory and Method. Madras: Cre-A.
Coming to Terms with Folkloristics. *Man,* 25:531.

1991

Never Try to Teach a Pig to Sing: Still More Urban Folklore from the Paperwork Empire (with C. R. Pagter). Detroit: Wayne State University Press.
The Blood Libel Legend: A Casebook in Anti-Semitic Folklore (editor). Madison: University of Wisconsin Press.
The Psychological Study of Folklore in the United States, 1880–1980. *Southern Folklore,* 48:97–120.
Bruno Bettelheim's Uses of Enchantment and Abuses of Scholarship. *Journal of American Folklore,* 104:74–83.
On the Possible African Origin of *Jigaboo. Midwestern Folklore,* 17:63–66.
The Mobile SCUD Missile Launcher and Other Persian Gulf Warlore: An American Folk Image of Saddam Hussein's Iraq (with C. R. Pagter). *Western Folklore,* 50:303–322.
The 1991 Archer Taylor Memorial Lecture. The Apple-Shot: Interpreting the Legend of William Tell. *Western Folklore,* 50:327–360.

1992

Introduction. Géza Róheim, *Fire in the Dragon and Other Psychoanalytic Essays on Folklore.* Princeton: Princeton University Press, pp. ix–xxvi.

dietary preferences (think sausage and chocolate), to Shakespearean plays, to the Genesis account of the Flood, to the New Testament account of Christ's life, to more traditional folkloric topics, like the study of fairy tales and proverbs. My purpose in this introductory essay is to impose some order and pattern on this imposing corpus by drawing out some of the consistent themes that have guided Dundes' work. The starting point of any such analysis, however, must be the man himself.

FIRST AND FOREMOST A FOLKLORIST

Alan Dundes (b. 1935) is first and foremost a folklorist who happens to be in a department of anthropology and who happens to be psychoanalytically inclined. His earliest degrees (B.A. and M.A.T.) were in English from Yale, his Ph.D. was in Folklore from Indiana, and his first job was in a department of English. In 1963 he came to the Department of Anthropology at UC Berkeley and since then has set about promoting folklore in a number of ways. He established and runs an interdisciplinary program in folklore at both the undergraduate and graduate level (the program awards an M.A.). His course in folklore, only a very small part of which is psychoanalytic in content, is regularly mentioned in student guides as one of the half-dozen or so most enjoyable and informative courses at Berkeley. He has edited or coedited several books whose function in each case has been to bring together a series of articles on one particular folklore topic, including Afro-American folklore (Dundes, 1972), the Evil Eye (Dundes, 1981a), the Cinderella story (Dundes, 1982a), the Oedipus tale (Edmunds and Dundes, 1983), sacred narrative (Dundes, 1984a), the legend of the Wandering Jew (Hasan-Rokem and Dundes, 1986), the Flood myth (Dundes, 1988a), and Little Red Riding Hood (Dundes, 1988b). Another of his concerns has been the collection and documentation of forms of folklore which are common in modern industrial societies but which are generally ignored by professional folklorists. Thus he has coedited books dealing with the photocopied materials that regularly appear on office bulletin boards (Dundes and Pagter, 1975, 1987, 1991) and has written several articles on various "sick joke" cycles that appear, diffuse widely, and then die out (see Dundes, 1987a). In between his writing and his teaching, he is forever flying off to some distant city, on this or some other continent, in order to ignite an interest in folklore in groups little exposed to this subject. Finally, there is the Berkeley Folklore Archives, which is modeled on the Folklore Archives at Indiana University.

The Folklore Archives at Berkeley have been built up over the past 25 years in conjunction with Dundes' undergraduate course on folklore. Every student in the course has to collect 50 different items of folklore, each written up in a standardized format. The format requires the collector to give the text or description of the item itself, the time and place of collection, and information on the informant's ethnicity. Collectors are also encouraged to elicit "folk interpretations" of the item collected from informants *and* to present their own interpretations. When turned in, these items are filed according to genre by archivists. By now there are tens of thousands of items on file. An index exists, and the archives can be searched by students at Berkeley, by professional folklorists, and in fact by any scholar who wants to use them. About half the items have been gathered from informants raised in the United States and the other half from informants raised outside.[1]

Dundes' concern with folklore derives in part from a genuine affection for the material he studies. Simply put, he likes to be a part of the folklore transmission process. One of the things that makes his class so appealing is the gusto and humor with which he discusses the many items of folklore that are part of each lecture. Even when discussing *blaisons populaires* (i.e., ethnic slurs) Dundes is able to disarm his class sufficiently that they can appreciate the logic that underlies this material without taking offense when their particular ethnic or religious group comes under the gun (as inevitably happens). Some of the playfulness that is a part of his course often carries over into his scholarly texts. This is seen most succinctly in the titles given to his more recent books, which betray his personal predilection for the pun as a form of humor, as in *Cracking Jokes* (1987a), *Parsing Through Customs* (1987b), and *Folklore Matters* (1989a).

If I have dwelt upon Dundes' commitment to folklore, it is oiiy as a prelude to asserting that his status among anthropologists and folklorists likely rests upon his work on behalf of folklore in general. It does *not* rest upon his psychoanalytic contributions. Indeed, many folklorists and anthropologists only tolerate his psychoanalytic stance because he is so good at all the other things he does as a folklorist. He has directly influenced some scholars to imitate his merging of psychoanalysis and folklore, but the number of such scholars is small. Many of them are represented in this study. Part of the reason that Dundes' own theoretical work has not had a wider impact is that he is forever sending distinct messages to two separate audiences, folklorists and psychoanalysts, and neither audience cares much for the message being sent.

---

[1]See Niles (1989) for a more detailed discussion of the Berkeley Folklore Archives.

TWO CORE MESSAGES

Alan Dundes' core message for folklorists is simple: Folklore is often the result of the sorts of psychological processes discussed by Freud. To those already committed to psychoanalysis, this will hardly seem problematic, but it is precisely that to most folklorists. A century ago, folklorists were concerned almost entirely with collection, classification, and "origins" (as in "where did this item of folklore originate?"). Although these same concerns continue to dominate the work of many folklorists, most modern folklorists now routinely make a concern for "meaning" a part of their analyses. Unfortunately, even a quick perusal through recent issues of virtually any journal of folklore reveals that "meaning" to most folklorists means the *conscious* meaning attributed to an item of folklore by informants. Jump-rope rhymes about babies being tossed down elevator shafts, fairy tales in which fathers cut off their daughters' hands, jokes about why cucumbers are better than men, myths in which male culture-heroes create the world using mud—the idea that such folk traditions might actually be popular because they reflect *unconscious* concerns is simply beyond the ken of most folklorists.

At times the insensitivity of folklorists and anthropologists to cues that literally scream out for psychoanalytic interpretation serves as a grim reminder of just how limited has been the influence of psychoanalytic thought in some areas. Consider the case of the Palio of Siena. Although this famous horse race has been the subject of any number of commentaries, most of these have been concerned only with documenting the historical development of the race. If the race was "interpreted" at all, it was seen sometimes as simple cultural survival, sometimes as a means of fostering solidarity within the various Sienese neighborhoods that sponsor the horses, and sometimes simply as a means for bringing in tourists. Yet this is a race in which (1) the riders are adolescent males who are given the stretched phalluses of unweaned calves as whips to be used on their horses *and* against each other, (2) members of the winning *contrada* (neighborhood) often suck a pacifier while marching along in the victory parade, and (3) members of the losing *contrada* are expected to take a purge. Despite the quite explicit appearance here of imagery that is at once infantile, phallic, and excremental, no one prior to Dundes and Falassi (1975) had thought to view the Palio through a psychoanalytic lens or even to focus on the details just mentioned in trying to explain the appeal and importance of the Palio to the people of Siena.

As Dundes (1989a) has himself noted over and over again, folklorists have not just "not accepted" his psychoanalytic interpretations; they have rejected them out of hand and with some degree of vehemence. In his own words:

> As a realist, I have to confess that my psychoanalytic bias is not shared by many of my folklore colleagues. That is putting it mildly. Let me rephrase the issue. Most folklorists are actively repelled by the application of psychoanalytic theory to folklore. They typically denigrate or ridicule any interpretation with a psychoanalytic cast to it [p. viii].[2]

Remember, this is from a person who loves folklore.

Only occasionally and in passing has Dundes sought to explain the source of this very vehement rejection of his work. He suggests, for example:

> There are dozens of psychoanalytic readings of fairy tales, most of which are totally ignored by literal-minded folklorists frightened and evidently greatly threatened by any thought that fairy tales might have a symbolic import [Dundes, 1988b, pp. 19–20].

and again:

> One reason for the resistance of literal-minded folklorists to the psychoanalytic approach to folktales might have to do with a basic fear of discovering why they are so utterly fascinated by the content of such folktales [Dundes, 1987c, p. 54].

Such remarks, I think, fall just short of insight. At one level, folklorists likely reject psychoanalysis for the same reason that most people reject psychoanalysis: It is a science whose core purpose is to bring to consciousness things that are unacceptable to the conscious mind. But I think that there is a second reason as well operative in this particular case. If folklorists fear anything from psychoanalysis it is not likely an explanation of why they *like* folklore materials, but why they like to *do* folklore. After all, what do most folklorists do? Despite Dundes' often-repeated claim that folklorists *should* be concerned with both collection and interpretation, most folklorists are fascinated only with

---

[2]For a detailed consideration of particular American folklorists and the nature and extent of their aversion to psychoanalytic theory, see Dundes (1991).

endless collection and classification. And what would the standard psychoanalytic perspective on people dominated by a concern for "orderliness" and the classification of minutiae be? It seems obvious: Folklore, as traditionally practiced, represents the concerns of what Freud called the "anal personality" writ large. In fact, Dundes (1962a) himself very early on recognized this affinity between the anal person-ality and professional folklore activities. The anal-erotic/anal-sadistic origins of a passion for folklore are, I suggest, the truth about themselves that folklorists would have to confront if they took Dundes' work seriously.

Dundes' second audience is composed of psychoanalysts. Here his analyses are better received, partly because the application of psycho-analysis to folk material is not in itself novel. As Dundes (esp. 1985a) has often made clear, Freud, Rank, Abraham, Jones, and a number of their successors analyzed myths, tales, legends, fairy tales, and the like. Even so, Dundes also has a core message for psychoanalysts who study folklore and it is simply this: Folklore always exists in *multiple* versions. The very nature of the process by which items of folklore are passed along—oral transmission or imitation—allows items of folklore to be changed and modified. The result is variation, and to ignore this variation is to lose a great deal of valuable information. This message, which will seem elementary and obvious to folklorists, is routinely ignored by psychoanalysts.

Dundes' harshest criticisms in this regard are directed against those psychoanalysts who analyze fairy tales using the Grimm collection (Dundes; 1987c), which means almost all the psychoanalysts who have looked at fairy tales. His first point about the Grimm tales is that they are not folktales at all since they were never in oral circulation. On the contrary, they are explicitly "composite" tales that were put together by the Grimms from the different tales they had collected. But his more important point is that each tale in the Grimm collection exists in dozens of variant forms. There is no particular reason to believe that these other versions, which are routinely ignored by psychoanalysts, are any less meaningful than the Grimm versions on which psychoanalysts have expended so much interpretive energy. What is particularly aggravating in all of this, at least to Dundes the folklorist, is that every university library contains two easily accessible reference tools, Thompson's *Motif-Index of Folk-Literature* (1955–1958) and Aarne and Thompson's *The Types of the Folktale* (1961), that could easily be used to locate several different versions of a given tale. Unfortunately, Dundes has made as little headway in converting psychoanalysts to the use of folklore scholarship as he has made in converting folklorists to psychoanalysis. Though there are exceptions, most psychoanalysts continue to analyze *the* story of Little Red Riding Hood using only the Grimm version, *the* story of Moses using only the Old Testament version, *the* story of Oedipus using only Sophocles' version, etc. — even though *all* these stories exist in multiple versions.[3]

Nevertheless, although Dundes has not inspired many psychoanalysts to imitate his careful attention to variation in folklore, psychoanalytic audiences do not react to his work with hostility. On the contrary, to the extent that they become aware of his work, most psychoanalysts tend to react favorably. This volume itself is evidence of that. It is for this reason that most of what follows is written with a psychoanalytically inclined audience in mind.

DUNDES' USE OF PSYCHOANALYTIC THEORY

Dundes (1987b, p. x) has said that the application of psychoanalytic theory to folklore is his major intellectual goal as a folklorist. This is true enough as far as it goes, but somewhat misleading. There is actually very little "psychoanalytic theory" in Dundes. Indeed, for all practical purposes he relies mostly on the theoretical arguments that Freud presented early in his career, notably in *The Interpretation of Dreams*. Dundes' genius lies in his encyclopedic familiarity with folk materials and in his ability to use a few simple psychoanalytic ideas to discern previously undiscovered patterns in these materials, even if they have been pored over by dozens of earlier scholars.

In particular, Dundes relies heavily on Freud's suggestion that dreams represent the disguised gratification of unconscious wishes. Applied to the study of folklore, this means that myths, tales, and so on are popular to the extent that identification with the central characters allows for the vicarious and disguised gratification of unconscious wishes. This hypothesis (and it is just that, a hypothesis) does not derive from the suggestion that folktales are "collective dreams" or any such nonsense. Rather it derives from the fact that folklore can be *changed* in the course of transmission. This means that as an item of folklore is passed along from person to person and from generation to generation, it can come to be shaped by the unconscious beliefs and desires typical of a particular

---

[3]Thompson's *Motif-Index* is the best source for locating variants of the Grimm tales. For an overview of the variant forms of the Oedipus story see Edmunds and Dundes (1983). For variants of the Moses story see Carroll (1987).

cultural group in a way that, say, a fixed literary form (like a novel) cannot.

Many of the specific analyses that have been guided by this "wish-fulfillment" hypothesis are fairly straightforward. Thus Dundes sees the folktale about George Washington chopping down his father's cherry tree as reflecting the disguised gratification of a son's desire to castrate the father (Dundes, 1971, pp. 26–28). Urban legends about a grandmother who dies while on a trip with her son's family and whose corpse is then lost reflect a youth-oriented society's desire to be rid of the older generation (Dundes, 1971, pp. 33–34). A jump-rope rhyme about wrapping up a baby and throwing it down an elevator shaft is about a girl's wish to eliminate unwanted siblings (Dundes, 1976, pp. 1507–1508). The ballad of John Henry, the "steel-drivin' man," is less a part of black American folklore than a part of *white* American folklore, since it portrays the black male as whites want him to be: strong, docile, doggedly loyal to his white boss, and even willing to die doing the white man's work (Dundes, 1976a, p. 1518). The association of the Holy Grail (in legend) with sexual imagery and with nourishment suggests to Dundes that the Grail is a mother symbol; this means that stories about the quest for the Grail are popular because they gratify every son's oedipal desire for the mother (Dundes, 1962b). "Dead baby" jokes became popular in the 1960s and 1970s because changes in sexual behavior and more public discussion about abortion and contraception led to increased anxieties about pregnancy; this engendered the desire that babies not be born, which is gratified by telling jokes about babies that are dead (Dundes, 1979a). But there is one particular application of the wish-fulfillment hypothesis that recurs more often than any other in Dundes' work and it is worth singling out.

MALE BIRTH-ENVY

Dundes' (1962c) analysis of the Earth Diver myth found in many North American Indian societies, though still widely cited as an exemplar in the psychoanalytic study of myth, is in many ways atypical of his later work. There is, for instance, a long introductory section containing the ponderous citation of previous anthropological pronouncements on myth, even though most of the discussion here is ultimately irrelevant to the particular myth being studied. Also missing from this early article is the meticulous concern for variation that would later become a hallmark of Dundes' articles. Thus, although he does mention in passing that the Earth Diver myth exists in many different versions, his analysis pays little attention to this variation and focuses instead on a "summary" version of the myth that itself was never in oral circulation. On the other hand, the theoretical interpretation he finally delivers laid down a formula that he would use over and over again.

In its summary form, the Earth Diver myth is about a culture-hero who has a variety of different animals dive into the primeval waters to secure a bit of sand or mud. Most of the animals fail, but finally one succeeds. From the bit of sand or mud brought up dry land is formed. For Dundes, the appeal of the myth lies in the fact that it allows for the vicarious gratification of a male's birth-envy. Drawing upon the work of earlier psychoanalytic investigators, Dundes suggests that males universally envy the female capacity to give birth. Unable to give birth in reality, they gratify this desire in fantasy. The Earth Diver myth is one such fantasy.

Why the myth's emphasis on "creating" from sand or mud? Here Dundes draws upon Freud's early work on infantile sexuality. One of the very first questions that the young child asks, said Freud, was the question Where do babies come from? One of the child's first answers to this question is the "cloacal theory of birth," which holds that babies are excreted through the anus like feces. The cloacal theory is quickly abandoned, but the memory of it remains in the unconscious and it is therefore available in the creation of fantasy material. Because both females and males defecate, the cloacal theory of birth is especially attractive to males who want to create birth fantasies. For Dundes, "mud" or "sand" are only slightly disguised feces symbols. A myth that has the present world being created from mud or sand at the instigation of a male culture-hero is thus a myth whose content has been shaped both by male birth-envy and the imagery of the cloacal theory.

Dundes has gone on to pursue this male birth-envy theme in a number of quite diverse contexts. It is a theme, for instance, that underlies his interpretation of male initiation rites in Australian aboriginal societies (Dundes, 1976b). Like many earlier commentators, Dundes suggests that such rites were male birth fantasies because (1) their purpose was to cause boys to be reborn as men, and (2) this birth (unlike their "first" birth) was totally under the control and direction of older males. He went beyond earlier commentators by noting that we could understand many of the otherwise puzzling details surrounding these ceremonies if we saw them as male birth fantasies that had been shaped specifically by memories of the cloacal theory of birth. This is why these ceremonies were associated with the use of bullroarers (whose sounds were the symbolic equivalence of flatulence), with men who covered themselves with mud or clay (feces again), and with a number of myths that make explicit reference to excrement.

Dundes (1983b) also made use of his male birth-envy argument (sans any reference to the cloacal theory of birth) in his discussion of the *couvade,* the tendency of males in some societies to simulate the symptoms of pregnancy and birth when their wives are pregnant and give birth. In couvade societies a man might take to bed when his wife becomes pregnant, simulate labor, or require a "rest period" after his wife gives birth. Dundes suggests that through such behaviors men are trying to participate in the birth processes at least as regards outward manifestation in order to gratify their unconscious desire to give birth. Here again, his argument is by no means novel, because others have interpreted couvade behavior in much the same way. But Dundes then uses this discussion of the couvade to provide an interpretation of the two Creation accounts in the biblical book of Genesis, which *is* novel. In the first Creation account in Genesis, for instance, the explicitly male God *rests* on the seventh day. But why, asks Dundes, should an omnipotent God need to rest? His answer: A male God is seen to rest after "giving birth" to the world for the same reason that a man practicing couvade rests after his wife gives birth. In both cases, a male is trying to imitate behavior that would more normally be associated with females who give birth. In the second account of Creation (which is historically the earlier account) the birth-envy theme is even more explicit: Not only is the Creator God a male, but it is specifically stated that the first woman was created from a body part (a rib) of the first man. It is a story, in short, which reverses the usual ordering: Instead of males being born from a female, the female is born from a male.

Taken collectively, Dundes' series of studies on male birth-envy is likely that portion of his work that has the greatest implications for the future development of psychoanalytic theory. After all, the dominant theoretical emphasis in psychoanalysis has always been upon female envy of males, notably upon a female's envy of the male's penis. Yet Dundes (1985a) argues that "penis envy" themes occur infrequently in folklore. This means that the pattern that emerges from a consideration of the folkloric data, namely, a strong emphasis on male birth-envy with little emphasis on penis envy, is very much the *reverse* of the pattern that has always characterized psychoanalytic theory.

PROJECTIVE INVERSION

In discussing the processes by which unconscious wishes shape folklore, Dundes has come to privilege *projection,* and in particular, what he calls *projective inversion.* In Dundes' terms, simple projection involves establishing a one-to-one structural similarity between an unconscious desire and some folkloric belief or action. Thus, a son's desire to castrate the father becomes a story about a son who chops down his father's tree; a desire to spread American-style free enterprise throughout the world at any cost (to others) comes to be reflected in a TV show in which a spaceship called the *Enterprise* flits about the universe converting or destroying alien cultures; a desire to be rid of the burdens of caring for the elderly comes to be reflected in an urban legend about a grandmother who dies and whose corpse is lost; and so on.

Projective inversion, by contrast, occurs when person A's attitude toward person B becomes (in folklore) a situation in which B, or someone like B, has that same attitude toward A. In connection with masculine wishes, the process that Dundes is calling projective inversion has already been discussed (simply as "projection") by leading psychoanalysts. In discussing "birth of the hero" stories, for instance, Otto Rank suggested that the son's wish to eliminate the father often became—in myth and legend—a father or father-surrogate's wish to eliminate the son. This was why, said Rank, so many birth-of-the-hero stories start with the son being threatened with death by his own father or a father-surrogate (like a king). Dundes' special contribution has been to demonstrate that projective inversion is far more common in folkloric traditions than was previously thought.

Consider for instance his analysis of the literary versions of the *King Lear* story (Dundes, 1976c). of which the Shakespearean version is only one example. Dundes first criticizes most previous commentators for ignoring the folkloric origins of *Lear.* In fact, the story of Lear seems based in large measure on a folktale usually identified as "Love like Salt." The defining plot element involves a king who asks his three daughters to declare their love for him. The third daughter, the king's favorite, responds that her love is like salt. This reply angers the father, and that daughter is banished. In the folktale, the third daughter usually ends up married and reconciled with her father. A careful consideration of other elements in "Love like Salt" leads Dundes to conclude that it is a weakened (i.e., sanitized) form of an even more popular tale whose defining element is a father who wants to marry his own daughter.

At this point Dundes offers his interpretation: The popularity of the folktale on which the Lear story is based, and thus by extension the popularity of the Lear story itself, derives from the fact that it reflects the gratification of the *daughter's oedipal desire for her father*. His argument is that "desire for the father" in the daughter's unconscious becomes, through projective inversion, "father's desire for his daughter" in the folktale. Many psychoanalytic readers, I think, might balk at this point. After all, wouldn't it be just as reasonable, and certainly more parsimonious, to see a folktale in which a "father desires his daughter" as reflecting — simply — the incestuous desires that develop in fathers toward their daughters? Actually, there is a critical step in Dundes' reasoning that precludes this possibility, and it is a step that is easy to miss.

Consider: Why do we take it as obvious that, say, *Hamlet* or *Oedipus Rex* — to the extent they are concerned with oedipal desires at all — are concerned with the *son's* oedipal desires? Presumably because the central character in each case is a son. But who is the central character in *King Lear*? In Shakespeare's version, and indeed in most of the literary versions, it is without question Lear. But in the particular folktales on which the Lear story is based the central character is just as unquestionably the *daughter*. It is this fact, Dundes argues, that makes it clear the underlying story is concerned with the *daughter's* desires, not the father's.

The argument Dundes developed in his "King Lear" article was later expanded by considering in detail one of the folktales on which (in his reconstruction) the Lear story was based. This was "The Maiden Without Hands" (Dundes, 1987c). In the Grimm version of this tale, a miller is tricked into promising his daughter to the Devil in marriage. The daughter evades the marriage, but the Devil, frustrated, demands that the father cut off her hands. The deed is done and the girl wanders into a forest. There she meets a king who has silver hands made for her and who takes her as his own wife. How to make sense of all this?

Dundes starts by noting that this is a good example of the dangers inherent in relying entirely on the Grimm canon in studying folklore, because the Grimm version of this tale is strikingly atypical of the tale as it appears in oral circulation. Indeed, in most versions of the story the Devil does not appear at all and it is, as already noted, the *father* who seeks his own daughter in marriage. Further, in a substantial number of versions, it is the daughter who cuts off her own hands.

To explain this tale Dundes offers the same hypothesis he had offered earlier: the tale expresses a daughter's desire for her father, which becomes, through projective inversion, a father's desire for his daughter.

One advantage of this interpretation, he suggests, is that it offers a fairly straightforward explanation of why it is the *daughter* who is punished (by having her hands cut off). After all, if Dundes is correct, it is the daughter who is guilty of the incestuous wish that is being expressed.

The need to compare the literary versions of a story (whether it is about King Lear, Oedipus, Little Red Riding Hood, or whomever) with the preexisting folktales from which the story derives is a recurrent theme in Dundes' work. One pattern that consistently emerges when he does this is that in moving from the folktale to the literary version there is an intensification in the process of *disguise*. This is presumably because the literary versions of a story are more likely to be influenced by the middle-class notions of morality characteristic of those who write such stories and those who read them. Consider the "punishment of the daughter" element, which is so explicit in "The Maiden Without Hands." In most literary versions of the Lear story "the favored daughter cuts off her hands" element becomes simply "the favorite daughter commits suicide." In Shakespeare's version, the distortion is carried even further, and it is Goneril, not Cordelia (the favorite) who is associated with suicide.

There are weak points in Dundes' analysis, to be sure. Even granting that his hypothesis explains the popularity of the *folktale* versions of Lear, how does it explain the popularity of the *Shakespearean* version? Distortion though it may be of the folk tradition, Shakespeare's *King Lear* seems clearly a *father*-centered story. Isn't it likely that whereas the folktale may have been popular because it reflects the disguised gratification of a daughter's incestuous desires, *King Lear* has become one of the most popular of Shakespeare's plays because it reflects the disguised gratification of a *father's* incestuous desires? Still, this is carping.

The bulk of Dundes' arguments seem at least as convincing, if not more so, than anything else that has been offered in connection with *King Lear*. Even aside from his specific arguments, his analysis lays the groundwork for a new approach to literary creations. Far more than previous commentators, he demonstrates clearly and in a precisely documented manner the folkloric context of *King Lear,* and he shows how an appreciation of this context offers possibilities to the psychoanalytic imagination that would otherwise be unavailable.

Dundes (1989b) also sees projective inversion as central to an understanding of the Blood Libel legend, one of the most pernicious and harmful folktales in the Western tradition. The core plot of this legend suggests that one or more Jews murder a Christian child in order to obtain blood for use in a religious ritual (e.g., to mix it with unleavened bread or to make matzos). This story has been in oral circulation from the 12th century right up until the present. In the first part of his essay Dundes reviews systematically the different versions of the Blood Libel legend, the opposition to the legend by some church leaders, the way it has nevertheless become the basis of local Christian festivals, and the trials that have been instituted against particular Jews as the result of the legend. Although the legend is pure fantasy without any basis in reality, there have even been some folklorists who have given credibility to its historicity. Only after this lengthy initial review does Dundes set out to explain why such a fantasy should have originated.

Anti-Semitism is a topic that has interested psychoanalysts from Freud on, because it has seemed obvious that such a virulent hatred could not persist across the centuries in various cultures unless it was fed by continuous psychological processes. At one level, the Blood Libel legend is fed by the processes that feed anti-Semitism in general. But, Dundes notes, this in itself does not explain the specifics of the legend. Why it is always a *young* child, usually a *boy,* who is killed? Why the emphasis on *mixing blood with unleavened bread?* The key for Dundes lies in two apparent anomalies. The first is that the consumption of blood is expressly prohibited in Judaism, yet the legend explicitly has Jews mixing blood with bread. In this connection, Dundes calls attention to the fact that the mixing of blood and bread, although foreign to Judaism, is very much a part of the Christian tradition, because Christians universally consider the bread and wine consumed during the Eucharistic ritual to be the body and blood of Christ. The second anomaly has to do with timing; in most versions of the Blood Libel legend, the ritual murder occurs in association with Easter or with a Jubilee Year, both of which are *Christian,* not Jewish, festivals. These anomalous elements suggest to Dundes that the legend likely reflects *Christian* concerns associated with the *Christian Eucharist,* which have been *projected* onto Jews.

Dundes' eventual argument goes like this: Though the Eucharist is central to Christian ritual, the underlying logic of the Eucharist requires that Christians devour the body and blood of Jesus Christ. Theological rationalizing aside, this is ultimately a cannibalistic act that must recurrently produce guilt. Christians avoid this guilt by creating a fantasy in which this act, or one very much like it, is committed not by themselves but by Jews. Remember that in Christian mythology Jesus Christ was both *Jewish* and the *son* of God. This means that through projective inversion Christians consuming a Jewish son (= Christ) can become Jews consuming a Christian son, which is in fact the core of the Blood Libel legend. Once we realize that the Blood Libel is a Christian

fantasy that derives (through projective inversion) from Christian concerns surrounding the Eucharistic ritual, then we can understand the
anomalous details, such as why it involves the mixing of blood and bread
(just as the Eucharist implies the mixing of blood/wine and bread) and
why it is associated with Christian festivals.

One last example of Dundes' use of projective inversion involves
psychoanalysts and psychoanalysis. Consider the pattern mentioned
earlier: The folkloric evidence would suggest that male envy of the
female capacity to give birth is far more widespread and far stronger than
female envy of the male's penis, and yet psychoanalysts have always
tended to reverse this pattern by emphasizing female penis envy far more
than male birth-envy. Why? For Dundes (1985a) it "could conceivably"
result from projective inversion. Unwilling to confront their birth-envy,
male psychoanalysts transform "I envy women" into "women envy men."
The result is an emphasis on penis envy. It is at the very least an
interesting hypothesis, and one that should be considered carefully by all
male psychoanalysts.

CULTURAL STUDIES

Another ongoing concern of Dundes the folklorist has always been to
convince his anthropological colleagues that the study of a society's
folklore is a useful way of discovering the values and orientations that
pervade that society. To put it more simply, the analysis of *folklore*
provides useful insights into *culture*. One of the best known of his
cultural studies is probably "The Number Three in American Culture"
(Dundes, 1968). In the first part of this essay he notes that although
many cultures seem characterized by a tripartite emphasis, this is by no
means a cultural universal. There are a number of cultures in which
"four" is clearly the dominant number pattern, and some in which the
dominant number pattern is "five." That said, Dundes embarks upon a
formidable listing of elements in American culture that are characterized
by a tripartite organization. Dundes ranges over topics as diverse as folk
speech, traditional games, professional sports, public entertainments,
naming conventions, mealtime behavior, clothing habits, technological
formulas, ways of thinking about social organization, religion, kinship
distinctions, and even the logic of theories developed by American
anthropologists and archaeologists. In each case, he provides example
after example of tripartite organization.

Dundes' analysis here represents what for some is the greatest strength of his analysis of culture and for others is the greatest weakness: his tendency to overwhelm his readers with seemingly endless examples of folkloric items that seem consistent with the arguments that he makes. The sheer number of such elements is indeed impressive, but the fear is always that he has been selective and that other investigators, focusing on other aspects of (in this case) American folklore, could come to different conclusions. In the end, it is an empirical matter, and as of this date no one (as far as I know) has countered Dundes by demonstrating that a different focus would result in different conclusions.

There was very little psychoanalysis in this "number three" article (which is probably why it has been reprinted so often). Only in the closing paragraphs does he point to Freud's suggestion that the number three has phallic significance given the tripartite organization of the male genitalia, and even this is raised only in a tentative and halting manner. His next major study of American culture, however was quite different. In this study Dundes (1978a) tackled football.

Football is among the most popular of all American sports. Why? Football (at least the game that Americans call "football") has never been that popular in Europe. Again, why? Dundes starts, as usual, by reviewing previous theories (football as aggression, football as a male initiation ceremony, etc.). Each theory has merit, he concludes, but does not explain why football is more popular than other team sports. He then builds up his own theory in stages. First, it seems clear that there is a great deal of sexual imagery in the game. There is, for example, the structure of the game itself (kicking a ball through a precisely defined spot), as well as the sexual connotations of many of the phrases used (e.g., making a pass, going all the way). Still, he concedes, such sexual imagery is present in several sports. What most distinguishes football is the presence of clear and explicit *homosexual* imagery. The game, after all, is played between two opposing teams of males who are each trying to get the ball into their opponents' "end zone" before their opponents get it into their "end zone." It is a game in which the nature of the equipment worn emphasizes the male physique by giving players wide shoulders, enlarged heads, narrow hips, and prominent bulges in the genital region. It is also the only game in which male players spend a considerable amount of time bent over with their buttocks presented upwards, thus simulating a position associated with anal intercourse. Finally, it is a game in which males display patterns of intimate physical contact (like bum-patting) that would be considered entirely inappropriate anywhere else.

It is easy to stop at this point in Dundes' argument. People who play or watch football can be outraged at the association with homosexuality; those with an antijock bias can be pleased. But to stop here misses the core of the argument. Dundes nowhere suggests that football players or football fans in the United States are more "homosexual" in their underlying orientation than anyone else in the world. Rather, he argues that males *universally* establish an early cathexis with their fathers (as with their mothers). This creates a predisposition for males everywhere to derive pleasure from physical contact with members of their own sex. It is, however, a feature of American culture, homophobic as it is, that public displays of physical contact between nonrelated males, even if not overtly sexual, are strongly discouraged. That is far less true in European cultures, where physical contact between males in public is tolerated if not encouraged. Football is popular in the United States but not in Europe, therefore, because it allows for the vicarious discharge of the early homosexual cathexis that in Europe is discharged in other ways. At one level, then, the "football" analysis is just another application of the wish-fulfillment hypothesis; at another it is an attempt to relate a folk tradition (the American predilection for football) to a cultural difference between the United States and Europe.

Quite often Dundes has investigated U.S. culture by focusing on jokes and joke cycles. Thus he has suggested that both "elephant" jokes (Dundes and Abrahams, 1969) and "wide-mouth frog" jokes (Dundes, 1977) reflect racist attitudes in this country; that "Jewish-American Princess" jokes (Dundes, 1985b) and "cucumber" jokes (as in "Why are cucumbers better than men?") (Dundes, 1987d)[4] reflect female discontent with the attitudes and behaviors traditionally associated with gender roles in this society; and that "light bulb" jokes (as in "How many Californians does it take to screw in a light bulb?") (Dundes 1981b)[5] reflect concerns about sexual impotence and a loss of U.S. influence in the modern world. Dundes (1976d) has also used a variety of American folk materials, including jokes, urban legends, and children's games and rhymes to demonstrate the pervasiveness of male chauvinism in American culture.

But the United States is not the only culture that Dundes has sought to study via folklore. One of his most important works is a book

---

[4]Some typical responses to Why are cucumbers better than men?: "The average cucumber is at least six inches long"; "Cucumbers stay hard for a week"; "A cucumber won't tell you size doesn't count"; "You only eat cucumbers when you feel like it"; "No matter how old you are, you can always get a fresh cucumber"; etc.

[5]The usual response to this particular light bulb joke: "Californians don't screw in light bulbs, they screw in hot tubs."

demonstrating that much of Germanic culture seems pervaded with anal themes, including here an emphasis on orderliness, a preoccupation with excretion, and an attraction toward items that are only barely disguised feces substitutes (Dundes, 1984b). He has linked variations in the design of a folk toy[6] to cultural differences in the perception of personal space and the availability of food (Dundes, 1989c). Other cultural studies include his analysis of Turkish boys' verbal dueling rhymes (Dundes, Leach, and Özkök 1970) the *piropos* found in Spanish-speaking societies,[7] and the potlatch practiced by Indian societies of the Pacific Northwest (Dundes, 1979b).

But the most daring of Dundes' "cultural studies" have been those in which he has used folk traditions to reconstruct the culture of ancient societies. He has argued (Dundes, 1980a) for instance, that surviving folk traditions about the Evil Eye reflect two distinct and important cultural orientations that prevailed in the Indo-European and Semitic societies of the ancient world. These two beliefs were (1) that society was characterized by "limited good" and (2) that "wet" was associated with life and "dry" with death. Similarly, the final section of his "The Hero Pattern and the Life of Jesus" (Dundes, 1980b) is really an attempt to show that the Jesus story reflects a recurrent feature of Mediterranean societies, namely, the need to separate boys from the world of women in which they were raised and bring them into the world of men. Under this interpretation, the Crucifixion becomes a symbolic reflection of a rite of passage, in which a Son is mutilated and degraded, only to be resurrected and reborn into the world of his Father. It is not exactly an interpretation calculated to please everybody, but entirely plausible and certainly imaginative.

FOLKLORE AND THE VALIDATION OF PSYCHOANALYTIC INTERPRETATION

Psychoanalytic interpretation, whether of a dream or a myth or whatever, almost always involves postulating an equivalence between an unconscious image and some conscious symbol. This equivalence flows

---

[6]The toy is a hand-held platform on which are several wooden chickens, usually attached to a wooden pendulum by strings. When the platform and the pendulum are rotated, the chickens peck against the platform's surface.

[7]A *piropo* is a type of verbal remark made by a male to a female in a public place; most have sexual themes. Often they are ostensibly complimentary but implicitly sexual; in other cases, they are overtly and aggressively sexual.

inexorably from the premise that what is found in the unconscious are desires and fears that are unacceptable to the conscious mind. When for a variety of reasons such desires and fears are pushed toward consciousness, they are disguised in order to avoid the discomfort that would result if the conscious mind confronted them directly. Replacing the images associated with these desires and fears with their symbolic equivalents is part of this process of disguise. But a problem faced by all psychoanalytic investigators (whether they choose to confront it or not) is that the symbolic equations they so glibly postulate in their interpretive work are often rejected by the educated public. In considering this problem Dundes has suggested that folklore might profitably be used to provide independent evidence of these equations.

The basic idea here is not entirely new. In *Dreams in Folklore* (written circa 1911, but not published until 1958) Freud and Oppenheim suggested that the "dream interpretations" that appear in folklore often validate the equivalences postulated by psychoanalytic investigators. For instance, in one of the tales they analyze a husband dreams of a demon who promises him a foolproof way of maintaining his wife's chastity. The demon gives the husband a ring to wear on his finger and says that as long as he wears it his wife cannot sleep with any other man. The man awakes and finds that he has pushed his finger into his wife's vulva. It is difficult to imagine what sort of evidence could more convincingly establish the reasonableness of a "vulva = ring" equivalence, at least in the minds of those telling this particular story. Freud and Oppenheim demonstrate that other dream interpretation episodes that appear in folktales similarly seem to validate the equivalences posited by psychoanalysts.

Dundes (1985c) has built on this early work by suggesting other ways that folk materials can be used to validate these equivalences. He calls attention, for example, to a folk cartoon that has appeared in a variety of locations throughout North America, showing an Indian snake charmer playing his flute and causing a snake to rise; the snake, however, is the charmer's own penis. Another widespread cartoon shows a dentist just after extracting a man's tooth; the tooth is pulled out, all right, but it is attached to the man's genitalia, which have also been pulled out. Dundes argues that cartoons like these validate (in the sense only of "make more reasonable") the "snake = penis" and "tooth extraction = castration" equivalences that have often been used by psychoanalysts in their interpretations.

Dundes (1985c; 1987c) has also suggested that symbolic equations can be validated by paying close attention to what is, after all, a defining

characteristic of folklore—variation. He specifically directs our attention
to the substitutions that occur across *allomotifs*. Allomotifs are analogous incidents across different versions of the same tale. Thus, if most
versions of a particular tale have a king who threatens to cut off the
hero's head, but some have the king threatening to cut off the hero's
pecker then this suggests that "pecker" has been substituted for "head"
(or vice versa) during the process of oral transmission. Such a substitution, Dundes argues, provides independent evidence in support of the
familiar "penis = head" equation used by Freud and any number of
other psychoanalytic investigators.

CONCLUSION

Readers who have come this far will note that I have not been especially
critical in reviewing Dundes' work. This is not because I find his work
flawless. On the contrary, I think that Dundes' exuberance and helter-
skelter style sometimes lead to assertions that are not as well supported
by his own evidence as he would have us believe. I also think that in some
cases the data he presents can be accounted for in a more parsimonious
manner, even while staying within the psychoanalytic perspective (see for
instance Carroll, 1984). None of this, however, detracts from the
incredible range of insights that he has offered over the past few decades,
or from his ability to develop new and original interpretations of familiar
materials, or from the conclusion that Alan Dundes is one of the most
consistently creative minds at work in the field of either anthropology or
folklore. Furthermore, his many talents are by no means dried up.
Almost certainly he will be producing at least three good articles (or
books) a year for some time to come. And no matter how much his critics
try to muddy the waters or thunder and rail, Alan Dundes will always
come from behind and win the Grail.

BIBLIOGRAPHY

AARNE, A. & THOMPSON, S. (1961), *The Types of the Folktale*. Helsinki: Academia
  Scientiarum Fennica.
CARROLL, M. P. (1984), On the psychological origins of the Evil Eye: A Kleinian view.
  J. Psychoanal. Anthropol., 7:171–187.
_____ (1987), "Moses and Monotheism" revisited—Freud's personal myth? *Amer. Imago*,
  44:15–35.
DUNDES, A. (1962a), On the psychology of collecting folklore. In: *Analytic Essays in
  Folklore*. The Hague, Netherlands: Mouton, 1975, pp. 121–129.
_____ (1962b), The father, the son and the Holy Grail. In: *Analytic Essays in Folklore*.
  The Hague, Netherlands: Mouton, 1975, pp. 151–162.

_____ (1962c), Earth-Diver: Creation of the mythopoeic male. In: *Analytic Essays in Folklore*. The Hague, Netherlands: Mouton, 1975, pp. 130–145.

_____ (1968), The number three in American culture. In: *Analytic Essays in Folklore*. The Hague, Netherlands: Mouton, 1975, pp. 206–225.

_____ (1971), On the psychology of legend. In: *Analytic Essays in Folklore*. The Hague, Netherlands: Mouton, 1975, pp. 163–174.

_____ (1972), *Mother-Wit From the Laughing Barrel: Readings in the Interpretation of Afro-American Folklore*. Englewood Cliffs: Prentice Hall.

_____ (1975), *Analytic Essays in Folklore*. The Hague, Netherlands: Mouton.

_____ (1976a), Projection in folklore: A plea for psychoanalytic semiotics. In: *Interpreting Folklore*. Bloomington: Indiana University Press, 1980, pp. 33–61x.

_____ (1976b), A psychoanalytic study of the bullroarer. In: *Interpreting Folklore*. Bloomington: Indiana University Press, 1980, pp. 176–198.

_____ (1976c), "To love my father all": A psychoanalytic study of the folktale source of *King Lear*. In: *Interpreting Folklore*. Bloomington: Indiana University Press, 1980, pp. 211–222.

_____ (1976d), The Crowing Hen and the Easter Bunny: Male chauvinism in American folklore. In: *Interpreting Folklore*. Bloomington: Indiana University Press, 1980, pp. 160–175.

_____ (1977), The curious case of the wide-mouth frog. In: *Interpreting Folklore*. Bloomington: Indiana University Press, 1980, pp. 62–67.

_____ (1978a), Into the endzone for a touchdown: A psychoanalytic consideration of American football. In: *Interpreting Folklore*. Bloomington: Indiana University Press, 1980, pp. 199–210.

_____ (1978b), *Essays in Folkloristics*. Meerut, India: Ved Prakash Vatuk.

_____ (1978c), The hero pattern and the life of Jesus. In: *Interpreting Folklore*. Bloomington: Indiana University Press, 1980, pp. 223–261.

_____ (1979a), The dead baby joke cycle. *Cracking Jokes*. Berkeley: Ten Speed Press, 1987, pp. 3–14.

_____ (1979b), Heads or tails: A psychoanalytic study of Potlatch. In: *Parsing Through Customs*. Madison: The University of Wisconsin Press, 1987, pp. 47–81.

_____ (1980a), Wet and dry, the Evil Eye: An essay in Indo-European and Semitic worldview. In: *Interpreting Folklore*, Alan Dundes. Bloomington: Indiana University Press, pp. 93–133.

_____ (1980b), *Interpreting Folklore*. Bloomington: Indiana University Press.

_____ (1981a), *The Evil Eye: A Folklore Casebook*. New York: Garland.

_____ (1981b), Many hands make light work, or caught in the act of screwing in light bulbs. In: *Cracking Jokes*. Berkeley: Ten Speed Press, 1987, pp. 143–149.

_____ (1982), The symbolic equivalence of allomotifs in the Rabbit-Herd (AT 570). In: *Parsing Through Customs*. Madison: The University of Wisconsin Press, 1987, pp. 167–177.

_____ ed. (1983a), *Cinderella: A Casebook*. New York: Wildman Press.

_____ (1983b), Couvade in Genesis. In: *Parsing Through Customs*. Madison: The University of Wisconsin Press, 1987, pp. 145–166.

_____ ed. (1984a), *Sacred Narrative: Readings in the Theory of Myth*. Berkeley: University of California Press.

_____ (1984b), *Life Is Like a Chicken Coop Ladder: A Portrait of German Culture Through Folklore*. New York: Columbia University Press.

_____ (1985a), The psychoanalytic study of folklore. In: *Parsing Through Customs*. Madison: The University of Wisconsin Press, 1987, pp. 3–46.

_____ (1985b), The J.A.P. and the J.A.M. in American folklore. In: *Cracking Jokes.* Berkeley: Ten Speed Press, 1987, pp. 62–81.

_____ (1985c), The American game of "smear the queer" and the homosexual component of male competitive sport and warfare. In: *Parsing Through Customs.* Madison: The University of Wisconsin Press, 1987, pp. 178–196.

_____ (1987a), *Cracking Jokes.* Berkeley: Ten Speed Press.

_____ (1987b), *Parsing Through Customs.* Madison: The University of Wisconsin Press.

_____ (1987c), The psychoanalytic study of the Grimms' tales with special reference to "The Maiden Without Hands" (AT 706). In: *Folklore Matters.* Knoxville: The University of Tennessee Press, 1989, pp. 112–150.

_____ (1987d), 97 reasons cucumbers are better than men. In: *Cracking Jokes,* Alan Dundes. Berkeley: Ten Speed Press, pp. 82–95.

_____ ED. (1988a), *The Flood Myth.* Berkeley: University of California Press.

_____ (1988b), Interpreting Little Red Riding Hood psychoanalytically. In: *The Brothers Grimm and Folktale,* ed. James M. McGathery. Urbana: University of Illinois, pp. 16–51.

_____ (1989a), *Folklore Matters.* Knoxville: The University of Tennessee Press.

_____ (1989b), The ritual murder or Blood Libel legend: A study of anti-Semitic victimization through projective inversion. *Temenos,* 25:7–32.

_____ (1989c), A folk toy as a source for the study of worldview. In: *Folklore Matters,* Alan Dundes. Knoxville: The University of Tennessee Press, pp. 83–91.

_____ (1991), The psychological study of folklore in the United States, 1880–1980. *South. Folklore,* 98:97–120.

_____ & ABRAHAMS, R. D. (1969), On elephantasy and elephanticide: The effect of time and place. In: *Analytic Essays in Folklore.* The Hague, Netherlands: Mouton, 1975, pp. 192–205.

_____ & FALASSI, A. (1975), *La Terra in Piazza.* Berkeley: University of California Press.

_____ , LEACH, J. W. & ÖZKOK, B. (1970), The strategy of Turkish boys' verbal dueling rhymes. In: *Parsing Through Customs.* Madison: The University of Wisconsin Press, 1987, pp. 118–144.

_____ & PAGTER, C. R. (1975), *Urban Folklore from the Paperwork Empire.* Austin: American Folklore Society.

_____ & _____ (1987), *When You're Up to Your Ass in Alligators: More Urban Folklore from the Paperwork Empire.* Detroit: Wayne State University Press.

_____ & _____ (1991), *Never Try to Teach a Pig to Sing: Still More Urban Folklore from the Paperwork Empire.* Detroit: Wayne State University Press.

EDMUNDS, L. & DUNDES, A., EDS. (1983), *Oedipus: A Folklore Casebook.* New York: Garland.

FREUD, S. & OPPENHEIM, D. E. (1958), *Dreams in Folklore.* New York: International Universities Press.

HASAN-ROKEM, G. & DUNDES, A., eds. (1986), *The Wandering Jew: Essays in the Interpretation of a Christian Legend.* Bloomington: Indiana University Press.

NILES, J. (1989), The Berkeley Contemporary Legend Files. In: *The Questing Beast: Perspectives on Contemporary Legend, Volume IV,* ed. G. Bennet & P. Smith. Sheffield: Sheffield Academic Press, pp. 103–111.

THOMPSON, S. (1955–1958), *Motif-Index of Folk-Literature,* 2nd ed., 6 vols. Bloomington: Indiana University Press.

2

Gallus as Phallus: A Psychoanalytic Cross-Cultural Consideration of the Cockfight as Fowl Play

ALAN DUNDES

The cockfight is one of the oldest, most documented, and most widely distributed traditional sports known to man. It has been reported in ancient India (Sarma, 1964; Bhide, 1967; Chattopadhyay, 1973), ancient China (Cutter, 1989a,b), ancient Iran (Modi, 1911), and ancient Greece (Witte, 1868). From Greece, cockfighting moved to Rome, as mosaics attest (Magaldi, 1929). The earliest recorded cockfight in China dates from 517 B.C. (Cutter, 1989a, p. 632; 1989b, p. 10), which would make cockfighting at least 2500 years old. (See also Danaë, 1989, p. 34, who suggests that cockfighting existed before 2000 B.C.) The antiquity of cockfighting in India is attested by a specific reference in the *Kama Sutra* (3rd century A.D.), Chapter 2 of Part I, where young women are advised to study some 64 arts, of which number 41 includes "The rules of cockfighting," the clear implication being that a woman would be more pleasing to men who are vitally interested in such activities (Vatsyayana, 1963, p. 14).[1]

There is some consensus that the cock itself (and perhaps the cockfight) may have originated in southeast Asia (Peters, 1913, p. 395; Tudela, 1959, p. 14), where it diffused to China, India, and eventually Iran and on to classical Greece and Rome before moving to Western

---

[1] I am indebted to Rafaela Castro Belcher and Margot Winer for their bibliographical surveys of cockfighting compiled in my folklore theory seminars in 1976 and 1986 respectively. For additional references, I am grateful to Jim Anderson, Caroline McCullagh, Judy McCulloh, Dan Melia, and Herb Phillips. I thank folklore archivist Almudena Ortiz for her assistance in translating several Spanish idioms, and my student Mariella Jurg for translating several passages from Dutch to English.

Europe and thence to the Caribbean. The cock may have come to the
New World as early as the second voyage of Christopher Columbus in
1493 (Tudela, 1959, p. 15). From Asia, the cockfight spread eventually
nearly throughout the Americas. The cockfight, however, is by no means
universal, as it seems never to have *spread* to any great extent to native
North and South America or to sub-Saharan Africa.

Once popular in much of western Europe, including England
(Pegge, 1773; Egan, 1832; Boulton, 1901), Scotland (Beattie, 1937);
Ireland (Beacey, 1945; O'Gormon, 1983), and Wales (Peate, 1970),
cockfighting is still to be found in the north of France (Demulder, 1934;
Cegarra, 1988, 1989), in Belgium (Desrousseaux, 1886, 1889, pp.
115-124; Delannoy, 1948; Remouchamps and Remacle, 1949), and in
Spain (Justo, 1969; Marvin, 1984). Nowhere is cockfighting enjoyed
more than in southeast Asia, as is confirmed by reports from Borneo
(Barclay, 1980), Celebes (Kaudern, 1929, pp. 337-348), and Java (Serière, 1873, pp. 92-10; Kreemer, 1893; Soeroto, 1916-1917), Malaysia
(Wilkinson, 1925), the Philippines (Bailey, 1909; Lee, 1921; Lansang,
1966; Guggenheim, 1982), Sarawak (Sandin, 1959), Sumatra (Scheltema,
1919), and, of course, Bali (Eck, 1879; Knight, 1940; Bateson and Mead,
1942; Geertz, 1972; Picard, 1983). Cockfighting is equally popular in the
Caribbean (Challes, 1972), for example, in Martinique (Champagnac,
1970; Affergan, 1986); in Haiti (Paul, 1952; Marcelin, 1955a,b); in Cuba
(Wurdemann, 1844, pp. 87-93; Hazard, 1871, pp. 191-195), and in
Puerto Rico (Alonso, 1849, pp. 77-93; Dinwiddie, 1899; Cadilla de
Martinez, 1941; Calderin, 1970; Feijoo, 1990). There are cockfight
enthusiasts throughout Latin America, for example, in Argentina
(Mantegazza, 1916, pp. 69-71; Saubidet, 1952, pp. 345-356); Brazil
(Leal, 1989); Colombia (Léon Rey, 1953); Mexico (Mendoza, 1943); and
Venezuela (Armas Chitty, 1953-1954; Acosta Saignes, 1954; Marquez,
1954; Perez, 1984; Cook, 1991, pp. 79-94).

In the United States, cockfighting is technically banned in most
states. Nevertheless, we have published accounts of cockfights from
California (Beagle, 1968); Connecticut (Liebling, 1950); Florida
(Vogeler, 1942); Georgia (Hawley, 1987); Louisiana (Del Sesto, 1975;
Hawley, 1982; Donlon, 1991); New York (Hyman, 1950); North Caro-
lina (Roberts, 1965; Herzog, 1985); Tennessee (Cobb, 1978; Gunter,
1978), Texas (Braddy, 1961; Tippette, 1978); Utah (Walker, 1986);
Vermont (Mosher, 1989, pp. 96-102); and Virginia (Anderson, 1933;
Carson, 1965, pp. 151-164), among others.

Some of the abundant literature devoted to cockfighting includes
detailed discussions of the various "rules" that prevail in different locales

(cf. Eck, 1879; Nugent, 1929; Saubidet, 1952, pp. 354–356; Marquez, 1954; Champagnac, 1970, pp. 58–65; Herzog, 1985; Harris, 1987). Other writings are concerned with the elaborate intricacies of breeding and caring for fighting cocks—one source noted 253 different names of breeds and cross-breeds, and this list included only English-language designations (Nugent, 1929, p. 79; see also Jull, 1927; Finsterbusch, 1980). A number of how-to manuals are incredibly specific and include the minutiae of recommended regimen right down to the details of diet (see, e.g., Phillott, 1910; Feijoo, 1990).

The cockfight has been a source of inspiration for a host of poems and short stories (Fraser, 1981; Cutter, 1989b) as well as paintings (Tegetmeier, 1896; Bryden, 1931; Gilbey, 1957; Marçal, 1967, pp. 350–351; Cadet, 1971, pp. 159–165). There is, for example, an entire Irish novel based on cockfighting (O'Gormon, 1983; for an American novel, see Willeford, 1972). Cockfighting has its own folk speech, which has led to the compilation of cockfight slang glossaries (Jaquemotte and Lejeune, 1904; Mendoza, 1943; Saubidet, 1952, pp. 345–354; León Rey, 1953; Marcelin, 1955b; Perez, 1984, pp. 17–78). In English, too, the cockfight has provided a rich set of metaphors for everyday life. The phrases "to turn tail," "to raise one's hackle(s)," and "to show the white feather" are some of the most familiar (Scott, 1957, pp. 118–119). Similarly, to be "cocky" or "cocksure" or to be "cock of the walk" (Gilbey, 1957, p. 24) and perhaps "to pit" someone against another presumably derive ultimately from the lexicon of cockfighting. There is one etymology, possibly a folk etymology, for the word "cocktail," that supposedly comes from "cock ale" or a liquid concoction designed to serve as a tonic to strengthen fighting cocks (Nugent, 1929, p. 80). It is also tempting to ponder the possible metaphorical associations of the "cock" found in guns (as in "Don't go off half-cocked") or in pipes where cocks regulate the flow of liquids (or gases). Among the more esoteric cockfighting traditions that have been studied are the names of fighting cocks in Brazil (Teixeira, 1992) and the folk art motifs used to decorate the carrying boxes used in northern Utah (Walker, 1986, pp. 39–41).

Most considerations of cockfighting invariably cite the classical instance of Themistocles, who was leading his Athenian army against the Persians in the fifth century B.C. when he chanced to see some cocks fighting. His alleged, but oft-quoted, remarks were: "These animals fight not for the gods of their country, nor for the monuments of their ancestors, nor for glory, nor for freedom, nor for their children, but for the sake of victory, and that one may not yield to the other" (Pegge, 1773, p. 137). This impromptu speech supposedly inspired and rallied the troops of Themistocles. (The standard source is Aelian, *Varia Historia* 2:28; cf. Bruneau, 1965, p. 107.)

Particular techniques are found in specific local cockfighting traditions. Some of these seem to be quite ancient. For example, there is an arcane system of cockfighting lore in the Philippines that suggests that there are definite times of the day that favor cocks of a particular color (Guggenheim, 1982, p. 11). This set of associations of calendar and cock color is almost certainly related to a complex "cock almanac" reported in south India (Saltore, 1926–1927, pp. 319–324).

The most common form of cockfight involves a one-on-one confrontation between two equally matched cocks, a battle that may be interspersed with standard periods of respite. Yet there is considerable variation within the one-to-one scenario. For example, a 19th-century account of cockfighting in Cuba summarizes some of the alternatives:

> There are various modes of fighting: *Al cotejo* — that is, in measuring, at sight, the size or spurs of both chickens. *Al peso* — or by weight, and seeing if the spurs are equal. *Tapados* — where they settle the match without seeing the chickens, or, in fact, "go it blind." *De cuchilla* — when they put on the artificial spurs, in order to make the fight sharper, quicker, and more fatal. *Al pico* — when they fight without any spurs [Hazard, 1871, pp. 192–193].

There were other, more elaborate forms of cockfighting. These include the battle royal and the Welsh main, once popular in England. We may cite an 18th-century description of these special forms of cockfighting:

> What aggravates the reproach and the disgrace upon us Englishmen, is those species of fighting which are called the Battle-royal, and the Welsh-main, known nowhere in the world, as I think, but here; neither in China, nor in Persia, nor in Malacca, nor amongst the savage tribes of America. These are scenes so bloody as almost to be too shocking to relate; and yet, as many may not be acquainted with the horrible nature of them, it may be proper, for the excitement of our aversion and detestation, to describe them in a few words. In the former an unlimited number of fowls are pitted; and when they have slaughtered one another for the diversion, dii boni! of the otherwise generous and humane Englishman, the single surviving bird is to be esteemed the victor, and carries away the prize. The Welsh-main consists, we will suppose,

of sixteen pair of cocks; of these the sixteen conquerors are pitted a second time; the eight conquerors of these are pitted a third time; so that, incredible barbarity! thirty one cocks are sure to be most inhumanly murdered for the sport and pleasure, the noise and nonsense, nay, I must say, the profane cursing and swearing, of those who have the effrontery to call themselves, with all these bloody doings, and with all this impiety about them, *Christians* [Pegge, 1773, pp. 148–149; see also Boulton, 1901, pp. 189–190].

As the unmistakable tone of the preceding passage reminds us, a large part of the mass of writings devoted to the cockfight concerns the question of whether the sport should be banned on the grounds of excessive cruelty to animals. According to one source (Powel, 1937, p. 191), the Society for the Prevention of Cruelty to Animals insists that the cockfight "is a blot on civilization's fair escutcheon." Typical strategy of the humane protest against cockfighting consists of simply describing cockfights in gory detail:

In almost every fight at least one cock is seriously mutilated or killed. In about half of the fights, more or less, *both* birds are maimed beyond further use if not killed. Eyes are gouged out, abdomens slit and slashed until the birds are anguished monstrosities, legs and wings are broken. But so long as a bird can and will keep facing towards the opposing cock he is left in the pit and cheered for his "courage" [Anon., 1952, p. 11; cf. Hawley, 1989].

Of course, the cockfighting community has fought back. One of their common arguments is that cockfighting is much less cruel than other sports, less cruel, for example, than boxing, in which men may be maimed or even killed. In England, cockfighting, which is illegal, is compared to foxhunting, which is legal, by one cocker as follows: "Cockfighting isn't as unfair as foxhunting, you see. One of my cocks has a 50–50 chance of winning. What chance has a fox got when there are fifty hounds chasing him? A million to one shot of getting away" (Penrose, 1976, p. 236). Another standard argument is that cocks are naturally inclined to fight. And that man is only facilitating or expanding on what occurs by itself in nature. Even the use of gaffs or blades is defended on the grounds that they are "used solely to end a fight quickly, and the winner will then return to his harem to propagate his species whilst the loser will die the death he has chosen" (Jarvis, 1939, p. 378). Incidentally, there are many different types of gaffs, for instance "brike special, skeleton, split socket, bayonet, jagger, regulation, and hoisters" (Jones, 1980, p. 144).

Another argument put forth by cockfighters is "that it is impossible to make a cock fight an adversary if the bird does not wish to fight. . . . If at the particular moment the joy of battle is not in him, neither skill by the 'setter' nor insult by the adversary will make him fight. The game-cock is never an unwilling gladiator" (James, 1928, p. 140). Yet another popular argument is that people raise chickens to be slaughtered for food—think of all the fried chicken franchises in the United States alone. Is that more cruel to the species than cockfighting? Cockfighters are wont to point out that chickens raised for market may be slaughtered when they are anywhere from eight to ten weeks of age. In contrast, a gamecock

> will not even be fought before he's one year old and during that one year, he will receive excellent care. . . . Many are retired to stud after only three or four wins. The question seems to be whether it is less cruel for the cock to be killed by a man rather than by another cock [Tippette, 1978, p. 274; see also Allred and Carver, 1979, p. 59].

Despite continuing efforts to ban the cockfight, there are places where cockfighting is legalized. In the north of France near the Belgian border there are 32 authorized "gallodromes" (Cegarra, 1989, p. 671). Even in places where cockfighting is officially illegal, it thrives.

While the vast majority of the written reports of cockfighting tends to be purely descriptive and not the least bit analytic, there is a small body of literature that seeks to interpret the cockfight. Of these, unquestionably the most famous is Clifford Geertz's (1972) "Deep Play: Notes on the Balinese Cockfight." This essay marks a turning point in the history of cockfight scholarship. All modern writing on the subject is directly or indirectly derived from Geertz's discussion of the Balinese material. Geertz argued in his interpretation of the cockfight "the general thesis is that the cockfight, and especially the deep cockfight, is fundamentally a dramatization of status concerns" (p. 18). According to Geertz,

> What sets the cockfight apart from the ordinary course of life . . . [is] that it provides a metasocial commentary upon the whole matter of assorting human beings into fixed hierarchical ranks and then organizing the major part of collective existence around that assortment [p. 26].

Geertz thus interpreted the cockfight exclusively in terms of Balinese social organization or social structure.

Geertz's reading of the Balinese cockfight has attained the status of a modern classic in anthropology (Watson, 1989) although it has received some criticism (Roseberry, 1982; Parker, 1985; Schneider, 1987). Anthropologist James A. Boon (1977), an expert on Balinese ethnography who is understandably reluctant to criticize one of his former mentors, remarked that "Geertz does not survey the range of Balinese cockfights; rather he telescopes repeated observations into an ideal-typical description of a choice elaboration of the form in one village area" (p. 33). More severe is Vincent Crapanzano (1986), who although very admiring of Geertz's "interpretive virtuosity" (pp. 53, 75) contends that Geertz offered his own subjective interpretation of the Balinese cockfight. Moreover, Crapanzano argues, Geertz presented little or no empirical evidence in support of *his* interpretation (pp. 72–75). Crapanzano concludes there is "no understanding of the native from the native's point of view. There is only the constructed understanding of the constructed native's constructed point of view" and that Geertz's "interpretation is simply not convincing" (p. 74; see also Fine, 1992).

Crapanzano's critique is echoed by Jacobson (1991), who maintains that Geertz made assertions unsupported by ethnographic data.

> Yet no evidence presented warrants conclusions about how Balinese think or feel about themselves or their society. Whereas the language and rules of the cockfight are described in detail, perceptions are simply attributed to Balinese. In short, Geertz develops his interpretation of the interpretive function of the Balinese cockfight by stating and restating his claims without providing data that substantiate them. He presents no evidence for accepting his reading of the "text" [pp. 52–53].

Unlike Crapanzano and Jacobson, anthropologist Scott Guggenheim (1982) has himself made an ethnographic study of a cockfight, in this case in the Philippines. Guggenheim agrees with Geertz that cockfighting is a "cultural performance" (p. 29), but he disagrees that the cockfight provides an indigenous or native model of social structure or status hierarchy. In some ways, Guggenheim argues, the cockfight in the Philippines is "strikingly blind to social reality" and the cockfight as folk model "skews social reality" (p. 29). In this context,

> There is, for example, no mention of women, despite women's prominent role not only in household management, but in mar-

keting agriculture, wage-earning labor, professional occupations, and politics. Nor does it say very much about what all those high ranking people do to deserve their positions, besides buying expensive chickens [p. 29].

The theoretical issue here, with respect to the role and function of folklore in culture — and the cockfight is an example of folklore: it is a traditional game or sport — is that the old-fashioned Boasian notion of "folklore as culture reflector," which wrongly assumed a one-to-one relationship between folklore and culture is inadequate. Folklore, to be sure, does articulate and sometimes enforces the norms of a culture, but it also, often at the same time, offers a socially sanctioned *escape* from those norms. This is what Bascom (1954) called the paradoxical double function of folklore (p. 349). To the extent that folklore involves fantasy, and I believe that it does to a very great extent, the literal one-to-one relationship posited between folklore and culture automatically assumed by a majority of anthropologists and folklorists is doomed to failure as a methodological principle designed to illuminate the content of folkloristic phenomena. Just as anthropologists inevitably assume that myths provide a "charter" for belief in social organization, à la Malinowski's literal, antisymbolic theory of myth, so Geertz and others wrongly interpret the cockfight as a charter or articulation of social structure, status hierarchy in particular. Guggenheim (1982) is on the right track in pointing out that the cockfight in the Philippines hardly qualifies as a model of normal Filipino social structure — why are women left out of the cockfight, he asks? But like other anthropologists who have considered the cockfight, he fails to appreciate its obvious and overt symbolism.

Although Guggenheim pays the usual social anthropological lip service to symbolism, his conclusions show that he too has missed the basic underlying significance of the cockfight: "Taken as a symbolic system, cockfighting successfully couples individual self-identity and self-esteem, social and political loyalties, and even aesthetic satisfaction to an elegant and exciting event" (p. 30). How do Geertz's and Guggenheim's interpretations of the cockfight compare with other anthropological analyses of the same event? Del Sesto (1980) sees the cockfight as "a symbolic representation of man's continual struggle for survival, as displays of courage and bravado in the face of adversity, and as attempts to understand the meaning and suffering of death" (p. 275). Parker (1986) claims that "the cockfight can be seen as a contest that is totally concerned with violence, competition, and aggression" (p. 26). Several ethnographers have sensed the importance of the masculine elements inherent in the cockfight. Marvin (1984), in his study of the Andalusian cockfight, sees it as a confirmation of male values:

> In all conversations concerning the cockfight those involved with the event emphasized that it was *una cosa de hombres* (a men's thing). It is a totally male-oriented event, the audience is almost totally male, the birds which fight are male and the virtues which are extolled are male virtues [p. 64].

Marvin concludes, "The cockfight, though, is a celebration in that it is an event which extols certain aspects of masculinity" (p. 68).

This view is echoed by Leal (1989), one of the few women to analyze the cockfight. In a superb ethnographic account, she also suggests that "cockfighting is a celebration of masculinity where men, through their cocks, dispute, win, lose and reinforce certain attributes chosen as male essence" (p. 210). This report from Brazil reaches conclusions similar to those of another female ethnographer who investigated cockfighting in northern France near the Belgian border. The latter confirms the masculinity aspect: "cockfights represent only one exclusive part of human society, that of the virile element" (Cegarra, 1988, p. 55). Similarly, Danaë in his magisterial survey of cockfighting worldwide concludes with a discussion of cockfighters as an esoteric masculine society (1989, pp. 227-247). Affergan in his study of cockfighting in Martinique claims it is an outlet for male identity and aggression by male members of an oppressed group (1986, p. 120) while Kimberley Cook in her analysis of cockfighting in Venezuela sees it as a "ritualistic form of aggression" where men vie to gain public recognition of their virility (1991, pp. 89-90).

All those interpretations of the cockfight, in my opinion, are flawed to some extent. Perhaps the most obvious methodological weakness is the failure to employ a comparative, cross-cultural perspective. The quintessential anthropological credo of cultural relativism notwithstanding, it is always a mistake to study data from one particular culture as if it were peculiar to that culture if comparable, if not cognate, data exist in other cultures. The cockfight is found outside of Bali, the Philippines, Louisiana, Tennessee, Brazil, northern France, Martinique, and Venezuela. Hence any would-be interpretation of the cockfight based on data from just one of these locations is bound to be inadequate. Let us assume, strictly for the sake of argument, that Geertz's interpretation of the Balinese cockfight as a "native" representation of Balinese status concerns is correct. If so, what, if anything, does this tell us about about the possible significance of the cockfight in all of the other many cultures in which the cockfight occurs? Balinese social structure is not to be found in Puerto Rico or Belgium. The point is that if an item of folklore has cross-cultural distribution, it must be studied from a cross-cultural perspective, especially if one is interested in possible symbolic aspects. This does not mean that the cockfight necessarily means the same thing in all of its cultural contexts — although this cannot be ruled out a priori. The study of a cross-cultural phenomenon in just one cultural context is clearly a limited, partial one. In that sense, all previous studies of the cockfight have been limited and partial.

Along with the plea for a larger comparative perspective to view the cockfight, I suggest that the cockfight itself cannot be understood without being seen as an exemplar of a more comprehensive paradigm involving male gladiatorial combat. There are many forms of male battle running the gamut from simple children's games to all-out war. It is my contention that the cockfight can best be analyzed as part and parcel of that paradigm.

Accordingly, let us begin our consideration of the cockfight as an instance of the broad category of male competitive games and sports. I believe one can discern a common underlying symbolic structure shared by most if not all such activities. It might be useful to distinguish three basic variants with respect to the nature of the participants. The first would be human male versus human male. This category includes fencing, boxing, wrestling, tennis, badminton, and ping-pong and such board games as chess and checkers. By extension, it could also subsume male team sports such as football, soccer, hockey, lacrosse, basketball, and so on. The second category would be human male versus male animal. Perhaps the classic illustration of this category is the bullfight. The third category would be male animal versus male animal. Here the obvious example is the cockfight.

It is my contention that all of those games and sports are essentially variations on one theme. The theme involves an all-male preserve in which one male demonstrates his virility, his masculinity, *at the expense of a male opponent*. One proves one's maleness by feminizing one's opponent. Typically, the victory entails (no pun intended!) penetration. In American football, the winning group of males get into their opponents' "end zones" more times than their opponents get into their end zones (see Dundes, 1987, pp. 178–194). In the bullfight, the battle of man against bull is to determine whether the matador penetrates the bull or whether the bull's horns penetrate the matador. The penetrator comes away triumphant and with his masculinity intact; the one *penetrated* loses his masculinity. In the case of the bullfight, the expertise and skill of the matador can be rewarded with different degrees of symbolic castration of the bull. The bull, if penetrated cleanly and dextrously, may have his hooves, ears, or tail cut off to be "presented" to the successful matador.

The cockfight, despite its great antiquity and its continued popularity into the 20th century, has never been properly understood as male phallic combat. Despite an enormous literature devoted to the cockfight ranging from vivid descriptions to purported analyses, there is to my knowledge no single discussion that takes adequate account of the symbolic nature of the contest. I should like to test my hypothesis that the cockfight is a thinly disguised symbolic homoerotic masturbatory phallic duel, with the winner emasculating the loser through castration or feminization. I believe that the evidence for this interpretation is overwhelmingly abundant and cross-cultural in nature. Nevertheless, it seems to me that the symbolic meaning of the cockfight is not consciously recognized either by those who participate in the event or those who have written about it. The sole exception is Cook's chapter on cockfighting on the island of Margarita off the coast of Venezuela in her 1991 doctoral dissertation when she remarks "that when two individual men fight cocks and one loses, the loser assumes a feminine role" (1991, p. 98; see also Affergan, 1986, p. 119. Baird [1981–1982, p. 83] claims that among the ancient Greeks the cockfight symbolized homosexual rape.)

Let us first consider the gallus as phallus. In all of the many essays and monographs devoted to cockfighting, only a few actually comment on the phallic nature of the cocks. Scott (1941) in a paragraph in his survey volume *Phallic Worship* does mention the phallic significance of the cock (p. 262), but in his full-length history of cockfighting (Scott, 1957), he drew no inferences from this. In Geertz's (1972) essay, which was first presented at a conference held in Paris in October of 1970, we are told:

> To anyone who has been in Bali any length of time, the deep psychological identification of Balinese men with their cocks is unmistakable. The double entendre here is deliberate. It works in exactly the same way in Balinese as it does in English, even to producing the same tired jokes, strained puns, and uninventive obscenities [p. 5].

It is a pity that Geertz was not a bit more ethnographically specific here inasmuch as he failed to give even a single example of the "tired

jokes" and "uninventive obscenities." Tired jokes and uninventive obscenities constitute valuable folkloristic data that any journeyman folklorist fluent in the language would have almost certainly recorded. Geertz
(1972) does cite Bateson and Mead's (1942) contention that the Balinese
conception of the body "as a set of separately animated parts" allows
them to view cocks as "detachable, self-operating penises, ambulant
genitals with a life of their own" (p. 5), but then claims that he does "not
have the kind of unconscious material either to confirm or disconfirm
this intriguing notion." Again, one regrets his failure to collect the jokes,
puns, and obscenities available to him. So, although Geertz did nomi-
nally acknowledge that cocks "are masculine symbols *par excellence*"
among the Balinese, this fact did not play a major part in his interpretation of the cockfight as a whole.

The English word "cock," meaning both rooster and phallus, is the
subject of wit among cockfighters in the United States. According to
Hawley (1982), "One Florida informant was heard to say 'My cock may
not be the biggest, but it's the best in this county." Apparently such
double meanings were so common as to make older cockers use the term
"rooster" in mixed company (p. 105; see also Baird, 1981).

Among the various surveys of the folklore of cocks (e.g., Gittée, 1891;
Fehrle, 1912; Rasch, 1930; and Coluccio, 1970), only a few bother to
mention the cock as a symbol of virility (Castillo de Lucas, 1970, pp.
363-364; Cadet, 1971, p. 109). The phallic associations of the rooster,
even apart from its apparent potential for magical resuscitation in
cockfighting, explains why the cock was a logical, if not psychologically
obvious, choice as a symbol for resurrection (Modi, 1911, p. 112).
Resurrection, if understood as reerection, or even in the narrow Christian sense of rising miraculously from the dead, is perfectly understandable in cockfight terms. There are numerous reports in the cockfight
literature of a cock, apparently totally vanquished and lying motionless,
somehow managing to recover sufficiently to arise and earn a victory
over its opponent. This phallic symbolism would help explain why the
cock is so often found atop penile Christian architectural constructions
such as church towers, often in the form of weather-vanes which
pointedly mark wind direction (see Callisen, 1939; Kretzenbacher, 1957;
Cadet, 1971, pp. 166-168, 199-204; see also Forsyth, 1978 and Baird,
1981-1982). The same rationale would illuminate the occurrence of a
cockfight motif on sarcophagi and other funerary monuments (Bruneau,
1965, p. 115; Forsyth, 1978, pp. 262-264).

Occasional comments indicate that cockfighting is analogous to
sexuality. In a Filipino cockfighting manual we are told, "An ideal cock

must be able to top a hen several times before letting her get up, because sex and gameness complement each other. . . . Indeed, no other sport has as much connection with sex as cockfighting" (Lansang, 1966, pp. 41, 59, 139). The explicit anthropomorphic projection upon roosters and chickens in the Philippines is such that a strict double standard is maintained. Cocks are expected to indulge themselves, but hens are considered to be "sexually promiscuous" (p. 151), and breeders must keep close watch over hens in the barnyard "because the hen is a natural whore" (p. 140).

Similar male chauvinism is found in other descriptions of chickens and roosters:

Females are strongly sexual and thus impulsive. Their actions are instinctively generated by feelings, and they need the presence of a male. They are amorous. Nature made them so and provided that their actions be governed by their sexual impulses. Males are cooler in disposition and have developed a different brain. They act according to logic. Females act impulsively [Finsterbusch, 1980, p. 166].

Hard to believe that these are descriptions of chickens and roosters, and not humans!

It is likely that the symbolic equation of cock and human phallus exists regardless of whether or not the term for "rooster" in a given culture refers explicitly to the male organ. In Spanish and Portuguese, for example, we are told that this verbal equation does not exist. However, in Brazil, a "tea of cock's spurs is recommended for sexual potency" (Leal, 1989, p. 241). In an Arabic tract from the 13th century we learn, "If you take a cock's blood and mix it with honey, and place it on the fire, and apply the mixture to the penis of a man, it will increase his virile power as well as his sexual enjoyment" (Phillott, 1910, p. 91). Moreover, if a woman ate a cock's testicles after intercourse, she greatly increased her chances of becoming pregnant (Smith and Daniel, 1975, p. 54; Hawley, 1982, p. 106). In other words, the customs and belief system make the connection between rooster and phallus perfectly clear. There are also numerous winged phallic amulets in the shape of cocks (Baird, 1981-1982, p. 84).

The sexual component is alluded to only en passant by most writers on cockfights, if it is mentioned at all. In an essay in *Esquire,* Crews (1977) remarked that when a man's cock quits in the pit, he suffers profound humiliation, *When a man's cock quits!* Yes, that's part of the ritual, too.

Perhaps the biggest part. A capon — a rooster that has been castrated to improve the taste of the meat — seldom crows, never notices hens, and will hit nothing with spur or beak. But a game fowl is the ultimate blend of balls and skill, all of which is inextricably bound up with the man who bred it and fed it and handled it in the pit (p. 8). Attributing "balls" to cocks is not all that unusual. In Andalusia, for example, according to Marvin (1984, p. 66), men may say admiringly of an especially aggressive cock "tienes los cojones de ganar bien [it has the balls to win well]" (p. 65). The same idiom is found in Nathanael West's account of a cockfight in *The Day of the Locust* when the Mexican cocker Miguel praises a red rooster: "That's a bird with lots of cojones" (West, 1950, p. 123). One difficulty in "proving" the sexual component of the cockfight lies in the fact that such a component is largely unconscious. Consequently, it is not easy to obtain informant confirmation of the symbolism through interviews. Wollan (1980) phrased the problem as follows:

> How much of this symbolism is present in modern cockfighting, and how much of it would be understood by cockers themselves, is difficult to say. How to research the topic is equally puzzling. Conversation promises to yield little information about cockfighting as a symbol, and certainly nothing about its sexual dimensions. Hence, interpretation of a sort not commonly done, certainly not in fashion in the social sciences, would seem indispensable [p. 28].

Hawley, whose 1982 Florida State doctoral dissertation in criminology sought to define cockfighters as a deviant subculture, claimed that in his field experience "sexual entendre was encountered infrequently. . . . However, the implicit sexual nature of the activity was omnipresent" (p. 104). Still, he admitted, "Sexual animism was definitely the most difficult cultural theme to study in any fashion systematically or haphazardly . . . a ticklish subject to study in the field under the best of conditions" (pp. 107, 147). Hawley himself does not doubt "the significance of the cock as a symbol of aggressive, male-oriented sexual behavior." In his words, "The cock is, to all appearances, a walking unselfconscious set of eager genitals . . . the cock represents male sexuality raised (or lowered) to the most primitive extremity." But, Hawley remarks, "the obvious sexual significance of the cock is characteristically ignored by the cocking fraternity in all but the most casual and relaxed settings" (p. 121). Hawley might have added the anthropological and folkloristic fraternities as well.

Yet the sexual symbolic significance of the "cock" is attested by countless bawdy jokes. One exemplar can stand for many: Q. What is the difference between a rooster and Marilyn Monroe? A. A rooster says "Cock-a-doodle-do." Marilyn Monroe says "Any cock'll do." It may or may not be relevant that St. Augustine in his interesting fourth century discussion of cockfights discusses them in a paragraph that begins with a consideration of the sexual organs of animals which one cannot bear to look at (Russell, 1942, p. 95).

If we accept the premise that the gallus can symbolically be a phallus, and if we provisionally accept the possibility that there is an underlying sexual component in the cockfight, we must next emphasize that the cockfight is an all-male event. Women do not usually attend cockfights. An early 18th-century account of cockfighting in England specifically remarks that "ladies never assist at these sports" (Saussure, 1902, p. 282). Geertz (1972) even bothers to comment that "the cockfight is unusual within Balinese culture in being a single-sex public activity from which the other sex is totally and expressly excluded" (p. 30n). Even in those cultures where women are permitted to observe cockfights, they are not active participants and do not handle the cocks. Some women resent their virtual exclusion from the world of cockfighting, and they resent as well the extraordinary amount of time their male companions devote to that world. From northern France we have a report of a female reproach that carries an overt sexual connotation: "He holds his cocks more often than he holds me" (Cegarra, 1988, p. 58). Also from northern France, we find a distinction between women who may kill chickens as part of preparing food and men who are involved in cockfights. The fighting cock is a wild animal whose death, necessarily violent, is symbolic. The arming of cocks for battle is an affair of men, not women, and should not be confused with the domestic household requirement of killing chickens for food (p. 59)

The separation from women in cockfights is also signaled by the fact that the roosters themselves are not permitted access to hens during the period immediately preceding a cockfight. This form of quarantine is surely analogous to the modern-day football coach's forbidding his players to spend the night before a game with their wives or girlfriends, or to a bullfighter's sexual abstinence the night before a bullfight. Here is an account of the training of roosters in the Texas–Mexico area:

The most important experience of the young stag commences when his trainer moves him from his solitary cage and places him in a hennery. There he bosses his harem of hens, living and learning the

meaning of his cockhood. Later, when the trainer takes him away
from the pullets, the cockerel turns into a bird of Mars. Now he has
a lust to fight, his lust arising from his strong sex drive [Braddy,
1961, p. 103].

In another account from Texas, we are informed, "They have had no
food this morning, and for two weeks have been penned up and deprived
of female company" (Gard, 1936, p. 66).

In the Philippines, "it is a mistake to release your stag in a place where
too many hens are kept, for so many hens make him tread often, and
much treading greatly debilitates a bird and makes him feeble when he
comes to fight" (Lansang, 1966, p. 61). We learn that in Martinique
sexual abstinence during the cocks' training is strict and that one makes
a concerted effort to keep hens away from the cages in which the cocks
are contained the evening before or the day of the cockfight for fear the
cocks will dissipate their energies (Affergan, 1986, p. 114). In the north
of France, too, keeping the cock in isolation away from females is
suppose to increase his aggressivity tenfold (Cegarra, 1989, p. 673).

In Brazil, cocks

> are not permitted sexual intercourse for long periods before
> fighting. . . . It is believed that sexual abstinence will give it the
> strength and will to fight, and that decreased sexual activity will
> create better quality semen. The underlying assumption is that
> sexual intercourse or even contact with a female will turn the male
> into a weaker being [Leal, 1989, p. 238].

In some traditions, the handler as well as the cock must abstain from
heterosexual intercourse. In the Philippines, "sex should be avoided
before going to the cockpit; the man stupid enough to have sex before a
match will be ignominiously humiliated when his bird runs away."
However, "Sex is heartily recommended for after the fight, when men no
longer need conserve their vital energies" (Guggenheim 1982, p. 10).

The renunciation of heterosexuality in conjunction with the cockfight
seems to support the idea that the cockfight is an all-male, or homosexual, affair. Thus, if the gallus is a phallus and if there is a sexual
component to the cockfight, it is a matter played out between two sets of
males: roosters and men. In this sexual battle, one begins with *two* males,
but ends with *one* male and *one* female. Is there any evidence to support
this contention? In Malaysia, the term used for matching two roosters
for a forthcoming fight may be relevant. "The stakes are all deposited

with a stake-holder (who receives a percentage for his good services); and the cocks are plighted or 'betrothed' to one another by the simple ceremony of allowing each bird one single peck at its rival" (Wilkinson, 1925, p. 65). The curious idiomatic usage of the word "betrothal" – the author does not provide the Malay native term – for the matching of two male cocks is significant. They are mates, analogous to heterosexual humans, but the fight is to determine which one will be the male and which the "female." In Bali, according to Bateson and Mead (1942), "In speaking of real courtship, the Balinese liken the behavior of boy and girl to that of two cocks straining toward each other with their heads down and their hackle feathers up" (p. 172). That the Malay term and Balinese image are not flukes is corroborated by a parallel custom in Martinique in which the two cocks to be paired in combat are said to be joined in "marriage" (Champagnac, 1970, p. 72; Affergan, 1986, p. 115).

In one of the finest ethnographic accounts of the cockfight to date, Leal (1989) describes the crowd's cheers during a typical Brazilian bout.

During a fight every movement of the cock is followed by the crowd's cheers of "go ahead! Mount him! [*Monta nele! Trepa nele!*]." Inasmuch as to *mount* or *to climb* (trepar) are also expressions commonly used to refer to sexual intercourse, usually implying the man's position in the sexual act, the crowd's cheers are not only metaphorical [pp. 217–218].

Here is certainly incontrovertible evidence supporting the equation of "gallus as phallus." Leal even recorded a folk poem that confirms the already explicit erotic significance of "mounting":

Quien tuviera la suerte	Who would have the luck
que tiene el gallo	that the cock has,
que en medio de la juria	that in the middle of the fight
monta a caballo.	to be mounted on a horse
	[p. 218]

The allusions to courtship, marriage, and mounting do underscore the sexual nuances of the cockfight, but what evidence is there to support the proposition that the loser in a cockfight is deemed a female?

In a cockfight, sometimes a cock will freeze in the face of a feared opponent. This so-called tonic immobility (Herzog, 1978) might simply be a desperate defense mechanism, that is, playing dead to prevent the dominant cock from attacking further. More commonly, a cock that loses its nerve may choose to flee. In an account from Texas, we are told:

> When a beaten gamebird decides to withdraw from the battle, he lifts his hackle, showing to the spectators the white feathers underlying his ruff. This act gave rise to the famous expression "showing the white feather," which symbolizes cowardice [Braddy, 1961, pp. 103–104].

In the north of France, a cock that flees, crying, is immediately declared to have lost if his opponent is standing (Demulder, 1934, p. 13). Such flight and such crying are deemed cowardly acts. In Belgium, too, a cock that starts crying is declared vanquished (Jaquemotte and Lejeune, 1904, p. 226). In the mid-19th century, the pioneering Italian anthropologist and sexologist Paolo Mantegazza, perhaps best known for his Frazerian survey, *The Sexual Relations of Mankind* (1916), visited Argentina, where he described a cockfight. He remarked on the different ways the fight could end. One way involved an exit from the arena "siempre abierta para los cobardes" [always open for cowards] in which a bloody and beaten rooster might sing, calling for aid from the hens of his harem (p. 69).

There is even better evidence that winning in a cockfight is associated with masculinity, whereas losing is considered to belong to the realm of the feminine. In Venezuela, one may hear a spectator yell, "Vamos, como tu padre! [Let's go, like your father!]" to exhort a cock to do better (Marquez, 1954, p. 45); in Brazil, during a cockfight one may hear comments referring to the losing cock along the lines of "the mother's blood is showing" (Leal, 1989, p. 216).

In Colombia, a cock that runs away is thought to cry like a chicken (León Rey, 1953, p. 93). In Mexico, to be a "gallo-gallina," a rooster-hen, is to be a coward or homosexual (Mendoza, 1943, p. 123). In Venezuela, there is a general folk belief that a rooster who "clucks" like a chicken is a sure sign of an imminent disgrace (Acosta Saignes, 1954, p. 39). In Andalusia, too, a cock may lose a fight by fleeing from its opponent while making a low clucking sound. This is called "canta la gallina," which may be translated as "the hen sings" (Marvin, 1984). Anthropologist Marvin astutely observes, "What should be noted here is not only does the bird flee but it also makes what is perceived to be the sound of a hen, a female. This behavior is regarded as reprehensible, for the cock is not acting as a true male" (p. 64). Here is prima facie evidence that the loser in the Andalusian cockfight is considered to be a chicken rather than a rooster, a female rather than a male. In Borneo, we find a possible parallel; we are told that "occasionally the bird was "chicken," and ran after the first scuffle (Barclay, 1980, p. 18) although it is not altogether certain whether "chicken" is a native-language term in Borneo or not. The placing of it in single quotes suggests, however, that it might be. Of course, in American folk speech, to be "chicken" is to be cowardly, especially among a group of male peers.

The feminization of the loser in a cockfight cannot really be disputed. In Martinique, there is a proverb "Kavalie vol a dam," which presumably has a literal meaning of "a cavalier flies to a lady [dame]." The proverb refers to the fact that there must always be an adversary for a cock, but, more important in the present context, that a good cock never hesitates to fly toward his opponent (as does a man toward a woman). The winning cock affirms his maleness, his virility, while the loser is forced to take the female role with a strongly negative connotation. It is clearly preferable to be a true female than a false (effeminate) male (Affergan, 1986, p. 119). Also in Martinique we find the idiom "faire la poule" (to be chicken) applied to a cock who cowers in front of an opponent, refusing to fight (Champagnac, 1970, p. 35). Leal (1989) reports that in Brazil, if a losing rooster attempts to run from the pit *"crying like a chicken [cacarejando feito galinha]*," this would constitute the worst kind of dishonor to the cock's owner and supporters since "symbolically at that moment the cock and the men become females." *Chicken* is a slang term for both "loose woman" and coward (p. 211). Such data support our contention that the losing cock in a cockfight becomes feminized, becomes a chicken.

Other details of the cockfight take on new significance in the light of the argument here proposed. These details include specific techniques designed to stimulate or revive a wounded cock. Prefight preparation sometimes involved inserting stimulants in prescribed orifices. For example, in Bali, according to Geertz (1972), red pepper might be stuffed down a cock's beak or up its anus to give it spirit (p. 6). Guggenheim (1982) reported that in the Philippines "sticking chili up the anus" (p. 10) was thought to increase the cock's "natural ferocity." In Belgium, just before a fight a cock might be given a piece of sugar soaked in cognac (Remouchamps and Remacle, 1949, p. 65).

Another prefight ritual is reported from Haiti. There, in order to convince the judge that no poison has been placed on a particular cock's spurs—poison that would unfairly eliminate the opposing cock if it entered its bloodstream—the cock's handler will suck the spurs of his cock and perhaps also the beak and neck of his bird as well (Marcelin,

1955b, p. 59). For the same practice in the Philippines, see Roces, 1959, pp. 65-66; for Martinique, see Affergan, 1986, p. 115. There also the cock is forced to drink the water in which he is bathed. This is similar to a technique in southern Louisiana where an official uses a wet cotton ball to wipe the metal gaffs after which he squeezes water drops into the cock's mouth (Donlon, 1991, p. 106). In Venezuela, Cook (1991, p. 92) notes the poison is applied at the last minute, right before the fight starts because otherwise the cock with the poisoned spur might accidentally scratch itself.

This practice is reasonable enough, but a similar one used to resuscitate wounded cocks during a fight requires a different rationale. In Bali, during breaks in the fight, handlers are permitted to touch their birds to revive them. The handler "blows in its mouth, putting the whole chicken head in his own mouth and sucking and blowing, fluffs it, stuffs its wounds with various sorts of medicines, and generally tries anything he can think of to arouse the last ounce of spirit which may be hidden somewhere within it" (Geertz, 1972, p. 9). An earlier account of cockfighting in Bali confirms that the handlers try to revive their cocks' "ardour by petting, massage or by blowing into their beaks" (Knight, 1940, p. 81), This means of "sucking the wounds of an injured cock is one of the oldest prescriptions for healing a bird" (Smith and Daniel, 1975, p. 86). A physician traveling in Cuba in the mid-19th century confirmed the practice as he reported seeing owners "sucking the whole bleeding head repeatedly" (Wurdemann, 1844, p. 92). The technique continues to be popular and is reported from Tennessee (Gunter, 1978, p. 166; Cobb, 1978, p. 92) and Texas (Braddy, 1961, p. 105) among other places. Literary critic Stanley Edgar Hyman (1950), describing a cockfight he attended in Saratoga Springs, New York, in the summer of 1949, noted the following:

> For centuries, it has been the custom for the handler during the breaks in the fighting, to wipe the blood out of his chicken's eyes on his mouth—a procedure that undoubtedly goes back to the ancient ritualistic origins of the sport, which are to be found in cock sacrifice and blood-drinking [p. 101].

Hyman, of course, presented not one shred of documentary evidence for his hypothetical ritual origin of the practice. He was well known for his ardent advocacy of "myth-ritual" theory, according to which all folklore was supposedly a survival from an original ritual of some kind (see Bascom, 1957). In some versions of the practice, the handlers blow water on the wounded cock, but some cockfighters preferred the licking system "because of the supposed healing power of human saliva" (Cobb, 1978, p. 92). An informant at a New York state cockfight claimed that cold water is dangerous for the birds' systems but that "human saliva not only is just the right temperature but is well known to have effective germicidal properties (Hyman, 1950, p. 101).

After a fight is over, a handler may attempt to apply a more conventional disinfectant to the cock's wounds such as tincture of iodine, but one old tradition (in Belgium and in England) insists that it is preferable to urinate on the wounds immediately after the combat on the grounds that urine is the best of disinfectants (Remouchamps and Remacle, 1949, pp. 75–76; Scott, 1957, p. 49). There are also reports that a cock should be fed urine. Scott (1957) remarked, "I well remember a famous exhibitor telling me some thirty years ago that the secret of getting birds into perfect show condition was to feed them on wheat which had been steeped in urine" (p. 42). In Brazil a handler "will put the cock's entire head inside his mouth in a desperate attempt to revive the cock for the coming round" (Leal, 1989, pp. 237–238). Leal has offered an ingenious interpretation of the exchange of bodily fluids between man and cock (p. 244). The man gives his body fluids saliva and urine to the cock while the cock gives his blood to the man: "Man's fluids (food, saliva, urine) become cock's fluids (semen and blood)" (p. 246). Still, the act of sucking the cock's whole head seems to require further explanation. In Venezuela, for instance, the practice is called "mamar el gallo" (Olivares Figueroa, 1949, p. 186) which might be translated as "sucking the cock"—"mamar" being the same word used for babies' nursing; mamar as in mammary gland, and ultimately the term "mama."

Hawley (1987), in his description of cockfights in the southern United States writes, "The handlers try to revive the weakened birds by various seemingly bizarre methods: taking the bleeding bird's head into his mouth to warm it and drain blood from its lungs" (pp. 22–23). Hawley (1982) mused about this practice in his unpublished doctoral dissertation, not in print.

Occasionally the seemingly bizarre resuscitative behavior in which handlers indulge during cockfighting has been observed to be the source of some coarse, jocular, and sometimes disapproving commentary from spectators and informants. As one might expect, when a handler puts a wounded cock's head in his mouth to suck out the blood, he is indeed engaging in behavior that some would find highly fraught with sexual implications. Since, according to

informants, this maneuver is highly efficacious in reviving fatigued
birds, perhaps the sexual *entendre* is unwarranted. It is, nonetheless, a disconcerting sight for the unitiated to behold [p. 106].

There is another curious technique sometimes employed to revive a
wounded cock. A Georgia informant, for example, after remarking,
"I've seen guys put a whole chicken's head in their mouth," went on to
describe another practice, "And one trick I've seen . . . they will blow
that chicken in his vent, you know, if he's about dead or about cut down
or something. They'll blow him back there to try to help him get a little
air and get him cooled off" (Anon., 1984, p. 483). A striking parallel to
this practice is reported from south India. Among the people of Tuluva,
we learn that

> sometimes, the beaten cock will again be encouraged to fight, by its
> owner, who, after taking it to a place near by, will pour cold water
> over its head or will air it through the anus. . . . The method of
> airing through the anus is a very curious one, and they say cocks,
> once beaten, if they survive this process of resuscitation, generally
> strike down cock after cock in the combat, much to the pride of
> their owners [Saltore, 1926–1927, p. 326].

According to anthropologist Peter Claus (1992, personal communication), who has carried out extensive fieldwork among the Tulu, the Tulu
handlers still engage in this technique of reviving an injured or fatigued
cock. In fact, blowing in the cock's anus is even used jokingly as a
metaphor in everyday life. For example, if a student were tired and
nervous about a forthcoming examination, a friend might facetiously
volunteer to blow in his anus to inspire him to put forth greater effort in
studying for the exam. There is apparently an analogous procedure
employed with cattle in India. Gandhi (1929) in his autobiography spoke
against "the wicked processes . . . adopted to extract the last drop of
milk from . . . cows and buffaloes" and even went so far as to claim that
it was this very process of "phooka" [blowing] that had led him to give
up drinking milk altogether [pp. 245, 474].

In our attempt to demonstrate that the cockfight is a homoerotic male
battle with masturbatory nuances, another important facet of the event
must be considered. As Guggenheim (1982) put it, "Whatever the social,
psychological, or political reasons why people attend cockfights, any
cocker will say the main reason he goes is to bet" (p. 19). In the Celebes,
"Cock-fights are always connected with betting" (Kaudern, 1929, p. 340).
Geertz (1972), after an initial overview of the generic Balinese cockfight,

gave considerable detail of the intricate betting system employed by the participants and observers of the cockfight. Geertz failed to note that betting accompanies cockfights in almost all parts of the world where cockfighting occurs. This omission is one consequence of his failure to consult other ethnographic reports of the cockfight, even those concerned with the phenomenon in Bali (Eck, 1879; Knight, 1940) or nearby Java (Kreemer, 1893; Soeroto, 1916–1917), another area studied by Geertz. Usually the betting is one-to-one, that is, one person will call out a bet and another person will accept it (Parker, 1986, p. 24). In this way, the betting scenario mirrors the one-on-one action of the fighting cocks. A cocker turned academic describes betting in his thesis as follows: "Betting at cockfights is an overt expression of machismo. The larger the bet the bigger the man. . . . In a cockfight the betting opponents are in a face-to-face confrontation, a man-against-man contest so to speak" (Walker, 1986, p. 49).

While one may well applaud Geertz's (1972) poetic insight that the cockfight's "function, if you want to call it that, is interpretive: It is a Balinese reading of Balinese experience; a story they tell themselves about themselves" (p. 26), one may not agree with Geertz about what that story is. Is the Balinese cockfight simply an extended metaphor for the Balinese social status hierarchy? And what is the connection between the gambling behavior of the Balinese (and others) and the cockfight proper? Had Geertz or other anthropologists been at all familiar with the psychoanalytic theory of gambling, he might have been better able to relate the two sections of his essay: the cockfight and the betting on the cockfight.

Ever since Freud's brilliant (1928) paper on "Dostoevsky and Parricide," the psychoanalytic community has been aware of the possibility that gambling is a symbolic substitute for masturbation. "The passion for play is an equivalent of the old compulsion to masturbate; 'playing' is the actual word used in the nursery to describe the activity of the hands upon the genitals" (p. 193). Actually, Ernst Simmel (1920) had previously suggested that "the passion for gambling thus serves auto-erotic gratification, whereby the playing is fore-pleasure, the gaining orgasm, and the loss ejaculation, defecation and castration" (p. 353). Lindner (1953) discussed the gambling-masturbation equation with clarity:

> Now gambling and masturbation present a wide variety of parallels — Both are repetitive acts, both are compulsively driven, and the nervous and mental states accompanying the crucial stages in the performance of each are almost impossible to differentiate [p. 212].

A characteristic of gambling that is perhaps most reminiscent of masturbatory activity is the "inability of the gambler to stop" (Fuller, 1977, p. 28) even when winning. Here we cannot help but be reminded of the Filipino manual on cockfighting that warns against "holding-handling" the cock in public, as "handling is habit-forming and once acquired, it is hard to get rid of" (pp. 97-98). As we shall seek to demonstrate, both the cockfight itself and the gambling that accompanies it are symbolic expressions of masturbatory behavior.

It should be noted that not all psychiatrists agree with the Freudian hypothesis of a masturbatory underpinning to compulsive gambling. However, for every psychiatrist who says, "In my experience with compulsive gamblers I find no support for Freud's formulation that compulsive gambling is a replacement for compulsive masturbation" there is one who reports, "What I had found, in my one patient [a gambler], to be the core of the psychopathology—the struggle against masturbation the content of his unconscious masturbation fantasies" (Niederland et al., 1967, pp. 180, 182). Fuller (1977), in the most extensive survey of the psychoanalytic study of gambling to date, concurs that masturbation may underlie it, but he argues that there is an anal component as well (to the extent that gamblers play with money—a fecal symbolic substitute).

The somewhat eccentric Wilhelm Stekel (1924) regarded sexuality as the most important component of gambling, and he used a bit of folkloristic evidence, a proverb, to support his contention. The proverb "Glück in Spiel, Unglück in der Liebe" (p. 240; see also Greenson, 1947, p. 74), unquestionably a cognate of the English proverb "Lucky at cards, unlucky in love," does suggest a kind of limited good. There is only so much luck (= sexual energy). If one uses it up in gambling, for example, playing cards, then there will be insufficient for heterosexual lovemaking. There is some clinical evidence to support this conclusion. It involves a compulsive gambler who fell in love. "He had abandoned gambling during the 18 months of his involvement, and resumed it when 'the love' was discarded" (Galdston, 1960, p. 555). This view that there is a finite amount of sexual capacity, or perhaps of sexual fluid, is reminiscent of old-fashioned views of masturbation. The idea was that all the ejaculations resulting from masturbation decreased the amount of sexual fluids available for heterosexual acts. The connotations of the German word "Spiel" in the proverb, analogous to the English word "play," do include explicit allusions to masturbation (see Borneman, 1971). The proverb might then be rendered, "Lucky in masturbation, unlucky in (heterosexual) love." (This discussion of the proverb is mine, not Stekel's.) The proverbial equation might also be relevant to the alleged connection between gambling and impotence. The argument is essentially that the "excitement of gambling and the symbolic equivalents for sexual release built into many games serve as a substitute for sexual relationships" (Olmsted, 1962, pp. 104–105, 120).

According to Bolen and Boyd (1968), "Latent homosexual manifestations are present in the antifeminine aspect of the gambling hall where there is relative exclusion of women and 'antifeminine vocabulary' (i.e., queens [in card games] are referred to as 'whores')" (p. 622; see also Greenson, 1947, pp. 64–65). Greenson (1947) had this to say about the homosexual component of gambling:

> The fellow gamblers are cohorts in homosexual activities. Gambling with other men was equivalent, in the unconscious, to comparing penises with other men; winning meant having the largest penis or being the most potent. Excitement together often represented masturbation [p. 74].

Greenson was speaking in general about gambling and not with reference to the cockfight, but his comments do seem applicable to the cockfight. The allusion to penis comparison cannot help but remind us of the care with which cocks are weighed—in the United States, the cocks are matched on the basis of weight down to ounce distinctions. Bateson and Mead (1942) note that in Bali "before the fight each man holds the other man's cock so that he can feel the enemy cock's strength and make sure that it is not much stronger than his own (p. 140). In this context, the cockfight might be construed as a metaphorical performance of a phallic brag session: "My cock is stronger than yours" or "My cock can outlast yours." This view is confirmed by a statement made by a cocker who wrote a thesis on cockfighting in Utah:

> As a man's own penis or cock is the staff of his manhood so by extension is his fighting cock an extension of himself. The man whose cock lasts the longest and thus wins the fight is judged the better man. A man's own sexual prowess is largely judged by how long he can maintain an erection. The obverse helps prove this statement. A man who is plagued with premature ejaculation is someone to be pitied and given professional counseling. Thus by association a man who has a battle cock with staying power, pride and fights to the end is macho indeed (Walker, 1986, pp. 59–60).

Bergler (1957), expanding on Freud's analysis of gambling, argued that "the unconscious wish to lose becomes . . . an integral part of the gambler's inner motivation" (p. 24; see also 1943, pp. 379, 381; Fuller,

1977, p. 88). The logic, in part, is that if gambling is really symbolic masturbation, then the participant should feel guilt for this act and should expect to be punished by a parent or parental surrogate. Bergler (1943) even goes so far as to speak of the gambler as a "naughty" child who expects punishment after performing his forbidden act (p. 386). According to this logic, the gambler is obliged to play until he loses because losing constitutes a form of punishment by an external authority, that is, fate.

The question is: to what extent, if any, is it legitimate to interpret the cockfight (and the gambling that accompanies it) as a symbolic form of male masturbation? Here we may turn to the relevant ethnography to find an answer to this question. Time and time again, we read reports of how much time a cock handler devoted to grooming and stroking his bird. In the Philippines, we learn, "the cock is handled and petted daily by his master" (Lansang, 1966, p. 140). Bailey (1909) described a cock tied on a wagon in the Philippines as being "unremittingly fondled" (p. 253). Again from the Philippines, a how-to primer for cock handlers warns against excessive handling or stroking of the cock, especially in public. "You can do the holding-handling at home as much as you desire." But the prospective cock handler is told in no uncertain terms that "handling" is habit forming and once acquired, hard to get rid of (Lansang, 1966, pp. 97-98). The grooming behavior found in the Philippines is by no means unique. In Martinique, "the cock is the object of a veritable loving passion on the part of its master, who caresses, fondles, kisses it and tells it sweet words" (Affergan, 1986, p. 119).

What about Bali? Knight (1940) reported, "You may be sure to find any [male] member of the village community from the age of fifteen up to eighty using any leisure moments toying with and fondling their birds" (p. 77). Bateson and Mead (1942) described Balinese behavior in similar detail:

> The average Balinese man can find no pleasanter way to pass the time than to walk about with a cock, testing it out against the cocks of other men whom he meets on the road. . . . Ruffling it up, smoothing it down, ruffling it up again, sitting among other men who are engaged in similar toying with their cocks—this passes many hours of the long hot afternoons [pp. 24-25].

Long before Geertz (1972) described the Balinese cockfight, Bateson and Mead (1942) had remarked, "The evidence for regarding the fighting cock as a genital symbol comes from the postures of men holding cocks, the sex slang and sex jingles, and from Balinese carvings of men with fighting cocks" (p. 140). Yet, despite this insight and such commentaries accompanying photographs as "Many men spend hours sitting, playing with their cocks" (p. 140), Bateson and Mead stop short of calling the cockfight itself a form of mutual symbolic masturbation. On the other hand, according to Olmsted (1962) "Bateson and Mead have remarked on the fact that in Bali, cocks are first taken to, and held and petted and fondled at just about the time that masturbation must be given up as 'babyish' . . ." (p. 181). This observation (which unfortunately is not documented by Olmsted) clearly suggests that cock grooming is a direct substitute for masturbation (see Figure 1). In a fascinating gestural comparison, Bateson and Mead (1942) claim that a mother "may ruffle the penis [of a baby] upward with repeated little flicks, using almost the exact gesture that a man uses when he ruffles up the hackle feathers of his fighting cock to make it angry" (p. 131).

Even Geertz (1972) could hardly avoid the overt behavior of the Balinese:

> Whenever you see a group of Balinese men squatting idly in the council shed or along the road in their hips down, shoulders forward, knees up fashion, half or more of them will have a rooster in his hands, holding it between his thighs, bouncing it gently up and down to strengthen its legs, ruffling its feathers with abstract sensuality, pushing it out against a neighbor's rooster to rouse its spirit, withdrawing it towards his loins to calm it again [p. 6].

Geertz never once mentioned the word "masturbation," nor do any of the other post-Geertzian analysts of the cockfight except for Cook in her 1991 doctoral dissertation who calls "the careful cleaning, stroking, bouncing and constant handling that fighting cocks receive from their owners" a form of "symbolic masturbation" (1991, p. 98).

For those skeptics who may not be able to see the possible symbolic meaning of a handler's massaging the neck of his cock, I call their attention to the fact that in American slang "to choke the chicken" is a standard euphemism for masturbation and that a "chicken-choker" is a male masturbator (Spears, 1990, p. 33).

Once the masturbatory underpinnings of the cockfight are recognized, many of the details of the cockfight can be much better understood. For example, there is a common rule that the handler can touch his own bird, but should at no time touch the opponent bird. In Tennessee, for

Figure 1

From a "home movie" taken by Berkeley anthropologist Herb Phillips in 1976, we see one of a group of Balinese men in a village not far from Den Pasar. All the men are sitting with their prize cocks. The sequence of images of one person shows clearly how (and, just as importantly, *where*) the cock is held as well as the typical series of hand grooming movements. The reader may judge for himself or herself whether the movement of the hands up and down the cock's neck is in any way suggestive of an autoerotic act. (I thank Professor Phillips for sharing this footage and especially Lowie Museum of Anthropology photographer Gene Prince for managing to transfer these images from 8 mm movie film to conventional black and white photographic form.)

example, "when a cock hangs a gaff in its opponent, the informant stated 'never touch another guy's bird' "(Cobb, 1978, p. 93). Ostensibly the rule is to prevent someone unethical from harming the opponent bird, but symbolically it suggests that one is expected to handle only one's own phallus. The same rule is reported in the Philippines. When cocks are being matched, we are told, "don't let anyone hold your cock to avoid regrets later" (Lansang, 1966, pp. 96, 179). Filipinos in California adhered to same code: "You never do that, touch someone else's bird" (Beagle, 1968, p. 29).

Typically, cocks are kept in covered baskets right up until the time they are scheduled to enter the pit. The cock is *exposed* at the last minute for everyone to admire (and to encourage betting). After the exposure, the opposing cocks are juxtaposed so that they are in striking or pecking distance of one another (so as to stimulate them to want to fight). We can now more fully appreciate the possible symbolic significance of the particular means handlers use to resuscitate flaccid cocks. By taking the cock's head into their mouths and sucking on it and blowing on it, we would seemingly have an obvious case of fellatio. Normally, it is considered demeaning for a male to indulge in such behavior — at least in public. It is worth recalling that the term of choice in Anglo-American slang for someone who performs such an act is "cock sucker." (The reference to "blowing" may carry a similar symbolic association. It is interesting that an Irish description refers to a handler who "put his bird's head into his own mouth to revive it. It used to work all right but whether he was sucking or blowing, I could not decide" [Crannlaighe, 1945, p. 512]. Also relevant may be the gambler's custom of 'blowing' on dice before throwing them.)

Additional ethnographic evidence alludes to oral-genital acts. In Brazil, the cockpit may have a bar or restaurant adjacent where drinks and barbecued beef are available. Leal (1989) reports that men may joke along the lines of "We are eating your cock" even though chicken is not served there (p. 232). Such specifics of joking behavior (of the sort Geertz, 1972, mentioned but failed to record) is absolutely critical for a full understanding of the symbolic significance of the cockfight. According to Leal (1989), "Jokes are made about *mounting [trepar]* or *eating (comer) someone's cock* (that is to say, the cock's owner) in the cockfight situation. Both words, *trepar* and *comer,* in Brazilian Portuguese are used for coitus while *cock* can stand for man, although not for a man's genitals" (p. 241).

Another piece of ethnographic data from Brazil bears on the connection between cockfighting and masturbation.

When a good quality cock leaves the pit badly hurt there is a general commotion and his owner or handler carefully examines his wounds. As soon as the cock is better, the handler checks the cock's sexual organs to see if they have been affected: with the cock supine the man gently rubs behind the cock's leg in the direction of its testicles. If the cock ejaculates and the sperm contains blood, it is considered that the cock is seriously hurt and will not be able to fight again (Leal, 1989, pp. 239–240; see also Finsterbusch, 1980, p. 245).

In a novelistic account of a cockfight set in northern Florida, massaging a cock's testicles is deemed a foul disqualifying that cock. The explanation: "You rub a cock's balls and you take every speck of fight right out of him. It's a deliberate way of throwing a fight" (Willeford, 1972, pp. 180–181).

Usually, the masturbatory aspects of the cockfight are not quite so overt. An 1832 account of a cockfight in England describes one individual attending a cockfight:

> He was trying to look demure and unmoved . . . but I was told that he was a clergyman, and that he would be 'quite up in the stirrups' when the cocks were brought in. He forced himself to be at ease; but I saw his small, hungry, hazel eyes quite in a fever — and his hot, thin, vein-embossed hand, rubbing the unconscious nob of his umbrella in a way to awaken it from the dead — and yet all the time he was affecting the uninterested, incurious man! [Egan, 1832, p. 151].

Fuller (1977) remarked that sometimes, especially in fictional accounts of gambling, "the masturbatory element erupts through its defenses" (p. 101), which seems to apply to the abstemious clergyman attending a cockfight and rubbing the nob of his umbrella.

The present argument also illuminates the fact that cockfights are illegal in many countries. No doubt being outside the law makes cockfights more exciting for those participating. In other words, it is illegal to play with cocks in public; hence, one must do it *sub rosa,* in secret. That authorities ban cockfighting but then allow it to take place in secret locations seems to confirm its symbolic value. Masturbation is typically proscribed by parents, but masturbation occurs nonetheless. We can now better appreciate Geertz's description of a Balinese cockfight. "This process . . . is conducted in a very subdued, oblique, and even dissembling manner. Those not immediately involved give it at best but disguised, sidelong attention; those who, *embarrassedly,* are involved, attempt to pretend somehow that the whole thing is not really happening" (Geertz, 1972, p. 8, my emphasis).

Other symbolic inferences can be drawn from the notion that the cockfight may be a sublimated form of public masturbation. Harris (1964, p. 515) quoted earlier psychoanalysts who suggested that orgasm and death might be symbolically equivalent. We know that even in Shakespeare's day not only did "cock" mean "penis" (Partridge, 1960, p. 88), but "to die" meant to experience orgasm (p. 101). So, metaphorically speaking, if one's cock dies, one achieves orgasm. In the cockfight, if one's cock dies and the opponent's does not, one loses money as well; that is, one is punished for reaching orgasm in an all-male environment in a mutual-masturbation duel. The bleeding of the losing cock further strengthens the image insofar as there is a visually empirical loss of fluid for all the world to see. Of course, the winning cock may bleed as well. Presumably both masturbators lose fluid at the end of the cockfight, the difference being that the winner is not punished, but rather is rewarded for outlasting his opponent, the loser. He has masturbated but remains alive, perhaps to masturbate on another occasion. That a particularly strong cock may fight again and again demonstrates the "repetition compulsion" aspect of cockfighting (and masturbation).

If the cockfight does represent symbolic masturbation with grown men playing with their cocks in public, all the details from the grooming behavior to the gambling make sense. The grooming, involving the heavy use of the *hands* is analogous to shaking dice, shuffling cards, or pulling the handles on slot machines (one-armed bandits). Although Geertz (1972) made passing reference to "a large number of mindless, sheer-chance type gambling games (roulette, dice throw, coin-spin, pea-under-the shell)" (p. 17), it was actually Bateson and Mead (1942) who reminded us that the dice thrown at a cockfight are "spun with the hand" (p. 143). The cockfight involves not only the risk of injury to or the loss of one's cock, but also the loss of money wagered on the fight. Losing would constitute "punishment" for indulging in symbolic masturbation while winning would permit great elation as having masturbated and gotten away with it. The Balinese say "Fighting cocks . . . is like playing with fire only not getting burned" (Geertz, 1972, p. 21). As Lindner (1953) put it, winning confirms the gambler-masturbator's feelings of omnipotence (p. 216). To be rewarded for masturbating is surely flying in the face of convention. In most cockfights, however, there are more losers than winners.

If a gambler's losing is a form of symbolic castration, as Freudians suggest (Fuller, 1977, p. 102), then betting in a cockfight would exactly parallel the symbolic infrastructure of the cockfight itself. If one's cock loses by being put out of commission or by being killed, this would be a symbolic instance of castration. (One is reminded of Cicero's quip in *Pro Murena* when in trying to ridicule Zeno's Stoic teachings such as the idea that all misdeeds are equal, he remarked "The casual killing of a cock is no less a crime than strangling one's father" [Cicero, 1977, p. 263].) If one had bet on one's cock and lost, the castration would be corroborated and confirmed. If, on the other hand, one's cock prevails, one avoids the immediate threat of castration and if one wins the bet on one's cock, one does the same thing symbolically speaking.

From the foregoing analysis, one can see that the link between the cockfight and the betting associated with it is much less obscure. *Both* the cockfight *and* the betting are related to male masturbation. We can, then, also better understand why women are not welcome at cockfights. Geertz (1972) noted that the cockfight was unusual in Balinese culture "in being a single-sex public activity from which the other sex is totally and expressly excluded" (p. 30*n*). But he offered no explanation whatsoever for this. If men are competing in public with their cocks, one can easily appreciate why they prefer to do so without women present. In terms of the thesis of this essay, the whole point of the phallic competition is to "feminize" one's opponent. This symbolic feminization becomes less meaningful in the presence of actual women.

We may now have insight into some of the first reports of cock-fighting in England and western Europe. According to most histories of cockfighting, the sport seems to have emerged among adolescent school-boys, a custom that goes back to the middle ages (Anon., 1888, p. 812; Demulder, 1934, p. 13; Vandereuse 1951). This schoolboy tradition of cockfighting continued into the early 20th century (Cegarra, 1988, p. 56). Often there would be a series of elimination bouts, with the schoolboy owner of the winning cock called Roi du Coq, King of the Cocks (Vandereuse, 1951, p. 183). There were related customs in which a rooster was beheaded (Vandereuse, 1951, p. 197; see also Coluccio, 1970, pp. 75–76) or a group of boys threw sticks at a rooster suspended between two trees. The boy whose stick delivered the death blow was proclaimed king (Vandereuse, 1951, p. 199). Given the symbolic analysis of the cockfight proposed here, it seems perfectly reasonable for it to be popular in all-male secondary schools.

One more element in the totality of cockfighting is, I believe, worthy of mention. It concerns the breeding of roosters. Many of the treatises on cockfighting offer advice about how best to produce a "game" cock. One old Georgia informant reported:

> Those chickens were raised — most of 'em came from one hen and one rooster. They single mated 'em. They'd take the offspring from that and test 'em in the pit to see whether they suited them or not. If they did, then they'd take six full sisters and the sisters' father or grandfather and they'd breed all those hens. That's what they call inbreeding and line breeding [Allred and Carver, 1979, p. 52].

In one of the many books devoted to cockfighting, we find an alternative term: "Full blood" mating. " 'Full blood' mating was approved; father with daughter, mother with son, brother with sister" (Gilbey, 1912, p. 89). The oedipal implications of such breeding practices are obvious enough. "You can only try your hens single breeding them and keeping exact records of their sons' performances, and when you come across a true-blooded hen, do not hesitate to breed the choicest son back to his mother" (Finsterbusch, 1980, p. 165). According to this same source, "when fowls are bred in, it can be done in two forms: 1) In a vertical sense, i.e., from parents to offspring and grandparents to grandchildren, or 2) in horizontal sense, i.e., from sister to brother or inter-cousins" (p. 140).

In a cockfighting novel, we are told that a cock bred from a father and a daughter "usually runs every time," whereas "those bred from mother and son have the biggest heart for fighting to the death" (Willeford, 1972, p. 39). Breeders may well argue for the genetic efficacy of such inbreeding, but from a psychoanalytic perspective — in which breeders might be said to identify with their cocks (and their behavior), such breeding might constitute wishful thinking as well as fantastic acting out. The point is that such fantasies would not be at all inconsistent with masturbation.

With all of the rich ethnographic detail available in print concerning the cockfight, it is surprising to read what anthropologists have written about it. The refusal to acknowledge the existence of clear-cut symbolic data can only be attributed to what might generally be characterized as an antisymbolic stance among social and cultural anthropologists. So-called symbolic anthropologists are among the chief examples of those espousing what I would term an antisymbolic stance. Symbolic anthropologists unfortunately define symbolism very narrowly, typically limiting it to matters of social structure.

Although some authors (e.g., Hawley, 1989) have observed a "sexual subtext" in the cockfight, they are quick to say that "sometimes a cockfight is just a cockfight or a gaming opportunity, and not an implicit homoerotic struggle" (p. 131). Hawley, for example, differs with "animal rights activists, who see cockfighters (and hunters and gun owners) as 'insecure about their masculinity' " (p. 131). A cocker who temporarily turned academic to write a thesis about cockfighting in northern Utah remarked (Walker, 1986, p. 28): "Most leave a cockfight as emotionally and physically spent as if they had engaged in extreme sexual activity. I am not saying the release is sexual, but the physical and emotional release is very similar." Geertz (1972), after dutifully noting phallic elements, totally ignored them in his analysis of the Balinese cockfight as being a metaphor for concerns about status and hierarchy.

Leal (1989), notwithstanding her splendid ethnographic documentation of the phallic nature of the Brazilian cockfight, declines to interpret it along such lines. Says Leal:

We can see the cockfight as a play of images where ultimately what is at stake is masculinity, not cocks, not even "ambulant penises" as Bateson, Mead or Geertz suggested. . . . I wonder if the equation cocks = penises is not an oversimplification, immediate to English-speaking people. . . . In my understanding, phallus itself is a sign invested with the meaning of manliness and power: androcentric cultures ascribe power to the ones who have penises. In contrast to Bateson and Mead, Geertz does not limit his analysis to the cock as a phallic symbol; masculinity and status concern are his main points [p. 220].

Thus Leal falls back to a nonphallic reading when she says, "Without doubt, cockfighting is a dramatization of male identity" (p. 227). Her position is stated clearly enough:

The association men/cocks, which seems to be self evident in cultures that have the word *cock* as a signifier for penis, is not an obvious one in gaucho culture. I am not denying the semantical association man/cock; rather I am suggesting that in cockfighting situations, the meaning of cock imagery cannot be reduced to the notion of male genitals [p. 240].

For Leal, if a man is able to "perform the tasks and rites which assure masculinity he becomes a *man;* he acquires the *phallus,* which means he gains prestige and power" (p. 240). It should be noted that in northeast

Brazil—far from where Leal carried out her fieldwork—little boys' genitals can be called "pintinho [little chick]" in contrast to adult men's, which are often called "galo [rooster]" (Linda-Anne Rebhun, 1992, personal communication). Still, Leal's view is echoed by Marvin (1984), who in his ethnographic account of cockfights in Andalusia noted, "Unlike Bali, in Spain there is no identification of men as individuals with their cocks" (p. 63). Certainly the data from English is more explicit. One thinks of the slang term "pecker" for penis, for example. In a cockfight where both cocks are wounded, it is the one who is still able to "peck" his opponent who is declared the winner. The pecker wins!

My own view is that it is not an oversimplification found exclusively among English-speaking people to equate cocks and penises, especially in view of the ample evidence of that equation available wherever cock-fighting exists. The data from Bali and from Brazil are exceptionally explicit, even though both Geertz (1972) and Leal (1989) tend to dismiss the obvious phallic implications of their data in favor of interpretations that favor emphases on "status" and "prestige and power." Indeed, it is my opinion that it is an oversimplification of the cockfight to claim that it is only about status hierarchy and prestige.

The predictable tendency of social anthropologists to interpret virtu-ally all aspects of culture solely in terms of social structure and social organization is easily discernible in previous readings of the cockfight. The combination of the bias toward social structure and the bias against psychoanalytic symbolic interpretation has prevented anthropologists from understanding the explicit implications of their own ethnographic data. It is ironic and paradoxical that social anthropologists—as well as conventional folklorists—invariably condemn Freudian interpretations as *reductionistic,* whereas in fact it is social anthropologists who are reductionists. They reduce all folkloristic phenomena (such as myths and cockfights) to reflections of social structure.

Geertz (1972) and those anthropologists who have followed his basic approach to the cockfight have erred in not being comparative in perspective, in failing to see the cockfight as a form of mutual mastur-bation or a phallic brag duel, in not offering a plausible explanation as to why women are unwelcome at cockfights, and, above all, in mis-reading the overall symbolic import of the cockfight with its paradig-matic aim of feminizing a male opponent either through the threat of castration (via the gaff or spur) or by making the losing cock turn tail to be labeled a female "chicken."

Psychoanalysts, to my knowledge, have not considered the cockfight. Ferenczi (1913) did discuss the case of a five-year-old boy who very much identified with roosters (to the extent of crowing and cackling) but who was also at the same time very much afraid of roosters. Ferenczi suggested that the boy's morbid dread of cocks "was ultimately to be traced to the threat of castration for onanism" (p. 212).

Is there any evidence of symbolic castration in the traditional cockfight? I argue that all those versions of the cockfight which involve the attachment of sharp metal spurs (also called heels or slashers) to the cock's feet add a castrative element to the sport. Some cultures forbid the use of such armor, in which case the natural spurs of the rooster may serve a similar purpose. Placing spurs on one's cock essentially entails arming a phallus. It is, in my view, symbolically equivalent to competitive kite-fighting in southeast Asia and elsewhere, where a young man will attach pieces of broken glass to his kite string. He does so with the hope that his kite-string will sever that of his opponent. In kite-fighting, the initial action is get one's kite up (a symbolic erection), but this is quickly followed by the battle to cut one's opponent's kite off. Bateson and Mead (1942, p. 135) noted that kite-fighting is a form of "vicarious conflict" analogous to cockfighting, but did not explicitly mention castration. In cockfighting, one puts sharp blades on one's cocks to cut down one's opponents' cocks. If the gallus is a phallus, then cutting a cock could properly be construed as symbolic castration. There is an anecdote about a Javanese official who was employed by the Dutch government which lends credence to this interpretation. When asked by the Dutch authorities to take action against illegal cockfights, he did not want to betray his own people and refused to do so. Instead, he proposed to castrate the cocks so that they would not wish to fight. No one paid any attention to the new rule because the men felt that if they castrated their cocks, they themselves would be castrated as well (Serière, 1873, p. 101).

If my analysis of the cockfight as a symbolic, public masturbatory, phallic duel is sound, one should be able to understand why participants might be reluctant or unable to articulate consciously this symbolic structure. In effect, the cockfight is like most folklore fantasy: its content is largely unconscious. If the participants consciously realized what they were doing, they would in all probability not be willing to participate. It is precisely the symbolic façade that makes it possible for people to participate in an activity without consciously understanding the significance of that participation.

Less forgivable and understandable is the utter failure of anthropologists and folklorists to decipher the symbolic significance of the cockfight. Anthropologists can presumptuously label their superficial ethnographic descriptions of the cockfight as "deep," but calling "shallow" deep does not make it so. Perhaps psychoanalytic anthropologists and folklorists should not really complain. If conventional anthropologists and folklorists actually understood the unconscious symbolic dimensions of human behavior—such as that consistently demonstrated in the cockfight—there would be far fewer challenges for psychoanalytic anthropologists and folklorists to take up.

BIBLIOGRAPHY

ACOSTA SAIGNES, M. (1954), Introducción al estudio de la gallina en el folklore de Venezuela. *Tradición,* 6 (15):29–46.

AFFERGAN, F. (1986), Zooanthropologie du combat de coqs à la Martinique. *Cahiers Internationaux de Sociologie,* 80:109–126.

ALLRED, K. & CARVER, J. (1979), Cockfighting. *Foxfire,* 13:50–61, 151–172.

ALONSO, M. A. (1849), *El Gibaro: Cuadro de costumbres de la Isla de Puerto-Rico.* Barcelona: D. Juan Oliveres.

ANDERSON, R. L. (1933), Chicken-fight. *Amer. Mercury,* 30:111–115.

ANON. (1888), Fighting-cocks in schools. *Chambers's J.,* 65:812–814.

———— (1952), Your taxes support cockfights. *National Humane Rev.,* 40 (11):10–11, 25.

———— (1984), Cockfighting. *Foxfire,* 8:385–487.

ARMAS CHITTY, J. A. DE (1953–1954), Las riñas de gallos en el Oriente del Guárico. *Archivos Venezolanos de Folklore,* 2–3:149–158.

AXON, W. E. A. (1899), Cock-fighting in the eighteenth century. *Notes & Queries,* 9th Series, 4:62–64.

BAILEY, G. H. (1909), The cockpit and the Filipino. *Overland Monthly,* 54:253–256.

BAIRD, L. Y. (1981), O.E.D. Cock 20: The limits of lexicography of slang. *Maledicta,* 5:213–223.

———— (1981–1982), Priapus gallinaceus: The role of the cock in fertility and eroticism in classical antiquity and the Middle Ages. *Stud. Iconogr.* 7–8:81–111.

BARCLAY, J. (1980), *A Stroll Through Borneo.* London: Hodder & Soughton.

BASCOM, W. R. (1954), Four functions of folklore. *J. Amer. Folklore,* 67:333–349.

———— (1957), The myth-ritual theory. *J. Amer. Folklore,* 70:103–114.

BATESON, G. & MEAD, M. (1942), *Balinese Character: A Photographic Analysis.* New York: New York Academy of Sciences.

BEACEY, P. (1945), Prelude to a cockfight. *The Bell,* 11:574–576.

BEAGLE, P. S. (1968), Cockfight. *Saturday Evening Post* 241, no. 17 (August 24):28–29, 76–77.

BEATTIE, G. (1937), The Scottish miner and his game-cock. *The Scots Magazine,* 14:213–217.

BERGLER, E. (1943), The gambler: A misunderstood neurotic. *J. Criminal Psychopathol.,* 4:379–393.

———— (1957), *The Psychology of Gambling.* New York: Hill & Wang.

BHIDE, V. V. (1967), Cock in Vedic literature. *Bharatiya Vidya,* 27:1–6.

BOLEN, D. W. & BOYD, W. H. (1968), Gambling and the gambler: A review and preliminary findings. *Arch. Gen. Psychiat.,* 18:617–630.

BOON, J. A. (1977), *The Anthropological Romance of Bali 1597–1972.* Cambridge: Cambridge University Press.

BORNEMAN, E. (1971), *Sex im Volksmund.* Reinbek bei Hamburg: Rowohlt Verlag.

BOULTON, W. B. (1901), *The Amusements of Old London,* Vol. 1. London: John C. Nimmo.

BRADDY, H. (1961), Feathered duelists. In: *Singers and Storytellers,* ed. M. C. Boatright, W. M. Hudson & A. Maxwell. Dallas, TX: Southern Methodist University Press, pp. 98–106.

BRUNEAU, P. (1965), Le motif des coqs affrontés dans l'imagerie antique. *Bulletin de Correspondance Hellénique,* 89:90–121.

BRYDEN, H. A. (1931), Cock-fighting and its illustrations. *The Print Collector's Quart.,* 18:351–373.

CADET, A. (1971) Le Coq. *Société d'Etudes Folkloriques du Centre-Ouest: Revue de Recherches Ethnographiques,* 5:99–112; 144–168, 199–210, 292–308.

CADILLA DE MARTINEZ, M. (1941), De los gallos y sus peleas. In: *Raices de la Tierra.* Arecibo, PR: Tipografia Hernandez. pp. 145–166.

CALDERIN, G. G. (1970), El gallo de pelea. *Isla Literaria,* 10–11 (junio y julio):16–18.

CALLISEN, S. A. (1939), The iconography of the cock on the column. *Art Bull.,* 21:160–178.

CARSON, J. (1965), *Colonial Virginians at Play.* Williamsburg: University Press of Virginia.

CASTILLO DE LUCAS, A. (1970), El gallo: Simbolismo refraneado de su preferente figura en la alfarería popular. *Revista de Etnografia,* 14:361–367.

CEGARRA, M. (1988), Les coqs combattants. *Terrain,* 10 (avril):51–62.

———— (1989), Les combats de coqs dans le nord de la France. In: *Anthropologie Sociale et Ethnologie de la France,* ed. M. Segalen. Bibliothèque des Cahiers de l'Institut de Linguistique de Louvain 44, Vol. 2. Louvain-La Neuve: Peeters, pp. 671–676.

CHALLES, M. DE (1972), Cockfighting in the 19th century Caribbean. *Caribbean Rev.,* 4(4):12–14.

CHAMPAGNAC, A. (1970), *Coqs de Combat et Combats de Coqs à la Martinique.* Alfort: Maisons-Alfort.

CHATTOPADHYAY, A. (1973), Cocks in ancient Indian life. *J. Oriental Instit.,* 23:197–201.

CICERO, (1977) Pro Murena. In: *Cicero in Twenty-Eight Volumes.* Vol. 10. Cambridge: Harvard University Press, pp. 167–299.

COBB, J. E. (1978), Cockfighting in East Tennessee. In: *Glimpses of Southern Appalachian Folk Culture,* ed. C. H. Faulkner & C. K. Buckles. Misc. Paper No. 3, Tennessee Anthropological Association, pp. 175–196.

COLUCCIO, M. I. (1970), El gallo. *Revista de Etnograia,* 14:59–81.

COOK, H. B. K. (1991), Small town, big hell: An ethnographic study of aggression in a Margariteño community. Unpublished doctoral dissertation in anthropology, University of California, Los Angeles.

CRANNLAIGHE, P. O. (1945), Cock fighting. *The Bell,* 19:510–513.

CRAPANZANO, V. (1986), Hermes' dilemma: The masking of subversion in ethnographic description. In: *Writing Culture,* ed. J. Clifford & G. E. Marcus. Berkeley: University of California Press, pp. 51–76.

CREWS, H. (1977), Cockfighting: An unfashionable view. *Esquire,* 87(3):8, 12, 14.

CUTTER, R. J. (1989a), Brocade and blood: The cockfight in Chinese and English poetry. *Tamkang Rev.,* 19:631–661.

———— (1989b), *The Brush and the Spur: Chinese Culture and the Cockfight.* Hong Kong: Chinese University Press.

DANAË, O. (1989), *Combats de Coqs: Histoire et Actualité de l'Oiseau Guerrier.* Paris: Editions L'Harmattan.

DEL SESTO, S. L. (1975), Roles, rules, and organization: A descriptive account of cockfighting in rural Louisiana. *Southern Folklore Quart.*, 39:1–14.

_____ (1980), Dancing and cockfighting at Jay's Lounge and Cockpit: The preservation of folk practices in Cajun Louisiana. In: *Rituals and Ceremonies in Popular Culture*, ed. R. B. Browne. Bowling Green, OH: Bowling Green University Popular Press, pp. 270–281.

DELANNOY, R. (1948), *Coqs de Combat et Combats de Coqs dans le Nord de Pas-de-Calais*. Paris: R. Foulon.

DEMULDER, R. (1934), Coqueleux et combats de coqs dans le nord de la France. *Revue de Folklore Français*, 5:8–14.

DESROUSSEAUX, A. (1886), Les combats de coqs en Flandre. *Revue des Traditions Populaires*, 1:338–339.

_____ (1889), *Moeurs Populaires de la Flandre Française*, Vol. 2. Lille: L. Quarre.

DINWIDDIE, W. (1899), *Puerto Rico: Its Conditions and Possibilities*. New York: Harper & Brothers.

DONLON, J. G. (1991), Leisure Most Fowl: Cock Fighting in a Cultural and Historic Milieu. Unpublished master's thesis in Leisure Studies, University of Illinois.

DUNDES, A. (1987), *Parsing Through Customs: Essays by a Freudian Folklorist*. Madison: University of Wisconsin Press.

ECK, R. V. (1879), Schetsen uit het Volksleven (I. Hanengevecht). *De Indische Gids*, 1:102–118.

EGAN, P. (1832), *Book of Sports and Mirror of Life*. London: T. T. & J. Tegg.

FEHRLE, E. (1912), Der Hahn im Aberglauben. *Schweizerisches Archiv für Volkskunde*, 16:65–75.

FEIJOO, L. J. R. (1990), *Apuntes sobre el arte de castar gallos de pelea*. Puerto Rico: Taller Gráfico Gongolí.

FERENCZI, S. (1913), A little chanticleer. In: *First Contributions to Psycho-Analysis*. London: Karnac Books, 1980, pp. 204–213.

FINE, G. A. (1992), The depths of deep play—The rhetoric and resource of morally controversial leisure. *Play & Culture*, 5:246–251.

FINSTERBUSCH, C. A. (1980), *Cock Fighting All Over the World*. Hindhead U.K.: Saiga.

FORSYTH, I. H. (1978), The theme of cockfighting in Burgundian Romanesque architecture. *Speculum*, 53:252–282.

FRASER, H. M. (1981), The cockfight motif in Spanish American literature. *Inter-Amer. Rev. Bibliog.*, 31:514–523.

FREUD, S. (1928), Dostoevsky and parricide. *Standard Edition*, 21:173–194. London: Hogarth Press, 1961.

FULLER, P. (1977), Introduction. In: *The Psychology of Gambling*, ed. J. Halliday & P. Fuller. New York: Penguin, pp. 1–114.

GALDSTON, I. (1951), The psychodynamics of the triad, alcoholism, gambling and superstition. *Mental Hyg.*, 35:589–598.

_____ (1960), The gambler and his love. *Amer. J. Psychiat.*, 117:553–555.

GANDHI, M. K. (1929), *The Story of My Experiments with Truth*, 2 vols. Ahmedabad: Navajivan Press.

GARD, W. (1936), Rooster fight. *Southwest Rev.*, 22:65–70.

GEERTZ, C. (1972), Deep play: Notes on the Balinese cockfight. *Daedalus*, 101(1):1–37.

GILBEY, J. (1957), Cockfighting in art. *Apollo*, 65:22–24.

GILBEY, W. (1912), *Sport in the Olden Time*. London: Vinton.

GITTEE, A. (1891), De Haan in de Volksverbeelding. *Volkskunde*, 4:154–166.

GREENSON, R. R. (1947), On gambling. *Amer. Imago*, 4(2):61–77.

GUGGENHEIM, S. (1982), Cock or bull: Cockfighting, social structure, and political commentary in the Philippines. *Pilipinas,* 3(1):1–35.

GUNTER, C. R., JR. (1978), Cockfighting in East Tennessee and Western North Carolina. *Tennessee Folklore Soc. Bull.,* 44:160–169.

HARRIS, H. I. (1964), Gambling addiction in an adolescent male. *Psychoanal. Quart.,* 33:513–525.

HARRIS, J. (1987), The rules of cockfighting. In *Hoein: The Short Rows,* ed. F. E. Abernethy. Dallas: Southern Methodist University Press, pp. 101–111.

HAWLEY, F. F. (1982), Organized cockfighting: A deviant recreational subculture. Unpublished doctoral dissertation in criminology, Florida State University.

_____ (1987), Cockfighting in the pine woods: Gameness in the new south. *Sport Place,* 1(2):18–26.

_____ (1989), Cockfight in the cotton: A moral crusade in microcosm. *Contemp. Crises,* 13:129–144.

HAZARD, S. (1871), *Cuba with Pen and Pencil.* Hartford, CT: Hartford Publishing Company.

HERZOG, H. A., JR. (1978), Immobility in intraspecific encounters: Cockfights and the evolution of "animal hypnosis." *Psycholog. Record,* 28:543–548.

_____ (1985), Hackfights and derbies. *Appalachian J.,* 12:114–126.

_____ & CHEEK, P. B. (1979), Grit and steel: The anatomy of cockfighting. *Southern Exposure,* 7(2):36–40.

HYMAN, S. E. (1950), Department of amplification. *The New Yorker,* 26(11) (May 6th): 100–101.

JACOBSON, D. (1991), *Reading Ethnography.* Albany: State University of New York Press.

JAMES, L. (1928), The ancient sport of "cocking." *Natl. Rev.,* 92:138–143.

JAQUEMOTTE, E. & LEJEUNE, J. (1904), Vocabulaire du coquelî. *Bull. Société Liegeoise de Littérature Wallonne,* 45:225–230.

JARVIS, C. S. (1939), Blood-sports and hypocrisy. *Cornhill Mag.,* 159:368–378.

JONES, R. (1980), Chicken fighting is a hobby. *Foxfire,* 14:143–150.

JULL, M. A. (1927), The races of domestic fowl. *Nat. Geogr. Mag.,* 51:379–452.

JUSTO, E. (1969), Las peleas de gallos. *Revista de Dialectologia y Tradiciones Populares,* 25:317–323.

KAUDERN, W. (1929), *Ethnographical Studies in Celebes.* IV. The Hague: Martinus Nijhoff.

KNIGHT, F. C. E. (1940) Cockfighting in Bali. *Discovery.* 2nd Series. 3, no. 23 (February): 77–81.

KREEMER, J. (1893), De Javaan en zijne hoenders. *Mededeelingen van wege het Nederlandsche Zendelinggenootschap,* 37:213–225.

KRETZENBACHER, L. (1958), Der Hahn auf dem Kirchturm. *Rheinisches Jahrbuch für Volkskunde,* 9:194–206.

LANSANG, A. J. (1966), *Cockfighting in the Philippines (Our Genuine National Sport).* Atlag, Malolos, Bulacan: Enrian Press.

LEAL, O. F. (1989), The Gauchos: Male culture and identity in the Pampas. Unpublished doctoral dissertation in anthropology, University of California, Berkeley.

LEE, F. (1921), Filipinos' favorite Sport. *Overland Monthly,* 77:20–22.

LEÓN REY, J. A. (1953), Riñas de gallos y vocabulario de gallistica. *Revista Colombiana de Folklore,* 2:79–96.

LIEBLING, A. J. (1950), Dead game. *The New Yorker,* 26, no. 6 (April 1):35–45.

LINDNER, R. (1953), The psychodynamics of gambling. In: *Explorations in Psychoanalysis,* ed. R. Lindner. New York: Julian Press, pp. 197–217.

MAGALDI, E. (1929), I "Ludi Gallinarii" a Pompei. *Historia,* 3:471–485.

MANTEGAZZA, P. (1916), *Viajes por el Río de la Plata.* Buenos Aires: Universidad de Tucumán.

———— (1935), *The Sexual Relations of Mankind.* New York: Eugenics Pub.

MARÇAL, H. (1967), O galo na tradição popular. *Revista de Etnografia,* 9:345–408.

MARCELIN, M. (1955a), Jeu de coqs. *Optique,* 13:35–41.

———— (1955b), Termes de gagaire ou de combat de coqs. *Optique,* 20:51–59.

MARQUEZ, L. G. (1954), *Reglamento del Club Gallistico de Caracas.* Caracas: Tip. Londres.

MARVIN, G. (1984), The cockfight in Andalusia, Spain: Images of the truly male. *Anthropolog. Quart.,* 57:60–70.

MCCAGHY, C. H. & NEAL, A. G. (1974), The fraternity of cockfighters: Ethical embellishments of an illegal sport. *J. Pop. Cult.,* 8:557–569.

MENDOZA, V. T. (1943), Folklore de los gallos. *Anuario de la Sociedad Folklorica de Mexico,* 4:115–125.

MODI, J. J. (1911), The cock as a sacred bird in ancient Iran. In: *Anthropological Papers.* Bombay: British Indian Press, pp. 104–121.

MOSHER, H. F. (1989), *A Stranger in the Kingdom.* New York: Doubleday.

NIEDERLAND, W. G. ET AL. (1967), A contribution to the psychology of gambling. *Psychoanal. Forum,* 2:175–185.

NUGENT, W. H. (1929), Cock fighting today. *Amer. Mercury,* 17:75–82.

O'GORMON, M. (1983), *Clancy's Bulba.* London: Hutchinson.

OLIVARES FIGUEROA, R. (1949), Gallos y galleros. *Diversiones Pascuales en Oriente y Otros Ensayos.* Caracas: Ardor, pp. 179–191.

OLMSTED, C. (1962), *Heads I Win, Tails You Lose.* New York: Macmillan.

PARKER, G. L. (1986), An outlet for male aggression: The secret fraternity of the southern cockfighter. *Tenn. Anthropolog.,* 11:21–28.

PARKER, R. (1985), From symbolism to interpretation: Reflections on the work of Clifford Geertz. *Anthropol. & Humanism Quart.,* 10:62–67.

PARSONS, G. E., JR. (1969), Cockfighting: A potential field of research. *N.Y. Folklore Quart.,* 25:265–288.

PARTRIDGE, E. (1960), *Shakespeare's Bawdy.* New York: Dutton.

PAUL, E. C. (1952), *"La gaguère" ou le combat de coqs.* Port-au-Prince: Imprimerie de l'Etat.

PEATE, I. C. (1970), The Denbigh cockpit and cockfighting in Wales. *Trans. Denbigshire Historical Soc.,* 19:125–132.

PEGGE, S. (1773), A memoir on cock-fighting. *Archaeologia,* 3:132–150.

PENROSE, B. (1976), Blood in the suburbs. *The Listener,* 95:236.

PEREZ, O. A. (1984), *La Pelea de Gallos en Venezuela: Léxico, Historia y Literatura.* Caracas: Ediciones Espada Rota.

PETERS, J. P. (1913), The cock. *J. Amer. Oriental Soc.,* 33:363–396.

PHILLOTT, D. C. (1910), Murgh-Nama. *J. Asiatic Soc. Bengal,* 6:73–91.

PICARD, M. (1983), En Feuilletant le "Bali Post": A propos de l'interdiction des combats de coqs à Bali. *Archipel,* 25:171–180.

POWEL, H. (1937), The game cock. *Amer. Mercury,* 41:185–191.

RASCH, J. (1930), De Haan in het volksgeloof. *Eigen Volk,* 2:216–221.

REMOUCHAMPS, E. & REMACLE, L. (1949), Les combats de coqs. *Enquêtes du Musée de la Vie Wallonee,* 4:40–80.

ROBERTS, B. S. C. (1965), Cockfighting: An early entertainment in North Carolina. *N. C. Hist. Rev.,* 42:306–314.

ROCES, A. R. (1959), *Of Cocks and Kites.* Manila: Regal.

ROSEBERRY, W. (1982), Balinese cockfights and the seduction of anthropology. *Soc. Res.,* 49:1013–1028.

RUSSELL, R. P. (1942), *Divine Providence and the Problem of Evil: A Translation of St. Augustine's De Ordine.* New York: Cosmopolitan Science and Art Service.

SALTORE, B. A. (1926–1927). Cock-fighting in Tuluva. *Quart. J. Mythic Soc.,* 17:316–327.

SANDIN, B. (1959), Cock-fighting: The Dayak national game. *Sarawak Museum J.,* 9:25–32.

SARABIA VIEJO, M. J. (1972), *El juego de gallos en Nueva España.* Sevilla: Escuela de Estudios Hispanoamericanos de Sevilla.

SARMA, I. K. (1964), The ancient game of cock-fight in India. *Quart. J. Mythic Soc.,* 54:113–120.

SAUBIDET, T. (1952), *Vocabulario y Refranero Criollo.* Buenos Aires: Editorial Guillermo Kraft.

SAUSSURE, C. DE (1902), *A Foreign View of England in the Reigns of George I & George II.* London: Murray.

SCHELTEMA, J. F. (1919), Roostam, the game-cock. *J. Amer. Folklore,* 32:306–323.

SCHNEIDER, M. A. (1987), Culture-as-text in the work of Clifford Geertz. *Theory and Soc.,* 16:809–839.

SCOTT, G. R. (1941), *Phallic Worship.* London: Laurie.

―――― (1957), *The History of Cockfighting.* London: Skilton.

SERIÈRE, V. DE (1873), Javasche volksspelen en vermaken. *Tijdschrift voor Nederlandsch Indië,* 4th Series, 2(1):81–101.

SIMMEL, E. (1920), Psycho-analysis of the gambler. *Internat. J. Psycho-Anal.,* 1:352–353.

SMITH, P. & DANIEL, C. (1975), *The Chicken Book.* Boston: Little, Brown.

SOEROTO, N. (1916–1917), Hanengevechten op Java. *Nederlandsch-Indië Oud & Nieuw,* 1:126–132.

SPEARS, R. A. (1990), *Forbidden American English.* Lincolnwood, IL: Passport Books.

STEKEL, W. (1924), *Peculiarities of Behavior,* Vol. 2. New York: Liveright.

TEGETMEIER, W. B. (1896), Sport in art: Cockfighting. *Magazine of Art,* 19:408–412.

TEIXEIRA, S. A. (1992), *A Semantica Simbolica dos Nomes de Galos de Briga, Bois, Prostitutas, Prostitutos e Travestis. Cadernos de Anthropologia* No. 8. Porto Alegre: PPGAS.

TIPPETTE, G. (1978), The birds of death. *Texas Monthly,* 6:163–165, 271–277.

TUDELA, J. (1959), Los gallos de dos mundos. *Amerikanistische Miszellen. Mitteilungen aus dem Museum für Völkerkunde in Hamburg,* 25:14–20.

VANDEREUSE, J. (1951), Le coq et les ecoliers (anciennes coutumes scolaires). *Folklore Brabançon,* 23:182–208.

VATSYAYANA, (1963), *Kama Sutra: The Hindu Ritual of Love.* New York: Castle.

VOGELER, E. J. (1942), Cock fighting in Florida. *Amer. Mercury,* 54:422–428.

WALKER, J. L. (1986), Feathers and steel: A folkloric study of cockfighting in northern Utah. Unpublished master's thesis in history, Utah State University.

WATSON, R. J. (1989), Definitive Geertz. *Ethnos,* 54:23–30.

WEST, N. (1950), *The Day of the Locust.* New York: New Directions Books.

WILKINSON, R. J. (1925), *Papers on Malay Subjects: Life and Customs, Part III. Malay Amusements.* Kuala Lumpur: F.M.S. Government Press.

WILLEFORD, C. (1972), *Cockfighter.* New York: Crown.

WITTE, J. DE (1868), Le génie des combats de coqs. *Revue Archéologique,* N.S. 17:372–381.

WOLLAN, L. A., JR. (1980), Questions from a study of cockfighting. *Bull. Center Study of Southern Culture & Religion,* 4 (2):26–32.

WURDEMANN, J. G. (1844), *Notes on Cuba.* Boston: Munroe.

3

Folklore and Psychoanalysis: Another Look at "The Boyfriend's Death"

MICHAEL P. CARROLL

The vast majority of the items on file in the Berkeley Folklore Archives (BFA) have been collected by students taking Alan Dundes' undergraduate course on folklore. The format used by the BFA, like that used by most folklore archives, requires students to present the text of each item collected along with some information (mainly age, gender, and ethnicity) on the informant who provided the item. But BFA format goes beyond most other formats in that it also encourages student-collectors to solicit *informant explanations* of each item ("what the item means to them"; something Dundes calls oral literary criticism) and to present as well their *own explanations* of each item.

Sometimes these explanations have been borrowed from someone else. In many cases, for instance, students offer an explanation that is obviously based on one of Dundes' lectures. But in other cases these explanations, from both informants and collectors, seem more clearly to be explanations they have developed for themselves on the spur of the moment. In these cases, we have something very close to "free association," which can be a valuable source of data for psychoanalytically inclined investigators. In this essay I want to illustrate how this sort of "folk commentary," when merged with Dundes' general approach to folklore, can provide new insight into a folk narrative that has been the subject of several earlier investigations.

THE BOYFRIEND'S DEATH

Urban legends are folk narratives that are transmitted orally, localized in a place or setting familiar to those telling the story, and considered to have actually occurred in the recent past. Such narratives are very much a contemporary form of folklore,[1] one in which the general public is very much interested.[2] Some of these narratives are overtly humorous; this alone might account for their wide popularity. Others are quite gruesome, dealing as they do with young boys castrated in shopping centers, women drivers threatened by knife-wielding assailants, children murdered in their beds while their babysitter sits nearby, etc.[3] My concern here is with one of these gruesome legends, typically called The Boyfriend's Death (hereafter TBD).

The basic structure of TBD goes like this:

1. Two teenagers, a boy and girl, drive to a secluded area and park.
2. The boy (always the driver) later tries to start the car, without success.
3. He tells the girl to stay in the car while he goes for help.
4. The boy does not return, and during the night the girl hears the sound of something brushing against, dripping onto, or hitting the car.
5. When morning comes, a policeman arrives and tells the girl to leave the car without looking back.
6. She gets out but violates the injunction and does look back.
7. She sees her boyfriend's dead body near the car.

Existing discussions of this particular legend are not particularly useful for anyone who wants to conduct a fresh investigation, mainly because they provide only a very small number of complete texts. In Linda Dégh's (1968) consideration of TBD, for instance, she makes reference to 19 different versions of the legend on file in the Folklore Archives at Indiana University, but presents the full text for only two of these. Similarly, TBD is discussed both by Barnes (1966) and Brunvand (1981), but here again each author presents only two full texts. The value of the

---

[1]Since "urban legends" are not restricted to urban areas, the term "contemporary legend" would seem a more appropriate label for these narratives. In fact, "contemporary legend" is the label used by British folklorists. In North America, however, "urban legend" is preferred, and I have honored that preference here.

[2]In part the great popularity of urban legends is evident from the fact that such legends are so widely known in our society. But their popularity is also evident from the fact that books dealing with these narratives do so well with the general public. It is rare, for instance, to find a well-stocked bookstore serving the general public that does not have one at least one of Jan Brunvand's (1981, 1984, 1986, 1989) books on urban legends in its "Myth/Folklore" section. Because Brunvand's books are almost entirely descriptive, the public's interest is clearly in the legends themselves, not in their analysis.

[3]Texts of all these legends, and a variety of others that involve gruesome events, can be found in already mentioned books by Brunvand.

folklore collections maintained at places like Berkeley and Indiana lies precisely in the fact that these collections permit scholars access to texts that are not available—and cannot be made available, given the constraints of publication—in published sources.

Looking through the texts of TBD on file in the Berkeley Folklore Archives, it seems apparent that there are three common variants of this legend, something that has not been clearly indicated in previous discussions. These variants (labeled here TBD_1, TBD_2, and TBD_3) are defined by the condition and position of the boyfriend's body at the end of the story.

In the most common variant, TBD_1 (of which there are 42 versions in the BFA), the boyfriend's body is hanging by the neck from a tree limb just above the car. The sound that the girl heard during the night was the sound of his feet brushing against the car roof as the body swayed in the breeze. The following are typical endings in TBD_1:

She starts walking and naturally looks back and sees her boyfriend hanging from a tree, his feet scraping against the top of the car [female informant, 1969].

She turned and there she saw the guy she was with, hanging from a limb of a tree by a rope around his neck above the car. His feet were dangling and the wind is what had caused his feet to hit the roof of the car all night [male informant, 1971].

Her eyes move from the car to the tree above and there is her boyfriend hanging by the neck and his feet had been dragging across the roof of the car all night long [female informant, 1979].

She looks up and sees her boyfriend hanging from the tree and his legs were swaying in the wind and hitting the top of the car [female informant, 1986].

In the second variant, TBD_2 (of which there are 23 versions in the BFA), the boyfriend is hanging upside down from the tree limb and the girl had heard his hands (or fingernails) brushing against the roof. The following are typical TBD_2 endings:

Above the car is her boyfriend hanging upside down, his arm softly brushing the top of the car [female informant, 1974].

There he was, dead and hanging upside down from the tree above the car, his nails scratching on the roof [female informant, 1975].

He was hanging from a tree by his feet, and his arm was dragging on the roof of the car [female informant, 1979].

He was dead and hanging upside down above the car, his fingernails scraping the roof of the car [female informant, 1981].

Finally, in TBD$_3$ (of which there are 13 versions in the BFA) the boyfriend has been decapitated:

The head of her boyfriend was suspended with a string from a tree branch, right outside the car. The bumping noise which she heard and thought were tree branches, was her boyfriend's head bumping against the windshield [male informant, 1962].

She sees the body of the boy on top of the car and the tapping noise that she heard was the sound of his blood dripping onto the trunk. His head had been cut off [female informant, 1974].

She gets out of the car. On the radio antenna of the car is her boyfriend's head, and the wind in the night was making it bump against the roof of the car [female informant, 1984].

All these endings are gory and horrifying, but then this is precisely the sort of material that has always proven amenable to psychoanalytic investigation.

FOLK INTERPRETATIONS

Teenage sexuality is almost certainly the underlying theme in TBD. Partly this is made clear by the opening incident: a teenage couple drive to a secluded place to park. Occasionally the text of the legend will say explicitly that they did this in order "to neck" or "to make out." In most texts, however, sex is *not* mentioned explicitly, presumably because the sexual nature of the event is too obvious to merit comment. What most of all establishes a link between TBD and teenage sexuality are the *explanations* of this story offered both by informants and collectors.

The most common explanation offered, for example, sees TBD as a *cautionary tale,* concerned mainly with discouraging teenagers from going to secluded locations for sexual purposes. For example:

> This story seems to fit the category of stories to scare young girls away from parking situations [female collector, 1970].

> He [informant] thinks that the story is supposed to make kids see that they shouldn't go off on lonely streets at night to neck in the car [1974].

> Sharon [informant] believes this story was meant to keep teenagers out of the hills by scaring them [1979].

> Nancy [informant] says that moralistically it could mean you shouldn't go out and fool around at night. It's dangerous to fool around at night [1980].

> The message to young women is clear: don't go out with boys who might try to compromise you [female collector, 1985].

Another commonly offered explanation is similar to this first one, but is more likely to see TBD as reflecting the fears and anxieties that teenagers, especially teenage girls, associate with heterosexual dating. For example:

> It is really directed or addressed to the girls and is an attempt to scare or warn them about the dangers and anxieties involved in dating [female collector, 1974].

> Its main purpose was to scare me and my friends. Of course, the question can be asked, "What were we scared of?" Was it the murderer,[4] or was it boys and the dating scene that we would soon be entering into? [female informant, 1979].

---

[4]While the decapitation element in TBD$_3$ seems to imply murder, explicit attributions of "murder" and "suicide" occur with roughly equal frequency across all three variants of TBD. Most versions—of any variant—make no explicit mention of either murder or suicide.

This transition from all-girl Friday night outings to the dating ritual with one boy causes a certain amount of anxiety. This anxiety gets projected and exaggerated in tales like this [female collector, 1976].

As a 16-year-old, my eyes were opened to the true horrors of dating! [female informant, 1975].

ANOMALY

Though these "folk explanations" offered by informants and collectors[5] can be used to provide evidence of a strong psychological association between TBD and teenage sexuality, they fail as *explanations* because they do not explain the most distinctive feature of the narrative: why it is that the *boy,* not the girl, meets such a gruesome end. After all, ours is a society in which young females have traditionally been more subject to sexual restrictions than young males. Furthermore, the fact that girls but not boys can get pregnant would suggest that in general teenage girls would be more likely to experience anxiety about sexual activities than teenage boys. If the narrative *were* primarily a cautionary tale designed to reinforce sexual norms or a vehicle for expressing anxiety, then you might expect that it would be the *girl* who suffers the most. Yet just the reverse happens.

Occasionally, those hearing the story will perceive that having the *boy* meet a gruesome end seems anomalous. The following remarks, for instance, were supplied by three different collectors:

This legend, as many other adolescent based legends, plays on the fear of dating experienced by teenagers. . . . However, in this case, rather than the boy taking the opportunity to turn the misfortune into a romantic encounter, he gets killed. I am, frankly, not quite sure what this implies, but there seems to be a message somewhere [female collector, 1972].

The legend's irony is that the guy is murdered when we expect that it is more likely that the girl will be harmed [male collector, 1974].

---

[5]I might add that most previous scholarly commentators, like most informants and student collectors, have also seen TBD as a cautionary tale or as a vehicle for expressing anxieties. See Brunvand (1981); Barnes (1966).

> This story seems to be of the sort warning girls about sex and dates, but the strange ending is perplexing. . . . The story seems to focus more on the boy than the girl, so I can't help but think that the story is commenting about him more than the girl [male collector, 1985].

So: why does the boy get killed and not the girl?

WISH-FULFILLMENT

I take it as self-evident that folk narratives would not be told and retold unless they were in some way gratifying to those who were transmitting them. Following Freud and Dundes, I also suggest that most folk narratives are gratifying because they allow for the vicarious and disguised fulfillment of unconscious wishes. With this in mind, the key to understanding the underlying appeal of TBD lies precisely in the anomaly mentioned above.

In actual practice, as already suggested, females are more likely to suffer as a consequence of teenage sex than males. TBD is thus a fantasy in which this "real life" situation is *reversed*. In contrast to what happens in real life, TBD presents a situation in which the unpleasant conse-quences that might follow upon teenage sex fall most heavily upon the *boy*. Such a fantasy should appeal most of all to young girls, and the evidence indicates that it does. Most of the informants from whom the narrative was collected were female, and informants routinely mentioned that TBD was a favorite at "slumber parties" attended by girls in their early teens.

Seeing TBD as reflecting a reversal of real life helps to explain other features of the narrative as well. For instance, it has long been a folk belief among North American teenagers that teenage boys often "run out of gas" in deserted areas in order take sexual advantage of their dates. Whether or not this actually happened to any substantial degree is not important; what is important is that most North American teenagers believe that it happens (or at least used to happen) with some frequency. That this folk belief about "running out of gas in order to take sexual advantage of females" is somehow associated with TBD is occasionally made clear by the remarks of both collectors and informants:

> Deliberately running out of gas, or otherwise having a car break down, is a common ploy used by males to be alone with their dates [female collector, 1972].

Running out of gas is the classic way of getting a girl alone, so a guy can make his move [female informant, 1979].

He [informant] says that it seems to be a deterrent story about guys and girls that go "parking" and "run out of gas," which is a popular excuse for couples who wish to be alone in a car together in the dark [1984].

But what folk commentators overlook when making this connection is that the narrative *reverses* the temporal ordering of events associated with this "common ploy": In the narrative the couple necks and *then* the boy tries to start the car, only to find that it won't start because it is out of gas or some such thing. Under the interpretation I am offering, this reversal of the temporal ordering associated with the "running out of gas" motif is a consequence of the general emphasis on the reversal of real life that enables TBD to gratify the wishes of young teenage girls.

There remains one element in TBD that needs to be explained, and that is the unusual nature of the boyfriend's death in all three variants.

LANGUAGE AND THE MAKING OF FOLK NARRATIVES

Because folk narratives are transmitted orally, they can be changed. It seems obvious that at least some of these changes will be shaped by the psychological associations that the narrative evokes in the minds of those who hear it. Some earlier investigators have suggested that *phonetic similarity* in particular plays a key role in this process. In the 19th century, for instance, Max Muller argued that *homonymy,* the fact that several different words in a language can share a common phonetic root, was utilized during the process of oral transmission in order to "enlarge" the kernel-story around which a myth formed. His favorite example was the Greek myth of Daphne and Apollo. In the most common variant of that myth Apollo pursues the wood nymph Daphne with lustful intentions. Daphne flees, but rapidly loses ground and calls upon the goddess Gaia for aid. Just as Apollo catches up with Daphne, Gaia changes the nymph into a laurel tree. Ever since, the myth relates, the laurel has been sacred to Apollo. But why, Muller asks, is Daphne changed into a *laurel* tree rather than some other type of tree? For Muller, the answer lay with the fact that the Greek words for "Daphne" and for "laurel" share a common phonetic root. This phonetic similarity, he argued, established a psychological association between "Daphne" and "laurel," which in turn made it likely that something about a laurel tree would be incorporated into a story about a person named Daphne.[6]

Freud too recognized that the mind made use of phonetic similarities in constructing fantasies. In tracing back the chain of psychological associations that gave rise to the content of particular dreams, he often found that the dreamer's mind had played upon phonetic similarities in disguising the wish that gave rise to the dream being analyzed. He suggested, for example, that the reference to "Italy" which appeared in one patient's dream resulted from the phonetic similarity between *gen Italien* and *Genitalien* [genitals] (Freud, 1900). Dozens of other examples, all involving psychological associations established by phonetic similarity, can be found scattered throughout *The Interpretation of Dreams*.[7] Dreams are not folklore, of course, but *jokes* are, and in his work on jokes Freud argued that phonetic similarities were quite often used in constructing jokes. For Freud, the mind's use of phonetic similarities was especially important in constructing a joke's ending, in which the normally repressed that underlies the joke is suddenly thrust into the conscious mind of the listener.

Alan Dundes is one of the few modern folklorists who has picked up on the suggestion that the psychological associations formed by phonetic similarity play an important role in shaping the content of orally transmitted material. Consider, for example, Dundes' (1980a) analysis of Tale Type 311, Rescue by the Sister. A common variant of this tale goes like this:

1. Two sisters, one after the other, are taken by an ogre to his subterranean castle and forbidden to enter one particular room.
2. They disobey and an egg or a key becomes bloody.

---

[6]For Muller a story about someone named Daphne *had* to be the core of this particular myth. His overarching hypothesis was that most Indo-European myths had started out as metaphors about the sun and the moon and that they became stories only when their original meaning had been forgotten. "Daphne", he argued, had originally meant only "dawn," and so the story of Apollo chasing Daphne had started life as nothing more than a metaphor describing how the sun's ray's chased away the dawn. But putting his "solar" interpretations aside, and focusing only on what Muller called homonymy, the myth-making process in this case could easily have started with something far simpler: the cultic belief that the laurel was sacred to Apollo. Given such a cultic belief, the phonetic similarity between "laurel" and "Daphne" could easily have given rise to a story in which a person named Daphne played a central role in establishing that cultic practice. For more on Muller and his solar mythology, see Carroll (1985).

[7]See especially the entries under "play upon words" and "verbal ambiguity" in Freud (1900).

3. The ogre kills them by decapitation.
4. The youngest sister eventually enters the room and finds the decapitated bodies of her sisters.
5. The dead sisters are resuscitated, and all the girls escape.

For Dundes the "getting into a special place" element is a reference to heterosexual vaginal intercourse.[8] The underlying concern of the tale, however, is specifically with a young girl's anxieties about "defloration." Such an interpretation, first of all, would explain why the central character is a young *girl*. It also explains why a "spot" appears on an egg or a key: For Dundes this is a symbolic representation of the blood that is often associated with the rupture of the hymen during the first experience of vaginal intercourse. But what about the decapitated heads of the heroine's sisters?

In most psychoanalytic discussions, including Freud's, decapitation is taken to symbolize castration. Dundes, by contrast, argues that the key to understanding the "decapitated heads of the sisters" element lies with an association formed by phonetic similarity. The heroine's sisters are (like her) "maidens," and so their heads are in effect "maiden heads." But "maiden heads" is phonetically similar to "maidenhead," a term commonly used to designate the hymen. In short, the "maiden heads" which appear in the tale, like "spot appears on key or egg," symbolize a young girl's anxieties about the rupturing of her hymen during her first experience of heterosexual vaginal intercourse.

This particular tale aside, Dundes has in a number of other contexts made the same general point: The psychological associations that shape folklore traditions are often psychological associations that have been established as the result of phonetic similarities.[9] I suggest that this is precisely what has happened in the case of TBD as well.

"NECKING"

So far I have argued that the TBD is best regarded as a female fantasy that reverses real life. But a literal reversal of real life, however, is not

---

[8]Though Dundes' does not mention it, there is another variant of Tale Type 311 in which the "sisters forbidden to enter special room" element is replaced by "sisters forbidden to eat a human bone" element, which seems an even more obvious representation of heterosexual intercourse. If allomotifs are indeed psychologically equivalent, as Dundes (1987a,b) has argued, then this second variant provides additional support for his interpretation of this tale.

[9]See for instance Dundes' (1980b) analysis of Evil Eye beliefs.

possible. Urban legends are told as stories that have actually happened, which means that such legends cannot violate the natural order of things (at least not too much). In this case, it means that the legend cannot portray the boyfriend as getting pregnant. The result: he dies instead.

Now consider the three variant endings to TBD: In one case the boyfriend is hung from a branch and his feet brush against the car's roof as he sways in the breeze, in another he is hung by the feet, in the third he is decapitated. A common element in both the first and third variants is that the boyfriend's death is associated with damage to his *neck*. But "necking" is one of the folk terms most often used by informants and collectors alike to describe the sexual activities that initiate the narrative[10] (the other two such terms being "making out" and "parking"). I suggest that the phonetic similarity between "necking" ($=$ the sexual activity) and "neck" ($=$ the body part) makes it likely that during the process of oral transmission something about a "neck" would be incorporated into a fantasy concerned with reversing the real life consequences of "necking." That "something" is that the boyfriend's death comes to be associated with damage to his neck.

Damage to the neck is *not* well developed in TBD_2. Indeed this variant is the one least consistent with my interpretation. Still, "hanging upside down" from a tree does seem generally consistent with the emphasis on reversal that pervades TBD. Furthermore, damage to the boyfriend's neck does occasionally appear in TBD_2, for example:

She saw her boyfriend tied upside down from the tree, *with his throat cut* . . . (male informant, 1969).

They told her not to turn around, but she did, and her boyfriend was hanging by his feet from a tree *with his throat cut* . . . (male informant, 1970).

She turns around to see Tom murdered, *his blood drained from the throat* . . . (male informant, 1980).

Panicking, she jumps up and out of the car to find her boyfriend hanging upside down from the tree *with his head almost cut off* (male informant, 1975).

---

[10]According to Partridge (1974), "necking" has been used in the United States to designate this sexual activity at least since the 1920s.

Even here then, as in TBD$_1$ and TBD$_3$, necking can lead to a death associated with neck damage.

URBAN LEGENDS AND SOCIAL CONTEXT

Dégh (1968) noted that TBD first began to circulate widely in the late 1960s. This was a period of great change for American teenagers, particularly in regard to sexual activity. Attitudes toward sex became more positive and less restrictive, and this was followed — in the late 1960s and early 1970s — by changes in sexual behavior. Dundes (1979) has argued that this increase in sexual activity brought with it an increased concern about the consequences of sexual activity. For women this meant an increased concern about possibly getting pregnant and having to have an abortion. Dundes sees the emergence of the "dead baby" joke cycle as a response to this increased concern about pregnancy and abortion.

That the TBD should become popular specifically in the late 1960s, then, seems consistent with the interpretation of that legend that has been developed here. By the late 1960s, in other words, unlike the 1950s, the issue was less one of anxiety about sex and more one of anxiety over the consequences of sex. For women, this increased anxiety over the consequences of sex would naturally lead — I suggest — to the unconscious wish that males (not themselves) might suffer the most as a result of sexual intercourse. If unconscious wishes do structure the content of folklore during the course of oral transmission, then this particular unconscious wish, held in common by a great many women, would work to produce a folk narrative in which it *is* the male, not the female, who suffers the most following sexual activity. For the reasons already given, TBD is just such a narrative.

None of this is to deny that TBD may have been constructed by borrowing and rearranging motifs from earlier legends. The opening scene in TBD, for instance, was almost certainly borrowed from "The Hook," an urban legend that was widely popular in the 1950s.[11] In the end, however TBD, in all its variants, was very much a product of the particular social context in which it emerged.

CONCLUSION

One of my goals in this article been quite limited: to discover the appeal of a particular urban legend. But there has been a second goal as well: to

---

[11]For a discussion of "The Hook" see Brunvand (1981); Dundes (1971).

demonstrate that the methodology that Alan Dundes has been urging on folklorists and psychoanalysts for three decades is not at all idiosyncratic, but rather is a methodology easily imitated by anyone who has a minimal familiarity with, say, *The Interpretation of Dreams,* and who has access to folkloric materials. Notice that my analysis of TBD has at every point been structured by the two things that I identified in the *Introduction* as being the defining features of Dundes' approach to folklore, namely: (1) the belief that folk narratives are appealing because they represent the disguised fulfillment of unconscious wishes, and (2) the methodological injunction to pay careful attention to folkloric variation. In this particular case I also made use of the "contextual" information that Dundes the folklorist insists be gathered alongside the text of any particular item of folklore, as well as Dundes' emphasis on the role played by phonetic similarity in establishing the psychological associations that shape oral traditions.

My own wish, then, not at all disguised, is that this volume will serve less to commemorate Alan Dundes' work than to promote a wider use of his methodology. The result would work to the benefit of both psychoanalysis and folklore.

BIBLIOGRAPHY

BARNES, D. R. (1966), Some functional horror stories on the Kansas University campus. *South. Folklore Quart.,* 30 (Dec):305–318.

BRUNVAND, J. H. (1981), *The Vanishing Hitchhiker.* New York: W. W. Norton.

———— (1984), *The Choking Doberman and Other "New" Urban Legends.* New York: W. W. Norton.

———— (1986), *The Mexican Pet.* New York: W. W. Norton.

———— (1989), *Curses! Broiled Again!* New York: W. W. Norton.

CARROLL, M. P. (1985), Some third thoughts on Max Muller and solar mythology. *Europ. J. Sociol.,* 26:263–290.

DEGH, L. (1968), The boyfriend's death. *Indiana Folklore* 1:101–106.

DUNDES, A. (1971), On the psychology of legend. In: *American Folk Legend: A Symposium,* ed. W. Hand. Berkeley: University of California Press, pp. 21–36.

———— (1979), The dead baby joke cycle. *West. Folklore* 38:145–57.

———— (1980a), Projection in folklore: a plea for psychoanalytic semiotics. In: *Interpreting Folklore,* A. Dundes. Bloomington: Indiana University Press, pp. 33–61.

———— (1980b) [orig. 1976], Wet and dry, the Evil Eye: An essay in Indo-European and Semitic worldview. In: *Interpreting Folklore,* A. Dundes. Bloomington: Indiana University Press, pp. 93–133.

———— (1987a) [orig. 1982], The symbolic equivalence of allomotifs in the rabbit-herd (AT 570). In: *Parsing Through Customs: Essays by a Freudian Folklorist,* A. Dundes. Madison: The University of Wisconsin Press, pp. 167–177.

———— (1987b) [orig. 1985], The American game of "smear the queer" and the homosexual

4

When a Lingam Is Just a Good Cigar: Psychoanalysis and Hindu Sexual Fantasies

WENDY DONIGER

PART I: THE PROBLEM

Dreams and Myths

Stories from ancient India present a great boon to psychoanalysts trained in the Freudian, Western tradition. The blatant sexuality of Hindu myths has often been noted. Aldous Huxley once said that an intellectual was someone who had found something more interesting than sex; in Indology, an intellectual need not make that choice at all. Fantasies that depth psychology speculates might exist in the minds of infants or young children are actually attested to in the recorded literature of Indian adults. Thus the Hindu stories seem to corroborate Freudian hypotheses about infant sexuality.

But at the same time, the Hindu myths raise broader questions about the very nature of symbolism, particularly the symbolism of dreams. In order to formulate tentative answers to these questions, we must begin by attempting to clarify the distinction between dreams and myths. Why do we think there is a connection between dreams and myths at all? There are several good reasons. First of all, Freud himself suggested the connection (Freud, 1900, pp. 386–389). Second, many traditional cultures have suggested the connection, in both directions: shamans and holy men claim to have had dreams which then become the substance of myths; people who wish to have significant dreams "incubate" them in temples and shrines where myths are told; and people incorporate into their dreams many of the cultural symbols that they have learned from myths. Third, we ourselves can see direct connections between certain phenomena that occur in myths and in dreams but not, usually, in other cultural expressions, the sorts of things that we now call "surreal": transformations (people turning into animals, etc.), distortions of time and space, people flying, and so forth.

On a continuum of narrative forms, myth mediates between the entirely personal, or solipsistic, of which the dream is the quintessential example, and the entirely general, or abstract, of which a logical syllogism is the quintessential example. Dreams are private; a myth is a dream that has gone public. Dreams are made to be forgotten, myths to be remembered. People possess myths, but dreams possess people. The myth is the secondary elaboration that attempts, always in vain, to recapture the dream. And since it can never succeed, it generates an infinite number of failures (Lévi-Strauss, 1963, 229) — or iterations, with significant changes, rather than repetitions, literally the same (to use Lacan's terms). We might say that a dream is to a myth as a penis is to a phallus: Neither a dream nor a penis is ever available to us unmediated, without the veil of language and symbolism; each hovers behind the symbol (i.e., the myth or the phallus) to give it meaning.

In his response to my book, *Dreams, Illusion, and Other Realities* (O'Flaherty, 1984), Sudhir Kakar pointed out the importance of this distinction, drawing his own distinction between "real" dreams (the product of the unconscious), imaginative creations (the product of conscious thought, a category that would include myths), and "invented dreams," elaborate literary creations that are presented by the texts as the dreams of one or another character (which draw upon both conscious and unconscious thought and thus mediate between dreams and myths). In the words of Kakar (1984):

These dreams [recorded in the Sanskrit myths] are not even the invented dreams one is familiar with from literature and which stand midway between real dreams and imaginative creations. Invented dreams in literature can indeed be interpreted by paying very close attention to their context, to the dreamer's feelings and thoughts at waking and to the associations of the audience or the analyst (in place of the missing associations of the dreamer, as in analytical practice). All these techniques which succeed in interpreting dreams in literature, at least to the analyst's satisfaction, simply do not succeed with the Indian dreams. From the psychological viewpoint, they are not dreams but imaginative creations, conceits in the service of the metaphysical narrative . . . in spite of their formal similarities to what we today call dreams [p. 363].

In the more technical psychoanalytical sense, the myth cannot have latent content on a personal level; only the people who respond to the myth have, each his or her own, latent meanings for the myth, in the strict sense of the term. But a myth has a latent *cultural* meaning that the culture as a whole may mask. Out of context, anything can symbolize anything; the context of a dream is provided by the personal associations of the individual dreamer, and the context of a myth by the associations of the culture. And because the culture is embodied in people, we must search for the associations of the culture in the cumulative glosses offered by a group, rather than by an individual, within the culture. We can do this by looking at a group of other myths (as Claude Lévi-Strauss advises us to do), commentaries on the myths (as classical philology advises us to do), and the broader data or "thick description" supplied by other cultural expressions (as Clifford Geertz advises us to do).

The hermeneutics of suspicion—the belief that a text can mean something other than what the author thinks it means, a hermeneutic derived directly from Freud—prevents us, however, from simply asking members of the culture what they think the symbol means. Many Hindus, for instance, will argue that the *lingam* has nothing whatsoever to do with the male sexual organ, an assertion blatantly contradicted by much of the material that we will soon examine. The gloss offered from within the culture must be accepted as a truth, but only a partial truth. We must also find other, more indirect cultural contexts, such as the patterns formed by other myths, or the rituals associated with the myth, or other evidence of how the myth is used in society.

Because the interpretation of symbols (such as phalluses) depends in part on the context supplied by the culture (as group dreamer), cross-cultural investigation may produce a disharmonious clash of symbols: It may well be that Hindu children, whose relationship to their parents is different from that of Viennese Jewish children, will not wield their phallic symbols in the ways that Freud anticipated. But the implicit gloss supplied by the context that one myth, one variant, constitutes for another, does seem to validate Freud's arguments about the processes, the mechanisms by which dreams and myths make use of symbols. The clue lies in the range not of content but of process (LaCapra, 1991). Thus, for instance, the fact that the vaginas in one variant of the Indra myth are replaced by eyes in another variant, or indeed that one variant actually *says* that the eyes replaced the vaginas, is good evidence for the process of upward displacement. But it is by no means a foregone conclusion that eyes or vaginas have the meaning for Hindus that they have for Freudians. The signifiers remain the same, but what is signified may be very different. Despite these shifts in what is actually signified, however, the process of signification is something that Freud has taught us to recognize, and that we can recognize in Benares as well as in New York. Thus, the inversion and condensation that are at the heart of Freud's theory of the interpretation of dreams and Lévi-Strauss' inter-pretation of myths (*pace* Lévi-Strauss' anti-Freudian protests) are clearly at work in the Hindu myths. The processes, therefore, may well be universal even if the contents are not.

The Manifest Latency of Unsymbols

If, then, we accept, with these modifications, a basic correspondence between the symbolic processes of dreams and the basic symbolic processes of myths, we are left with a problem. The blatant sexuality of Hindu myths challenges us to refine the Freudian assumption that a symbol *always* hides something else. Indian texts seem to express sexual violence in an unmasked form; things that are latent, symbolized by other things, in the West are manifest, symbolized only by themselves, in many Indian texts. Or so it seems. One might well ask: If all this is manifest, what is latent? What is it that these stories reveal and conceal? If what is on the surface is sex, what is below the surface? What implications do these stories have for Freudian and post-Freudian theories of sexual symbolism?

There are three possible approaches to the challenge posed by the manifest latency, as it were, of Indian myths. First, we can say that they have nothing to do with dreams, nothing to do with the unconscious, at all, and leave it at that. If we reject this option, as I think we must, and instead acknowledge the relationship, however attenuated, between dreams and myths, we are left with two more options. We can jettison either the Freudian assumption that a symbol always hides something else or that what the symbol always hides is sexual. In the first case, we can argue that some elements of dreams or myths are simply not symbolic, that they stand literally for themselves; indeed this is the case for some, though not for all. But if we wish to argue that some dreams and myths do indeed contain symbols (and I can hardly see how we can fail to do this), we must ask what it is that they symbolize. Let us examine these last two options.

In the introduction to *The Trial(s) of Psychoanalysis,* Françoise Meltzer (1987) writes:

> There is the famous anecdote about Freud: upon being reminded by a disciple that to smoke cigars is clearly a phallic activity, Freud, cigar in hand, is said to have responded, "Sometimes a good cigar is just a good cigar." The anecdote demonstrates, it seems to me, a problematic central to psychoanalysis: the discipline which insists on transference and, perhaps even more significantly, on displacement as fundamental principles, ultimately must insist in turn on seeing everything as being "really" something else. Such an ideology of metamorphosis is so much taken for granted that unlike the rest of the world, which generally has difficulty in being convinced that a pipe, for example, is not necessarily a pipe at all, psychoanalysis needs at times to remind itself, in a type of return to *adaequatio,* that it is possible for a cigar really to *be* a cigar [p. 1].

And on the cover of the book, under a Magritte-like cigar, is the caption: "Ceci n'est pas un cigare." A cigar is a cigar when you strike a match to it and smoke it. In a dream, when you dream of picking up a cigar and then have an orgasm, that cigar is not a cigar.

Yet even Freud's cigar may have been more than just a cigar; this episode is said to have taken place only a year after Freud's cancer of the mouth had been diagnosed, and in this context the cigar may well have symbolized for him death rather than sex (Gilman, 1991). Moreover, the anecdote in question is highly apocryphal, and seems rather to represent secondary revision on the part of Freudians (or even anti-Freudians) than the words of Freud himself. Whether Freud himself was ever so critical of Freudian symbolism is, on the face of it, unlikely. But the enduring popularity of the apocryphal anecdote (like the popularity of the equally apocryphal Jungian anecdote of Kékulé and the dream of the ouroboros that gave him the clue to the arrangement of the six carbon atoms in the benzene ring) tells us something worth knowing about the doubts of the post-Freudian tradition.

Not only a cigar, but even a phallus, may symbolize itself. Perhaps it would be better to say that a symbol always does symbolize something else, but that not all stories or images are symbolic. Some would argue that, at times, a dream or a myth can simply express itself, symbolizing nothing (as Shakespeare's Macbeth said of our lives: "A tale told by an idiot, full of sound and fury, signifying nothing"). The nonsymbolic aspects of presumed symbols have long bedeviled psychoanalysts: "As somebody (Bernfeld?) once remarked, an aeroplane is a symbol of erection, and the fact that one can also use it for going from Paris to Berlin is merely incidental" (Róheim, 1970, p. 156; O'Flaherty, 1985, p. 115).

If, as Adler is said to have remarked, everything is a symbol of intercourse except intercourse, what is intercourse a symbol of? And does this pose the same sort of problem for Indian mythology that it poses for Western psychoanalysis?

One way to account for the blatancy of sexual symbols in Indian myths is simply to argue that the Hindus invented our psychiatric myths better than we did, as well as earlier. This was what Claude Lévi-Strauss argued, perversely, *against* Freud. He pointed out that there is a "convergence between psychoanalytic and mythic thought," and, more particularly, that Freud's theory of the primeval oedipal conflict (expressed in *Totem and Taboo;* Freud, 1913) was like a myth of the Jivaro, a South American Indian tribe (Lévi-Strauss, 1989, p. 172). "As we can see," he remarks, "the Indians even had psychoanalysts!" And he goes on to emphasize the complete convergence of Jivaro myths and Freudian theories by remarking, tongue firmly in cheek, "How wise are the Americans in calling psychoanalysts 'head-shrinkers,' thus spontaneously associating them with the Jivaro!" (p. 186).

The convergence, Lévi-Strauss argues in the same work, is evident in the founding myth of incest:

> It is *Totem and Taboo* in its entirety that, well ahead of Freud, the Jivaro Indians anticipated in the myth that for them plays the part of a Genesis: societies arose when the primitive horde split into hostile clans after the murder of the father whose wife had committed incest with their son. From a psychological point of view the Jivaro myth offers an even richer and more subtle plot than *Totem and Taboo* [p. 186].

This rather tautological and certainly unfalsifiable argument (see Doniger, 1989) is somewhat reminiscent of Philip Roth's suggestion that Jews don't need Freud, so patent are their oedipal relationships with their mothers. Speaking of a boy who had hanged himself, the women friends of his mother say, "You couldn't look for a boy more in love with his mother than Ronald!" Roth (1969) comments on this:

> I swear to you, this is not bullshit or a screen memory, these are the very words these women used. The great dark operatic themes of

human suffering and passion come rolling out of those mouths like
the prices of Oxydol and Del Monte canned corn! . . . No, you
don't have to go digging where these people are concerned — they
wear the old unconscious on their *sleeves!* [p. 108].

Thus we can outsmart ourselves if we try to apply a hermeneutics of
suspicion to material that is innocent. Discounting this argument, which
would discard Freud as redundant, merely duplicating the Jivaro (and,
by implication, the Hindu) texts, I would argue, on the contrary, that
such texts are corroborative. But we must use them with caution.

The blatant Hindu images, which Prakash Desai has termed "unsymbols," appear in many cultures. Thus a man in Jonathan Swift's
Gulliver's Travels so hated symbols that he kept a wheelbarrow full of the
real things to point to when he wished to refer to them. And the poet
Yehuda Amichai remarked, when told that Jerusalem was a symbol, that
it was a symbol with a sewer system. Within the Hindu myths,
"unsymbols" do, as Freud and Lévi-Strauss pointed out, mask the
meaning by fragmenting it, inverting it, obfuscating it, and obsessively
repeating it, never the same. Symbols may sometimes be blank or
censoring, but sometimes they simultaneously fragment and reassemble
with other, related meanings. A disguise is going on here, too. But is it
disguising something besides the fear of the sexual act that is often the
specific, manifest focus of the myth?

This brings us back to the second half of the syllogism, the Freudian
assumption that when a symbol does hide something, what it always
hides is sex. When is a phallus not a phallus? When it is a phallic symbol.
This was a bone of contention between Freud and Jung for many years.
As Jung (1974) wrote:

Unfortunately, Freud's idea of sexuality is incredibly elastic and so
vague that it can be made to include almost anything. . . . Take,
for instance, the so-called phallic symbols which are supposed to
stand for the *membrum virile* and nothing more. Psychologically
speaking, the *membrum* is itself . . . an emblem of something
whose wider content is not at all easy to determine [p. 105;
O'Flaherty, 1985, pp. 115-116].

The mind boggles at the thought of what *Jung* regarded as "vague" in
Freud, when he himself would only define the referent of the phallus as
"something whose wider content is not at all easy to determine." Freud
acknowledged that genital language often masked much broader issues

of sexuality, itself conceived as a force that encompassed far more than genital activity. Freud also referred to a phallus as a "simulacrum," paving the way for Lacan's distinction between the penis (as part of the body, signified) and the phallus (as a word, a signifier).

One Man's Obscenity Is Another Man's Divinity

In India, what is obscene may be something else—something that is symbolized by a simple, everyday thing like a phallus. It might be something like death—for, as we shall see, a phallus or vagina is often a lethal weapon—or god. What is signified (with its symbols that signify it) in the beginning may be sex, but then it is religion that is signified (by sex and its symbols, as well as by the symbols of religion), and finally, in a kind of second naïveté, sex is signified by religion and its symbols, which is in turn signified by sex and its symbols, as well as by the symbols of religion . . . until we find ourselves in an infinite *mise en abîme,* and it is impossible to distinguish between signified and signifier. In "unpacking" the symbolic image, one must beware of taking theology too seriously, but one must also beware of taking sexuality too seriously.

It is notoriously difficult to isolate the sexual signifiers or signifieds of sacrifices. An Upanisadic text likens the depositing of semen in the woman to the depositing of the oblation in the sacred fire, in a passage giving practical, ritual instructions for taking back the seed from a lover whom the husband hates (implying, perhaps, that there is another category not discussed here, a lover whom he does not hate . . .)

> If a man's wife has a lover whom he hates, he should spread out a row of reed arrows, their heads smeared with ghee, and sacrifice them, in inverse order, into a vessel of fire, saying, "You have made a libation in my fire! I take away your breath, your sons, your cattle, your sacrifices and good deeds, your hope and your expectations. You have made a libation in my fire, you [Mr. X]."
> If a Brahmin who knows this curses a man, that man dies impotent and without merit. Therefore one should not try to get on "joking terms" with the wife of a learned Brahmin [*Brhadaranyaka Upanisad* 6.4.12; O'Flaherty, 1980, p. 10].

Is the sacrifice itself, the pouring of butter into a pan of fire, derived from a sexual metaphor in the first place? Is this text imposing a sexual meaning on a nonsexual sacrifice, or bringing out the meaning that underlies the sacrifice in the first place?

When a friend of mine, a Catholic priest, attended a Jewish ceremony of circumcision for the first time, he was horrified to discover that they actually cut the child's penis. "I thought it was *symbolic!*" he exclaimed, no doubt recalling his own tradition that substituted wine for the blood of Christ. But of course the circumcision *is* symbolic, not of the cutting of the child's penis (which actually happens) but of the child's initiation into the tribe of Israel. And the communion wine, on the other hand, need not be so very symbolic. When Catholic missionaries encountered the Maya in Yucatan, in the 16th century, they were horrified to discover that after the Maya had been converted to Christianity they adapted their former ceremonies of human sacrifice to include a *real* crucifixion (O'Flaherty, 1988, p. 117). The Inquisition regarded this barbarism as a "mock crucifixion," but it was in fact a *real* crucifixion, as the Mass was not. Here again, one culture's symbol is another culture's reality—and, at another level (e.g., circumcision), its symbol.

The ease with which symbols vibrate between the theological and the sexual was delightfully demonstrated in the context of a Tantric Indian ritual that Sudhir Kakar (1982) tried to understand:

> In my own conversations with tantriks, I sometimes had the impression that they deliberately (and mischievously) used the multivalence of tantrik terminology to befuddle the perhaps too-earnest outsider. Whenever the term *ananda* came up in a text . . . and I translated it as "supreme bliss," I was told to forget all the mystical balderdash since *ananda* was the pure and simple pleasure of intercourse. If I took the concrete meaning . . . then I was invariably chided for my literal-mindedness, since the word in that particular context just happened to stand for "enlightenment" [pp. 156–157].

Is sex a euphemism for god? Or is god a euphemism for sex? Or both? This is the cross-cultural challenge to Freudian universalism: It may be that what is latent for us may be manifest for them, and vice versa. Can we learn from them, therefore, about our latent fantasies, or about theirs? Can we take what is manifest in their myths not only as symbolic of something latent in their culture (whatever that might be), but of something latent in ours, or, even better, of something *manifest* in ours? If we can draw parallels between the latent content of our dreams and their myths, does this imply that there are some universal latent cultural contents that arise out of universal human situations? For example, do individual members of different cultures experience their genitalia in ways similar enough (despite being differently mediated by different cultures) to inspire similar group fantasies (myths) of vulnerability and sexual mutilation? The answers to these questions can only be sought by a close examination of the myths, to which we must now turn.

PART II: THE EVIDENCE OF THE MYTHS

Preinfantile and Infantile Sexuality: Freud in Sanskrit

Indian texts speculate not only on infantile fantasies but on sexual fantasies even *before* the womb, when the soul-to-be-reborn has left its last body (that of a dying person) but has not yet entered its new body, and hence is called an "intermediate-state-being." As McDermott (1976) relates:

> The Oedipal character of [the Buddhist] analysis would do justice to Freud: driven by karma, the intermediate-state being goes to the location where rebirth is to take place. Possessing the divine eye by virtue of its karma, it is able to see the place of its birth, no matter how distant. There it sees its father and mother to be, united in intercourse. Finding the scene hospitable, its passions are stirred. If male, it is smitten with desire for its mother. If female, it is seized with desire for its father. And inversely, it hates either mother or father, which it comes to regard as a rival. Concupiscence and hatred thus arise in the [unborn creature] as its driving passions. Stirred by these wrong thoughts, it attaches itself to the place where the sexual organs of the parents are united, imagining that it is there joined with the object of its passion. Taking pleasure in the impurity of the semen and blood in the womb, the [intermediate state being] establishes itself there. Thus do the [elements of matter] arise in the womb. They harden; and the intermediate-state being perishes, to be replaced immediately by the birth existence [pp. 171–172].

Thus Buddhist embryology corroborates the Freudian hypothesis that *very* young male children experience lust for the mother and antagonism toward the father. After that, it is mere child's play, as it were, to speculate on sexual fantasies *within* the womb. A passage from the *Brhaddevata* states:

> The sage Brhaspati tried to rape Mamata, the wife of his brother Utathya, when Mamata was pregnant. But the unborn embryo protected his mother by kicking out the intruding penis, shouting, "Get out, uncle! There's only room for one in here, and I was here first!" The infuriated rapist cursed the embryo to be blind; the child was born as Dirghatamas ("Long Darkness") [4.11–15].

The myth of Dirghatamas corroborates the Freudian hypothesis that a young male child is threatened by the sexuality of the father with his mother and that the father retaliates with physical aggression against the child. The direction of the aggression, from father to son rather than from son to father, has been characterized as typically Indian (Ramanujan, 1983). The aggression results in the child's mutilation—here, blinding, which, Freud hypothesized, stands for castration, through upward displacement. We will return to other examples of upward displacement in Hindu myths.

There are many other Hindu stories about the sexuality not of embryos but of very young children. In one variant of the myth of Brahma's incest with his daughter, the daughter desires her father as he desires her; then, to purify herself, she immolates herself in a fire and obtains the boon that she will be reborn as Arundhati, the epitome of the chaste wife, that her husband will be merely a "close friend" to her, and, finally, that any man who looks upon her with desire will become impotent. Moreover, she officially establishes the moral law that creatures before adolescence will not be subject to desire (*Siva Purana* 2.2.5–7, O'Flaherty, 1973, pp. 64–65, 118–119; 1980, p. 105). Arundhati extricates herself from the immediate situation by being reborn as a child, and, moreover, as a child explicitly protected from any possibility of the infant sexuality from which she has suffered in such a blatant way. In addition to this, she protects herself by defusing her potential aggressors, not by turning them into children but by the equivalent (albeit more drastic) measure of unmanning them. In discussing this myth, Sudhir Kakar comments (1978) on "the castration fantasy of turning all men into eunuchs in the Arundhati myth" (p. 90) and on the daughter's "fantasied erotic wishes toward her father, and her later repudiation of these wishes by transforming them into their opposite, aloofness and chastity" (p. 69).

The question of the justice of childhood guilt is explicitly challenged in the great Sanskrit epic, the *Mahabharata*. In this story, a sage named Mandavya is wrongly supposed to have participated in a robbery and is impaled on a stake. But this is not the end of him:

> The Brahmin seer remained on the stake for a long time. Though he had no food, he did not die. He held fast to his vital breaths and summoned together the seers. . . . He said to the ascetics, "Whom can I blame? For no one but me is guilty." The king had him taken down from the stake. But since he was unable to pull the stake out of him, he cut it off at its base. And so the sage went about with the stake still inside him. As he moved around with the stake in his neck, ribs, and entrails, he started to think, "The stake could be used as a pole to carry flower baskets." By means of this asceticism he conquered worlds that were hard for other people to conquer; and people used to call him, "Tip-of-the-stake Mandavya."
>
> Then the Brahmin . . . scolded [Dharma, the moral law incarnate], saying, "What *was* the bad deed that I did, without knowing what I had done, a deed which has earned me such a fruit of retribution?" . . . Dharma said, "You stuck blades of grass up the tails of little butterflies, and this is the fruit that you have obtained from that karma, ascetic." Tip-of-the-stake Mandavya said, "*When* did I do this? Tell me the truth." To this question the king of dharma replied, "You did it when you were a child."
>
> Then Tip-of-the-stake Mandavya said, "For a rather small offence you have given me an enormous punishment. . . . I will establish a moral boundary for the fruition of dharma in the world: no sin will be counted against anyone until the age of fourteen . . ."
> [*Mahabharata* 1.101; O'Flaherty, 1990, pp. 51–53; Goldman, 1985].

We may see masked sexual symbolism in the impalement (a homosexual violation) and the cutting off of the long stake (a castration), though we should also notice what the Indian tradition makes of this episode: In a kind of reverse castration, Mandavya feels that he has *gained* something, has been given a stake that, however shortened, he still seems to regard as an extension of himself, a useful superpenis, as it were. The childhood guilt that inspired the episode of anal intercourse gives way to the fantasy of the large penis of the grown man.

The Fatal Phallus of Indra

This fantasy of the parental penis is glorified in a cycle of stories about Indra, the king of the gods, beginning in a text composed in 900 B.C. that rivals anything ever written by the Marquis de Sade. It is the earliest (and most extreme) example that I know of the myth of the vagina dentata, and in a starkly oedipal situation. It exemplifies a blatant oedipal conflict and vivid, repeated instances of upward displacement of sexual mutilation, from the genitals to the head. The story has three episodes, which tell how Indra's son Kutsa (consciously or unconsciously) impersonates Indra in order to sleep with Indra's wife, Kutsa's mother; how Indra sends his grandson in his place to seduce and destroy a dangerous woman with multiple sexual organs; and how Indra impersonates another man in order to sleep with that man's wife, and is therefore cursed with multiple sexual organs.

Here is the first episode:

Kutsa Aurava ("Thigh-Born" [as we would say, "Sprung of his loins"]) was made out of the two thighs of Indra. Just as Indra was, so was he, precisely as one would be who is made out of his own self. Indra made him his charioteer. He caught him with his wife, and when he asked her, "How could you do this?" she replied, "I could not tell the two of you apart." Indra made Kutsa bald; but Kutsa wrapped a turban around his head and went to her; still she could not tell them apart and again Indra caught her with Kutsa. Then Indra bound Kutsa and made him a wrestler [*Jaiminiya Brahmana* 3.199–200; O'Flaherty, 1985, pp. 74–75].

The myth implies that Kutsa plays upon his physical resemblance to impersonate Indra; rather, that is the justification that Indra's wife gives for sleeping with Kutsa as well as with Indra. Making Kutsa bald deprives him of the hair that is so often a symbol of semen, the seed in the head, through upward displacement. The oedipal implications of the result of the physical resemblance of father and son need not be labored. Thus the story of Indra and Kutsa enacts the fantasy of incest, and the fear and guilt of its ultimate punishment.

The second myth in this sequence is about Indra and a son of Kutsa, a story as blatant about the physical sexual act as the first episode was blatant about the oedipal conflict:

Long-tongue was a demoness who used to lick up the oblations with her long tongue. Indra sent the son of Kutsa to seduce her. But Long-tongue turned him down, pointing out, "You have just one penis, but I have 'mice' on every limb, on this limb and on that limb. This won't work." When Indra gave him penises on every limb, he succeeded in seducing the demoness. They lay together. As soon as he had his way with her, he remained firmly stuck in her. He summoned Indra, who ran against her and struck her down with his thunderbolt and killed her [*Jaiminiya Brahmana* 1.161–163; O'Flaherty, 1984, pp. 102–103].

The woman in this myth is a grotesque nightmare image of the devouring sexual woman; her excessive sexual organs are referred to euphemistically (which is unusual in Sanskrit mythology, which usually calls a spade a spade, and a vagina a *yoni*) as "mice." But in Sanskrit, "mice," in the dual, is sometimes used to designate the two testicles of a man. Thus Long-tongue is a "male" woman, the woman with a phallus (Róheim, 1945). The long tongue with which Long-tongue licks up the oblation is a phallus; but it is also the organ of language (*langue* in French, or "tongue" in English, meaning both "a part of the mouth" and "language"). So, too, the phallus itself, as Lacan tells us, is a word, a "tongue" in the second sense of the word. Long-tongue's excessive vaginas provide a precedent not only for the (female) *vagina dentata* of several demonic figures in Hindu mythology (*Skanda Purana* 1.2.27–29; O'Flaherty, 1975, pp. 252–261) but also for the (male) long tongue of Kali (who is thus depicted on many icons).

In another variant of this myth, Indra himself is said to have penises on every limb — another way in which he is "indistinguishable" from his grandson and son (*Kausitaki Brahmana*, 23.7.5–12). But in later mythology, Indra has not multiple penises but multiple vaginas, and he gets them, in the final episode in this cycle, when he assumes the form of a certain sage in order to commit adultery with the sage's wife: when the sage catches him, he curses Indra to have a thousand vaginas on his body (which literally emasculates him, or at least enfeminizes him, and may therefore be roughly equivalent to a castration). Later, this curse is modified and reduced to merely having a thousand eyes on his body, a stunning example of upward displacement (*Kathasaritsagara* 17.137–148). But in other variants of the myth, Indra is actually castrated (and later restored with the testicles of a ram) (*Ramayana* 1.47.15–31). Indeed, in one variant of the story, from the *Padma Purana,* Indra gets the vaginas *and* the eyes *and* the castration:

Gautama cursed Indra, saying, "Since you have acted in this way for the sake of the female sexual organ, let there be a thousand of them on your body, and let your penis *(lingam)* fall." Then Indra praised the goddess in her aspect of Indraksi ("Eyes of Indra"), and she said, "I cannot destroy the evil created by a sage's curse, but I can do something so that people will not notice it: you will have a thousand eyes in the middle of the female organs, and you will have the testicles of a ram" [1.56.15–53].

Looking at the history of the story, we can see that the myth that changes Indra's vaginas into eyes is reversing the course of time; in fact, Indra (like several other Vedic gods) was originally said to have thousands of eyes (*Rig Veda* 1.23.3, 10.90.1, 10.81.3). This was then the source of a myth that gave him (through downward displacement?) first thousands of penises and, finally, thousands of vaginas that were later turned (back) into eyes. Nor is this a single, perverse image; it is a famous story, that is even satirized in a Sanskrit farce (Ksemendra, *Desopadesa*), in which a whore says, "I wish I had as many vaginas *(bhagas)* as Indra; I could make a thousand times as much money as I'm making now."

The Archetypal Phallus of Siva

But when Indra's thousand eyes are turned into vaginas, and then again into eyes, what is the foreground and what is the background? For Hindus, the phallus in the background, the archetype (if I may use the word in its Eliadean, indeed Bastianian, and non-Jungian sense) of which their own penises are manifestations, is the phallus (called the *lingam*) of the god Siva, who inherits much of the mythology of Indra (O'Flaherty, 1973). The *lingam* appeared, separate from the body of Siva, on several occasions: At the time of creation, the flame *lingam* arose out of the waters of chaos, stretching up to the sky and down to the bottom of hell, infinite in both directions; then Siva himself tore it off his body when he was disillusioned with human creation; finally, the sages in the Pine Forest castrated Siva and caused his *lingam* to fall to the ground when he had seduced their wives. On each of these occasions, Siva's wrath was appeased when gods and humans promised to worship his *lingam* forever after, which, in India, they still do.

Indeed, certain texts, like the *Skanda Purana* (8.18–19), argue that all human beings are naturally designed to be the worshipers of Siva and his wife Parvati; the clear proof of this is the fact that all men have the *lingam,* and all women the *pinda* (the vagina, the image of Parvati). But the manifestation itself may sometimes be understood only in terms of the archetype. As related by Gupta (1980), the great Vedantic sage Ramakrishna described what he called his madness: "When I experienced that divine madness, I used to worship my own sex-organ as the Siva-phallus" (p. 491). The archetypal *lingam* reappears in Paul Scott's *Staying On* (1977). Mr. Bhoolabhoy, an Indian Christian, deplores the near certainty that he is about to make love once more to his horrid wife:

> "Indeed I am lost," he thought. "She will make me do it. I am not a Christian at all. I am a Hindu and she is my goddess. Every orgasm is an offering to her, and every erection is a manifestation in me of *Shiva-lingam.*" He shut his eyes so that he could not see his idol. He tried to conjure a different image. It would not come [p. 243].

Thus the archetypal Hindu image casts its inexorable siren spell on the would-be convert.

In a short story by the contemporary Marathi writer Vilas Sarang (1990), the hero is transformed, not into a cockroach or a nose, in the manner of Kafka or Gogol, but into an appropriately Hindu variant. The story begins: "I awoke one morning from strange dreams and found myself transformed in my bed into an erect phallus. My head was round and smooth, with a small slit at the top. Completely hairless, it rested upon the pillow, while the rest of my straight, round body stretched out on the bed beneath the covers" (p. 99). His girlfriend screamed and ran away (though her friends in the dormitory remarked, "O my God, what a prick!" "Man, so big!" "Latika, where did you find such a big one?"), and he eventually hopped out of the city to the countryside. There the villagers decided that he was "The *lingam* of Shiva," a "self-created," natural *lingam*. They built a hut for him, worshiped him with flowers, and prayed to him. He spoke to them and told them his myths, beginning with the story of his creation as part of the body of Siva. The people continued to worship him, and one woman in particular, Rakhmabai, massaged him at night: "I [] became more and more excited, so that in the end I was possessed with a wild desire to send a burning jet of semen leaping from my mouth. But I knew that couldn't be. All that would emerge from my mouth would be words, words, words" (p. 108). Rakhmabai, who was childless, begged him for a drop of his seed, but he replied, "It will be possible only when I am reunited with Lord Shiva." Indeed, this became an obsession with him:

Yet I felt a certain sadness. It was not a good thing that Lord Shiva broke off his *lingam* and threw it away. Without doubt, the chaos that was now the hallmark of life on earth was the result of Lord Shiva's wrathful act. If I could be reunited with my lord, peace and love would prevail upon the earth. When would that be? When would I rejoin my lord? [p. 108].

He ceased to speak to his devotees, and became depressed. "And then, one night, I suddenly underwent another transformation; I lost my state of erection, and collapsed limply to the floor. I, who was over five feet tall, was now reduced to two feet" (p. 109). Rakhmabai carried him away, at his request:

She held me in her arms like a child, and stepped out of the temple. After walking a long way in the dark, she placed me on a large rock in a deserted spot. She tore off a large stretch of cloth from the end of her sari and wrapped me in it; thus she protected me from ants and crows and other creatures of the wild [p. 109].

Grafted onto the hilarious and obscene Kafkaesque fantasy is a Hindu myth that leads to a strange conflation of sexual and theological despair. The penis is first severed from the father, then detumesces into impotence, and is finally abandoned by the mother — the failed mother, who leaves him among wild animals, like so many mutilated heroes (including Oedipus).

Oedipus and Krsna

If Siva is the castrated father and Indra is the unhappy oedipal father, Krsna is the happy oedipal child. Indeed, there is a notorious battle between Krsna and Indra in the first book of the *Mahabharata,* in which Indra tries, in vain, to rain on the parade (more precisely, the forest fire) that Krsna has ignited; Indra floods it with showers of the rain that is his semen, but Krsna picks up a great mountain and shuts out the rain. Krsna's adventures begin like those of Moses and Jesus and Oedipus and other heroes (Dundes, 1990): his uncle, Kamsa, the king, tries to kill him, and Krsna is raised, among animals, by foster parents who are cowherds. In the early mythology of Krsna, the cowherd women (Gopis) are at once maternal and erotic in their relationship with him; they function simultaneously as his nurses and his lovers (Masson, 1974; see also

Goldman, 1978; Ramanujan 1983). But as the myth of Krsna and the
Gopis develops in late medieval times, Hindus begin to feel uncomfortable with the merging of the female roles of nurse and mistress in the
Gopis. And as both the erotic and the maternal aspects of the Gopis
become heightened and exaggerated, the erotic aspect is expressed in the
image of the lethal whore and the maternal aspect in the image of the
nurturing Madonna of the Freudian paradigm.

Let us look at two examples of this dichotomy, beginning with the
paradigmatic evil wet nurse, the demoness Putana:

> The horrible Putana ("stinking"), a devourer of children, was sent
> by Kamsa to kill his nephew, Krsna. She wandered through cities,
> villages, and pastures, killing infants. One day she came to Krsna's
> village, and by her magic powers she assumed the form of a
> beautiful woman. She saw the infant Krsna there on the bed.
> Though he kept his eyes closed, he still knew that she was an ogress
> who killed children. She whose wicked heart was concealed by
> sweet actions like a sharp sword encased in a scabbard, took him
> onto her lap, as one might pick up a sleeping deadly viper,
> mistaking it for a rope. Krsna's mother was overcome by her
> splendor, and, thinking her to be a good woman, stood looking on.
>   Then Putana took the baby on her lap and gave him her breast,
> which had been smeared with a virulent poison. But Krsna,
> pressing her breast hard with his hands, angrily drank out her life's
> breath with the milk. The ogress, with agonizing pain in her
> breasts, opened her mouth, stretched out her arms and legs, tore
> her hair, and fell lifeless on the ground. Then she resumed her true
> form. Her mouth was full of terrible teeth as large as plough-shafts
> [*Bhagavata Purana* 10.6.1-20, 30-44; O'Flaherty, 1975, pp.
> 214-15].

Putana's outer form, which gives milk, appears to be maternal, beautiful, divine, and nourishing, but her true inner form, which gives poison,
is nonmaternal, hideous, demonic, and devouring. It is worth noting that
the child, as well as the ogress, has a sweet exterior and a violent inner
nature, and that the mother, by being taken in by the masquerade,
exposes her son to the danger and can be said to be indirectly responsible.
Even the good mother is not really a good mother.

During the same historical period when Putana came to symbolize the
fatal dichotomy between the Madonna and the whore, one particular
cowherd woman, Radha, took on the role of erotic partner, without

entirely relinquishing her older role as wet nurse. As Hindus became increasingly uncomfortable about this combination, Krsna himself split into two, most dramatically, in a variant of the myth told in Bengal:

> One day Krsna's father gave the infant Krsna to Radha to care for; Radha was at the peak of her full voluptuous beauty. She took the child and carried him away; passionately excited, she embraced and kissed him again and again. Then, through Krsna's power of illusion, suddenly the baby vanished from her lap, and she saw instead a handsome, dark blue youth in the prime of life. They made love passionately, indulging in every sort of love-play; but suddenly Krsna ceased to be a youth and became an infant again. Deeply disappointed, Radha handed the baby back to his father [*Brahmavaivarta Purana,* 4.15.1-181; O'Flaherty, 1980, p. 103].

Radha is required to fulfill two roles—nurse and mistress—that she herself feels to be incompatible (for the text stresses her unwillingness to play the role of nurse). This tension leads her to fantasize that the troublesome infant becomes a handsome lover, and because the infant happens to be the lord Krsna, he is able to use his own power of illusion to fulfill her fantasy. Thus she is able to integrate her own dual nature by splitting into two the object of both of her female roles. In this way, the deus ex machina allows the Hindu myth to fantasize a happy solution to the potentially destructive conflation of the maternal and the erotic. But even in the myth this solution cannot last forever; the reality principle reasserts itself, and Radha is left holding the baby—until his father takes him back.

A more thoroughly satisfying oedipal encounter is attributed to the son of Krsna, named Pradyumna:

> When Pradyumna was six days old, he was stolen by a demon who threw him into the ocean. There he was swallowed by a large fish, which was caught and brought to the demon's palace. Now, the demon's wife supervised all the cooking, and when the fish's belly was cut open, she saw inside it a magnificent young boy. As she wondered who he was and how he had come to be inside the belly of a fish, a sage told her the story of the child's birth. She took care of the boy, and she was so deluded by his extraordinary beauty that she came to love him passionately even when he was still a child. When he came to young manhood, she taught him all the magic that she had. But when the boy realized how ardently attached to

him she was, he said, "Why are you acting like this, instead of acting like a mother?" Then she said to him, "You are not my son; that terrible demon stole you from your father, Krsna, and threw you into the ocean, where a fish swallowed you. I took you out of the fish's belly, but your own mother is still weeping for you." Pradyumna eventually killed the demon and married the demon's wife [*Visnu Purana* 5.27.1–31; O'Flaherty, 1984, pp. 99–100].

This is still in essence the "family romance" that Freud wrote about. Several versions of the story express the woman's qualms; one version creates yet another double, a wet nurse, to spare the demon's wife the awkwardness of being both mistress and nurse, and in another the demon catches his wife and Pradyumna *in flagrante delicto* and says to her, "You crazy whore, have you lost your mind, making love with your son?" But, unlike the Sophocles/Freud variant, this is a truly satisfying fantasy: "I can have sex with my mother because she turns out not to be my mother."

PART III: THE CONCLUSION

The Happy Ending

The story of Pradyumna is, I would argue, a clearer window into the subconscious than the most obvious Western parallel, Sophocles' *Oedipus the King*. Sophocles' Oedipus myth is not the best example of suppressed oedipal longings; it accounts only for self-deception ("I didn't know it was my mother"; recall the lame argument of the mother of Kutsa: "I couldn't tell the difference; I thought it was my husband, not my son"). In so doing, it masks and diffuses the guilt of a conscious violation of a sexual taboo. As Sophocles himself has Oedipus say in the sequel, *Oedipus at Colonus,* if someone was trying to kill you, would you first ask him if he was your father, or would you attack? (lines 991–994). The Hindu story of the son of Krsna and the demon's wife is a much more convincing wish-fulfillment: The boy thinks it *is* his mother and is enormously relieved to discover it isn't. In a way, one might say that the tale of Pradyumna provides a happy ending for Sophocles' tragedy, that it cleans it all up and makes it come out nicely. This is *Oedipus Rex* as it might have been retold by Melina Mercouri in the film *Never On Sunday,* in which she plays a whore in the Athenian port of Piraeus who gives all the Greek tragedies a happy ending: everyone goes to the seashore.

Indeed, one major respect in which Hindu myths differ from Freudian stories is the fact that Hindu myths (though not Hindu epics), by and large, have happy endings. There is no real tragedy, perhaps because rebirth always gives you a second chance; it doesn't end with death. Or because of the twist of illusion: It really didn't happen; it really doesn't matter. The myth makes the listener feel better by releasing all the worst fears of his or her own psyche, showing that even these fears can be transcended if you understand rightly. Moreover, taken in their *own* context, the threatening materials embedded deep in the Hindu myths are made distant and safe to talk about by being told in ritual contexts or group readings, as they almost always are, deflecting their impact from the individual to the group. The dream becomes safe when it becomes a myth, and the culture as a whole can diffuse and disperse the terror. This may be one reason why sexual fears that are masked in dreams may appear so blatantly in myths: Once the power of the fear has been displaced onto the group as a whole, it is no longer necessary to displace it by burying it (making it "latent") in manifest symbols. Thus Hindus, too, have discovered *The Uses of Enchantment* (Bettelheim, 1977). To this extent, the Hindu myths might well be taken as evidence in support of Freud's argument that all dreams, even apparent nightmares, are wish-fulfillments. Or, rather, we might say that the myth represents the wish-fulfillment of a dream (Steinberg, 1991).

But even when the story actually ends with all wrongs righted, all wounds healed, the amount of wrongs and wounds depicted along the long, long road to the happy ending leaves a Western reader with a bitter aftertaste of tragedy. It may be that the happy ending in Hindu myths is made possible by a kind of denial that removes the latent content. Many of these stories are embedded in texts describing rituals guaranteed to procure immortality for the ritualist, or myths guaranteed to procure immortality for the listener. What is repressed in these tales of blatant sexuality may be the knowledge that the ritual will fail, that even if you listen to the myth you will die. What is repressed may be the denial of the denial of death.

Thus the Hindu myths are, on one hand, less censored than ours in certain areas that make possible the open expression of sexual violence and the violation of sexual taboos, but are, on the other hand, perhaps more censored in the area of certain denials, such as the denial of death, that make possible the happy ending. For, as Freud taught us, there is no happy ending.

BIBLIOGRAPHY

A. Sanskrit Texts

Bhagavata Purana, with the commentary of Sridhara. Bombay, 1832.
Brahmavaivarta Purana. Poona, 1935.
Brhadaranyaka Upanisad. Bombay, 1913.
Brhaddevata of Saunaka. Cambridge, MA, 1904.
Desopadesa of Ksemendra. Delhi, 1953.
Jaiminiya Brahmana. Nagpur, 1954.
Kathasaritsagara of Somadeva. Delhi, 1970.
Kausitaki Brahmana. Wiesbaden, 1968.
Mahabharata. Poona, 1933–69.
Padma Purana. Poona, 1893.
Ramayana. Baroda, 1960–75.
Rig Veda. Oxford, 1890.
Siva Purana. Benares, 1964.
Skanda Purana. Bombay, 1867.
Visnu Purana. Calcutta, 1972.

B. Secondary Sources

BETTELHEIM, B. (1977), *The Uses of Enchantment.* New York: Vintage Books.
DONIGER, W. (1989), Structuralist universals and freudian universals. *Hist. Religions,* 28:3, February, pp. 267–281.
DUNDES, A. (1990), The hero pattern and the life of Jesus (1976). Reprinted in *In Quest of the Hero.* Princeton, New Jersey: Princeton University Press, 1990, pp. 179–223.
FREUD, S. (1900), The interpretation of dreams. *Standard Edition,* 4 & 5. London: Hogarth Press, 1953.
_____ (1913), Totem and taboo. *Standard Edition,* 13. London: Hogarth Press, 1955.
GILMAN, S. Personal communication. September 16, 1991.
GOLDMAN, R. P. (1978), Fathers, sons and gurus: Oedipal conflict in the Sanskrit epics. *J. Indian Philos.,* 6:325–392.
_____ (1985), Karma, guilt, and buried memories: Public fantasy and private reality in traditional India. *J. Amer. Oriental Soc.,* 105:3, pp. 413–425.
GUPTA, M. (1980), *The Gospel of Sri Ramakrishna,* trans. Swami Nikhilananda. Mylapore, India: Sri Ramakrishna Math.
JUNG, C. G. (1974), *Dreams,* Trans. R. F. C. Hull. Princeton, New Jersey: The Bollingen Foundation.
KAKAR, S. (1978), *The Inner World.* Oxford: Oxford University Press.
_____ (1982), *Shamans, Mystics, and Doctors.* New York: Alfred A. Knopf.
_____ (1984), Paper presented at the annual meeting of the American Academy of Religion in Chicago, December, 1984. Cited in the second edition of O'Flaherty (1985), pp. 363–364.
LACAPRA, D. Personal communication. September 16, 1991.
LEVI-STRAUSS, C. (1963), *Structural Anthropology.* New York: Basic Books.
_____ (1989), *The Jealous Potter.* Chicago: University of Chicago Press.

MASSON, J. L. (1974), The childhood of Krisna: Some psychoanalytic observations. *J. Amer. Oriental Soc.,* 94:454–459.

McDERMOTT, J. P. (1976), Karma and rebirth in early Buddhism. In: *Karma and Rebirth in Classical Indian Traditions,* ed. W. D. O'Flaherty. Berkeley, California: University of California Press, pp. 165–192.

MELTZER, F. (1987), Introduction: Partitive plays, pipe dreams. In: *The Trial(s) of Psychoanalysis,* ed. F. Meltzer. Chicago: University of Chicago Press, pp. 1–7.

O'FLAHERTY, W. D. (1973), *Asceticism and Eroticism in the Mythology of Siva.* London: Oxford University Press.

_____ (1975), *Hindu Myths.* Harmondsworth: Penguin Books.

_____ (1980), *Women, Androgynes, and Other Mythical Beasts.* Chicago: University of Chicago Press.

_____ (1984), *Dreams, Illusion, and Other Realities.* Chicago: University of Chicago Press.

_____ (1985), *Tales of Sex and Violence.* Chicago: University of Chicago Press.

_____ (1988), *Other Peoples' Myths: The Cave of Echoes.* New York: Macmillan.

_____ (1990), *Textual Sources for the Study of Hinduism.* Chicago: University of Chicago Press.

RAMANUJAN, A. K. (1983), The Indian Oedipus. In: *Oedipus: A Folklore Casebook,* ed. L. Edmunds & A. Dundes. New York & London: Garland Publishing, pp. 234–266.

ROHEIM, G. (1945), Aphrodite, or the woman with a phallus. *Psychoanal. Quart.,* 14:350–390.

_____ (1970), Telepathy in a dream. In: *Psychoanalysis and the Occult,* ed. G. Devereux. New York: International Universities Press, pp. 146–157.

ROTH, P. (1969), *Portnoy's Complaint.* New York: Random House.

SARANG, V. (1990), Anil Rao's metamorphosis. In: Vilas Sarang, *Fair Tree of the Void.* Delhi, India: Penguin Books, pp. 99–109.

SCOTT, P. (1977), *Staying On.* London: William Heinemann.

SOPHOCLES. *Oedipus at Colonus.*

_____ *Oedipus the King.*

STEINBERG, M. Personal communication. September 16, 1991.

5

Of the Usurper's Ears, the Demon's Toes, and the Ayatollah's Fingers

M. OMIDSALAR

Among the many important contributions of Professor Dundes to psychoanalytic folkloristics is a body of penetrating studies on folk narrative. In these papers, as in his other work, Dundes is concerned not only with identification of the narrative in the context of world folklore, but also with its cultural and unconscious meanings (Dundes, 1975, 1980a, 1980b). It is Dundes' use of psychoanalytic interpretation to attain the unconscious meaning of a given item of folklore that has designated him as the foremost "Freudian folklorist" of our time. It is perhaps fitting, therefore, to offer the following psychoanalytical study of a rumor emanating from an old political legend to my learned mentor as a token of my respect and gratitude.

With the Iranian revolution, and especially the hostage crisis in 1979, Iran became the most recognizable Middle Eastern country in America. Soon Iranians and their leader, the Ayatollah, claimed their place in the American folk tradition, especially jokelore (Mulcahy, 1979; Glagovsky, 1980; Aman, 1982; Rad Hayrapetian, 1983; Dundes, 1981; Carnes, 1989). As early as 1979, urban legends and rumors with Iranians as the dramatis personae, began to circulate. One such legend, dealing with the Shah's medical visit to New York, alleged that the monarch was not there for cancer treatment, as officially stated, but rather for plastic surgery, which was to give him a new appearance. This story implied that an unknown volunteer was being operated on in order to assume the likeness of the deposed ruler, so that the Shah could stay safely in America (Dresser and Schuchat, 1980). A similar rumor, versions of which were found among the Iranian expatriates as well as their

American hosts, alleged that the Ayatollah is an impostor. According to this item, the true Ayatollah has *four* fingers whereas the religious leader of Iran has *five*. The Iranian version of this rumor assigns *six* fingers to the true Ayatollah, suggesting that the man who ruled Iran with only five fingers on his hands was an impostor. Both of these rumors fall under the motif number F552.1.1, "hands with unusual number of fingers."

I have collected numerous versions of the Iranian form of this item in Los Angeles during the period 1988 to 1990. Among my informants have been one former university chancellor and professor of Persian literature, a well-known Persian poet, a number of retired businessmen, and younger male and female professionals. In accordance with my informants' wishes, I will not provide further details regarding their identities.

Let us consider the rumor now. It is not a narrative per se. It is simply stated in the form of an assertion. A typical version says: "Some believe that this guy is not even the true Ayatollah, because the true Ayatollah has six fingers, while this one has only five." Nothing is known about the characteristics of the extra finger. Its shape, coloration, and location on the hand remain a mystery. What matters, it seems, is the fact of its existence. The American form of the rumor provides no more details. It asserts that the impostor has four fingers instead of five (Dresser and Schuchat, 1980). Neither the Iranian nor the American informants are concerned with the whereabouts of the "true Ayatollah," although they both agree that the man who served as the spiritual leader of Iran was an impostor.

Given the existence of this rumor, the present study seeks to establish two points. First, that the notion of the impostor with some bodily defect can be traced to at least the fifth century B.C.E. in Iran. Second, that the bodily defect attributed to the Ayatollah-impostor reveals certain concerns and anxieties common to the cultural groups who foster and perpetuate it. Furthermore, it provides a means by which these groups focus hostility and aggression upon an adversary (Decotterd, 1988).

Alan Dundes has already suggested that at least two steps are necessary in the proper analysis of narratives. These are *identification* and *interpretation* (Dundes, 1975). Identifying a folk narrative involves "a search for similarities" and seeks to place it in the context of other related and ancillary narratives. It is essentially an objective and empirical process. Interpretation of folklore items, however, is more subjective and speculative. All interpretation must of necessity follow identification in order to be fruitful. It is with this insight in mind that we shall approach the rumor about the Ayatollah in Persian and American oral traditions.

I. IDENTIFICATION

It is not unusual for rumors to grow out of more elaborate narratives such as legends (Dégh and Vazsonyi, 1971). The rumor with which we are concerned in this chapter is based on an interesting legend about a royal impostor. This legend has a long history in Iran (König, 1938). Its earliest written form is the Behîstûn inscription of King Darius the Great (521–486 B.C.E.). The inscription, which is basically Darius' political biography, tells how a certain magian or priest by the name of Gaumâta usurped the throne of Persia. Darius' account is as follows: The Emperor Cambyses (559–529 B.C.E.) had a brother by the name of Bardiya, whom he had secretly killed. Gaumâta somehow found out about this royal secret, managed to pass himself off as the slain Prince Bardiya, and ascended the throne in the absence of Ambyses, who was busy campaigning in Egypt. According to Darius' version of events, the impostor evidently manages to fool everyone, including the members of the royal family, because the people flock to his side, and he firmly establishes himself as the sole ruler of the realm. Meanwhile, Cambyses conveniently dies in Egypt. Darius, who was an officer serving with Cambyses' army in Egypt, mysteriously finds out that the man ruling in Iran is not the true heir to the throne of Cyrus. Where or how he gains this knowledge is not stated in the inscription. He simply asserts the matter in fine royal form.

Spurred on by aristocratic indignation at the takeover of the royal throne by an impostor, Darius rushes back to Iran, secures the cooperation of seven other aristocrats, finds the usurper in a northern castle, kills him, and takes over the throne (Kent, 1953). Darius goes on to consolidate his power by defeating several challenges to his authority. According to his own inscription, Darius fights, captures, and kills nine kings, six of whom he accuses of having been impostors. It seems to me that if six out of nine rebellious kings were in fact impostors, then the practice of seizing power by impersonating someone else was much more common then than it has been any time since. Gaumâta the Magian was one of these impostors whose story seems to be at the base of the modern rumor about the Ayatollah.

It has already been demonstrated that Darius may have in fact killed Bardiya, the true heir to the throne of Cyrus, by accusing him of being an impostor in order to take over the Empire (Bikerman and Tadmore, 1978; Calmeyer, 1987; Demandt, 1972). In addition to the arguments presented in Bikerman and Tadmore's essay, one may perhaps suggest a complementary psychoanalytical explanation. The names Gaumâta and Bardiya have a similarity of meaning that may be significant. Gaumâta means "bull size" or "big as a bull." Bardiya, however, is derived from the Old Persian stem bard- ("to be high"), which is related to New Persian burz ("high, tall"), and means something like "tall of stature or size." Ctesias' Greek rendition of the prince's name is tanudzarches which in Persian meant "bigbody" (Gershevitch, 1979). Thus, it seems that the sense of both names has to do with greatness of size or bulk. If so, then is it not possible that Darius, having killed the true prince whose name meant something like "big man," betrayed his crime by unconsciously inventing a name for the alleged impostor with a similar meaning to the meaning of the name of his victim? If this argument is true, then the king has fallen victim, in his inscription, to what is commonly called a "Freudian slip," and has thus betrayed his crime of regicide in this manner.

In his study of the alleged impostor Guamâta, Professor Gershevitch suggests that the similarity between the names of Bardiya and Gaumâta merely implies an actual likeness in appearance between the prince and the Magian (Gershevitch, 1979). Although I fully agree with Professor Gershevitch's learned philological discussion, I find the literal interpretation of this narrative unacceptable, on the ground that a scenario in which a priest walks off the street and assumes the throne of Persia is manifestly absurd. To get back to our story, Darius says nothing in his inscription about how he came to discover the true identity of the "usurper." It is Herodotus to whom we have to turn for details on this event.

According to Herodotus' account, after taking over the throne Gaumâta the Magian (called Smerdis in the Greek text) sought to ensure the continued success of his fraud, by preventing communication between the ladies of the imperial harem and other close associates of the king. His remarkable physical similarity to the slain Bardiya fools everyone for a time. However, there is one slight difference between him and the prince whom he impersonates, and that is he lacks ears; they were cut off as punishment for a crime that he had once committed. One of the ladies of the harem discovers this unusual feature and promptly informs her father, an aristocrat who had already suspected foul play, of the state of affairs (Herodotus, Bk. III:68–70). One should remember that ancient Iranian tradition prohibited anyone with a bodily defect, especially those who lacked a bodily member, from assuming the offices of kingship or priesthood. It has been reported, for example, that the Sasanid monarch King Qobâd (448–531 c.e.) could not proclaim his second son Jam, who was both brave and well loved by the aristocracy, to be his successor because the latter was blind in one eye (Fûlâdpûr and Rabî î, 1990, p. 19; Procopius, 1961, I:11:6). To sum up, two points are significant in the Greek account. First, that political authority was usurped by an impostor. Second, that the impostor lacked a body part.

Let us now consider our third piece of data. Alexander H. Krappe was the first to point out the similarity between, and the relationship of, Herodotus' story of the False Smerdis and the Talmudic account of Solomon and Ashmedai (Krappe, 1933). Rejecting H. Varnhagen's view that suggested an Indic origin for the tale of Solomon and Ashmedai (Varnhagen, 1882), Krappe argued that "The story is of Persian-Mesopotamian provenance, having developed out of the New Year ritual" (pp. 260, 265–266). The figure of Ashmedai in the Jewish tradition is believed by some scholars to be based on an Iranian demon (Shaked, 1984). The tale of Ashmedai and Solomon is set forth in the Talmud of Jerusalem (350 c.e.). In the book of Tobit Ashmedai is called the prince of demons (III:8; VI: 14). He teaches King Solomon the whereabouts of a certain worm called *shamir*, which could bore through stones and which the king needed for the building of the temple.[1] According to the Haggadic version of the legend, later adopted by Moslem religious texts, Ashmedai tricks Solomon, throws him 400 parasangs from Jerusalem, and rules in his place by assuming the likeness of the king (motif K1934.1, "impostor [magician, demon] takes the place of the king"). During his rule, the demon Ashmedai, much like his Iranian counterpart Gaumâta, admits none of the close associates of Solomon into the court. This goes on for some time until the demon's lecherous behavior brings about his downfall. Against Jewish law, he tries to sleep with some of the ladies of the harem while they are menstruating. He goes even further, by attempting sexual intercourse with King Solomon's mother. The queen mother, understandably alarmed by this odd conduct, voices her objections by proclaiming "thou art not my son."

The role of the women of the court in revealing the identity of the impostor is not limited to the queen mother's outrage at the demon's

---

[1]According to the *Shâhnâmah*, the national epic of Iran versified in the 10th century based on much older material, vanquished demons build great palaces and other buildings for King Jamshîd, who after the conversion of Iran to Islam is identified with Solomon.

amorous advances. Solomon's wives inform everyone that the king never takes off his shoes. This bit of information makes everything quite clear, because as everyone knew in those days, demons had cock's feet, and thus lacked toes (cf. Motifs: G303.4.5.3.2, "Devil's footprints without toes"; G303.4.5.3, "Devil has horse's foot"; G303.4.5.3.1, "Devil detected by his hoofs").

A number of similarities are apparent in the Greco-Persian and the Judeo-Moslem versions of the legend of the impostor. In both narratives it is the ladies of the court who discover the true identity of an impostor who by virtue of his physical similarity to a legitimate ruler somehow manages to take over the throne. Furthermore, in both cases the discovery is based on the impostor's lack of bodily appendages. These appendages are ears in the Greco-Persian version, and toes in the Judeo-Moslem version.

The structural similarity of the bodily deficiency of the impostor in these ancient legends and the allegedly fake Ayatollah in the modern rumor is self-evident.

Before we begin our analysis of the American and Iranian versions of this rumor, the reader must remember that in the American version of the story the true Ayatollah has only four fingers, while in the Iranian version he has six. Thus, both rumors consider the spiritual leader of Iran, who was digitally intact, to have been an impostor.

II. ANALYSIS

The key to the analysis of this narrative is found in the Ayatollah's fingers. However, because the Greek form of the legend involves the impostor's ears, let us briefly consider the symbolic meaning of ears before turning our attention to the Ayatollah's fingers. In the Greek version of the legend, motif Q451.6 "ears cut off as punishment " (cf. motif S168 "mutilation: tearing off ears") is the mechanism of recognition of the impostor. Ears are overdetermined symbols insofar as they may symbolically stand for both male and female genitals. Such motifs as T541.14 "birth through ear"; T517.3 "conception through ear"; and A112.7.1 "god born from mother's ear" testify to the validity of the interpretation of the ears as symbolic female genitals or wombs. The phallic symbolism of the ears may be inferred from motifs such as: Q451.6.1 "ears cut off as punishment for adultery"; Q451.6.0.1 "fairy bites off ear of ravisher"; and more explicitly F304.4.1 "flesh struck from ravisher's ear." Ears and fingers in the narrative of the legend with which we are concerned are what Dundes has called "allomotifs," that is, motifs which may functionally and symbolically stand in for one another in different versions of a given narrative (Dundes, 1987). In the legend of the impostor, fingers, toes, and ears are allomotifs. Because fingers and toes are linguistically similar (see the following), and in the interest of brevity, I shall not discuss the symbolic meaning of toes, and proceed to concentrate instead on fingers.

Although the symbolic significance of the finger may be obvious to the psychoanalytically informed reader, it is always advisable to provide relevant cultural evidence in order to demonstrate that such symbolic interpretations have a basis in the culture's own data (Dundes, 1987). Furthermore, by so documenting one may avoid the charge of "mechanical symbol translation" so often leveled against psychoanalytical interpretations of literary and historical data.

Apart from the obvious symbolic meaning of the finger that is self-evident in such gestures as "giving someone the finger," one can find ample evidence in world folklore supporting the equation finger = phallus. Consider the following motifs: T26.1, "Finger cut because of absorption in the charms of the beloved"; T511.6.2, "Conception from eating finger bones"; G303.1.5, "Adam creates five devils by wetting five fingers with dew and shaking them behind him"; *A1724.1, "Animals from severed fingers of woman"; T333.2, "Tempted man burns his finger"; F715.1.3, "River from man's finger (and its obvious urinary signification)"; C911, "Golden finger as sign of opening forbidden chamber"; and many others (Thompson, 1955–1958, s.v. "finger"). In the Puranas, Prajapati creates progeny from his right thumb, while in a Sri Lankan story Viṣṇu splits his right hand and takes out a prince (O'Flaherty, 1980). In the classical Greek account of the castration of Attis, his little finger remains alive to indicate that the castration is incomplete (cf. Dundes, 1980). According to medieval Persian and Arabic sources, a castrated man's fingers will become crooked (Qazwînî, 1983; al-Bayhaqî, 1961).

Let us now consider the word finger in terms of comparative philology. It has been observed that "there is no inherited group pointing to an Indo-European word for 'finger'" (Buck, 1949, pp. 239–240; see also the words "thumb" and "penis," pp. 240–241 and 258–259). Furthermore, there is often no clear distinction made between finger and toe on one hand, and finger and thumb, on the other. Toes are often referred to as "foot fingers" just as the thumb is called the "large finger." In Persian, for instance, there is no word for toes, which are called simply angusht-e pa, meaning "fingers of the foot." Now, whereas the etymological origin of these words is unclear or at least debatable, there is no shortage of other interesting and relevant data about them.

Consider for instance the case of the middle finger. The form "middle finger" is a translation of the Latin *medius (digitus)* and Greek *mesos daktulos*. These names however, are "cover words" shielding some "repudiated and repressed colloquial terms" (Thass-Thieneman, 1973, I:272). The German name of the middle finger, *der namenlose Finger* ("the nameless finger"), suggests that the original name of this finger has been bypassed for some reason. This reason, it has been suggested, is associated with its significance in antiquity. In ancient Greece the middle finger is charged with the most "opprobrious crimes" (Thass-Thieneman, 1973, I:272). Called *impudicus, infamis,* and *famosus* in Latin, the middle finger has some uncomely qualities.

The phallic characteristics of the finger from a linguistic point of view have been demonstrated for some time now (Thass-Thieneman, 1973). In rabbinical Hebrew, the word for "finger" is used with the meaning of *membrum virile* (Delcor, 1976), while in Persian usage, the "twenty-first finger" is a metaphor for the phallus (Hedâyat, 1990). The most authoritative lexicon of the Persian language, *Lughat Nāmah-yi Dihkhudâ* lists the entry *angusht-i shikam* (literally, "stomach finger") as a metaphor for penis (Dihkhudâ, 1959, s.v. *angusht*). In Persian practice it is the thumb rather than the middle finger that is used in the obscene gesture of "flipping the finger." In the chapter dealing with the anatomy of hands and arms in a Persian medical text composed in the 12th century C.E., it is stated that "Persians call the thumb *the male finger*" (Jurjânî, 1976, p. 22). There is a famous Persian joke about a little boy who is very good in class, and his female teacher offers to reward him by granting him a favor. The little boy asks the lady to close her eyes and allow him to place his *finger* in her *navel*. The teacher agrees, and once the boy finishes enjoying his reward, the teacher, ever striving to educate, tells him *where* he placed his finger was not her *navel*. The little boy answers, it is O.K., because *what* he placed there was not his *finger*.

Please note that it is not some zealous psychoanalyst who is assigning a phallic identity to the finger in the cultural data presented here. It is, rather, folklore and linguistic data that clearly imply the finger/phallus equation, data developed by those who did not experience the benefit and indoctrination of psychoanalytic training, and who therefore lacked "bias" and indoctrination. My interpretation of the finger as a possible phallic symbol in this context is also not a mechanical symbol translation imposed on the narrative by myself, but one which is inherent in the cultural perception of this member.

Now we can proceed to suggest that if the finger/phallus symbolic equation is correct, then the Ayatollah's missing finger in the American version of the rumor is an expression of the American fantasy of castrating or subduing the Iranian leader. After all, no political leader in modern memory offended and injured American pride and manhood as severely as did the Ayatollah. Now, if the Ayatollah has offended the virility of the American nation by symbolically castrating it through invading its embassy (i.e., entering American territory by force; penetrating the motherland), and by burning its flag, etc., then it stands to reason that Americans will retaliate by doing the same to the Ayatollah in fantasy. Hence in the American version of the rumor the Americans' desire to remove at least one of the Ayatollah's bodily extremities has led to the creation of the four-fingered Ayatollah. Not only has the Ayatollah *been cut down to size* and rendered harmless, but he has also been made to conform to a more acceptable American/Christian ideal of a religious leader who is not a menacing temporal force, but a person completely concerned with spiritual matters.

Other data from American folklore clearly demonstrate a desire to castrate the Ayatollah. Consider the following graffito, recorded in New York and collected in 1979: "No matter where you are// From Brooklyn to Niagara Falls// Let's take an A-Bomb// And blow off Khomeini's balls" (Mulcahy, 1979, p. 276). Furthermore, if the religious leader of Iran was an impostor, as the American rumor alleges, then does it not logically follow that the true Ayatollah, if not killed, must have been kidnapped and kept somewhere against his will? And doesn't his fate bear a remarkable similarity to that of the American hostages who were kept by their Iranian captors (allegedly the Ayatollah's men) for over a year? And is it not fitting punishment for a hostage taker to be taken hostage?

Let us now consider the Persian form of the rumor. According to this version, the true Ayatollah has six fingers, which means that the impostor lacks one.[2]

Given the finger/phallus equation, the impostor of the Iranian imagination who lacks a finger is deficient, whereas the true Ayatollah

---

[2]It should be noted that Americans are not the only group who wish to symbolically castrate the Ayatollah. Dr. Heda Jasson informs me that she has collected the four-fingered Ayatollah legend from Iranian Jews who immigrated to Israel. The form of the legend among the Iranian Jews, a non-Moslem group which like Americans was assaulted by the appearance of the Ayatollah, in principle agrees with the American version rather than the Moslem Iranians' version. This is because the Persian Jews, unlike their Moslem countrymen, can oppose the Ayatollah without any anxiety.

who has six fingers is a superphallic being endowed with more of what a common man may boast. His superphallic characteristic, symbolically expressed by his extra finger, is justified insofar as he is a father figure par excellence. That is, the true Ayatollah has both political and religious authority, and is therefore the potent father of the superego.

The superphallic nature of the "holy man" qua father is well supported in classical and modern Persian texts. In the interest of brevity, I will present only one charming example from the classical Sufi literature. The reader should be aware that such examples can be easily multiplied. In a 13th-century mystical Persian text which deals with the biography of the great mystic Sheikh Ahmad of Jâm, (1049-1141 c.e.), this holy man, appropriately nicknamed *zhindah pîl* ("raging elephant"), when in his 80s asks for the hand of a 14-year-old maiden in marriage. The girl's mother energetically disagrees, arguing that a man of such advanced age can hardly make a suitable mate for her youthful daughter. A miraculous event during which the old sheikh rescues the girl from certain death causes the parents of the young lady to consent to the marriage. During the wedding night "the Sheikh had intercourse with her sixty times [lit: entered her 60 times], saying: 'If it were not that I don't want to harm your health, I would have had intercourse with you one hundred times, so that your mother would never [again dare] say: Ahamad [i.e., the Sheikh] is old'" (Ghaznavî, pp. 202-204). As I hope this example demonstrates, there is more than holiness to a holy man. Therefore, the true Ayatollah's superphallic characteristic, symbolized by his extra finger, should not be surprising.

There is an extra dimension of meaning in the form of the rumor found among the anti-Ayatollah Persians. These individuals are Shi ite Moslems and have great reverence for their religious institutions and beliefs. Ayatollahs, as symbols of spiritual authority and interpreters of the divine scripture, have been revered and emulated by Iranian Shi ites since the conversion of the country to Shi ism., After all, the title Ayatollah [from Arabic *âyat allâh*] means "sign of God." It is thus emotionally difficult, in some instances even traumatic, for a Shi ite Persian to think of a grand Ayatollah as an impostor or a fake.[3] The

---

[3]Another Iranian rumor about the Ayatollah alleges that he is not Iranian at all, but a citizen of India. This rumor relies for evidence exclusively on the last name of one of the Ayatollah's brothers, who was known as Mr. Hindi, which in Persian means "Indian." The obvious implication of the rumor is that the population is not only trying to deny the fact of the Ayatollah's Iranian citizenship, but also to make opposition to him morally acceptable, by turning him into an "other" or a "foreigner." The theme of the foreigner

psychic tension aroused by these Persians' opposition to their spiritual leader is resolved by means of a compromise according to which the spiritual leader of Iran must become an impostor. In other words, driven by a need to maintain their allegiance to an acceptable religious patriarch, they create in the fantasy world of folklore one who is not only legitimate but superlegitimate, and thus endowed with great paternal authority.

This greater paternal authority of the imaginary Ayatollah is symbolically expressed by his sixth finger. The six-fingered Ayatollah of the Iranian imagination turns the real Ayatollah into an impostor, who can therefore be opposed without moral or religious objection. There remains, however, one question: If the person who served as the spiritual leader of Iran was an impostor, does that not imply that the true Ayatollah, six fingers and all, has either been killed or is being kept somewhere against his will? Does this not turn him into a weak individual who is overcome or manipulated by unknown forces, as in the American version of the rumor? The special place held by the concepts of martyrdom and occultation in Iranian "folk Shi'ism" overcomes the apparent contradiction. If the true Ayatollah is killed, then he has received martyrdom in the same manner as his ancestor Imam Husayn, the grandson of the Prophet Muhammad. This immediately places the Ayatollah in the company of a man who is easily one of the two most sacred personages of Iranian folk Shi'ism.

If, however, he is not killed and has simply disappeared, then he enjoys another prestigious boon. The Shi ites believe that the 12th Imam, a descendant of the Prophet Muhammad, is alive and lives in the state of occultation. He will some day come and fill the world with justice and good, after it has been overwhelmed with evil. Thus, the model of the spiritual leader in the state of occultation is not one that would imply either helplessness or defeat. It is a ready-made cultural model that bestows greater sanctity and spirituality insofar as it pairs the "hidden" Ayatollah with the most sacred living saint of the Shi'ite tradition (i.e., the "hidden" Imam). The fact that the Ayatollah, like the hidden Imam, is a descendent of the Prophet Muhammad reenforces the matter. In that sense, the "true" Ayatollah of the Persian variant of the rumor has a completely different significance than that implied in the American version.

---

as the source of all evil can be traced in Iranian lore and literature since at least the beginning of the Iranian epic tradition.

III. CONCLUSION

The modern rumor featuring the two Ayatollahs with varying numbers of fingers on their hands is the outcome of the reworking of an ancient legend that has often been employed in Iran during periods of political upheaval involving a crisis of legitimacy. The ancient legend is identified as the legend of a usurper who assumes the reigns of authority by pretending to be the legitimate ruler of the realm. He is discovered because of a slight physical difference which exists between him and the legitimate ruler. This slight physical difference is the impostor's lack of a bodily appendage. A rumor based on this ancient legend seems to have surfaced at a period of great political and social upheaval, which for a time linked Persian and American societies in an emotionally charged atmosphere.

The psychological conflict aroused in the minds of anti-Ayatollah Iranians and their American hosts were then resolved and mastered in fantasy; through the production of this rumor about the Ayatollah group agression was focused against an acceptable object. This acceptable object of group aggression was an imaginary Ayatollah, whom the Americans managed to wishfully castrate; the Persians at the same time opposed the actual Ayatollah, without committing a moral and religious transgression, by believing him to be a pretender. The rumor served the double purpose of gratifying tabooed wishes or frustrated aggressions, and at the same time reaffirmed cultural values and beliefs.

One of the functions of folklore is to make possible ways of satisfying forbidden desires that cannot be gratified in reality. Thus folklore alleviates anxiety and avoids the pain and tensions of reality. In this sense it has a therapeutic effect. There is an American joke, once told to me by my mentor Alan Dundes, which states: "Neurotics build castles in the air, psychotics live in them, and the psychiatrists collect the rent." Folklore offers its therapeutic services free of charge.

BIBLIOGRAPHY

AL-BAYHAQÎ, I. M. (1961), *Al-Mahāsin wa al-Masāwī*, ed. M. A. Ibrâhîm. Cairo, Egypt: N.P., 2 vol.
AMAN, R. (1982), Kakalogia. *Maledicta*, 6:290–315.
BIKERMAN, E. J. & TADMORE, H. (1978), Darius, psudo-Smerdis, and the magi. *Athenaeum*, 56:239–262.
BUCK, C. D. (1949), *A Dictionary of Selected Synomyms in the Principal Indo-European Languages*. Chicago: University of Chicago Press.

CALMEYER, P. (1987), Greek historiography and Achaemenid reliefs. In: *Achaemenid History: The Greek Sources: Proceedings of the Groningen 1984 Achaemenid History Workshop,* ed. H. Sancisi-Weerdenburg & A. Kuhrt. Leiden, Netherlands: Nederlands Institut voor het Nabije Oosten, pp. 11-26.

CARNES, P. (1989), American political jokes: The Iranian example. *Motif: Internat. Rev. Research in Folklore Lit.,* 9:3-7.

DÉGH, L. & VAZSONYI, A., (1971), Legend and belief. *Genre,* 4, no. 3:281-304.

DECOTTERD, D. (1988), Gossip, rumor, and legend: A plea for a psychological and cross-cultural approach. In: *Perspectives on Contemporary Legend III,* ed. G. Bennett & P. Smith. Sheffield, England: Sheffield Academic Press, pp. 239-241.

DELCOR, M. (1976), Two special meanings of the word *yd* [yad] in biblical Hebrew. *Religion d'Israel et Proche Orient.* Leiden, Netherlands: Brill, pp. 139-150.

DEMANDT, A. (1972), Die Ohren des falschen Smerdis. *Iranica Antiqua,* 9:94-101.

DIHKHUDÂ, A. A. (1959), *Lughatnâmah.* Tehran, Iran: Majlis.

DRESSER, N. & SCHUCHAT, T. (1980), In search of the perforated page. *West. Folklore,* 39, no. 4:301-306.

DUNDES, A. (1975), The study of folklore in literature and culture: Identification and interpretation. In: *Analytic Essays in Folklore,* ed. R. M. Dorson. The Hague, Netherlands: Mouton, pp. 28-35.

_____ (1980a), Projection in folklore: a plea for psychoanalytic semiotics. In: *Interpreting Folklore,* ed. A. Dundes. Bloomington: Indiana University Press, pp. 33-62.

_____ (1980b), To love my father all: A psychoanalytic study of the folktale source of *King Lear.* In: *Interpreting Folklore,* ed. A. Dundes. Bloomington: Indiana University Press, pp. 211-223.

_____ (1987), The symbolic equivalence of allomotifs in the rabbit-herd (AT 570). In: *Parsing Through Customs: Essays by a Freudian Folklorist,* ed. A. Dundes. Madison: The University of Wisconsin Press, pp. 167-178.

FÛLÂDPÛR, H. & RABÎ Î, H. (1990), The tale of Mazdak and Qobâd revisited. *Iran Nameh,* 8:1:1-47 (English abstract: 1-3 of the English section).

GERSCHEVITCH, I. (1979), The false Smerdis. *Acta Antiqua Academ. Scient. Hungar.,* 27, no. 4:337-351.

GHAZNAVÎ, M. (1967), *Maqâmât-i Zhindah Pîl: Ahmad-i Jâm,* ed. H. Mo'ayyad. Tehran, Iran: BTNK.

GLAGOVSKY, D. (1980), Elite maledicta. *Maledicta,* 4:148.

HEDÂYAT, S. (1990), *Tûp-e Morvârî,* ed. M. J. Mahjoob. Spånga, Sweden: Arash.

JURJÂNÎ, I. [died 1136 C.E.] (1976). *Zakhīrah-yi Khwārazmshāhī,* ed. Sà îdî-ye Sîrjânî. Tehran, Iran: Intishârât-i Bunyâd-i Farhang.

KENT, R. G. (1953), *Old Persian: Grammar, Texts, Lexicon.* New Haven: American Oriental Society.

KÖNIG, F. W. (1938), *Der falsche Bardija: Dareios der grosse und die Lügenkönige.* Wien, Austria: Gerold & Co.

KRAPPE, A. H. (1933), Solomon and ashmodai. *Amer. J. Philol.,* 54:260-268.

MULCAHY, D. (1979), Graffito. *Maledicta,* 3, no. 2:276.

O'FLAHERTY, W. D. (1980), *Women Androgynes and Other Mythical Beasts.* Chicago: University of Chicago Press.

PROCOPIUS (1961), *History of the Wars,* ed. & trans. H. B. Dewing. Cambridge, MA: Harvard University Press.

QAZWÎNÎ, Z. M. (1983), Ajâyib al-Makhlûqât. ed. N. Sabûhî. Tehran, Iran: Markazî.

RAD HAYRAPETIAN, J. (1983), Political humor: Its function and significance in the Iranian revolution. *Folklore Mythol. Stud.*, 7:24-40.

SHAKED, S. (1984), Iranian influences on Judaism: First century B.C.E. to second century C.E. In: *The Cambridge History of Judaism,* 2 vols., ed. W. D. Davies & L. Finkelstein. Cambridge: Cambridge University Press, pp. 308-326.

THASS-THIENEMAN, T. (1973), *The Interpretation of Language,* 2 vols. New York: Aronson.

THOMPSON, S. (1955-1958), *Motif-Index of Folk-Literature.* 2nd ed., 6 vols. Bloomington: Indiana University Press.

VARNHAGEN, H. (1882), *Ein indisches Märchen auf seiner Wanderung durch die asiatischen und europäischen Literaturen.* Berlin, Germany: Weidmannsche Buchhandlung.

6

Spatial Symbolism in Southern Spain

STANLEY BRANDES

It is obvious that all child's play is influenced by a desire that constantly dominates children — the desire to be big and to do what big people do.

— Freud, *Beyond the Pleasure Principle*

In the mid-1970s, having just carried out fieldwork in a southern Spanish town, I found myself perplexed by the meaning of an elaborate annual parade. I turned for help to Alan Dundes. With typical quick insight, he remarked that the costumed processional figures known as Giants *(Gigantes)* and Big-Heads *(Cabezudos)* — the subject of my research at the time — reminded him of parents and children. All I needed was this suggestion for the symbolic connection to become obvious (Brandes, 1980). The Giants, I discovered, had many qualities that could be associated with parents, and the Big-Heads acted and looked much like children. But the contrasting feature that came to interest me most was that of size: The Giants were tall and the Big-Heads short. It seemed that tallness, at least in this parade, was connected symbolically to social superiority, whereas shortness implied the opposite. The more I considered the matter, in fact, the more convinced I became that this symbolic association could be applied generally, that it was not limited to the parade alone.

I wish to thank Alan Dundes and Maurice Apprey for useful comments on an earlier version of this paper.

Up and down, high and low, tall and short—these vertically ordered spacial dimensions seem to provide metaphors for opposing moral, social, and other qualities in Western civilization as elsewhere. Historian Carlo Ginzburg believes that not even the opposition between right and left, which we know to have nearly ubiquitous symbolic value (Needham, 1973), is as universal as the opposition between high and low. Says Ginzburg (1976), "It is significant that we say that something is 'high' or 'superior'—or conversely 'base' or 'inferior'—without considering why what we most praise (goodness, strength, and so on) must be located high" (p. 31). The so-called upper classes are rich and powerful; poor laborers and lumpenproletariat belong to what we call the lower classes. Heaven is located up high; hell down low. Good people are high-minded; evil ones are base. We could multiply similar examples from our own language *ad infinitum*. Moreover, according to Ginzburg "every civilization located the source of cosmic power—God—in the skies" (p. 32). Although this statement, if explored thoroughly, might prove exaggerated, we do frequently find that powerful rank is symbolized by high spatial situation. One has only to consider the Japanese custom of bowing, whereby the higher-status individual ideally remains more elevated than his or her inferiors; or seating arrangements in Balinese household courtyards, wherein numerous pavilions, each mounted on sandstone of a different height, provide "a hierarchy of sitting places" (Belo, 1948, p. 156). It may even be that in societies throughout the world, as in the United States, it is considered desirable for husbands to be taller than their wives. Ideal relative height is no doubt an only partially conscious means for people to acknowledge and express male superiority.

In Monteros, the name I have given to the Andalusian settlement where I carried out fieldwork for about a year and a half between 1975 and 1980, social divisions of all kinds—between men and women, Gypsies and non-Gypsies, children and elders, rich and poor—are expressed largely in terms of highness and lowness. Monteros is a typical Mediterranean agro-town of some 7000 inhabitants, located in the center of the olive-growing region of southeastern Spain. The town's social structure is not unlike that which prevails—or at least until recently prevailed—throughout most of rural Andalusia. There are, first of all, class divisions and prestige hierarchies based on occupation, living standards, and moral reputation. In particular, the distinction between day laborers and large-scale landowners is what dominates the town's economic profile. Further, people in Monteros display a good deal of sensitivity to the qualities that they believe distinguish men from women.

There exists a salient gender consciousness, with members of each sex striving to conform to culturally appropriate, gender-specific codes of conduct. Then, too, the distinction between young and old, in Monteros as everywhere else in southern Spain, is one that occupies people's attention. As they mature into responsible adults, boys and girls are motivated to conform to distinct expectations at different stages of childhood.

If we examine how the people of Monteros articulate these basic divisions of class, gender, and age in their folklore and expressive culture, there emerges a pervasive metaphoric association between relative height and other qualities. Tallness indicates positive values — wealth, power, control — whereas lowness represents the opposite — poverty, weakness, and submission. This spatial symbolism resonates throughout Monteros folklore and informs people's interpretations of masculinity and femininity, upper- and lower-class behavior, as well as qualities associated with youth and maturity.

SPACE AND SOCIAL INEQUALITY
IN MONTEROS

Consider just a few of the many ways in which social inequality is expressed through spatial metaphors in Monteros. First let us return to the parade of Giants and Big-Heads, which opens the town's main four-day fiesta each September. The Giants consist of two representations of monarchs — king and queen — who form a couple, as parents do. Supported on 15-foot slender frames and carried by young men hidden beneath lengthy robes, these figures are dignified in bearing, as is appropriate to their status. They march through town in a controlled, graceful manner. Every once in a while, though, they depart from their regular movements and unaccountably bounce around. From the point of view of the town children, for whose benefit the parade of Giants and Big-Heads is enacted, the size and behavior of the Giants are like those of parents. Like parents, the Giants are big, dominating, and controlled. Like parents, too, they occasionally and unpredictably descend from gracefulness and self-discipline into foolishness and disarray.

The Big-Heads, by contrast, are numerous (in the mid-1970s there were 14). As they consist of young men dressed in costume, who don papier-mâché masks, they are of human height, that is, short of stature relative to the towering Giants. Moreover, their papier-mâché heads are disproportionately large for their bodies, the way children's heads are in comparison to those of adults. The Big-Head costumes imitate a wide range of foreigners and fantasy figures: black Africans, Asians, Moors, cartoon characters, anthropomorphic animals, witches carrying broomsticks, and others. As they wend their way along the processional route, they display clumsiness, spontaneity, rowdiness, and aggressivity. They rush around in unpredictable directions, bopping children with their sawdust-filled stockings and engaging in partly humorous, partly hostile antics. In all this behavior, they provide children and others in the audience with an image of how not to behave.

The Big-Heads manifest above all dangerous instinctual activity. This quality is most evident in the way they wield the sausage-shaped stockings. These objects are known colloquially as *porras,* or "clubs." Aside from this object's physical resemblance to the penis, there is the fact that the term *porra* and its derivatives are used in Monteros to refer to the male organ. The phallic symbolism of the object is evident. When the Big-Heads attack the crowd with the *porra,* they are not only symbolically exposing the penis but are also asserting their masculinity through the penis' aggressivity. Linguistic evidence further supports this interpretation of Big-Head phallic representation. In Monteros the word *cabeza* ('head') is associated with the male organ. The foreskin, for example, is called the "head of the penis" *(cabeza del pijo).* And men jokingly state that "We men have two heads; when the lower one gets erect, you lose the one above!" *(Cuando se endurece la de abajo ¡se pierde la de arriba!).* The young men who play the Big-Head role in the annual parade are in a way symbolic penises, aggressively asserting their masculine potency.

The Giants are the only figures explicitly designed to represent familiar people, that is, Europeans. For traditional, rural Andalusians, non-European peoples are as removed from daily experience as are wild beasts. While the Giants represent the ideals that children should strive to emulate, the Big-Heads provide a simultaneously frightening and laughable visual image of outsiders and wild, supernatural beings. These are, of course, beings that lurk inside of all of us, instinctual beings, but ones that nonetheless are deemed inferior in character to the socially and morally superior Giants. In the parade of Giants and Big-Heads, the tall Giants are clearly associated with that which is desirable; the short Big-Heads symbolize dangerous qualities which, outside the confined context of ritual, are best suppressed. The Giant and Big-Head figures therefore demonstrate above all how conceptions of rank and age are represented spatially in secular ritual performance.

Gender distinctions, too, are symbolized through vertical ordering in

Monteros religious ceremony. Take the most prominent Roman Catholic ceremony, the Mass, for example. In 1976, I calculated that only 20 percent of the townspeople receiving holy communion were males, and many of these were preadolescents. There are no doubt a number of explanations for this curious phenomenon, among them the prevalence of male anticlericalism in Monteros, as throughout Andalusia (see, e.g., Gilmore, 1984; Kaplan, 1977; Mintz, 1982). Additionally, however, informants claim that men refrained from partaking of this sacrament because of what they considered to be the feminizing manner in which it was administered.

Until the 1980s, the preferred (and for decades before that, the required) method of taking communion was for the parishioner to kneel in front of the priest and open his or her mouth in silent anticipation. The priest would then hold the communion wafer up high, and quietly say, "The body of Christ," thereby transforming it into sacred substance. Finally, he would place it in the parishioner's mouth. Some townsmen claim that to take communion in this fashion is essentially to lower yourself before another man, the priest. In Andalusia, the act of lowering oneself is nothing short of humiliating, a public demonstration of subjugation and inferiority. Consequently, the occasional man who did want to take communion might keep one knee raised in symbolic protest against a more complete expression of self-humiliation. A woman would never keep one knee raised during Mass, whether at communion or at any other time. In fact, so much more of the Mass than just communion requires kneeling that it is possible that men, for this reason, among others, viewed the entire ceremony as emasculating.

Religious processions in Monteros display the same spatial meanings as do Mass and the parade of Giants and Big-Heads. For example, as a penitential act, many women will walk barefoot in procession; a few even crawl on their knees. In a survey of Monteros processions that I took in the mid-1970s, I found that fully a quarter to a third of the participating women walked barefoot, whereas only two or three men out of several hundred did so on any given occasion. Although several women went so far as to crawl on hands and knees, never did I see a man assume this posture. When I asked about this differentiation by gender, friends in Monteros assured me that anybody who wants to—who has the will, as they put it—can crawl or walk barefoot in a procession; the participant's sex is irrelevant. Nonetheless, the distinction in actual practice is obvious: Women carried out these penitential acts and men did not. What is more, it was working-class women, those from the least prestigious and powerful families in town, who tended to walk barefoot or crawl. These acts were considered beneath the dignity of those from the commercial or property-owning classes, who considered them superstitious. In processions, the most elevated segments of society, socially speaking, did what they could to keep themselves elevated spatially. Neither men nor those women with pretentions to high social rank would deign to lower themselves in a public act of religious contrition.

A final example of spatial differentiation comes from the olive harvest, which takes place between December and March. During this season, the town empties out as laborers are transported by the vanful to the surrounding groves. In Monteros, during the period I carried out my fieldwork, all harvesting took place by hand. Machinery, though cheaper and more efficient, was said to cause permanent damage to the trees, a serious consequence considering that olive trees are capable of fine fruit-bearing over the course of literally hundreds of years.

The olive harvest is carried out through a division of labor that is immediately evident: Men, standing erect, strike the olive branches with poles while women, kneeling under the trees, pick the fruit from the ground. It is impossible to rely on either history or biology to explain this dichotomy. To state that men and women adopt distinct roles because they have inherited them from the past is merely to beg the question of how the custom originated. Nor does supposedly superior masculine strength account for the division of labor; men and women alike acknowledge that being on one's knees all day takes greater fortitude than hitting the branches with poles. In fact, during my residence in Monteros, a male labor shortage (caused by migration to cities and foreign countries) made it necessary for several women to adopt the male harvesting role. Although this was the first time anyone could remember such an event occurring, everyone agreed that the women performed as well as or better than the men on their crew.

It was a large-scale landowner, an educated and reflective person, who provided me with the most satisfying explanation of the division of labor at the olive harvest. He offered a four-part account. First, he said, women and men have always enacted this particular division of labor, so they have no motivation to change; second, women are the ones who normally clean the floor — sweeping, scrubbing, and the like — an act parallel to what occurs at the olive harvest; third, these distinct economic roles are metaphoric equivalents of male moral superiority and female inferiority, qualities which naturally accord men a spatially higher place than women in the harvesting scheme; and, finally, olive harvesting is a metaphor of coitus, with the men on top, dropping their seed onto the women below. (In support of this latter interpretation, we might suggest that for men to stand during the olive harvest, in other words to remain erect, and to hit the branches with sticks, is for them to assert masculine potency.) Whether or not this landowner is correct, he at least provides an insider's view that is consonant with the spatial symbolism prevalent in other areas of Monteros life: Higher-ranking individuals occupy physically higher realms than those lower down in the hierarchy of power and prestige.

CHILDREN'S GAMES

The spatial symbolism that emerges in the parade of Giants and Big-Heads, Mass, religious processions, and the olive harvest is also evident in children's games. This association is particularly evident in boys' games, the category about which I collected most information during the 1970s. The games demonstrate a regular pattern: The player who succeeds in mounting another, getting on top of another, rising above another, wins. All these games, as we shall see, incorporate those elements of symbolic homosexuality that Alan Dundes has identified for men's and boys' games in the United States and elsewhere (Dundes 1978, 1985). The games not only provide a safe, circumscribed arena in which close physical contact among pubsecent and adolescent men can occur. They also serve as an outlet for young boys' needs to assert their burgeoning masculinity through symbolic feminization of a male rival. To demonstrate these assertions, let us examine the separate games and game strategies in turn.

Echar Pies

The pattern emerges clearly in one of the most frequent ways by which individual players or team captains choose who is to go first. The most common technique is for players to *echar pies* (literally, "to cast out feet"). Two competitors, usually team captains, but often just a pair of competing individuals, face each other at a distance of some two meters. (At this stage of the game, nobody takes account of precise measurement.) They slowly begin to walk toward one another, each competitor taking a step in turn. As they proceed, each player situates the heel of one foot exactly in front of and touching the toe of the other. In the majority of instances, when the players meet, the foot of one player will overlap the foot of the other. The player whose foot lands on top presses his foot against that of his opponent. He then makes sure that the foot which lands on top, when placed flat on the ground with ankle twisted so that it is perpendicular to its normal position, fits in the space between his other foot and his opponent's losing foot. If these conditions are met, the player whose foot lands on top proclaims, *¡Monta y cabe!* ("It mounts and it fits!"). With this proclamation, the player whose foot mounts the other's wins the right to go first. If, however, there is a space between the foot of one competitor and that of the other that is narrower than the width of a boy's foot, the two players have to return to their original positions and start over again.

Echar pies conforms to the general Monteros pattern of superiority being attributed to him or that which is relatively high, spatially elevated. However, there is more at stake symbolically than just elevation. I refer specifically to the winner's exclamation, *¡Monta y cabe!* The verb *montar* ("to mount") has a number of meanings in Monteros. It refers most prominently to the male role in coitus; during sexual intercourse, men and male animals in general are said to "mount" females. In the only sexual act considered normal in Monteros, men do actually mount or get on top of their partners. But quite aside from this literal interpretation, mounting, both sexually and in game-playing, is seen in Monteros as an act of domination. It therefore follows that he whose foot "mounts" another's should be the player to go first.

Jugar a Churro

Mounting is a common theme in Monteros games. In an exclusively male team game known as *jugar a churro* ("playing churro," a churro being a long skinny pastry), also known as *jugar a los churros* ("playing churros"), two boys by common consent are named captains. They *echar pies* for the right to get first choice as to team player, with each captain alternately choosing players after that. Someone volunteers to assume the impartial role of *madre,* or "mother"; hence, there has to be an odd number of players, because teams are of equal size. Often, I am told, the *madre* will be someone who arrives on the scene late and needs a justification to participate after teams have already been chosen.

Once the teams are formed, the captains *echar pies* again to see which team will assume the submissive, less desirable role of *mula,* or "female mule." To form the *mula,* the *madre* stands against a lamppost or wall, facing outward. A member of the opposing team bends forward, burying his head in the *madre*'s stomach. The other members of his team attach themselves to one another in a long line, each boy bent forward and wrapping his arms around the waist of the boy in front. The boys' backs form a platform; the whole formation is known as the *mula.*

Members of the *madre*'s team now proceed to "mount" the *mula,* doing so by running from behind a base line and jumping on top of "her." All sorts of rules at this point come into play to determine which team wins. The members of the *madre*'s team (unlike the *mula,* this team has no special denomination) must all try to get on top of the *mula.* Thus, those who mount first try to position themselves as far forward as possible, a difficult task because players must remain at the spot where they land when they leap onto the *mula.* According to the rules, team members can mount atop one another too, thereby creating tiers of players, all sustained by the *mula.* As each mounter runs, he must call out, *¡Churro!* He can also shout this term just prior to leaping. Forgetting to say the word at all means that his team automatically loses. The team also loses if a player's feet touch the ground while leaping and mounting. At the same time, should the *mula* cave in — that is, should the team on bottom lose grip of one another and collapse to the ground — the *mula* loses. For this reason, it is often the strongest or heaviest mounter who goes last. This player is supposed to land hard on the *mula* just at the point that it is carrying the greatest weight, thus causing it to collapse.

If the *mula* fails to cave in, a self-appointed representative of the *madre*'s team raises a certain number of fingers in a predetermined signal. Any one of the players constituting the *mula,* his head of course bent toward the ground, instantly guesses which signal that might be, that is, how many fingers his opponent is holding up. The *madre,* who faces both teams, acts as impartial observer and declares whether the player has guessed correctly. If he has guessed correctly, the two teams change roles, the players who mounted now becoming the *mula.* If not, the teams assume the same roles as before.[1] To be among the *mula* is a physically trying, undesirable role. The object of the game is to mount, never to be mounted. The *madre,* unless "she" quits, continues to play as long as the game stays in effect or someone else assumes the position.

---

[1] Sutton-Smith (1972) reports an 1890 version of this hand signal game which he collected in New Zealand. Opie and Opie (1969) report numerous contemporary versions of the game from the north and midlands of England, and cite evidence of it from the 18th and 19th centuries. There are also pictoral representations of the game (e.g., in Bruegel's children at play, dated 1560) as early as the 16th century. The game I report here is clearly a version of what Brewster (1965) calls "How Many Horns Has the Buck?" a guessing game of widespread distribution, ranging from India to Argentina to Turkey. He traces the game back to Roman antiquity, and in 1938 even discovered it being played in Indiana.

Informants claim that this game is *más bruto* ['rougher'] than most, and that therefore it is confined to adolescent boys or those nearing adolescence. Neither girls nor younger boys participate. This information provides a critical context with which to interpret the symbolic meaning of the game. For one thing, the game forces boys who are struggling to assert their budding manhood actually to assume feminine roles, those of the *madre* and the *mula*. Within the safe, confined context of the game, boys therefore implicitly accept the feminine component of their personality, which they otherwise fear. We may assume that the game helps them to overcome that fear in more or less the same way that children in the United States can master their fear of ghosts, witches, and wild animals by donning the costumes of these dreaded beings on Halloween.

As for the *madre,* "her" main function is twofold: first, to act as a physical buffer between the players and the lamppost, so as to protect them from possible injury; second, to serve as impartial witness. In both these ways, the *madre* in the game parallels the real-life mother, who provides nurturance and protection and at the same time ideally cares for all her children without prejudice or favoritism. The real-life mother, as much as the mother in the game, must remain unbiased. The name *mula* is far from arbitrary, given that, among the people of Monteros as much as in the animal kingdom, females are the ones who get "mounted." It is therefore not too farfetched to interpret the game as one in which adolescent boys, still under the surveillance and protection of the mother, struggle to mount rather than be mounted, to assume the dominant, superior role rather than be forced into the potentially humiliating, and physically less comfortable, role of *mula*. In this game, the boys strive to position themselves in an attacking or mounting position in order to avoid being the object themselves of symbolic homosexual attack. This is a spatial expression of sentiments that appear in Monteros male folk speech as well (Brandes, 1980).

From another point of view, *Jugar a churro* incorporates a split female figuration. The mounted mule symbolizes one side of the split, at once the denigrated female figuration, the dominated female below, and the feminized male subject to attack from behind. The "mother" in the game represents the other side of the split female figuration. Femaleness in the game is not all denigrated. The mother is witness to transgression (i.e., the symbolic homosexual attack from behind), but she is also protector and guardian. To the extent that she enacts her role as fair, unprejudiced, nonjudgmental observer, the mother fosters the positive identification of pubescent and adolescent boys with women. In the end, the game reinforces a dual image of females — as dominated sex objects, on one hand, paragons of purity and goodness, on the other — that prevails throughout much of the Spanish-speaking world, including southern Spain (Dundes and Suárez-Orozco, 1984).

Jugar a Maisa

The word *maisa,* untranslatable, refers to this game alone. It is essentially a version of leapfrog, which is played mainly, if not exclusively, by boys. One boy, again known as the *mula,* bends down with his hands on his knees, and another jumps over him. The jumper uses his companion's back as a springboard and tries to land in front of him. At this point, both players squat with their hands on their knees and a third boy leaps over them, landing in front of them and squatting as they do. With each leap, players position themselves far enough in front of the player just behind so that the next person can jump over each person's back one at a time. Players do not attempt to leap over several people at once. When all the players have had a turn, the first boy rises and leaps over the rest, and the game continues in chain fashion until the players tire.

Although this game is theoretically noncompetitive, it incorporates an unmistakable element of aggressivity. As reported to me, occasionally the player squatting on the ground — that is, the *mula* — gets kicked in the backside by the leaper.[2] This act, if nothing else, demonstrates at least the strategic superiority of the player on top. As in *jugar a churro, jugar a maisa* places the spatially higher player in a position of dominance over the spatially lower one. In both games, too, the player in the inferior position keeps his back to the one above. The squatter, with backside in a vulnerable, exposed position, is, once again, called by a feminine and symbolically feminizing term, *la mula.* As in *jugar a churro,* this game suggests that in order to avoid symbolic, feminizing homosexual attack from behind, the players must place themselves in an attacking or mounting posture.

La Salavica del Nene

This game had gone out of fashion in Monteros by the 1970s. However, older and middle-aged informants remembered it from their childhood.

---

[2]In a parallel Cape Verde version of leapfrog reported by Brewster (1953) "each player may kick the 'frog' [i.e. the player squatting on the ground] in the buttocks with his right foot as he jumps" (p. 105).

It thus constituted part of the formative experiences of many of the adult men residing in town at the time I carried out my Andalusian fieldwork.

La Salavica del Nene translates literally "The Young Boy's Little Saliva." The game, an elaboration of leapfrog, begins with players selecting among themselves for the least desirable role, again that of *la mula*. The selection takes place by one player hiding a pebble in one hand, putting his hands behind his back, and having the other players guess which hand it is in. (This process is called *echar la china*—"toss the pebble.") Players who guess correctly are absolved from having to become the *mula*. If all guess correctly, the player holding the pebble becomes the *mula*. Otherwise, the last player to guess incorrectly must assume that undesirable role.

The game is like leapfrog except that as each player jumps, he spits, with his saliva landing on the ground. The object is for the player who follows to spit such that his saliva lands on top of the saliva of the first player. If the saliva lands where it should, the first player loses and assumes the role of *mula*. If it does not land where it should, the second player becomes the *mula*. Saliva, in this game, becomes a metonymic equivalent of the players themselves. Just as players mount the mula, the saliva of one player has to mount that of the previous player. The item on top—be it player or saliva—is the dominant entity, the winner. The result is not only symbolic domination through the covering of one boy's saliva by that of another. An actual mixing of bodily fluids also occurs in the game. This feature, together with the feminization of the player on the bottom, is consonant with an interpretation of the game as an expression of symbolic homosexual union and rivalry.

Jugar a los Santos

Throughout Spain, matchsticks are made of wax and come in little cardboard boxes, with pictures on one side. These pictures are referred to as *santos,* or "saints," probably because saints were originally portrayed on the boxes. The name of this game thus translates literally "to play at saints." Like *La Salivica del Nene,* this game had become obsolete by the time of my fieldwork. Nonetheless, adult men in the 1970s were familiar with it from their childhood. It was exclusively a male game; boys were the ones who collected *santos.*

The object of the game is to increase your collection of matchbox pictures. One by one, each player places his *santo* against a wall and lets it fall freely to the ground. If your *santo* lands on someone else's, you take possession of that person's card. After each player has a turn, there is another round, this time with a second player letting his *santo* fall to the ground first. With each round, a different player thereby becomes vulnerable to having his *santo* taken by someone else. If, in the course of the game, you lose all your cards, you can borrow more from a companion. Otherwise, you have to retire from the game. To choose the first player of all, a *santo* is placed on the ground. All players then let their *santos* fall. The player whose *santo* lands closest to the original one goes first.

Here again is a game in which to be on top is to win, only this time it is a card, rather than saliva or a person, which is the winning entity. Significantly, the verb used to describe what happens when one *santo* lands on another is *montar*—"to mount." In another version of this game bearing the same name, matchsticks rather than *santos* are placed against a wall and then let fall to the floor. The rules and symbolism of this version are identical to those in which cards are used.

El Lapo

This game, again exclusively a boys' pastime, utilizes the knee bone from an animal such as a pig, dog, or cow. The bone is curved, with knobs at both ends. For purposes of the game, the convex side of the bone is called the *panza,* or "belly," because that in essence is its shape. The concave side is referred to as the *oyo,* or "hole," also for its form. There are usually five or six players, who take turns flipping the bone in the air and letting it fall on a table. According to the position in which the bone lands, the players assume certain imaginary roles.

There are three such roles that are assumed at any given moment, although the players change roles rapidly with each toss of the bone. If the bone falls "belly up" *(panza arriba),* you are "saved" *(te salvas).* If it falls with the hole, or concave side, facing up *(oyo arriba),* you are punished *(te castigan).* If it falls to one side, you are selected king *(rey),* and if it lands on the opposite side, the mirror image of the *rey* side (the two sides are identifiable by certain bone markings), you are named hangman *(verdugo).* The punishment meted out is administered by whipping, and the instrument used is a belt. *Lapo,* the name of the game, in fact means "whip" or "blow." The "king" determines the severity of the punishment, that is, the number and strength of lashings which the unlucky player, who tosses the bone hole up, is to receive. The "hangman" administers the punishment.

As each player flips the bone, he assumes the role that fate has decreed, and the previous person in the role relinquishes it. Hence, a player who administers the punishment at one moment might be on the receiving end the next. This built-in feature of the game moderates the kind of treatment each victim is expected to suffer. The general idea, according to informants, is to administer as hard a whipping as you can without risking retribution against yourself at a later stage in the game. As in the other games we have analyzed, one of this game's goals is obviously to avoid being treated with destructive aggression by assuming the role of aggressor one's self.

The spatial dimension of *el lapo* is of special interest here. If the bone lands belly up, that is, protruding vertically, you are saved; if it lands with the hole facing up, however, you lose, in that you are punished. Convexity is obviously more highly valued than concavity. Concavity victimizes. In fact, one of the most famous proverbs in the Spanish language states, *El muerto al hoyo y el vivo al bollo* ("To the hole [i.e., to the grave] with the dead, and the roll [i.e., bread] to the living"; Arora, 1980). Being placed below ground, that is, in a very lowly spatial position, is therefore associated with death.

In Monteros, as throughout Andalusia, not all the dead are buried, however. The wealthiest townspeople place their deceased relatives in so-called *nichos,* or "niches," which are aboveground compartments faced with marble or stone that usually line one or two sides of the cemetery and appear in the aggregate like a giant beehive. *Nichos* for the elite, graves for the commoners: even in death, social superiority receives spatial expression, with the rich being situated higher than their economic inferiors.

CONCLUSION

In Monteros, rank and prestige clearly receive both metaphoric and actual spatial representation. A wide range of ritual and religious activities, including the parade of Giants and Big-Heads, Holy Mass, and practices associated with burial of the dead, all demonstrate the association between highness and superiority, on the one hand, and lowliness and inferiority, on the other. The same can be said of the sexual division of labor: women, whom Andalusians have traditionally considered to be morally and socially inferior to men (see, e.g., Brandes, 1980, 1985; Gilmore, 1986), work close to the ground at the olive harvest, while men's harvesting activities are carried out while standing. In children's games, particularly boys' games, the players who climb or jump to the top and stay there are the winners, while those at the bottom lose. Likewise, in games that involve tossing or dropping objects of one sort or another, the thing that lands on top wins. All of these cultural manifestations in Monteros reflect the near-universal association of the high with the good, the powerful, and the strong and the association of the low with weakness as well as with social and moral inferiority.

Nobody has done better to explain these spatial meanings than Percy Cohen. Asks Cohen (1980), "Why is higher . . . superior?" (p. 58). His answer: "All men have experienced childhood; and all children have experienced adults as more powerful, more prestigious, and more advantaged than they are; all children have also experienced adults as higher than they are and have come to recognize or, at least, to suppose that greater height has much to do with greater advantage. . . ." As Martha Wolfenstein has demonstrated with reference to juvenile jokes and joking (1978), children yearn to be big, to be like their parents. During their lengthy period of early development, children experience parents hovering over them, walking effortlessly as they themselves must crawl and falter. Parents are both competent and large; the two qualities undoubtedly become inextricably associated in children's minds. As Cohen says, "children are aware, as they grow up, that being taller, or 'more grown up,' means having more self-governing access to things and services and more power to control and to withhold, as well as to give, in their dealings with those who are less 'grown up' " (p. 58).

This is not to say that the origin of social differentiation lies in the size difference between children and their parents. It does mean, however, that adults interpret all sorts of ranking—economic, moral, political, ethnic, and the like—in terms of the earliest and most fundamental system of social differentiation they know: the one established within the nuclear family, in which strong, powerful, accomplished people are tall; and weak, submissive, awkward people are short. Short family members, the children, strive to be like their superiors. This universal desire provides perhaps the single most effective motivation for children to develop motor and cognitive skills.

Andalusian culture, like many others, has encoded the meanings of high and low, of bigness and smallness, in such a way that they resonate with the experience of childhood. In and of themselves, the expressions *clase alta* ("upper class") and *clase baja* ("lower class") do not evoke childhood memories. But it is the experience of childhood that makes such semantic formulations understandable and intuitively true; at the very least, the child's perspective on his or her social world makes it unproblematic that wealth and power should be associated with great height and that poverty and powerlessness should be associated with being close to the ground.

Each culture will develop its own specific expressions of the same basic spatial metaphor. In Monteros, and throughout traditional Andalusia, relative height is associated with a host of social distinctions, including that between men and women. Hence, it is considered emasculating for a man to lower himself, be it during Mass or at the olive harvest. For the same reason, sexual domination as well as competition in childhood play are represented through females being situated in a lower position than males. The children's games that we have analyzed are mainly a reflection of a pervasive spatial metaphor with which players are already intuitively familiar. However, it is probable that the games reinforce popular representations of gender by repeated demonstration of the message that females are on the bottom, that they are the losers, and that superiority and domination is achieved by rising to the top.

Spatial metaphors in Andalusia are hardly unique; they represent but one specific complex of analogies that make sense and are culturally shared because they coincide with childhood realities. If nothing else, the symbolic analysis of verticality in southern Spain should reinforce the opinion of those who believe that symbols are not arbitrary. We do conceive of the world in terms of common human experiences, although different cultures usually provide distinctive linguistic and behavioral expressions of those experiences.

BIBLIOGRAPHY

ARORA, S. L. (1980), "To the grave with the dead . . .": Ambivalence in a Spanish proverb. *Fabula,* 21:223–246.

BELO, J. (1948), The Balinese temper. In: *Personal Character and Cultural Milieu,* ed. Douglas Haring. New York: Syracuse University Press, pp. 148–174.

BRANDES, S. (1980), *Metaphors of Masculinity: Sex and Status in Andalusian Folklore.* Philadelphia: University of Pennsylvania Press.

_____ (1985), Women of southern Spain: Aspirations, fantasies, realities. *Anthropol.,* 9:111–128.

BREWSTER, P. G. (1953), *American Nonsinging Games.* Norman, OK: University of Oklahoma Press.

_____ (1965), Some notes on the guessing game, How many horns has the buck? In: *The Study of Folklore,* ed. Alan Dundes. Englewood Cliffs, N.J.: Prentice-Hall, pp. 338–368.

COHEN, P. (1980), Psychoanalysis and cultural symbolization. In: *Symbol as Sense: New Approaches to the Analysis of Meaning,* ed. Mary LeCron Foster & Stanley Brandes. New York: Academic Press, pp. 45–68.

DUNDES, A. (1978), Into the endzone for a touchdown: A psychoanalytic consideration of American football. *West. Folklore* 37:75–88.

―――― (1985), The American game of "smear the queer" and the homosexual component of male sport and warfare. *J. Psychoanal. Anthropol.*, 8:115–129.

―――― & SUAREZ-OROZCO, M. (1984), The *piropo* and the dual image of women in the Spanish-speaking world. *J. Amer. Folklore*, 10:111–133.

GILMORE, D. D. (1984), Andalusian anti-clericalism: An eroticized rural protest. *Anthropol.*, 8:31–44.

―――― (1986), Mother-son intimacy and the dual view of women in Andalusia. *Ethos*, 14:227–251.

GINZBURG, C. (1976), High and low: The theme of forbidden knowledge in the sixteenth and seventeenth centuries. *Past/Present* 73:28–41.

KAPLAN, T. (1977), *Anarchists of Andalusia, 1868–1903.* Princeton: Princeton University Press.

MINTZ, J. R. (1982), *The Anarchists of Casas Viejas.* Chicago: University of Chicago Press.

NEEDHAM, R. (1973), *Right and Left: Essays on Dual Symbolic Classification.* Chicago: University of Chicago Press.

OPIE, I. & OPIE, P. (1969), *Children's Games in Street and Playground.* Oxford: Clarendon Press.

SUTTON-SMITH, B. (1972), *The Folkgames of Children.* Austin: University of Texas Press.

WOLFENSTEIN, M. (1978), *Children's Humor: A Psychological Analysis.* Bloomington: Indiana University Press.

7

"Sweet Dreams, My Daughters": An Alaskan Eskimo Bedtime Story

RUTH MCDONALD BOYER

This presentation begins with a story told by a histrionic Inuit mother/grandmother residing in a Yukon Delta village in June of 1973. The audience consisted of three of the teller's five daughters, myself, and, for a very brief period, a young grandson and his male playmate. It was designated as a "fairy tale" by the narrator, to much noisy denial by the younger women, who insisted that it was history, that the events had actually occurred in a neighboring community. The dignified old woman stated flatly that this was untrue and proceeded regally with the "fairy tale." Translation was done by the daughter whom I knew best.

The grandmother explained that she was telling a bedtime story, one recounted on arctic winter evenings with the avowed intent of lulling youngsters to sleep. This particular tale was long, taking all day to recount, and in a life situation would have been a serial, a "cliff-hanger," continuing over many nights.

Following the presentation of the story herein (interrupted from time to time by notes concerning Eskimo reactions), certain theoretical comments will be made, primarily involving the "burnt child" reaction syndrome (Boyer, DeVos, Borders, and Tani-Borders, 1978), which this example of expressive culture seems strongly to reinforce. The ways in which the story duplicates metaphorically the family's psychological dynamics within common aspects of the greater Alaskan Inuit culture will be obvious.

The story began. Narrator and audience were grouped in a small bedroom. I was honored with a wooden box for a chair; the other three intent listeners sat close together on the floor. The eight-year-old son of one daughter was playing outside with a friend. After two or three sentences, the elderly mother abandoned her introduction, and leaning back on the cushions of the bed where she presided, she recited emotionally certain sad trials of her own life.

"I have not always lived here. I lived in another small village until my husband died. Then I came here to be with two of my daughters. All my life I wanted a son — but no, all I had was five girls." The last sentence was stated in a resigned but melancholy tone. Three times she had adopted boys, some as old as eight years, whose parents (related to her husband) were "giving them away." The first two died, and the third, now adult, is no longer with her. "I really needed a son to provide food for all the womenfolks." Again she commenced the story she had elected to tell, changing her tone when appropriate to story events, gesturing with hands and arms, beating against a wooden box with her fist for dramatic emphasis. She was a master at her craft.

THE HISTORIC FAIRY TALE (ABBREVIATED)

"Way up north, there was this young woman who grew up with her mother. The mother had five children — all girls. The husband was dead. So they lived alone.

"That mother tried hard to feed her daughters by fishing those little white fish, those tomcods [Grandmother demonstrated their short length].

"All during the winter she went out fishing for tomcods.

"All winter [repeated several times].

"She went fishing those tomcods in the wintertime in order to provide her children with food.

"One time during the winter they had this blizzard, a snow blizzard, with the wind blowing and the snow blowing — like a sandstorm in the wintertime. And during that winter the mother came home with less and less fish. She hunted all day and sometimes she would get only five little tomcods.

"One day the little fish she brought home were only two. She went out again, every day [last sentence repeated]. She hunted for fish. And one day she hunted all day and came home with nothing.

"The next day and for several days after that, she hunted, but she got nothing." [Throughout the story, the listeners had mournful mien, clucking their sadness at the diminishing fish supply.]

"And the next day, and for several days after that, she hunted and never got anything. She went out every day, every day, and the blizzards kept on and on and on, and she never caught anything.

"So her oldest daughter began to feed her sisters. She let them chew on pieces of seal skins, on the scraps from making mukluks. She had them chew on them in order to have something to eat, little pieces of sealskin. While the mother was hunting, the oldest daughter fed them, letting her younger sisters chew on these. The mother went out hunting every day all winter long [last sentence repeated several times].

"One time their mother came home and the oldest daughter was listening for her, and one time when she came home, the mother opened this window. They had this window up in the ceiling, the window that's made of sealskin. The mother opened the window, the window they had up on the ceiling.

"In the house they had a bench on one side where all the children slept. The mother slept on the other side. The four older girls were sitting on one end of their sleeping bench; the youngest girl was at its other end. And their mother, after she opened the window, she came down through the door with an armful of wood, and when she came down with the wood, she built a fire in the middle of that house, and she put her pot over the fire. She had this pot made out of stone that was ground into little pieces and mixed with some kind of clay and was made into a pot, and she put that over the fire. She put that over the fire. She put some water in the pot and put it on the fire.

"They used to have big wooden plates or pans. After she put a big wooden pan on the floor, the mother got up. She went to her youngest girl that was sitting at the other end of the bed. She took her by the arm and took her to the middle of the floor. Then, after she took her to the middle of the floor, she started to take off her clothes, and then she killed the little girl, the youngest daughter.

"And the mother, after she killed the little girl, she cut her body up and cooked the body, cooked it in the pot [sentence repeated].

"And this oldest, her oldest daughter was very upset. Her youngest sister being killed and cooked up.

"The mother watched what she was cooking, and when she thought it was cooked, the mother ate it all by herself — not the children [much moaning by the listeners].

"Of course, the older daughter was very upset by this. And her mother would not talk to her any more.

"Then, in the evening, they went to bed. This oldest daughter was very upset. She couldn't sleep all night. She was thinking that maybe the mother was going to do the same thing to all her children. She couldn't sleep all night. But finally, sometime during the night, she fell asleep for a little while. When she woke up her mother had already left, gone out hunting. And whenever she comes home after that, she ate what was left of the little girl. After she came home, she ate what's left, just herself. And when she left to go hunting, the oldest daughter fed her sisters little bits of sealskins, cut from mukluks, cleaning them and then feeding them to her sisters.

"Finally, the mother finished eating the little girl. She went out hunting. Her oldest daughter was worried that when the mother came home again, one of her sisters would be killed once again.

"This one time, the mother came home again. Before she came in, she opened the window above, up there, and she came in through the door, and like before, she had wood in her arms. She brought wood inside and put it on the floor. These sisters were sitting on the bed, the older one at one end, and the youngest one on the opposite end, just like before. The mother made a fire, just like before, and then she went to her youngest daughter, the next to youngest, took her by the arm and took her to the middle of the floor — like before. Again she took off her clothes and then she killed the little girl. After she killed the little girl, she put her in this big wooden pan, and she cut up the body and put it in the pot.

"The oldest daughter was very, very upset — more than before.

"And the mother cooked the body, and when it was cooked, the mother ate it all by herself.

"Every day the mother went out hunting. While the mother was gone, the oldest daughter fed the children with scraps of skins. She would have them chew on skins and some sinews too — in the daytime — while the mother was hunting. Then, in the evening, they all went to bed. This time the oldest daughter couldn't sleep all night, all through the night ["couldn't sleep all night" repeated several times].

"In the morning, the mother got up, got ready, and went hunting again. These children were three now. Three children left. And the mother went out hunting every day, and the oldest daughter kept feeding her sisters with scraps of sealskins and sinew, every day.

"And these blizzards were every day. Every day blizzards went on and on and on, every day. Every day there was snow and storm, blizzards.

"Every day, when the mother comes home, she would eat part of this, of her little girl, all by herself. She wouldn't give any to her other children. Then one day, she came home and she finished the food which was left — of her little girl. She finished it that evening. Then the next day, she went out hunting again. When the girls got up, their mother was already out hunting. The oldest girl kept feeding her two other sisters who were left scraps of sinews and skins—and she fed herself too.

"One evening their mother came home. She listened. She heard the girls from the outside. The three of them were sitting on the bed. And then they heard her. They saw her take the window off. The oldest daughter got really scared that her mother was going to kill one of them again.

"The mother came in again with her arms full of wood. She had stopped talking to her children. She never talked to them—no more. The oldest daughter continued to feed her sisters—to keep them going.

"The three girls were sitting there on the bed when the mother came in with wood in her arms. The mother filled her pot with water and put it over the fire. Then she went over and got the third little girl. She did just like before. She took off her clothes and cut up the body and cooked it for herself. Their mother ate all of her by herself.

"Now the oldest sister was very, very upset. There were only two left now. She didn't sleep all night. All night she did not sleep.

"Then, the day after that, after their mother went out hunting, the oldest daughter started thinking about leaving their home. She knew that if they stayed, they will die. They would die, she knew.

"Even if they left their home, she knew they would die. . . . They would die.

"The blizzards went on and on [Repeated versions of the blizzard accompanied by appropriate movements and sounds from the listeners].

"So the older girl started to pack things for her sister and herself. She started to pack before her mother came home. After she got ready, she dressed her sister as warmly as she could, and she herself too, and they went out of their house. The older sister took a piece of stick which she can use as a walking stick or cane.

"When they went out, the snowstorm was so bad they couldn't see anything. Not a thing. The only thing they could see were their own feet on the snow. Nothing else [phrase repeated]. They started walking. She took her sister by the hand. They walked and walked and walked all day through the snow.

"Then pretty soon, she started to see that it was getting dark. When she realized it was getting dark, she made a hole in the snow like a cave. She sat down there and had her sister sit on her lap. She saw there was ice on the bottom of the hole. She put that stick in the snow, and she talked to the stick, as to a person. She told her to guide them where there is other people. She told the stick to guide them." [Note that if the foregoing "her" is not merely an error in translation, and indeed the hopefully beneficent stick was accurately ascribed feminine gender, we can speculate that the girl still had *hope* concerning the goodness of things female. On the other hand, if the pronoun should have been "him," perhaps the elder sister felt a need for help from a male, perhaps it was a plea to a father figure. Unfortunately, the phallus later will bend, becoming disappointingly impotent and as dangerous as a mother.]

"While they were sitting there, her sister fell asleep. Then pretty soon, she fell asleep. When she woke up, it was starting to get daylight. She gave her sister a little piece of skin to chew on. She did the same. She looked at the stick that she had put firmly straight up in the snow. The stick had bent down a little bit sideways. So she followed the direction the stick was pointing. The girls started walking through the snow. They started walking, and they walked and walked and walked. The snow was blowing [sentence repeated]. They walked and walked.

"After they walked all day, when she realized it was getting dark, she did the same thing, that second night. She made a cave. She dug the snow. She found there was ice under the snow. After she made that hole, she sat down like the night before and had her sister sit on her lap. Then she put her stick straight into the snow, and again she talked to the stick, asking it to lead them toward the land because there was still ice under the snow where they were.

"When she woke up in the morning, she looked at her stick. It had bent down a little more than the night before. When they got up, she had her sister chew on some skins. She did the same thing as the day before. They started walking toward the direction the stick was pointing. And they walked all day. There was still a snowstorm, a blizzard going on." [Several minutes went by while the walking and blizzard were described in repetitive fashion as the listening chorus nodded and intoned.]

"They couldn't see anything. But she knew it was starting to get dark, so she did the same thing as before, making a cave in the snow. But this time on the bottom of the snow, she found land. There was ground under the snow, not ice. When she saw that there was ground under the snow, she was happy. She sat down as the night before. She put her stick into the snow and talked to the stick.

" 'My stick, my stick, please lead us toward the place where there are some people in the morning.' For the first time in a long, long time, that night the sisters slept all night — for the first time.

"When they woke up, it was daylight, and the blizzard wasn't as bad as before. It was a little better. When she got up, she started going in the direction where her stick was pointing, like before. They started walking. They walked all day.

"Pretty soon, she started noticing that there were some hills on the ground. They went over to these hills. When they got to the top of the hill, she looked down and she saw that there was a village near the river, and in the middle of the village was a *kusgih* [bathhouse/ sweat house/ men's house/ ceremonial room].

"When the girls went over this hill, they hid among the trees and they watched to see if there were people in the village, but they saw nobody. Nobody was around. Nobody could be seen. So after watching, staying there, watching for some people, she decided to have the younger sister go down to the *kusgih* to see if there were any people in there. The younger sister went down. The older sister stayed behind and watched. She saw her sister go into that *kusgih*. Then, after a while, the older sister who stayed behind, she saw some people coming out of the *kusgih*. They were eating her sister's body.

"When the sister saw that these people were eating her sister's body, for the first time, she cried. She bent down on her knees and she cried. She cried when she heard the people talking there must be another one that was with her sister. She heard the people saying that they were going to go out. They were going to look for her.

"When she saw these people, she talked to her stick. She asked the stick why it had led them to this kind of people, people who eat other people. And she was telling the stick not to have these people find her. It was like praying to the stick.

"Then she watched the people. They were coming closer to where she was hiding. They came close, but they did not find her. They decided to go back to the *kusgih*. They went inside. They did not find her [relief expressed by listeners].

"After they went in, the girl stayed for a long time where she was. She was scared that somebody might see her if she tried to go out, tried to go away from that place. Finally, she decided to crawl on her hands and knees. She went over the hill behind the village, away from the village.

"Then she started walking all by herself. She thought that now it didn't matter where she went because if she had stayed with her mother, her mother would have killed her and eaten her and she would have died anyway — if she went back to her mother or anyplace. She knew that she was going to die.

"By this time she had walked to the end of the day. She did not make a hole in the snow as before. She was mad at her stick because the stick had led her to this kind of people and she talked to the stick. *Why* had it led her to the people who eat people?

"She slept all night. When she woke up in the morning, she saw that her stick had fallen flat in the snow, on the ground, flat. It had fallen flat. So she walked and walked. All day she walked. Then she came to another hill. She went over the hill and stopped to look down. She saw at the bottom of this hill, she saw that there was a river down there. And there was only one house—only one house [phrase repeated].

"She decided to go down to this house and go inside—whether she gets killed or not—to see who is in there. So she went down to the house to go in.

"When she came to this house, she saw there was a little storehouse where they keep fish and food for winter. She saw there was a *kusgih*. She went to the house and tried to make some noises to make sure if there were people inside. Nobody came out. After making noises, she saw that nobody came out and so she went in through the door, and around through the tunnel and up through the door hole, and she saw in this room that there were five beds—two on each side and one on the third side, five beds altogether in the room.

"She saw that there was nobody in this house. But she saw that there were some men's clothes in there—only men's clothes. She went into this house and she didn't care now, even if they killed her or not, whoever lived in that place. She went in and sat near the door. She was sitting there. While she was sitting there, finally, she heard some noises outside. Then she heard this person coming in through the tunnel and then she saw this person go up into the house through this hole and this person looked around. This person saw her. She saw it was a man. This man asked her why and from where she came, she being alone as a woman. He wanted to know where she came from.

"After he came in, he told the woman that he was living with his four other brothers, that they were all living in that house—five brothers and they needed a woman to live with them. He told her he wanted her to live with them. He told her the five brothers go out every day to hunt, and then the eldest brother usually comes home early to cook meals for his younger brothers, and he wanted her to stay with them."

At this point in the story, the two boys who had obviously been listening quietly just outside, opened the door a crack—then wider, crept in, sitting on the floor next to the entry. Grandmother and daughters bridled, the younger women making a tense, clawing gesture toward the face of the grandson. The boys were assuredly not welcome. They looked frightened and made a hasty retreat. Grandmother continued with her tale.

"Then this man decided this woman should be *his* wife. And while they were there, one of his younger brothers came home and he said he was glad that there was this woman who came to live with them.

"Those men started coming home one right after the other, those four brothers and finally the youngest one was the last one to come home — the youngest brother.

"This youngest brother, when he came in, well, he was — the woman saw that he was kind of mean and rough. He was telling the woman that he did not like her. He told her mean things — like she smells. He was mean.

"The oldest brother told the woman not to mind his youngest brother, that he is always like that, rough and mean, and he told her not to mind anything — to pay no attention. He told her the men were happy to have a woman in their house to take care of the skins, to take care of the food.

"He also told her never to put anything in front of the youngest brother's face, never to hurt him by moving toward his face roughly, by snatching at his face." [At this point the teller of the tale made the clawlike gesture with her fist and the listeners drew back and made sounds of alarm.]

"Then the four brothers went hunting. The youngest one stayed at home with the woman. He stayed behind to help the woman with the seals. Soon he started to treat her rough, pushing her, taking things roughly from her hands. And soon, this lady was getting irritated and she was getting mad at the boy for being so nasty and rough to her. She had this *ulu,* this knife with a rounded edge, a rounded blade, an Eskimo knife *ulu.* In those days they were not made of steel, they were made of stone. She had that kind of *ulu* in her hand. And then she got mad. She got mad [indignation on the faces of the listeners, as they murmured displeasure]. "She kind of tried to scare him in his face with this knife.

"The young man fell backward. He fell back, but she did not touch his face with the knife. After he fell backward, she went over to see him, and she saw that his face was cut in half. But she didn't touch him with her knife. But he was dead [more murmuring from listeners].

"Then she went to this man. She tried to get him up to see if he was alive. But he was dead. He was dead. She was thinking what to do. Finally she went outside. She didn't know what to do. She went to this little house where they kept food and fish. This little storehouse was up above the ground. It had supports to keep it high off the ground. She opened the door to this storehouse, and when she opened the door, she saw inside this house, this fish house, that there were lots of reindeer skins rolled and tied. She decided to take the boy, this young man's body out to the fish house. She unrolled one of these big reindeer skins. She put the body inside. She rolled it inside the skin and tied it all up. Then she put it on the bottom of the stack of reindeer skins. All the other skins she put on top of it to cover it. Then she went back to the house.

"After a while her husband, the oldest brother, came home. He asked her where his youngest brother was. So the woman told him that after they left, he had decided to go out hunting too. Finally the other brothers came home in the evening. They all waited for him. They waited for the youngest brother to come home. They waited. They waited. They waited all evening for him to come home.

"But he didn't come home, the youngest brother. They waited all night. All night long they waited, but he didn't come home, so in the morning the brothers decided to go out to look for him. It was in the wintertime, and they decided to go out and look for him. This was winter. But since that time, they went out every day looking for their brother instead of hunting. Every day, every day, they went looking.

"Pretty soon it was springtime. Then one day this oldest brother decided to go out under this fish house to fix his bow and arrow. He was sitting under this fish house. He sat there. Pretty soon something dripped on his shoulder. He felt something dripping, drop, by drop, by drop, on his back. Pretty soon he was beginning to wonder what was dripping on his back. He reached behind him with his hand, and he saw that there was this kind of bloody stain on his hand. He looked up to the floor. He saw through this crack that there was this bloodstain coming through this wooden floor. Lots and lots and lots of blood, coming through this crack. And when he saw all that blood dripping through this crack, he decided to go into the fish house and take a look. He opened the reindeer skins that were rolled up inside. He opened the last one and he found the body of his youngest brother.

"Then he went back into their house. He went to his wife. He asked her why she didn't tell him about his youngest brother. He had told her before never to hit him with anything in front of his face." [While this part of the story was told, a mosquito began buzzing around the faces of the listeners. They immediately bared their claws and snatched at it with the gesture previously described.]

"The man asked her why she didn't tell him about it earlier, before. But he told her it was all right now. Everything was already done; they couldn't do anything else. Everything was going to be all right.

"Then he told her she should not be afraid of anything that may happen to her.

"After they found out their brother was dead, they buried him. And in the summer they started hunting again. They hunted reindeer. But they never caught any. Only one, sometimes one. They never had a really good hunt like they had had before.

"Then one day the oldest daughter was alone at home. Her husband and his brothers went out hunting in the daytime. She was sitting there sewing on some skins, and while she was sewing there, she saw this little bird up there, landing around the top window.

"This little bird kept making noises. It wouldn't go away. Finally she decided to talk to the bird, and she told the bird that if the bird has anything to say to her, to talk to her in a way she can understand. So, after she talked to the bird, finally, it made some noises with its beak on the wood on the side of the window. The woman looked up and saw that this bird had a human face. The bird talked to the lady. The bird told her that these four other brothers are now preparing a place for her outside in order to get revenge for their youngest brother's death.

"Then this bird talked to the woman, giving her instructions to make a sewing bag out of skins, and to make some designs on it like birds from the ocean, or some kind of animals from the ocean on the sewing bag. The bird told her that when she finished the bag, to hide it either under her sleeve or under her long mukluk legs, and to do whatever the men wanted her to do—not to be afraid—like if they want to take her out someplace.

"The bird also told the lady if they take her out, they will take her to this place, and before they throw her into this place, they are going to kill her. She is to tell them she has something to show them before she dies. It was this sewing bag that she made. And then the bird flew away.

"As soon as it was gone, the lady started making this sewing bag with the special designs, the animal designs from the ocean—the birds and seals, to make it as fancy as she could. She finished it before the brothers came home. Before they came home, she tried to cook a meal for the brothers. When they came home, she served them. She put some food in their wooden plates. They sat on the floor and ate with the plates in their laps—not at the table.

"When they finished their meal, the oldest brother, her husband, told her that she has never gone anywhere, not any place, since she came there. He told her that when they go out tomorrow, that they are going to take her with them, when they go out hunting.

"The next day, her husband, the oldest brother, told her to get ready for a trip. So she got all ready. She put on her waterproof sealskin boots. She got all ready to go out with them. After they got all ready, she put the sewing bag under her sleeve. That's what she did. Then they went out to go. They left and they went out toward the land, not toward the ocean.

"Her husband took her by the arm. They started walking out. His brothers were right behind her, walking, walking, walking with them. While they were walking, the woman started hearing a noise like a pounding sound. She started hearing noises like pounding. Like somebody knocking. Pretty soon the noise got louder and louder." [Grandmother began pounding on a wooden box by her bedside in order to demonstrate the increasing sound.]

"Then, while they were walking along, the woman saw that way ahead of them there was this great big hole in the ground and on the side of the hole there was this reindeer body dead on the side of this great big hole, lying on the ground by the side of this hole. Then, as they got closer to this big hole in the ground, they got to it, close to it. This woman looked down, and saw in this hole in the ground, that there were lots of — lots and lots of worms, maggots. They were making this knocking, loud sound, this pounding-like sound [more demonstrations from tale teller].

"Then when they got there, her husband took her by the arm; the other brother took her other arm, and the others were all around her. They told her that she made them look for their brother all winter long and that now they were going to put her in that hole.

"The two other brothers held her, and the other brothers that were not holding her, they went to the reindeer body. They threw it into this hole — to those worms. In a minute it went down under the worms. Then, right away, the bones of the reindeer were coming up.

"This woman, whose oldest brother is her husband, she told him that before they throw her in the hole, that she has something to show them which she made. The woman took this sewing bag out of her sleeve, the one she made with all the designs from the animals from the ocean on it. She unrolled it and put it up for them to see. These brothers were so amazed with the designs on that sewing bag that they let go of her. They grabbed the bag. They looked at the bag with the designs on it. Seals and birds from the ocean.

"This bird had told her that while they are looking at this bag — the bird had given her instructions to hold her arms up, to reach for something, grab for something. So while they are interested in this bag, she lifted up her arms and grabbed something, and pulled it down toward her. Then she got on it, whatever it was — it was like a swinging bar — this thing she got on is something like a swing.

"When these brothers noticed she wasn't on the ground, they tried to reach up. They reached up and jumped for her, but they couldn't catch her. Then when they saw they couldn't catch her, her husband started begging her to come down. He told her that they were not going to do anything to her even if she came down. He begged her to come down and be his wife again.

"But she didn't come down. So, pretty soon, they got mad. They got mad at each other. They started throwing each other in this hole — the oldest one too — all of them. All four of them went into the hole. They pushed each other, and they pushed each other and finally, the last one of them fell.

"That is the end of the story."

COMMENTS

Sweet dreams, my daughters. No matter how deceitful, how dreadful mothers and husbands and villagers are, no matter that they try to murder you, magic will save you eventually. Go to sleep.

First of all, the suspenseful narration begins with a mother with five daughters and no sons, a situation mirrored dramatically in the teller's life. This introduction demonstrates clearly the "remembering" of a tale by an individual who unconsciously makes changes based on his or her psychological environment (Boyer, 1964, 1979).

The tale is replete with traits familiar in Alaskan Eskimo culture and recorded frequently in the literature (Hippler and Wood, 1977): difficult survival situations, starvation, occasional cannibalism, homicide, ostracism (in this case by a mother's silence), instability of emotional ties between marriage mates (Burch, 1975; Lantis, 1960), and fragility within the mother-child relationship. Burch's depiction of primarily ideal and traditional kinship ties and the care of babies includes the statement: "Eskimos absolutely could not stand to hear an infant cry" (pp. 132–133). Foulks (1972) likewise speaks of instant child gratification. We suggest that yielding to a baby's demand so immediately might well involve more than adoration of the child; instead, it may involve adult gratification. Burch makes no mention of teasing of infants and toddlers, which was striking to both Briggs and the author (whose fieldwork observations were for a short time only). Teasing will be addressed shortly.

Again, themes and motifs common in Inuit folklore[1] abound in our

---

[1] Hall's analysis of Nunivak tales is interesting in this regard. Nanogak's (1983) story *Kopilgok* duplicates many of the themes and motifs described in the grandmother's bedtime story (but omits the cannibalistic sequence): the splitting of a brother-in-law by means of a slashing *ulu*, prompted by his teasing; noisy worms eating animal/human

presented tale. Motifs other than those noted previously involve the magic of objects; punishment for the violation of taboo; a lake of worms; the supernatural savior (often animal or bird with human features), and the orphaning of the victimized youngster who has no kin to lend physical or psychological support. Eskimo culture often suggests that there is weakness in both sister-sister and brother-brother dyads; what support they give each other is subject to failure. So, as is usually the case, this story does not lack educative value in terms of expectations.

Eskimo socialization practices create doubts as to interpretation by a young child. This uncertainty may once have had a valuable function; it could create a sense of caution in hazardous situations such as hunting with partners (although males often depended on cohunters' skill and bravery to get them out of dangerous situations). It behooved a man to choose as a hunting partner an alert, reliable individual seasoned in the hazards of life. Who then would this be? A brother? Perhaps the best of the risky choices.

Childrearing among Eskimos is contradictory in its messages. "We love children" is verbalized frequently. Some activities appear to reinforce this ideal. However, underlying the acclaimed affection is considerable ambiguity, reinforced by the teasing games that continue in duration to the point of the child's tears. Pretending to injure the child is considered great fun (Briggs, 1970, 1979a,b, 1991). The clawlike gesture-that-killed in the plot of the tale is seen within Alaskan everyday life; sometimes it is innocuous to humans, as in the killing of the mosquito, but it is also a means of disciplining youngsters. What does it mean? Will the face be clawed, or is it mere play? Teasing? The youngsters and I were taken aback. The women's reaction was an abrupt, spontaneous movement. It consisted of a lurching forward of the upper body, an extension and snatching action of the entire arm, with the hand palm-down and shaped like a claw, nails bared for action. Briggs (1979a, 1979b) describes the motion among Canadian Eskimos: "reaches out . . . with exaggerated clutching gesture, fingers clawed and tensed" (p. 394; p. 7).

I suggest now that we look at the bedtime story as a form of teasing that is malicious because it gives double messages. Its alleged purpose is to dull the excitement of the day and lull a child to sleep. The *only*

---

remains; the intervention of a supernatural force; the magic of pretty handwork; the reversal of the husband's threat so that he himself is devoured. Nanogak was a renowned story teller representing both Alaskan and Copper Inuit cultures. The plot is undoubtedly common throughout Eskimo culture.

sleep-promoting features are actually the tale's length, the repetitive phrases such as "every day, every day, every day," and finally, the rescue of the eldest daughter by a supernatural force. Its plot describes mostly a nightmare, one in which five sisters are threatened with catastrophe until there is only one, one who faces death and cannibalism in her turn. The story's potential for instillation of anxiety, fear, and doubt veiled behind "kindly" intentions is obvious—even though one conscious purpose may be nothing more than a desire to keep children quiet. The comforting aspect is destroyed by the brutal plot—a vicious, effective example of teasing (giving and snatching away). How better to indicate ambivalence? Just *try* to sleep in peace, my daughters.

We should note, however, that the young women were eager to hear their mother relate the tale, even though they noisily disagreed with her as to the historical possibilities. It was a story familiar to them. Throughout the recital, they made sounds appropriate to the story line, oohing and aahing and making clucking "how dreadful" sounds. The milieu (and perhaps the attraction) was that of the horror film. The women already knew its terrors, but could not resist listening. Further, they often interrupted the sequence of the tale to inquire about their mother's comfort. She ignored them. But upon completion of her performance, she claimed to love her children. In the same breath she complained bitterly that her daughters never did anything for her, cared nothing for her—yet she loved them.

Related to this transient changeability might be what Boas noted in Inuit folklore as early as 1904: "A very peculiar trait of Eskimo tales is the sudden springing up of hatred between men who had been the best of friends, which results in treacherous attempts on life" (p. 10), the change in attitude being based on trifling reasons.

The carniverous maggots (worms) deserve special mention. They are a motif found in other Alaskan Inuit tales (Hall, 1975, Lucier, 1958). Hall (p. 433) presents a theory of Lantis (1953, p. 133) suggesting that the image of these human-consuming worms in a lake may involve food anxiety "because blowfly maggots ('worms') ate a considerable amount of food in aboriginal times." On another level, we should consider the possibility that these maggots eating the dead (or killing them through their devouring nature) may be a variant of Eskimo cannibalism (of course involving food shortages). One aspect of this may consist of a wishful expression to obtain the life and power of the slain being. Thus construed, on a psychoanalytic level, the reconstitution of the maggot may express an unconscious desire for timelessness, that is, a longing of the child to be at one with the mother by ingesting her (Boyer, 1992).

Beyond the foregoing comments, space does not permit further analysis of various features in the story. Instead, let us turn to the tale as a reinforcement of what Bruno Klopfer termed the "burnt child reaction" (Klopfer et al., 1956, p. 292) as referred to at the beginning of this article, and described further by L. B. Boyer (Boyer et al., 1978) who used Rorschach protocols to substantiate many of his arguments.

Klopfer found the burnt child reaction to indicate the existence of intense early emotional gratification followed by severe early emotional trauma. The emotional responses of the individual are seriously inhibited, thus interfering with close emotional ties and relationships in later life. An examination of Inuit socialization indicates the existence of the necessary ingredients for such a syndrome. A very brief outline of practices follows.

There is close physical and emotional contact between the Eskimo mother and baby. This relationship was even more apparent in the past when the nude infant was held against the naked back of the mother while the child was held within her parka. The child was fed on demand. However, there were frustrations.

Although the mother is reported not to tolerate a baby's crying, this was apparently true only during her waking hours. Briggs (1970) pointed out that a sleeping mother is almost impossible to rouse, and that an infant's screams were ignored by other adults in the room. This was observed also in Alaska. Before a child is a toddler, teasing by adults has already begun.

Objects may be held toward the youngster and then retracted; burning matches, for example, may nearly be grasped before they are blown out by the adult holder. A shiny cigarette lighter may be hidden the moment the child is about to touch it. All young Eskimos hear the bedtime and other tales that speak of catastrophe.

As I have noted, Briggs' writings about Canadian Inuit stress the prevalence of teasing games, or "morality plays," which have themes of death, possession, and sibling rivalry. How *prevalent* the viciousness of this form of "play" is among the people of the Yukon Delta has not been documented. The writer visited only one village. However, the Inuits' Rorschach protocols suggest its possibility (Boyer et al., 1978). Play is frustrating and discipline is fearful, at least when the claw is used.

Eskimo children are encouraged to nurture their baby siblings; they are prompted also to play with and often to torture baby animals, although both kinds of infant are represented as fragile. Prior to maltreatment, animals may be played with as though human. Toward other humans, a child must learn to be pleasant and inconspicuous, without antagonistic display.

Sibling rivalry is intense and often unresolved. Some mothers openly commented to me about hatred among their children. In a personal communication by telephone (1991) Arthur Hippler described Eskimo drinking behavior in urban Fairbanks and Anchorage. When emotional control is weakened by alcohol, deep-seated hostility manifests itself in brutal behavior between sibling-surrogates. Among Eskimos of past times, with the arrival of the new baby, the intense physical intimacy between the mother and the older child comes to an abrupt end. There is no room in the parka for two. The infant will then receive intense gratification while the toddler fusses. The younger child retains the mother's devoted (although often ambivalent) and primary attention.

The Rorschach tests mentioned previously bore out the belief that the Alaskan Inuit, both children and adults, fear too spontaneous and affective interactions. Mature concerns tend to be lacking. According to Boyer et al. (1978) "it seems reasonable to assume that the individual is as insecure with internalized object relationships as with relationships with external objects" (p. 44). There is shallowness and wariness of affect.

In other words, the Eskimo child has been burnt in early childhood. Tales such as "Sweet Dreams, My Daughters" are heard from earliest infancy throughout adulthood. They reinforce the doubts and anxieties taught by kin through games and other interactions of a cruel, teasing nature camouflaged by loving overtones. Cultural norms must be followed, or there is the threat of ostracism. Go to sleep, my darling, but heed the lake of maggots.

BIBLIOGRAPHY

BOAS, F. (1904), The folk-lore of the Eskimo. *J. Amer. Folklore,* 17:1–13.
BOYER, L. B. (1964), An example of legend distortion from the Apaches of the Mescalero Indian Reservation. *J. Amer. Folklore,* 77:118–142.
_____ (1979), Folktale variation in the service of defense. In: *Childhood and Society: A Psychoanalytic Study of Apache Personality.* New York: Library of Psychological Anthropology, pp. 136–151.
_____ (1992), Verbal communication, May.
_____ DE VOS, G., BORDERS, O. & TANI-BORDERS, A. (1978), The "Burnt Child Reaction" among the Yukon Delta Eskimos. *J. Psycholog. Anthropol.,* 1:7–56.
BRIGGS, J. L. (1970), *Never in Anger: Portrait of an Eskimo Family.* Cambridge, MA: Harvard University Press.
_____ (1979a), *Aspects of Inuit Value Orientation.* Mimeo. Canadian Ethnology Service Paper No. 56, Ottowa: National Museums of Canada.
_____ (1979b), The creation of value in Canadian Inuit society. *Internat. Social Science J.,* 31:393–403.
_____ (1991), Mazes of meaning: The exploration of individuality in culture and of

culture through individual constructs. In: *Psychoanal. Study Soc.*, 16:111–154. ed. L. B. Boyer & R. M. Boyer. Hillsdale, NJ: The Analytic Press.

BURCH, E. S. JR. (1975), *Eskimo Kinsmen: Changing Family Relationships in Northwest Alaska.* The American Ethnological Society Monogr. 59. St. Paul, NY: West Publishing Co.

FOULKS, E. F. (1972), *The Arctic Hysterias of the North Alaskan Eskimo.* Anthropological Studies No. 10. Washington, D.C.: American Anthropological Assn.

HALL, E. S. (1975), *The Eskimo Storyteller: Folktales from Noatak, Alaska.* Knoxville: The University of Tennessee Press.

HIPPLER, A. E. (1991), Verbal communication, June.

_____ & WOOD, J. R. (1977), *The Alaska Eskimos; A Selected, Annotated Bibliography.* Fairbanks: Institute of Social and Economic Research, University of Alaska.

KLOPFER, B., AINSWORTH, M. D., KLOPFER, W. & HOLT, R. H. (1956), *Developments in the Rorschach Technique.* Vol. II. New York, Chicago, San Francisco, and Atlanta: Harcourt, Brace & World.

LANTIS, M. (1953), Nunivak Eskimo personality as revealed in the mythology. *Anthropol. Papers Univ. Alaska* 2, No. 1.

_____ (1960), *Eskimo Childhood and Interpersonal Relationships: Nunivak Biographies and Genealogies.* University of Washington Press: Seattle, WA.

LUCIER, C. (1958), Noatagmiut Eskimo myths. *Anthropol. Papers Univ. Alaska,* 6:89–117.

NANOGAK, A. (1983), Kopilgok (Worms). In: Nanogak, A. *More Tales from the Igloo.* Edmonton, Canada: Hurtig Publishers, pp. 53, 56.

8

A Phantom Fairy Tale, Among Others, Along Sigmund Freud's Intellectual Itinerary[1]

LAWRENCE M. GINSBURG

Only think of fairy tales and of the many daring products of the imagination, which are full of meaning and of which only a man without intelligence could say: "This is nonsense, for it is impossible" (Josef Popper-Lynkeus as quoted by Sigmund Freud, 1923, pp. 262–263).

Sigmund Freud presented a lecture on "The Aetiology of Hysteria" to the Society of Psychiatry and Neurology in Vienna on April 21, 1896. Richard von Krafft-Ebing, who chaired the lecture, commented afterwards: "It sounds like a scientific fairy tale" (Schur, 1972, p. 104). Despite the humiliating reproach, Freud was not dissuaded from drawing upon the literature of fairy tales in the development of his theoretical formulations. He utilized *The Emperor's New Clothes,* by Hans Christian Andersen, as a model for interpreting embarrassing dreams of being naked (Freud, 1900). In "The Occurrence in Dreams of Material from Fairy Tales," Freud (1913a) illustrated how certain motifs furnish a crucial starting point in reconstructing childhood memories. Characters found in children's stories popularized by the Brothers Grimm suffused the beginning phases of his treatment of Sergius Pankejeff (The Wolf Man), who became the subject of a famous case history.

[1]For her guidance and assistance, I am especially grateful to my wife, Sybil A. Ginsburg, M.D., who is a member of the Faculty of The Psychoanalytic Institute at the New York University Medical Center in New York City as well as Clinical Associate Professor of Psychiatry at the State University of New York Health Science Center in Syracuse, New York.

1. LITERARY STIRRINGS[2]

Ernest Jones (1957) speculated about Freud's aspirations of becoming a novelist[3] while he was a young man:

> We may, however, be pretty sure that had Freud's destiny not taken him along the path it did his creative faculties would have found a literary expression. He is said to have told someone that as a young man he had thought of becoming a novelist. The only slight contemporary allusion to such an idea is in a letter Martha Bernays (April 1, 1884). "Here's a surprise for you. Over and again—I don't know how!! many stories have come into my mind, and one of them—a tale in an oriental guise—has recently taken a pretty definite shape. You will be astonished to hear that I am becoming aware of literary stirrings when previously I could not have imagined anything further from my mind. Shall I write the thing down, or would it embarrass you to read it? If I do so it will be only for you, but it will not be very beautiful. Also I have very little time just now. Still I believe that if the train of thought comes back it will really get done by itself. In that event I will write it, and you will chuckle to yourself without saying a word about it to anyone" [p. 418].

According to Peter J. Swales (1983), Freud's literary "train of thought" ultimately found expression in a fairy tale which he recited for the benefit of Theodor Reik:

> It seems to me very possible, indeed quite probable, that the Oriental "fairy tale" which Freud narrated to Theodor Reik many years later was the very same Oriental story as that which, on April

---

[2]Freud was awarded the Goethe Prize by the City of Frankfurt-am-Main in 1930 as a "personality of established achievement whose creative work is worthy of Goethe's memory" (Freud, 1930, p. 206). See Appendix A for the complete text of the official citation.

[3]After receiving an inquiry about her father's use during his later life of the term *Doppelgänger,* Anna Freud (1971) replied: "There is no difficulty in explaining what my father meant when he used the word *Doppelgänger.* He often spoke about the fact that poets and writers in their own way come to the same conclusions about human nature as he had to fight for in painstaking analytic work with patients. In this sense, therefore, the novelist is the double *(Doppelgänger)* of the analyst" (July 11 letter to Jeffrey B. Berlin quoted by J. B. Berlin & E. L. Levy, 1978, p. 110).

1, 1884, he announced to his fiancée having conceived and was contemplating writing down [pp. 18n.-19n.].

The thematic context of the fairy tale[4] "in an oriental guise" was, of course, quite relevant to his prenuptial mentality on April 1, 1884.

2. DIE TRÄUMLEITER: EIN MÄRCHEN (S. ANDREAS, 1832)[5]

The above title (i.e., *The Dream Ladder: A Fairy Tale*) has been indexed in *The Letters of Sigmund Freud to Eduard Silberstein, 1871–1881,* edited by Walter Boehlich (1990). It was initially referenced in the August 15, 1877 letter from the 21-year-old Freud to the 7½-month-younger Silberstein after the following passage:

> Your sister Mina came to visit us last Sunday and we all went to the Prater. She looks very well, seems to be growing quickly, and, during the first half of her stay here, was more unruly than ever. Later she calmed down. Among other things, she drew up a list of books in my room of which you may make her a present. Andreas's fairy tales, Auerbach's *Auf der Höhe.* — A very strange creature. Still, it seems a characteristic of your family to suffer from a surfeit of energy until you are fifteen, and, all in all, that is not a bad sign [p. 164].

The 19th-century publication does not appear in any of Freud's bibliographies, nor did he ever refer to the author in his other writings or published correspondence. It seems unlikely, however, that Freud neither read nor absorbed the books[6] which left his personal library in the hands of Mina Silberstein.

---

[4]See Appendix B for the fairy tale related to Reik by Freud whose introductory comments supposedly referenced it as "a fairy tale I once read—where was it?" (Reik, 1956, pp. 19–20).

[5]Credit for locating an accessible copy of the "elusive" fairy tale belongs to Martha Hsu, North European Studies Bibliographer at Cornell University in Ithaca, New York. It was reprinted in *Hessisches Album für Literatur und Kunst,* ed. Franz Dingelstedt (1838). See publication history in attached bibliography. Available on request is an English translation by Louis R. Wonderly, Jr., a doctoral candidate in the Department of German Studies at Cornell University in Ithaca, New York. The material is available from Dr. Lawrence Ginsburg, 820 University Building, Syracuse, NY 13202.

[6]The second book, entitled *Auf der Höhe* ("On the Heights") by Berthold Auerbach, is a novel written and published in German in 1865 and thereafter translated into English.

3. EROTIC FANTASIES AND BOOKWORMS

Freud's feigned loan of the two books owned by him to a younger sister of a contemporary male figure is thematically reminiscent of certain sexual fantasies whose painful effects he had partially repressed. Among the disguised principals in Freud's *Dandelion Meadow* defloration screen memory were himself, his older nephew John, and John's younger sister Pauline during their early childhood in Freiberg.[7] The *Botanical Monograph* dream[8] led to another of Freud's screen memories involving himself and his sister Anna as the principal male and female figures. In Freud's words (1900):

> I had been five years old at the time and my sister not yet three; and the picture of the two of us blissfully pulling the book to pieces (leaf by leaf, like an *artichoke,* I found myself saying) was almost the only plastic memory that I retained from that period of my life [pp. 172ff].

He thereupon equated his "favorite hobby" (i.e., "learning out of monographs") with a "passion for collecting and owning books" dating back to the time "when I became a student" (pp. 172ff). A "verbal bridge" (See Section 4) enabled Freud to associate his seemingly disparate chains of thought with one another:

> (The idea of "favorite" had already appeared in connection with cyclamens and artichokes.) I had become a *bookworm.* I had always from the time I first began to think about myself, referred this first passion of mine back to the childhood memory I have mentioned. Or rather, I had recognized that my childhood scene was a "screen memory" for my later bibliophile propensities [pp. 172ff].

---

[7]The texture of Freud's infantile Garden of Eden and its parallels to the Bible story of Adam and Eve, as retrospectively viewed by him, has been examined elsewhere (Ginsburg, L. M. & Ginsburg, S. A., 1992; pp. 285–308).

[8]Freud (1900) reminded himself that on the morning before his Botanical Monograph dream, he "had seen a *monograph* on the genus Cyclamen" displayed in a bookshop. After recalling that cyclamens were his "wife's favorite flower," he reproached himself "for so rarely remembering to *bring* her *flowers,* which was what she liked" (p. 162).

A major theme in Freud's analyses of both of these screen memories was the confluence of flowers with his incestuous fantasies involving the defloration[9] of a younger female relative.

At 16 years of age, Freud (1872a) had confided in Eduard Silberstein about his infatuation with the nearly 13-year-old Gisela Fluss in whose family's Freiberg home[10] he was then vacationing for the second consecutive summer as a guest of her older brother Emil. After returning to Vienna 3½ weeks later, Freud (1872b) addressed a letter to his 5-month-younger host with whom he had been friends since their early boyhood. The adolescent Freud summed up his "whole flirtation" with Emil's younger sister Gisela by enigmatically quoting "Goethe's line: 'A fairy tale' . . . it was once upon a time' " (p. 421).

As a young adult, on the other hand, Freud's concern for the educational growth of Mina Silberstein had been poignantly articulated in a letter he sent to Eduard Silberstein during August of 1876.[11] In Freud's letter written a year later and excerpted at the beginning of Section 2 of this chapter, he designated Silberstein as his surrogate donor of the books Mina had ostensibly "borrowed." Perhaps, the indirect manner in which Freud finalized his gift of the two books reflects his struggle against the possible germination of further defloration fantasies.

4. RELATIONSHIPS BETWEEN FAIRY TALES AND SCREEN MEMORIES

In 1913, Freud wrote:

> It is not surprising to find that psychoanalysis confirms our recognition of the important place which folk fairy tales have acquired in the mental life of our children. In a few people a

---

[9]In 1918, Freud offered *The Taboo of Virginity* for publication. He theorized that one of the consequences of defloration is an unleashing of "an archaic reaction of hostility towards" the deflowerer, "which can assume pathological forms that are frequently enough expressed in the appearance of inhibitions in the erotic side of married life. . ." (p. 208).

[10]See paper cited in footnote 7 for discussion of the erotic courtship and defloration fantasies engendered by native folk customs in the Moravian milieu revisited by Freud during his adolescent years.

[11]During his teenage years, Freud had not only "helped his sisters with their studies," but had also "exercised some censorship over their reading, telling them what they were too young to read; when his sister Anna was fifteen, for instance, she was warned off Balzac and Dumas" (Jones, 1953, p. 20).

recollection of their favorite fairy tales takes the place of memories of their own childhood; they have made the fairy tales into screen memories [p. 281].

"The Psychopathology of Everyday Life," since its initial publication, has been subtitled: "Forgetting, Slips of the Tongue, Bungled Actions, Superstitions and Errors" (Freud, 1901, p. vii). Subsumed under the "Forgetting" category in the 1901 and 1904 editions were successive chapters entitled "The Forgetting of Proper Names," "The Forgetting of Foreign Words" and "Screen Memories." The last such chapter was subsequently redesignated "Childhood Memories and Screen Memories."

In post-1904 publications of "The Psychopathology of Everyday Life," Freud's editors incorporated many of the handwritten notes they had found in his interleaved copy of the 1904 edition. One such addendum about screen memories was inserted after a paragraph about the use of "verbal bridges" that abetted the resurrection of a patient's screen memories "from the later years of childhood" (p. 49). Following the "verbal bridges" terminology appearing in post-1904 volumes, Freud's editors inserted a significant footnote, to wit:

Dr. B— —showed very neatly one Wednesday that fairy tales can be made use of as screen memories in the same kind of way that empty shells are used as a home by the hermit crab. These fairy tales then become favorites, without the reason being known. . . [p. 49ff].

The analogy seems more ascribable to Freud than to the unknown "Dr. B— —" because it is one that he often used himself. The nervous system of the fresh-water crab had been his primary research interest during the summer of 1880 (Clark, 1980). Letters written by him to Theodor Reik during 1928 ("I am at present in a bad state of transition, still unable to do anything and compelled to hide like a crab that changes its shell")[12] and either 1929 or 1930 ("At present I am in my most helpless state, comparable to a change of shell, and have to hide") illustrate such usage (Freud, 1928b, p. 647; 1929–1930, p. 649).

---

[12]The German word for both "crab" and "cancer" is *Krebs*. After 1923, when the existence of Freud's cancerous condition became known to him, his usage of the word for "crab" operated as a double entendre.

5. "THE INTERTEXTUALITY" OF FREUD'S EARLY READING AND LATER WRITING

Riccardo Steiner (1988) has reconstructed a number of intellectual "trains of thought," from the Romantic period in German literature, about dreaming, which led to Freud's way of contemplating the unconscious:

> In one sense they refer to tracks, traces, the simple underlinings in red pencil made by Freud himself and now to be seen in books which he managed to salvage and bring with him to London when he fled Vienna just before the Second World War burst upon the world. In another sense, these "tracks" consist of the bibliographical references which Freud meticulously, if somewhat long-sufferingly, supplied right from the first edition of the *Traumdeutung* [p. 415]. . . . What we do not have, however, and what for a considerable time we will not have, is a plausible reconstruction — based on what might unfashionably be called the sources, the more or less proximate ancestors, the companions Freud met on the road and who traveled with him on the adventure which brought him to compose his masterpiece — of the way in which the *Traumdeutung* and other of Freud's works achieved their final shapes and structures. And for those who prefer the terminology of modern semiotics, we should discuss "the intertextuality" of the *Traumdeutung* . . . [p. 417].

The correlation of graphic art in certain books read by Freud as a preadolescent with his subsequent work has been previously noted (L. M. Ginsburg and S. A. Ginsburg, 1987). Robert R. Holt (1988) considered some possible effects of three books that Freud presumably read "during the second decade of his life" (pp. 167–168). Holt attempted to elucidate the assimilative tendencies of Freud's creative thought as an affirmative attribute:

> Human memory is not like a tape recorder, preserving for literal replay a basically faithful record of experience, though exceptional people called eidetics do have somewhat comparable capacities. In his youth, Freud himself was such a person, who could retain a virtually photographic image of pages of a book quickly scanned. Since the capacity is so rare, especially in adults, when we encounter word-for-word similarities between earlier and later

published works, we generally find it more credible that some kind
of cheating has taken place, including that deliberate copying
known as plagiarism — certainly not at issue here. . . . All writers
have their "sources" and "influences." To discover antecedents of a
great thinker's formulations in books he read is more a work of
homage than of detraction, or at least it should be [p. 189].

While Theodor Reik (1956) wrote about Freud's "astonishing memory, a memory which in his earlier years was almost photographic" (p. 7),
he also observed that "Freud who overestimated the scope of my reading,
often asked me for the source of a passage from literature" (p. 641).
Examples of such requests are contained in a series of dated and undated
letters from Freud to Reik, encapsulated in part as follows:

Today I write simply to ask you for a bit of information out of your
superior literary knowledge. The question: Where in Schiller or
Goethe is the well-known maxim: "He who has art and science has
also religion," etc.? My notion that it was in the *Xenien* has not
proved correct. Goethe's maxims in verse perhaps? . . . [1928a]
The famous story of the mandarin *(tuer son mandarin)* comes from
Rousseau, after all. Could you tell me without going to too much
trouble where it is to be found? . . . . [1929a] Please don't bother
yourself any longer about the "inch of nature" and forgive me for
having bothered you with it. I've done without the quotation. No
one was able to locate it. Where I could have picked it up remains
a mystery, for it is hardly likely to be of my own coining. Since,
besides Shakespeare, I used to read only Milton and Byron, there is
still the possibility that it might be found in Byron. But please do
not look for it, and accept my best thanks for your trouble [1929b].
[See Reik, 1956, pp. 646–648 for full text.]

The second of Freud's unremembered sources, which is excerpted
above, became the subject of a series of essays written by Reik (1965).
Reik contrasted Freud's first inquiry about the "famous story of the
mandarin" with its reemergence in another context 14 years afterwards
(pp. 23–42). In accounting for Freud's "regression to an abandoned
literary puzzle," Reik compared the psychological differences between "a
healthy man" at the time of his initial concern and "the same man whose
life is threatened by a dangerous disease" (pp. 28–30) when the mistaken
reference subsequently reasserted itself. "Literary detective work" about

the origins of Freud's scholarly sources was not limited, as Reik remarked, to "who wrote Shakespeare's plays" (p. 29).

Reik (1956) recalled an occasion when he had written a review of an article published by a German psychiatrist about Hamlet. Reik shared a draft of his proposed review with Freud. In it, he "had accused the author of plagiarizing articles by Otto Rank and Ernest Jones on the problem of Hamlet" (p. 630). In his December 13, 1913 letter, Freud (1913b) criticized Reik's prospective review for ventilating "a superfluous suspicion" which was "very likely a case of cryptomnesia. If not, it is in no way permissible to repeat discoveries made thirteen years ago" (p. 631).[13]

6. A PREPSYCHOANALYTIC SOUVENIR ABOUT DREAM MEANINGS

Although dream remembrances are a common element in fairy tales, a paradigm for the dream-process itself is hardly ever found in such literature. *The Dream Ladder: A Fairy Tale* looks like an exception to the rule. Its curious title seems to invite the author's audience to join him in scaling atmospheric layers in which their dream processes are presumably heightened. Andreas overcame the peculiarity of his subject matter with a unique style of expression in the form of idyllic prose and poetry punctuated with dramatic metaphors. Durable visual images were created by him to encompass his extraterrestrial discourse about dreaming.

What intellectual debt, if any, did Freud owe to the "resurrected" fairy tale in conceptualizing his dynamic model for understanding the nature of dreaming and dreams? An historian of dream interpretations in such prepsychoanalytic literature could justifiably conclude that fairy tales which survive over the generations do so because of an inherent capacity for satisfying the unconscious conflicts and emotions of their intended

---

[13]Harry Trosman (1976) has referenced Freud's self-doubts about the absolute originality of his own theories. "I am very ready to give up the prestige of originality," wrote Freud (1937) in *Josef Popper-Lynkeus and The Theory of Dreams,* "especially as I can never be certain, in view of the wide extent of my reading in early years, whether what I took for a new creation might not be an effect of cryptomnesia" (p. 245). Freud (1920) came to realize a half century after reading the collected essays of Ludwig Börne "at 13 or 14 years of age" that he clearly remembered them except for the one which must have influenced his theory of "free association" (p. 265). Cryptomnesiac episodes described by Else Frenkel-Brunswik and Friedrich W. Nietzsche shared a common denominator with Freud's, according to Trosman (op. cit.) who concluded that "the original perception for the later cryptomnesiac experiences occurred" during their early adolescence (p. 250).

audience. Like Freud, he might study the overlapping spheres in children's comprehension of fairy tales and, to paraphrase Bruno Bettelheim (1976), agree that "fairy tales are *unreal* but not *untrue*" (p. 73).

How the psychological vernacular of the Romantic movement in adult German literature had an impact on Freud's work has been the subject of detailed study (Steiner, 1988) as have the scientifically oriented discoveries of Jean Martin Charcot, Pierre Janet, and Richard von Krafft-Ebing (Sand, 1992). Of much earlier vintage were the philosophical assumptions of Plato and Aristotle, which, in several instances, presaged Freud's development of his own theories.[14]

The transcendentalism animating Freud's cultural heritage is manifested quite vividly in *The Dream Ladder: A Fairy Tale*. A number of its thematic currents and crosscurrents resonate in 20th-century schools of psychological thought such as the Jungian theories of the archetype, the collective unconscious, and analytic metapsychology. Andreas' fairy tale provides the modern reader with a generic profile of 19th-century perceptions about the nature of dreaming and dreams. The converging and diverging "highways, byways, and detours" of the intellectual realms through which Freud, among others, navigated are readily discernible in their prepsychoanalytic context.

EPILOGUE

After publication of the initial edition of "The Interpretation of Dreams," Freud turned more and more to the links between different psychic and cultural productions. In his "Preface to the Third Edition of 1911," he speculated about future editions:

> I may even venture to prophesy in what other directions later editions of this book—if any should be needed—will differ from the present one. They will have on the one hand to afford closer contact with the copious material presented in poetry, in myths, in linguistic usage and in folklore; while on the other hand they will have to deal in greater detail than has here been possible with the relations of dreams to neuroses and mental diseases [pp. xxvii-xxviii].

---

[14]Prominent examples were Platonic dualism (i.e., the manifest dream, which is tangible and observable, is afforded a lesser degree of "reality" or "truth value" than "latent" or unobservable dream thoughts) and the Aristotelian supposition that dreaming is simply the continuation of our mental activity into the state of sleep.

In a footnote at the end of the very same edition, Freud mentioned the work of Prof. David Ernst Oppenheim in connection with folkloric dreams and stated that the appearance of a paper on the subject was soon anticipated.

Oppenheim had previously sent Freud a reprint of an article about folklore, dedicated to him and containing references to psychoanalytic observations, whereupon Freud wrote a solicitous response on October 28, 1909, in part, as follows:

> We are lacking in academic training and familiarity with the material. Thus we are looking about for an enquirer whose development has been in the reverse direction, who possesses the specialized knowledge and is ready to apply to it the psychoanalytic armory that we will gladly put at his command—a native enquirer, as one might say, who will be able to achieve something quite other than we who are intruders of another species. Can it be that you are willing to be this man we are longing for? What do you know of psychoanalysis? And have you the leisure and inclination to plunge into it more deeply for these ends? Forgive me if I am mistaken and have interpreted the signs too far [p. 14].

Almost a half century elapsed before Oppenheim's collection of folk dreams (a preponderance of which are Slavic in origin) emerged in print with Freud's collaborative introduction, commentaries, interpretive observations, annotations, and concluding statements.

Freud himself was not shy about analyzing fictional dream material. *Delusion and Dreams in Jensen's "Gradiva"* (1907) is an example of the serious attention Freud gave to authors whose fantasies about the mysteries of the unconscious corroborated his own findings. The narrative and poetic paradigms found in the "elusive" fairy tale by Andreas await their definitive analyses by a current generation of "enquirers."

SUMMARY

Sigmund Freud respected fairy tales as a genre for portraying the fantasy realms of a culture. The timeless struggles they memorialize often paralleled the unconscious human concerns of his own patients. He recognized that fairy tales often cast a mysterious spell whose remarkable power is retained long beyond the first two decades of life. At 21 years of age, Freud's personal library included a copy of *The Dream Ladder:*

A Fairy Tale, which was first published in 1832. Despite the ostensible simplicity of the theme that its title suggests, the modern reader is presented with a number of prepsychoanalytic narrative and poetic paradigms about the dream process itself. It merits further study in addition to other fairy tales whose analyses still resonate in 20th-century schools of psychological thought.

APPENDIX A
1930 CITATION FOR THE GOETHE PRIZE[15]

"By strictly scientific methods, and at the same time boldly interpreting the parables coined by poets, Sigmund Freud has beaten a path to the driving forces of the mind, and thus created the possibility of recognizing the origin and structure of the forms of civilization and of curing many of their diseases. Psychoanalysis has revolutionized and enriched not only medical science, but also the inner world of the artist and the pastor, the historian and the educator. Sigmund Freud has gone beyond the dangers of self-dissection and beyond all the differences between intellectual trends, to lay the foundations of a new cooperation of the sciences and a better mutual understanding between nations. As the earliest beginnings of Freud's search into the mind go back to a reading of Goethe's essay "Nature," so in recent years as well, the Mephistophelian urge, encouraged by Freud's method of research, mercilessly to tear apart all veils, appears as the inseparable companion of Faust's insatiability and his reverence for the sculptural-creative forces slumbering in the unconscious. All outward marks of honor have up to now been denied to the great scholar, writer, and warrior Sigmund Freud, although the revolutionary influence of his work was more in tune with the spirit of the times than that of any other living man. After carefully weighing everything for and against, the board of trustees wishes to show, with this honor, the value it sets upon Freud's ideas as a transition to a world of values cleansed of obsolete notions and strengthened anew."

APPENDIX B

"A barber in the Orient, let us say Bagdad, often heard his customers talking of a beautiful princess in a faraway land who was held captive by

---

[15]Official Proclamation of Lord Mayor of Frankfurt-am-Main is quoted in footnote 289 at page 334 of *Sigmund Freud: His Life in Pictures and Words,* ed. E. L. Freud, L. Freud & I. Grubrich-Simitis. New York: Harcourt Brace Jovanovich (1978).

a wicked wizard. The brave man who would free the princess was promised both her hand and a great kingdom. Many knights and princes had set out upon the adventure, but none had succeeded in reaching her. Before the castle in which the beautiful lady was imprisoned there lay a vast, gloomy wood. Whoever crossed this wood would be attacked by lions and torn to pieces. The few who succeeded in escaping these lions were later met by two terrible giants who beat them down with cudgels. Some few had escaped even this danger and after years of travail had reached the castle. As they rushed up the stairway, the wizard's magic caused it to collapse. It was said that one brave prince had nevertheless managed to ascend into the castle, but in the great hall where the princess was enthroned a fierce fire raged which destroyed him.

The adventurous barber was so deeply impressed by these tales of the beautiful princess that by and by he sold his shop and set out to liberate her. He had singular good fortune; he escaped the wild beasts, overcame the giants, and survived many other adventures, until at last he reached the castle. He strode over the stairway, although it toppled beneath him, and plunged intrepidly through the roaring flames that were threatening to consume the hall. At the end of the great hall he could dimly see the princess. But as he rushed across the room and drew near the figure, he saw a gray old woman supporting herself on a cane as she sat, her face full of wrinkles and warts, her hair drawn back in sparse, snow-white strands. The brave barber had forgotten that the princess had been waiting 60 years for her deliverer."

BIBLIOGRAPHY

ANDREAS, S. [?] (1832), Die träumleiter: Ein märchen. Reprinted in: *Hessisches Album für Literatur und Kunst,* ed. F. Dingelstedt. Cassel, Germany: J. J. Bohné, 1838, pp. 203–222. [The original reference is indexed in a number of bibliographies. According to the *Gesamtverzeichnis des deutschsprachigen Schrifttums (GV) 1700–1910* (Vol. 4, p. 191), it was published in 1832. The *Allegemeines Bucher-Lexikon* (Wilhelm Heinsius, Leipzig, 1836) contains a corresponding entry. Both bibliographies list the initial *S* for the author's first name. The *Goedekes Grundriss zur Geschichte der deutschen Dichtung, Neue Folge* (Band I, p. 246) indicates that the existence of a copy of the original publication is unverifiable. It also points out that the identity of the author's first name is uncertain although the cited reprint contains the initial *S* before the author's last name. The author's birthdate and date of death are likewise listed as unknown. According to Walter Boehlich, his German edition of *The Letters of Sigmund Freud to Eduard Silberstein, 1871–1881* footnoted Freud's reference to "Andreas" as "presumably S. Andreas." Boehlich's translator (Arno Pomerans) apparently reexamined the clarity of Freud's handwriting to determine if it might have been misread as "Andersen" rather than "Andreas." Freud (1901) later found himself susceptible to such an unconscious revision ("slip of the pen") of a cited author's name ("Buckrhard" instead of "Burckhard") in such a fashion that the misspelled name itself formed what he came to classify as a "switch-word" (pp. 117–118, 275–276)].

AUERBACH, B. (1865), *On the Heights,* trans. F. E. Bunnett. New York: Burt (n.d.)

BETTELHEIM, B. (1976), *The Uses of Enchantment: The Meaning and Importance of Fairy Tales.* New York: Alfred A. Knopf.

CLARK, R. W. (1980), *Freud: The Man and the Cause.* New York: Random House.

FREUD, A. (1971), July 11 letter to Jeffrey B. Berlin quoted by J. B. Berlin & E. J. Levy. In: On the letters of Theodor Reik to Arthur Schnitzler. *Psychoanal. Rev.,* 65:109–130.

FREUD, S. (1872a), August 9 letter to Eduard Silberstein quoted by H. Stanescu (1971). In: Young Freud's letters to his Rumanian friend, Silberstein. *Israel Ann. Psychiat. Related Discipl.,* 9:195–208.

_____ (1872b), September 4 letter to Eduard Silberstein quoted by H. Stanescu (1971). In: Young Freud's letters to his Rumanian friend, Silberstein. *Israel Ann. Psychiat. Related Discipl.,* 9:195–208.

_____ (1876), Undated August letter to Eduard Silberstein. In: *The Letters of Sigmund Freud to Eduard Silberstein, 1871–1881,* ed. W. Boehlich. Cambridge, MA: Harvard University Press, 1990, pp. 9–10.

_____ (1877), August 15 letter to Eduard Silberstein. In: *The Letters of Sigmund Freud to Eduard Silberstein, 1871–1881,* ed. W. Boehlich. Cambridge, MA: Harvard University Press, 1990, pp. 9–10.

_____ (1900), The interpretation of dreams. *Standard Edition,* 4 & 5. London: Hogarth Press, 1953.

_____ (1901), The psychopathology of everyday life. *Standard Edition,* 6. London: Hogarth Press, 1960.

_____ (1907), Delusion and dreams in Jensen's *Gradiva. Standard Edition,* 9. London: Hogarth Press, 1959.

_____ (1909), October 28 letter to David Ernst Oppenheim in Addendum to Preface. In: *Dreams in Folklore,* ed. B. L. Pacella. New York: International Universities Press, 1958, pp. 13–16.

_____ (1913a), The occurrence in dreams of material from fairy tales. *Standard Edition,* 12. London: Hogarth Press, 1958.

_____ (1913b), December 13 letter to Theodor Reik. In: *The Search Within,* ed. T. Reik. New York: Grove Press, 1956, p. 631.

_____ (1918), The taboo of virginity. *Standard Edition,* 11:191–208. London: Hogarth Press, 1957.

_____ (1920), A note on the prehistory of the technique of analysis. *Standard Edition,* 18. London: Hogarth Press, 1955.

_____ (1923), Josef Popper-Lynkeus and the theory of dreams. *Standard Edition,* 19:259–263. London: Hogarth Press, 1961.

_____ (1928a), Undated letter to Theodor Reik. In: *The Search Within,* T. Reik. New York: Grove Press, 1956, p. 646.

_____ (1928b), September 13 letter to Theodor Reik. In: *The Search Within,* T. Reik. New York: Grove Press, 1956, p. 647.

_____ (1929a), October 20 letter to Theodor Reik. In: *The Search Within,* T. Reik. New York: Grove Press, 1956, pp. 647–648.

_____ (1929b), November 18 letter to Theodor Reik. In: *The Search Within,* T. Reik. New York: Grove Press, 1956, p. 648.

_____ (1929–1930), Undated letter to Theodor Reik. In: *The Search Within,* T. Reik. New York: Grove Press, 1956, p. 649.

_____ (1930), The Goethe Prize. *Standard Edition,* 21. London: Hogarth Press, 1961.

_____ (1937), Analysis terminable and interminable. *Standard Edition,* 23. London: Hogarth Press, 1964.

_____ & OPPENHEIM, D. E. (1911), *Dreams in Folklore,* ed. B. L. Pacella. New York: International Universities Press, 1958.

GINSBURG, L. M. & GINSBURG, S. A. (1987), A menagerie of illustrations from Sigmund Freud's boyhood. *The Psychoanalytic Study of the Child,* 42:469–486. New Haven, CT: Yale University Press.

_____ (1992), Paradise in the life of Sigmund Freud: An understanding of its imagery and paradoxes. *Internat. Rev. Psycho-Anal.,* 19:285–308.

HOLT, R. R. (1988), Freud's adolescent reading: Some possible effects on his work. *Freud Apprais. Reapprais.: Contribut. Freud Stud.,* 3:167–192.

JONES, E. (1953), *The Life and Work of Sigmund Freud,* Vol. 1. New York: Basic Books.

_____ (1957), *The Life and Work of Sigmund Freud,* Vol. 3. New York: Basic Books.

REIK, T. (1956), *The Search Within.* New York: Grove Press.

_____ (1965), *Curiosities of the Self.* New York: Farrar, Straus & Giroux.

SAND, R. (1992), Pre-Freudian discovery of dream meaning: The achievement of Charcot, Janet, and Krafft-Ebing. In: *Freud and the History of Psychoanalysis,* ed. T. Gelfand & J. Kerr. Hillsdale, NJ: The Analytic Press, pp. 215–229.

SCHUR, M. (1972), *Freud: Living and Dying.* New York: International Universities Press.

STEINER, R. (1988), "Paths to Xanadu . . ." Some notes on the development of dream displacement and condensation in Sigmund Freud's "Interpretation of Dreams." *Internat. Rev. Psycho-Anal.,* 15:415–454.

SWALES, P. J. (1983), *Freud, Martha Bernays, and the Language of Flowers: Masturbation, Cocaine, and the Inflation of Fantasy.* New York: Privately published paper.

TROSMAN, H. (1976), The cryptomnesic fragment in the discovery of free association. Monograph 34/35. Freud: The fusion of science and humanism. In: *Psychological Issues,* 9(2/3):229–253.

9

Black Hamlet:
A Case of "Psychic Vivisection"?

SAUL DUBOW

Wulf Sachs' *Black Hamlet* is, as the subtitle explains, an account of "The Mind of an African Negro Revealed by Psychoanalysis." First published in 1937 and republished in 1947 as *Black Anger,* it is a remarkable work (Sachs, 1937, 1947a). Judging by contemporary accounts, *Black Hamlet* had a considerable impact and enjoyed a wide readership when it was first published. I have not been able to trace more than a couple of reviews in academic journals, but there are reports of its having been translated into Swedish, German, French, and Czech. Subsequently, however, it seems to have slipped from historical memory, perhaps because it does not fall conveniently within conventional disciplinary boundaries like psychology, anthropology, and history. With the notable exception of Ranger (1970) and, most recently, Vaughan (1991), historians have made little use of its suggestive possibilities as a documentary source.

The origins of *Black Hamlet* date back to the end of 1933 when Wulf Sachs, a doctor and psychoanalyst, met "John Chavafambira" in a slumyard in downtown Johannesburg, which he calls "Swartyard" (but which is in fact Rooiyard, New Doornfontein). Sachs does not refer to the woman anthropologist who introduced him to "John" by name, though it is equally clear that the individual referred to must be Ellen Hellman, a young anthropologist from the University of the Witwaters-

I am grateful to Bob Edgar for sending me material concerning Sachs, and also to Terence Ranger and Baruch Hirson for suggesting various leads. Bill Epstein, Jacqueline Rose, and L. Bryce Boyer read the text with care and made useful comments.

rand. Hellman was then in the process of researching a master's thesis on the slumyard. John Chavafambira was an important informant, performing a vital mediating role between Hellman and the Rooiyard community. At the instigation of Max Gluckman, director of the Rhodes-Livingstone Institute, Hellman's (1948) work was finally published as *Rooiyard: A Sociological Survey of an Urban Native Slum Yard.* This pioneering study of the process of proletarianization and the interwar conditions of urban African life bears the strong imprint of "culture contact" theory, an approach that came to exert a dominant influence on South African social anthropology from the mid-1930s.[1]

Hellman's *Rooiyard* contains a detailed case history of John Chavafambira in the appendix. There is also a photograph of John, closely resembling the pencil sketch of him at the beginning of *Black Hamlet* (Fig. 1). Other material has subsequently come to hand that helps to corroborate the existence of a man whose precise identity is deliberately concealed by Sachs. Aside from the photograph, the most intriguing independent evidence comes from the private diary of Ralph Bunche, the African-American political scientist (and subsequently a leading United Nations diplomat) who visited South Africa in 1937–38 as part of his training in the methodology of anthropological fieldwork. Bunche met John on two occasions in Orlando township in the company of Sachs and Hellman. He was suspicious of John's credentials as a healer, and described him in his diary with evident distaste as "a beady-eyed, sly and cunning-looking fellow, with pouting lips and a head pointed on top. Medium stature. Shows a very good memory. Probably not at his best in English because of a limited vocabulary. Very temperamental and addicted to Kaffir beer" (Edgar, 1992, p. 166).

Sachs' account of John tells the complex story of a Manyika healer-diviner who moves from eastern Zimbabwe to Johannesburg in 1921, living mainly in the slumyards of Doornfontein and in the townships of Sophiatown and Orlando. For historians of this period *Black Hamlet* offers a unique insight into the interwar experience of black Johannesburg and the pattern of proletarianization that drove Africans from the entire southern African region to the industrial areas of the Witwatersrand. As an attempt to understand the complex pathology of South African race relations, *Black Hamlet* is greatly in

---

[1]Earlier versions of this study were published in article form in *Africa* VIII, 1, 1935, and in *Bantu Studies,* XIX, 3, 1935. Hellman's work was intended to parallel, in the urban context, the research then being undertaken by Monica Hunter (Wilson) in the Eastern Cape. For Hunter's work, see Hunter, M. (1934), The study of culture contact. *Africa,* VII: 335–350; Hunter, M. (1936), *Reaction to Conquest.* London: Oxford University Press.

Figure 1
John Chavafambira in *Rooiyard* (Hellman, 1948).

advance of its time. However, it remains a document *of* its time. That too is part of its fascination.

The period covered here—the early 1930s to the second world war—coincides with the era in which racial segregation in South Africa was entrenched both in law and fact. In 1936 Prime Minister J.B.M. Hertzog's Native Bills were finally enacted, having been more or less constantly on the parliamentary agenda for a decade. The principal effect of this legislation was to abolish the residual nonracial franchise provisions in the Cape and to confirm the unequal division of land in South Africa between blacks and whites. Urban segregation was reinforced by the 1937 Native Laws Amendment Act, which considerably strengthened the government's capacity to evict from urban areas those Africans who were not actively involved in "ministering to the needs" of whites.[2]

South Africa's recovery from the 1929–32 depression was stimulated by a boom in the gold mining economy, which led to a large inflow of

---

[2]These points are dealt with at length in Dubow, S. (1989), *Racial Segregation and the Origins of Apartheid in South Africa, 1919-36*. London: Macmillan.

capital. This in turn stimulated the growth of manufacturing industry, whose development was further accelerated during the war. Employment for Africans in secondary industry almost doubled between 1936 and 1945, while the urban African population increased by some 50% to reach 1,689,000. The war years witnessed a revival of urban political radicalism, frequently taking the form of transport boycotts, industrial strikes, and squatter movements. In industry the power of organized African labor was increasingly registered. The African National Congress, which had been largely quiescent for over a decade, was revived from the early 1940s by a group of dynamic and youthful new leaders, and it began to reorient itself as a mass organization committed to the realization of popular democracy. Buoyed by the wartime anti-Fascist alliance, the Communist Party also came to enjoy unprecedented levels of support.

The social ferment that was unleashed by these processes was nowhere experienced so dramatically as in the Witwatersrand region, South Africa's industrial powerhouse and center of the mining industry. It was on the Witwatersrand, too, that the rapid process of proletarianization was experienced most acutely. The social geography of Johannesburg was in constant flux as accommodation became increasingly scarce. Unrestrained urbanization, coupled with government attempts to clear slums within the center of the city, hastened the growth of vast new squatter encampments on the periphery of the city.[3]

It was in the context of this bewildering social change that *Black Hamlet* was conceived and written. Its author, Wulf Sachs, was born in Lithuania in 1893. He trained at the Psychoneurological Institute in St. Petersburg, Russia (under Pavlov and Bechterev), at the University of Cologne, Germany, and at London University, where he took a degree in medicine. In 1922 Sachs emigrated to South Africa with his family and began to practice as a general practitioner in Johannesburg. His interest in psychology was intensified by the experience of working with black schizophrenic patients at the Pretoria Mental Hospital from 1928. In 1929–30 Sachs traveled to Berlin where he came into contact with Freud and underwent psychoanalysis.[4] Returning to South Africa, Sachs gave a

---

[3]There is a large historical literature on this period. A useful way into the area is Hirson, B. (1949), *Yours for the Union: Class and Community Struggles in South Africa, 1930–1947.* London: Zed Books.

[4]Sachs' daughter believes that her father received analysis from Abraham Brill, the Austrian-born American psychoanalyst and long-time associate of Freud. According to Ernest Jones, Brill visited Freud in 1929 and Sachs' analysis might have taken place at this time. It should be remembered that clinical psychoanalysis was in that period usually brief and, by today's standards, quite superficial. On Brill's movements at this

series of lectures on psychoanalysis that were organized by Professor Hoernlé of the Wits philosophy department. These lectures formed the basis of an introductory book on psychoanalysis to which Freud himself contributed a commendatory foreword.[5] Sachs pioneered psychoanalysis in South Africa in the face of considerable skepticism and hostility. In 1946 he became the first training analyst in South Africa and played a leading role in the creation of the SA Psychoanalytical Training Institute. His sudden death in 1949 at the age of 56 was unexpected and came at the height of his creative powers.

By all accounts Sachs was a highly energetic and cultivated man, who gathered an enthusiastic circle of students and followers around him. He was also an enlivening influence in the cosmopolitan cultural life of the Johannesburg Left. Sachs' naturally combative nature often brought him into opposition with established institutions. He was a member of the South African Zionist Federation but often came into conflict with the organization and was regarded as something of a maverick. According to Hellman (1949), his "Zionism and his Socialism were inextricably linked." He supported Zionism because of his belief that Jewish nationalism should be given expression in the form of a Jewish state. But he was also an internationalist who remained committed to the maintenance of the Jewish diaspora. During the war Sachs became increasingly involved with progressive political and social issues. In 1943 he became editor and leading spirit of *The Democrat,* a politically independent, socialist-oriented review, which provided incisive analysis both of domestic and international politics, as well as the arts.

For the majority of white South Africans, then as today, black South Africa was scarcely understood outside of the master-servant relations that governed daily interaction. Wulf Sachs and Ellen Hellman were part of the small professional and academic intelligentsia that sought to understand these dynamics, and at times to influence their direction. In the case of Sachs, the process of discovery involved an exploration of self, though this is not always made explicit. Thus, *Black Hamlet* represents a psychological and anthropological engagement with

---

time, see Jones (1957, pp. 155, 320). The recently published diaries of Freud suggest that Sachs spent a period of six months in Berlin in 1929–1930 during which he received some form of analysis from Reik. Michael Molnar's annotations indicate that Freud, Anna Freud, and Jones were well disposed to Sachs and were "intrigued" by the idea of a South African study group under his leadership (see Freud, 1992, pp. 173, 215–216, 294).

[5]Sachs, W. (1934), *Psycho-Analysis. Its Meaning and Practical Applications.* London: Cassell.

"the other," but it is also an account of the way in which two very
different individuals confront and attempt to understand each other and
themselves.

JOHN'S STORY

Sachs first met John after having been asked by Hellman to treat John's
wife Maggie, who was crippled by severe pain in her legs. As a trained
herbalist and diviner *(nganga)*, John shared with Sachs an interest in
medicine and psychology. Sachs was eager to find out whether psychoanalytic tools were universally applicable across different cultures. For
his part, John desired to gain a working understanding of European
medicine. This congruence of interests formed the basis of an intriguing,
if fraught, collaboration between the two men. Over a period of two and
a half years Sachs psychoanalyzed John by means of free association.
During this time, Sachs claims to have visited practically every place
spoken of by John and to have talked to many of the persons he
mentioned. Each morning John walked the short distance between his
lodgings and Sachs' consulting room. The proximity was important,
because this meant that Sachs did not have to pay John's busfare. Sachs
(1937) explains:

> In my case, it would have been disastrous to introduce money into
> our relationship. Our work had to be carried out in an atmosphere
> of friendliness and mutual interest: a kind of interchange of
> medical knowledge. For the final part of my studies, it was essential
> that John should become so attached to me that he would be willing
> to give me information and not to sell it. And even when a time
> came when he had to be helped financially, I never did so directly,
> but through a third person, usually the anthropologist who had
> first introduced us [p. 14].[6]

John Chavafambira (or Chawafambira) — if that is indeed his name —
was born near Umtali (now Mutare) in eastern Zimbabwe, around 1904.
A "pure Manyika," he came from a long tradition of well-known
diviner-herbalists. John's father died when he was about three years old.
In accordance with established custom, John's mother, Nesta, subse-

---

[6]It is striking that Sachs was so consciously intent on keeping their relationship free of
financial complications. My own feeling is that John must nevertheless have been aware
of Sachs' potential as a benefactor. As the account shows, at certain critical moments
Sachs came to John's aid with material help.

quently married Charlie, his father's brother, who was also a diviner. After a childhood spent as a shepherd and some two years' education at mission school, John returned to his kraal (village) in 1915 (Hellman, 1948).[7] In accordance with the wishes of his deceased father he was now given instruction in the various arts of traditional doctoring by Charlie. But he undertook to refrain from practicing his medicine until he reached a more mature age. Between 1917 and 1918 John worked as a nurse in charge of small children and as a "kitchen boy" in Umtali. He returned to his kraal during the postwar influenza epidemic, which killed his mother in 1918. Between 1919 and 1921 John found domestic employment in Salisbury and Bulawayo, and in 1921 he left for Johannesburg.[8]

Thus far John's story is unremarkable: He fitted into a network of labor migrancy in which many young Manyika workers traveled to South Africa, often finding employment as waiters or domestic servants (Ranger, 1989). John's particular experience, however, marked him out from the beginning, for on the journey south he underwent a spiritual encounter that was to have a profound impact on his future. Its importance is reflected in the fact that it formed the subject of the very first day of his analysis with Sachs. The dynamics that it set in motion provide the basis for an understanding of the narrative structure of the book as well. It is with this episode that we too must therefore begin.

Just over the South African border in the northern Transvaal, John encountered a small community that was greatly suffering from prolonged drought. This, together with the wretched and lifeless feel of the village, suggested that its inhabitants might be at odds with their *midzumu* (ancestral spirits). Their plight persuaded John to abandon temporarily his vow not to practice medicine, and he agreed to assist in "smelling out" the malevolent spirits. As the ritual progressed, John felt the presence of his father, who promised that rain would come. That night he was awakened by lightning and strong rain. The lightning occurred during a dream, which he interpreted as meaning that he would become a famous and wealthy doctor and that he would replace his uncle Charlie when he became older. Next morning the unfortunate villagers surprisingly greeted him with suspicion and displayed no gratitude— despite the fact that he had brought them rain.

---

[7]There is a discrepancy between Hellman and Sachs on this point, the latter claiming that Charlie forced John to leave school in 1917 and that his training as a healer occurred while he was at school.

[8]Hellman (1948, p. 118) says he "entrained for Johannesburg." Sachs (1937, p. 17) maintains he had no money for the train fare and walked from Manyikaland to the South African border.

John soon became aware of a young, beautiful woman whom he involuntarily spoke to in his own Manyika language. The woman disclosed that it was she who was responsible for bewitching the kraal and that she was avenging the death of her father and the poisoning of her mother and brothers. Her father had been killed for insisting that she marry a fellow Manyika rather than an elder of the kraal who wished to take her as a third wife. (In a dream that John subsequently revealed to Sachs and that has a major bearing on the story as a whole, he admitted that he had inadvertently forgotten to ask the girl her *mutopo* [clan name]. To sleep with someone sharing the same *mutopo* was tantamount to incest.) John was horrified by her story and appalled that the young woman had "got hold" of him. At this point the spirit of his mother appeared, and reassured him that the girl-witch was only obeying her *midzumu* and was therefore not to be blamed.

John repeated his ritual on the following two nights and on both occasions it rained. During one of these storms his father again came to him. He instructed John to leave the kraal immediately, without saying good-bye or taking the cattle he was owed for his services. John's father warned him that his blood was "too hot" and that it was confusing his thoughts. He therefore reiterated that John should refrain from practicing medicine for the time being.

At this point Sachs expresses some skepticism, remarking that it is difficult to "discern truth from fiction in this romantic story." But he relates it in considerable detail, both because of the symbolic importance that John attached to the experience, and because of the light it sheds on John's psychological make-up and future life. The beguiling image of the young Manyika witch, the spiritual dream presence of father and mother, and the misery of the bewitched villagers, were an enduring influence and remain with him to the end of the book. It also provides the point of departure for Sachs: Henceforth, he adopts a narrative approach, preferring to "give the story of [John's] life in chronological order instead of in the disconnected manner in which I encouraged him to talk to me" (Sachs, 1937, p. 31).

According to Sachs' account, John reached the town of "P— —" (Potgietersrus or Pietersburg) after leaving the bewitched village, without going on to Johannesburg as he had originally intended.[9] There he found work in the kitchen of a seedy commercial hotel owned by a Mr. Kaplan.

---

[9]In *Black Anger,* Sachs (1947) names the town as Pietersburg. Hellman (1948), on the other hand, says he arrived at Johannesburg and went to the Registry Office, which arranged work for him in a Potgietersrus hotel.

John maintained a somewhat aloof attitude from the rest of the hotel staff, though he did form a friendship with a Zulu chambermaid named Maggie whose mother lived near Pietersburg. Despite Maggie's physical disability and her plain appearance, the relationship grew. His interest in her was largely determined by a mixture of compassion and professional concern. Maggie finally won his affection by contriving to make John jealous of a rival suitor. At Maggie's suggestion they obtained leave and departed for her village, a few hours' walk from the hotel. After complex negotiations and a considerable interval of time, *lobola* (bridewealth) was arranged and the two were married.[10] John was much taken by Maggie's mother Mawa, whose graciousness and beautiful hands reminded him of his own mother. But he took an immediate dislike to her husband George, considering him to be stupid and gross.

Following the marriage John returned to his work in the hotel. Already at this stage he felt trapped into marriage with a woman he did not love and a father-in-law he detested. Resentful at Maggie's indolence and isolated from his fellow workers as the only Manyika in the town, John became dispirited. Maggie's failure to produce a child after a year of marriage was considered a severe embarrassment, but she succeeded in becoming pregnant after going through an elaborate fertility ceremony organized by her father, George. The birth of a son was welcome, but it failed to improve John's state of mind, and he experienced various premonitions of evil.

John's resentment of the humiliations of domestic service in the hotel manifested itself in a generalized feeling of anger toward whites. One evening, a middle-aged woman resident returning from the bathroom accused John of attempted rape when he bent to pick up her fallen gown. Because her obsessive fear (or desire—as Sachs suggests) of being attacked by men was well known by the hotel proprietor and its domestic staff alike, the woman's story was not believed. Nevertheless, the proprietor felt obliged to dismiss John without a reference, in spite of the fact that he believed in his innocence. (Notably, a very similar story is enacted in Lionel Rogosin's 1959 film *Come Back, Africa,* which reinforces the archetypal nature of this very South African story.)

John took the train from Pietersburg to Johannesburg in the company

---

[10]The marriage was neither solemnized in church nor registered in church. *Lobola* was fixed at four cows and eight goats. In view of the difficulties of getting stock from Manyikaland, John was persuaded—much against his will—to pay £25 with an initial installment of £12. John was disturbed by the idea of paying cash because this did not seem to be in the spirit of marriage. He also claimed that Maggie's father was a constant drain on his resources and that he actually paid more than the full *lobola* price.

of Maggie and his child. It was 1927. He described vividly his impressions
of arriving among the throng of passengers at the station. In particular,
he was horrified by the wretched appearance of a group of black
prisoners, handcuffed to each other, who were being escorted by police
from the court to the jail. Within a week of his arrival fellow countrymen
had obtained for him a job as a waiter in a boarding house, where he
appears to have worked until 1930. Maggie refused to live in the
unnamed location because of its distance from town. John therefore
found her a room in a yard in Doornfontein, near the city center. During
this time Maggie gave birth to another son, but John visited her only
occasionally (though he did provide financial support). He drifted into
an unsatisfactory relationship with Edith, a colored housemaid at the
boarding house where he worked. John was homesick and yearned above
all for his dead mother Nesta. The absence of Maggie was, however, a
compensation, and he was fascinated by Johannesburg, taking time to
explore it in detail on foot.

Hellman (1948) records that John attended night-school during this
period, attaining "considerable proficiency in reading and writing, both
in his home tongue and in English" (p. 118). Though he found Edith
unattractive, he grew to admire and respect her intelligence. She was a
film enthusiast and showed him photographs of movie stars. John was
particularly intrigued by a photo of Paul Robeson, whose wealth and
evident acceptance by whites came as a revelation. It led him to fantasize
briefly about going to America, where he would sing Manyika songs and
achieve success.

A visit to Edith's sick mother evoked John's sympathy, and he
persuaded her to see a healer he had recently met. However, he was
outraged by the callous and unprofessional conduct of the doctor.
Greatly troubled by the case, John threw the bones and successfully
treated her swollen legs. Thus he was forced to admit his true vocation to
Edith for the first time. This event precipitated John's decision to take up
medicine once more. At this stage, too, the boarding house gained a
harsh new proprietor whom John greatly disliked. His decision was
confirmed following a hospital visit during which he was disturbed by the
lack of intimate contact and knowledge between doctor and patient. In
the meantime he began to prepare himself by studying medicine and
making contacts with healers. At this point Maggie left her Doornfontein
quarters in order to be closer to his work. He resented her presence and
realized that becoming a *nganga* would free him from her constant
attention and sexual demands. In a dream his father at long last gave him
the signal to commence his work. His success at treating a sick girl gave

him a tremendous feeling of confidence, and he resolved to leave his employment as a waiter and to recommence work as a *nganga*.

John now moved to a room in Jeppe, where he lived with Maggie and their children. For Maggie (who spoke independently to Sachs) this year was her happiest since marriage. John's practice flourished, his affection for Maggie was rekindled, and they had another child. Their room became a center of social activity in which long discussions were held about the difficulties of life, "the cruel oppression of the white people" and the nature of religion (Sachs, 1937, p. 113). Tembu, one of the new members of this social circle, exuded a sense of natural authority, and John regarded him with awe. He was particularly impressed by the fact that Tembu had refused to adopt a "white" name for the convenience of employers.

Some time during 1930 John left for Kroonstad on business. Maggie did not hear from him for three months, nor did she receive any money from him. During this period Maggie had a brief affair with a young miner, but she soon grew anxious that John would find out. Fearful of the consequences, she returned to her parents' village. When John returned he found his room locked and empty. Their neighbors had also left, having been expelled by the municipal authorities in terms of the 1923 Urban Areas Act. John soon found out about his wife's infidelity but, according to Sachs, treated the affair with indifference.

In 1931, after experiencing considerable difficulty in finding living quarters, John moved to Rooiyard. According to Ellen Hellman, who describes the yard in great detail, it consisted of a total of 107 rooms arranged in a rough triangular shape, with a double line of back-to-back rooms in the center. The whole yard, accommodating 376 inhabitants in 1933, was served by only six latrines, and was therefore both highly congested and insanitary. The alleyways were cluttered with tins used for the illegal brewing and storage of beer, which formed an important part of the domestic economy. But despite the crowded squalor of the common areas, Hellman (1948) remarks on the care with which the interiors of most rooms were kept. John rented a room here for 30 shillings a month. Maggie soon joined him there but, unlike most of the women and in spite of John's urging, she refused to brew beer for sale.

John first met Hellman and Sachs in 1933. At this time Rooiyard was on the municipal authorities' "insanitary" list, and there were constant rumours of its impending closure.[11] The threat of imminent eviction, coupled with the widespread practice of illegal beer brewing and

---

[11]Rooiyard was finally demolished in 1934.

prostitution, meant that Hellman's constant presence and prying questioning was treated with considerable suspicion by the community. According to Hellman (1948), the white landlord was also deeply resentful of her presence and helped to fuel suspicion against her.

The belief that Hellman was a spy was a source of inner turmoil for John. He informed Sachs (1937) of the community's suspicions toward "that rich young woman who comes here in her grand motor-car . . . [and] asks questions all the time; silly questions about what we eat, how many children we have, what money we earn, and so on" (p. 132).

John had himself been fearful of Hellman's presence and had participated in denouncing her. But by the time he confided this to Sachs, he had already rejected the notion that Hellman was a spy. It was Tembu who was responsible for persuading John that Hellman was not a threat. According to Sachs (1937), Tembu had said that the woman was merely studying African life:

> He told me, Doctor, that we are to the Europeans still a mysterious people, though they know us for hundreds of years. These students come to us not because they care for us, but because they want to write books about us. In the Milner Park [by which he referred to the Witwatersrand University] the white young men and women study to be doctors, lawyers. They learn about nature, about butterflies and flowers and stones, and they also study us Africans. When they want something from us, they are kind, speak to us nicely. But in their own houses they treat the blacks like slaves, not better than the others [pp. 133–134].

Despite this cynical indictment of Johannesburg's white liberal intelligentsia, Tembu assured John that Hellman was trustworthy. Indeed, she might even be of great help. This assurance changed John's opinion of Hellman and from then on he became one of her supporters — even helping to defuse a potentially dangerous situation one Saturday night when Hellman and Sachs decided to experience Rooiyard's drunken revelries at first hand.[12] In time, Hellman came to depend more and more on John as an informant, and in return she began to help him financially. John's changing attitude to Hellman typified his ambivalence

---

[12]For a discussion of the vibrant slumyard culture of which this was a part, see Koch, E. (1983), Without visible means of subsistence: slumyard culture in Johannesburg 1918-1940. In: *Town and Countryside in the Transvaal,* ed. B. Bozzoli. Johannesburg, S.A.: Ravan Press, pp. 151-175.

to whites in general, a feeling that extended to Sachs as well. He regarded whites with distrust and fear, but he was also fascinated by the knowledge and power they represented.

It was at the very moment that John's ambivalent feelings toward Hellman were being resolved in her favor that he met Sachs and commenced "analysis" with him. At first John was cautious and for a month he did not admit he was a practising *nganga,* though he stated that it was his ambition to become one. Sachs came to realize that John had agreed to enter into analysis, not in order to please him, but as a means of extracting information about "European" medicine and whites in general. Sachs was struck by the way in which John copied his own analytic technique, asking questions and listening for long periods without interruption, even when Sachs used words he could not have been familiar with. Finally, John persuaded Sachs to give him pills, tablets, and mixtures with which he could experiment.

Despite the warnings of friends that he should avoid contact with whites and their medicine, Sachs (1937) felt that John was already strongly under his influence and that, "unknown to himself, civilization had penetrated into his innermost being" (p. 140). For John, this tension was the source of severe inner conflict that, according to Sachs, was revealed in John's dreams and in the contradictory feelings of love and hate he manifested toward his analyst.

One Saturday night, as John was struggling to resolve these conflicting feelings, he wandered into central Johannesburg, where he was summarily arrested—with no explanation—for being in the streets at 11 P.M. without a special pass. Unable or unwilling to pay a fine, he was duly sentenced to a month's imprisonment. John regarded his trial with a mixture of horror and fascination. For most Africans arrest was regarded as an inevitable part of life in the cities. But this knowledge did not in any way diminish John's sense of humiliation. He found it "infinitely degrading" to be publically shackled to another man.

John spent his sentence as part of a convict road-gang. He collapsed with a recurrence of the lung complaint he had suffered as a result of the 1918 influenza epidemic and was hospitalized for six weeks. Sachs found him there by chance. The hospital and its forms of treatment aroused intense interest in John, and he bombarded Sachs with detailed questions during his recovery. In particular, it brought into sharp focus different explanations of the aetiology of disease. For instance, John expressed disbelief toward the concept of infection, holding to the idea that illness must have an identifiable source. He resolved these problems in a pragmatic fashion by accepting that African and white methods of medical treatment each had their respective place: Africans, he decided, ordinarily became ill as a result of the will of ancestors, evil-doers, or bad luck, whereas whites were afflicted by diseases, the origins of which were unknown. In the cities, however, Africans were susceptible to illness from both sources. It was therefore perfectly acceptable to be eclectic in the use of different forms of treatment.

When John's health improved, Sachs took him back to Rooiyard. His practice continued to flourish, but it soon became apparent that the authorities were determined to close down the yard. This was toward the end of 1933. The residents, urged on by the white shopkeeper and landlord, sought to blame this disaster on John and his white associates. His position soon became untenable: ostracized as a result of his connections with Sachs and Hellman, John decided to leave. At one point he guiltily related a dream in which Sachs became identified with a detective who had (in reality) accused him falsely of the murder of newborn twins for the purposes of witchcraft. John repeated a warning he had often been given: "Never trust a white man. He is like a puff-adder in the dust, that strikes backwards " (Sachs, 1937, p. 154).

Sachs (1937) says that he encouraged John to voice his hostility toward whites in general and himself and Hellman in particular. But the respect and confidence that, in the past, had allowed John to overcome his fear had weakened. And he remained "obstinately silent, or answered in monosyllables" (p. 154). During this near breakdown in the relationship, Sachs sought to persuade John that "hatred, like love, cannot be conquered: it must emerge in one form or another" (p. 155). Ultimately, Sachs managed to regain John's confidence and the months that followed were the most successful period of their relationship.

For John, however, times were difficult. His practice deteriorated, having been interrupted by prison, illness, and the hostility of the Rooiyard residents. Manyika patients suddenly remembered that he had not gone through the initiation ceremony that was necessary to be fully qualified as an *nganga,* and there were also accusations that his drugs had lost their healing power. Stories of his unsuccessful treatments began to gain currency and were seized upon and spread by his competitors. Increasing harassment by police, tax officials, and health inspectors made Rooiyard more difficult than ever to live in. He was also feeling deeply estranged from Maggie. More and more, he became absorbed with the idea of escaping to Manyikaland. Sachs and Hellman's offer to pay for the costs of removing his family to Maggie's parents' kraal helped to resolve the frustrated sense of indecision from which he was suffering:

"He was like a hunted animal, pinned in a corner, who is suddenly shown a way of escape" (Sachs, 1937, p. 181).

Sachs did not hear from John for several months and finally decided to track him down at Maggie's village in the northern Transvaal. John and Maggie greeted Sachs warmly, though they were in the midst of considerable family difficulties. Mawa, Maggie's mother, was in a state of severe depression, which Sachs (1937) diagnosed as "manic-depressive insanity," expressing itself in "cycles of excitement and melancholia" (pp. 186–187). The brave and vital woman described by John had "sunk into a condition of unalleviated apathy and despair" so that "only her emaciated casket remained" (p. 183).

When John had first arrived, he had found Maggie's family in a state of destitution, having been apparently abandoned by George. In a relatively short time, however, John was able to establish a medical practice, and the children soon began to recover from starvation. But Mawa's psychological state had not improved. John threw the bones to establish who was responsible for poisoning Mawa and how the poison had entered her body. There was talk that George and his second wife had ill-treated Mawa. This second wife was known as a witch, and John and Maggie became convinced that it was she who was responsible for Mawa's insanity. But they feared her, and without Mawa's cooperation, it was in any case impossible for John to be of assistance.

The problem came to a head about a month later when Mawa, now in a phase of aggressive "maniacal excitement," strangled her own four-year-old daughter. Arrested and found guilty of murder, Mawa was committed to an asylum (probably in Pretoria). John stayed there with one of the warders, a man named N'komo, whose handling of, and sensitivity toward, the mental patients, Sachs regarded with the utmost respect. Through N'komo, John became interested in many of the patients, blaming the institution and the cruelty of whites for their predicament. He became "carried away by his fantasies of helping the suffering black humanity," desiring to lead the inmates in the destruction of the hospital and "the whole white superstructure that places such bitter and intolerable burdens upon the black man" (Sachs, 1937, p. 192).

Sachs (1937) was struck by John's new-found assertiveness: "Beneath the armor of servility, meekness, and cowardice I saw a will to help and a readiness to sacrifice. I saw at these moments the emergence of a new John" (p. 192). In practical terms, John was only able to throw the bones for the inmates. But Sachs was nonetheless impressed by his capacity to gain their confidence and to extract information from them. John was far more successful in this respect than Sachs himself, and Sachs began to wonder whether "it wouldn't be advisable, from a psychological point of view, to employ *ngangas* in the treatment of insane natives" (p. 193).

John's efforts were ended, however, when one of his patients attacked him with a knife, accusing him of being in league with the white doctor — Sachs — and taking away his blood. John interpreted this incident as being an expression of his *midzumu*'s anger, "a warning to refrain from betraying his own nation" (Sachs, 1937, p. 194). Not only had he betrayed his profession to Sachs, he had also betrayed it to Hellman who, as a woman, was "unclean" and outside of the medical profession. Fearing that John was on the verge of a nervous breakdown, Sachs sedated him and took him back to Johannesburg.

Now living in Sophiatown, John resumed his career. He resolved to keep away from whites — including Sachs — as well as to refrain from attending the political meetings with which he had been peripherally involved. (Tembu, among others, had recently been imprisoned in connection with such activities.) But John did not find satisfaction in the company of those whose social life revolved around drinking and carousing. He felt that he belonged neither to "these uncontrolled, stupid people," nor to educated African circles and their clubs, and not either to white people. As a *nganga* he should remain aloof, devoting himself only to his practice.

Nevertheless, John's contact with Sachs did not cease entirely. Together, they visited a *ngoma* named Emily, who had gained a considerable reputation for effecting remarkable cures. At first, John was highly suspicious of her abilities, but he gradually developed a close relationship with her. Sachs also gained Emily's confidence. He diagnosed her as suffering both from "extreme hysteria" and also from a serious disorder that caused her to be grossly overweight. John's difficult relationship with Emily had a disastrous end. In the midst of a trance while treating a patient, she was rudely awakened by two policemen raiding for illegal liquor. This caused Emily to suffer a fit from which she collapsed and died. John was deeply disturbed by the news and blamed her death on "the white people."

The purveyor of this sad news was a Malawian named Mdlawini who was being treated by Emily at the time of her death. John became convinced that it was this man who had been Maggie's lover when he was working in Kroonstad in 1930. He also became convinced that it was this betrayal that had caused his medicines to lose their potency and, by extension, his subsequent problems. John took revenge by telling Mdlawini his life was under threat, warning him that his enemy would probably take on the form of a ghost. He instructed Mdlawini to be on guard and to keep a weapon next to him at night.

Again, disaster struck. Greatly disturbed by John's warning and by his experience of Emily's dreadful death, the Malawian obtained an assegai and kept it next to him in his communal quarters. That night he was suddenly awakened by a vague shape that touched him and then lay down. Panicked by the appearance of the enemy forecast by John, Mdlawini struck out at the shape with his assegai, killing him soundlessly. Mdlawini, who is described by Sachs as a "raw, illiterate native," was soon arrested. Fortunately for John (who attended the trial together with Sachs) his own involvement was not disclosed. But the four months between preliminary examination and trial caused John great anxiety. And when Mdlawini was sentenced to life imprisonment for murder, John reacted dangerously by proclaiming the injustice of white justice outside the court.

That same evening John's friend and mentor Tembu called on Sachs to inform him that John had been arrested for intervening in an incident in which a young boy was being beaten by a policeman. Sachs felt uncomfortable at the (unspoken) imputation that he was somehow responsible for John's predicament. The profound sense of inner turmoil experienced by Sachs had a cathartic effect, causing him to review his role as a psychologist and his understanding of John's personality. As Sachs (1937) described it, "I tried for the first time to see John the human being and not the subject of psychoanalytical studies. It seemed to me that in spite of my sympathy and external freedom in relationship with him, he nevertheless had remained chiefly a psychoanthropological specimen: the main aim had been to collect his dreams, his fantasies, and find out the workings of the primitive unconscious mind" (p. 227).

Sachs concluded that John had behaved in a self-destructive fashion ever since the onset of Mawa's insanity and that this self-destructive urge might be the result of John's abrupt severance from Sachs himself. To abandon any patient "in the state of a so-called positive transference" might have serious consequences for their mental health. But Sachs realized that he had not taken appropriate precautions with John because "John had been to me only a subject of experiment, and the whole analysis nothing more than a case of psychic vivisection." As Sachs (1937) reread his voluminous notes, a "new man separated himself from the pages [he] was reading. The human: the real John" (pp. 227–228).

Early the next morning, Sachs went to Tembu, desiring to find out openly just what Tembu thought of him. At this point Sachs (1937) notes that he always found interaction with "educated natives" difficult: "they never spoke to the point, they always hinted, made indirect references, were always too polite and obliging" (p. 230). But Sachs was determined to establish whether he was held to be responsible for John's predicament and whether he was suspected of being a spy. In the event, Tembu's welcoming attitude allowed Sachs to adopt a more circumspect approach. But he nevertheless inquired whether Tembu and his friends regarded him as being "a real friend of the Africans," honest in his relations with John, and trustworthy. After a silence and endless introductory apologies one of the men answered. He said that he had recently visited a white in order to discuss the new Native Bills, which, "by abolishing the Cape franchise, are depriving us of the last vestige of human rights."[13] At this, the white host protested indignantly. After asking for the toilet, the host directed him to the servants' quarters outside and a "a dirty, foul-smelling latrine. On our way there we had to pass a similar place in the house. It was clean, well-kept, not like the other. I ask you, Doctor: What are we to think?" (p. 231).

John's case was heard in the magistrate's court and he was fortunate to escape with a fine. Believing that John, in his present state, should not remain in Johannesburg, Sachs conferred with Hellman and the advocate responsible for the defense of the Malawian, Mdlawini. Together, they decided that John should leave the country, fearing that he had committed a criminal offense "by practicing witchcraft with dire results" (Sachs, 1937, p. 233). John agreed with this plan, and Sachs decided to drive him back home to his village in Manyikaland. Meanwhile, Maggie and their three children returned unexpectedly to Johannesburg from Pietersburg. Initially, John was pleased to see his family. But he was soon driven to despair by the anger unleashed on him by Maggie and her (justified) suspicion that John was seeking to abandon her once again.

Eventually, after much hard bargaining, John left with Sachs, accompanied by Daniel, his son. During the long trip north to Zimbabwe, John was grimly withdrawn. At the border he was even more morose, gazing malevolently at the white border officials. That night, John awoke Sachs with the startling revelation that he had killed Maggie. In a fit of rage after having accused Maggie of consistently conspiring to ruin his life, he had placed poison (which he had obtained from Sachs' room) in her tea. She had gone into a deep, motionless sleep, and he had left her for dead. But Sachs burst out laughing when John handed him the bottle labeled "poison." It emerged that the poison was merely a sleeping aid and that

---

[13]The reference to the "new native bills" refers to the remodeled segregationist legislation that emerged from secret parliamentary select committee in 1935.

no harm could have come to her. However, in spite of his relief, Sachs was stunned by the realization that John had intended to kill his wife. At the same time, he was pleased to discover (1937) "that the old John, lacking courage and endurance, was disappearing, and that there was steadily growing within him self-assertion and the instinct to fight his own way through life. Unnoticed by himself and others, John had become ready for revolt" (p. 240).

John's relief engendered a new mood of optimism in him and he began to take an excited interest in the journey. A visit to the ruins or Great Zimbabwe filled him with a feeling of "possessive pride." At Rusape, the administrative center of Makoni district, he met a number of acquaintances, including his sister Edna. Further on, close to his village, John took Sachs on a roundabout route, pointing out the steep hill, topped by enormous trees, where his grandfather was buried. When they eventually arrived at their destination, John was greeted by two women family members, who began to cry hysterically.

Charlie was not present when they arrived, but when he did return the enmity between "the flabby, wrinkled, dirty, and dissolute old man" and John became immediately clear (Sachs, 1937, p. 250). John was particularly hurt that Charlie ignored his son, Daniel. He felt acutely the tension between his urban and rural identities. This feeling was exacerbated by constant barbed remarks made by Charlie to the effect that John had forgotten the taboos and restrictions of the kraal. Rumors soon began to circulate that John had returned to replace Charlie, and many people came forward with complaints and stories of the old man's incompetence and maliciousness. Just as he had dreamed, John became infatuated with a beautiful young girl, a stranger to the kraal. At last he had someone to supersede the image of the Manyika witch that had obsessed his thoughts since he left his home 15 years before.

Meanwhile, the village divided into two opposing camps, with the women solidly behind John, and a number of young men—potential rivals—seeking to strengthen Charlie against him. Eventually, John confronted his stepfather, who was forced to agree to initiate him as a *nganga*. This tension was echoed by wider political stirrings, which coincided with a severe drought. Demands by a tax inspector for arrears, as well as outstanding rent, raised the specter of the inhabitants' removal to an official government reserve. There were stories of bloodshed in the Zambian copper mines to the north, and reports of a general revolt throughout Manyikaland. Controversy surrounded the activities of an old man named Johannes, who lived in the mountains and led a breakaway religious sect—one of many independent churches expressing

African disillusionment with the unfulfilled promises of traditional mainstream Christianity.[14] The threatened implementation of the 1930 Land Apportionment Act, in conjunction with other forms of state intervention involving restrictions on peasant access to land, may also have contributed to the general climate of uncertainty and fear.[15]

In Sachs' view these circumstances had a galvanizing effect on John, who was able to link his own personal desire for self-assertion with a desire to liberate his people. The village was seized by an overwhelming sense of expectancy and collectively refused to pay tax. The anger of the *midzumu* manifested itself when a six-month-old child, after failing to respond to Charlie's medicines, was secretly taken to a neighboring *nganga,* who declared that the child was doomed because his two upper teeth were cutting before his lower teeth. The child would have to be killed, otherwise disaster would befall his parents and the clan as a whole. Seizing an opportunity to deflect criticism from himself, Charlie demanded the sacrifice of the baby. The father, however, refused to countenance the sacrifice, saying that he would appeal to "the white man's law" should any harm come to his son. In response, the village — with the brave exception of John — ostracized them. During a meeting (at which John was not present) Sachs himself declared that he would report any murder to the government. Charlie, realizing the situation, prudently declared that the ancestors had spoken to him in the night and that it would be sufficient to rub special herbs on the child's gums. Moreover, he said that John's initiation should proceed.

The tension in the village did not abate, however, and when a fire broke out in the local school, open revolt erupted against Charlie. It was decided that John should succeed Charlie as the *nganga* in three days' time. Meanwhile, Charlie should teach John the art of poisoning in accordance with his oath to John's father. Faced with this pressure,

---

[14]This may well have been Johana Masowe, founder of the Apostolic Sabbath Church of God. According to Daneel, he preached a radical and apocalyptic message from the early 1930s, proclaiming the imminence of the day of judgment and that government and established churches were of the devil. His main influence was in the area between Rusape and Umtali. See Daneel, M. L. (1971), *Old and New in Southern Shona Independent Churches, Vol. 1.* The Hague, Netherlands: Mouton, pp. 339–340. Prof. Terence Ranger has pointed out to me that Masowe fits the description of Johannes but that Masowe was not an old man in the 1930s. He suggests that Johana Maranke, a leading Manyika preacher and dissident, might also be the model for Johannes. For an important discussion of the independent African churches in rural Mashonaland, see Ranger (1970), chap. 9.

[15]Ranger, T. O. (1985), *Peasant Consciousness and the Guerilla War in Zimbabwe.* London: James Currey, chap. 2.

Charlie acceded to the villagers' demands. At this point Sachs decided to leave the village, fearing that if some form of revolutionary outbreak should occur, the authorities would hold him responsible. John was feeling depressed and frustrated at the continuing intrigue of his enemies. Aware of rumors circulating that he was a police spy, Sachs moved to the house of a local trader, planning to return to Johannesburg as soon as the initiation ceremony was complete. The ceremony duly took place as planned, with Sachs watching events from a distance. But even as he was confirmed as the new *nganga,* John began to experience a sense of regret, wondering whether he should have returned and whether he would be happy in his new position.

At this point Sachs took his leave. Some 300 miles away, however, he suffered an accident and was forced to stay in a small village—close to where John had met the bewitched people on his first journey south—in order to wait for the arrival of spare parts from Johannesburg. After almost a week, he unexpectedly met John and Daniel on the main road, both of whom were utterly exhausted. It transpired that John had spent a wildly passionate night with his bride. After making love, he explained that their marriage would be officially ratified in the morning, and he asked what her *mutopo* (clan sign) was. When she answered "Soko" (monkey)—his own sign—he realized that he had unwittingly committed the incestuous crime he had so often been warned of in his dreams. Only witchcraft could explain his failure to ask the basic question one always asked of strange women when first meeting them.

Distraught, John sent her away. Although he could remedy matters by the sacrifice of oxen and goats, he would always be ridiculed as the *nganga* who became so civilized in the towns that he had become intimate with a girl before asking her *mutopo.* The only thing he could do was to run away again. On the road with Daniel a troop of monkeys appeared. John took this as a positive sign. But a car came by driven by three whites, one of whom picked up a stone to throw at the mother monkey. John intervened to stop the young man from throwing the stone, but he was physically assaulted in the process. His headwound was not serious, and he expressed pride at having been able to stand up for his *mutopo.*

According to Sachs, John now experienced a new kind of self-resolution. He had freed himself of the image of the Manyika woman who had bewitched the village some 15 years' ago. He had saved the monkey and was therefore at peace with his ancestors. It was now possible to return to Maggie, to educate his son "for life as it is now, and not as it was when I was a boy," and to resume work as a waiter (Sachs, 1937, p. 279). John, according to Sachs, had finally arrived at a position whereby he could reconcile the past with the future, kraal life with life in the town. In Sachs' (1937) view, John had finally realized that "the black and the white people must work together. Given that, the future of his son was assured. But, without it, it would be bare and purposeless indeed" (p. 280).

SACHS' INTERPRETATION

The major analytical device that Sachs deploys in order to understand John is the syndrome he calls "Hamletism." This he describes (1937) as "a universal phenomenon symbolizing indecision and hesitancy when action is required and reasonably expected" (p. 176). Following the psychoanalytic interpretation of Shakespeare's *Hamlet* offered by Freud and Ernest Jones, Sachs rejects the idea that Hamlet suffered from an inborn lack of decisiveness. Rather, his temporizing is the consequence of an unresolved Oedipus complex, which is reactivated by the death of the Danish king and the marriage of Gertrude to Claudius.

In Sachs' view (1937), the tragedy of *Hamlet* is "common to all humanity" and therefore "appeals to men of all races and nations" (p. 177). In the case of John Chavafambira, for example, John, though not a prince, is the son and heir of a famous *nganga*. His father dies in mysterious circumstances and there is a suspicion that Charlie, his uncle, is responsible for poisoning him. As in the Hamlet story, the position of the deceased father is usurped by the uncle. Just as Hamlet was unable to separate himself from Gertrude, so John is unable to relinquish Nesta. (For Sachs, this is confirmed by John's evident devotion to his mother as well as a dream related by John in which he sleeps with her.) Like Hamlet, John is unable to form a successful relationship with a woman and never falls fully in love. John's preferred explanation is that the demands of his medicine were too strong. But according to Sachs, John's devotion to his medicine arises out of his desire to usurp Charlie. Thus, John's interest in psychoanalysis is held to be motivated by a wish to gain the knowledge necessary to overcome Charlie. Moreover, in the case of both Hamlet and John, repressed inner desires conflict with a sense of duty to custom and tradition.

Sachs' objectives in *Black Hamlet* are twofold: to show that the structure of the "native mind" is identical to that of whites, and to demonstrate this similarity in terms of the universal applicability of Freudian analysis. In the context of prevailing views about race in the 1930s, the idea of extending the notion of Hamletism to the analysis of a black man would have seemed odd or even perverse. Notably, Sachs (1937) is cautious about advancing the analogy between Hamlet and John, acknowledging that the reader might find the comparison unacceptable: "John's tragedy, at first glance, may seem far beneath Hamlet's, and one is justified in ridiculing at the start any comparison between John the witch doctor and Hamlet the Danish prince" (p. 178). Thus Sachs does not attempt to ennoble John in virtue of a direct comparison with Hamlet. He merely states that both manifest a similar psychological condition.

Quite aside from the question of the universal applicability of Freudian analysis, the claim that blacks and whites shared identical mental structures was highly contentious at this time. Many South African researchers seriously doubted that the mental capacities of blacks and whites were equivalent.[16] Endless speculations by amateur anthropologists, administrators, missionaries, etc., about the "nature of the native mind" suggested that Africans thought differently from Europeans. In South Africa, the popular writings of social Darwinists sought to prove that blacks were fundamentally irrational, that their mental capacities were "arrested" at the onset of puberty, or that they were unable to free themselves as thinking individuals from the restrictive collective representations of communal society. Within the wider colonial psychiatric community, there existed, as Vaughan (1991) shows, a definite belief that African insanity was different in type from white mental illness. This was considered to be reflective of the existence of basic differences in the mental structures of "normal" whites and blacks.

Sachs first challenged such notions in a paper he delivered to the 1933 meeting of the South African Association for the Advancement of Science. Based on his study of 100 schizophrenic black patients at the Pretoria Mental Hospital, he concluded (1933) that "the delusions and hallucinations of the insane native were in structure, in origin and, partly in content, similar to those of the European" (p. 710). From this, he surmised that "if the mind of the native in his abnormal state operates on the same principles and finds the same modes of expression as in the case of the European, then the working principles of the mind in the normal state must also be identical in both cases" (p. 713).

---

[16]My current research project is on the history of the scientific idea of race in 20th-century South Africa. For a discussion of the concept of relative intelligence between different races, see, for example, Dubow, S. (1991), Mental testing and the understanding of race in twentieth-century South Africa. In: *Science, Medicine, and Cultural Imperialism,* ed. T. Meade & M. Walker. New York: St. Martin's Press, pp. 148–177.

Black Hamlet sought to explore the "working fundamental principles of the mind in its normal state." If this project was not in itself entirely original, Sachs' choice of psychoanalysis as the method of investigation certainly was. He refrained from making the easy generalizations born of casual anthropological observation. And he rejected the validity of the empiricist forms of investigation undertaken by fellow researchers (e.g., conducting mental tests or attitude surveys), maintaining (1937) that these did not lead to "any appreciable understanding of the black man" or to a true "insight into the mind" (p. 11).

Allied to the Hamlet syndrome, Sachs argues that John, like many other Africans, suffers from a tragic inability to cope with the rational demands of modern Western life. In this respect Sachs is less free of the conventional views on "native mentality" current at the time. In his view, John oscillates between close identification with and violent rejection of himself. These conflictual feelings are heightened by the difficult role John is forced to play as an intermediary between Sachs and Hellman on one hand, and the suspicious residents of Rooiyard on the other. A sense of acute conflict emerges most graphically at the point when the closure of Rooiyard appears imminent. It is introduced by a description (Sachs, 1937) of an uncontrolled outburst on the part of John, who rails against the impending eviction of Africans from Rooiyard—and becomes even more enraged when Sachs and Hellman suggest that the provision of alternative "location" accommodation is evidence that the intentions of the authorities are essentially "humane" (pp. 173–174). John is moved to fury: "You say the white people want to help us. Who will believe it? Who will believe the white devils? Tembu was right. The devil is not black; the devil is white like all of you. The white people want to suck our blood and throw us away. You say they want to help us, but I say they want to get rid of us! Well, let them give us back our land, then we will gladly go away, live by ourselves, away from you all. We don't want white devils" (p. 174).

To the modern reader this may seem an articulate and appropriate response, given the circumstances. But Sachs (1937) sees it as emblematic of John's psychological inadequacies. He is critical of John's passionate effort "to explain the reason of segregation as he had learned it from Tembu and others" and accuses John of incoherence. "Suddenly, he stammered, tried to recover himself, stopped. . . . But words failed him. And, with the first sign of failure, as usual, he collapsed as suddenly as he flared up" (p. 174).

Sachs goes on to interpret this incapacity in terms of a general conception of the psychological problems faced by Africans in their attempt to negotiate the gulf between rural and urban life. Like many other Africans, John's rural upbringing and education tragically failed to equip him with the willpower or perseverance necessary for achievement. "Renunciation and flight were John's choice in any situation requiring strength of will and endurance of pain." Sachs extends this analysis by arguing that John had not reached the stage of personality development achieved by healthy humans beings who manage to avoid emotional extremes and are able to modulate their reactions in accordance with what is appropriate to a given situation. In common with most other Africans, John was hopelessly caught between "the clash of his two worlds." The conflict between rural and city life meant that Africans were forced to live a psychological "double life" caused by the strain of reconciling competing moral codes, religious beliefs, and modes of life (Sachs, 1937, pp. 174-175). In John's case, this conflict was particularly severe. On one hand, "he loved the white man's life, loved civilization, wanted to be like Tembu, the civilized African." But on the other hand, "he was bound by his profession to his past, for he was destined to perpetuate his father, the great *nganga*" (p. 175).

To sociologists and anthropologists of the time, this analysis would have struck a familiar chord. The developing anthropological school of "culture contact" pioneered by Malinowski—of which Hellman was a leading exponent in the urban context—was grappling with "the changes which had occurred in a Native culture as a result of European contact influences" (Hellman, 1948, p. 3). Liberals like Hellman and Sachs, who sought to establish a common society in South Africa, tended to take a sanguine view of the interaction of African and Western culture. But behind them was a weight of conservative opinion (as exemplified in the British colonial doctrine of indirect rule) that sought to avoid the perceived threat to social order posed by "detribalization." Similar anxieties strongly informed the growth of segregationist ideology in South Africa at this time. Psychiatrists and psychologists in colonial Africa expressed these fears in terms of the so-called deculturation thesis. This view suggested that African psychopathology resulted from an inability to cope with the breakdown of "tribal" restraints, and the strains imposed by the demands of Western education and cultural values (Vaughan, 1991).

Sachs can be seen to be seen as lending broad support to the general paradigm of "deculturation" or "detribalization," though he cannot easily be associated with the conservative implications of that frame-work. Rather than using the notion of competing cultural forms as the basis of social differentiation, his real sympathies are with the creation of an integrated, common society. And, while he manages a remarkable degree of empathy with the values represented by "tradition," he does not exoticize John or demean the medicine he practices. On the contrary, he is highly receptive to what would be seen today as "alternative" psychological therapy. Moreover, although Sachs admits to a sense of discomfort in his relations with "educated" Africans, he does not reject them or their aspirations. Indeed, he is acutely aware that John's overpowering inner conflict and sense of frustration is greatly exacerbated by efforts on the part of whites to "keep him down, withholding emancipation under the pretext that two thousand years separate the African from the European. When the African strives to become Europeanized, he is told to stick to the traditions of his fathers; but when he does so, adhering to the barbarous traditions and customs of kraal life, he is pointed out as a savage. No way is open to him. He is forced to seek a compromise. Few succeed in achieving it" (Sachs, 1937, p. 175).

A key question that the reader of *Black Hamlet* needs to bear in mind at all times is whose voice we are hearing. At the outset Sachs (1937) assures us that he is telling John's story "in normal, as opposed to the broken, though fluent English in which it was told to me. Nevertheless, it is John's story, unaltered in its essence" (p. 15). How far we can accept this claim is difficult to say. Sachs (1947b) once referred to *Black Hamlet* as a "literary form of psychoanalytic biography containing all the facts revealed during analysis, but without too many scientific interpretations and interpolations" (p. 5). Sachs had originally elected to write the story in the form of a novel; indeed, a manuscript entitled "African Tragedy: the Life of a 'Native Doctor'" is in existence.[17] However, Sachs decided that the fictional form would miss the true story and that it would not be believed by his readers. On the other hand, he did not want to present John's story as a psychoanalytic case history, fearing that its readership would be restricted to academics. Thus, he decided to retain the novel form by reconstructing John's life "in the way he lived it, and not in the way he told it to me" (p. 5).

The fact that John's story is mediated by Sachs raises a host of difficult issues. In the first place, the distinction between the subject's account and the analyst's interpretation is often blurred. At a simple empirical level, the problem of verifying Sachs' claims is complicated by the fact that he deliberately obscures names and details in an effort to protect John's confidentiality. As far as the essential framework of the

---

[17]Sachs, W. (n.d.) African tragedy: The life of a native "doctor" (ms.). University of the Witwatersrand, Manuscripts Department, Cullen Library, A2120.

story is concerned, corroborating evidence is provided by Ellen Hellman's anthropological case study of John—though one should remember that she relied, by her own admission, on Sachs' notes. Sachs' references to contemporary events fit in well with the historical record. And there can be no doubt of John's existence: There is a picture of him in Hellman's monograph, Ralph Bunche records having met him, and Sachs' surviving daughter, Eileen Newfield, recalls his visits to the family home.

More problematic is the question of authorial interpretation. As an avowed pioneer of Freudian analytical techniques in South Africa, Sachs' agenda is to demonstrate the universality of psychoanalysis. In this respect John serves both as source and as receptacle for Sachs' ideas. Though the Hamlet analogy is striking and perhaps even convincing, it also functions as a grid through which John's evidence is forced. The structure of the narrative, which begins with the death of John's father and concludes with John's challenge to his uncle and the successful resolution of his inner turmoil, is almost too neat and has a novelistic quality about it. Can we take at face value, for example, Sachs' final conclusion in *Black Hamlet* (1937) that John was at last able "to reconcile the past with the future, life in the kraal with that in the town"? Was his determination to educate his son Daniel symbolic of "this new attitude towards his life"? Did John really realize at last "that the black and the white people must work together"? (p. 280).

Answers to these questions—which would otherwise remain hanging—are suggested by the update to the story in *Black Anger*. Here we find that the rosy ending provided in *Black Hamlet* was never realized. In *Black Anger* we learn that, immediately following their return to South Africa from Manyikaland, John was arrested and imprisoned for carrying a "lethal weapon"—a bicycle chain legitimately given to him by Sachs. He is released when Sachs pays his fine, but then Sachs becomes ill and does not see John for several months. When contact is reestablished in 1938 John is discovered living in abject poverty in "Blacktown" (probably Orlando in present-day Soweto) together with Maggie and the children. In the interval his practice has deteriorated, he is drinking heavily, and he has become involved with a gang of young petty thieves. Even more shocking, as far as Sachs is concerned, is the fact that John has compromised his hitherto impeccable professional standards as a *nganga* by cynically throwing the bones in a way calculated to maximize his own financial reward.

In this dangerous situation, Sachs seeks to redeem John and to reestablish his professional status as a healer. He does so by supplying

John with aspirin, vitamins, and other basic medications to augment John's own forms of treatment. The collaboration between Sachs and John is evidently successful, and John's reputation is soon enhanced. By the end of *Black Anger,* which takes the story up to 1945, we are presented with a new optimistic resolution of John's life, in which he emerges as a reformed and politicized "New African."

I shall return to this presently. Meanwhile, more needs to be said about the way in which John is revealed to us through Sachs. One way to approach this is to understand *Black Hamlet* as a confrontation between two essentially unlike men who nonetheless have a common interest in coming to terms with each other. The relationship between the two is manifestly not the usual one of analyst and client: The unconventional analytical techniques employed by Sachs (such as his frequent interventions in John's life and his interviews of John's associates) rule this out from the start. The relationship is maintained because both men have a reciprocal interest in drawing from each other's medical knowledge. For his part, Sachs wishes to explore the universality of Freudian analysis. In the process, he becomes increasingly absorbed by the psychological techniques employed in "traditional" medicine. Conversely, John is fascinated by the tools of Western medicine. He is attracted by the evident curative power of its scientific pharmacopia, but is disgusted by the atomized and dehumanized nature of its practices. In particular, he is dismayed by the disregard shown by hospital doctors toward the complexities of their patients' life histories and relationships. John is not troubled by the logical contradictions implicit in practicing both Western medicine and "traditional" healing. He is content to adopt an eclectic approach and seeks to bolster his own powers by learning from Sachs, in the belief that this will enhance his powers as a *nganga*— and also provide him with a crucial advantage over his uncle.

For Sachs, the relationship with John undergoes a significant shift. We have seen how he initially approaches John in the spirit of scientific curiosity, regarding him more as a "psychoanthropological specimen" than an individual human being. This arises from Sachs' earlier experiences at the mental hospital in Pretoria (1937) when he made the "startling discovery" that "the manifestations of insanity, in its form, content, origin, and causation, are identical in both natives and Europeans" (p. 11). Given standard scientific attitudes of the time toward "native mentality," one should not underrate the significance of this revelation.

As the relationship between the two men develops, Sachs' experiences a further revelation, namely, the realization that John is a human being like any other, and that his psychological make-up cannot be understood in isolation from the society that has produced him. The relationship is, however, by no means an equal one. Sachs acts as a father confessor, a repository of knowledge, and a mentor. He is manifestly a participant in John's life, but he remains an observer, sometimes condescendingly so. When Sachs learns from John, it is as a result of observation and intervention rather than of being taught. Sachs nonetheless learns a great deal from the relationship. He gains insight into his own work as an analyst and doctor, and he gains entry into aspects of black social life that are precluded to all but a handful of whites.

Most notably, it is through John that Sachs' own political consciousness develops. The political dimensions of the period dealt with in *Black Hamlet* are only alluded to in passing, but there are strong hints that, as a result of his acquaintance with John, Sachs himself becomes increasingly politically aware. Part of the fascination of *Black Hamlet* is the oblique, yet penetrating, psychological insights into the relations between black and white in pre–World War II Johannesburg. The well-meaning but often awkward contacts between white liberals and their African counterparts (through mechanisms like the joint council movement, the Institute of Race Relations, the churches, and the University of the Witwatersrand) are well known to historians of this period. Sachs' acute eye provides a striking psychological dimension to what is known through other more conventional sources about such institutions. The suspicion and hostility shown by ordinary slum-dwellers toward Hellman, for example, adds flesh to her own coded comments on this score in her Rooiyard monograph. Also revealing is the outburst of Tembu and his friends against the hypocrisy of the white liberal who invites them as guests to discuss the injustice of the Native Bills—but then shows them to the latrine in the servants' quarters.[18]

Even by today's standards of "reflexive" anthropological investigation, Sachs is conscious—if not consistently so—of the unequal power relations between observer and observed. His recording of Tembu's acid remarks about the intentions of Wits academics who study Africans in the same way as they study butterflies and flowers is a poignant example. Sachs is remarkably honest about admitting to his unease in the company of "educated natives" (like Tembu) whose anger seems to manifest itself indirectly and in tones of deference. But he is nevertheless concerned to

---

[18]Note that Sachs informs us in *Black Hamlet* (1937, p. 231) that these words are uttered by a "coloured" associate of Tembu's, whereas in *Black Anger* (1947a, p. 233) they are attributed to Tembu himself.

"discover once and for all just what the civilized black man thought of me."[19] In the aftermath of John's arrest after the trial of Mdlawini, Sachs professes to having been irritated by Tembu's hint that he is somehow responsible for John's predicament. He defends himself with an air of self-righteousness, declaring, "There was no need to instruct me in my duties to my fellow-men: I, of all people, who had constantly proclaimed my deep interest in the natives. Indeed, I had even been victimized because of this interest. I had been compelled to leave a consulting-room in a fashionable block of flats, outwardly on some trivial pretext, but actually I suspected because John and other natives came often to visit me there."[20]

Like Sachs, John is also troubled by the world of the African elite symbolized by Tembu, though for different reasons. Sachs recounts how John is in awe of Tembu and desperate for his friendship, but remains critical and resentful at the same time. John is embarrassed when he meets Tembu at the guest-night of a sophisticated club where Africans speak English and dress in "European" fashion. He feels out of place and is hurt by Tembu's apparent neglect of his presence. (In *Black Anger* this ambivalence appears to be resolved, with John appearing more comfortable in the presence of the "educated" Africans Sachs claims to have introduced him to.)

Through John, Sachs has the opportunity to gain access to a sphere of black political activity that would normally be precluded to whites. Together, they attend a meeting protesting against such issues as the poll-tax, the pass laws, and the land act. Both Sachs and John are evidently impressed by the eloquent address of a speaker (enigmatically referred to as "one of the greatest black men in Africa") who advises the meeting against feelings of bitterness and revenge, encouraging Africans instead to strive for education and "the fruits of civilization" (Sachs, 1937, pp. 168–169). John's passionate response to these sentiments lead him to attend "Communist meetings in preference to others because there the speeches took on a more fiery character." But John was skeptical of the claim that in Russia all were treated alike and found it difficult to envision a society in which there was no distinction between rich and poor, black and white. Rather, he was attracted to the idea, adapted

---

[19]Sachs, 1937, p. 230. cf. Sachs, 1947a, p. 222, which drops the reference to Tembu as a "civilized black man."

[20]Sachs, 1937, p. 224. Note that in *Black Anger* (1947a, p. 218), Sachs amends this to: "There was no need to instruct me in my duties to my fellow-men. I had been fulfilling them as well as I knew how for a long time. I had even been victimized. . . ."

from traditional Christianity, that "All of us were born good; but the white people made us bad with their cruelty and oppression, and also through our sorcerers and poisoners" (p. 170).

In Sachs' view, John experiences a gut response to racial injustice but is unable to formulate a coherent political analysis of its causes. Sachs records John's frustration at his inability to articulate political ideas with the analytical rigor of Tembu. And on numerous occasions he is critical of John's impulsive, undirected response to white oppression. At the same time, it is through John that Sachs' understanding of the daily humiliations suffered by black South Africans at the hands of whites is sharpened.

John first experiences a sense of generalized anger toward whites while working at Kaplan's hotel in the northern Transvaal. He soon comes to resent his servile status and the capricious demands made upon him by the customers. The incident in which he is unfairly accused of the attempted rape of a white woman brings these as yet unfocused feelings to the fore. None of the hotel staff — management included — are inclined to believe the fantasies of the woman. But John is naive enough to believe that his innocence will be vindicated. He fails to comprehend, as his fellow workers do, that whatever the rights of the situation, the mere fact that he, a black man, is accused of an assault on a white woman entails a presumption of guilt.

On arrival in Johannesburg John is appalled to see a wretched line of handcuffed black prisoners being publically marched through the streets by armed white police. The injustice of this spectacle is profound, and John at last begins to understand the advice of the waiters at the hotel who warned him of being taken in chains to prison. Throughout John's time in Johannesburg it is the routine injustice and degradation of black life in a white city that he finds intolerable. His general response is to avoid conflict and to retreat within his own world. But when confronted by brutality, he reacts impulsively and, it seems, irresponsibly. He first lands in prison for being on the streets of Johannesburg at night without a pass. According to Sachs, John did not even realize the nature of his "crime" until he reached the police station, and he finds himself being marched along the streets in just the same sort of prison procession that had so horrified him earlier. In court he is curiously detached and, though fearful, he retains a curiosity about the arcane proceedings of the judicial system.

John's next major brush with officialdom occurs during the trial of the Malawian who mistakenly murdered his friend, having been terrified by John's warnings that his life was under threat. Although there is a distinct danger that John's own incidental role in the tragic event will be revealed, he insists on attending the trial, albeit in a considerable state of agitation. When the Malawian is convicted and sentenced to life imprisonment, John can no longer contain his outrage. Outside court, he begins to declaim hysterically against "the white man's place of justice," and it is only with difficulty that John's friend Simon is able to calm him down. Later that evening, however, John is arrested for intervening in an incident in which a young African boy is beaten by a policeman. In the ensuing trial he is fortunate to escape with only a fine.

These incidents, taken together with numerous other examples of John's mistrust of whites, are described by Sachs in considerable detail. Sachs' own analysis is that John reacts in bouts of uncontrolled anger alternating with helpless submission. Sachs regards John's inability to formulate a considered political response (like Tembu) or to acquiesce pragmatically (like his friend Simon) as an indication of a certain lack of maturity. He suggests that John has strongly self-destructive tendencies, which are only curbed when external agents (like Sachs himself) intervene on his behalf.

CRITICAL EVALUATION

Assuming that Sachs is correct in his analysis of John's unpredictable behavior and erratic bouts of rage, the way in which this is described and interpreted remains problematic. It is dependent on Sachs' view that, through the process of therapy, John's anger is channeled into more creative directions. For example, the incident in which John attempts to poison Maggie is seen by Sachs (1937) as a positive action, to the extent that it indicates a departure from "the old John, lacking courage and endurance" and the emergence of a new spirit of "self-assertion and the instinct to fight his way through life" (p. 240). According to Sachs, this event symbolizes John's new readiness for "revolt" — which is how Sachs characterizes the final section of *Black Hamlet,* in which John returns to Zimbabwe in order to confront Charlie.

It is difficult to avoid the suspicion that this progressive view of John's evolution toward greater self-realization and direction, has more to do with Sachs' own perception of the therapeutic process than the reality of John's life. Related to this is the possibility that the account we are given of John's life reflects Sachs' own growing comprehension of the nature of racial oppression in South Africa. In this sense, it seems that Sachs is projecting his own political radicalization onto his interpretation of John.

There is a considerable amount of evidence to support this reading. At the start of Sachs' investigation, his purpose is motivated by a wish to discover whether the workings of the human mind are identical in blacks and whites. But as the book progresses, Sachs becomes aware that John's life has to be "interrelated with the general condition of life in South Africa." Moreover, as Sachs becomes more closely acquainted with John, his interests broaden to encompass "the whole native community." John is no longer simply the subject of investigation, but the means toward a wider exploration. In practical terms he acts as Sachs' assistant, helping him to establish contact with other African "patients" and gaining their confidence. In this way Sachs (1937) claims—with some justification—to have arrived at a "deeper insight" into African life as a doctor and psychologist, than many anthropologists (p. 199).

Sachs' growing sensitivity to the social and political context in which his psychological investigations take place is indicated by a number of minor but significant alterations in the text of *Black Anger*. (The very change of title in the new edition is revealing.) These alterations are not major in themselves, but together they indicate Sachs' greater awareness of John both as an individual and as a social agent. They also remove some of the more patronizing aspects of Sachs' narrator persona.

The first alteration occurs at the very beginning of the revised edition. It has already been noted that *Black Hamlet* begins with Sachs' account of his work with Africans at a mental institution and his discovery that the manifestations of insanity are identical in both blacks and whites. In *Black Anger* this is introduced by an unattributed quotation from a typical South African to the effect that blacks are "gentle, happy savages" who cannot possibly be treated as equals. For Sachs, the only way to get through this type of irrational white fear is "to get to know the blacks not as blacks but as human beings." This, he now claims, is his motivation for working at the black mental institution. And although Sachs (1947a) repeats his discovery that insanity takes an identical form in blacks and whites, he no longer refers to this as "startling" (p. 3).[21] Thus, from the outset of *Black Anger* one is aware that Sachs is subtly rewriting the history of his own investigation to reflect a less condescending and more politically committed attitude.

Corroborating evidence is not difficult to find. In *Black Hamlet* the subject of the book is introduced as "an ordinary native man, a witch doctor, whom I shall call John." He is referred to by his first name

---

[21]Note that the term "African" in *Black Hamlet* is replaced by the more politically resonant "black" in *Black Anger*.

throughout, and it is only well into the account that his surname is first mentioned. *Black Anger,* however, immediately refers to John by his surname, Chavafambira. This subtle change seems to imply a greater measure of respect and acceptance accorded by the author of the book to its subject.

A number of paragraphs in the original that may be construed as patronizing on the part of Sachs are excised in the second edition. One glaring example is the section in *Black Hamlet* in which Hellman and Sachs explain to an angry John that the government's motivation in removing the occupants of Rooiyard is "for the sake of the Bantu people" and that "decent quarters" were being provided in the locations. In *Black Anger* the reference to the provision of better quarters no longer appears and the statement itself is not attributed to Sachs or Hellman (Sachs, 1937, p. 173; 1947a, p. 167). Another example occurs when John is quoted as telling Sachs, "I can see that you, Doctor, really love the natives. You want to know how they really live and what they think. I tell so to my patients and people. They will like you when they meet you." In *Black Anger* this is amended to: "I can see that you, Doctor, are a true friend of ours. I say so to my patients and people. They will like you when they meet you" (1937, p. 200; 1947a, p. 193).

As a final example, we may note the difference in the two accounts as to how, following John's appearance in court for interfering with a policeman, it was decided that John should leave for Zimbabwe with Sachs. In *Black Hamlet* the decision is taken on John's behalf by a self-appointed "council" consisting of Sachs, Hellman, and an advocate. The process of this decision is taken entirely out of John's hands, and Sachs pretentiously compares their efforts to save John with "the partisans of Dreyfus, or similar cases where the saviour of one innocent man symbolizes the integrity of the whole of society." In *Black Anger,* Sachs simply advises John to go back to Manyikaland, and there is no reference either to Dreyfus or to a collective decision taken on his behalf (Sachs, 1937, pp. 232–233; 1947a, p. 224).

The most important difference in the two accounts is in their endings. As was mentioned earlier, *Black Hamlet* concludes with John's realization that Daniel should be educated and that black and white people ought to work together. In *Black Anger,* however, there is no mention of interracial cooperation, and the need to educate Daniel is qualified by a statement that "decent schooling was almost unattainable for the Africans" (Sachs, 1937, p. 280; 1947a, p. 271). The final section of the book, entitled "Revolt," is now considerably rewritten with much additional material. It takes the narrative from their return from Manyikaland to Sachs' departure for the United States in 1945.

Sachs (1947a) begins this section with an assertion that "John had long ago ceased to be merely an object of study." He had never been regarded as a patient, and "within the limits of his grim reality John was a relatively well-adjusted individual. His deficiencies were not characterological; they were the product of his whole life situation, a situation produced by the society in which he lived. John's greatest need was not to know more of his repressed unconscious, but to know the society he lived in, to recognize its ills and to learn how to fight them" (p. 275).

This is a remarkable statement, indicating a significant shift from Sachs' earlier emphasis on John as an inadequate personality suffering from deep inner psychological torment, to a new assessment of him as someone who is essentially a victim of the sociological conditions in which he lives. The transition is perfectly explicable in terms of Sachs' own intellectual and political development, but it sits uneasily with the earlier analysis of John's inner conflict as a rural African inadequately prepared for life in an urban environment. My concern in pointing to some of the differences in the two versions is not to catch Sachs out, or to suggest which is more correct. Rather, it is to indicate that Sachs' account of John in both versions cannot possibly be divorced from his own conceptions as analyst and author. Sachs' understanding of South Africa changes between the writing of *Black Hamlet* and *Black Anger,* but he continues to project his own views onto John. The essentially unequal nature of the relationship between the two men does not alter significantly. And Sachs is no less ready to intervene directly in John's life. Not only does he reconstruct John's life retrospectively, he does so prospectively as well.

Upon discovering John in his piteous condition in Soweto, Sachs once again sets about restoring his confidence and direction. Significantly, the breakthrough appears to come when Sachs arrives with a copy of the newly published *Black Hamlet*. He then proceeds to read the book to John, inviting him to make comments as they go along. Sachs reports that the book made a "tremendous impression" on John. He also indicates that John was "puzzled" by some of the psychological interpretations offered in the text. But Sachs does not reveal whether this surprise was coupled with understanding born of self-recognition. Nor does he provide us with a satisfactory account of John's reaction to being the subject of a book (Sachs, 1947a, p. 283).

As well as reading the printed text of *Black Hamlet* to John, Sachs provides him with various medications (such as aspirin, tonics, and vitamins) for the purpose of treating patients. Sachs refers to this as "a sort of collaboration" and insists that John refers those patients with serious physical illnesses back to him. As a result of this cooperation,

John's medical practice is reestablished on a sound footing. Sachs does not explicitly claim that he is the instrument of John's recovery, though he does attribute it to "the analytic situation as a whole," the implication being that their discussions around the reading of *Black Hamlet* somehow play a cathartic role (Sachs, 1947a, p. 294).

By 1940 John's life is transformed. We see him surrounded by the "educated, cultured Africans" (such as N'komo) Sachs had introduced him to, and acting responsibly as a community leader. John attempts to mediate (unsuccessfully) in a tense situation between Basuto and Shangaan workers in the Benoni location ("Vandi"); he intervenes in a dispute between the Sofasonke Party and the Vigilance Committee in neighboring "Shantytown" (Orlando); and he addresses meetings and provides advice during the 1944 Alexandra ("Nandi") bus boycott. The victory of the boycotters in this epic struggle is experienced by John as "his own personal achievement" (Sachs, 1947a, p. 323).[22] And when, in 1945, Sachs says good-bye to John before leaving for a period of research and teaching in the United States, he reports that John is filled with hope, and "looking beyond to a new vision—a bond with his people in America" (p. 324). It is thus with the image of John as a motivated, politically conscious, and psychically independent individual that *Black Anger* concludes.

One must surely read the final section of *Black Anger* with a measure of skepticism. It is a highly compressed, almost hurried account of some eight years and is written in an instructive style. (Notably, one of the most didactic speeches—Tshakdada's account of the "new African"—is closely modeled on an article written by Herbert Dhlomo in Sachs' journal, *The Democrat*).[23] Like its earlier version, *Black Anger* ends on an upbeat note with a sense of resolution, but it is altogether less convincing. In *Black Hamlet* the nature of this resolution is psychological: John has, through the process of his analysis with Sachs, come to terms with the destructive conflicts inherent in his personality, and we are led to believe that he is prepared to return to Johannesburg, educate Daniel, and work for interracial understanding. *Black Anger* proves that this outcome was not realized, and John instead becomes hopelessly enmeshed by his life-situation as a black person in South Africa. The

---

[22]For more on the Alexandra bus boycotts see articles by Stadler and Lodge (1981) in: *Working Papers in Southern African Studies, Vol. 2,* ed. P. Bonner. Johannesburg, S.A.: Ravan Press, pp. 228–257, 258–303.

[23]Dhlomo, H. I. E. (1945), Racial attitudes: An African view-point. In *The Democrat,* 17 November 1945.

suggestion at the conclusion of *Black Anger* is that John's further contact with Sachs and his discovery of himself as a political agent is a more lasting form of personal liberation with implications for society as a whole. Thus Sachs (1947a) ends *Black Anger* by saying: "And thus it was that this story, which was to have been read by a limited number of scientists, became the story of John the man, written to be read by everyone" (p. 324).

CONCLUSION

The story of *Black Hamlet* and its update, *Black Anger,* is capable of sustaining multiple readings and interpretations. In this paper I have concentrated on the interaction between the two principal figures, John Chavafambira and Wulf Sachs. I have sought to explain the complexity of their relationship by counterposing their shared professional and intellectual interests against their differing motivations and objective life situations. In order to contextualize their relationship I have located the story in the context of the history of the migration of rural Africans to South Africa's mining and industrial heartland in the first decades of this century; the dynamic social, cultural, and intellectual milieu of urban Johannesburg in the 1930s and 40s; and the broad political processes that conditioned the uneasy and tentative nature of black–white contact at this time. An understanding of this context significantly enhances our appreciation of the circumstances under which the protagonists of our story engage with each other. But the individuality of both is never wholly subsumed by the structural forces that operate upon them.

Black Hamlet and *Black Anger* may perhaps be read most appropriately as a political parable or allegory. The books tell, in novelistic form, the story of John's awakening *through* Sachs (i.e., both via the author's narrative voice and as a consequence of his active agency). This contradiction lies at the heart of our interpretive difficulties. It sets up a series of ambiguities, the essence of which was captured in the unwitting remark by a reviewer who claimed that Sachs "found John a simple native, and he left him a man. . . . For John Chavafambira, whose story this is, is transformed in the course of it from an abused and ignorant native into a militant leader of his people" (Dunham, 1947).

This gloss is perhaps a telling indication of how contemporary audiences might have understood the message of the story. As readers today, however, we are left with a number of unanswered and possibly unanswerable questions: in particular, whose story *is* this? who is transformed, and by whom?

Black Hamlet can perhaps also be understood as an expression of a deep ambivalence within Sachs himself. This highly imaginative and creative figure was unable to resolve the tension between his passionate advocacy of psychoanalysis and his growing awareness that South Africa's problems were rooted in structural inequalities that could only be addressed politically. One consequence of this tension is that *Black Hamlet* is inadequate as a purely psychoanalytic study—a point nicely captured by Sybille Yates (1938), who reviewed the book for the *International Journal of Psychoanalysis*. She argued that Sachs had not succeeded from the psychoanalytic point of view: "[C]ertainly he has used the method of free association, but from what can be gathered, the transference situation was hardly dealt with. In fact the writer reproaches himself that he has not been concerned over 'John' as a patient, but only as a subject of research. No true psychoanalysis can be done under these conditions" (p. 251).

Yates was undoubtedly correct about the technical deficiencies of the work from the psychoanalytic point of view. She was also justified (1938) in arguing that the book was mainly of interest "as a sociological study of the Negro problem in South Africa" (p. 252). What Yates did not appreciate, however, is that even if the "transference" is not demonstrated, a form of "countertransference" is more clearly evident. It is demonstrated in relation to Sachs' political and intellectual development, and to the extent that John becomes the vehicle for Sachs' own changing conceptions of South African society. Sachs himself is inscribed in the "John" of Black Hamlet, a figure who is an individual in his own right as well as a collective or composite symbol of hope for the future.

These complexities underline a fundamental ambivalence within Sachs himself, which blunted his effectiveness both as a pioneer of psychoanalysis in South Africa and as a political activist. This contradiction was incisively brought out in the obituary to Sachs carried by the *International Journal of Psychoanalysis:* "The conflict in himself between the thoughtful investigator and the revolutionary, though it may have enriched his personality, weakened his fervor as a revolutionary and blunted his perceptions as a scientist. But he who was so energetic was not in haste to make big social changes: he was an educator of the free, not a guide for slaves."[24]

---

[24]Obituary in the *International Journal of Psychoanalysis* XXXI, 4, 1950:288–289. See also *The Democrat Monthly,* July 1949:13–16.

BIBLIOGRAPHY

DANEEL, M. L. (1971), *Old and New in Southern Shona Independent Churches, Vol. 1.* The Hague, Netherlands: Mouton.

DHLOMO, H. I. E. (1945), Racial attitudes: An African viewpoint. In: *The Democrat,* November 17, 1945.

DUBOW, S. (1989), *Racial Segregation and the Origins of Apartheid in South Africa, 1919-36.* London: Macmillan and New York: St Martin's Press.

_____ (1991), Mental testing and the understanding of race in twentieth-century South Africa. In: *Science, Medicine, and Cultural Imperialism,* ed. T. Meade and M. Walker. New York: St. Martin's Press.

DUNHAM, B. (1947), Review of *Black Hamlet.* In: *Book Find News,* August, 1947.

EDGAR, R. (1992), *An African American in South Africa: The Travel Notes of Ralph J. Bunche, 28 September 1937-1 January 1938.* Athens, Ohio: Ohio University Press.

FREUD, S. (1992), *The Diary of Sigmund Freud 1929-1939. A Record of the Final Decade.* ed. M. Molnar. London: The Hogarth Press.

HELLMAN, E. (1948), *Rooiyard. A Sociological Survey of an Urban African Slum Yard.* Cape Town: Oxford University Press.

_____ (1949), Dr. Wulf Sachs: A tribute. *The Zionist Record,* July 1, 1949.

HIRSON, B. (1949), *Yours for the Union: Class and Community Struggles in South Africa, 1930-1947.* London: Zed Books.

HUNTER, M. (1934), The study of culture contact. *Africa,* VII: 335-350.

JONES, E. (1957), *Sigmund Freud: Life and Work, Vol. 3.* London: Hogarth Press.

KOCH, E. (1983), Without visible means of subsistence: slumyard culture in Johannesburg 1918-1940. In: *Town and Countryside in the Transvaal,* ed. B. Bozzoli. Johannesburg, South Africa: Ravan Press, pp. 151-175.

LODGE, T. (1981), "We are being punished because we are poor": The bus boycotts of Evaton and Alexandra, 1955-1957. In: *Working Papers in Southern African Studies, Vol. 2,* ed. P. Bonner. Johannesburg: Ravan Press, pp. 258-303.

OBITUARY TO W. SACHS in the *International Journal of Psychoanalysis* XXXI, 4, 1950: 288-289.

RANGER, T. O. (1970), *The African Voice in Southern Rhodesia 1898-1930.* London: Heinemann.

_____ (1985), *Peasant Consciousness and the Guerilla War in Zimbabwe.* London: James Currey.

_____ (1989), Missionaries, migrants and the Manyika: The invention of ethnicity in Zimbabwe. In: *The Creation of Tribalism in Southern Africa,* ed. Vail. London: James Currey, pp. 118-150.

SACHS, W. (1933), The insane native: An introduction to a psychological study. *S. African J. Science,* 30:706-713.

_____ (1934), *Psycho-Analysis. Its Meaning and Practical Applications.* London: Cassell.

_____ (1937), *Black Hamlet: The Mind of an African Negro Revealed by Psychoanalysis.* London: Geoffrey Bles.

_____ (1947a), *Black Anger.* New York: Grove Press.

_____ (1947b), The mind of a witch-doctor. *Book Find News,* August.

_____ (n.d.), African tragedy: The life of a native "doctor." Unpublished manuscript. University of the Witwatersrand Manuscripts Department, Cullen Library, A2120.

STADLER, A. (1981), A long way to walk: Bus boycotts in Alexandra, 1940-1945. In:

Working Papers in Southern African Studies, Vol. 2, ed. P. Bonner. Johannesburg: Ravan Press, pp. 228–257.

VAUGHAN, M. (1991), *Curing Their Ills: Colonial Power and African Illness.* Cambridge: Polity Press.

YATES, S. L. (1938), Review of *Black Hamlet. Internat. J. of Pyscho-Anal.,* 19:251–252.

10

A Psychoanalytic Study
of Argentine Soccer[1]

MARCELO M. SUÁREZ-OROZCO

If one were to make a list of major social events in which millions of men, in most corners of this earth, invest curiously large amounts of affective energy, the soccer spectacle would most likely occupy a comfortable place among the 10 top such events. Despite this, a glance at the scholarly works on the psychosocial nature of the soccer spectacle shows an alarming lack of coherent documentation and insight into the dynamics of the cathexis the soccer fan so intensely invests in the soccer show.

As a child growing up in Argentina, I became a captive of the addicting webs of the soccer spectacle. It is perhaps this early involvement I had with the game that led me to search for the tools in anthropology, folklore, and psychology needed to unravel the meaning of this show, which (as my distorted retrospection now tells me) had such a narcotizing effect on me as a child.

The first inkling of the questions I raise here was perhaps formulated when, as a child, I was taken most weekends to the soccer stadiums

[1]An earlier and shorter version of this essay appeared in *The Journal of Psychoanalytic Anthropology* Vol. 5(1):7–28. It was then, as it is now, dedicated to Alan Dundes. The essay won the first (1986) *Ruth Boyer Award for Excellence in Psychological Anthropology* annually awarded to a graduate student in the Department of Anthropology at the University of California, Berkeley. I am indebted to Professor Stanley Brandes and Professor Howard Stein for their insightful comments and suggestions. Marcelo Mario Suárez-Orozco, a recovering soccer fan and author of many books and articles in psychological anthropology, is Fellow at the Center for Advanced Study in the Behavioral Sciences, Stanford, and Associate Professor of Anthropology, UCSD.

by neighbors to join others in passionately rooting for our home team. Although then, in my frantic shouting and mimicking of the older fans, I had no clear idea of what was really going on, I must have had the first real feeling of social belonging. My soccer cult continued when I was a bit older, and I was allowed (not without frowns from my parents) to go to the stadiums, no longer with a guardian, but now with my own adolescent friends. Soon we all recognized the real dangers in going to a stadium, where up to 20,000 fans for each of two rival teams gathered to root and thus (at least in theory) help their teams win. However, the emotional involvement, the delirious and unrestrained shouting, the ritualized exchange of insults between fans of the same and opposite teams, their vicious throwing of bottles and stones at each other, and the general state of dissociation bring to attention (even to the eye of an untrained adolescent) the fact that much more than mere rooting for the victory of one's team is occurring in soccer stadiums throughout Argentina (and probably in other places of the world, where the soccer phenomenon has reached equivalent dimensions). My parents' frowns were thus not without reason.

The questions this paper explores include: Why are hundreds of thousands of men attracted to soccer stadiums every weekend all over Argentina? What force is there in the soccer spectacle that addicts men, possessing them during the 90 minutes in which 22 players, 11 for each team, try to kick a ball—in its ancient form a pig's bladder (Mafud, 1967), sometimes stuffed with hair (Pickford, 1940)—into the rival team's goal more times than that team kicks it into their goal?

SUFFICIENT REASONS

Scholarly works on the psychosocial nature of the soccer spectacle have for the most part been conducted by either European (both British and Continental) or Latin American researchers.[2] These writers have proposed a wide array of sufficient reasons to explain what, in the professional soccer game, attracts millions of fans to the stadiums every weekend all over the globe where soccer has become a central sociological event. In this section of the paper, I shall review these proposed sufficient reasons and briefly evaluate their strengths and weaknesses in explaining the unusual behavior of fans at the stadiums.

Buytendijk, in his *Le Football: Une Etude Psychologique* (1952), argues that spectators seek sensationalism in the soccer stadium. This after-the-fact statement is inherently circular and does not satisfactorily

---

[2]With, of course, exceptions, among others Yale sociologist Janet Lever (1969, 1972).

explain what underlies the fans' seeking it in the first place. Buytendijk also argues that fans seek diversion from the pressures of everyday life. At first glance, no one would disagree with this line of argument; however, it does not address why it is that the fans overwhelmingly seek the soccer game and not, for example, polo or other diverting shows to the degree they follow soccer. Nor would any person who has seen a considerable number of soccer spectacles really believe his proposition that soccer is pressure free.

A quick glance at the statistics of tragic violence on the stadiums (Taylor, 1969, 1971a,b) would convince even those who have never seen a professional soccer game that the opposite is true.

Buytendijk further argues that the game offers fans a sense of common belonging with their fellow fans and their beloved players. Regrettably, he does not document the specifics of structural scapegoating the "other" as a means of defining one's group. This aspect of scapegoating, or more precisely, projecting in the psychoanalytic usage of the term, as I shall later document, appears of central importance in the Argentinian soccer stadium as a means of defining not just one's group but also one's masculinity. Interestingly, and in accordance with Foster's (1979) image of "limited good and machismo" (p. 130), the fan must define his manliness at the expense of that of other fans. But as we shall see, this is only the tip of the psychodynamic iceberg. Last, Buytendijk views soccer as offering the fans an opportunity to be experts, at least in this area of their existence, due to the well-known and rather simple rules that govern the game. Although this view of the "cerebral fan" does have some validity, the affective and irrational involvement of the fan in the game is, in my opinion, a far more fundamental underlying factor that must be accounted for if we are to understand the basic dynamics of the fan's behavior.

Da Silva (1970) views spectators as inherently voluble and emotional, and he argues that any frustration will automatically lead to aggression, "the most frequent being verbal aggression directed toward the athlete, who becomes an easy and readily available scapegoat" (p. 307). Because he fails to document specific instances of verbal aggression toward the athlete,[3] and as my data indicate that the most frequent form of verbal aggression is not so much toward the players as toward the rival team's

---

[3]Da Silva does, however, present the case of a soccer player who was referred to him with "a serious psychological problem" due mainly to his being sensitive to "the shouting of the rooters" (p. 309). However, the author fails to include a description of what it was that the rooters shouted that had such an impact on the player's psychological functioning.

fans, at least in the Argentinian case, we must question the validity of his *ex cathedra* statement.[4] Further, I must note that the frustration-aggression psychological hypothesis of Dollard, Doob, Miller, Mower, and Sears (1939) inherent in da Silva's argument can be seriously questioned in its ability to explain aggression in the soccer field. Consider Hopcraft's (1968) discussion of the problem of violence in and around the British soccer stadiums: "Initially it seemed possible to align the vandalism directly with the disappointment of supporters who had traveled far to see their side go down. Later on it became clear that the result of the game had no causative effect on this kind of behavior at all: win, lose, or draw, there could be trouble or there could be none" (p. 183). Again, dissociative, irrational behavior with no apparent causes appears to be a recurring theme of the behavior of both British and Argentinian fans, and I have no reason to believe that Brazilian fans differ that much.

For da Silva (1970), aggression in the stadium provides fans "a catharsis and an outlet not only for the spectator's sportive frustrations, but also for his economic and even existential anxieties" (p. xxx). Again, he regrettably fails to outline and illustrate the dynamics of the catharsis. Further, his implied understanding that it is the violent nature of the spectacle that attracts fans to the stadiums is really an oversimplification of the complex dynamics of the spectacle. I shall briefly evaluate more critically this hypothesis.

Freud's student, Helene Deutsch, brilliantly explored the relationship between castration fears, associated in their genesis with oedipal rivalry, and the attraction males have for soccer. Briefly, she viewed (1926) soccer as a mechanism used, even by nonmarkedly neurotic individuals, for the "projection of a source of anxiety into the outside world and discharge of the anxiety" (p. 226). Later I shall more thoroughly explore Deutsch's thesis in the context of our understanding of the symbolism of the game itself. Suffice it to say here that from her argument it logically follows that one reason, among many others, that millions of males are attracted to stadiums every weekend is the possibility the game offers them to "project" themselves into their idols, with whom they obviously identify, and with them vicariously to master "the ball," and by extension their own masculinity. I shall return to this point.

Dunning and Elias have done more than any other English-speaking

---

[4]Note that I am not arguing that verbal aggression toward the athletes is not common in Argentina; what I am arguing is that it may not be "the most frequent" form of verbal aggression found in the stadiums.

scholars to document the history and sociology of soccer.[5] Dunning (1967) views soccer as an institutionalized means of channeling aggression: "Many of the more brutal practices of earlier times were rooted out, but the chances for participation in a physical struggle were not eliminated entirely" (p. 884). By extending his logic we can infer that the fans are attracted to the show, at least in part, to take pleasure in watching the "physical struggle" between the teams. The idea of fans taking sadistic pleasure in watching the violence on the field and around them is shared by Hopcraft (1968), who sees soccer as being an essentially conflictual sport: "People enjoy watching violence, and they are fed it in children's comics, in pop music, and by cinema and television. When it occurs on the football terraces there is relish as well as condemnation in the way the seated ranks and the newspapers respond to it" (p. 185).

Although this is partially true, it does not explain why fans are addicted to soccer and not to other more violent games.

Later, Elias and Dunning (1970) argue that the spectacle and color of professional soccer functions as a relief from the constraint and control of civilization. Fans are perceived as searching for excitement in "unexciting societies." No one would really question this argument, but the question still remains, why soccer and not other "colorful" spectacles?

Frankenberg (1957) views soccer as a symbol of village prestige and unity in the face of the outside world, in the community he studied in North Wales. Soccer is viewed as a functional, cohesive bond that provides the community a sense of common destiny and belonging, especially when relating to the outside. This may be true for the rather remote village he studied, but in my opinion it would be a mistake to extend this rather romantic view of the game to the rest of world soccer. The inherent conflictual nature of the game (Hopcraft, 1968; Taylor, 1969, 1971a,b) makes the extension of Frankenberg's observations in North Wales to soccer generically untenable.[6]

---

[5]See Dunning (1971), a selection of readings on the sociology of sport, which provides the student of theoretical works on soccer the best single location of articles dealing with the historical development and sociology of British soccer. See also Dunning and Elias (1971) for a well-documented historical account of the development of the game in England from the early Middle Ages to the end of the 19th century. A careful description of the most significant structural changes in the developing game is the central feature of this sociological survey.

[6]It would be naive not to recognize that intragroup conflict and violence are active aspects of the soccer spectacle. I myself have witnessed countless times fans rooting for the same team exchange insults and fists over who the real star of their team was, how the team should be aligned, or who the captain should be.

Lever, in her theoretical works on soccer in Brazil, describes the game as "the opium" (1969) of the Brazilian people and more generally as "a Brazilian way of life" (1972). However, "to make such a statement is not to give an explanation of why some seek opiates and others do not" (De Vos, 1978, p. 7), an insightful comment on Marxists' views of religion. And the same applies to our research problem: Why do fans seek the soccer and not other "opiates"?

Mafud, in his *Sociologia del Futbol* (1967), views the game, following Buytendijk (1952), as a basic regression from culture to nature. The game attracts crowds, in the eyes of this Argentine sociologist, for a different set of reasons. First, borrowing from Buytendijk, soccer is pictured as a diversion, allowing men, both players and fans, to escape everyday reality. Second, the game offers fans and players alike an opportunity to discharge aggression by structuring groups against each other. And third, in Mafud's reasoning, the game attracts crowds by offering them a *chivo emisario* (p. 111) or "scapegoat" into which to project *la propia culpa, el propio miedo, la propia agresividad sobre el otro o sobre los otros* (one's own guilt, one's own fear, one's own aggression into the other or the others).[7] Although he briefly discusses the mechanics of scapegoating, his examples are few, and clearly do need further elaboration to prove his hypothesis to be useful.

Others, for example Patrick (1963), a victim of 19th-century unilinear evolution theorizing, sees games such as soccer as offering a devolutionary return to savagery, thus allowing the "higher centers" of the brain to momentarily rest. Mender (1956) views games such as soccer as intensifying human vitality. Dundes (1978) reports the following views of ancient soccer: "The ancestral form of football, a game more like rugby or soccer, was interpreted as a solar ritual—with a disc-shaped rock or object supposedly representing the sun"[8] (p. 76) and also "as a fertility ritual intended to ensure agricultural abundance" (Ibid.). Pickford (1940, 1941) in his rather romantic historical studies of the origin and development of the game, sees it again as a constructive use of aggression. Reaney (1916), in her doctoral thesis, views the popularity of soccer in the fact that the game brings into play the primitive instinct of propelling a missile toward an aim (the goal). Schwartz (1973) reviews what he considers to be the most important determinants of spectator sports. For him, the pleasure of observing excellence hypothesis, the need for excitement hypothesis, and the release of tension hypothesis are probably

---

[7]All translations are mine.
[8]Dundes refers to Johnson (1929).

the most important in determining fans' attendance at the stadiums. However, Schwartz grimly concludes, these hypotheses remain to be tested.

The problem with all of the preceding views on soccer's popularity as being due primarily to its acting as an outlet for aggression has been correctly outlined by Dundes (1978) in his psychoanalytic study of American football: "It is insufficient to state that football offers an appropriate outlet for the expression of aggression" (p. 76). It would be an oversimplification "to single out violence as the sole or even primary reason for the game's popularity" (Arens quoted in Dundes, 1978). As other, far more violent sports do exist in Argentina (boxing, wrestling, etc.), and are far less popular than soccer, Dundes' objection applies also in our case.

Stokes' ingenious study points, in my opinion, to a more fruitful area of research by looking at the symbolism inherent in the game itself. His psychoanalytic study of ball games views soccer specifically as a stage in which oedipal fantasies are acted out in a disguised, egosyntonic way. Each team is perceived as defending the symbolic maternal vagina (goal) from the aggressive father (rival team). At the same time, the teams are seen as trying to conquer new lands (women), thus developmentally moving from infancy to adulthood. In Stokes' own words (1956):

> When football teams canter out of the natal tunnel beneath a stand, the crowds applaud, surrender to them the field of play. Then, each team defends the goal at his back; in front is the new land, the new woman, whom they strive to possess in the interest of preserving the mother inviolate, in order, as it were, to progress from infancy to adulthood: at the same time, the defensive role is the father's; he opposes the forward of youth of the opposition [p. 187].

His theoretical bias made him, in my view arbitrarily, perceive the goals as either the symbolic maternal vagina or the symbolic vagina of the "new woman." This view is contrary to my data, which in fact show that the goal, which each team defends at its back, is symbolic of the players' masculinity. However, Stokes' symbolic interpretation opens new avenues to arrive at the possible psychosocial meanings of the game.

Two other important works on soccer must be evaluated before we move on to our own analysis. Veccia, in his "Sunday Orgasm" (1976), states *ex cathedra* that soccer can be viewed as dramatizing collective unconscious impulses of a sexual and aggressive nature. This is easily detected, Veccia argues, in the game's symbols and in the spectator's emotions. The conduct of the athletes, officials and spectators is interpreted as having a sexual content, with specific sexual meaning. The author further argues that voyeurism, deindividuation and interaction are the three most important factors that induce spectators to attend soccer stadiums. His failure to illustrate his imaginative points with even a single datum makes his propositions mere speculations.

In what remains the best researched monograph on the soccer phenomenon in Europe, Vinnai (1973) reviews the most salient features of the spectacle, emphasizing its relation to the larger society. Vinnai views the soccer game as providing a stage for the fans to observe the inherent nature of their working hours. "Here, twenty-two sportsmen provide the thousands on the terraces with routinized performances paralleling those of working hours" (p. 39).

Thus, for Vinnai the soccer spectacle appears to fulfill the same function myths serve in the views of Lévi-Strauss (1973): It is a stage upon which the inherent contradictions of life are enacted in a disguised form. This view is in direct contradiction to most of the scholars discussed above, who view the game as offering both players and fans an escape from reality. Furthermore, for Vinnai (1973) the spectacle has become a mere capitalistic plot, preventing the working classes from directing their energies to their true enemy, the bourgeoisie. "The same holds for the struggle for a better life, but the pseudoactivity of football canalizes the energies which could shatter the existing power structures" (p. 90). He concludes: "Sport, which has long belonged to the realm of unfree activity, is also a part of the system of capitalist mass culture, designed to keep the victims of the alienated industrial apparatus under close control" (p. 14). This Marxist view of soccer, which reduces the game to a mere mirror of the struggle of the classes, fails to address the issues of meaning and value that both players and fans attach to the game. Further, Vinnai's etic construct does not really address the obvious problem of why fans should get such orgasmic pleasure, as they in fact do, in observing their own tragic struggle being enacted.

THE SPECTACLE AND THE UNCONSCIOUS

In this section, I shall describe and interpret soccer stadium ethos as revealed by both its folklore and game symbolism. An emphasis will be placed on the former, with the intention of explaining why it is that fans are so emotionally involved with the soccer spectacle. Further, an insight into the meaning of the symbols inherent in the game itself will help us understand why the game triggers such peculiar fantasies and behavior from the fans.

I have chosen to discuss fans' folklore following the proposition endorsed and elegantly documented by Dundes (1976) that folklore is unconscious and that "among its functions, folklore provides a socially sanctioned outlet for the expression of what cannot be articulated in the usual direct way" (p. 1503). Dundes goes on to argue, "It is precisely in jokes, folk tales, folk songs, proverbs, children's games, gestures, etc., that anxieties can be vented " (p. xxx). The Argentinian fan, as will be documented, has plenty of anxieties to vent, especially about his masculinity.

Thus, borrowing from Geertz (1973), a "thick description" of the "deep" aspects of the Argentinian soccer spectacle, including fans' folk songs and verbal duels, may help us uncover the possible underlying dynamics that motivate men to go to stadiums and what the spectacle may tell us more generally about Argentinian male psychology.

A typical journey to the soccer stadium starts characteristically after the big Sunday lunch, when the average working-class fan is picked up by the *barra,* the "gang," who are of course all fans for the same team.[9] The soccer show is, for all practical purposes, an all-male spectacle; only males play it professionally,[10] and the overwhelming majority of the fans are male.[11] With this point in mind, I turn to a description of a typical day at the soccer stadium. As *la barra*[12] meets, they will immediately begin a passionate discussion of how their team should line up, guess

---

[9]In Argentina first division games are played Sundays and the less important, but also spectacular, second division games are played Saturdays.

[10]I must note that very early in the game's history the English Football Association excluded women from playing the game. In 1946 the Association exhorted its members to "take steps to prevent clubs letting their grounds or otherwise creating opportunities for female players to participate in irregular football matches" (quoted in Vinnai 1973, p. 75).

[11]In the smaller, less-known stadiums, I would argue, soccer is essentially an all-male affair, with all-male fans. Women are sporadically seen in the more modern and bigger stadiums, but almost always accompanied by men, and typically in the expensive *plateas,* or covered seats under a roof, the best section of the stadium. This more expensive, rather small section, reserved for officials and the upper classes that occasionally find amusement in the spectacle, is separated from the larger terraces by wire fences. Note that for all practical purposes women are not "real" fans, and go to the stadiums by and large to find exotic amusement.

[12]*La barra* are usually neighbors who have most likely grown up together. Their beloved team has been at times (usually of victory) a source of group cohesion, but when disaster strikes and their team loses, in-group conflict is sure to occur. Fights over team issues may break lifelong friendships, especially among the most emotional fans.

who of their beloved stars will first score a goal, and perhaps anticipate in paranoid fashion that the referee for today's match has probably been "bought" by the rival team.[13] The moral integrity of the referee will surely be a topic of discussion on the way back home from the game if one's team lost in a close match.

By now, as they get closer to the stadium, they will begin to be increasingly excited, especially as they join other *barras* of their team and, waving the team's precious flag, chant lines such as:

Soy de Boca	*soy de Boca,*	*de Boca yo soy.*
(I) am of Boca,	(I) am of Boca,	for Boca I am.

"Boca" is the name of their team. As they eventually meet *barras* from the opposite team, the chanting will get louder. Cursing and ritualized insulting will automatically start. The more elaborated songs and insults will not start until the fans for both teams are inside the stadium and the game has begun.

Once inside the stadium the more verbal and more fanatic rooters[14] will lead their *barras* to the terraces in back of one of the two goals, facing directly the barras of the other team, who traditionally will be in back of the opposite goal. Facing each other, on opposite sides of the soccer field, separated by its length, thousands of fans will loyally join their fellows in chanting, insulting, and humiliating the rival team's fans, the rival team's players, their coach and owner, the game's referee, and, when felt necessary, the players of one's own team. The neutral spectator will avoid the heated polar ends of the stadium and will most likely buy the more expensive ticket for either the safer *plateas* (covered roof) along the lateral side of the stadium, or will find a seat in the uncovered portion, along the opposite lateral side to the *platea,* thus facing the *platea,* and having to his right hand and to his left hand the fans of each of the two playing teams. Although this type of more neutral, less fanatic observer does have a role in the soccer spectacle, for obvious reasons of space I will discuss only the folklore of the more active fans, who, due to their larger numbers, form a more relevant group to this study.

THE MACHO ETHOS

With this more or less typical background setting in mind, we can now begin to document soccer stadium folklore. The pregame peak of fans'

---

[13]I myself have countless times observed and participated in all three of these hypothetical topics of conversation among fans.

[14]Sometimes called the "owners" of the *barra* rooting for a given team.

dissociation will reach its more notable degree as the players of both teams emerge from an underground tunnel. At this point the fans will compulsively shake their team's flag and throw clouds of confetti, and sooner or later the fans for one of the two teams, let us call them team A, may chant this commonly heard song at the beginning of games:

Vamos a ganar,	*vamos a ganar*
We will win,	we will win
Porque sino	*los vamos a vejar*
Because if not	we will rape them

This song is particularly common at the beginning of games that are, in one way or another, decisive and which one's team has to win at all costs lest catastrophe should follow. So, this song is used to warn the fans and the players of the other team that if one's team does not win this critical game they will rape the members of the rival team. Of course, almost never do such homosexual rapes actually occur. Nevertheless the chant is an important datum, as it represents a vehicle to threaten the rivals to put them in the shameful position of a passive recipient of a homosexual encounter. Thus, indicating that if they cannot attain power (victory) on one level by winning the game, they will have to assert their superiority on other levels: by homosexually overpowering their rivals with rape. This need to assert one's masculinity at the expense of victimizing the other appears to be a recurring pattern in soccer stadium folklore. But before further speculating on this theme, let us search in the data for more convincing evidence.

To the above threat the enraged fans of the other team (let us call them team B) may respond with the following statement about the nature of their team:

No tenemos a Maradona,	*no tenemos a Filliol*
We do not have Maradona,	we do not have Filliol
Pero sí tenemos huevos,	*huevos para salir campeon.*
But yes we have eggs,	eggs to come out champion.

Freely translated, this means "we do not have Maradona playing for us, we do not have Filliol playing for us, but yes, we do have the balls, the balls it takes to come out champions." In other words, even though they do not have Mr. Maradona playing on their team, the recently disgraced in a drug-related scandal but once loved and respected star of Argentine soccer (nicknamed "the white Pelé"), or the almost equally famous goalkeeper Mr. Filliol, they do have the hyperphallusness (*los huevos,* i.e., "balls") that is, in their estimation, required to win the championship and by extension that very game.

A concern with the attributes and power inherent in possessing a hyperphallic sexual organ is also evident in other aspects of Argentinian folklore. For example, a big compliment paid to Juan Domingo Peron (nicknamed *el macho* by his loyal *Peronistas*) was that he had a sexual organ that was bigger than a whole ham. As this song indicates:

> *La poronga de Peron*
> The prick of Peron
>
> *Es más grande que un jamon*
> Is bigger than a ham

In their view Peron, the true macho, was a great man in part because he had a great phallus, bigger than a whole ham. Both songs thus mirror the Argentinian popular belief, held by many men, that a "real macho" must be endowed with a large penis, which in turn is a metaphoric source of power. In the soccer stadium we can see this occurring: Although the fans admit lacking great players, their team and they themselves do have *huevos* (eggs = "balls"), which are the ultimate symbol of masculinity, superiority, and courage. The inherent power derived from their phalluses will enable them to subjugate all rival teams and thus eventually win the championship.

If the two hypothetical teams playing our typical game were really mismatched, a song such as the following may be heard:

> *Señor Armando, Señor Armando*
> Mr. Armando, Mr. Armando (club's owner)
>
> *A su cuadrito lo cogemos caminando*
> To your little team we fuck walking

Freely translated: "Señor Armando, we screw your little team effortlessly." I myself heard this song at the Banfield Club stadium some years back when the home team, a rather small and second-rate team, was facing the powerful, most-feared of the nation's teams, owned by Mr. Armando. The Banfield (in reality a little team) fans began nervously to sing to the owner of the powerful Boca Juniors team, Mr. Armando, how their team was "screwing his little team," not even playing hard but just casually "walking" the field.

This song, I argue, is of importance, as it illuminates several theoretical issues. First, the song shows how in the unconscious mind of the fan, as revealed by this folklore item, the game itself symbolizes a homosexual encounter. Thus the "Mr. Armando, we play better soccer than your little team" becomes "We screw your little team."[15] This point will be of importance in refuting Stokes' (1956) proposition that the goals in the soccer stadium symbolize the "maternal" and "new woman" vaginas. In fact, in Argentina at least, the folk themselves in their projective symbolic systems associate the goals with their masculinity, more specifically their *culos* (the backside). I shall briefly return to this critical point.

A second critical process that appears to recur in the Argentine data, which the above song beautifully illustrates, is the process of "projective inversion" as described by Dundes (1976). For Dundes, projection in the psychoanalytic sense occurs in two distinct ways. Direct projections, in folklore, are "more or less direct translations of reality into fantasy." But projective inversion occurs with those "human problems which evidently require more elaborate disguise" (p. 1521). In our last song we have a clear example of projective inversion. The fans for the lesser team — who undoubtedly fear, like all other fans in Argentina do, the powerful Boca Juniors' team and fans — project, in an inverted disguise, their own well-founded fears of being "screwed" in the stadium by their rivals.[16] Thus, the unconscious fear "you are going to screw us" becomes the pseudoaggressive, egosyntonic "we will screw you effortlessly."

Back to our stadium. At this point of the heated verbal exchanges, Boca's fans may want to warn Banfield's fans not to step over the line and remind them who they are:

> *Hinchada, hinchada, hinchada hay una sola*
> Fan, Fan, Fan, there exists only one
>
> *Hinchada es la de Boca que le rompe el culo a todas*
> It is the fan of Boca that breaks the ass of all

---

[15]Please note that no a priori theoretical categories are being imposed on the data; they just emerge.

[16]Boca Juniors Club fans are feared perhaps more than any other fans, due to their reputation, most likely deserved, of being more violent, destructive, and in general more aggressive than most other fans.

which freely translates, "Real fans are Boca's, who fuck and tear open the anuses of all other fans." This song, in its evident manifest content, indicates that the fans, and obviously by extension, real men, real machos, are Boca's, who in fact, as noted previously, have a reputation for being hypermanly machos, because they are superphallic (i.e., they have "balls"). They are superphallic because they not only force others fans into a passive-recipient homosexual encounter, but also they "tear the anuses open" (*romper:* to tear open or to break) of all other male fans of any and all teams. Another song articulating this fantasy was chanted in Argentina during the 1978 Jules Rimet soccer World Cup. In order to make it to the final rounds, the home team of Argentina had to score a decisive victory (victory by *goleada,* i.e., by scoring many goals) over the Peruvian national team. As they approached the stadium Argentinian fans deliriously chanted,

> *Salta, salta, salta, pequeño canguro*
> Jump, jump, jump, little kangaroo
>
> *hoy a los Peruanos les rompemos el culo*
> today we break the ass of the Peruvians

which freely translates into "Today we will tear open the anuses of the Peruvians."

Beneath such sadistic fantasies, an interesting picture develops that will enable us to explore a dimension of machismo that has largely been ignored by social scientists who have studied the macho syndrome. Machos, as illustrated in their collective fantasies, are sadists who tear open the anuses of other men. Chapman (1967) notes, "Moreover, in many instances the sexual sadist has profound doubts about his sexual adequacy and masculinity, and he attempts to assuage these doubts by exaggerated aggressiveness in his sexual activities" (p. 206). Although, of course, in our folklore data we are dealing with sadistic *fantasies,* and Chapman is describing the psychiatric profile of practicing sadists, nevertheless his point offers us a tool to explore the possible meanings of this aspect of macho behavior.

The important point is that in fact the macho, as documented by his unconscious fantasies, has "profound doubts about his sexual adequacy and masculinity," and these doubts are evident in his paranoid fear of being anally penetrated by other machos. This important point on the psychology of the hypermanly macho, which has emerged from my data, escaped the eyes of other social scientists working on the macho syndrome in other parts of the world (Bolton, 1979; Gilmore and Gilmore, 1979; Chinas, 1973; Fromm and Maccoby, 1970; Foster, 1979). Bolton, for example, describes the macho "ethos" (p. 318) as a set of beliefs, values, attitudes, emotions, and behavioral patterns found most commonly in Latin America. I would add that machismo in Latin America was inherited from Spain. Brandes' (1980) superb documentation of masculine metaphors in southern Spain as well as Gilmore and Gilmore's shallower interpretation of the ontogenesis of machismo in an Andalusian town corroborate my argument.

According to Bolton (1979), for a male to qualify as a true macho, he must "be assertive, powerful, aggressive, and independent" (p. 319).[17] A rather similar profile to our Argentine macho fans. Bolton further argues that a macho competes with other machos, as for example in trying to outdrink them. And there is also the well-known fact that a true macho must dominate his women. However, Bolton fails to discuss the salient feature of machismo, inherent in the Argentine data, that the hypermanly macho is *afraid of being homosexually attacked by other machos.* The macho fear of being anally penetrated is not just limited to my data. As Brandes (1980) reports, "The threat of anal penetration" (p. 95) is an important male concern in southern Spain, which in fact is part of a larger Mediterranean preoccupation (Dundes and Falassi 1975; Dundes, Leach, and Özkök, 1970; Miner and DeVos, 1960) naturally inherited in Latin America.

Fromm and Maccoby (1970), in their study of a Mexican village, also appear to have overlooked the homosexual dimension of the macho syndrome. For them "machismo indicates an attitude of male superiority, a wish to control women and keep them in an inferior position" (p. 16). The point to be made is that the macho, who spends so much psychic energy in maintaining his women in an "inferior position," with all the status anxiety this brings along, must at all times guard his own *mas* (male) *culus* (anus) (Dundes, 1978, p. 87) or "masculinity" from the perceived phallic threat of other males.

Foster (1979) also fails to discuss the possible homosexual aspects of machismo, although he does discuss his idea of the image of "limited good and machismo" in the Mexican village he studied (p. 130). We must not assume that because these eminent social scientists fail to report the possible homosexual dimensions of the hypermanly behaviors of machos, the syndrome must therefore not exist in Mexico. It is interesting to note that the Mexican Nobel-poet and essayist Octavio Paz, in his now

---

[17]My data do not tell us how "independent" Argentine macho fans are.

classic humanistic portrait of Mexican national character, does briefly discuss the possible homosexual components of the Mexican macho. Paz (1961) notes: "It would not be difficult to perceive certain homosexual inclinations also, such as the use and abuse of the pistol, a phallic symbol which discharges death rather than life, and the fondness for exclusively masculine guilds" (p. 82). Of course it is not "difficult to perceive" such homosexual inclinations. What *is* difficult is to understand how and why these inclinations arose in the first place—a topic beyond the scope of this chapter, or to document and interpret how and *why* these tendencies, which seem to be in direct contradiction to all other aspects of macho ethos, surface in their expressive life.[18]

With this understanding in mind, let us return to the soccer spectacle to further document how these homosexual preoccupations surface. A most common song, heard only after one's team has scored a goal, will help us elucidate how the fans themselves, in their unconscious, view the game itself in symbolic terms. This one-liner goes:

> *Oh, oh, oh, por el horto*
> Oh, oh, oh, through the asshole
>
> *Oh, oh, oh, por el horto*
> Oh, oh, oh, through the asshole

Thus, after their team has scored a goal the fans, in orgasmic joy, chant how their team has just put the ball "through the asshole," meaning of course the goal, of the rival team. Here we have further unequivocal evidence that, in the fans' folkloristic free associations, the goals do not in fact symbolize vaginas, as Stokes (1956) asserted, but in the Argentine case they symbolize the *horto* (asshole) of the opposite team. The game, thus, can be viewed not so much as a stage in which oedipal fantasies are acted out, as Stokes suggested, but rather as a stage in which macho homosexual fantasies are acted out, particularly in their need to put other males down, very specifically in the shameful recipient role in a homosexual encounter (perhaps due to an exaggerated fear of being penetrated).

But let's take a more elaborate song to illustrate this basic process.

---

[18]See Gilmore and Gilmore (1979) for an attempt to describe the ontogenesis of machismo in southern Spain, as a "reaction formation against unresolved bisexuality" (p. 283). Amazingly, they fail to report the macho's fear of being anally penetrated, which Brandes (1980) reports in the same region of southern Spain.

Ya todos saben que Brasil está de luto
Now all know that Brazil is mourning

Son todos negros, son todos putos
Are all niggers, are all faggots

which freely translates, "By now all know that Brazil is mourning, they are all a bunch of niggers, they are all a bunch of faggots." An informant of mine heard this song during the 1978 Jules Rimet soccer World Cup played in Argentina. As the Brazilian team, then the natural rival of the Argentine national team, was eliminated from entering the finals, the Argentinian fans all over the joyous city of Buenos Aires took to the streets singing this song. Again, as in other cases, more than one function and meaning can be extracted from the chant. At the surface level the song mirrors the eternal national rivalries between Argentina and its northeastern neighbor, Brazil.[19] Also, at a deeper level of analysis the song nicely illustrates the Freudian process of projecting onto the outside thoughts and affects of a taboo nature that originate within the self. So, again at the surface level, the chant functions to put down the Brazilians by calling them *putos* (faggots), and thus assign them to the passive, recipient role in a homosexual encounter. At the deeper level of meaning we see how these machos' "unresolved bisexuality" (Gilmore and Gilmore, 1979, p. 283) and potential recipient homosexuality is projected onto the rivals.

An important culturally constituted issue in the construction of (homo)sexuality in the Spanish-speaking world surfaces in these songs and the phenomena they relate to. According to Latin American folk definitions male homosexual behavior is only the behavior of a *passive recipient* in a homosexual encounter (i.e., he who is anally penetrated). According to this folk view, the penetrator may not be considered, or indeed consider himself a homosexual, as long as he remains the *active* partner in the sexual act. Note the monumental significance of this folk belief and practice in the context of the AIDS epidemic and its specific impact on the Hispanic population. Many Hispanic males, thinking that AIDS is a problem affecting mainly homosexuals, may think that as long as they are the penetrators and not the penetrated in a homosexual act, they need not to worry about the disease!

Many soccer chants relate to homosexual themes. An interesting psychodynamic process is at work in this next song:

---

[19]Of course, this song also reflects Argentinian racial prejudice.

Soy de Boca, soy de Boca . . . que puto yo soy.
(I) am of Boca, (I) am of Boca . . . what (a) faggot I am

I myself heard this song at the Boca Juniors Club stadium during a national soccer championship season. This game was a most important one, as the mighty Boca Juniors team, then leading all teams, was facing the second most respected team that season, San Lorenzo de Almagro Club. The San Lorenzo de Almagro fans began singing, "I am for Boca, I am for Boca . . ." thus puzzling the whole stadium, especially Boca's fans, who began wondering why the San Lorenzo fans began, all of a sudden, to root for their rivals. Then the second part of the song was chanted and everything became clear. "I'm for Boca, I'm for Boca . . . what a faggot I am." This song was perceived by all as being so creative that even the most loyal of Boca's fans nervously laughed and even applauded its ingenuity.

The song is important for our thesis, as it clearly shows how machos' fears of "turning into passive homosexuals" surface in their folkloric fantasies.[20] The song is in fact saying that Boca's fans are a bunch of passive homosexuals, unlike us (San Lorenzo fans) who are "straight," *but could possibly turn into passive homosexuals if we were to become fans of the wrong team (Boca).* At the surface the song serves to put Boca's fans down; at the deeper level the internal taboo and anxiety-producing thought of being a passive homosexual is projected onto "the other," in this case, interestingly, within the self (of every macho), which is a potential homosexual were that foreign I to become a fan of the wrong team. It is precisely a paranoid fear that other machos might see this vulnerable potentiality for passive homosexuality that determines, of course unconsciously, much of the macho's well-known hypermasculine behavior.

To the above song, Boca's fans may eventually reply:

La copa, la copa, se mira y no se toca
The cup, the cup, is seen and is not touched

---

[20]There is an important difference between these two roles (passive vs. active), at least for Latin men. Professor Alessandro Falassi pointed out to me in a personal communication how the homosexual film director Pier Paolo Pasolini was murdered by the male prostitute he picked up. Apparently the "active" male prostitute was enraged when, after the prostitute had been the aggressive "giver," Pasolini demanded that the prostitute now be the passive "recipient." At that point, the male prostitute, apparently disgusted with the idea, is said to have killed Pasolini. *Puto* implies passivity.

meaning, "The cup, our cup, can be seen but not touched." This song can be seen as reflecting the pride the Boca Juniors fans have in the fact that their team has won, and thus possesses, the last national championship cup. However, it is also immediately clear that the cup is a symbol that stands for other things. First and foremost, the cup symbolizes victory and superiority, which in the Argentine cultural context equals power, which in turn equals virility or masculinity. So the song now reflects through the symbolic equivalence cup = victory = macho an exhibitionist wish to expose one's masculinity, which can "be seen" but never "touched" (i.e., penetrated) in any way. The fear of being homosexually penetrated, as reflected by our data, is the basic psychodynamic process at work, which is surprisingly similar (although cultural differences do exist) to the syndromes described by Miner and De Vos (1960) on Algerian males and by Dundes et al. (1970) on Turkish boys.

This next song gives us a good summary of a macho's views on homosexuality.

Sol y luna, sol y luna
Sun and moon, sun and moon

Sol y luna, sol y luna
sun and moon, sun and moon

La poronga de Armando
The prick of Armando (name of Boca's owner)

En el culo de Labruna
In the ass of Labruna (name of rival team's owner)

What are some 20,000 of Boca's hypermanly fans saying with this song? Obviously they think that the sexual organ of the owner of their team, Mr. Armando, belongs up the anal orifice of the coach of the rival team (Mr. Labruna), thus mirroring how true machos, like Mr. Armando, beloved by the fans of his team and even nicknamed "the Peron of soccer," with his powerful organ, or *poronga,* penetrates Mr. Labruna. I must repeat that in the macho worldview it is fine to engage in homosexual acts as long as one's role is the active, penetrating aggressor and not the passive, feminine recipient. The song, of course, is consciously aimed at debasing the rivals to the lowest, most humiliating level. This is also evident in the manifest content of this next song:

Ahora, ahora, nos chupan bien
Now, now, they suck us well

Las bolas los de Lomas de Zamora
The balls of Lomas de Zamora

meaning, "Now, the Lomas de Zamora fans suck well our balls." By inviting the Lomas de Zamora fans and players to engage in oral sexual intercourse with them, they automatically (in their own eyes) put them in the lowest role imaginable to a macho, performing fellatio on another man. And that is precisely what machos fear.

Another common strategy found in the Argentinian soccer stadium verbal duels is to put the rivals down by calling them "animals." Relevant to our thesis is the fact that this animal is almost always a chicken, which in the Argentinian cultural context is loaded with specific symbolism, as found in the next song:

Mandarina, Mandarina, Mandarina, Mandarina
Mandarin, Mandarin, Mandarin, Mandarin

Me parece que los de River
It appears to me that those of River

Son todos unas gallinas.
Are all chickens.

which freely translates: "Mandarin, Mandarin, it appears to me that River's fans are a bunch of chickens." The song, in its manifest content, shows how River's fans are dehumanized and symbolically made into animals — interestingly enough, female animals.

In Argentina, *gallina* is not used to refer to women, but very specifically to cowards, who in theory stand in binary opposition to the machos (see Paz, 1961). Furthermore, in Argentine humor, another genre of folklore, the *gallina* is typically the ideal prey for the sex-hungry macho. Indeed, the *gallina* is the object of countless jokes, because it is the most preferred sexual partner of the lonesome gaucho, an archetypical macho.

Lack of contact with females for extended periods of time seems to drive the gaucho to bestiality, preferably with a *gallina*. The following joke confirms how the *gallina* — which never directly refers to women but only to passive cowards — is in fact a recipient of macho sexual penetration. A gaucho, after having been in the deserted pampas for an extended period of time, returns to the city and goes directly to a house of prostitution. There the owner tells him: "Go to room #1, open the door, put your prick next to the red light, and have sex." The young, desiring gaucho religiously follows the instructions, goes into the dark room, puts his phallus in the hole next to the red light, and after having an orgasm, the gaucho cries, "Tell me you loved it!" The reply is "ki-ki-ki," the supposedly onomatopoeic voice of a *gallina,* or chicken.

A real macho sees nothing wrong in engaging in bestial or homosexual intercourse[21] so long as he "gives" but does not "receive." The *gallina* motif did not just appear at random in the above song, but forms a whole cycle of folksongs in Argentinian soccer stadiums.[22]

CONCLUSIONS

In this chapter I have attempted to document the thesis that machos in Argentina are attracted to the soccer field in order to find a collective therapeutic outlet for their taboo thoughts regarding the fear of being debased into a passive, emasculated role. This is most evident in the fans' fantasies of penetrating or being anally penetrated by other males. It is the very symbolism of the game that, in my view, triggers all these homosexual fantasies that surface in the folkloristic free associations. In the game 11 men from each team protect the goal at their back from the penetration of the aggressive rivals. As my data have shown, the goals are highly symbolic of the players', and by extension the fans', anuses. Each time "the ball" penetrates one's goal, the fans' and players' own masculinity is at stake.

In soccer, as opposed to rugby or to American football, we can infer that the ball is unconsciously experienced as an inherently dangerous and dirty object. The players must never touch the ball with their hands during the game (except for the goalkeeper—in his restricted area—and by any of the players when the ball gets out of the field of play), under penalty of foul play. R. W. Pickford (1941) noted this symbolism when he wrote, "In 'soccer,' the player seems afraid that he will dirty or

---

[21]Please note that I do not imply they are equivalents.

[22]For example: *Aunque sean campeones, aunque sean campeones, siguen siendo unas gallinas, la puta que los pario.* (Even though they may be champions, they are still a bunch of chickens, the sons of bitches.) Or: *Cuide señora su gallinero, porque esta noche vamos a afanar una gallina para el puchero.* (Madam, take care of your chicken coop, because tonight we will steal a *gallina* for the stew.) There are many others.

endanger himself by touching the ball with his hand" (p. 283). Then he goes on to argue how naturally persons with unconscious desires to "spurn them (the ball) with his feet or to use them as weapons of attack, he may fall in love with 'soccer' " (p. 283). Regrettably, the author fails to make the critical connection between the player's own "fears" of his "balls," more specifically his underlying *fear of castration,* and the player's pseudoaggressive use of this phallic symbol, the soccer ball, to penetrate the rival's goal, at the rival's back.

We may now return to Deutsch's (1926) psychoanalytic views of the game to show how in fact the previous connection, which Pickford failed to make, is of critical importance for an understanding of how the symbolism inherent in the game directly affects the surfacing of the fans' homosexual aggression. Deutsch bases her thesis on the analysis of a patient suffering from impotence, anxiety states, and depression. The patient could only feel "full of power" by playing ball games such as soccer. Clearly the patient felt better turning from passivity to active control of the "ball." Deutsch concludes that soccer must offer a mechanism for "the projection of a source of anxiety into the outside world and discharge of the anxiety" (p. 226).

From Deutsch's case study we can see how, in the game, a fear of castration is projected onto the ball and is symbolically mastered by the player and (by extension) the cathected fan. This fear of castration is evident in the symbolism of the game and is also present in the *no me rompas las bolas* ("Do not break my balls") cycle in Argentine folklore. This latter body of male folklore is rich with metaphors articulating and venting castration fears. Documenting this cycle is, however, beyond the scope of this chapter.

This castration threat appears to be at the root of machos' obsessive fears of being anally penetrated by other males. Miner and DeVos (1960), in their study of Algerian males, endorse this psychodynamic point: "The fear of retreating into passive homosexuality is one of the dangers besetting an individual who retreats from genital masculinity in the face of subconscious castration threat" (p. 141).

The macho's excessive fear of being penetrated represents an unconscious and forbidden wish, which is at times disguised in the form of egosyntonic projective inversions. Further, this form of pseudoaggression has been shown to be connected to an underlying fear of homosexuality (Chapman, 1967). The other side of such an obsessive fear is, of course, a taboo wish.

These intrapsychic conflicts are enacted in disguised forms within the soccer spectacle. The conflicts are found in the game symbolism and in its structural equivalents: the fans' folk songs and the verbal duels.[23] The game symbolism evokes the fantasies so eloquently articulated in the songs and verbal duels reviewed here: In the game, as in the songs, you use your ball to get it into the other team's backside. It is precisely this anxiety-venting nature of the spectacle that is critical for understanding the addiction effect the soccer show has for hypermanly machos, at least in the Argentinian case.

BIBLIOGRAPHY

ARENS, W. (1975), The great American football ritual. *Natur. History,* 84:72–80.

BOLTON, R. (1979), Machismo in motion: The ethos of Peruvian truckers. *Ethos,* 7(4):312–342.

BRANDES, S. (1980), *Metaphors of Masculinity.* Philadelphia: University of Pennsylvania Press.

BUYTENDIJK, F. J. J. (1952), *Le Football: Une Etude Psychologique.* Paris: Desclée de Brouwer.

CHAPMAN, A. H. (1967), *A Handbook of Clinical Psychiatry: An Interpersonal Approach.* Philadelphia: J. Lippincott Company.

CHINAS, B. (1973), *The Isthmus Zapotecs: Women's Roles in Cultural Contexts.* New York: Holt Rinehart & Winston, Inc.

DA SILVA, A. R. (1970), The role of the spectator in the soccer player's dynamics. Contemporary Psychology of Sport: Proceedings of the Second International Congress of Sport Psychology. Chicago: The Athletic Institute, pp. 307–310.

DEUTSCH, H. (1926), A contribution to the psychology of sport. *Internat. J. Psycho-Anal.,* 7:221–227.

DEVOS, G. (1978), Selective permeability and reference group sanctioning: Psychocultural continuities in role degradation. In: *Major Social Issues.* ed. J. Milton Yinger & Stephen J. Cutler. New York: The Free Press, pp. 9–24.

DOLLARD, I., DOOB, L. W., MILLER, N. E., MOWER, O. H. & SEARS, R. R. (1939), *Frustration and Aggression.* New Haven, CT: Yale University Press.

DUNDES, A. (1976), Projection in folklore; a plea for psychoanalytic semiotics. *Mod. Lang. Notes,* 91:1–1S33.

_____ (1978), Into the endzone for a touchdown: A psychoanalytic consideration of American football. *West. Folklore,* 37:75–78.

_____ & FALASSI, A. (1975), *La Terra in Piazza: An Interpretation of the Palio of Siena.* Berkeley & Los Angeles: University of California Press.

_____ LEACH, J. & ÖZKÖK, B. (1970), The strategy of Turkish boys' verbal dueling rhymes. *J. Amer. Folklore,* 83(329):325–349.

DUNNING, E. (1967), The concept of development: Two illustrated case studies. In: *The Study of Society: An Integrated Anthology,* ed. P. I. Rose. New York: Random House, pp. 879–893.

---

[23]I again concur with Dundes (1978), where he puts forth the convincing argument that in both American football and in male verbal duelings, the object is "to put one's opponent down; to 'screw' him while avoiding being screwed by him" (p. 81). The same applies to my data.

————, ed. (1971), *The Sociology of Sport; A Selection of Readings.* London: Frank Cass & Co.

———— & ELIAS, N. (1971), *The Making of Football.* London: Frank Cass & Co.

———— & ———— (1970), The quest for excitement in unexciting societies. In: *The Cross-Cultural Analysis of Sport and Games,* ed. G. Luschen. Champaign, IL: Stipes.

FOSTER, G. (1979), *Tzintzuntzan: Mexican Peasants in a Changing World.* Rev. Ed. New York: Elsevier North Holland.

FRANKENBERG, R. (1957), *Village on the Border: A Social Study of Religion, Politics and Football in a North Wales Community.* London: Cohen of West London.

FROMM, E. & MACCOBY, M. (1970), *Social Character in a Mexican Village: A Sociopsychoanalytic Study.* Englewood Cliffs, NJ: Prentice-Hall.

GEERTZ, C. (1973), *The Interpretation of Cultures.* New York: Basic Books.

GILMORE, M. & GILMORE, D. (1979), "Machismo": A psychodynamic approach (Spain). *J. Psychol. Anthropol., 2*(3):281-299.

HOPCRAFT, A. (1968), *The Football Man: People and Passions in Soccer.* London: Collings.

JOHNSON, B. W. (1929), Football: A survival of magic? *Contemp. Rev., 135:* p. 228.

LEVER, J. (1969), Soccer: Opium of the Brazilian people. *Transaction, VII*(2):3.

———— (1972), Soccer as a Brazilian way of life. In: *Games, Sport Power,* ed. G. P. Stone. New Brunswick, NJ: Globe, pp. 1-17.

LEVI-STRAUSS, C. (1973), The structural study of myth. In: *High Points in Anthropology,* ed. P. Bohannan and M. Glazer. New York: Alfred A. Knopf, Inc., pp. 409-428.

MAFUD, J. (1976), *Sociologia del futbol.* Buenos Aires: Editorial Americalee.

MENDER, S. (1956), *Das Ballspiel im Leben der Volker.* Berlin: Verlag: Aschendorff.

MINER, H. & DEVOS, G. (1960), *Oasis and Casbah: Algerian Culture and Personality in Change.* Ann Arbor, MI: University of Michigan.

PATRICK, G. T. W. (1963), The psychology of football. *Amer. J. Psychol., 14:*368-381.

PAZ, O. (1961), *The Labyrinth of Solitude.* New York: Grove Press, Inc.

PICKFORD, R. W. (1940), The psychology of the history and organization of association football. *Brit. J. Psychol., 31:*80-93.

———— (1941), Aspects of the psychology of games and sports. *Brit. J. Psychol., 4:*279-293.

REANEY, M. J. (1916), The psychology of the organized group game. *Brit. J. Psychol., Monogr.* Suppl. IV.

SCHWARTZ, J. M. (1973), Causes and effects of spectator sports. *Internat. Rev. Sport Sociol., 3-4*(8):25-45.

STOKES, A. (1956), Psychoanalytical reflections on the development of ball games, particularly cricket. *Internat. J. Psychoanal., 37:*185-192.

TAYLOR, I. R. (1969), Hooligans: Soccer's resistance movement. *New Soc., 7*(2):4-206.

———— (1971a), Football mad: A speculative sociology of football hooliganism. In: *The Sociology of Sport: A Selection of Readings,* ed. E. Dunning. London: Frank Cass & Co., pp. 352-374.

———— (1971b), Soccer consciousness and soccer hooliganism. In: *Images of Deviancy,* ed. S. Cohen. Harmondsworth, Middlesly: Penguin Books, pp. 134-164.

VECCIA, S. (1976), Sunday orgasm. *Internat. J. Sport Psychol., 7*(1):3-39.

VINNAI, G. (1973), *Football Mania: The Players and the Fans; the Mass Psychology of Football.* London: Ocean Books.

11

Interpretation by Allomotifs

BENGT HOLBEK

One of the best known of all traditional fairy tales is that of "The Forgotten Fiancée." It may be told in the following manner:

A man and his wife cross a bridge after sundown. Their carriage suddenly stands still and a troll comes up. He will release them only if they promise him what the wife is carrying under her apron. They must do so. In due time she gives birth to a son, who must then go to the troll when he is 12 years old.

The boy is given three tasks, each to be completed before sundown on pain of death. The first is to clean a sheepcote that has not been cleaned for 24 years. He cries because the task is impossible. The girl who brings his food promises to help if he will be faithful to her. He promises and she sets the dung fork working by magic. Next he is to fell a large stand of wood, and when the girl has done this for him, he is to plow and harrow the land he has cleared, sow it with rye, harvest, thresh the grain, and bake three loaves, all before sundown. He succeeds, thanks to the girl.

She says the troll is angry now, and they decide to flee together. First she spits at three places and when the troll's wife dreams that they have fled and calls, the spittle answers. The fourth time she realizes that they are gone and sends the troll to catch them. The girl turns herself into a bush and the boy into a rose on the bush. The troll is deceived and returns empty-handed. His wife explains the deception and sends him off again. This time the girl turns herself into a church and the boy into a priest and the troll is again deceived. The third time the troll's wife goes herself. The girl turns herself into a pond and the boy into a drake, but she is not deceived. She lies down to drink the pond dry, but she bursts and they are saved.

The boy goes to his parents' home and the girl warns him not to let anyone kiss him. But his mother kisses him while he sleeps and when he wakes up he has forgotten his fiancée. After some time he is engaged to be married to another girl.

When his first fiancée realizes that he is not coming back to fetch her, she takes lodging with an old woman and works as a seamstress. In preparation for the wedding, the farmhands at the boy's farm want to have new shirts sewn. They go one by one to the seamstress. When they express their wish to sleep with her, she is apparently willing enough, but she tricks the first into spending all night holding on to a latch, the second into holding on to a fire tong, and the third into chasing a calf all night.

When the bridegroom is to drive to church, the doubletree breaks and all substitutes break, too. The first farmhand tells about the latch and is sent to borrow it. Next, the pole breaks and they have to borrow the firetong. Finally, the carriage is stuck and they must borrow the calf. In return the girl is invited to the wedding. She insists on sitting next to the bridegroom.

At the wedding feast, she feeds her doves three times. Each time the male takes more grain than the female and each time she cries, "You fail her as my sweetheart failed me!" The bridegroom recognizes her and marries her instead of the other girl.

In this chapter I shall attempt to interpret this tale on the basis of principles set forth in my *Interpretation of Fairy Tales* (1987). Briefly, my contention is that tales of this kind should be read not as texts that have been composed once, thereafter to be more or less faithfully reproduced, but as utterances in a highly specialized language. Those who want to master this form of expression must learn not only its "grammar," but also its "words," the stock of compositional material from which they are to select according to what they want to express. The traditional storyteller is neither repeating by rote nor composing entirely anew, but is rather like the craftsman who uses a traditional form of expression with individual skill.

When Vladimir Propp (1928a) published his *Morphology of the Folktale,* he made the first attempt to define the range of this skill. The various "functions" in his syntagmatic model could be filled with material that seemed to vary according to its own rules. One chapter of his book, which was dedicated to a study of these rules, was excised by the editor and appeared separately (Propp, 1928b). It describes the transformations to which narrative material is subjected—reduction, amplification, intensification, weakening, and various kinds of substitution and assimilation—but does nothing to explain why these transformations take place. This is where Alan Dundes' (1982, 1984) theory of allomotifs comes in. He had introduced the term already in 1962, when he also introduced "motifeme" as a substitution for Propp's "function," but he did not unfold its interpretive potential until two decades later (1982):

> If . . . we examine the various allomotifs which can fill a specific motifemic slot . . . we may gain access to implicit native formulations of symbolic equivalences. If A and B both fulfill the same motifeme, then in some sense is it not reasonable to assume that the folk are equating A and B. In other words, allomotifs are both functionally and symbolically equivalent [p. 92].

I used these ideas in my *Interpretation*. A brief comparison of a number of versions of AT 530, "The Princess on the Glass Mountain," showed that it made no structural difference whether the princess had been placed on top of the glass mountain by a dragon, a troll, the Devil himself, or her father, from which I concluded that dragons and other monsters were the motifemic equivalents of fathers; in other words, they functioned in the same way, and it would be reasonable to assume that they were also symbolic equivalents (Holbek, 1987). It would of course be ludicrous to assume that fathers were symbolic expressions of monsters, whereas the opposite makes excellent sense. Mention of the father as the one who desires the princess may be less than felicitous, not to say outright tabooed, and the storyteller circumvents the problem by selecting a suitable threatening figure from his or her array of allomotifs. Comparing motifemic equivalents could, then, point the way from symbolic expression to "clear text" in which no attempt is made to veil the sensitive matter, (i.e., constitute the first step in interpretation).

Encouraged by this little investigation and by Dundes' papers, I went on to make a more detailed study of the allomotifs in AT 433B, "King Wivern" (Holbek, 1987). It turned out that Dundes' concept could become a powerful analytical instrument when combined with my revised version of Propp's syntagmatic model, which put the definition of the motifemic slot on a firmer basis. An impressive number of enigmatic characters and other tale elements could be linked to features of the real world (which is one reason why I dislike the term "tales of magic"; what we find in these tales is symbolic play with reality, not serious magic). But two other observations from that study are relevant for the present argument: First, not all folktales are equally well told; second, one must be alert to the possibility that a substitution by a new allomotif not only implies a new shade of meaning, but also may introduce new meaning. In my study of "King Wivern" I found that a constant process of small-scale creativity could be documented. Each of those narrators who had made use of this particular narrative material had her (in one case: his) own ideas as to how it should be used and the analysis would have to take this into account.

In a recent study of "Snow White," Steven S. Jones (1990) has criticized my insistence on including the narrators when studying the tales: "if we are concerned with the appeal and significance of a given folktale, then examining the various versions of that tale can stand alone and can be most illuminating" (p. 10).

But is that in fact what we should really be concerned with? If I conceive of fairy tales as utterances in a specialized language, the implication is that I must study the "speaker" as well as the "language." Literary texts are deliberately produced to stand by themselves, but folklore texts can be fully understood only in their context — indeed, the notion of a "folklore text" is a *contradictio in adjecto:* It is produced, objectified, by a folklore collector (followed, perhaps, by an editor), and thereby removed from the soil in which it grew. Bogatyrev and Jakobson long ago (1929) clarified this fundamental distinction between folklore and literature, but seemingly to no avail; students of literature still fail to grasp it (see also Holbek 1987, pp. 39–43). What I am concerned with, then, is not "a given folktale" as such, but the function of these tales in the traditional communities that produced them.

In order to test Dundes' theory of allomotifs further I shall in the following section concentrate on the versions of AT 313 recorded by the Danish folklore collector Evald Tang Kristensen in Jutland in the period 1868–1905. There are several reasons for choosing such a corpus. First, the focusing on a limited area and period is necessary if we want to obtain an impression of the range of variation that could be at a narrator's disposal in a given cultural area. Second, the area and period chosen are characterized by relative uniformity as regards material culture, social organization, popular traditions, language, religion, and internal communication. In the third place, I have limited myself to the tales recorded by a single highly skilled collector who knew his informants' culture intimately; his original recordings, which were made while he was listening, not afterwards, have been preserved in the Danish Folklore Archives, Copenhagen, along with detailed information about the storytellers and their background.

The catalogue of Tang Kristensen's folktale records (referred to in the following by ETK + No.) contains references to 42 records of AT 313, 313A, and 313C, the tale of "The Forgotten Fiancée" and its cognates. Eight of these will be disregarded here: some belong to other tale types and contain only minor elements of AT 313; some are fragmentary; and there is one instance of the same tale having been recorded twice from the same informant.

ETK No.	Sex of informant	I	II	III	IV	V	VI	VII
44	m	x		x	x	x	x	x
163	f	x		x	x	x	x	x
266	m	x	x	x	x	x	x	x
267	f	x	x		x	x	x	x
392	f	x	x	x	x	x	x	x
418	f	x	x		x	x	x	x
449	m	x	x	x	x			x
492	m	x		x	x	x	x	x
649	m	x	x	x	x	x	x	x
672	m	x	x	x	x	x	x	x
727	m	x		x	x	x	x	x
928	f	x	x	x	x	x	x	x
931	f	x	x	x	x	x	x	x
1017	m	x	x	x	x	x		x
1089	f	x	x	x	x	x	x	x
1202	f	x	x	x	x			x
1328	m	x	x	x				x
1342	f	x	x	x	x	x	x	x
1408c	f			x				
1674	f	x		x	x	x	x	x
1679	m	x	x	x	x	x		x
1762	f	x	x	x				x
1771	m	x	x	x	x			x
1797	f	x	x	x	x			x
1856	m	x		x				
1865	f	x		x	x	x	x	x
2004	f	x	x	x	x	x	x	x
2024	m	x		x				x
2068	m	x		x				x
2149	m	x		x	x			x
2242	m	x	x	x	x	x	x	x
2461	f	x		x	x		x	x
2486	m	x	x					x
2514	m	x	x	x	x	x	x	x

We have, then, 34 records. What Belmont has observed in her study of the French versions of this tale type (1985) is true of the Danish ones as well: Aarne's (1930) division of the material into three subtypes is not locally valid.

I have divided the narrative sequence into seven segments. It would have been possible to use the five-move format I developed in my *Interpretation* (1987), but as I am here dealing with a single tale type, it is possible to define more concrete analytical units (as also done by Jones, 1990, in his analysis of "Snow White"). Before entering on this analysis, it is worth noting that the distribution by sex of narrator is almost even, there being 17 male (ETK 449 and 492 were told by the same man) and 16 female narrators, which is remarkable, considering that male informants in general account for approximately 65% of the tales recorded by Tang Kristensen.

In the following, I shall discuss the tale segment by segment according to the Roman numerals in the composite version summarized above.

I. How does the boy get into the monster's power? The material falls into ten groups:

a. Married couple stopped when crossing bridge after sundown, must promise unborn son to get free: 649, 672, 1089, 2004;

b. King (and queen) get into monster's power in woods, must promise unborn son to get free: 1017, 1674, 2242;

c. Merchant (fisherman) out sailing, ship seized by troll, must promise (unborn) son to get free: 449, 1202, 1679, 1797;

d. Two kings fight, loser to give winner his son: 266, 267, 931;

e. King borrows money from troll, must send son as payment: 2514;

f. Rich man (married to witch) buys or adopts boy: 163, 492, 727, 1771;

g. Boy accidentally caught by troll: 928, 1762, 2149;

h. Boy gets into troll's power when searching for abducted sister or princess: 1856, 2024, 2486;

i. Boy seeks / has job with troll: 44, 392, 418, 1328, 1342, 1865, 2461;

j. Events take place in boy's own home: 2068.

With the exception of one version (j), all relate that the boy is away from home and in the monster's service (and power). He went there of his own accord in seven versions (i), all others agree that he got there by trickery, foul play or brute force, or because his parents had economical difficulties. The boy is nearly always described as the victim, but he goes willingly and in good cheer, whereas his parents are often unhappy and sometimes (unsuccessfully) try to avoid handing him over.

I shall now assume as a working hypothesis that all of these motifs except (j), which are motifemically equivalent (they lead to the same result), are also symbolically equivalent. It is immediately apparent that (i) is an expression in "clear text" without any attempt at circumvention or symbolization. I shall assume that the other motifs express the same basic event, but overlaying it with various shadings of meaning and at the same time softening the impact of the basic event. Why would anyone attempt that?

At this point, one must take into account where and among whom the tale is told. It is a fact that in a traditional peasant community like that of 19th-century Jutland, most children had to leave home to serve with strangers, often at a tender age if their parents were too poor to support them. This motif is clearly present in (e) and (f) and is also implied elsewhere—in ETK 1649, the monster gives the merchant power to conquer a pirate's ship (i.e., rewards him financially, after he has promised to give his son away). The same motif is found in various forms in the introduction to a great many other tales, and I do not doubt that at this point the tales reflect real feelings associated with a boy's departure from home. It is told in quite a number of tales that he is too young to leave, and resentment against his parents for kicking him out of the nest prematurely would not be unexpected. But such feelings are tabooed, and that is, I believe, the reason why the departure must appear to be forced from the outside. The boy's resentment can then be directed against the outside world as personified in the monster, and his attachment to his parents is not tainted. Or, to put it another way, he avoids the feeling of guilt that would have been associated with hating his parents. It is no fault of theirs that they do not have the strength to withstand a monster with preternatural powers.

There is another aspect to segment I: The boy is presented as a prince (b, d, e, and one version of h), but he has little to show for it. The most likely explanation is that this feature is a product of the ubiquitous "family romance" first described by Freud (1909), the notion that one's real parents are of much higher status than the poor couple with whom one grew up.

The beginning of the boy's career is thus characterized by dreaming and unrealistic imagination. He is cast into the outside world without being prepared for it.

In 22 out of 34 versions of segment II, the boy is now given a series of impossible tasks to perform, usually three. Not only the amount of work is enormous, but the implements are inadequate (sieve for carrying water, leaden axe for felling trees, enormous dung fork for mucking out), the materials are insufficient (three grains of barley for brewing, sticks or playing cards for building) and there is magic afoot as well (the dung flies right back into the stables, the firewood returns to the forest, every stone taken away from the field is replaced by ten more stones). The most frequent tasks are:

a. Cleaning out sheepcot / stables: 266, 392, 672, 928, 931, 1089, 1328, 2004;

b. Building barn / house / palace: 266, 931, 1017, 1342, 1797, 2004;

c. Cutting down forest: 418, 672, 1342, 1679, 1771, 1797;

d. Breaking in / watering dangerous magical horses: 266, 267, 418, 449, 931, 1679;

e. Emptying well / lake: 418, 1089, 1679, 1771;

f. Recognizing girl (fiancée) among others looking exactly like her: 649, 931, 1017, 1202;

g. Sowing grain, harvesting, threshing, baking loaves in one day: 449, 1679, 1771;

h. Brewing beer out of a few grains: 392, 928, 2242.

The other tasks, if less frequent, are just as bad. Nearly all of them — except (f) — are enormously exaggerated, virtually Herculean, versions of the tasks farmhands would be expected to perform. There can be little doubt that this part of the tale describes the reactions of a very young and inexperienced farmhand to the demands of a stern master. But instead of admitting his own lack of skill and strength the boy projects his feelings onto his surroundings (projections of this kind occur frequently in fairy tale beginnings).

A few of the tasks mentioned belong to the female sphere. In ETK 2242, the boy is to brew 15 hogsheads of good beer, to bake bread and cakes out of 15 barrels of flour, and to roast the meat of numerous calves, deer, and roes. Curiously enough, this version was told by a man, but one may suspect that it came to him in a form shaped by a female storyteller. Apart from this and a few other instances, segment II is clearly laid in a men's world. Nevertheless, a woman plays a prominent role in it.

There is no way the boy can perform the tasks heaped upon him by the monster. In many versions he sits down to cry instead of working, which confirms our impression of him as a boy who has been sent away from home prematurely. But he wins the support of a girl who is in the monster's power already. In some versions, he gains her support by the method known from innumerable tales of swan maidens or seal maidens: She is bathing together with her sisters; he steals her garments and only gives them back after she has promised to help him. In other versions, he finds her at a place where he is forbidden to go, but in most versions, she is simply part of the household when he arrives. Who is she?

    a. Monster's daughter: 44, 163, 266, 267, 418, 449, 492, 727, 931, 1017, 1202, 1408c, 1679, 1771, 1865, 2149;

    b. Maidservant: 392, 649, 928, 1328, 1342, 2461, 2514;

    c. Abducted princess / girl: 1674, 2024, 2486;

    d. Boy's own sister: 1856;

    e. No information: 672, 1089, 1762, 1797, 2004, 2068, 2242.

The records do not offer any obvious reason to suspect any tabooed matter; but it must be observed that the young couple is almost invariably pursued when they leave the monster's home. Exceptions are ETK 267 and 418, in which the girl is manifestly the warlock-king's own daughter, and 2486, in which she is an abducted princess. She may not be the monster's own daughter in every tale in groups (b) and (e), but she is treated as if she were. With few exceptions, then, these tales seem to relate of a boy who falls in love with his master's daughter, as in so many other fairy tales. It is expressed in "clear text" in ETK 44 and may elsewhere be assumed. The strange task of recognizing the girl he loves in a flock of girls looking exactly alike may be regarded as a test of his feelings.

The apparently magical help he receives from the girl may be interpreted in the light of what I have described in my *Interpretation* (1987) as "contraction": the slow, steady processes of growth, travel, and work are never described in fairy tales. Instead, they are telescoped into instantaneous transformations of a miraculous character. What the girl really teaches him is patience and endurance. It is said in some versions that she tells him to sleep while she sets the implements working. I take this to mean that she teaches him not to lose courage beforehand, not to lose heart when he thinks of all the work he will have to do.

In most versions, she exacts a promise of faithfulness from the boy before she will help him. One may view this in the light of events in segments I and IV: He is immature and her parents may have good reason to doubt his reliability. But there seems to be more to it.

The preternatural character of the master is signaled already in the first segment of the tale: he often emerges from the forest, from under the bridge, from beneath the sea, or he defeats the boy's father by magic; when the boy is to enter his service, he is taken down under the bridge or into the sea, or he has to travel through seven kingdoms. The master is called troll, dwarf, warlock-king; his wife is a witch, and they demonstrate magical powers accordingly. The fleeing couple is saved in some cases by crossing water (which trolls cannot do), in others by seeking refuge in a churchyard or by crossing the border to "Christian land" ("the Holy Land" in French versions). In other words, the troll and his realm represent an out-group of some sort. It cannot be defined further, because its prime characteristic is that of *not* being one's in-group. This reflects, I think, the rather parochial worldview of the traditional peasant who has little reason or occasion to travel and regards all outsiders with suspicion. Again, the tabooed, but very real, feeling (of hostility against outsiders) is masked and made to seem justified.

That feeling is apparently mutual. The troll wants the boy for his laborer, not as a prospective son-in-law. Some versions assert that he flees because the troll resents his ability to perform the most difficult tasks, but many more versions indicate that what really causes the flight is that the relation between the two youngsters is discovered. What the tale seems to portray is, then, the uneasy relations between two groups (perhaps two families) who need each other economically but will not accept marital bonds (the Romeo and Juliet situation).

In segment III the young couple flee. This is a regular part of the tale, omitted only in a few cases. One version (ETK 1408c) actually consists of little more than the flight. A prince comes to woo a princess, but her mother, the queen, is a widow, and she tells her daughter to go on playing with her dolls a while longer because she wants the prince for herself, which causes the young couple to flee. This is an original form and an excellent demonstration of the point that we cannot without further ado transfer observations from one version of a given tale type to another. In this case, the mother is envious of her daughter's sexual attractiveness and will not yet give up her own desires. This motif is known from numerous other fairy tales, and its presence may also be detected in a few other versions of this tale, but it has only become the central theme in this version. The narrator was a master who could transform the traditional narrative material to create a tale that expressed what she herself had on her mind.

The flight is missing only from ETK 267, 418, and 2486, and it is not described in ETK 492, but apart from that, it assumes the two classical forms defined by Aarne (1930), "Transformation Flight" (24 versions) and "Obstacle Flight" (6 versions). Before the flight begins, the girl often employs a gimmick to gain time: She places three answers, usually by spitting, on the door, the hearth, and the bed. The troll's wife wakes up because she has dreamed that they have fled, calls, and is deceived three times by the answers. The purpose of this little ploy is of course to induce suspense, but it also serves to characterize the opponents: The girl is crafty, circumspect, and innocent-appearing; the powerful troll and his cunning wife are duped. This is in keeping with the theme of secret love in the preceding segment of the tale and with the transformations, the purpose of which is to deceive the trolls further.

The transformations usually occur in a series of three; sometimes there are fewer. Perhaps this is on purpose or due to forgetfulness. They are as varied as the tasks and all of them cannot be enumerated here, but broadly speaking, there are three groups of transformations, which occur more or less regularly in the following order:

a 1. Two trees or flowers: 44, 649 (twice), 672, 931, 1797, 2461;

a 2. Tree (bush) and flower: 449, 1679, 1771, 2004;

a 3. Tree and bird: 392, 1089, 2068;

a 4. Old man leading cow: 44, 1408c, 1865;

b 1. Church and priest: 392, 449, 727 (church and plumber on roof), 1017 (monastery and monk), 1202, 1408c, 1679, 1762, 1771, 1797, 2004 (church and owl in belfry light), 2068 (church and wedding procession), 2514;

b 2. Mill and miller: 266, 931, 2149;

c 1. Duck and drake (in pond or at sea): 44, 163, 449, 727, 1089, 1202, 1342, 1408c, 1679, 1762, 1797, 1865, 2149, 2461, 2514;

c 2. Duck and old woman coaxing it: 266, 649, 672, 931;

c 3. Duck and pond: 392, 1771, 2004, 2068.

The main theme of the transformations is inconspicuousness, and it nearly always works well the first two times. The pursuers are duped, but when they return to the abode of the troll or witch, the illusion is explained to them and they are sent off again. The third time, the troll or witch goes himself or herself, and this time no illusion can help the fugitives. If they have not by then succeeded in getting into "Christian land" or into a church (churchyard) or across water, they must rely on their ability to remain uncaught in the pond or sea. The troll/witch tries to coax them to the shore or make them swallow bait with strings attached, but in vain, and as a last resort, the pursuer tries to drink the pond or sea dry, but bursts in the attempt.

The "Obstacle Flight" occurs in only six versions (ETK 928, 1328, 1674, 1856, 2024, 2242) and the tradition is much more uniform than that of the "Transformation Flight." When the flight is discovered, the pursuer, who is a troll in all versions, tries to overtake the fugitives three times, but is foiled each time because the boy, at the girl's instigation, throws a small object behind him which turns into a great obstacle. The most common obstacles are (1) a forest, (2) a mountain, and (3) a lake. But whereas the troll can cut down the forest and dig his way through the mountain, the lake proves his undoing, either because he tries to drink it dry and bursts, or simply because he is drowned.

Motifemically, the "Obstacle Flight" occupies the same position as the "Transformation Flight," for which reason it must be taken into account in the interpretation. The tale roles are the same and so is the outcome, but where the theme of the transformations clearly was inconspicuousness, illusion-making (which could, however, be penetrated by the cunning opponent), that of the "Obstacle Flight" rather seems to be stubborn obduracy: the fugitives rely on massive denial. It is interesting that in this subtype of the tale, which emphasizes force and will, the opponent is consistently the troll (the witch's cunning does not enter into the picture) and most of the informants are male.

It is well known that space and time in fairy tales cannot be measured according to our standards. The boy performs three tasks and with that, he has spent 14 years at the troll's; or he takes service with a troll next door and has to cross a sea to get home. Distance and duration are used in these tales to indicate feelings, not objectively measurable reality, for which reason I submit that the "flight" does not mean that the fugitives travel a great physical distance — as in the case of the glass mountain (AT 530 and elsewhere), which does not in my view indicate physical elevation, but social distance between the princess at its top and the boy at its foot. In other words, I think the flight means that the girl separates herself from her parents in an emotional sense, but it does not follow that she also does so in a physical sense. The time comes in the life of all parents when they lose their children to future spouses and they often find it difficult to accept this and fight it to the bitter end. In the case of boys, this may assume the form of deeds of great derring-do (dangerous expeditions, slaying of dragons etc.), but it seems that in this tale, the roles are reversed: It is the girl who advises and helps the boy, who organizes their flight, and finally overcomes their pursuers. I think the underlying reality is easily deduced from the changing emotional pattern: the girl ends up being rid of her parents and attached to the boy — and it makes no difference, motifemically speaking, whether the troll and the witch are drowned (or otherwise killed) or deprived of their magical power in other ways.

Many of the transformations take on a new meaning when seen in this light. Most of those in group (a) seem to indicate innocence; the source of symbolism is often the vegetable kingdom. But group (b) is of a more suggestive character; it describes buildings (which may symbolize the human body) and someone moving about inside, and similar images may appear in group (c). A list of transformations in which one of the fugitives becomes a "milieu" and the other something or someone within it or supported by it will look like this:

	"Milieu": Girl	"Milieu": Boy
Tree, flower	1679, 1771, 2004	449
Tree, bird	392, 1089	2068
Field, bird		1202
Field, pig	2149	
Log, sawyer	266	
Mill, miller	2149	266, 931
Church, priest	392, 1408c, 1679, 1771, 2514	449, 1202, 1762, 1797
Church, plumber	727	
Church, owl	2004	
Monastery, monk	1017	
Church, wedding procession		2068
Smithy, apprentice	1342	
House, old woman		727
Pond, duck	392, 2004	1771, 2068

In an earlier study of a single version of this tale, ETK 1342 (Holbek 1987), I noted that "the sexual implications of these symbols are obvious" (pp. 516–521); but they seem less obvious in the light of the data presented here. A comparison version by version is, however, illuminating: the narrators of ETK 392, 727, 1017, 1089, 1342, 1408c, 1679, 2004, 2149, and 2514 consistently support my view, whereas it is to a limited extent (one transformation each) contradicted by the narrators of ETK 266, 727, 931, 1762, 1771, and 1797. Only ETK 449, 1202, and 2068 are consistently opposed to it. I conclude from this that sexual symbolism is implied in many, but far from all, versions of the tale; some narrators perhaps have overlooked it, or it means nothing to them. In this case, it would be interesting to inspect a much larger sample to see whether the tendencies I think I have observed in Kristensen's material are general or accidental. The information assembled by Aarne (1930) pays no attention to the question of sex.

Nearly all versions of the "Transformation Flight" subtype end with the ducks sailing in water, just as five out of the six versions of the "Obstacle Flight" subtype end with water as the decisive obstacle. I have argued elsewhere (1987) that water symbolizes life, the feminine life principle in particular, see also Dundes' (1980) observation that the opposition between dry and wet often seems to signify the opposition between death and life. But in the present context, it is possible to specify this interpretation a little differently: the water is the element that protects the *young*. Their pursuer(s) cannot enter it, they try to drink it all and burst, or they fall into it and are drowned. ETK 1679 contains an illuminating remark made by the girl when she is about to turn herself into a duck: "The witch cannot take me in the water, it has not beenbewitched." I think the water symbolizes the girl's own life. The witch and the troll belong to the preceding generation. They may hold sway for a while, but sooner or later they must inevitably succumb to their successors. Ultimately, they cannot control their fate. This interpretation is not contradicted by the versions in which the fleeing couple reach "Christian land" or a churchyard or turn into a church against which the troll crashes to his death: the Church and the Christian world represent *our* in-group, in which evil attempts to curb *our* (the young couple's) wishes come to nothing—an egoistic worldview perhaps, and possibly not quite consistent with the doctrine of the Church, but functional within the compass of the fairy tale world.

With this episode, the first half of the tale is concluded. Many fairy tales display a kind of hiatus at this point: The love relation has been established, now it is to be realized. The opposition to it may emanate from two sources, her family and his. In this case, her family is out of the picture and his moves onto the stage.

In segment IV the boy forgets the girl. One might have expected him to bring her to his parents, just as one might have expected the dragon-slayer to accompany the princess to her home after having killed the dragon (AT 300), but that almost never happens. I believe the reason is that the girl has not moved in any physical sense. She has distanced herself definitively from her parents, but she is still with them after the boy has left or perhaps has been sent home in disgrace after the affair was discovered. She beseeches him not to forget his true love and warns him against temptations, but to no avail. This episode, which occurs in 27 out of 34 versions, may take the following forms:

a. He falls in love with another girl: 266, 267, 392, 727, 928, 931, 1017, 1771, 1797, 2242;

b. His mother kisses him and he forgets: 449, 649, 672, 1089, 1342, 2004;

c. He eats and drinks and forgets: 44, 266, 267, 931, 1674, 1865;

d. Red hound licks him and he forgets: 163, 418, 2514 (the hound turns into a girl with whom he falls in love);

e. He is distracted in other ways: 492, 1202, 1679, 2149, 2461.

These are allomotifs, they fill the same motifemic slot. Where it is not mentioned explicitly, it is implied in what follows that the boy becomes engaged to another girl, often at his mother's instigation. There is nothing extraordinary in this. The tale stem from a culture in which marriages, particularly of those who were to inherit the farm, were regularly arranged by parents.

It has been noted previously that the boy was far from being mature and independent. This is apparently still the case. As soon as he returns to his mother's sphere of influence, he is again under her sway. The old bonds between him and his family are reasserted and he willingly accepts the arrangements his mother wants to make. The girl who appears at this point of the tale or later on has no face, no character of her own, she is merely the expression of his mother's will. All the allomotifs seem to mean the same: The dutiful son accepts the role prepared for him by his family, his mother above all.

But in segment V his first love goes on existing. She takes lodging with an old woman and pretends to be her daughter, or she returns to her real mother from whom the troll had stolen her, or she builds a house of her own. We do not know that she has actually left the home of her childhood, but we now see her from a new vantage point, from the perspective of the family to which the boy belongs. He lives at a farm or a manor-house and she lives in a cottage. Obviously she is not a suitable partner for the young gentleman.

In 20 versions, three young men in succession are now lured to her house, ostensibly to have new shirts sewn for the impending wedding, but really to spend a night with her. They usually serve at the farm where the young man is being groomed for the wedding, and in four cases (ETK 44, 727, 1679, and 2242) he himself is the last of her visitors.

Their intentions are frustrated, however. The girl always manages to get to bed first, and when her would-be lover has undressed down to his shirt, she suddenly remembers chores undone, almost invariably the following: (1) closing the door with a latch, (2) banking the fire by means of the fire tong, (3) chasing the little red calf in. The first lover is left pulling at the latch all night, the second fumbling with the fire tong all night, and the third chasing the calf all over the landscape.

It lies near at hand to interpret these events as symbols of sexual frustration, especially considering that the young men are in fact so frustrated. There is no reason to attempt any exact interpretation of the three symbols, although it should be noted that they all pertain to the sphere of female work, within which the men are evidently powerless. But it is significant that four versions of the tale mention the bridegroom as the last of the would-be lovers. Belmont (1985) informs us that this is frequently the case in French tradition, and I would reason that he is at least motifemically equivalent to the other visitors. In other words, it

250 BENGT HOLBEK

seems probable that he is still strongly attracted to his first love even on the verge of marrying another. But now she repudiates him: she will be wife, not concubine. I have endeavoured to show (1987) that this is a regular feature in fairy tales. The spoilt young man (or woman, as the case may be) tries to have his (her) cake and eat it, but this conduct is not acceptable in the universe of fairy tales.

In segment VI the tale becomes easier to penetrate toward the end, as is often the case in this genre. The veils, or most of them, have fallen. If it is accepted that the three farmhands who went to visit the girl in the cottage are nothing but the bridegroom's aliases, the meaning of this segment of the tale clearly is that he cannot go anywhere or achieve anything without assistance from the girl he really loves. At every turn, he is confronted with his need for her.

The wedding ceremony in the church is of no account. Among the peasants to whose culture this tale belonged, the consummation of the wedding in bed was the point of no return. The bridal couple would be ceremonially led to their bedroom by all the guests, and only when they emerged from it next morning were they in truth married. Strangely enough, one of our versions (ETK 727) diverges at this point. The bridegroom regains his memory, but regrets that it is now too late to go back on the word he gave in church. All he can do is set his former sweetheart up in style. That is evidently a modernization made by a narrator who was not comfortable with the traditional view of wedding customs. In all other versions that include segment VI, the purpose clearly is to prepare the stage for the showdown in VII. It is characteristic of this genre that the protagonist, who has been the driving force up to this point, now has to let the future spouse take over. She—in other tales: he—can get no further. The protagonist is the outsider, often poor and unprepossessing, who is waiting outside the gate of the palace to be summoned by the future spouse or his (her) parents. It is an indication of the continued lack of independence and initiative of the boy that even at this point, it is his mother who has to invite the girl to the wedding feast, if she has not herself demanded a place next to the bridegroom in return for her assistance.

Finally, in segment VII the girl makes the boy remember her. This happens in 26 out of 34 versions. The dominant motif is the feeding of the doves (21 versions), in which the allomotifs are: she tells her story (ETK 163, 1679), kisses him (ETK 449—a reversal of the effect of his mother's kiss), and shows him her half of a broken ring (ETK 1771). An elegant amalgamation with AT 403 is found in ETK 1797, in which the girl, still in duck shape, comes into the kitchen through the gutter and says that she can return only twice more; the boy recognizes her and she reverts to her own shape.

Some versions do not have this motif. In ETK 1856, the boy has gone in search of his sister, and there is of course no wedding between them. In ETK 1408c, the emphasis is on the escape from the witch, who wanted the boy for herself. In ETK 2068, the boy and the girl flee together from *his* house and they return when the witch, who slandered and persecuted them, has died. In addition, a few tales move directly from the flight to the wedding.

What is above all worth noting in this segment of the tale is the deliberate use of symbols. There is no doubt what the feeding of the doves means, as the girl explains it. In ETK 1771, the boy goes on to tell the wedding guests a story: I once had a cupboard, but the key to it was lost. I had a new one made, but then I found the old one and it fits better. Which of the two keys should I retain? Everyone says: The old one, and he replies: Then I shall also keep my first love. This motif also appears in versions from other countries; it clearly belongs to tradition. Examples like these — and there are of course many others — show that we need not hesitate to assume a regular translation of narrative material from "clear text" to symbolic expression and back again, as Dundes suggests. The present study indicates that the narrators have made these substitutions quite frequently. Nor do we have to assume that they made them unconsciously, as depth psychologists tend to think. Fairy tales are, after all, as opposed to dreams, products of the conscious mind (cp. Holbek 1987).

Summing up, I think it may be concluded that interpretation by allomotifs is efficient. The use of this analytical tool within the frame of a Proppian syntagmatic model enables the analyst to *trace the process of symbolization back to its source, the emotional stresses and conflicts in the traditional community* that produced tales of this kind. By studying the tales in this way we gain an insight into a culture that would otherwise have been completely impenetrable to the modern scholar. At the same time we get an answer to two questions that have vexed folktale scholarship since its inception. One is that of origins: Did these tales originate in a particular period, area, and social class? The answer clearly is that there has been a continuous and widespread creativity on a small scale. Every narrator who has taken up one or more of these tales has probably contributed a little and it would be vain to look for ultimate origins, because the last generations of storytellers were in all probability no less creative than their forebears hundreds or thousands of years ago. The vast majority of the fairy tales are intimately associated with the structures and institutions of traditional peasant communities, and they may be as old as peasant culture itself. The second question concerns the "wonderful tenacity of tradition" on which so many writers have commented. It would be wonderful indeed if it was a question of *remembering* tales created very long ago. But if they are regarded as being intimately associated with the problems and concerns of the storytellers themselves and of their audiences, then it becomes clear that they are constantly nourished by the soil in which they grow. The storytellers need not *remember* what the tales are about, just as the shoemaker does not have to reconstruct from memory what a foot looks like: reality is around him constantly, all he has to do is look. Similarly, I believe, the traditional storytellers could go on taking inspiration from the life of the community of which they themselves were part. In the case of "The Forgotten Fiancée," it was not even once necessary to look for sources of inspiration outside traditional peasant life. The problem rather lies in admitting that it could produce and uphold an artistic form of expression as sophisticated as the classical fairy tale.

ABBREVIATIONS

AT + No.: type No. in Aarne & Thompson, 1961.
ETK + No.: catalogue No. in Catalogue No. 7, folktales recorded by Evald Tang Kristensen, in *Dansk Folkemindesamling* (Danish Folklore Archives), Copenhagen, signature: DFS 1929/43.

BIBLIOGRAPHY

AARNE, A. (1930), *Die magische Flucht. Eine Märchenstudie.* FFC No. 92. Helsinki, Finland: Academia Scientiarum Fennica.
_____ & THOMPSON, S. (1961). *The Types of the Folktale.* FFC No. 184. Helsinki, Finland: Academia Scientiarum Fennica.
BELMONT, N. (1985), Orphée dans le miroir du conte merveilleux. *L'Homme,* 93:59–82.
BOGATYREV, P. & JAKOBSON, R. (1929), Die Folklore als eine besondere Form des Schaffens. In: *Donum Natalicium Schrijnen* (pp. 900–913). Nijmegen/Utrecht, Netherlands.
DUNDES, A. (1980), *Interpreting Folklore.* Bloomington/London: Indiana University Press.
_____ (1982), The symbolic equivalence of the allomotifs in "The Rabbit Herd" (AT 570). *Arv,* 36 (1980):91–98.
_____ (1984), The symbolic equivalence of allomotifs: towards a method of analyzing folktales. In: *Le Conte, Pourquoi? Comment? Folktales, Why and How?* ed. Geneviève Calame-Griaule et al. Paris, Ed. du CNRS, 1984, pp. 187–199.
FREUD, S. (1909), Family romances. *Standard Edition,* 9:237–241. London: Hogarth Press.

HOLBEK, B. (1987), *Interpretation of Fairy Tales. Danish Folklore in a European Perspective.* FFC No. 239. Helsinki, Finland: Academia Scientiarum Fennica.

JONES, S. S. (1990), *The New Comparative Method: Structural and Symbolic Analysis of the Allomotifs of "Snow White."* FFC No. 247. Helsinki, Finland: Academia Scientiarum Fennica.

PROPP, V. JA. (1928a), *Morfologija skázki.* Leningrad. *(Morphology of the Folktale)* 2d. rev. ed. Austin/London 1968: Publications of the American Folklore Society, Bibliographical & Special Series, 9.

———— (1928b), Transformacii volšebnych skazok. *Poètika 4,* 70–89. (Transformations of the wondertale.) In: idem, *Theory and History of Folklore.* Manchester, England, 1984, pp. 82–99.

12

The Forging of the *Sampo* and Its Capture: The Oedipus Complex of Adolescence in Finnish Folklore[1]

TOR-BJÖRN HÄGGLUND

"The creation of the *Sampo*[2] and its elevation to the status of a possession of the Finnish nation," Julius Krohn has stated, "has, without Lönnrot consciously intending or noticing it, risen to become the central theme of the Kalevala" (Setälä, 1932, p. 18). When gathering the songs that make up our national epic and combining them into an integral whole, out of a personal belief in the genuineness of this ancient tale of heroism, Lönnrot used the *Sampo* poems as the nucleus for his composition, placing Lemminkäinen alongside the true heroes, Väinämöinen and the smith Ilmarinen. Lönnrot departed from the folktale, or chose to supplement it, in that he viewed the Kalevala as representing the struggle between two peoples. And, he says in his introduction to the original version, "Almost all the epic songs depict two peoples whose relations are not especially harmonious. One we may call the people of Pohja and the other the people of Kalevala. . . . This is the bond or connection that binds the Kalevala songs together, that they tell us how Kalevala gradually prospered, to vie with Pohjola and eventually emerge as victor" (Lönnrot, 1928 p. xxx). Lönnrot recorded his first *Sampo* song at Akonlahti in 1832, and it was in 1835 that he was able to publish the

---

[1]An earlier version of this paper was published in *Scand. Psychoanal. Rev.*, 1985, 8:159–180.
[2]The word *Sampo*, which does not mean anything in particular in Finnish, has been given many different interpretations. However, it is a symbol for an object which the heroes of the Finnish epos Kalevala long for and which would become a source of happiness for them.

whole of his "Kalevala, or Ancient epic songs of Karelia from the early times of the Finnish people."

Lönnrot found something important in the *Sampo* songs for this nation, which was moving toward independence, and for its blossoming national romantic movement, something to raise the spirit of the individual in his smallness, and the people greeted it with rapture. The Kalevala of Lönnrot does not correspond exactly to the folk songs, departing from them perceptibly at certain points, but it does furnish a genuine connection with the message of the ancient epic songs, even though he has romanticized the spirit of combat to some extent. The Kalevala was published at a time when Finland was preparing for independence from the yoke of the neighboring powers. In other words, the nation was preparing for the same ordeal as faces every adolescent when striving for freedom from dependence on his or her parents and the world of childhood fantasy.

The *Sampo* songs have been spared from all forms of cult. They contain mystic and religious elements, but it is their purely poetic aspect that comes to the fore (Setälä, 1932). And they also contain many folk themes, as Setälä points out:

> Firstly one should mention the emphasis on the work done to gain every achievement. The forging of the *Sampo* itself is a labour which is acknowledged in both the *Sampo* songs proper and in those that tell of the competition for the hand of the maiden of Pohjola. . . . There are other elements of folk-tale origin in the *Sampo* songs, the making of the *Sampo* from the bones of a lamb, the point of a swan's feather, the milk of a farrow cow, a grain of barley, the scraps from a distaff, etc. . . . Similarly, the turning of the *Sampo* would seem to have originated from the magic mills of the folk-tales. . . . It is typical of folk stories that the heroes can change into animals whenever they please . . . and the appearance of barriers in the path of pursuers or anyone striving to reach a definite spot is another notable folk-tale element. This is represented in the *Sampo* poems, especially by the hurling of flint and tinder in the path of the boat carrying the wife of Pohjola. A common theme in tales of competition in love is that of the girl hiding amongst the stars of the sky, the trees of the forest, the grains of sand on the seashore or the fish in the sea, so that the young man has to seek her out by counting the objects among which she is hidden. . . . We encounter a vast eagle and other legendary birds, and even a dragon, all of which are the property of

epic songs and folktales. . . . Nor is the customary witch far away, since the wife of Pohjola at one point binds birch branches to her arms as wings and flies with them; or the beautiful maiden, whose fairness of skin is described in quite fairytale terms "through her flesh, the bone is seen, through her bone, the marrow." There are other points in the *Sampo* songs which one might suspect of being borrowed from folk-tales, but this is sufficient for one story [pp. 435–436].

Thus, it is possible to approach the *Sampo* songs psychoanalytically and interpret them in the manner of a folktale. In earlier interpretations of such tales, I have set out from the assumption that the tale does not describe real events or real human relations but instead the individual's inner world. The characters then stand for the various sides and features of the personality of the principal participant, the narrator or listener, which are externalized through these characters (Hägglund & Hägglund, 1976). Examined in this light, the folktale allows people the opportunity to externalize the conflicts between different sides of their own personality in the characters and events that are portrayed. They can then appreciate the situation over again from an external point of view and be subjected to new influences, before they internalize it again, in a slightly different form than earlier. In this way, use is made of the splitting and projection of things and feelings to the external world for the purpose of coping with growth and development, an extremely powerful feature during the period of regression and growth in adolescence (V. Hägglund, 1983).

THE MESSAGE OF THE EPIC SAMPO SONGS

The cornerstone of Lönnrot's epic consists of a *Sampo* song of 366 verses sung for him by Ontrei Malin, or Malinen, at Vuonninen in the parish of Vuokkiniemi in 1833 and published in his shorter epic *Väinämöinen*. In 1834 he made a new excursion into the province of Viena and recorded a further *Sampo* poem of 407 stanzas as recited by Arhippa Perttunen at the village of Latvajärvi, also in Vuokkiniemi *(Finnish Folk Poetry Epic)*. Nothing further came up after these two poems that required any departure from the original outlines, all the other versions encountered being variations on these or on the same theme.

The introduction to the *Sampo* song tells how a hunchbacked or split-eyed Lapp shoots the horse on which Väinämöinen is riding—a

"blue elk" (Ontrei), or a "straw-hued stallion," "a horse the color of a
pea-stalk" (Arhippa). Väinämöinen falls into the sea and drifts away,
and according to Ontrei and some other versions creates the world
(Setälä, 1932).

> there he wandered for six years
> stopped there for seven summers
> wandered as a spruce
> as a log from a pine-tree

> he prayed to Ukko*
> and worshipped Pavannainen (Arhippa).

Then a great wind stirred up by Ukko

> bore old Väinämöinen
> to dark Pohjola (Arhippa).

Väinämöinen complains that

> "I've swum to strange lands
> to quite unknown doors."

to which the crone of Pohjola replies with the proposal

> "So what will you give me
> if I take you to your own lands
> there to hear your own cock crow
> far from these strange lands
> these quite unknown doors?"
> If you shaped a new *Sampo*
> worked a brightly worked cover
> from one feather of a swan
> from one piece of a distaff
> one snippet of wool
> the milk of a barren cow
> from one barley grain" (Arhippa).

Another version of this is

---

*The chief of gods in Finnish mythology.

"Come now old Väinämöinen
should you forge a *Sampo*
from two bones of a lamb
from three grains of barley
or even from half of that
then would you gain for wages a maiden" (Ontrei).

Väinämöinen promises that if the wife of Pohjola will take him back to
his own land, he will send Ilmarinen, the smith, "who will forge the
Sampo." This she does, and Väinämöinen by singing creates a golden-
branched spruce tree and in it a marten with a golden breast. He tells
Ilmarinen that there is a wondrous maiden in Pohjola, renowned through
all the land

"through her flesh the bone is seen,
through her bone the marrow" (Ontrei).

The man who forged the *Sampo* could have this maiden for his own. But
Ilmarinen realizes that Väinämöinen has promised to send him in
exchange for his own self, to save his own skin. Then Väinämöinen lures
him into the golden-branched spruce tree to catch the marten and "to
meet with a squirrel," high into the sky. He then raises a mighty wind. "It
stirs the air into a rage" and sends him on his way to Pohjola. The harlot,
the wife of Pohjola—or according to Lönnrot, Louhi*, the wife of
Pohjola—has him begin to forge the *Sampo:* "she fed the man till he was
bloated, gave him to drink in plenty, and laid him down beside the
maiden."

Then the smith Ilmarinen
by day he built the *Sampo*
and by night courted the maid
then the smith Ilmarinen
fashioned the *Sampo*
brightly worked the bright-covered
but the maid was not courted (Arhippa).

The wife of Pohjola was delighted with it and gave her daughter to
Ilmarinen, who took her to his home.

---

*The mistress of Pohjola, or Northland, in the epic songs of the Finns. She commands fog
and wind, sends diseases and wild beasts.

The smith Ilmarinen's hand
was in a bright-worked mitten
the other on the maid's breasts
his foot in a German boot
the other between her thighs
as he came from Pohjola (Arhippa).

On his return Ilmarinen announces

See now, old Väinämöinen
there is now a *Sampo* in Pohjola:
now there's ploughing, now there's sowing
now will grow all manner of things;
but the *Sampo* is shut away
behind nine stout locks
with its roots laid down
nine fathoms deep (Ontrei).

Väinämöinen then proposes that they should set out to capture the
Sampo, a desire that no doubt arises out of the affluence it can produce
for its owners and which Väinämöinen and Ilmarinen would not willingly
allow others to enjoy. They decide to take a third man with them as well.
Presumably in an attempt for greater coherence in his narrative, Lönnrot
places the third major hero of the Kalevala, Lemminkäinen, in this role.
The Viena version names this third person as Vesi Liito, the son of Laito,
who brings with him boards for the sides of the boat, whereas Arhippa's
ballad names him as Iku Tiera, the son of Niera and the foremost among
Väinämöinen's friends. On reaching Pohjola, Väinämöinen sings the
people of the village to sleep.

Then he took out sleeping-darts
sent the wicked folk to sleep
oppressed the pagan people (Arhippa).

Then *they* use a plough to uproot the *Sampo.*

But the *Sampo* would not move
its roots were rooted in the earth.
Then the old Väinämöinen
ploughed the roots of the *Sampo*

with a hundred-horned ox
a thousand-headed sea-worm
bore the *Sampo* to his boat
and placed it in his vessel (Arhippa).

Thus the *Sampo* is carried to the boat and they set out on their return
journey. Ilmarinen asks why Väinämöinen does not sing now that he has
taken the *Sampo,* but he replies that it is still too early to rejoice and
sends his companion as a lookout. There is nothing to see. Then an ant
bites a crane on the leg and causes it to squawk, which awakens the
people of Pohjola (Ontrei). In the other version:

An ant, a ballocking boy
pissed on the leg of a crane
in dark Pohjola.
The crane let out a great squawk
screeched out in an evil tone
the whole of Pohjola woke
the evil realm was awake (Arhippa).

The awakened village, with the wife of Pohjola at their head, give chase
in a boat with a hundred rowlocks in which

a hundred were the men rowing
with the turning of a thousand oars (Ontrei).
        or
a hundred men armed with swords
a hundred men for shooting (Arhippa).

But the lookout sees this, and Väinämöinen flings flint and tinder into
the sea to form a crag, on which the boat from Pohjola will run aground:

Then the old Väinämöinen
saw his doom coming
his day of distress dawning:
he fumbled in his pocket
he groped about in his purse
found a tiny piece of flint
a little scrap of tinder
pitched them right into the water

cast them into the sea
straight over his right shoulder
under his left arm.
He himself uttered these words:
"A crag was formed in the sea
a hidden isle spirited
stretching eastward for ever
westward without end
on and on to Pohjola
upon which the craft would be jammed
and the boats would be caught!" (Ontrei)

The wife of Pohjola rises up on the wings of a skylark, "ascends on a bunting's wings," but Väinämöinen slashes the bird across the claws with his paddle so that only the little finger is left. He suggests to the wife of Pohjola that they should divide up the *Sampo* "on the point of that misty cape," but she will not agree to this. Then he sifts the mist with his sieve and wishes "the miserable land of Pohjola, the great wastes of Finland" ploughing, sowing, moons, and suns. The wife of Pohjola in turn threatens his patches of cultivated field with hailstorms (Ontrei).

According to other versions, the wife of Pohjola gives chase almost from the beginning in the guise of a bird (Setälä, 1932)

And then that wife of Pohjola
made of her claws
made of herself a fierce bird
set he elders to row
herself sat at the stern
at the helm of birchwood.

In this interpretation, the whole fine ship in which the wife of Pohjola set out was only a flying bird. In the same way, the Finnish versions speak mostly of a bird of Lapland or Turja's eagle. On other occasions, the bird in whose form the crone of Pohja flew, is referred to in fabulous terms as a wyvern. In some versions, she even binds birch twigs together as wings and takes a pine branch as a tail, or has birch branches as her tail and a man's tunic as her wings. Indeed, the notion of flying on birch wings occurs so frequently that this can scarcely be only a passing reference. In other words, she is pictured as flying on birch branches, just like other witches.

As they fight over the *Sampo,* the branches collapse and fall into the sea.

Old Väinämöinen himself
raised a paddle from the sea
his oar from the waves
smote the eagle on the claws
the wyvern upon the toes.
One nameless finger was left
to seize the *Sampo*
to carry off the bright-covered.
Then the old Väinämöinen
took up his own sword
took in his right hand
from its scabbard on his left.
Then he shattered the *Sampo*
the bright-covered brightly flashed
upon the clear stretch of sea
the open water.
And the wind lulled them
and the soft breeze shifted them
about the blue sea:
washed all the other pieces
up on the seashore
up on the sea-slush.
The gap-toothed crone of Pohja
carried the cover home to Pohjola.

INTERPRETATION OF THE EPIC
SAMPO SONGS

Folkloristic studies of the *Sampo* songs have tended to concentrate on the question of the geographical location of Pohjola. This is of no relevance for its psychoanalytical interpretation, however, any more than is the fact that the capture of the *Sampo* may be associated temporally with other journeys of pillage. From the point of view of the growth of the individual, Pohjola may be regarded as an internal landscape, which is referred to in the poems as a "strange land," where people are said to move about "at quite unknown doors" or "at unknown gates." The information most commonly given in the poem is that the journey took place

right into far Pohjola
to the man-eating village
the village that drowns heroes.
(Simana, *Finnish Folk Epic,* pp. 122–127)

Certainly Pohjola is mostly referred to as a "village", or even "the eternal village", but in many cases, it is felt sufficient to say only "the man-eating place" (Setälä, 1932, p. 500). Regarded psychoanalytically, the journey took place into a childhood world of fantasies ruled by the phallic mother, the crone of Pohja, a witch, and where the child's life and growth are threatened by a man-eating female. This figure in Finnish folk-tales may be taken as an incarnation of jealousy, born in the sauna and capable of being destroyed by burning in the sauna. There is a clear connection here with the feelings aroused by the naked human body (Hägglund and Hägglund, 1984). Thus, this is a journey into the world of childhood fantasies and the child's consciousness of the mysteries of the sexual inner space of the mother's body. I have discussed this mystery earlier as being the greatest of all riddles for the child of oedipal age: where do children come from, and what really happens hidden in the mother's inner space. Being unable to understand this mystery, unable to share it with his mother, as the father does, the son develops a phallic defense mechanism against his jealousy and ignorance, which consists of frightening, aggressive phallic-narcissistic fantasies, the frightening and aggressive nature of which the young Oedipus projects to his phallic mother (Hägglund, Hägglund, and Ilkonen, 1978b). The regression in early adolescence leads the boy to return to these phallic-oedipal fantasies of his childhood. The journey to Pohjola thus symbolizes well the adolescent boy's return to the oedipal conflicts of his childhood.

The *Sampo* song in fact begins with the slit-eyed Lapp shooting Väinämöinen's horse, the man's phallic protection, whereupon Väinämöinen slips into the sea and drifts there for six years. The boy's childhood phallic protection against his sexual mother, whom he fears and envies, collapses, and he finds himself in a state of adolescent regression for six years. It is in this state of regression that Väinämöinen creates the world, a new world to replace that of his lost childhood. Left helpless with the oedipal solutions of his childhood, he prays to his father, Ukko, for help until such time as he has the courage to face the crone of Pohjola, his phallic mother, once the wind raised by Ukko has driven him up onto the shore of Pohja, to a cabin warmed and cleaned out specially for him. Now he begins to resolve the mystery of motherhood all over again, but this time by the means available to an adolescent rather than a child.

In order that the boy should be allowed to return from Pohjola to his own world, the crone of Pohja demands that he should fashion a *Sampo,* or in many versions of the songs a *new Sampo.* It has to be made out of common, everyday materials, but using only very small amounts. What is this *Sampo* which is supposed to bring happiness? This is a question that has puzzled scholars constantly, and numerous explanations have been put forward by academics, artists, and representatives of organized religion. In his book *Sammon arvoitus* (The Riddle of the *Sampo*), Setälä (1932) goes through a number of these explanations. In his footnotes to the New Kalevala, Lönnrot refers to the *Sampo* simply as "a bringer of fortune to the land, a source of happiness," while in his dictionary of 1877 he merely defines it as "a still unexplained miraculous object producing good fortune." The *Sampo* is normally conceived of as a concrete object, for example a mill, which generates affluence and riches for its owner, although it has also been thought of as a living creature and even a maiden. Mythologists have tried to see the *Sampo* songs as a variation of the symbolism of day and night, as representing a struggle between light and darkness, in which the *Sampo* is a heavenly body giving out light (Setälä, 1932). It has also been interpreted as a magic drum, and one theosophical explanation associates the name with the Sanskrit word *samboo* or *samboodha,* meaning the highest knowledge or wisdom. The name has also been likened to the Tibetan word *Sangfu,* meaning the "secret source" (of all happiness).

All the above interpretations come close to the present argument, that the *Sampo,* which does not mean anything in particular in Finnish, is merely a secret pseudonym referring to the human body, and more precisely to its rebirth during the period of adolescent regression. In other words, the *Sampo* stands for the creation of the *image of the sexually active human body* and its release from the bonds of the childhood imagination so that it can bring happiness and well-being to the independent adult, in contrast to the dependence on his mother characteristic of childhood. Laufer (1968, 1982) observes on the basis of a clinical series, that one of the most important problems and tasks for the adolescent is to free his sexually active body from the possession of his mother. The child feels that his mother owns his body and is responsible for his well-being. Clinical experience suggests that adolescence, and especially the fantasies of its regression period, represent a struggle with the mother for possession of the young body. Guided by his regressive fantasies, the adolescent views his mother as the mother figure of his various stages of childhood development, as a mother who nurses him and cares for him, as a witch who threatens him, or as someone who is trying to seduce him erotically (T-B Hägglund, 1977). It is only once he has externalized the various mother images of his early development in the form of his present mother or other currently relevant female figures that he is able to work through his regressive fantasies and resolve anew using the improved methods available in adolescence. Above all, it is the oedipal fantasies of childhood that are externalized in his existing parents and other authorities, and it is only their reformulation that can make it possible to resolve the oedipal situation at the adolescent level. This is what the *Sampo* legend seems to describe.

When the crone of Pohja demands that Väinämöinen forge the *Sampo* as the price for his release, he does not yet feel capable of this. In other words, he is not yet master over his erotic body to the extent that he could fashion a *Sampo* and obtain the daughter of the house as his sexual companion. Thus Väinämöinen offers his better developed contemporary, Ilmarinen, in his place. He can be seen as falling back upon his peers and adolescent culture in order to gain the upper hand over his phallic, oedipal mother. Ilmarinen succeeds in fashioning the *Sampo* and returns from Pohjola "one hand on the maiden's breasts and one foot between her thighs." Together, the young men had accomplished what one alone was incapable of doing, being still tied to his mother by the bonds of childhood. Ilmarinen had worked himself free from the bondage of his oedipal mother, but the outcome of his labors, the *Sampo,* remained with the crone of Pohja, so that Väinämöinen was in effect still left dependent on his phallic mother, the crone herself. He now proposes a raid to recover the *Sampo,* that is, he removes the image of his sexual body from the possession of his phallic mother in secret while she is asleep, being aided in this by other young men. Incapable of forging a *Sampo* of his own, his attention and his heart are still entirely bound up in his mother, and so, as a fine singer, a magic-phallic son, he engages the aid of his peers to capture for himself the erotic pleasure and well-being that he cannot achieve through the normal course of breaking free from his oedipal mother.

The crone of Pohja, from whom the young men steal the *Sampo,* would thus seem to correspond to Väinämöinen's image of his oedipal mother. His urethro-phallic impulses nevertheless awaken her like "an ant, a ballocking boy, pissing on the leg of a crane" and he is led into a confrontation with his phallic mother. He fights like a fairy-tale hero against the dragon Louhi, the harlot of Pohja. He takes his sword and "smites the wyvern across the toes, so that only one nameless finger was left to carry the *Sampo.*" This finger, the ring finger, symbolizing erotic union, remains unsevered. This may be interpreted as suggesting that in spite of the might of his phallic mother and his own still greater strength, Väinämöinen is unable in the course of the phallic contest to sever the erotic union between them, in the form of his childhood images. This proved impossible to achieve by phallic means.

The *Sampo* falls into the sea and shatters into pieces, which are washed up onto the shore, all except for the cover, which the crone carries home with her to Pohjola. This may be understood as signifying that following the phallic struggle between mother and son over possession of the young man's sexual body, the topic itself is dispersed and repressed to the unconscious, to the depths of the sea. Some part of it remains with the mother and the rest drifts around, to reappear at random.

The *Sampo* songs do not tell us or advise us how the act of breaking free from the oedipal mother of childhood should be accomplished during adolescence. They tell us only of the conflict experienced by one adolescent as he tries to solve the problem for himself. The gaining of independence from the mother figure of his childhood is just as great a mystery for the adolescent as is the inner space of the mother. The *Sampo* songs do not contain any sexual male with whom the mother shares her sexuality and with whom the adolescent boy can identify, as is normally the case. Normal, successful growth is not a subject for folk poetry or songs, any more than it is for literature, for all of these find their inspiration in mutual conflicts, without which they would be felt to be too prosaic. If the *Sampo* song does indeed describe the emergence of an adolescent's image of his own sexual body in the form of the conflicts and alterations associated with the fashioning of the *Sampo,* they are truly songs of creation. On this subject, Setälä (1932) states that "One part of the *Sampo* songs, the early part concerned with the beginning of the world, can evidently be regarded as a song of creation . . . but in any event, the possibility should also be borne in mind in the final account of the origins of the poems, that the whole work may be a song of creation" (p. 441).

THE OTHER HEROES OF THE KALEVALA

Lönnrot intuitively included within the Kalevala parts of folktales that do not strictly speaking belong to the *Sampo* songs but which fit in well with them in their treatment of the unconscious conflicts experienced in adolescence. When he split the *Sampo* song, sung by the people as one integral work, and fitted other poetic material into it, his aim was to construct an epic with a single, continuous plot out of all the songs recorded among the Finnish people. Thus, the tale of Väinämöinen's attempts to woo the beautiful maiden of Pohja was placed in between parts of the *Sampo* tale, and the same is true of the story of the fashioning of the Golden Maiden, a poem that tells how one who is unlucky in love attempts to console himself by forging a bride for himself out of gold. Setälä (1932) believes that this poem is closely connected with the *Sampo* songs. Similarly, Lemminkäinen's journey to Pohjola, his death and return to life and his coming to the wedding at Pohjola are located in between parts of the original songs, just as Lemminkäinen himself is established as the third man in the capture of the *Sampo* in place of Vesi Liito, the son of Laito. Other interpolated tales are those of Väinämöinen's boat building, the journey to Tuonela*, the competition for the hand of the maiden, the labors and the fashioning of a sword. The poems of Kullervo, which are principally the songs "The Orphan," "Rutsa," and "Leaving for War" *(Finnish Folk Poetry Epic)* blended together, are again interpolated, whereas the end of the Kalevala bears no connection at all with the actual *Sampo* songs.

The interpolated poems such as "The Golden Maiden" and those concerned with Lemminkäinen and Kullervo would seem to be closely related to the *Sampo* topic. They all describe failure to break free of the childhood mother figure and establish a nonincestuous sexual relationship. In the song of the golden maiden, recourse is made to a substitute, whereas Lemminkäinen is portrayed as a phallic fighter and stealer of women who cannot attach himself seriously to any woman. He is bound by dependence on his mother, who follows him about, puts right his misdeeds and pieces him together again after his demise in the river of Tuonela. On his mother's advice, Lemminkäinen tries to escape the revenge of the people of Pohjola, (i.e., the power of his phallic mother) by fleeing to the same island to which his father had once escaped. There he falls into incestuous relationships with his sisters, the daughters of his own father. Thus Lemminkäinen too is a male character who has failed to forge his *Sampo,* to create an independent sexual body for himself.

If Lemminkäinen is bound to his childhood mother because she feeds his phallicism in a manner that draws them together, Kullervo is a prisoner of his own oedipal hatred of his father and his desire for

---

*The dead-land of Finnish mythology.

revenge. He kills his father, who is disguised in the person of his stepfather, murders the whole of his father's family, and destroys their house. He becomes involved with his sister, however, and finally perishes by his own sword. The Kullervo songs in the Kalevala, which it is not possible to recount here in detail, would seem to be comparable with Shakespeare's *Hamlet*. As far as his own inner motives were concerned, Kullervo had killed his father in the course of his childhood oedipal fantasies, and thus lost his opportunity for emulating and internalizing this "father-king." Later, in adolescence, he wanders about searching for revenge and destroying all the personal relationships that are of any importance to him, until at last he becomes preoccupied with the thought that if only he could change everything . . . and eventually destroys himself in the process.

Lönnrot's aim in uniting these folktales into one epic was to create a picture of two peoples in conflict one with the other. For this purpose, he placed the poems describing the competition for the hand of the maiden and the wedding feast in amongst the *Sampo* songs proper. As Setälä (1932) notes, the account of the wedding feast, made up "to a fair extent of the incantations of the wedding guests," included as it is within the story of the *Sampo,* has the quite particular effect of creating and maintaining an impression of two tribes, those of Kalevala and Pohjola, "which are now as it were united by the bonds of marriage" (p. 53). This aim of Lönnrot was nevertheless entirely at variance with the content of the *Sampo* song, as such, for the *Sampo* songs did not aim to describe union between Väinämöinen and the crone of Pohja but rather their separation one from the other.

THE OEDIPUS THEME IN FINNISH FOLK POETRY

The Oedipus theme may be seen as a feature running through Finnish folk poetry and affecting very many of the heroes of the Kalevala. This mingling of adolescent phallic-narcissistic bravado with dependence on and attachment to an overwhelming mother figure serves to depict the adolescent conflicts brought about by the Oedipus complex and the subject's unsuccessful attempts to gain dominion over his own sexual body. The forging of the *Sampo* is a great secret and a great mystery, and it is only this that can free the adolescent from his phallic mother. Once the *Sampo* has been fashioned for the crone of Pohja, however, and the bride obtained, both Väinämöinen, who represents the magic-phallic singing aspect in the song, and Ilmarinen, who represents the magic-phallic singing aspect in the song, and Ilmarinen, who represents the more advanced, skilful aspect, are overcome by jealousy of the maternal happiness and well-being that this source of good things brings with it. Looked at in this way, the adolescent's barrier to independence from his mother may be said to be his jealousy of his childhood mother figure. The child's jealousy of his mother's sexuality, her fertility and creative inner space, features that the young Oedipus was never able to share with his mother, are revived at the point at which the adolescent strives to free himself from his mother's bonds and sees this sublime state persisting in her. In other words, he cannot allow his mother this narcissistic value and happiness and leave her with her sexuality, her *Sampo*, to live her own life in the company of his father. This interpretation may be valid in spite of the fact that the father is not referred to explicitly in the *Sampo* legends other than in the sense that, while at sea, (i.e., in the unhappiness of his adolescent regression), Väinämöinen prays for help from Ukko.

The heart of the childhood Oedipus problem lies in the fact that the child was unable to comprehend the mystery of his mother's inner sexuality, which enabled her to produce children and to bind his father to her. Thus he remained a jealous outsider with respect to the sexual inner space union between his parents (Hägglund et al., 1978a, b). On the other hand, the child developed phallic-narcissistic fantasies regarding his own overwhelming phallic attraction and power as a defense against his own jealousy. Upon reaching the stage of adolescent regression, he is confronted once more by the same problem, and the *Sampo* songs and their interpolations seem to be concerned with precisely those conflicts that arise as a consequence of this unconscious Oedipus complex. The Oedipus theme as it appears in Finnish folklore can be separated into a number of subproblems as far as adolescence is concerned, that is, the Oedipus complex of childhood becomes predominantly that of Väinä-möinen, of Ilmarinen, of Lemminkäinen, or of Kullervo, depending on what part of the childhood smallness complex is felt by the adolescent Oedipus to be most problematical, although all the elements are naturally present to some degree or other in every boy's Oedipus complex.

Väinämöinen is unable to fashion a *Sampo* or to leave one behind to produce phallic-narcissistic value and happiness for his mother figure. He tries to outdo his phallic mother by phallic-narcissistic and magico-phallic means, and sacrifices his independent sexual body, in the form of the *Sampo*, in the process. Väinämöinen's downfall is his jealousy of his oedipal sexual mother.

Ilmarinen is able to fashion the *Sampo,* but cannot leave it with his phallic mother, and thus he sacrifices his sexual achievement, the maiden of Pohja. The forging of the golden maiden may be regarded as an attempt at compensation for this. Ilmarinen's downfall similarly lies in his jealousy of his mother's sexual inner space, which is capable of creativity and childbearing, a jealousy he attempts to deny by creating a bride for himself out of gold and silver. Although he succeeds in this, the result does not come up to his expectations and he rejects it. He has failed to give his mother figure credit for the fertility of her sexual inner space and attempts to wrench this from her by identifying himself with a child-bearing mother.

Lemminkäinen's complex lies in the fact that his phallic-narcissistic bond with his mother is so overwhelmingly satisfying that he rejects all other women and goes through the world as her phallic champion. His character exudes immaturity and boyish aggression; he is stuck in an oedipal maternal relationship. By contrast, Kullervo's complex is largely a matter of adolescent oedipal hatred and jealousy combined with revengefulness at the union prevailing between his parents and his own exclusion from it. He sets out to destroy everything and ends up by destroying himself.

The question still remains of whether it is possible to find a good father-figure relationship with which the boy of oedipal age can identify himself and with which he can form a union upon his release from dependence on his oedipal mother. No father figure occurs in these folk poems. Is it the case that such a character is lacking from Finnish folk culture in general, or is it that he merely remains too weak a personality by the side of the mother? Or was it felt unnecessary to sing songs about the successful achievement of adulthood and release from the maternal bonds? Probably all three of these alternatives are involved. Finnish folk literature contains many illegitimate, fatherless children, "serving-maid's children"; the Finnish woman is traditionally a strong personality by comparison with the man, and why, after all, should one weave songs of creation around successful unions and healthy growth, in which the individual's sexual body, as a source of narcissism and the satisfaction of the basic urges, is in one's own possession?

I am also inclined to think that the Oedipus father complex is secondary in nature to the jealousy and incomprehension aroused by the sexual inner space of the mother, for it is only when this is repressed to the unconscious that the father becomes the object of jealousy, in the manner proposed by Grunberger (1957, 1967). The narcissistic affront experienced by the small boy on account of the unapproachability of his mother's sexual inner space leads him at oedipal age to direct his narcissistic fury toward his father, and also, inasfar as he is able to bear the jealousy he feels toward his father, to identify with him. Thus, the oedipal problem is primarily a narcissistic problem of the form "How can I bear the union between mother and father when, as a small boy, I am unable to achieve the same union myself?" and "How can I bear the love mother shows for father when it is I who am born out of her?" In childhood, this fury is directed predominantly at the mother and the father is approached with fear, in the form stated by Grunberger "It is not true that I am incapable. It is he (my father) who is preventing me."

At the time of adolescent regression and development, this pattern is reversed, the narcissistic fury being turned upon the father whereas the mother becomes an object of fear, in the form "Father is old and incapable by comparison with me, but how can I free myself from mother's immeasurable power of attraction?" The adolescent at the regression stage feels that his mother controls his body and his sexual fantasies, and fears that she will interfere with his sexuality, because he cannot defend himself against his mother as he can against his father, with whom he can identify. His phallic struggle against his mother cannot secure his release, but rather binds him to this phallic-oedipal mother figure. He could do it if he were to exclude his mother's sexual body from the sphere of his fascination, but in order to do this he would first have to come to terms sufficiently with his jealousy of his mother's creative inner space, (i.e., his Väinämöinen and Ilmarinen complexes).

The tragedy of the Oedipus situation is above all narcissistic in character, and it is a tragedy common to both father and son, in that neither can reduplicate himself out of his own inner space. The difficulty they encounter in identifying with the mother and her creative ability to carry and give birth to a child may easily lead to a desire to possess the mother. Thus, the state of competition between father and son may at a deeper level be simply a desire to dominate the source of creativity and narcissistic value in the family. This reaches its climax at the stage of adolescent regression, when each has a body capable of attracting the mother sexually but the generation gap between them is not yet sufficiently great to lead their interests toward women of different generations. Although it is the son who is going through adolescence, the state of competition and the narcissistic vulnerability entailed in this affect them both. The mother is perceived unconsciously as a woman who controls their bodies and their fantasies with an erotic attraction that recalls the unconscious magic-phallic childhood images of witches. The phallic mother dominates both of them, father and son, and can easily be comprehended in the manner of the wife of Pohja, who rules over the whole of Pohjola—the erotic inner world of the male.

ADOLESCENT OEDIPAL FANTASIES

The oedipal fantasies of adolescence can be of three kinds, which may be superimposed upon one another and become intermingled in a manner that can cause extreme confusion in the mind of the adolescent, namely, development, independence, or protection fantasies. In my paper "Some Viewpoints on the Ego Ideal" (1980), I put forward the idea that the creative fantasies of adolescence may be a continuation of those of the transition phase in childhood, in which creative illusion progressed from the parts of the body of the mother and child to creative play and shared illusions on common topics. The masturbation fantasies of adolescence, on the other hand, are connected more with the conflict over who possesses, satisfies, and restrains the erotic body of the adolescent, and are therefore fantasies of power. The *development fantasies* of adolescence are creative fantasies concerned with what happens in the sexual inner space of the mother, how it works, how one can get into it, how it can be divided up, what kind of interaction can be established, etc. They are growth fantasies concerned with everything that the adolescent cannot yet know or feel but is trying to approach. Just as creative illusion is used to gain a knowledge of the unknown in the transition phase of childhood proposed by Winnicott (1953), so the adolescent can approach the sexual body, his own and that of his mother, by developing fantasies as one does of a transference object and by forming analysable illusions regarding it.

The *independence fantasies* are fantasies of power involving an internal struggle between desire, ego, and superego fantasies and an external struggle over who possesses the body of the adolescent, the adolescent himself or his mother, and who possesses the sexual body of the mother, the father, Oedipus, or the mother herself. The Finnish *Sampo* songs represent in the same way a struggle over who will fashion and possess the *Sampo*.

The third group of adolescence fantasies are the *protection fantasies,* which are primarily phallic-narcissistic in nature and are intended as a means by which the adolescent protects himself from the smallness complex. It is the complex that includes the whole narcissistic tragedy of the Oedipus complex, which for the boy implies that he is unable to give birth to children out of his own body, unable to understand how his mother does this, and unable to control or possess the creative sexual inner space of the female. He therefore constructs a mighty phallic-narcissistic shield against the resulting sense of jealousy.

The one common aim of all these fantasies is the question of how the image of the individual's sexual body can be integrated into his whole personality in order to meet the needs of this personality in terms of narcissistic values and human relations. It is a question of how the sexual body can be rendered independent and free of external constraints and domination, which is perhaps the most important requirement for achieving a healthy narcissism and good object relations.

THE FOLK POETRY OEDIPUS THEME IN THE EPIC OF A NATION SEEKING INDEPENDENCE

The heroes of the Kalevala are relatively pale characters for the principal figures in a national epic. They are not great conquerors or proclaimers of ideals. Instead, because the nucleus of the Kalevala is the legend of the *Sampo* as described above, its heroes are men engaged in a struggle against the overbearing power of a woman, the wife of Pohja, and this in spite of the fact that Lönnrot's aim was to depict a struggle between two peoples. Even so, the work performed an important function as a national epic in the service of Finnish independence. Could it be that the message of the *Sampo* poems did in fact instill itself into the hearts of a people themselves beset by a smallness complex, enabling them to work on their Oedipus complex relative to their great neighbors of that time?

On the one side was the eagle of Russia and the "Little Father," as the Czar was called, symbols that implied a dread of dominion and often arbitrary rule in the minds of the Finns of the day, while on the other side was "Svea-mamma," mother Sweden, as she was known. It was this country's language that dominated the intellectual and educational life of Finland, and the Sweden of that time was looked on as a prying, possessive mother figure who attached little worth to either the Finnish language or its culture.

For his own part, Lönnrot was brought up in the sphere of Finnish folk culture and refined by the Swedish school and university world that prevailed in Finland. He was a tenant farmer's son who studied medicine and gained his doctorate in the field of folk poetry. He must have experienced oedipal conflicts not only in his own private life, but also in the social and political state that prevailed in Finnish culture at that time. As an artist and man of vision, he created the Kalevala as a bridge between the message of the Finnish folk culture and the aspirations of the upper classes and intelligentsia of Finland. The act of breaking away from the family, becoming independent, and setting up a family of one's own has always been recognized as problematical and demanding in the eyes of ordinary people, who have then tended to alleviate the difficulties through the medium of folktales or poems that tell of the conflicts lying at the heart of human growth and development. Other devices that serve the same purpose include various rites such as initiation ceremonies.

Those brought up among the intelligentsia and in the educated world are well aware of the importance of a spirit of competition when striving for positions from which to influence the progress of their own country. Lönnrot was at home in both worlds and was able to combine the folk culture's desire for intellectual growth with the educated classes' desire to govern their own country and free it from foreign rule. He succeeded in combining these two aims, release from the smallness complex and release from oedipal conflicts, first in his own personality and then in the Kalevala, which evolved into a work that lent support both to the romantic nationalism of the age and also to the educated classes in their struggle for an independent Finland.

The outcome was that the Finnish people and their intellectual leaders were able to unite in their attempts to escape from the complex of smallness and dependence on others and to resolve their "oedipal" conflicts. Its success was short-lived, however, and terminated in the Civil War, which took the form of a class struggle between the upper classes and the people, in which the upper class, as victors, executed those brought up in the folk culture, their children both symbolically and in a physical sense, by their hundreds. Symbolically in the sense that those of modest means are the children of those who are more comfortably off, and physically in the sense that a large number of the "serving maid's children" were the illegitimate progeny of upper-class fathers and were filled with hatred and resentment toward this class as a whole. Thus, the oedipal conflict had assumed the proportions of an internal political problem within the one nation. A further interesting development is that the Kalevala has become with time the property of the educated circles, which ordinary people scarcely read at all. As a national epic, it is too far removed from their sphere of existence.

SUMMARY

This paper forms a continuation of an earlier discussion of "The Oedipus Theme in Finnish Folklore" (Hägglund and Hägglund, 1981). The major theme running through the Finnish national epic, the Kalevala, is that of the *Sampo*. The author interprets this poetic account of the fashioning and capture of the *Sampo* psychoanalytically as a metaphorical representation of the adolescent's struggle to free his own sexual body from the hegemony of his mother. Each of the heroes of the Kalevala, Väinämöinen, Ilmarinen, Lemminkäinen, and Kullervo, attempt to accomplish this in his own way, so that the analyst is able to distinguish a corresponding set of variations on the theme of the adolescent Oedipus complex.

Finally, the paper considers how a people suffering from a smallness complex can have collectively given expression to this Oedipus relationship toward their mighty neighbors. The significance of this national epic for the efforts of a nation on the road to independence to resolve its Oedipus complex toward its rulers of that time is reflected in an attempt to describe and resolve essential questions related to the Oedipus complex at the developmental level of the adolescent and by the mechanisms available to the adolescent.

BIBLIOGRAPHY

KUUSI, M., BOSKY, K. & BRANCH, M., ed. (1977), Finnish Folk Poetry Epic. Helsinki: The Society of Finnish Literature.
GRUNBERGER, B. (1957), Essai sur la situation analytique et le precessus guérison. In: *Le narcissisme: Essais de psychanalyse.* Paris: Payot, 1971, pp. 53–115.
────── (1967), L'oedipe et le narcissisme. In: *Le narcissisme: Essais de psychanalyse.* Paris: Payot, 1971, pp. 331–348.
HÄGGLUND, T-B. & HÄGGLUND, V. (1976), Mourning and death in fairy tales and folklore. *Psychiat. Fenn.,* 25–31.
────── (1977), On development and growth. *Psychiat. Fenn.,* 41–46.
────── HÄGGLUND, V. & ILKONEN, P. (1978a), Some viewpoints on woman's inner space. *Scand. Psychoanal. Rev.,* 1:65–77.
────── ────── & ────── (1978b), On the defensive nature of phallicity. In: *Dying: A Psychoanalytical Study With Special Reference to Individual Creativity and Defensive Organization.* New York: International Universities Press, pp. 89–108.
────── (1980), Some viewpoints on the ego ideal. *Internat. Rev. Psycho-Anal.,* 7:207–218.
────── & ────── (1981), The boy who killed his father and wed his mother: The Oedipus theme in Finnish folklore. *Internat. Rev. Psycho-Anal.,* 8:53–62.
HÄGGLUND, V. (1983), Narsismin kehitys nuoruusiässä (The development of narcissism in adolescence). Finn. Youth Psychiat. Soc. Yearbook No. 4, 17–31. Jyväskylä: Gummerus.
LAUFER, M. (1968), The body image: The function of masturbation and adolescence: Problem of the ownership of the body. *Psychoanal. Study of the Child,* 23:114–140.
────── (1982), The formation and shaping of the Oedipus complex: clinical observations and assumptions. *Internat. J. Psycho-Anal.,* 63:217–228.
LÖNNROT E. (1928), *Alkukalevala* (Primal Kalevala). Helsinki: Relander, Publications of the Society of Finnish Literature no. 178.
SETÄLÄ, E. N. (1932), *Sammon arvoitus* (The Riddle of Sampo). Helsinki: Otava.
WINNICOTT, D. W. (1953), Transitional objects and transitional phenomena. In: *Playing and Reality,* 1–25. London: Tavistock Publ., 1971.

13

Pierced by Murugan's Lance:
The Symbolism of Vow Fulfillment

ELIZABETH F. FULLER

As celebrated by the Tamils of Penang, Malaysia, the Thaipusam festival, which honors the god Murugan, son of the great Hindu deities Siva and Parvati, lasts for three days and is the most important festival of the year. On the first day Murugan is carried in procession from the center of George Town to a temple at the edge of the city that is owned by the Nattukottai Chettiars, a lineage group that claims high status as the sponsors of this procession. On the third night Murugan, represented as a god-king, completes the tour of his domain in a procession that lasts all night. The second day of the festival is Thaipusam, a day marked by a conjunction of astrological forces that make it especially auspicious for the worship of Murugan in pilgrimage temples that are associated with a tradition of devotional worship, known as *bhakti,* which rejects the role of *brahmin* priests and the institutions of caste hierarchy. On this day, several thousand Tamil devotees of Murugan fulfill vows they have made to him.

Devotees prepare for the day of vow fulfillment by observing a self-appointed regime of austerities, which includes chastity and fasting. This is believed to purify body and soul. On Thaipusam the pilgrims who are to fulfill vows rise early, bathe, and dress in ritual garments, loincloths or saris of cotton that have been dyed saffron yellow. They gather at small shrines throughout the city, where they construct small altars from the *kavatis* (wooden arches traditionally decorated with peacock feathers and an image of Murugan) that most devotees will carry with their offerings. Each devotee will then be put into a trance by a non-*brahmin* priest.

As the devotee begins to pray the priest waves incense while family and friends chant, *Vel, vel, vetri vel* (Lance, lance, victorious lance). Most devotees fall gradually into a state of composed dissociation: eyes closed and body relaxed. Sometimes, however, a devotee or bystander will start to dance wildly or take up a martial stance and confront bystanders, the priest, or invisible warrior spirits with a challenge to fight. Then the priest applies sacred ash to the forehead of the possessed person, and this usually terminates the outburst.

When devotees who are to fulfill a vow appear to be in a calm state of trance, the priest inserts into their flesh hooks (Figure 1) or a *vel* (a lance, the invincible weapon of Murugan). The devotees generally show no signs of pain, nor do they bleed. Both men and women may have their tongues pierced by a miniature *vel*. Men may also have hooks placed in the skin of their chest (and back, in some cases) so that offerings in the form of small pots of milk or limes may be hung from them. Some young men pull small chariots decorated with images of Murugan by means of hooks embedded in their backs. Others have both cheeks pierced by a full-sized replica of the god's lance (see Figure 2). These young men, typically accompanied by a group of friends including a drummer, perform the pilgrimage to Murugan by dancing to devotional music, which is played in stalls that have been erected along the pilgrimage route as an act of homage to Murugan.

Figure 1

Figure 2

After fulfilling their vows and awakening from trance, devotees appear to be preoccupied and little inclined to talk about their experience. They have no conscious memory of the thoughts or feelings that were associated with the fulfillment of their vow. This amnesia is explained by the belief that trance involves possession by Murugan. The analgesia of the trance state is accepted as a sign that Murugan has entered into or empowered his devotees and eliminated the pain that they would ordinarily feel. Some devotees described their mood as one of elation (Simons, Ervin, and Prince, 1988). Speaking in Tamil, participants call this experience of divine possession *arul,* a word that is usually translated as "divine blessing" or "grace"; when speaking in Malay, they call it *kemasukan,* a noun form of the verb "to enter," which refers to incidents of divine or demonic possession. There is a parallel here to the word "ecstasy," derived from the Greek *ekstasis,* which was used in ancient Greece for a trance in which either the soul left the body to unite with the divine, or the god dwelt inside a person, who thereby became an oracle (Lewin, 1950).

When asked why they insert hooks or spears into their bodies, devotees of Murugan usually respond by giving their reason for making a vow—their desire for a child, for example, or the wish to be cured of a life-threatening illness. They see the vow as a kind of contract: The devotee asks the god for a favor and in exchange promises to fulfill a vow on Thaipusam. The deity may or may not grant the devotee's request; in

either case, whether to induce the god to act or to repay him for a favor
obtained, the devotee is expected to fulfill the vow. However, many
devotees cannot provide a reason for their vow and simply reply that they
felt impelled to make a vow to Murugan.

Invariably, the devotees also cannot explain the symbolic meaning
of typical forms of vow fulfillment—for example, of piercing their
cheeks with the lance of Murugan or carrying pots of milk suspended by
hooks from their chests (Freud, 1907b). When pressed, they generally say
that a priest must be consulted to interpret the meaning of the rituals
performed (Diehl, 1956; Shulman, 1980).

Although the devotees of Murugan cannot provide an interpretation
of the symbolic acts performed as ritual vow fulfillment, they do help us
to understand their acts as they provide narrative commentary on
controversies among different groups of Tamils over the celebration of
Thaipusam in Penang, the authenticity of their own practices as compared to those of others, and especially as they refer to the legends that
tell of Murugan's deeds and his relations to other deities. As Dundes
(1976, 1985) has pointed out, symbolic communication is encoded in the
folklore of a culture. Legends, myths, tales, jokes, proverbs, ritual
practices, and so on, provide a store of images with shared associations
from which individuals may draw in symbolic communication. The dense
complexity of associations and layering of multiple meanings generated
by folklore allow people to elaborate individually specific meanings that
rest on culturally shaped understandings. In this chapter I explore the
realm of meanings that symbolic acts of vow fulfillment may express:
conflicts over sexuality and aggression, expressions simultaneously rebellious and submissive, and paradoxes of gender identity.

ASCETICISM AND POWER

The legend that associates Murugan with ascetic practices is a tale of
sibling rivalry that ends in the fantasy of the son who compels his father
to recognize his position as the newly constituted authority. Murugan
and Vinayagar,[1] the elephant-headed god who is his brother, both wish
to have a golden mango that the sage Narada has brought to their
parents. The brothers are told that they must compete to win the prize:

---

[1]In North India, where the elephant-headed deity is known as Ganesh, he is often
represented as the only son of Siva and Parvati. There are other important differences
in the representation of the gods in the North, where, for example, Ganesh has seven
wives and Skanda (Murugan) is a celibate warrior.

the first to go around the world will be given the mango. Murugan immediately mounts his peacock and sets forth, but Vinayagar, who rides a rat, sits down to think. Then he rises and, after circling around his mother (parents), demands the prize, explaining that his mother is all the world to him. His devotion to his parents is rewarded. When Murugan returns, he is outraged that his brother has been given the mango and, after stripping off the sacred thread of the high "twice-born" castes, he leaves the Himalayan home of the gods to go to the jungle hill-tracts of Tamilnadu in the southernmost part of the Indian subcontinent. In his retreat on a hilltop Murugan meditates and observes the austerities of an ascetic. His father, Siva, seeks him out there to persuade him to return home. Failing to induce his son to give up his ascetic life, Siva finally acknowledges the power of his son and says to Murugan, *Parani* (You are the fruit). The pilgrimage temple of Palani was founded to mark this recognition of the power of Murugan. The celebration of Thaipusam is the most important festival of the year at this temple and is the model for the Penang celebration.

Indian folklore abounds in tales of religious hermits, as well as demons (*asuras* and *raksasas*), who perform ascetic practices *(tapas)* with the aim of obtaining boons from the gods. In the *Mahabharata,* ascetics, empowered by their *tapas,* shake the throne of Indra, who sends down heavenly nymphs to distract them from their ascetic discipline. Ravana, king of the *raksasas* and antihero of the *Ramayana,* by performing ascetic practices forced Brahma to grant him boons that made him invulnerable and enabled him to assume any form he pleased. And the horrible man-eating *raksasa* Viradha, "wearing a tiger's skin, dripping with fat, wetted with blood, terrific to all creatures, like death with an open mouth" also obtained the boon of invulnerability from the gods through *tapas* (Dowson, 1961).

The theme of these tales is empowerment—by control of his (the hermits are invariably male) own desire, the ascetic is able to compel the gods to grant him a boon (Bhagat, 1976). Frequently, these ascetic practices are associated with fantasies of revenge for wrongs done to one by those who are more powerful; for example, Menninger (1938) cites the tale of a corrupt Raja who ordered the house of a *brahmin* destroyed and his lands confiscated. The *brahmin* retaliated by fasting at the palace gate until he died, after which he became an avenging ghost who destroyed the Raja. Menninger points out that this fantasy assumes that the (self-imposed) suffering of the ascetic will elicit feelings of guilt in the one who witnesses it "and thus force him to assume the moral but illogical obligation for it" (p. 110). Gandhi demonstrated the political efficacy of just such passive-aggressive asceticism in wresting power from the British.

One of the most well-known tales of asceticism[2] tells of the rivalry between the *kshatriya* warrior-king Visvamitra and the *brahmin* Vasistha. Defeated in battle, time and again, the warrior Visvamitra finally recognized that the spiritual power of a *brahmin* is superior to the physical prowess of the warrior and resolved to acquire spiritual power through ascetic discipline. He fasted and meditated day after day, but his first attempt was defeated when the nymph Menaka seduced him. His second attempt failed when he used his newly acquired powers to destroy the beautiful nymph Rambha, who also had been sent to distract him. Finally he succeeded in subjugating all the passions, lust, greed, and anger, and became a *brahmasari,* an exemplar of the ideal ascetic, and a *brahmin* by caste.

The moral of the tale is clear: the low and the weak prevail over the powerful by conquering their own impulsive and desirous natures and acquiring the virtues of the powerful. They fulfill the aims of their aggression by turning that aggression back against themselves. In the Hindu corpus of sacred texts the tale is told in a way that acknowledges the rivalry for status and power between *kshatriya* warrior-kings and *brahmin* priests who claim higher status in the caste hierarchy. Visvamitra ultimately prevails by becoming a *brahmin,* thereby providing further proof of the superiority of *brahmins.* What begins as a refusal to recognize the superiority of *brahmins* ends by acknowledging the traditional social order.

The connection between the stigma of caste and redemption through asceticism is made explicit in the *Mahabharata* when the sage Parasara says to King Janaka: "O King! those great-souled ones who have made themselves pure by austerities even though born of low parentage cannot be considered low, only because of their low birth" (Bhagat, 1976, p. 203). Visvamitra's renunciation of sexual desire and the aggressive impulses of the *kshatriya* warrior is interpreted as mastery over the "lower propensities" of his nature, which have determined his birth in a relatively "low" caste. Symbolically, ascetic practices conflates a rebellion against the social order of caste and a conquest of the self that involves a denial (or repression) of aggression.

Although the themes of guilt and atonement noted by Menninger are not absent from Indian tales of asceticism, the idea of penance is

---

[2]This tale appears in the *Mahabharata,* the *Ramayana,* the *Markandya Purana,* the *Harivamsa,* and the *Yoga-Vasistha.*

generally subordinated to that of empowerment and a protest against the socially imposed stigma of caste (Bhagat, 1976). The ascetic discipline of *yoga* specifies how sexual energy may be transformed into spiritual power (O'Flaherty, 1973; Danielou, 1964; Eliade, 1969; Obeyesekere, 1981). The term for ascetic practices, *tapas,* is derived from the Sanskrit root *tap,* which means "heat." *Kama* (desire) generates the heat of sexuality, which is dissipated in sexual intercourse. A man may concentrate this power through the self-control and sexual abstinence involved in ascetic practices. Thus spiritual power is also manifested as heat, as in the third eye of Siva, which can destroy by fire.

Paradoxically, in the Hindu view, ascetic practices offer as compensation for self-inflicted suffering enhanced sexual potency. The concentration of spiritual power allows the ascetic to indulge in sexuality without depleting his supply of energy. Thus Śiva, the ascetic paradigm, is worshipped in the form of the phallic *linga.* Kakar (1981) has suggested that the ascetic fantasy is a defensive one in which a denial of bodily needs is equated with denial of a need for supplies of love and gratification from others in the world, according to the formula, "I do not need anyone's love, nor do I need anything from the world, not even food" (p. 156). He points out that Siva's sexual energy is not directed toward an object; he has no desire for another. He is self-sufficient. By withdrawing from the world, the ascetic comes to believe that he no longer needs the love or approval of others.

The symbolic equivalence of self-mastery and mastery of the world has been noted by many scholars of yoga and Hindu asceticism. For instance, Eliade (1969) writes, "One always finds a form of yoga whenever there is a question of experiencing the sacred or arriving at complete mastery of oneself, which is itself the first step toward the magic mastery of the world" (p. 196; see also Masson, 1976; Menninger, 1938). And Kakar (1981) comments that Śiva, the ruler of the universe, who meditates in the Himalayas, embodies the ascetic ideal in which as Eliade (1969) puts it, "mastery of the self is equated with mastery of the world" (p. 196).

We can now also understand the startling association of asceticism with the disgusting, greedy, and rapacious demons, who are at the bottom of the divine hierarchy. The power and status of high castes are justified by their innate virtue and purity. Low birth is equated with the part of the self that feels sexual desire and desire for things in the world. This aspect of the self, represented symbolically by demons who embody lust, greed, and anger, must be mastered in order for the ascetic to become empowered.

THE DEMON DEVOTEE:
MASTERED BY MURUGAN

The legends associated with Thaipusam identify the worshiper who fulfills a vow by carrying a *kavati* with the demon Idumban, Murugan's chief devotee. The sage Agastya, who is venerated by Tamils for bringing literature, science, and Hindu ritual to South India, employed the demon Idumban to take two hills to Tamilnadu, one called Sivagiri in honor of Śiva, the other Saktigiri in honor of his spouse. The demon looped serpents around the hills and carried them suspended by a pole borne on his shoulder. Upon reaching the southern forests, he sat down to rest. When he wanted to resume his journey, he found he could no longer lift the hills. Investigating, he discovered a youth clad in a loincloth on top of the larger hill, who claimed the mount as his own. The demon attacked him, but the youth, whom he did not recognize as Murugan, quickly defeated him. Responding to the pleas of the demon's wife and the sage Agastya, Murugan brought Idumban back to life and made him guardian of the Palani temple located at the top of the hill. Thus the demon Idumban became the model for devotees who carry shoulder-borne *kavatis* to Murugan's temple on Thaipusam.

In folk belief, the *raksasas* or *asuras* are demonic beings who exist in perpetual revolt against the gods *(devas)*. According to tradition, Prajapati, the creator, formed the *devas* from higher life energies and the *asuras* from lower energies (Danielou, 1964). Originally the gods and the *asuras* were equally powerful, but their power was divided, with the gods exercising power by day and the *asuras* by night (Stutley and Stutley, 1977). The *asuras* therefore are believed to visit people at night in their dreams (Obeyesekere, 1981). Like the Titans of Greek mythology, these rebels against the high gods are associated with the angry resentment of those who are relegated to a position below the high and powerful and with repressed, forbidden wishes (Freud, 1900). For example, Obeyesekere writes of demon possession among Sinhalese and Tamils that when the priest diagnoses a woman's illness as "Kalu Kumara [a particular demon] *dosa* (sin), it almost invariably implies that the patient is afflicted by disturbing sexual impulses. By contrast, Mahasona, the demon of the cemetery, is related to problems of aggression" (p. 121).

According to the theology of Saiva Siddhanta, the *asuras* are said to personify the three *malas* or *pacas,* the forces that bind human spirits to this world: *anava* (ignorance), *karma* (the inevitability of action's fruit), and *maya* (worldly ensnarement) (Clothey, 1983). In texts on *yoga,* the progress of an ascetic is described as a battle between the gods and demons in which desires must be defeated so that the true ascetic, who is represented by Skanda (Murugan), may be born (Danielou, 1964). Shulman (1980), interpreting Tamil temple legends, explicitly links the demon-devotee with the inner demon that each devotee must defeat:

> The demon . . . symbolizes the evil within man (preoccupation with a false 'selfhood,' the lust for power, opposition to the divine ideals); this evil must be destroyed before redemption becomes possible . . . For the human devotee, this process need not culminate in actual death (as it does on the symbolic level for the demon devotee); it does, however, require a form of self-sacrifice [p. 320].

The theme of the demon-devotee who is subdued by Murugan and comes to be his honored servant also appears in the legend of Murugan's peacock mount. The demon Surapadma was granted the boon of immortality by Siva because of his great austerities. Surapadma then led a rebellion of the *asuras* against the high gods who ruled in the Himalayas. The gods finally realized that only a son of Siva would be able to defeat the rebellious demons and sent Parvati to seduce the god. When Murugan reached maturity, his mother gave him the *vel* for his conquest of the demonic forces. Murugan dispatched Surapadma's demon allies and also his two brothers, but the battle with Surapadma was prolonged because the demon took different forms in order to gain an advantage over the god. Murugan could not kill the demon because of the boon granted by Siva. Finally, Surapadma took the form of a tree, which Murugan split with his lance so that one part of the tree became a rooster and the other a peacock. Murugan placed the cock on his banner and made the peacock his vehicle (Clothey, 1978).

Like the demon, the devotees who fulfill vows on Thaipusam have been pierced with the lance of Murugan, vanquished by the god, and transformed into his faithful servant-devotees. Through ascetic discipline they have subdued the inner demon associated with aggression and sexuality.

OEDIPAL THEMES

For Saivite Hindu Tamils the divine family consists of Siva, his consort Parvati, and the brothers, Vinayagar and Murugan. The mythical biographies of the two sons of Siva and Parvati explore the conundrums of gender identity and sexuality from the different perspectives of the father-identified son and the mother-identified son.

Murugan was born of his father's seed without the participation of his mother. Parvati had been sent to Śiva's retreat so that a son would be born to fight against the rebellious *asura* Surapadma, but Siva, engaged in ascetic practices, did not respond to Parvati's seductive advances. Even after Parvati had secured Siva's attention through her own asceticism and they were married, no child was born. Finally, the dove obtained the seed of Siva, but because the seed was so hot, the dove dropped it into the river Ganga, who gave birth to six children. When Parvati gathered the children into her arms, they became one child with six heads. In this myth sexual intercourse between the parents is denied, and the son is identified exclusively with his father, expressing the wish-fulfilling fantasy that fathers may produce children as mothers do (Dundes, 1962). Siva's ability to ignore Parvati's advances also may allay anxiety about loss of control in the face of sexual temptation. Nevertheless, the myth suggests a fear of sexual contact with women.

Several commentators have suggested that oedipal conflict in Indian tales and myths has a different form from the Greek myth that we take to be paradigmatic. Ramanujan (1984) noted that "instead of sons desiring mothers and overcoming fathers (e.g., Oedipus) and daughters loving fathers and hating mothers (e.g., Electra), most often we have fathers (or father-figures) suppressing sons and desiring daughters, and mothers desiring sons and ill-treating or exiling daughters or daughter-figures" (p. 252). He cites a Tamil tale (Type 706) in which a stepmother desires her stepson (Kunalan), who rejects her advances. She accuses him of making improper advances to her (Potiphar's Wife motif, K 2111.1), and his father punishes him by blinding—emphasizing the theme of paternal hostility that Devereux (1984) has called the "Laius Complex." Similarly, in the *Mahabharata,* when Bhima renounces the kingdom and becomes a lifelong celibate so that his father may marry a fisher girl, the rivalry between father and son is resolved by the son's self-sacrifice and submission to his father. Later, however, Bhima gains renown for his superhuman strength, the consequence of his austerities. Thus, the Indian tale promises compensation to the submissive son. Similarly, in the story of Murugan, the son flees from the father and mother, whereupon his hostility is internalized and directed at the self through asceticism.

Murugan's ascetic withdrawal, which wins his father's acknowledgement of his maturity and autonomy, apparently frees the young god from his exclusive attachment to the mother so that he can woo the tribal maiden Valli. However, it is the goddess who is said to give the young god his invincible lance, the *vel,* with which he defeats the demon Surapadma. For this victory Murugan is rewarded by being made the general of the heavenly army. He also is given Deviani, the daughter of Vishnu, in marriage. This marriage between cross-cousins, for Deviani is said to be the daughter of Murugan's mother's brother, is the culturally preferred form of marriage among Tamils. However, it is Murugan's illicit liaison with the tribal maiden Valli, rather than his marriage to Deviani, that establishes Murugan as the divine lover, who like Krishna becomes a figure of devotional worship.

The legendary account of Murugan's love affair with Valli, much beloved by Tamils everywhere, is especially associated with the temple of Kataragama in Sri Lanka. Obeyesekere (1978, 1984) has explored this corpus for its oedipal themes. During the temple festival at Kataragama, Murugan (known here as Kataragama) is taken in procession to the temple where Valli Amma (Mother Valli) is said to abide. The purpose of the festival is for the divine couple to have sexual intercourse. When their union has been consummated on the third day, devotees celebrate by bathing in a nearby river in a climax of riotous erotic release. In Penang, as well, many Tamils say that Murugan is taken in procession to visit his wife (or mistress), but they also say that he returns on the third night under cover of darkness because he has not succeeded in having intercourse with her. In the Penang version shame and anxiety prevail.

Vinayagar, Murugan's brother, is the mother-identified son. The tale of Vinayagar's birth denies that any father participated sexually in the conception of this son, who is created by Parvati from the dirt that she washes from her skin mixed with unguents. Vinayagar is also given the wish-fulfilling fantasy of guarding his mother's chamber against his father's entry. However, when Siva is barred by the youth, he cuts off his head before he learns the boy's identity. Responding to Parvati's pleas that he restore her son to life, Siva says he will replace the boy's head with that of the first living creature he encounters. That creature is the elephant. In addition to the motif of decapitation, other signs of Vinayagar's symbolic castration are his "exaggerated but perpetually flaccid trunk" and a broken tusk (Courtright, 1985 p. 109). According to some legends, this injury was the consequence of eating the mango that was the reward for the son's devotion to his mother (Obeyesekere, 1984).

In a discussion of the importance of food metaphors for love in Tamil speech, the anthropologist Trawick (1990) evokes the emotional associations of the mango:

A mango was like a breast. You kneaded it between the palms of your hands until the pulp was a creamy juice, then you cut a small

hole at the tip and sucked out the juice. In our village, it was a sin
to cut down a fruit-bearing mango tree, just as it was a sin to kill
a pregnant cow. I cannot help but think it significant that the
mango tree was called *ma* [p. 97].

As Obeyesekere (1978) has pointed out, from a psychoanalytic point
of view Vinayagar is the castrated son, oedipally fixated on his mother
and unable to attain sexual maturity (see also Ramanujan, 1984). The
myths and legends about Vinayagar most popular in South India confirm
this interpretation. Throughout Tamilnadu images of Vinayagar are to
be found at public bathing places where he is said to be continually
looking for a woman as beautiful as his mother. Because he never finds
one, he remains a perpetual bachelor. Vinayagar's bulging potbelly is
said to be the result of his childish love of sweets and the overindulgence
of his mother. His satisfactions thus remain at the oral level. This is
depicted visually in the displacement upward of the phallic trunk onto
the (elephant) head.

Obeyesekere (1978) points out that in Sri Lanka and Tamilnadu the
mango, the prize awarded in the contest between Vinayagar and Murugan, is a symbol of the vagina. This interpretation is supported by a
variant of the legend found in the *Siva Purana,* which makes the prize a
bride (Courtright, 1985). Taken together the variants suggest that oral
satisfaction represented by food may be symbolically equivalent to
genital satisfaction. This allows for the expression of a consciously
unacceptable sexual desire for the mother in the sublimated form of a
desire for food. Kakar (1981) suggests that Vinayagar "embodies certain
'typical' resolutions of developmental conflicts in traditional Hindu
society. . . . In effect, the boy expresses the conviction that the only way
to propitiate the mother's demands and once again make her nurturing
and protective is to repudiate the cause of the disturbance in their
mutuality: his maleness" (pp. 101–102). In identification with Vinayagar,
the ascetic renunciation of sexual aims and aggressive impulses may
return the individual to an infantile state of dependency wherein he must
compel the attention of the gods passively through hunger, pain, and
suffering (Fenichel, 1953; Dundes, 1963).

However, in the diagnosis of pathology in the mythology of Vinayagar, we perhaps succumb to our own culturally given models of gender
and sexuality. In India the popular tale of the rivalry between Murugan
and his brother, the elephant-headed god, may be told from two points
of view, as exemplifying the superior cleverness of Vinayagar or in
identification with Murugan as the less-favored son who is ultimately

victorious in the rivalry with his brother. As told in the *Padma Purana,* when Murugan performs a pilgrimage and Vinayagar's devotion is rewarded with food, Parvati exclaims, "All the pilgrimages and sacrifices are not worth a sixteenth part of the worship of one's parents." In this text the rivalry between Vinayagar and Murugan is used as a metaphor for two different religious paths—devotion to one's parents and fulfillment of caste duty on one hand and the ascetic's path of self-denial and rejection of family responsibility on the other (Courtright, 1985). Either path may be advocated; both are respectfully acknowledged.

In India, as among the ancient Greeks, the expression of a son's hostile and rivalrous wishes toward the father is culturally disapproved and must be expressed in a disguised form. In Indian tales oedipal rivalry frequently appears to be displaced to a brother, as in the tale of the rivalry of Murugan and Vinayagar over the golden mango. While Indian epics celebrate male sibling cooperation as exemplified by Rama and his brothers, rivalry between brothers is a common theme in folk tales (Beck, 1986; see also Courtright, 1985). This substitution of brother for father appears natural in a culture where, when the father is dead or absent, the eldest brother stands in the position of father as the authority to whom respect and obedience are owed.

THE DANCE OF THE PEACOCK: SEXUAL CONUNDRUMS

The dipping, swirling dance of devotees of Murugan, who carry a *kavati* decorated with peacock feathers, is said to imitate the trancelike dance of the displaying male peacock. This association introduces the motif of sexual beauty and courtship into the worshiper's identification with the peacock/demon devotee. During the Thaipusam festival, especially on the day of vow fulfillment, there is a good deal of flirtation between young men who fulfill vows and young women who come, dressed in their finest saris and wearing gold bangles and chains, to watch the devotees whirl to the beat of the drums in a display of erotic exhibitionism that enacts the courtship dance of the male peacock (Menninger, 1938). For these youths, the ritual might be described as a rite of passage into manhood, during which sexual desires may be acknowledged and symbolically controlled at the same time. In the symbolic identification with the peacock, a person's emotionally based understanding of his sexuality is interwoven with themes already introduced—submission, rebellion, empowerment, and control over impulses.

In Hindu iconography, each of the male deities is associated with an animal vehicle. Siva rides Nandi, the bull; Vishnu rides the Garuda (a mythical figure with the beak and talons of a predatory bird and the body of a man); Murugan rides the peacock; and Vinayagar, the elephant-headed god, rides the rat. These animal vehicles can be seen as distinctive representations of the sexual energies of the gods. Śiva's bull, for example, is the male counterpart of the great Indian mother symbol, the cow, and the bull is used to plough the earth (mother). Vinayagar, who is represented as phallically crippled (his face distorted by the limp phallic trunk, his tusk broken off), rides the rat, which inhabits secret holes underground; whereas Murugan's vehicle, the male peacock, is frequently employed in Tamil poetry on love as a symbol of masculine beauty (Clothey, 1978; Shulman, 1980). The peacock thus aptly reflects the sexual energy of the young and handsome deity who is worshiped as the divine lover of the earthly tribal maiden Valli.

Female deities, however, are not always represented with animal mounts. The warrior goddess Durga, slayer of the buffalo-demon Mahisa; Kali, who wears a necklace of skulls; and the *Amman* (mother) goddesses of Tamil villages ride a lion (or sometimes a tiger). Although apparently a masculine symbol, the maned lion can also be interpreted as a frightening representation of the female genitalia that may castrate, and of the devouring mother (Freud, 1922). Durga appears to represent the danger of castration (Kinsley, 1986; Babb, 1975). In Tamil myths Mahisa, the buffalo-demon, is said to be her suitor. Durga is typically portrayed in the act of plunging her spear into the body of the buffalo from which a man is seen to be emerging. (This suggests that in ritual vow fulfillment to the goddess, the piercing of the cheeks with a spear by male devotees may have a different meaning than the same act performed in vow fulfillment to Murugan.)

In the image of Kali, the frightful, gaping mouth of the lion is repeated in the goddess's own gaping mouth and lolling tongue that drips with blood, and the emphasis seems to be on the dangerous, devouring mother (Chaudhuri, 1956). This is a motif that appears frequently in Indian folk tales. In a corpus of tales analyzed by Beck (1986), of 27 stories that describe mother–daughter relationships, 24 involve a mother who (inadvertently) eats the flesh of her own female offspring. In tales that feature the mother–son relationship, 50 percent depict episodes of aggression or hostility between them: a mother is shown to be a party to her own son's sacrifice, or is forced to eat him to avoid starvation, or comes to believe that he is an ogre.

As a symbol, the vehicle of the goddess provides a striking contrast to the animal vehicles of male deities, which suggest sexual energies that have been domesticated or brought under control. Significantly, the goddess usually is not represented with an animal vehicle in her benevolent form as Parvati, spouse of Siva. (When she is, the lion sleeps peacefully at her side.) This suggests that it is the unmarried goddess who is dangerous. As Kinsley (1986) puts it, "Independent in her unmarried state, Durga is portrayed as possessing untamed sexual energy that is dangerous, indeed deadly, to any male who dares to approach her" (p. 115). When the goddess is married, however, her sexual energies are controlled and subdued by her consort, and she is no longer felt to be threatening or dangerous.

THE AUSPICIOUS WIFE: SUBMISSION AND SELF-DENIAL

Sita, the chaste, loyal, and submissive wife of Rama, provides the model for the ideal Hindu woman, who is expected to be a devoted and respectful daughter and then to worship as a god the husband that her father chooses for her. Even when the actions of her husband endanger a woman's security or cause her hardship, she must never express anger at or resistance to his control. Powerless in the decisions that affect her life, through the virtue and self-sacrifice that she demonstrates as a wife and mother, she obtains supernatural powers to protect those she loves (Kakar, 1981).

Tales of the powers of auspicious women are frequently told or enacted during rituals of fasting and worship performed to safeguard the health and safety of a woman's husband and other male relatives. These rituals, which are called *nonpu,* have been described as "power events" in which a woman ritually becomes a goddess or appropriates some of the goddess' power (Reynolds, 1980). Thus women, like male ascetics, are granted through submission and self-sacrifice the compensation of supernatural powers.

However, when misfortune befalls a family, a woman may be blamed for her lack of virtue or failure to secure the gods' protection for her family through worship and fasting. The anthropologist Reynolds (1980) quotes an informant who told her that, "A woman at the death of her husband mourns not so much for the husband but for the status she has lost" because her husband's death reflects her own lack of virtue (p. 50). For Tamil women, hostility toward husband or children may be so frightening because of the supernatural powers attributed to women that such feelings or thoughts normally cannot be accommodated in conscious awareness. However, both dangerous sexual and hostile feelings do appear in spontaneous episodes of trance that are understood as demonic possession.

The tradition of *nonpu* culturally supports the tendency to control impulses thought to be dangerous by turning aggression into self-sacrifice and self-denial. Although such ritual fasting provides Tamil women with a culturally sanctioned way to demonstrate their desire to protect loved ones from danger and to reassure themselves that they embody the ideal of the virtuous wife and good mother, not the dangerous sexuality and malevolent violence of the unmarried goddess, it also reinforces their anxiety about the danger they pose to their children and husbands.[3] This anxiety on the part of both men and women appears to underlie the rituals of the festival of the *Amman* (mother) goddess, which have the purpose of transforming the malevolent goddess who has failed to provide for her children into her benevolent form, either by appeasing her appetite with offerings or by marrying her to the god (Moffatt, 1979; Beck, 1981) and also the forms of vow fulfillment chosen by women on Thaipusam.

THE APPEAL OF THE INFANT GOD

The offering that devotees bring to Murugan on Thaipusam is milk. Despite the fact that the Palani temple (and the temple in Penang modeled on it) is devoted to the worship of Murugan as an ascetic youth, on Thaipusam many devotees worship the god as an infant deity. Murugan is depicted in this form resting on a lotus in a pond recently added to the temple complex, and popular prints of the infant Krishna (who, like Murugan, is adorned with peacock feathers) are used to represent Murugan in the *kavatis* that women make. In the symbolism of the milk offering, the metaphor of maternal devotion is employed as an image of the devotees' love for Murugan (Lewin, 1950).

For an Indian woman the birth of a son is the culmination of her destiny (Kakar, 1981). As a bride, she enters the house of her husband a relative stranger, who may be resented as a potential rival by her new mother-in-law. She may deeply miss the comfort and support of her own mother and her natal family and resent her new role as one who is

---

[3]Kakar (1981) argues that because Hindu women turn aggression back against the self (in culturally approved ways through fasts and self-sacrifice) in a diffuse hostility of self-blame, they come to feel worthless, inferior, and bad.

expected to serve not only her husband but all of her new in-laws. All this will change when she gives birth to her first child, especially if that child is a son. She will return to her mother for the birth and also attain a new status in her husband's house. Most important will be the new possibility of fulfilling the wish to love and be loved.

The emotional bond between mother and son appears to be a deep one in which the ideal of unambivalent love is preserved by a denial of feelings of hostility on both sides. This is reflected in folk tales in which sons frequently express feelings of love and devotion for mothers (Beck, 1986; Ramanujan, 1984; Kakar, 1981). The most common mother–son story involves a son who rescues his mother from danger or rights an injustice done to her (Beck, 1986). In worshiping Murugan as an infant deity, then, a woman can be reassured about her essential goodness as an ideal mother and perhaps also enjoy the fantasy that the god as son will, when he reaches maturity, right the wrongs she suffers (Kakar, 1981).

THE DEVOTEE AS BELOVED OF THE GOD: FEAR OF AND IDENTIFICATION WITH FEMALE SEXUALITY

In devotional texts the sexual union of Murugan with Valli is developed as a metaphor for the experience of union with the divine. From a psychoanalytic perspective, women may thus identify with the lowly maid who is wooed by Murugan, who first takes the form of a sage (oedipal father) and then appears in his true form as a beautiful youth (Obeyesekere, 1978). On the other hand, men can identify with Murugan in his wooing of the dark, sensual tribal girl, the forbidden woman. Obeyesekere has pointed out that the appeal of this fantasy may be particularly strong because among Tamils, a man will ideally marry the daughter of his mother's brother, and this increases the likelihood that he will unconsciously equate his wife with his mother with the consequence that sexual desire is repressed.

However, men also sing devotional songs in the voice of Valli, the beloved of Murugan. Especially popular are songs of the poet Arunagirinatur, such as this one quoted in Zvelebil (1973):

Lord with the spear
. . .
in love embraced
in your merciful arms

Rescue
this daughter of the earth
where great poets stray
with your golden-rayed spear
. . .
rescue this woman with creeperlike waist
from being destroyed in sorrows

. . .
[p. 245].

In other songs Arunagirinatur expresses anxiety about women as seduc-
tresses who lure men into danger and begs Murugan to save him from
temptation.

Those women
with swaying breasts
lovely red hands
filled with bangles
as they jingle
with dark cloudlike tresses
where bees sing
and soft beseeching words like the *kuyil*
lovely as the five-colored parrots
their voices honey
fishlike eyes
vying
warm with fear
their forehead a crescent moon
By them I was lured
in their magical ways
into this sea of birth
Your slave am I
Help me reach the shore
of your brave noble feet
Conquer and bless me
[p. 243].

The fear of women and their sexuality expressed in this poem is easy to
understand, for Tamils believe that in sexual intercourse men lose *sakti*
(power/energy) to women through their semen. Women do not suffer the
same depletion because fluids are not exchanged. Tamil men, therefore,

may see women as devourers of energy and life-force (Daniel, 1980; Carstairs, 1958). As Kakar (1981) puts it, taking account of the images of malevolence associated with the goddess, the powers attributed to women, and the intensity of the mother–son bond:

> Underlying the conscious ideal of womanly purity, innocence and fidelity, and interwoven with the unconscious belief in a safe-guarding maternal beneficence is a secret conviction among many Hindu men that the feminine principle is really the opposite — treacherous, lustful and rampant with an insatiable, contaminating sexuality [p. 93].

Identification with Valli allows a man to avoid the dangers of sexual contact with a woman by taking a male deity as an object of sexual longing. It also may offer another kind of reassurance, in that the son who renounces his male sexuality is no longer a threat to his father in an oedipal rivalry for the mother (Fenichel, 1953). For these men the piercing of the (phallic) tongue (Jones, 1929) with a *vel* may be a symbolic castration that is meant to reassure the powerful representatives of the father — the god, high-caste leaders, and political authorities — that the rebellious son is not a threat. The male devotee's feminine self may then win the love of the god through submission, as a Tamil woman submits herself to her father and husband and thus wins their love. These devotees might then also see the lance of Murugan as a phallic implement that brings the devotee into sexual union with the god.

Some male devotees also show feminine identification by hanging small pots of milk from their chests (as artificial breasts) in fulfillment of a vow. Here we find an identification with the "good," asexual mother who offers oral (not genital) gratification and receives the love of the god because of her nurturing devotion.

Identification with the female, however, is likely to produce ambivalent feelings for men as well as for women due to the fear of an internal "bad mother" full of sexual and aggressive impulses that must be controlled, for the woman, like the animal and the demon, can represent the "lower self" of the devotee that must be mastered and punished. In this context, the symbolic attack on the body with the *vel* of Murugan may serve also to punish or subdue the body conceived as the feminine part of the self.

Women may also express a masculine identification when possessed by Murugan, for instance by piercing their tongues with a miniature *vel,* because this is normally a male form of vow fulfillment. However, because oral and genital images are condensed, this kind of vow fulfillment when done by women can also express an unconscious wish to be pierced with the phallic *vel,* the god's implement of power, or a desire to punish the greedy, devouring, and sexual self, thus denying that one is hostile and dangerous.

CONCLUSION

Ascetic practices are associated with a search for power. They also allow worshipers to respond to misfortune (seen as loss of the god's love) by self-punishment, or forestall punishment for unconscious desires and impulses that evoke guilt (Freud, 1907b), and compensate for feelings of low self-esteem due to low caste status. At the same time Tamil devotees of Murugan enact an inner drama in which the carnal "lower self," pictured as an animal, a demon, or a woman, which is characterized by uncontrolled desires, is mastered in identification with Murugan, the ascetic warrior. The most striking form of vow fulfillment, the piercing of the body with the lance of Murugan, represents a defeat of sexual and aggressive impulses, but also acknowledges a moral order and the social and political hierarchy associated with it.

What is revealed by an exploration of the myths and legends associated with Murugan and the Thaipusam festival is that ideas about caste and power, the nature of the inner world of the self, the dangers of sexuality, and the relations of men and women, as well as those of gods and demons, are deeply interwoven. Thus, the drama that each person enacts in ritual vow fulfillment is scripted by culturally given possibilities and psychologically structured understandings, but each person interweaves the themes and motifs in a uniquely personal representation of an inner self. The symbolism of the ritual allows devotees to enact, in a disguised form, feelings and wishes that must be denied. At the same time, vow fulfillment allows worshipers to demonstrate their newly attained purity and their special relation to the god who empowers them. Successful fulfillment of a vow raises a devotee's status in the eyes of self and society.

BIBLIOGRAPHY

BABB, L. (1975), *The Divine Hierarchy: Popular Hinduism in Central India.* New York: Columbia University Press.
BECK, B. (1981), The goddess and the demon: A local South Indian festival and its wider context. *Purusartha,* 5:83–136.
——— (1986), Social dyads in Indic folktales. In: *Another Harmony: New Essays on the*

Folklore of India, ed. S. Blackburn & A. K. Ramanujan. Berkeley: University of California Press, pp. 76–102.

BHAGAT, M. G. (1976), *Ancient Indian Asceticism.* New Delhi, India: Munshiram Manoharlal.

CARSTAIRS, M. (1958), *The Twice Born: A Study of a Community of High-Caste Hindus.* Bloomington: Indiana University Press.

CHAUDHURI, A. K. R. (1956), A psycho-analytic study of the Hindu mother goddess (Kali) concept. *Amer. Imago* 13:123–146.

CLOTHEY, F. W. (1978), *The Many Faces of Murugan: The History and Meaning of a South Indian God.* The Hague, Netherlands: Mouton.

―――― (1983), *Rhythm and Intent: Ritual Studies from South India.* Bombay, India: Blackie & Son.

COURTRIGHT, P. B. (1985), *Ganesa: Lord of Obstacles, Lord of Beginnings.* New York: Oxford University Press.

DANIEL, S. B. (1980), Marriage in Tamil culture: The problem of conflicting "models." In: *The Powers of Tamil Women,* ed. S. Wadley. Syracuse, New York: Syracuse University, pp. 61–92.

DANIELOU, A. (1964), *Hindu Polytheism.* New York: Pantheon Books.

DEVEREUX, G. (1984), Why Oedipus killed Laius: A note on the complementary Oedipus complex in Greek drama. In: Edmunds, L. & Dundes, A. *Oedipus: A Folklore Casebook,* New York: Garland Pub., pp. 215–233.

DIEHL, C. G. (1956), *Instrument and Purpose: Studies on Rites and Rituals in South India.* Lund, Sweden: Gleerups.

DOWSON, J. (1961), *A Classical Dictionary of Hindu Mythology and Religion, Geography, History and Literature.* London, England: Routledge & Kegan Paul, Ltd.

DUNDES, A. (1962), Earth-Diver: Creation and the mythopoeic male. *Amer. Anthropol.,* 64:1032–1105.

―――― (1963), Summoning deity through ritual fasting. *Amer. Imago,* 20:213–220.

―――― (1976), Projection in folklore: A plea for psychoanalytic semiotics. *Mod. Lang. Notes,* 91:1500–1533.

―――― (1985), The psychoanalytic study of folklore. *Ann. Scholarship,* 3:1–42.

ELIADE, M. (1969), *Patanjali and Yoga.* New York: Funk & Wagnalls.

FENICHEL, O. (1953), Trophy and triumph. In: *Collected Papers.* New York: W. W. Norton, pp. 141–162.

FREUD, S. (1900a), The interpretation of dreams. *Standard Edition,* 4&5. London: Hogarth Press, 1953.

―――― (1907b), Obsessive acts and religious practices. *Standard Edition,* 9. London: Hogarth Press, 1959, pp. 117–127.

―――― (1922), Medusa's head. *Standard Edition,* 18. London: Hogarth Press, 1955, pp. 273–274.

―――― (1930), Civilization and its discontents. *Standard Edition,* 21. London: Hogarth Press, 1961, pp. 64–145.

JONES, E. (1929), The madonna's conception through the ear. In: *Psycho-Myth, Psycho-History: Essays in Applied Psychoanalysis.* vol. 2. (Reprinted 1974.) New York: Hillstone, pp. 266–357.

KAKAR, S. (1981), *The Inner World: A Psychoanalytic Study of Childhood and Society in India.* Delhi, India: Oxford University Press.

KINSLEY, D. R. (1986), *Hindu Goddesses: Visions of the Divine Feminine in the Hindu Religious Tradition.* Berkeley: University of California Press.

LEWIN, B. D. (1950), *The Psychoanalysis of Elation.* New York: W. W. Norton.

MASSON, J. M. (1976), The psychology of the ascetic. *J. Asian Stud.*, 35:611–626.

MENNINGER, K. (1938), *Man Against Himself*. New York: Harcourt, Brace & Co.

MOFFATT, M. (1979), *An Untouchable Community in South India: Structure and Consensus*. Princeton: Princeton University Press.

OBEYESEKERE, G. (1978), The fire-walkers of Kataragama: The rise of Bhakti religiosity in Buddhist Sri Lanka. *J. Asian Stud.*, 37:457–478.

_____ (1981), *Medusa's Hair: An Essay on Personal Symbols and Religious Experience*. Chicago: University of Chicago Press.

_____ (1984), *The Cult of the Goddess Pattini*. Chicago: University of Chicago Press.

O'FLAHERTY, W. D. (1973), *Siva: The Erotic Ascetic*. Oxford: Oxford University Press.

RAMANUJAN, A. K. (1984), The Indian Oedipus. In: Edmunds, L. & Dundes, A. *Oedipus: A Folklore Casebook,* New York: Garland Pub., pp. 234–261.

REYNOLDS, H. (1980), The auspicious married woman. In: *The Powers of Tamil Women,* ed. S. Wadley. Syracuse, New York: Syracuse University, pp. 35–60.

SHULMAN, D. D. (1980), *Tamil Temple Myths: Sacrifice and Divine Marriage in South Indian Sawa Tradition*. Princeton: Princeton University Press.

SIMONS, R., ERVIN, F. & PRINCE, R. (1988), The psychobiology of trance. *Transcult. Psychiat. Research Rev.*, 25:249–284.

STUTLEY, M. & STUTLEY, J. (1977), *Harper's Dictionary of Hinduism: Its Mythology, Folklore, Philosophy, Literature, and History*. San Francisco: Harper & Row.

TRAWICK, M. (1990), *Notes on Love in a Tamil Family*. Berkeley: University of California Press.

ZVELEBIL, K. V. (1973), *The Smile of Murugan: On Tamil Literature of South India*. Leiden, Netherlands: E.J. Brill.

14

The Problem of Mourning
in Jewish History

AVNER FALK

The ethnic groups known as Hebrews, Israelites and Jews suffered heavy losses and group-narcissistic injuries throughout their history. They lost their Kingdom of Israel to the Assyrians in 722–721 B.C.E. They lost their Kingdom of Judah along with their sovereignty, their language, their Holy City of Jerusalem, and their Temple of Yahweh to the Babylonians in 587–586 B.C.E. They lost their Second Temple along with their Holy City to the Romans in 70 C.E. Half a million Jews were slaughtered by the Romans during the tragic Bar-Kochba revolt of 132–135 C.E. For eighteen centuries thereafter, with few notable exceptions, the Jews lived as a hated, despised, persecuted minority everywhere.

For many centuries the Jews lived in a kind of ahistoric time bubble. They lived more in fantasy than in reality, more in the past than in the present. They developed the myth of Jewish Election, the myth of Jerusalem as the center of the world, and the myth of the ten lost tribes of Israel living in a faraway land beyond the raging river *Sambation* (symbolizing the rage of the Jews at their own fate). The psychological function of these myths was to deny the unbearable Jewish reality. For 1,500 years, from Flavius Josephus in the first century to Bonaiuto (Azariah) de' Rossi in the 16th, there was no scientific chronological Jewish historiography (Yerushalmi, 1982). On the other hand there was a vast body of fantastic, mystical, mythical, and Messianic Jewish literature. The medieval Jews gave the nations and countries with which they came in contact obscure, anachronistic Biblical names that had nothing to do with these peoples and places: thus Rome was called *Edom,* Byzantium *Yavan,* Germany *Ashkenaz,* France *Zarephath,* Spain

Work on this chapter was begun during the author's Resident Scholarship at the Rockefeller Foundation's Study and Conference Center in the Villa Serbelloni, Bellagio (Como), Italy, in 1987. The author wishes to thank the trustees and officers of the Rockefeller Foundation for inviting him to their unique Center.

Sepharad, and Turkey *Togarmah.* The River Rhine was often called the Jordan River. This was a striking refusal to live in harsh reality; it was an escape into a glorified past.

The target of unconscious projections and externalizations everywhere, the Jews suffered from the perennial hatred of their host societies, from ritual murder and host desecration libels to executions, persecutions, discriminations, and massacres in Christian Europe throughout the Middle Ages. They were massacred by the Crusaders in 1096, expelled from several countries, and murdered by the Ukrainian Cossacks in 1648-1649. They were persecuted all over Europe. The Jewish self suffered severe damage. Finally, six million Jewish men, women, and children were slaughtered by the Nazis in the unprecedented Holocaust of the Second World War.

These losses were impossible to mourn properly. The psychological reactions included denial, viewing the present in terms of the past, and longing for Messianic redemption. Political Zionism sought to turn back the wheel of history, to restore the losses rather than to mourn them, and to mend the damaged Jewish self. It denied the demographic Arab reality of Palestine, proclaiming "a land without a people for a people without a land." The tragic Arab–Israeli conflict is one result (Falk, 1992). The "Land of Israel" is imagined by Zionist Jews as high above all other countries. Hence the Zionist terms *aliyah* (ascent) for immigration to Israel and *yeridah* (descent) for emigration from it. These terms are sheer psychogeographical fantasy. Other notions Israeli Jews swear by, such as The Jewish People, the Nation of Israel, the Land of Israel, the Chosen People, the Holy Land, the Holy City, the Diaspora, the Exile, are anachronistic myths based on a *denial* of the harsh reality of a small Jewish nation living in a sea of hostile Arabs. Like other nationalisms, Israeli nationalism is a defensive group narcissism.

The thesis of this chapter is that the Jews have not been able to mourn their historical losses and injuries. Instead, the defensive unconscious processes of denial, projection, externalization, and splitting have operated collectively. The Israeli Jews have not mourned their group losses properly, above all that of the six million Jews massacred by the Nazis during the Holocaust of 1941-1945, as well as the thousands of soldiers killed in their wars with the Arabs. This is seen in the very way the Israeli Jews commemorate their losses. The Hebrew ninth of Ab is a day of fast and mourning for both the First and Second Temples, as if they were both destroyed on the same date. Some Israelis wish to restore the losses by building the Third Temple on the site of the Muslim Dome of the Rock. The Nazi Holocaust is remembered on the Israeli "Memorial

Day for the Holocaust and Heroism," which commemorates the Warsaw Ghetto uprising, the partisans, and the other Jews who resisted the Nazis along with their six million Jewish victims, seeking to deny the unbearable fact that the masses of the European Jews were led like lambs to the slaughter. The "Memorial Day for the Fallen Israeli Soldiers" devotes only a few minutes to an actual silent commemoration, and is followed immediately by the very joyous celebration of the Israeli Day of Independence.

Psychogeographical fantasies and the refusal to mourn losses are common everywhere, but the special and tragic history of the Jews has made them key features of the Jewish mind. Whether or not group mourning is possible is a major question dealt with below.

PSYCHOGEOGRAPHY

We tend to view our earth anthropomorphically. The word *Geography* derives from the name of the Greek goddess *Gaia* (Earth). The Greek myth of *Kronos* (Harvest), who saved his mother-earth *Gaia* from her cruel husband *Uranos* (Heaven) by castrating *Uranos* with a *harpe* (sickle or curved sword) and throwing his phallus into the sea, from whose *aphros* (foam) *Aphrodite* was born, can be viewed as a *psychogeographical fantasy*. The myth of the giant *Atlas* carrying the Earth upon his shoulders begins with Perseus petrifying Atlas with the sight of Medusa's terrible snake-infested head, transforming Atlas' beard and hair into forests, his head into a mountain peak, his arms and shoulders into cliffs, his bones into rocks, indeed, his entire body into geographical entities.

We also tend to glorify and idealize our environment. Some people have lived on little islands but thought they occupied the whole world. Some Israelis firmly believe that their tiny country is the greatest, most beautiful, and most important of all and that Jerusalem is the center of the entire world. Medieval and Renaissance cartographers drew maps of California as a golden island. Explorers discovered America but believed they had discovered India.

Eliade (1959) discussed sacred space and sacred centers from the religious studies viewpoint. The term *psychogeography* has been used by Niederland (Stein and Niederland, 1989), Volkan (1979, 1988), and Stein (1984, 1987) to designate our unconscious emotional transference relationships to geographical entities. A group of people may be said to live in psychogeographical fantasy if they live in one place but act and feel as if they were living in another, if they believe in nonexistent countries and lost continents at the bottom of the sea, like Arcadia, Atlantis, El Dorado, and paradise islands, or wondrous tribes in faraway regions. The Hebrew myth of the Garden of Eden (Genesis 2–3) is one of the best-known psychogeographical fantasies. The unconscious process underlying such fantasies is the regressive displacement of our feelings about our Early Mother's body to the wonders of our Earth.

Yet, whereas some psychogeographical fantasies may be regressive, they also have an adaptive function (Róheim, 1943). Fantasy in general serves constructive, adaptive, and creative functions as well as defensive and maladaptive ones. Theodor Herzl's dictum, *Wenn ihr wollt, ist es kein Märchen* (If you wish, it is no fairy tale) is often erroneously rendered "If you will it, it is no dream." Herzl did convert his feverish fantasies into political Zionist reality (Falk, 1993). Whether or not Zionism and the creation of Israel were adaptive, or led to further tragedy, has yet to be determined.

LIVING IN THE PAST

A group of people may be said to live in psychohistorical fantasy if they live in a certain time but act and feel as if they were living in another. The rulers of the medieval "Holy Roman Empire" were acting as if the old Roman Empire had never been destroyed. As Voltaire put it, theirs was neither an empire, nor Roman, nor holy. The Temple Mount Faithful in Israel wish to destroy the Dome of the Rock on Jerusalem's Temple Mount and rebuild Solomon's Temple on its site. Some fanatical Muslim Arabs wish to restore the medieval glory of *Dar al-Islam*. Psychogeographical and psychohistorical fantasies may be benign, but they may also lead to great destruction, as was the case with the medieval Crusaders, or with Hitler's Third *Reich*. The Jews, with their often tragic history, have had more than their share of psychogeographical fantasies. In this chapter I shall attempt to trace the psychogeographical and psychohistorical fantasies that have characterized much of Jewish history.

THE JEWISH DENIAL OF HISTORY

Patai (1976), Yerushalmi (1982), Roskies (1984), and Ebel (1986) have pointed out the dramatic denial of painful history underlying the almost total absence of scholarly, chronological Jewish historiography over a period of 15 centuries following the destruction of the Second Temple by the Romans in 70 C.E. Reality had become too painful for the Jews. It consisted mainly of disaster, death, catastrophe, destruction, loss, persecution, massacre, and torture. Their denial of reality helped the Jews live in fantasy. They created for themselves an anachronistic, ahistorical, and timeless bubble, living in their idealized, glorified past rather than in their painful, humiliating, unhappy present. Throughout the Middle Ages the Jews lived in psychohistorical fantasies.

The Jews also lived in psychogeographical fantasies. After the fall of the Kingdom in Israel in 721 B.C.E., the Ten Tribes of Israel were exiled by the Assyrians and eventually assimilated by the various peoples of the Assyrian empire. This meant that 10/12 of the Hebrew people had been lost. The Jews could not reconcile themselves to this loss. Many centuries later they developed the fantasy that the Ten Lost Tribes of Israel were still living as Jews beyond a mythical river named *Sambation*. In the ninth century a deranged Jew calling himself Eldad the Danite showed up in Jewish North Africa and Spain, spreading tales about the Ten Lost Tribes of Israel that he had found in the heart of Africa and Asia. The Jews believed him fervently. In the 17th century Rabbi Manassas ben Israel of Amsterdam claimed that the Indians of North America were the ten lost tribes of Israel. It was a refusal to mourn and to give up the great loss.

The Hebrew name *Sambation* derives from the Greek *Sabbateion,* meaning "of the Sabbath." The myth had it that the River Sambation kept roaring and throwing up huge rocks and was impassable on every day of the week except the Jewish Sabbath (Saturday). Jews were forbidden to cross the Sambation. The Jews firmly believed in the mythical River Sambation. The "Sons of Moses" were said to dwell beyond it, in the "Land of the Blessed" (Ginzberg, 1967–1969, 4:317, 5:111, 6:407–409). Flavius Josephus placed the Sambation in Syria. The Jewish sages located it "beyond the Mountains of Darkness." The Roman historian Pliny placed it in Judea. The medieval Jewish scholar Nahmanides identified it with the River Habor (II Kings 17:6). Throughout Jewish history, despite the injunction, Jews fervently sought the Ten Lost Tribes of Israel. Psychologically, the roaring, raging river was an externalization of the roaring rage of the Jews at their defeat, destruction, and loss.

The ancient Jews gave the Roman Empire, and later Christian Europe itself, the collective name of *Edom,* the ancient Semitic people east of the Jordan River and the Dead Sea who had been traditional enemies of the Biblical Israelites. Later every Christian became known in Hebrew writings as an *Edomite*. The Greek word *christos* is equivalent to the Hebrew word *mashiah* (Messiah): both mean "anointed." The Christians, however, whose name would properly translate into Hebrew as *meshihiyim* (Messianics), are called *notzrim* (Nazarenes), an obvious denial of their key belief in Jesus as the Messiah.

The Byzantine Empire, which actively persecuted the Jews, was known among the medieval Jews as *Yavan,* the Hebrew name for Greece, which came from *Ionia,* and was itself a misnomer. France is still called in Hebrew *Zarephath* (I Kings 17:9, Obadiah 20), the name of a Biblical city near Sidon, in present-day Lebanon. Spain is still called *Sepharad* (Obadiah 20), an obscure Biblical place name which may refer to Sardis in Asia Minor. Germany was called *Ashkenaz* (Genesis 10:3), the Biblical name of a great-grandson of Noah, a grandson of Japheth. Turkey was called *Togarma* (Genesis 10:3), a Biblical brother of Ashkenaz.

Mesopotamia (Iraq), whether under Persian, Parthian, Neo-Persian, Byzantine, or Muslim Arab rule, was always called by the Jews *Babel,* the name of the ancient Biblical kingdom of Babylonia. The Babylonian Empire had ceased to exist in 538 B.C.E. with the Persian conquest of Cyrus the Great. The city of Babylon on the Euphrates River had ended in 275 B.C.E. when its inhabitants were moved to the new Seleucid Greek capital of Seleucia on the River Tigris. Yet the Jews of the Persian empire who lived in Mesopotamia continued to call themselves "Babylonian."

For 2,500 years, while The Land Between the Rivers (Mesopotamia) successively became Persian, Greek, Roman, Parthian, Neo-Persian, Arab, Ottoman, and British, the Jews clung to the anachronistic epithet of "Babylonian." Their great early medieval literary production, written in Aramaic and Hebrew, is known as the "Babylonian Talmud." The misnomer does not seem to have disturbed anyone. To this very day, organized Iraqi Jewry in Israel calls itself "the Babylonian Jewish community." This is a striking psychohistorical and psychogeographical fantasy. People are living in fantasy more than in reality, in the past more than in the present.

Similarly, the Palestinian Talmud, not a word of which was written in Jerusalem, is known in Hebrew as *Talmud Yerushalmi* or "The Jerusalem Talmud." The Jews were expelled from Jerusalem by the Romans after the disastrous Bar-Kochba revolt of 132–135 C.E. The city was renamed *Aelia Capitolina* and became a pagan Roman city forbidden to the Jews. The entire Palestinian Talmud was written outside Jerusalem, yet the Jews clung to the fantasy and named it after their lost city. This illustrates the great emotional power of psychogeographical fantasies.

When the Roman emperor Flavius Claudius Julianus (Julian the Apostate) fought the Sassanid Neo-Persian empire of Shahpur II and seized its capital of Ctesiphon in 363, destroying the nearby Jewish city of Mahoza as well, the Jews took the side of their Persian rulers and called the "Edomite" Julian their worst enemy. The Romans were soon defeated and Julian was killed. His successor, Flavius Claudius Jovianus (Jovian), was forced to conclude a humiliating treaty of surrender with Shahpur II, ceding Armenia and several Jewish cities to the Persians. The Jews rejoiced at the defeat of the hated "Edomites." This was pure psychogeographic and psychohistorical fantasy.

Jews still call their worst enemies *Amalek* (Genesis 14:7, 36:12; Exodus 17:8–16), a bitter ancient Biblical enemy of the Israelites. The epithet "Amalek" was given by the Jews to every major enemy in their history, from the Assyrians and the Babylonians through Haman the Persian in the Book of Esther to Adolf Hitler in our own time. The classical Hebrew saying "Remember what hath done to thee Amalek!" (Deuteronomy 25:17) still inspires hatred of the enemy. *Amalek* has become a Hebrew term for hated enemy and persecutor.

THE JEWISH INABILITY TO MOURN

What possible reasons could there be for such anachronisms? Why did the Jews cling for so many centuries to geopolitical entities that no longer existed? Why did they live in psychohistorical fantasy? Why did they live in the past rather than in the present, in fantasy rather than in reality?

Volkan (1979, 1988), Koenigsberg (1977), Mack (1983), Boyer (1986), Stein (1984, 1987), Stein and Niederland (1989) and myself (Falk 1974, 1982, 1983, 1987) have suggested that the powerful emotions evoked by borders, cities, countries, islands, oceans, rivers and other geographical entities, and their unconscious meaning in our minds, are derived from our very early perceptions of and feelings about our own body and that of our mother. Winnicott (1971) and Mahler et al. (1975) have studied the process of the infant's separation and individuation from its initial fusion with the mother. As the child is often unable to let go of its mother during this early process, so an entire people could not separate from its mother land.

The process of separation and individuation involves our earliest mourning of a lost object, our Early Mother. Every subsequent loss in our lives involves separation and must be mourned to be mastered. The problem of why, whether, and how people mourn their losses was first tackled psychoanalytically by Freud (1917). Pollock (1961, 1975, 1977, 1989), Rochlin (1973), Mitscherlitsch and Mitscherlich (1975), and Volkan (1981, 1988) have expanded his work. Dietrich and Shabad (1989) have pointed out the adaptive, creative, and regenerative role of mourning in our lives. Mourning occurs not only on the individual but also on the group level. The issue of lost objects, such as territory and sovereignty, in an ethnic group's history is passed on from one generation to the next. Each child learns about its people's great victories and great losses. *Nations often cannot mourn their historical losses, preferring to entertain fantasies of their recovery.* For each of us, the lost objects of our ethnic history become unconsciously fused with the lost objects of our personal history, beginning with our Early Mother.

Alexander and Margarethe Mitscherlich (1975) have shown the tragic consequences of the Germans' inability to mourn their great losses after the Second World War. I interpret the anachronistic attitude of Jewish literature and the almost total absence of chronological Jewish historiography between the first century and the 16th century as evidence of the Jewish inability to mourn. The Jews lived in the past. To them the fifth-century Sassanid Neo-Persian empire was identical with that of Cyrus the Great a thousand years earlier, and the Romans were identical with the traditional Edomite enemies of the Israelites.

As Ebel (1986) has written, time had been standing still for the Jews. They were psychologically protected by a timeless bubble. Current world events were viewed through the prism of Biblical heroics. They idealized their Persian rulers and denigrated their Roman enemies. When the Orthodox Byzantine emperor Theodosius II (401–450) persecuted the Jews of his realm, the Jews bitterly complained of the "Greek" tyrant. They fled Palestine and other Byzantine lands to Persia, where the tolerant Shah Yazdegerd I reigned (399–420). This monarch resisted the fanatical priests of the Zarathushtra religion. Persian Jewish tradition, or fantasy, has Yazdegerd marry the daughter of the "Babylonian" Jewish exilarch, known in Aramaic as *Resh Galuta.*

Neo-Persian (Sassanian) Shah Yazdegerd II (reigned 438–457), influenced by the Zoroastrian Magi, began to persecute the Jews, Christians, and other heretics in his realm. The Roman rule of *cuius regio eius religio,* meaning "he who rules, his is the religion," now became enforced upon the Jews. They were forbidden to recite major prayers like the *Shema Yisrael* (Hear, O Israel) and to light their Sabbath candles. In 540 Sassanid Shah Khosru I Nushirvan (531–579), who is called by many historians "the greatest monarch of the Sassanid dynasty," captured the great Seleucid-Byzantine city of Antioch and deported many of its Jews to his capital of Ctesiphon on the Tigris. The exiles, unable to mourn their loss, built a new city near Mahoza, which they called "New Antioch."

By 629 the victorious Muslim Arabs were invading the Neo-Persian empire, and by 642 the Byzantines had lost all of their erstwhile territories in the east. During the last decade of Neo-Persian (Sassanid) rule (628–637) there was great disorder and confusion in Persia. From 633 to 638 the Muslim Arab warrior Khalid ibn-al-Walid conquered Syria, Egypt, Iraq, and Persia for Islam. He was known as *Saif-Allah* (Sword of God). Finally the Neo-Persian empire was no more. The "Babylonian" Jews were now under Islamic Arab rule. The Umayyad Caliphs of Damascus ruled the great new Dar al-Islam (House of Islam).

The Hebrew word *Gaon* originally meant "The pride of Jacob and of Israel" (Nahum 2:2). It later came to designate the medieval "Babylonian" Jewish academy heads. Rabbi Saadiah ben Yoseph al-Fayumi *Gaon* (882–942) was the "Babylonian" head of the Jewish *yeshivah* (academy) at Sura. He was born in Upper Egypt. The Egyptian Jews had been thoroughly Arabized. Their names, language, and culture were Arabic. The use of the term "Babylonian" to denote Arabic-speaking Jews was sheer fantasy. As I have pointed out earlier, from Flavius Josephus in the first century to Azariah de' Rossi in the 16th century there was no scholarly, scientific or chronological Jewish historiography. For 15 centuries the Jews refused to live in external reality.

Some Jews still cannot mourn their ancient losses of land, holy city, temple, sovereignty, and territory. For many complicated reasons the Jews are still unable to mourn the Nazi Holocaust, and the psychological problems of modern Israel are partly derived from this tragic fact. The Israeli day commemorating the Holocaust is officially called "Memorial Day for the Holocaust and Heroism." *The heroism of the Warsaw Ghetto uprising and other resistance movements against the Nazis is used to mitigate the need to mourn.* I shall give further examples of this tragic inability to mourn below.

BIBLICAL NAMES FOR MODERN LANDS

After their terrible losses of land, holy city, temple, sovereignty, and nationhood in the first and second centuries, the Jews made up for their group narcissistic injuries with grandiose fantasies. One *Midrash,* or myth, developed during the time of the Talmud (third to fifth century) said that the Land of Israel was the Center of the World, Jerusalem was the Center of the Land of Israel, the Temple was the Center of Jerusalem, and the Shrine, or the Holy of Holies, was in the middle of the Temple (Ginzberg, 1967–1969, 1:12). This *ethnogeocentrism* was a form of psychogeographical fantasy. It helped the Jews survive their great losses without actually having to mourn them.

Following the great Muslim conquests of the entire Middle East, North Africa, and Spain in the seventh and eighth centuries, the Jews had to adjust to the new reality, and they developed new psychogeographical fantasies. On one hand they wished to merge with the new Muslim world; on the other hand they needed to set themselves apart from it, to establish their group boundaries, as the Group for the Advancement of Psychiatry (1987) puts it. The Jews of Yathrib (Medina) had been calling their annual *Yom Kippur* (Day of Atonement and Fast) by the Arabic name of *Ashura,* meaning the Tenth Day [of the Hebrew Month of Tishri, actually a Babylonian name]. This very name, *Ashura,* is now used by Shiite Muslims to designate *their* Day of Atonement and Fast for the martyrdom of Husain ibn-Ali, on the 10th day of the Muslim month of *Muharram.* On that day Shiites flagellate themselves until they draw blood.

The psychogeographical fantasies involved in medieval Hebrew place names such as *Sepharad* for Spain, *Zarephath* for France, and *Ashkenaz* for Germany were taken from obscure verses in the Old Testament (Genesis 10:3, I Kings 17:9, I Chronicles 1:6, Jeremiah 51:27, Obadiah 1:20) and had little or nothing to do with the European countries they designated. The name *Togarma,* a Biblical brother of Ashkenaz, was given to Turkey, which certainly was no brother of Germany. It was as if the Jews lived in a Biblical fantasy world, clinging to an irretrievable past. They refused to mourn their losses and wrote no chronological history of their people, as Yerushalmi (1982) has shown.

Campbell (1959) used the term "land-taking" in discussing the way immigrants to America tended to name their new homes after their old ones in Europe—New England, New Amsterdam, New Bedford, New Albany, New Bern, New Brunswick, New Jersey, New York—in order to make their new land feel like home. Many American cities carry Old World place names—Athens, Paris, London, Toledo, Bethlehem, Cairo. This may indicate that Americans also secretly long for the Old World. Phrases like "Remember the Alamo" and "Remember Pearl Harbor" indicate the refusal to mourn underlying the longing for revenge. But Americans are usually aware that they are talking about new places: they say "Athens, Georgia" or "Cairo, Illinois." *The Jews did not use the word "new" in naming the European countries after Biblical places; they actually thought and acted as if these were the Biblical places.*

THE KHAZARS AS JEWS

Judah Halevi (1075–1141) was one of the most famous Jewish poets of medieval Muslim Spain. He was a rabbi and an Arabic philosopher as well. One of his most important Arabic-language works was *The Book of Proof and Evidence in Defense of the Despised Faith,* known in Hebrew as *Sefer Hakuzari* (The Book of the Khazar), in which he emphasized the value of religious truths attained through intuition and feeling over that of philosophical and speculative truths achieved through logic and reason. This work put forth a philosophy of history based on the force of divine influence on world events. The book was constructed upon the story of a great people known as "the Kuzari" who had adopted Judaism as their religion after becoming convinced of its great value.

The people Judah Halevi had in mind were the Khazars (Chazars), a Turkic people who lived in Transcaucasia by the second century and later settled in the lower Volga region. During the seventh century they became a powerful and expansionist military force. Between the eighth and tenth centuries their empire extended from the Black Sea and Caspian Sea in the south to the Ural Mountains in the east and to Kiev in the west. The Khazar *nobility* embraced Judaism in the eighth century. They defeated and subdued the Volga Bulgars, the Crimean Tatars, and the eastern Slavs, and warred with Arabs, Persians, and Armenians. During the tenth century they allied themselves with the Byzantines against the Arabs. They were defeated by Duke Sviatoslav of Kiev in 965.

The Khazars were later believed to have been the ancestors of the East European Jews, even though the masses of those Jews had migrated east from "Ashkenaz" to Poland. Judah Halevi's psychogeographical fantasies about the Kuzari were matched in the 19th century by the fantasies of Chief Rabbi Samuel Kohn of Budapest, who thought the Khazars were related to the Magyars and that therefore Jews and Magyars were brothers (Falk 1993).

MESSIANIC YEARNINGS

Although the early Jewish Christians accepted the myth of Jesus Christ and embraced Jesus of Nazareth as their Savior, most Jews did not give up their Messianic longings. The Jews' yearning for the Messiah, Savior, and Redeemer who would lead them back to their Promised Land may be viewed as a longing for rebirth. The Messianic fervor that repeatedly gripped the Jews through the long centuries of exile and dispersion was another expression of their refusal to give up their losses, of their inability to mourn. Repeatedly throughout Jewish history, borderline and psychotic personalities proclaimed themselves to be the Messiah and were embraced by the Jewish masses as such (cf. Meissner 1990, 1992).

Jewish Messianism began with the fall of Babylon to Shah Cyrus the Great of Persia in 538 B.C.E., when the Jews viewed the Persian king as their Savior and Redeemer. Deutero-Isaiah explicitly called Cyrus "the Lord's anointed" (Isaiah 45:1), better translated as "Yahweh's Messiah." The Talmudic literature of the third to the fifth centuries invented two Messiahs, one "Messiah son of Joseph," the other "Messiah son of David." It repeatedly invoked the True Messiah, whom it called "Messiah son of David," making sure to distinguish him from Jesus of Nazareth.

In 711–718, after the Moorish conquest of Spain, the victorious and ambitious Arabs besieged Constantinople, the capital of the Byzantine Empire. Byzantine emperor Leo III the Isaurian (675/680–741) finally succeeded in repelling their last siege in 717–718. The Byzantine Jews were once again inspired by Messianic hopes. Many fled to Syria, which was ruled by Caliph Omar (Umar) II, denouncing the "Greek" despot. The Muslim Arabs were now viewed by the Jews as their saviors, despite the glaring discrimination against the Jews as *dhimmi* (protected people) in the *Dar al-Islam*.

One of the Byzantine Jewish exiles, whose name is variously given as Shirini, Sherini, Serene, Serenus, or Zonrias, proclaimed himself the new Messiah. Many desperate Jews flocked to his banner. Like Sabbatai Sevi nine centuries later, this seemingly psychotic Messiah advocated the abolition of many traditional taboos, including the incest one. There were two other Jewish Messiahs in eighth-century Persia, Abu Issa of Isphahan and Yudghan ar-Rai (the Shepherd) of Hamadan. Most of the self-styled Messiahs were seriously disturbed personalities. Their followers saw them as Redeemers and Saviors, a view which betrays the desperate need of the followers to idealize their leaders. Not all Jews followed these "Messiahs." It takes considerable emotional immaturity in the followers to cling to a delusional leader.

From 767 to 900 the great Karaite (Ananite) schism divided "Babylonian" Jewry. Anan ben David, the obsessional reformer who wished to do away with all Jewish oral tradition and law and return to the strict constructionism of the Torah, is said to have been influenced by the Messianic followers of Abu-Issa and Yudghan ar-Rai. He was rigid, ascetic, fanatical, and extremely stubborn, all of these qualities being unconscious defenses against the early feelings of helplessness. His followers were noted by their asceticism and by their longing for Zion, another display of the inability to mourn, to accept one's losses, and to adjust to the pain of life. In the 10th century a group calling itself "The Mourners of Zion" gathered in Jerusalem, mourning the destruction of the temple and praying for its restoration. Psychologically, they refused to truly mourn their losses.

Another Jewish Messiah was David Menahem Alroi (Alrohi) in 12th-century Islamic Persia, who collected around him a band of fanatical Jews in Baghdad, provoking the Persian rulers into having him assassinated. There was the 13th-century mystic Abraham Abulafia, who attempted to convert Pope Nicholas III to Judaism, was imprisoned for a month, made many attempts to establish himself as prophet and Messiah, and finally vanished. There was Isaac Sarfati of late 15th-century Turkey, who called upon the Jews of "Ashkenaz" to move to the wonderful country of "Togarma" where no one lacked for anything. Ottoman Turkey had become the Great Good Mother in the fantasy of many Jews.

After the fall of the Byzantine Empire to the Ottoman Turks in the mid-15th century and the great expulsion of the Jews from Spain in 1492 there arose a fervent Messianism among the Jews of Italy. It was led by the Jewish scholar and mystic Don Isaac Abrabanel, a self-styled herald of the Messiah who wandered throughout southern Italy in 1496–1498 announcing the end of the "Holy Roman Empire" and of the Christian "Edomites." He wrote Messianic tracts and predicted the Resurrection of Zion in the year 1531. Asher Lemlein, a German-Jewish mystic, proclaimed himself the Messiah's herald in 1502. He had numerous followers.

In 1524 a delusional Jewish vagrant named David Reubeni showed up in Venice, calling himself a member of the lost Israelite tribe of Reuben. He told the Jews of Europe there was a great Jewish kingdom in the Arabian Desert ruled by the lost tribes of Reuben, Gad, and Manasseh. Its king, he said, was his own brother Joseph. This sick man stirred a great Messianic movement among the Jews. He was given an audience by Pope Clement VII, to whom he offered military assistance against the Ottoman Turks. The Pope gave him a letter of recommendation to King João III of Portugal, the country that had expelled the Jews in 1497.

The Spanish and Portuguese *Nuevos Cristianos* (new Christians), or *conversos,* were Jews who had been forcefully converted to Christianity. Those among them who practiced Judaism covertly were known as *Marranos,* an obscure word meaning "convert," "swine" or "accursed." In Portugal a young Marrano visionary named Diogo Pires was seized by a fervent wish to join David Reubeni in his Messianic quest. When the latter turned him down, Pires converted back to Judaism, changed his name to Solomon Molcho, and went to Palestine, where he studied with the Jewish mystics at Safed.

In 1527 the German and Spanish armies of "Holy Roman Emperor" Charles V defeated Rome, besieging Pope Clement VII. Molcho saw this defeat as a divine sign of the imminent salvation of the Jews. In 1529 Solomon Molcho returned to Italy, where he was received by the Pope.

Molcho was seized by the Inquisition, but the Pope helped him escape. He walked the streets of Rome as the Messiah, weird-looking and fanatical. In 1530 David Reubeni was expelled from Portugal and went to Rome, where he met Solomon Molcho. Reubeni attempted to reach the Holy Land but was shipwrecked and washed ashore in Spain, where he barely escaped the Inquisition. He wound up in Venice, where the authorities were astute at exposing his delusions and expelled him. Molcho and Reubeni took turns at occupying center stage. Both had been able to sway the heart of the Pope. One of Molcho's enemies had denounced him to the authorities as an enemy of Rome and of Christianity. Molcho was sentenced to death but managed to escape to Germany in 1531. Finally, in 1532, Molcho was handed back to the Inquisition, tried, condemned to death, and burned at the stake. Reubeni was imprisoned and died in jail. This was the tragic end of one of the most famous Messianic episodes in Jewish history, an episode that provoked great excitement and following among the Jews.

During the late Middle Ages there were mass migrations of persecuted Jews from "Ashkenaz" to Poland. In 1648–1649 there were terrible massacres of the Polish and Ukrainian Jews by the Zaporozhian Cossacks led by *hetman* Bohdan Chmielnicki. The Eastern Orthodox Cossacks hated the Jews for being agents of the Catholic Polish lords who were enslaving them, as well as for having killed their Savior, Jesus Christ. Many Jewish survivors of the massacres became psychotic, killed themselves, or fled to other countries. Messianic longings once more overwhelmed the hearts of many Jews.

In 1665 a new Messiah appeared to the Jews by the name of Sabbatai Sevi (Shabbetai Tsevi). He was born in Turkey in 1626 and suffered from manic-depressive illness from his youth (Falk, 1982). He was a mystic who provoked the rabbis of his home town of Izmir to drive him out of town and who performed many bizarre acts, such as marrying the Book of the Torah (Holy Pentateuch). Nevertheless he was "discovered" in Palestine by Nathan of Gaza, a young hypomanic visionary and prophet, and declared to be the Messiah. By 1665 Sabbatai was known all over the Jewish world, with many thousands of disciples and hundreds of thousands of followers.

Within a year Sabbatai Sevi was seized by the Ottoman authorities, imprisoned, and forcefully converted to Islam. Still, many Jews continued to believe not only that he was their True Messiah, but that he was God Himself. The Sabbatean movement divided the Jewish world for a very long time. As Scholem (1973) has shown, it was the most important Messianic mass movement in Jewish history. Theodor Herzl, the founder and leader of political Zionism in the late 19th century, was also hailed as the New Messiah by many of his followers.

Messianic longings and fantasies developed in Jewish life following the great historical losses and group narcissistic injuries of the Jews: the destruction of the kingdom of Israel by the Assyrians in 721 B.C.E. with the exile of the Israelites, the destruction of the kingdom of Judah by the Babylonians in 586 B.C.E. and the exile of the Judaeans, the destruction of the Second Temple by the Romans in 70 C.E., the dispersion of the remaining Jews all over the ancient world, their expulsion from various Europeans countries such as England in 1290 and Spain in 1492, and their persecutions and massacres everywhere.

The Christian persecution of the Jews as a hated minority, upon which all unacceptable aspects of the group self of the host peoples were unconsciously externalized and projected, reinforced their tendency to live in fantasy. The Jews were either unable or unwilling to mourn their terrible losses adequately. The pain was too great, and they preferred to live in psychogeographical fantasy. From the first century to the 16th century they lived both in a protective psychohistorical bubble, with no chronological historiography of their own, and in psychogeographical fantasy.

POLITICAL ZIONISM AS REBIRTH FANTASY

The name *Zion* has an interesting history. It was originally a Jebusite stronghold on a hill in Jerusalem, which David captured and renamed the City of David (II Samuel 5:7-9). Later it came to designate the entire city of Jerusalem (Isaiah 1:27), the entire Land of Israel (Isaiah 35:10, Lamentations 1:4), and the Jewish people itself (Isaiah 51:16). Like the modern Mount Scopus, the present-day Mount Zion has nothing to do with the historical one. Gonen (1975) wrote a psychohistory of Zionism, which, though somewhat simplistic and reductionistic, still captures the fantastic flavor of political Zionism. It was in many ways a psychohistorical and psychogeographical fantasy. It was an attempt to turn back the clock of history and to recover the ancient losses of land, sovereignty, and nationhood rather than to mourn these losses.

The idealized and glorified fantasies of Theodor Herzl in his books *Der Judenstaat* and *Altneuland* and those of other early Zionists, about *Eretz Yisrael* (The Land of Israel), had little to do with the reality of Ottoman Palestine. Herzl wanted to turn the clock back on history and to build a fantastic modern land at the same time. It is a testimony to the emotional power of psychogeographical fantasies that his movement eventually led to the creation of the modern state of Israel. This state, however, is locked in a tragic violent conflict both with the Palestinian Arabs and with the Arab world at large (Falk, 1992).

The Hebrew term for immigration to Israel is *aliyah* (ascent), and the term for emigration from Israel is *yeridah* (descent). These terms betray the fantasy that Israel is a country set high above all other countries. *The Mother Land assumes the image of the Early Mother set high above the infant.* During the early days of Zionist settlement in Palestine, and especially during the Second *aliyah* of 1905–1914, the psychogeographical fantasies of the Jews about the "Land of Israel" were extended to its ancient Biblical components. The Jews of Palestine between 1905 and 1947 never called themselves Jews, only "Hebrews." There was "Hebrew" labor, the "Hebrew" University of Jerusalem, the "Hebrew" Revolt against the British, the "Hebrew" Technion of Haifa, the General Federation of "Hebrew" Workers in the Land of Israel. . . . Only the Jewish Agency for Palestine kept the word "Jewish" in its name because it had so been set up by the terms of the 1920 Treaty of San Remo.

In 1909 the new "Hebrew" city of Tel Aviv was founded near the Arab city of Jaffa. Its name was an awkward Hebrew rendering of Herzl's *Altneuland* (Old New Land). Because Jerusalem had a mixed Arab and Jewish population and most of the towns and villages around it were Arab, the name *Yehudah* (Judea), which in ancient times had designated the area around Jerusalem, was now given to the Jewish region surrounding Tel Aviv. This fiction persisted for over sixty years, until Israel became independent.

Similarly the name *Shomron* (Samaria), which had designated the area around Shechem (Nablus), was now applied to the Jewish area around Natanyah and Haderah, on the Mediterranean coast, halfway between Tel Aviv and Haifa. This fiction persisted throughout the British Mandate period (1920–1948) and even through the first 19 years of Israel's existence as a state (1948–1967). After the Six-Day War of 1967 the names Judea and Samaria were reapplied to the occupied West Bank. The psychological purpose, however, was still to deny the reality of the Palestinian Arab population and to believe that these are purely Jewish parts of *Eretz Yisrael* (The Land of Israel).

Some extreme right-wing Israelis have fantasies of expelling all Arabs from Israel and its occupied territories, which they call "The Whole Land of Israel" (Greater Israel). They refuse to call the Arab areas "occupied," insisting on calling them "liberated." Some dream of destroying the sacred mosques on Jerusalem's Temple Mount and of rebuilding the

Third Temple on that very site. Other Israelis may harbor such fantasies in their subconscious minds. Nationalistic psychogeographical fantasies can easily lead to war, as we have seen throughout human history. The inability to mourn underlies this tragic process (cf. Fornari, 1976). If nations could mourn, perhaps they could study war no more.

BIBLIOGRAPHY

BOYER, L. B. (1986), On man's need to have enemies: A psychoanalytic perspective. *J. Psychoanal. Anthropol.*, 9:101-120.

CAMPBELL, J. (1959), *The Masks of God: Primitive Mythology.* New York: Viking Press.

DIETRICH, D. R. & SHABAD, P., eds. (1989), *The Problem of Loss and Mourning: Psychoanalytic Perspectives.* Madison, WI: International Universities Press.

EBEL, H. (1986), Adapting to annihilation: Reviews of Yerushalmi (1982) and Roskies (1984). *J. Psychoanal. Anthropol.*, 9:67-89.

ELIADE, M. (1959), *The Sacred and the Profane: The Nature of Religion.* New York: Harcourt, Brace & Co.

FALK, A. (1974), Border symbolism. *Psychoanal. Quart.*, 43:650-660. Reprinted in Stein, H. F. & Niederland, W. G., eds. (1989), *Maps from the Mind: Readings in Psychogeography.* Norman: University of Oklahoma Press.

_____ (1982), The Messiah and the Qelippoth: On the mental illness of Sabbatai Sevi. *J. Psychol. Judaism,* 7:5-29.

_____ (1983), Border symbolism revisited. *Internat. Rev. Psycho-Anal.,* 10:215-220. Reprinted in Stein, H. F. & Niederland, W. G., eds. (1989), *Maps from the Mind: Readings in Psychogeography.* Norman: University of Oklahoma Press.

_____ (1987), The meaning of Jerusalem: A psychohistorical inquiry. *Psychohistory Rev.,* 16:99-113. Expanded version in Stein, H. F. & Niederland, W. G., eds. (1989), *Maps From the Mind: Readings in Psychogeography.* Norman: University of Oklahoma Press.

_____ (1992), Unconscious aspects of the Arab-Israeli conflict. *The Psychoanalytic Study of Society,* 17:213-247.

_____ (1993), *Herzl, King of the Jews: A Psychoanalytic Biography of Theodor Herzl.* Lanham, MD: University Press of America.

_____ (in progress), *A Psychoanalytic History of the Jews.*

FORNARI, F. (1976), *The Psychoanalysis of War.* Garden City: Doubleday.

FREUD, S. (1917), Mourning and melancholia. *Standard Edition,* 14. London: Hogarth Press, 1957.

GINZBERG, L. (1967-1969), *The Legends of the Jews.* 7 volumes. Philadelphia: Jewish Publication Society.

GONEN, J. Y. (1975) *A Psychohistory of Zionism.* New York: Mason/Charter.

GROUP FOR THE ADVANCEMENT OF PSYCHIATRY (1987), *Us and Them.* The Psychology of Ethnonationalism. New York: Brunner/Mazel.

KOENIGSBERG, R. A. (1977), *The Psychoanalysis of Racism, Revolution, and Nationalism.* New York: Library of Social Science.

MACK, J. (1983), Nationalism and the self. *Psychohistory Rev.,* 11(2-3):47-69.

MAHLER, M. S., PINE, F. & BERGMAN, A. (1975), *The Psychological Birth of the Human Infant: Symbiosis and Individuation.* New York: Basic Books.

316   AVNER FALK

MEISSNER, W. W. (1990), Jewish messianism and the cultic process. *The Psychoanalytic Study of Society,* 15:347–370.

_____ (1992), Medieval Messianism and Sabbatianism. *The Psychoanalytic Study of Society,* 17:289–325.

MITSCHERLICH, A. & MITSCHERLICH, M. (1975), *The Inability to Mourn: Principles of Collective Behavior.* New York: Grove Press.

PATAI, R. (1976), Ethnohistory and inner history. *Jewish Quart. Rev.,* 67:1–15. Reprinted in Patai, R. (1977), *The Jewish Mind.* New York: Scribner's.

POLLOCK, G. H. (1961), Mourning and adaptation. *Internat. J. Psycho-Anal.,* 42:341–361.

_____ (1975), On mourning, immortality, and utopia. *J. Amer. Psychoanal. Assoc.,* 23:334–362.

_____ (1977), The mourning process and creative organizational change. *J. Amer. Psychoanal. Assoc.,* 25:3–34.

_____ (1989), *The Mourning-Liberation Process.* 2 vols. Madison, WI: International Universities Press.

ROCHLIN, G. (1973), *Man's Aggression: The Defense of the Self.* Boston: Gambit.

RÓHEIM, G. (1943), *The Origin and Function of Culture.* New York: Nervous and Mental Disease Publishing Co. New York: Doubleday/Anchor 1971.

ROSKIES, D. G. (1984), *Against the Apocalypse: Responses to Catastrophe in Modern Jewish Culture.* Cambridge: Harvard University Press.

SCHOLEM, G. G. (1973), *Sabbatai Sevi: The Mystical Messiah.* Princeton: Princeton University Press.

STEIN, H. F. (1984), The scope of psycho-geography: The psychoanalytic study of spatial representation. *J. Psychoanal. Anthropol.,* 7:23–73.

_____ (1987), *Developmental Time, Cultural Space: Studies in Psychogeography.* Norman: University of Oklahoma Press.

_____ & NIEDERLAND, W. G., eds. (1989), *Maps from the Mind: Readings in Psychogeography.* Norman: University of Oklahoma Press.

VOLKAN, V. D. (1979), *Cyprus — War and Adaptation: A Psychoanalytic History of Two Ethnic Groups in Conflict.* Charlottesville: University Press of Virginia.

_____ (1981), *Linking Objects and Linking Phenomena: A Study of the Forms, Symptoms, Metapsychology, and Therapy of Complicated Mourning.* New York: International Universities Press.

_____ (1988), *The Need to Have Enemies and Allies: From Clinical Practice to International Relationships.* Northvale, NJ: Aronson.

WINNICOTT, D. W. (1971), *Playing and Reality.* Harmondsworth: Penguin.

YERUSHALMI, Y. H. (1982), *Zakhor: Jewish History and Jewish Memory.* Seattle: University of Washington Press.

15

Sensible Beasts: Psychoanalysis, Structuralism, and the Analysis of Myth

JOHN MORTON

But to eliminate the will altogether, to suspend each and every affect, supposing we were capable of this — what would that mean but to *castrate* the intellect?

— Friedrich Nietzsche
On the Genealogy of Morals, 12

LÉVI-STRAUSS AND PSYCHOANALYSIS

The basis for the psychoanalytic theory of symbolism was laid down by Freud at the turn of this century, but the classical statement on the matter came from Ernest Jones (1950), who in 1916 wrote, *"All symbols represent ideas of the self and the immediate blood relatives, or of the phenomena of birth, love, and death.* In other words, they represent the most primitive ideas and interests imaginable" (p. 102). "The self," he went on to say, "comprises the whole body or any separate part of it, not the mind," whereas the "relatives include only father, mother, brothers and sisters, and children." Birth, he suggested, refers to "begetting, or . . . being born oneself," whereas death can only be "the death of others" represented as "lasting absence." Finally, he stated that love should be understood only in terms of sexuality, as that concept is defined to include all the polymorphous aims of the body (p. 103). In short, Jones argued that what he called "true symbolism" is always concerned with basic questions of reproduction — and psychoanalysis surely still stands (or falls) by this claim.

In true symbolism, said Jones (1950), things symbolized are always unconscious: "the individual has no notion of [the symbol's] meaning, and rejects, often with repugnance, the interpretation" (p. 90). Claude Lévi-Strauss, the founder of French structuralism, is one man who falls under the category of "rejector," because he has persistently questioned the basis of the psychoanalytic conception of symbolism. Flatly (if only implicitly) rejecting Jones distinction between superficial symbolism, in which symbol and symbolized can be consciously articulated through access to the preconscious, and true symbolism, Lévi-Strauss (1972) has suggested that the psychoanalytic notion of the unconscious is no more than an extension of the preconscious, because, "as a reservoir of recollections and images amassed in the course of a lifetime," the preconscious "is merely an aspect of memory" (p. 203), and it is precisely this function of "container" that psychoanalysts give to the unconscious. But, says Lévi-Strauss, the unconscious must be opposed to the preconscious in these terms, because the former

> is always empty — or, more accurately, it is as alien to mental images as is the stomach to the foods which pass through it. As the organ of a specific function, the unconscious merely imposes structural laws upon inarticulated elements which originate elsewhere — impulses, emotions, representations, and memories . . . [T]he preconscious is the individual lexicon where each of us accumulates the vocabulary of his personal history, but . . . this vocabulary becomes significant . . . only to the extent that the unconscious structures it according to its laws and thus transforms it into a language [p. 203].

In spite of Lacan's attempt to incorporate structuralist laws of language into the Freudian unconscious, Lévi-Strauss has remained faithful to his critique. He has in particular been keen to show how his structuralist theory improves on psychoanalytic formulations in the area of mythology. So, for example, he states (1972) that the idea that mythology is necessarily related to repression leads too easily to "a clever dialectic [that] will always find a way to pretend that a meaning has been found" (p. 208); that the psychoanalyst who would study structures in myths tries "to explain types of categories by reducing them to contents which are not of the same kind and which, through the operation of a remarkable contradiction, are supposed to modify their form from without" (1981, p. 627); and that all Freudians can really be credited with in the analysis of myths is their partial deciphering of "the psycho-organic code," which is but one unprivileged code among many others (1988, pp. 186–187).

These claims are related to others that typify the fundamental differences between Lévi-Strauss and most Freudians. Psychoanalysis cannot do without the notions of "instinct" and "drive," which ensnare the discipline in the field of the body and its emotions. As Lacan (1979) has suggested, if a science is defined by its object, then that of psychoanalysis is desire. But according to Lévi-Strauss (1973a) "affectivity is the most obscure side of man": it "is refractory to explanation" and thus "*ipso facto* unsuitable for use in explanation" (p. 140). In the same work he goes on to say:

Actually, impulses and emotions explain nothing: they are always *results,* either of the power of the body or of the impotence of the mind. In both cases they are consequences, never causes. The latter can be sought only in the organism, which is the exclusive concern of biology, or in the intellect, which is the sole way offered to psychology, and to anthropology [p. 142].

So, for Lévi-Strauss, it is impossible to pass easily from mind to body, as psychoanalysts are wont to do, and Lacan himself is said to be in error for "sliding a metaphysics of desire under the logic of the concept, [which] deprives this logic of its foundation" (1981, p. 630). Lévi-Strauss has it that desire has no mental logic, yet Lacan and other psychoanalysts spend a great deal of time pursuing this chimera.

Here I propose to explore some of these arguments in relation to the field that Lévi-Strauss has made very much his own in anthropology— that of myth (see in particular 1970, 1973b, 1978a, 1981). Psychoanalysts have long interpreted myths in the same way as Freud originally interpreted dreams, and the field of mythology is thus an excellent testing ground for the relative adequacy of structuralist and psychoanalytic theories. By taking a number of myths from Aboriginal Central Australia I closely examine Lévi-Strauss's claim that the "psycho-organic code" cannot in any sense be privileged in a network of symbolic transformations. The analysis of the Central Australian myths shows, I believe, that this claim is false, even though one must concede to Lévi-Strauss that psychoanalytic interpretations of myth often stand in need of correction on this count.

In the final part of the chapter I assess the implications of the analysis for structuralist and psychoanalytic understandings of human subjectivity. I argue that while Lévi-Strauss, a self-confessed biological reduction-ist, would reduce his metaphysical notion of mind to a material brain (1966, pp. 263–264; 1972, p. 201; 1973a, p. 163; 1981, p. 689), psychoanalysts can, and should, call this limited conception of mental activity into question. Psychoanalysis, I suggest, implicitly or explicitly transcends a metaphysics of the mind (or brain) with a metaphysics of the soul (or body) (cf. Bettelheim, 1985). Thus, in keeping with myth itself, psychoanalysis retains the question of the relationship between the whole of the body and its nonmaterial agencies — a matter that Lévi-Strauss, for subjective reasons very much his own, refuses to acknowledge.

HUMANITY ENCHAINED

Throughout a large part of Aboriginal Australia, but particularly among Arandic groups and their neighbors in the center of the continent, we find myths that tell of the shaping of humanity from an original formless mass of embryonic beings. The first published Aranda version of such a myth comes from Gillen (1896).

Myth 1

Ages ago ancestors of the present race lived in the form of a great species of porcupine . . . called [*inapatua,*] which had no limbs or organs of sight, smell, or hearing, and which did not eat food. This animal, incapable of motion, presented the appearance of a man whose legs and arms were so shrunken and "doubled up" that mere indications of limbs were visible. A spirit called *Alkappera* came from the east . . . who, seeing these strange creatures, felt a great pity for them and, on examination, discovered that, with the aid of his magic knife, he could, by releasing from the curious mass of flesh the faintly outlined legs and arms, give these creatures the same shape as himself. Taking up one of the [*inapatua*] he quickly released the arm, adding fingers by making four clefts at the end of the arm; the legs were then released and toes added in like manner. The figure could now stand erect, the nose was formed and the nostrils bored with the finger; one stroke of the knife added the mouth, which was pulled open several times to make it flexible; eyes were formed by the simple process of incision and another stroke or two of the magic knife provided the new being with genital organs. The *Alkaperra* continued his operations until all the [*inapatua*] were converted into living images of himself. In this way the sexes were created with equal rapidity. Having finished his task the spirit called all the men and women together, endowed them with the gift of speech, and informed the men that the women were made for their use, with a view of increasing their numbers. It was ordained that the men, before taking wives, must undergo the ordeals of circumcision and subincision, and that they must hide from the women during recovery; these operations being performed on them at once. The men and women assembled were then divided into [marriage] classes . . . and were instructed in the marriage laws, which are observed at the present time [pp. 184–185].

Gillen and his collaborator Spencer give further elaborations on this story elsewhere. In *The Native Tribes of Central Australia* (1899) they state (Myth 2) that the earth was originally covered with salt water: when this water receded the *inapatua* were exposed. Two beings then descended from the western sky and shaped the *inapatua* in the manner already described.

The [*inapatua*] creatures were in reality stages in the transformation of various animals and plants into human beings, and thus they were naturally, when made into human beings, intimately associated with the particular animal or plant . . . of which they were transformations—in other words, each individual of necessity belonged to a totem . . . The same tradition relates that, after having performed their mission, the [beings from the sky] transformed themselves into little lizards called [*mangarkunjerkunja*] [pp. 388–389].

In *The Northern Tribes of Central Australia* Spencer and Gillen (1904, p. 150) briefly repeat this story, but they also reproduce another that is clearly related. The fragment that is of particular significance here runs as follows.

Myth 3

[Long ago a] man of the Unmatjera tribe arose at a place . . . in the Harts Range. At first he had the form of a little lizard called [*mangarkunjerkunja*] . . . ; then he looked at himself and said "Hullo, I have got bristles like a porcupine". At first he was stiff and could not walk, but he lay down all day long in the sunlight, and warmed himself and stretched his legs. After a time he looked at himself and saw that he was not a porcupine, but . . . a jew lizard. He still lay quiet, and, later on, again looked and saw on the ground beside him another little [jew lizard,] who had come from him, and he said "Hullo, that is all the same as me"; again and again he looked, with the same result . . . [until,] after a time, he saw one die, and said, "That is me dead . . ." For a long time he remained quietly in the one spot, and continually looked at himself until gradually he increased and became great in the flesh, and grew into . . . a great and wise man [p. 400].

The remainder of the story tells how the jew lizard man taught his method of reproduction to other totemic beings.

Spencer and Gillen also relate a second Unmatjera myth relevant to those already noted.

Myth 4

[Long ago] an old crow man . . . arose . . . from a [*tjurunga*, or sacred object,] and when he came out he looked at himself and said, "I think that I must be a hawk; but no — I am too black". Then he thought he was an eagle-hawk, but decided that he had too much wing; then he looked at his arms, out of which black feathers had sprouted, and said, "I am a crow." When the sun shone he sat out on top of a hill warming himself, and when it set he [returned home.] One day he saw . . . a lot of [*inapatua*] . . . He decided to go over and make them into men and women. He did this by means of his beak, and then returned to his camp and there made a . . . sacred stone knife, with which he intended to come back and circumcise them. Meanwhile, however, two old [perentie] lizard men had come . . . and, with their teeth, they both circumcised and subincised the men, and performed [introcision] upon the women . . . [pp. 399–400].

The Kaititj tell a similar story (Myth 5): here a pair of hawks replaces the pair of perenties. In addition, the hawks perform all the surgical operations without the interference of other ancestral beings (p. 153).

A final story about the *inapatua* may be found in the work of Carl Strehlow, who gives three very similar versions (Western Aranda, Kukatja and Matuntara). The following is a brief summary of the Aranda version (Strehlow, 1907; cf. 1908, pp. 4–5).

Myth 6

The earth was eternal, but covered by sea out of which several mountains towered. On the slopes of the mountains dwelt the *inapatua,* known also as the "grown-together people" on account of their limbs being still unseparated from their bodies and the fact that they were all joined together like a chain. Their eyes and ears were closed, and instead of true mouths they had minute openings on the face. The fingers of the hands were webbed and the hands themselves were balled and grown to their breasts. Their legs were drawn up, fetal fashion, to their bodies. One half of these beings were called "land-dwellers," the other half "water-dwellers," each division corresponding to a moiety or group of marriage classes. Iliingka, the sky god, commanded that a connecting mountain between sky and earth be flattened and that the pied butcherbird withdraw the expanse of sea that had hitherto covered the ground. As the sea and mountains disappeared, the *inapatua* settled at the banks of great waterholes and found there great nests on little islands. Great totemic beings rose from the ground and one of these, who was a fly-catching lizard *(mangarkunjerkunja),* eventually approached the *inapatua* and with a stone knife made them all into separate individuals. Then he took each one in turn, slit open their eyes, ears, mouths, fingers, and toes, and at the same time subincised or introcised them and taught them all the cultural arts. He stressed to each of these newly fashioned beings how they were to continue performing religious ceremonies and marrying strictly according to the rules governing moiety interaction. He then distributed all the people throughout the country [pp. 2–8].

AUSTRALIAN ZOEMES

These myths form more or less what Lévi-Strauss calls a transformation group or set: they are closely allied to each other, both structurally and thematically. They employ a number of different "codes," the most dominant of which is the zoological, and in this section of the paper I want to show how one can handle this dominant code in Lévi-Straussian terms by specifying the transformational relationships existing between "zoemes"—"animals given semantic functions" (Lévi-Strauss, 1988, p. 97). In due course, I will show how these transformations are related to a specifically psychoanalytic interpretation of the myths.

Consider first the term *inapatua,* which describes the chains of embryonic humanity. The word stems from *inapa,* which means "porcupine" (properly speaking, echidna), compounded with *atua,* which means man. Broadly, the sense of *inapatua* is "echidna people" and this is made quite explicit in Myth 1 (M1). The echidna also makes a conspicuous appearance in M3—but why?

Australian Aborigines, perhaps more than any other people, are well attuned to the "fetal" nature of reproduction, because they live in a continent of marsupials and monotremes. Marsupials, such as kangaroos and possums, give birth to their young in a very early stage of development and these young look similar to the *inapatua* insofar as they have relatively undeveloped limbs and sense organs. The echidna, a monotreme (egg-laying mammal), is perhaps the most remarkable Australian animal in this respect. It is born as "a curious little naked baby" (le Souef and Burrell, 1926, p. 371)—as a tiny hatchling of "rosy pink" and "translucent white" (Griffiths, 1978, p. 240). Only the head and forelimbs have any recognizable shape and most sense organs are virtually nonexistent. Given the terms in which Central Australian Aborigines construe primordial, embryonic humanity, it is thus no accident that the echidna, the most primitive of protomammals, should serve as a model.

In M3 the echidna has something of a confused identity: it is a (mistaken) transitional form between a *mangarkunjerkunja* lizard and a jew lizard. Lizards do, in fact, have prominent roles in many of these myths when, either as perenties or *mangarkunjerkunja,* they are operators who fashion humanity into proper human shape. Why is it, then, that these reptiles stand in a relationship of convertibility with the echidna people?

M3 suggests that reptiles make appearances in these origin myths because of cold-bloodedness. Here the jew-lizard man was originally immobile, but after lying in the sun he began to stretch his legs—and this discovery of his limbs not only parallels the *inapatua*'s discovery of their limbs, but also the actual manner in which reptiles are, so to speak, born with every dawn as they warm their cold blood in sunlight in order to become properly mobile. This warming up process, as we shall see, is a metaphor for *growth.*

Another name for the jew lizard is the bearded dragon. It gains this latter name by virtue of possessing numerous spines, both on its back and on its throat, where the impression of a full, dark beard is given. Echidnas, too, have spines and this no doubt partly accounts for the echidna's brief entry into M3, in which it stands between the *mangarkunjerkunja* and the jew lizard. As the myth makes clear, this double transformation from *mangarkunjerkunja* to echidna and from echidna to jew lizard implies growth toward adult status, and it is naturally the case that the appearance of body hair is taken to be a sign of approaching manhood in Central Australia. I will deal with the identification of the *mangarkunjerkunja* below, but it is sufficient to say for the moment that this lizard is small and without spines. In this it resembles juvenile jew lizards, which have no back spines and no "beard." It thus seems reasonable to assume that the echidna in M3 acts as a mediator between the *mangarkunjerkunja* and the jew lizard in a sustained image of maturation. Echidnas do not acquire *their* spines until many months after birth and their subsequent leaving of the mother's pouch, after which they are reared in secluded nests. Such nests were also the home of the *inapatua* in M6.

M4 describes a double transformation very similar to that of M3, except that it does so exclusively in ornithological terms. The key figure here is the crow, who first believes himself to be a hawk and then an eaglehawk before discovering his true identity. Feathers here take the place of the spines in M3, because it is the sprouting of these that finally settles the crow's self-appreciation. But the myth also introduces two other factors into the transformation—color and wing-size. The "hawk" in the myth is the black falcon, a bird that is easily confused with the crow when on the wing and which may "appear black, but most of its plumage is dark sooty-brown" (Frith, 1976, p. 133). The eaglehawk, or wedge-tailed eagle, is Australia's largest bird of prey, noted for its extensive wingspan and silky black plumage, like that of the crow. In the end, then, the crow's identity is settled by combining the limbs of the black falcon and the plumage color of the wedge-tailed eagle, although the myth marks this transition negatively: the crow cannot be a black falcon because it has the wrong color ("too black"); it cannot be the wedge-tailed eagle because it has the wrong wings ("too much wing").

However, the crow assumes his final identity in a positive way as well: he has a suitable beak with which to fashion the *inapatua* into full human beings—this after warming himself up like the jew lizard in M3. Black falcons and wedge-tailed eagles are both hunting birds, whereas the crow is primarily a scavenger: but all three birds are carnivorous and have beaks especially adapted to such feeding. As with most birds of prey, falcons and eagles have hooked beaks with which to tear flesh from their victims. The crow's beak, on the other hand, is long and straight "and can penetrate the carcasses of animals up to the size of sheep" (Frith, 1976, p. 578). Thus the suitability of the crow among these three black, winged creatures seems to stem from the fact that it alone possesses the instrument appropriate for fashioning humanity—a bill that can, as it were, constructively and penetratingly mold or sculpt, rather than destructively tear to pieces.

At this point M4 mentions the use of a stone knife for circumcision, subincision, and introcision, thus linking itself with M1, M2, M5, and M6. However, M4 is unique in attributing these initiatory ritual operations to the perentie lizards, who beat the crow to his task and perform the operations with their teeth. In M5 the perenties' place is taken by a pair of hawks, a fact that is linked to the close association in certain parts of Central Australia between black falcons and the origins of initiation. Discussion of this particular mythical axis, leading as it would to the analysis of other groups of myths concerning both black falcons and western native cats, is beyond the scope of this chapter (but see Morton, 1985). What is critical for the present discussion is the place of the perenties.

We have seen how M4 makes color (or absence of color: blackness) critical for distinguishing the crow. But the crow is, in the final analysis, unsuitable for performing genital operations on the *inapatua,* his place being taken by the perenties. Perenties are, in fact, very large lizards with a variegated skin pattern of fragmentary dark and light, which elsewhere in Central Australian mythology associates them with the night sky and the Milky Way (Morton, 1985, pp. 178–179, 186). This variegated pattern is also transformable into an ornithological code via the pied butcherbird (sometimes called the magpie—pp. 180–181), a bird with black and white plumage which is encountered in M6, where it mediates between both earth and sky, and sea and land. Evidently, then, the opposition of black and white, or of dark and light, is important in our understanding of these myths and this can be shown most clearly if we shift our attention to the *mangarkunjerkunja* lizard.

There are two conflicting species identifications for the *mangarkunjerkunja,* one given by Spencer and Gillen, the other by Strehlow. However, *mangarkunjerkunja* means no more than fly-catcher and it is quite likely that this name applies to different species at different times and in different places. We have seen, for example, how the name may be applied to the young jew lizard, yet both published identifications are different from this.

In *Across Australia* Spencer and Gillen (1912) say that:

One of the most interesting forms [of lizards] was a representative of the genus Physignathus *(P. longirostris)* . . . It is essentially a water lizard, spending its time on logs in and by the water . . . [It] is a very graceful, active creature . . . Its general body colour is light blue-grey, except along the back, where there is always a median line with a darker and lighter brown band on each side. It darts about with great rapidity, often standing up on its hind legs as it runs, and catches flies and other insects with wonderful dexterity, so much so that, in some parts, the natives call it [*mangarkunjerkunja,*] which means "fly-quick-quick" [p. 156].

Two things thus stand out about this little lizard—its coloration and its perambulatory habits in the vicinity of water. In respect of the latter we already know that the ability to stand upright is an important aspect of one of the *inapatua* myths (M1); we know also that the ability to move gracefully and quickly is linked to reptiles generally in relation to being warmed by the sun's heat (M3). Both these points are linked to the freeing of the *inapatua* and their consequent individuation and growth of the senses (M1, M2, M4, and M6). But how do such themes relate to coloration?

The *mangarkunjerkunja* is above all *divided* by its color: and its dissection matches the way in which the *inapatua* are themselves dissected. Probably no other type of animal in Central Australia would attract more attention in this respect, as there is a great variety of species recognizable from elaborate skin colors. Even within species there is tremendous color variation. The characteristic dorsal division is common to many types, including the one identified as *mangarkunjerkunja* by Strehlow (1908, p. 65), who names the species as *Ablepharus boutonii,* which is also known as *Cryptoblepharus boutonii,* or Bouton's snake-eyed skink. Ablepharus and cryptoblepharus mean "without eyelids" and "with concealed eyelids," respectively, and refer to the fact that the genus is characterized "by a fused, immovable lower eyelid forming a spectacle over the eye" (Cogger, 1979, p. 258). In a sense, then, this *mangarkunjerkunja* has eternally open eyes, which appears to match its function as revealer of the senses to the *inapatua*.

Bouton's snake-eyed skink is subject to great color variation, carrying a number of lateral striped areas around the circumference of its body. These alternate between light and dark. In recent years the species has been subdivided into four subspecies, the Central Australian type coming to be known as *Cryptoblepharus plagiocephalus*. This creature is a quite remarkable embodiment of opposites, because many of the stripes dissect the animal's sense organs (mouth, eyes, ears, and nostrils) and in addition pass over into each other by means of small dark and light spots that invade the light and dark bands respectively. As a kind of faunal embodiment of the principles of yin and yang, the *mangarkunjerkunja* thus completely encapsulates the contradictory principles of fission (metonymic relatedness) and fusion (metaphoric relatedness).

The significance of this embodiment is by no means self-evident, although a clue is given by the position of the perenties in M4. These lizards are preferred to the crow as performers of genital mutilations, but they are specifically contrasted to the crow in terms of their dappled appearance: the crow is all black, whereas the perenties embody both black and white. It seems, then, that a black/white dualism is somehow essential to the maturation of the *inapatua*.

The *inapatua,* apart from being circumcised, subincised, and introcised by way of initiation, are also given their senses. They are thus made able to see, as well as taste, touch, hear, and smell, what is going on in the world—although the position of Bouton's snaked-eyed skink in M6 suggests that seeing may well be a dominant metaphor in this repertoire (much as it is in English when applied to general understanding). If this is true, then the perenties would be more suitable than the crow for signifying maturity precisely because they appear "enlightened" in a world in which one may indeed "understand" or "see." It seems, in fact, that the key point about the opposition of dark and light in these myths is that the contrast is embodied as *discrimination* — as a *making sense* of things attendant on a process of individuation requiring separation of figure and ground.

What, then, are we finally to make of this collection of "zoemes" and their mutual convertibility? Clearly, the myths deal with a certain idea of growth in humanity's powers—growth that is at once connected to sensory perception and the development of the body, as well as to some of the most fundamental cosmological and sociological facets of the Central Australian Aboriginal world (sky and earth, fire and water, marriage classes and human reproduction). Within the scope of this general idea the stories transform themselves in just the way we would expect given Lévi-Strauss' treatment of similar mythical themes in North and South America (1970, 1973b, 1978a, 1981). But the fundamental question remains: do these transformational structures represent the limit of in-depth analysis?

ENTER PSYCHOANALYSIS

If these "zoemes" constitute a code, as Lévi-Strauss would have it, then psychoanalysts would perhaps be inclined to suggest that it is also a projection of a schema that is more basic and determinate. This schema is what Lévi-Strauss calls the "psycho-organic code": it is a *body schema,* or what Jones originally intended by his use of the term "self." But according to Lévi-Strauss (1988) it would be an error to privilege this "code" and say that it "conveys the 'better' meaning" (p. 186). "There is no more truth in one code than in any other. The essence of the myth . . . is founded on the property inherent in all codes: that of being mutually convertible" (p. 187).

As it happens, the *inapatua* myths have been interpreted by the psychoanalyst Róheim (1945, pp. 200–209), who situates them in a general understanding of Aboriginal myth and ritual. For Róheim, who conducted fieldwork in Central Australia in 1929, all Aboriginal religion betrays the indelible mark of a certain psychic truth, namely, that all life processes are dualistic, with two contrary trends: "the life process of growth, with the 'away from the mother' trend, and the fantasy process . . . of reestablishing the broken union" (p. 202). Thus, for Róheim, Aboriginal myths always indicate *sublimation* and are "transitional" in the sense since elaborated upon by Winnicott (1980).

In the case at hand Róheim (1945) concentrates on the helpless embryonic condition of the *inapatua* and the fact that, for the latter to progress toward a human condition, they have to be separated by various phallic instruments.

In these incomplete human beings and in the lizard that separates them we have the true key to Australian mythology. The infant starts life in . . . the *dual unity* organization. For the embryo really lives . . . an indissoluble unity with the mother. Birth causes the first cleavage in this unity, but certainly does not end it; indeed birth creates a dual unity: two who are yet one . . . Whereas the description of these unformed human beings is in some sense similar to that of an embryo, their state of being *not separated* symbolizes the dual unity of mother and child . . . *In the beginning there was the separation of mother and child and what separated*

*them was the phallos or the life impulse. All institutions originate
after this separation; culture is a reaction to it, a finding of mother
substitutes* [p. 202].

How, then, does Róheim support this reduction of the myths?
Róheim's analysis deals with a fuller set of myths than those handled
here, because he adds several other stories from elsewhere in Australia.
The other myths need not concern us now, even though it would certainly
be of interest to chart the transformations that they embody. What is
important is to understand that Róheim uses the broader context to
furnish mythical illustrations of a universal formula, of which Australian
totemic mythology is supposed to represent no more than a single case.
As he puts it (1945), "Totemism . . . is a defense organized against
separation anxiety . . . It represents our efforts to deal with the problem
of growing up . . . The path is Eros, the force that delays disintegration"
(pp. 249–250). Thus, for Róheim, the myths have to be handled as
"daydreams." When linked to ritual action they assist people to mature
and deal with reality: they are "transition myths" (p. 16), and all
transitions are "from the mother to the mother" by way of the "inter-
mediate object," which is always "the phallos" (p. 66). Here, then,
Róheim appropriates Aboriginal cosmology to bolster the cosmology
that is psychoanalysis: but to what extent is this justified?

The *inapatua* are characterized by a number of features: above all,
they are amorphous, without senses, and chained together. According to
Róheim this general state of fusion must signify union with the mother.
Although he produces little evidence for this, we know that he is in some
sense correct, because the *inapatua* are modeled on infantile echidnas in
need of mothering. But Róheim makes his statement about fusion with
the mother in an arbitrary way. What is more, he goes on to situate his
interpretation of the *inapatua* myths in a wider context by discussing
myths in which mothers and penises actually appear, as if this were proof
of his original interpretation. This procedure, which privileges certain
myths by citing them as the least repressed versions (cf. Róheim 1972, p.
84), is precisely the one which, according to Lévi-Strauss, leads to the
erroneous singling out of the "psycho-organic code."

In this respect there is no doubt that Lévi-Strauss' strictures should be
taken wholeheartedly into account. There simply is no warrant for
privileging particular myth variants this way, and all myths in a set have
to be regarded as equally valid statements of a theme. However, in spite
of Róheim's procedure, I do not think that his interpretation is necessarily inappropriate. I would argue, in fact, that any hypothetical

introduction of mothers or penises into the *inapatua* myths or cognate stories is largely irrelevant to the validity of Róheim's formulation, which must itself be treated mythically in much the same way as Lévi-Strauss has enjoined us to treat Freud's Oedipus (1972, p. 217) — as a transformation of other versions of a story. This way leaves open the question of the status of the so-called psycho-organic code, but before considering this question afresh, it is necessary to look closer at the institutional setting of the *inapatua* myths in order to see how Róheim's interpretation might function as a valid translation of the original mythic forms.

In a number of papers I have described the cosmology of Central Australian Aborigines and analyzed it in relation to both indigenous practice and psychoanalytic theory (Morton, 1987a,b, 1989a,b). These Aboriginal people describe the animation of the fetus in terms of what has come to be called spirit conception — the taking up of residence within the body of the fetus by a spirit child that has come from an ancestral being embodied in the environment by a religious object *(tjurunga)* made of stone or wood. The animation takes place at the time of quickening, the first sign that the child is entering into a true relationship with its mother, and the child is regarded as a corporeal instantiation of the ancestor, who is closely associated with a totemic species. The infant is identified with the same species — hence the child receives a name that is connected with the particular ancestral myths in question. However, it does not receive this name until considerably later than spirit conception.

The time from spirit conception through birth and up to the age when the child crawls and toddles is regarded as a consolidation of the ancestral spirit's new corporeal form. The consolidation is marked at about one year of age, when the ancestral spirit begins to enter into a relationship with the mother's own conception spirit or totem, which is said to look after the child in the same way as an active, caring mother. The infant's motility is the critical marker, because this signifies the encouragement and nurturing that has taken place in the previous year of postnatal life and the six months of postconception life in the womb. Naming, the fixing of the spirit in the child's body, and the relationship between this spirit and that of the mother all cohere when the child can readily leave the mother and explore the environment alone. Spencer and Gillen's remarks to the effect that the *inapatua* are "stages in the transformation of various animals and plants into human beings" has to be understood in this light. The *inapatua,* like crawling or toddling children, are *ripe for individuation,* having left behind their totemic embodiment in *tjurunga.*

Róheim is thus correct to see the *inapatua* as symbolizing the relationship of mother and child after birth rather than *in utero,* in spite of the *inapatua* being depicted as embryos. However, we have to be more explicit about what is meant by "mother" in this context. The *inapatua* are characterized in the myths as being indissolubly linked to their fellows: the unity is not, as Róheim would have it, strictly that of mother and child, but of a number of beings who are exactly alike in certain given and well-described respects. Their relationships to each other are *transitive* and this is the very mode of relating that characterizes children of about one year of age who are passing through what Lacan has called the mirror phase. Such children, although having a felt integrity based on their objective sense of body coordination, have no sense of perspective or any sense of "I" separate from any "you." Paradigmatically and primordially this relationship may well be formed in terms of the mother–infant dyad, but it is first of all a "frame of mind" whose function "is to establish a relation between the organism and its reality — or, as they say, between the *Innenwelt* and the *Umwelt*" (Lacan, 1977, p. 4). We are thus obliged to qualify Róheim's comments, without actually dispensing with them: psychoanalysis does not deal with *a* mother or *any* mother, but with *the* mother, and in this case *the* mother is the whole world in which the emerging subject sees himself reflected. Technically, the *inapatua* symbolize *the formation of the ideal ego.*

The *inapatua* have no identity or coordination that they can call their own: perception and motility occur without any sense of perspective, and the senses remain yet to be claimed. This, I suggest, is why the *inapatua* are characterized as having no eyes, ears, feet, hands, and so on. Children going through the mirror phase do, of course, have sensory contact with the world, but their situation is comparable to that depicted in the 115th Psalm:

> They have mouths, but they speak not:
> Eyes have they, but they see not:
> They have ears, but they hear not:
> Noses have they, but they smell not:
> They have hands, but they handle not:
> Feet have they, but they walk not:
> Neither speak they through their throat.

These words describe idols and the idolators who mirror their character. As McLuhan (1964) has said, there is an exact equivalence here between the Psalmist's notion of idol and the (primary) narcissistic object as conceived first in Greek myth and later appropriated by psychoanalysis. The subjective agency of primary narcissism is the ideal ego; the constant embracing of its image in another leads to what Lacan sees as alienation — in McLuhan's terms, to a "sense closure" or "displacement of perception" (p. 55). This, I suggest, is precisely why the *inapatua* are a closed chain of individuals unable to move and perceive *for themselves*. They are "numb," as the very name Narcissus (a cognate of "narcosis") suggests (p. 51).

Mirroring has a key role to play in the myths we have discussed. In M1 Alkappera felt pity for the *inapatua* and resolved to make them like himself; in M3 the main character constantly looks at himself as he evolves into a man; and in M4, too, the main character settles on his identity by looking at himself — after which he separates the *inapatua*. In fact, the general structure of the *inapatua* myths is "reflective", insofar as agents such as crows and lizards are there to make the *inapatua* into beings like themselves, that is, beings capable of *dividing*. In Róheim's estimation, that which divides is always "the phallos or the life impulse", although it seems to me that this is the point at which his formulation begins to go astray.

The problem with Narcissus was not that he loved himself: it was that he idolized his reflection without knowing that it was his own. Narcissus did not know how to "look to himself" like some of the characters in our myths, and this "looking to oneself" seems to embody a defining element of aggression instead of the all-embracing, self-closing system of love felt by Narcissus. Róheim arbitrarily identifies the phallus in the *inapatua* myths with Eros (or "the life impulse"), yet it is clear that the instruments involved are predominantly aggressive and associated with Thanatos (the will to destruction or the death instinct). From a superficial reading of the myths alone, then, we are entitled to question Róheim's interpretation at this point, though we have yet to replace it with anything better.

M3 describes as part of the process of self-reflection the witnessing of one's own death: it is this witnessing that prefigures the jew lizard growing into "a great and wise man." In the other myths a kind of partial death is necessary to individuate the *inapatua*, because in all cases the enchained beings are placed under the knife (or some similar instrument). At the same time, however, the knife that divides is wielded by animals that are themselves divided, and it touches the bodies of the *inapatua* in order to divide them. If this knife is a phallus, then, it undertakes the specific task of separating, and thus of distinguishing between figure and ground (or self and other).

In his original analysis Róheim (1945, p. 204) points out that an important aspect of the *inapatua* myths is the depiction of sexual difference or tension. This difference or tension is related to other divisions connected with marriage and reproduction, such that the myths begin to look very much like a statement on the nature of difference itself, in which color, animal species, and social groups are formally analogous. Yet the institution of difference is not taken for granted; it is something acquired by the *inapatua* as a result of coming under the knife of those who already possess this difference. It seems, in fact, that the possession of this knife (or some similar instrument) is the very mark of difference to be communicated.

At this point, then, one is bound to concede to a psychoanalytic interpretation of difference: difference is first of all sexual difference, as indicated in "the signification of the phallus" (Lacan, 1977, pp. 280–291). Without the introduction of this signifier there is no difference, and thus no culture, for the *inapatua*. It is not necessary here to reiterate everything psychoanalysis has discovered about "the signification of the phallus" during the narcissistic crisis that follows mirroring, but one should point out that individuation follows a number of stages in which intentional aggression becomes manifest in identification with one's rival. As Lacan states, "the Oedipal identification is that by which the subject transcends the aggressivity that is constitutive of the primary subjective individuation" (p. 23). It is, of course, aggressive intent that the *inapatua* must face in order to become individuals.

And so it is that the *inapatua* follow a path that leads them ultimately to initiation and symbolic castration—they are circumcised, subincised, and introcised, and then deemed fit to marry. This path cannot, as Róheim suggests, be constituted exclusively by Eros, "the force that delays disintegration." Indeed, it is this integrating force of Eros in primary narcissism that the phallus must negate and transform in order to fashion true men and women of the *inapatua* by penetrating the space between self and other. As Aborigines suggest, the mirroring child is named in order to *characterize* him, to make him into a *figure;* and he can only be made into a figure if he first emerges from the earth, from his *ground.* This is the fundamental nature of the division that he thereafter "embodies in black and white".[1]

---

[1]For Lévi-Strauss the principle of opposition (difference, discrimination) is the very basis of the human capacity to symbolize. He (1945) assumes this capacity as an a priori principle, refusing to be interested in its origins: "sociology cannot explain the genesis of symbolic thought, but has just to take it for granted in man" (p. 518). Though I cannot expand on the subject here, I take this to be a key difference between purely structuralist and psychoanalytically inspired understandings of the principle of opposition. The

THE MYTH OF THE DEATH OF MYTH

When Róheim claims that all transitions in Aboriginal mythology can be reduced to a journey *from* the mother *to* the mother, by way of the phallus, his statement can only make sense if the terms in question are taken as "archetypes." One might adopt a Freudian or Jungian position in relation to these archetypes (or imagines), but both of these would be rejected by Lévi-Strauss on the ground that any "libido" must lie outside of the mind.[2] The analysis here suggests that mythology fails to support this view. Logical transformations between myths do *not* exhaust the meaning of those myths, whose coherence cannot be divorced from their sensuous, practical, and moral settings. Indeed, although structuralist laws of transformation can be found in the myths, these clearly represent no more than a superficial level of analysis so long as they remain detached from the drive.

Lévi-Strauss (1970) partly defines myth as having "no obvious practical function." Rather, it represents mentation "when the mind is left to commune with itself and no longer has to come to terms with objects" (p. 10). This is why myth is a privileged arena for finding the laws of the unconscious.

> Myths are anonymous . . . When the myth is repeated, the individual listeners are receiving a message that, properly speaking, is coming from nowhere; this is why it is credited with a supernatural origin. It is therefore comprehensible that the unity of the myth should be projected onto a postulated center, beyond the conscious perception of the listener through whom for the time being it is merely passing, up to the point at which the energy it radiates is consumed in the effort of unconscious reorganization it has itself previously prompted [p. 18].

Psychoanalysts, who see such a close connection between myth and dream, can perhaps sympathize with this depiction of the mind in freeplay. What they surely cannot accept is the idea that mythic processes have "no obvious practical function" and that they do not "have to come to terms with objects."

---

position I am putting forward here, derived in the first instance from Lacan, has much in common with the Kleinian idea that symbolization originates in the subject's ability to feel hurt and adopt what Segal (1986) calls the "depressive position."

[2]For comment on the relationship between Jungian and Lévi-Straussian notions of symbolism and the unconscious see Chang (1984).

Lévi-Strauss has not only suggested that Freud's Oedipus story is a myth; he has also said that the psychoanalytic cure itself is a myth (1972, pp. 199, 202) and that psychoanalysis generally engages in a kind of magic (pp. 183–184). These remarks are not entirely critical and they are reminiscent of Freud's (1933) own claim that: "The theory of the instincts is so to say our mythology. Instincts are mythical entities, magnificent in their indefiniteness. In our work we cannot for a moment disregard them, yet we are never sure we are seeing them clearly" (p. 95). One cannot disregard Freud's "mythical entities" (Eros and Thanatos), along with others, like Narcissus and Oedipus, even in Lacanian "mythology," which describes the unconscious as "structured like a language" and startlingly reduces it to logical functions (see also Matte Blanco, 1975). One cannot disregard them because psychoanalysis is indeed a mythology, but a mythology that, in keeping with all previous forms, is oriented to the field of being, and not just to the field of thought.

Lévi-Strauss (1970) accepts that, insofar as the structural analysis of myth must "conform to the requirements of that thought and . . . respect its rhythm," then the analysis "is itself a kind of myth" (p. 6) – a "myth of mythology" (p. 12). But while myth is normally understood as a true *cosmology*, like the one that Freud built from his eternal battle between Life and Death (cf. Laplanche, 1976), the structuralist myth has only one ultimate reference: the structure of the mind (or brain). Mythology always deals with *agencies* (gods, spirits, souls, and the like) and transformations are always the results of these agencies being in tension. Yet Lévi-Strauss's cosmology has no agent. This is why Lévi-Strauss was in the forefront of the movement to exorcise subjectivity from social scientific discourse. For him (1970), not even *human* agency could be detected in myths: "I . . . claim to show not how men think in myths, but how myths operate in men's minds without their being aware of the fact" (p. 12).

Psychoanalysis locates anonymity in the id (or Lacan's Other): Lévi-Strauss sees it only as submersion in the collectivity. For Lévi-Strauss (1978b), there is no "I": "I never had, and still do not have, the perception of feeling my personal identity. I appear to myself as the place where something is going on, but there is no 'I', no 'me' " (pp. 3–4). But for psychoanalysts there is indeed an "I," even if it is alienated by the discourse of an ego. Lévi-Strauss (1981) has reacted strongly to this claim:

By substituting for the Self on the one hand an anonymous Other, and on the other hand an individualized desire (individualized, because, were it not so, it would signify nothing), one would fail to hide the fact that they need only be stuck together again and the resulting entity reversed to recognize underneath that very Self, whose abolition had been so loudly proclaimed [p. 630].

It is this very image of a two-headed coin to which Lévi-Strauss refuses currency, in spite of its obvious affinity with the Saussurean image of the sign. For Lévi-Strauss the individualization of anonymity within the body is not admissable, just as it is not admissable that the body has anything fundamental to do with the mind. Obviously, this maneuver is closely associated with the identity Lévi-Strauss posits between mind and brain.

Psychoanalysis on the whole resists biologism, but it surely cannot dismiss it entirely. If the discipline finds that the unconscious consists of representations, then it also finds that these representa*tives* of the drive. The unconscious is the system of primary process that allows human beings to think without thinking to think (Lacan, 1977, p. 166), to perform tasks without having to think *about* those tasks. It is, of course, the body that "works," and language, which is evidence of thought, is itself a task performed by the body. The opposition between consciousness and the unconscious cannot simply be that between content and structure, because this opposition is between *domains*. The dynamic between them consists in a dialectic between knowledge that is "superficial," "actual," and "detached" and knowledge that is "deep," "potential," and "committed." The latter is always "elsewhere," where the subject's "sense" is alienated from conscious understanding.

Metaphysical speculation has always explained humanity's alienation from itself in terms of its relationship with an agency *other than humanity* — God (or some equivalent term). Religion has always satisfied the requirement that "human being" gains its sense from some "Other Being," and myth is the Word of this "Being" — the language of some Other. Myth has always been first and foremost related to "matters of the heart," a conception quite radically different from a metaphysic that would deal with the mind only as "a matter of the brain." Thus, if Lévi-Strauss has presented us with a myth in his work, it is clearly a new kind of myth — one that would strangely deny its own mythic character. To reaffirm this character we need to give it some "other sense."

Badcock (1975, pp. 109–112) has suggested that we should take Lévi-Strauss at his word and treat his work as myth. We should, he suggests, analyze the myth in terms of its manifest and latent contents, where the latter can be seen to be the active repression of sensuous, bodily being, instinct, and the Freudian unconscious, and where the former is nothing other than a great metaphor for the age of cybernetics. The human mind, in Lévi-Strauss' hands, becomes an impersonal binary computer. But as von Sturmer (1987) has pointed out, there is yet more to this grand metaphor, because through it Lévi-Strauss does not really dispense with the subject at all, but instead reads all others through his own sense of subjectivity. Lévi-Strauss

> concludes . . . that in trying to understand the world, "the mind . . . only applies operations that do not differ in kind from those going on in the natural world itself" [cf. Lévi-Strauss, 1985, pp. 101–120]. This formulation takes us well beyond any notion of the psychic unity of man . . . It posits a Universal Unity. And it opens up the prospect of a "true religion" . . . in which adherents would be as terminals in a vast complex of computers [p. 108].

Lévi-Strauss' mythology, then, is a genuine cosmology, but not quite in the terms he presents it to us. In reducing the mind to the brain, and in reducing myth to a kind of universal brain linked by endless schemes of transformations, he has presented us with nothing less than a picture of the uniform and electronically mediated global village. It so happens that the problem of monoculture in the modern world is prominent in Lévi-Strauss' thinking: it is a trend he laments and deplores. And yet, in his transcendental brain, he has himself imagined that trend as intrinsic to the human condition, in the process managing to see an analogy between the cells of his own brain and the individual components of the society that surrounds him (1973c, p. 414). What McLuhan (1964) sees as the formula for the age of electronic gadgets is in fact also the formula of Lévi-Strauss' anthropology: "In the electric age we wear all mankind as our skin" (p. 56). But if humanity is but a seething surface, it is integrated at a deeper level by a kind of superintelligence—a brain, which, perhaps simultaneously perfect and flawed, like that of Einstein (Barthes, 1973, pp. 68–70), produces nothing but clever mathematical equations untainted by the dross of morality, conscience, and emotional engagement.

It is at this point that we are entitled to say that Lévi-Strauss' myth is really a kind of scientistic "antimyth," because it refuses to acknowledge its own subjective moral grounds. It is a myth that is supposedly completely objective and detached. Von Sturmer (1987) has noted that this objectivism possibly "represents a profound . . . misanthropy which only with difficulty can be kept under control" (p. 122), and this has been spelt out more clearly by Cuddihy (1987, pp. 151–162), Diamond (1981, pp. 292–331), and Pace (1983), who have all detected clear signs of an inauthentic (and perhaps specifically Jewish) "anthropology of ressentiment" in Lévi-Strauss' corpus. When not in the scientistic genre, talking up what is "good" about privileged objectivity and distance, Lévi-Strauss work is dominated by a combination of angry criticism levelled at his own civilization and a sad sense of loss at the passing of other worlds and their reduction to a global monoculture. And yet Lévi-Strauss has done nothing vital in relation to this problem. His outlook is "fundamentally nihilistic" (Pace, 1983, p. 199) and he clings to his sense of loss "as if it were his most valuable possession" (p. 198). Pace adds:

> Thus, Lévi-Strauss speaks not only about but also through the "primitive." And the message he sends is primarily one of loss mixed with anger. The source of these emotions is not clear . . . And, yet, this emotion seems so all-pervading that it must . . . have its roots in that substratum of experience we call psychology, perhaps in a childhood separation never fully integrated into the adult personality [p. 202].

Lévi-Strauss does not simply speak through the so-called primitive: he actively appropriates "primitive" discourse — myth. He claims myth as his own, yet reduces it to a nonenergetic, nonmoral, nonrelational field to be studied "in itself." In this maneuver we see, I think, the violence that is done to myth and the virtual aggression that lurks behind the facade of objectivity. As Schlesier (1988) explains, Lévi-Strauss, on his own admission, is an anthropologist who "plays with myths as the cat plays with mice" (p. 148). This is surely why Lévi-Strauss's myth is such a good one for our age, embracing as it does the moral affirmation of objectivism and denying its implicit contempt for the object. Such a structure of ressentiment can only be exhibited by individual subjects who fear their own unconscious roots and who have yet to symbolize adequately their childhood passages toward individuation.

Much like the *inapatua* of Central Australian myth, such people fail to claim their own senses, preferring instead to take refuge in any numbed sense that can be given to life by machinery. It is not for nothing that Lévi-Strauss denies his own pain in objective distance, so transforming his sense of marginality into a "prestigious immunity" (Diamond, 1981, p. 305), and it would appear that he is quite unable to embrace his own image in his myth. It is particularly interesting that although Lévi-Strauss repeatedly engages Freud and the myth of Oedipus (1969, pp. 490–492; 1972, pp. 206–231; 1977, pp. 21–24; 1988, pp. 185–206), he never tackles the problem presented by Narcissus. Narcissus, of course, solved his difficulty by killing himself: Lévi-Strauss (1966, p. 263) appears to prefer the murder of myth at the same time that he claims for himself a mythic intelligence imaged in a primary narcissistic play of mirrors.

CONCLUSION

The terms of Freudian metapsychology suggest that killing myth is bad psychoanalysis. As we have seen, the instrument of death can simply be nothing other than the image of the brain as the organ that thinks alone. Yet many stories, not just Freudian, suggest that there must be something rather more to thinking. *The Wizard of Oz,* for example, informs me that if I do not have a brain, then I may be an ineffective scarecrow with stuffing in constant danger of disintegration. But it informs me, too, that if I do not have a heart, then I am a completely empty tin man—well protected, but with nothing to protect. And finally, it informs me that, when heart and brain are out of touch like this, I become a sensible beast manqué—a lion, outwardly courageous, but in fact with no nerve. "Brain," "heart," and "nerve"—this is surely something more like a complete set of mythical terms for an adequate metaphysics of the mind. One cannot afford to be simple-minded about the location of thought: as the poet says, "Maybe all basic thought takes place in the blood around the heart, and is only transferred to the brain" (Lawrence, 1974, p. 107).

This statement cannot be any more remarkable than one that states that there is no "I" and that it is only the brain that thinks. It is, in the end, the greatest irony of Lévi-Strauss' work that his denial of subjectivity is based on a Cartesian materialism, in which his "organ of the symbolic function," the unconscious or the brain, can be nothing other than an ego (cf. Gould, 1978) or Self. This, at any rate, is what *The Wizard of Oz* teaches us, and it is at this point (though possibly this point only) that Lévi-Strauss' work strictly mirrors that of Jung rather than that of Freud or Lacan. But like any myth, it is partial—and it is partial to Lévi-Strauss' brand of universal, scientistic intelligence. This intelligence has nothing but contempt for the true claims of myth: as Lévi-Strauss (1981) says, "myths tell us nothing instructive about the order of the world, the nature of reality, or the origin and destiny of mankind" (p. 639).

We can end, therefore, with a recapitulation of the totemic myths from Central Australia and their promise of a certain destiny for mankind. Lévi-Strauss (1973a) has defined totemism as a way of identifying humans according to a natural model: Lacan (1977, p. 23), on the other hand, has identified it as being fundamentally concerned with the definition of the Other in opposition to the ego. Both views may be correct. The myths unfold an unconscious drama whereby to be human is to be *naturally* human along animal lines (cf. Urton, 1985). Some might say that animals do not use their brains, but that is surely not so. What animals are good at is synchronizing hearts *with* brains: this is much more difficult for a beast that is beset by the intervention of language and representation—and so humanity looks to animals for a genuine, even graceful, way to be. If in totemic myths human thought is constantly transformed, this can only be in response to a certain drive which it is in men's interests not so much to maintain as to discharge as a natural sense of morality. In the case of Lévi-Strauss, the lesson he has failed to learn in his refusal to claim his own subjectivity is indeed moral: "There where it was . . . it is my duty that I should come into being" (Lacan, 1977, p. 129). And as Freud (1933) originally said, recalling for us the withdrawal of the sea from mythical Central Australia to expose the *inapatua,* this "is a work of culture—not unlike the draining of the Zuider Zee" (p. 112).

No amount of structural analysis can take away from myth the fact that it symbolizes human destiny, and Jones' original definition of symbolism, whatever its shortcomings, is still a good one in all main respects. Wherever one encounters myth one will find ideas about Self and Other, about the Father and the Mother, about the Phallus and the Womb, and about Life and Death. Lévi-Strauss' denial of the validity of these archetypal terms does not stem from the character of myths per se, but from his own moral stand and the character of the myth he uses to bolster that stand. Some of us prefer other stories. If it is true, as Lévi-Strauss suggests (1966, pp. 267–269), that structuralism converges with mythic thought in seeing the world as a universe of messages, then the version of structuralism that comes from Freud, via Lacan, must surely restore to this thought the animism that was always intrinsic to it before Lévi-Strauss saw fit to perform an exorcism. We can claim to live in a soulless world; we can even continue to build an ersatz world through artificial intelligence: but in the end we suffer the same fate as our fellow creatures. We are, like echidnas, crows, and lizards, sensible beasts, even when we masquerade as numb, if not dumb, thinking machines.

BIBLIOGRAPHY

BADCOCK, C. R. (1975), *Levi-Strauss: Structuralism and Sociological Theory*. London: Hutchinson.
BARTHES, R. (1973), *Mythologies*. St Albans, Herts: Paladin.
BETTELHEIM, B. (1985), *Freud and Man's Soul*. London: Fontana.
CHANG, M. J. (1984), Jung and Lévi-Strauss: Whose Unconscious? *Mankind Quart.*, 25:101–14.
COGGER, H. G. (1979), *Reptiles and Amphibians of Australia*, 2nd ed. Sydney, Australia: Reed.
CUDDIHY, J. M. (1987), *The Ordeal of Civility: Freud, Marx, Lévi-Strauss, and the Jewish Struggle with Modernity*, 2nd ed. Boston: Beacon Press.
DIAMOND, S. (1981), *In Search of the Primitive: A Critique of Civilization*, 2nd ed. New Brunswick, NJ: Transaction.
FREUD, S. (1933), New introductory lectures on psychoanalysis. *Standard Edition*, 22:1–182. London: Hogarth Press, 1953.
FRITH, H. J., ED. (1976), *Reader's Digest Complete Book of Australian Birds*. Surrey Hills, N.S.W.: Reader's Digest.
GILLEN, F. J. (1896), Notes on some manners and customs of the Aborigines of the McDonnell Ranges belonging to the Arunta tribe. In: *Report on the Work of the Horn Scientific Expedition to Central Australia*, Part IV, ed. B. Spencer. Melbourne, Australia: Melville, Mullen & Slade.
GOULD, N. (1978), The structure of dialectical reason: A comparative study of Freud's and Lévi-Strauss' concepts of the unconscious mind. *Ethos*, 6:187–211.
GRIFFITHS, M. (1978), *The Biology of Monotremes*. New York: Academic Press.
JONES, E. (1950), *Papers on Psycho-Analysis*, 5th ed. London: Baillière, Tindall & Cox.
LACAN, J. (1977), *Écrits: A Selection*. London: Tavistock.
––––––– (1979), *The Four Fundamental Concepts of Psycho-Analysis*. Harmondsworth, Middlesex: Penguin.
LAPLANCHE, J. (1976), *Life and Death in Psychoanalysis*. Baltimore: The Johns Hopkins Press.
LAWRENCE, D. H. (1974), *Apocalypse*. Harmondsworth, Middlesex: Penguin.
LE SOUEF, A. S. & BURRELL, H. (1926), *The Wild Animals of Australasia*. London: George G. Harrap.
LÉVI-STRAUSS, C. (1945), French sociology. In: *Twentieth Century Sociology*, ed. G. Gurvitch & W. E. Moore. New York: The Philosophical Library.
––––––– (1966), *The Savage Mind*. London: Weidenfeld & Nicolson.
––––––– (1969), *The Elementary Structures of Kinship*. London: Eyre & Spottiswoode.
––––––– (1970), *The Raw and the Cooked: Introduction to a Science of Mythology 1*. London: Jonathan Cape.
––––––– (1972), *Structural Anthropology*. Harmondsworth, Middlesex: Penguin.
––––––– (1973a), *Totemism*. Harmondsworth, Middlesex: Penguin.
––––––– (1973b), *From Honey to Ashes: Introduction to a Science of Mythology 2*. London: Jonathan Cape.
––––––– (1973c), *Tristes Tropiques*. London: Jonathan Cape.
––––––– (1977), *Structural Anthropology: Volume II*. London: Allen Lane.
––––––– (1978a), *The Origin of Table Manners: Introduction to a Science of Mythology 3*. London: Jonathan Cape.
––––––– (1978b), *Myth and Meaning*. London: Routledge & Kegan Paul.

_____ (1981), *The Naked Man: Introduction to a Science of Mythology 4*. London: Jonathan Cape.

_____ (1985), *The View from Afar*. Oxford: Basil Blackwell.

_____ (1988), *The Jealous Potter*. Chicago: University of Chicago Press.

MCLUHAN, M. (1964), *Understanding Media: The Extensions of Man*. New York: Signet.

MATTE BLANCO, I. (1975), *The Unconscious as Infinite Sets: An Essay in Bi-Logic*. London: Duckworth.

MORTON, J. (1985), Sustaining desire: A structuralist interpretation of myth and male cult in Central Australia. Unpublished doctoral dissertation, Australian National University, Canberra.

_____ (1987a), The effectiveness of totemism: "Increase ritual" and resource control in Central Australia. *Man*, 22:453–74.

_____ (1987b), Singing subjects and sacred objects: More on Munn's "Transformation of Subjects into Objects" in Central Australian myth. *Oceania*, 58:100–18.

_____ (1989a), Singing subjects and sacred objects: A psychological interpretation of the "Transformation of Subjects into Objects" in Central Australian myth. *Oceania*, 59:280–98.

_____ (1989b), Mama, *papa*, and the space between: Children, sacred objects, and transitional phenomena in Aboriginal Central Australia. *The Psychoanalytic Study of Society*, 14:191–225.

NIETZSCHE, F. (1968), On the genealogy of morals. In: *Basic Writings of Nietzsche*. New York: Random House.

PACE, A. (1983), *Claude Lévi-Strauss: The Bearer of Ashes*. London: Routledge & Kegan Paul.

RÓHEIM, G. (1945), *The Eternal Ones of the Dream*, New York: International Universities Press.

_____ (1972), *The Panic of the Gods and Other Essays*. New York: Harper & Row.

SCHLESIER, R. (1988), Lévi-Strauss's mythology of the myth. *Telos*, 77:143–57.

SEGAL, H. (1986), Notes on symbol formation. In: *The Work of Hanna Segal: A Kleinian Approach to Clinical Practice*. London: Free Association Books.

SPENCER, B. & GILLEN, F. J. (1899), *The Native Tribes of Central Australia*. London: Macmillan.

_____ (1904), *The Northern Tribes of Central Australia*. London: Macmillan.

_____ (1912), *Across Australia*, 2 vol. London: Macmillan.

STREHLOW, C. (1907), *Die Aranda- und Loritja-Stämme in Zentral Australien: 1, Mythen, Sagen und Märchen des Aranda-Stammes*. Frankfurt am Main, Germany: Joseph Baer.

_____ (1908), *Die Aranda- und Loritja-Stämme in Zentral Australien: 2, Mythen, Sagen und Märchen des Loritja-Stammes, die Totemistischen Vorstellungen und die Tjurunga der Aranda und Loritja*. Frankfurt am Main, Germany: Joseph Baer.

URTON, G., ED. (1985), *Animal Myths and Metaphors in South America*. Salt Lake City: University of Utah Press.

VON STURMER, J. (1987), Claude Lévi-Strauss. In: *Creating Culture: Profiles in the Study of Culture*, ed. D. J. Austin-Broos. Sydney, Australia: Allen & Unwin.

WINNICOTT, D. W. (1980), *Playing and Reality*. Harmondsworth, Middlesex: Penguin.

16

Mythology into Metapsychology: Freud's Misappropriation of Romanticism

DAN MERKUR

The traditional histories endorse Sigmund Freud's (1914) acknowledgment that Karl Abraham "initiated the [psychoanalytic] researches into myths" (p. 36) by interpreting myths as though they were dreams. Never mentioned, so far as I can tell, are Freud's scattered remarks regarding another interpretive method that he applied to myth, on which the Freudian tradition did not build. In this method, Freud interpreted myths directly and not by analogy from the interpretations of typical dreams.

Freud (1985) announced the theory behind the technique in a letter to Wilhelm Fliess, dated December 12, 1897: "Can you imagine what 'endopsychic myths' are? The latest product of my mental labor. The dim inner perception of one's own psychic apparatus stimulates thought illusions, which of course are projected onto the outside and, characteristically, into the future and the beyond . . . *Meschugge?* Psychomythology" (p. 286).

In *On Dreams,* Freud (1901a) suggested that dreams were originally "regarded . . . as either a favourable or a hostile manifestation by higher powers, daemonic and divine" (p. 633). With the subsequent rise of science, however, "all this ingenious mythology was transformed into psychology." Freud expressed his position more clearly (1901b) in *The Psychopathology of Everyday Life.*

> *Because* the superstitious person knows nothing of the motivation of his own chance actions, and *because* the fact of this motivation presses for a place in his field of recognition, he is forced to allocate

it, by displacement, to the external world. . . . a large part of the mythological view of the world, which extends a long way into the most modern religions, *is nothing but psychology projected into the external world.* The obscure recognition (the endopsychic perception, as it were) of psychical factors and relations in the unconscious is mirrored—it is difficult to express it in other terms—in the construction of a *supernatural reality,* which is destined to be changed back once more by science into the *psychology of the unconscious.* One could venture to explain in this way the myths of paradise and the fall of man, of God, of good and evil, of immortality, and so on, and to transform *metaphysics* into *metapsychology* [pp. 258–259].

Freud suggested that mythology consists of projections onto the environment of what are actually divisions within the psychic apparatus. By reversing the projections, that is, by reinterpreting the tales in a reductive, psychologizing manner, metaphysics might be replaced by metapsychology. The classic example of this methodology is, of course, Freud's treatment of the legend of Oedipus. The Greeks regarded the tragedy of Oedipus as an ancient legend, but Freud reinterpreted it as a projection of a complex of unconscious structures within the psyche.

Freud provided two more examples. The capacity to seek delayed gratification, whose developmental acquisition is first consolidated around age five and one-half years, was the basis, Freud (1911) suggested, for the doctrine of reward in the afterlife. Again, in discussing the origin of sexuality, Freud (1920) turned to the *Symposium* of Plato, which has Aristophanes narrate a myth that human beings were originally eight-limbed, two-headed, double-torsoed, bisexual creatures, but were anciently sundered in two, since which time we each seek our other half.

These several instances illustrate but do not fully explain Freud's discussion of the method in *The Psychopathology of Everyday Life,* in which he introduced the term "metapsychology." Because he did not again use the neologism for over a decade, we cannot be certain about its meaning in 1901; but it is at least likely that he then referred, as he did later, to the portion of psychoanalytic theory that concerns the psychic apparatus. Freud's first model of the mind is conventionally termed "the topographic hypothesis." Published in *The Interpretation of Dreams* (1900), the hypothesis divided the psyche into the system *Preconscious* (which includes the "sense organ" of *Perception-Consciousness*), and the system *Unconscious.*

Are we to understand that Freud developed the topographic hypothesis by reinterpreting mythical metaphysics as projections of the psyche's internal structure? I believe so. The myths whose metaphysics Freud reduced to metapsychology belonged, I suggest, to German Romanticism.

Freud apparently encountered Romanticism after entering the University of Vienna as a medical student in 1873. From his first semester onward, Freud took courses with Ernst Brücke, whose Institute of Physiology he attended from 1876 until he left university in 1882. Brücke taught a blend of empiricism and *Naturphilosophie* (Bernfeld, 1949). Not to be confused with the "natural philosophy" of Galileo, Newton, Comte, and Darwin, *Naturphilosophie* or "philosophy of nature," is a technical term for a type of nature mysticism that descended from the Greek pre-Socratics through the Middle Ages to Paracelsus, and from the Paracelsian tradition to Goethe and German Romanticism (Faivre, 1987). Both the term *Naturphilosophie* and the characteristic form of the Romantic doctrine were introduced by the philosopher Friedrich Schelling (Schenk, 1979).

During Freud's first three years at university, all of his studies were preparatory for his intended career as a research scientist with the exception of six seminars with the philosopher Franz Brentano (1838–1917). An ordained Dominican priest, Brentano had left the priesthood in opposition to the introduction of the doctrine of papal infallibility. Empirical in his philosophy, he urged Freud to read Kant, Hume, and Feuerbach. He condemned the Romantics Schelling, Fichte, and Hegel as charlatans. In the spring of 1875, his seminar on the existence of God almost converted Freud to theism, but Freud finally resisted for fear of losing his way in occultism. Freud's relation to Brentano was close. He was a visitor at Brentano's home; in 1879, some years after the seminars, Brentano responded to a publisher's casual inquiry at a party by recommending Freud for a job of work as a translator (Merlan, 1945, 1949; McGrath, 1986). Brentano was not a Romantic, but he came of a Romantic family. He was the grandson of Goethe's boyhood friend, and the nephew of Clemens Brentano, a celebrated Romantic poet. An uncle by marriage, Friedrich Karl von Savigny, had been the teacher of both the brothers Grimm and J. J. Bachofen (Bernfeld, 1949; Campbell, in Bachofen, 1967). Franz Brentano was able not only to explain Romanticism in detail, but to refute it.

Romanticism was all over campus. Freud belonged to a philosophical discussion group that published a short-lived journal. The group was possibly composed of Brentano's students; but other members included

Josef Paneth and Siegfried Lipiner. Lipiner, whom Freud admired, knew and was regarded favorably by Friedrich Nietzsche, Richard Wagner, and Gustav Mahler; while Paneth, who was a close companion of Freud, lectured on Nietzsche's ideas and eventually befriended the philosopher (McGrath, 1986). Conversations with his fellow students account for the many striking parallels of Freud's theories and Nietzsche's philosophy (on which, see: Brandt, 1955), without challenging Freud's repeated denials that he ever read or studied the latter. Again, from 1873 until the society's dissolution in 1878, Freud was also an active member of the *Leseverein der deutschen Studenten* (Reading Society of German Students). The *Leseverein* was a politically active – and in its later phases, politically radical – German nationalist group that admired Schopenhauer, Wagner, and Nietzsche (Trosman, 1973; McGrath, 1967, 1986).

The extent and content of Freud's encounter with Romanticism remain unknown, but one matter more must be emphasized. Romanticism was not simply an artistic style and metaphysical philosophy. Lovejoy (1961) has richly documented German Romantics' references to an initiation into mystical experiences at the roots of their metaphysics. It is my hypothesis that Freud either received such an initiation or was privately taught to know its contents.

Some of Freud's Romantic attachments were enduring. Freud's friendship with Friedrich Eckstein began no later than 1873. Although Eckstein later became a leading figure in Viennese Theosophy, the friendship survived six decades. Articles by Eckstein were published in the *Almanache der Psychoanalyse* as late as 1930 and 1936; the articles claimed Leibniz and Plotinus, respectively, as the founders of the study of the unconscious (Webb, 1976). Also dating to Freud's student years was a friendship with Christian von Ehrenfels, who was later a professor of philosophy. Half a lifetime later, Freud (1908) cited Ehrenfels' book, *Sexualethik,* which had been published in 1907. In 1916, Ehrenfels proposed a Neoplatonic cosmogony in which God evolved from unconsciousness to consciousness (Webb, 1976). The proximity to Freud's later presentation of libido is intriguing. Freud (1920) wrote: "The attributes of life were at some time evoked in inanimate matter by the action of a force of whose nature we can form no conception. It may perhaps have been a process similar in type to that which later caused the development of consciousness in a particular stratum of living matter" (p. 38).

Freud's student interest in Romanticism ended in vehement renunciation and a brief turn to radical materialism. According to his disciple and biographer Ernest Jones (1953), "That this was a highly emotional reversal of attitude was demonstrated in a discussion in a students' society where he behaved very rudely to his philosophical opponents and obstinately refused to apologize; there was even for the moment some talk of a duel" (p. 43). Freud's opponent was Victor Adler, a chum from his Gymnasium days who had argued on behalf of Idealism (Webb, 1976).

So much for Freud's Romantic period. Its enduring legacy remains to be established. Romanticism was the source of both his penchant for analogical reasoning (Schenk, 1979) and his lifelong habit of personifying Nature (Trosman, 1973). Freud also shared Romanticism's tolerance for the irrational and preoccupation with the individual (Beres, 1965; Hillman, 1989). Again, Rudnytsky (1987) has demonstrated that a century of Romantic literary criticism had drawn attention to the *Oedipus Rex* of Sophocles and developed the distinctive reading that Freud took for granted. Freud did not come across the play by happenstance. Neither did he assess its contents, themes, and implied values on the basis of an unschooled reading. Where Sophocles had portrayed a pitiable wretch, helpless in the face of destiny, the Romantics valued the heroism of opposing fate, no matter how hopelessly.

A case might also be made that Freud's account of libido in *Beyond the Pleasure Principle* (1920), together with his articles on telepathy, represent lapses into Romantic mysticism. For example, Freud (1941) acknowledged "the real existence of psychical forces other than the human and animal minds with which we are familiar" (p. 177). The Romantic connection is uncertain, however, because Freud's views also resemble the Aristotelian concept of *nous,* the Active Intellect, to which Brentano (1867) had devoted a book. With the exception, then, of a point where Romanticism and Aristotelianism happened to converge, Freud's writings on psychoanalysis contain no evidence of his subscription to Romantic metaphysics. It is my suggestion that Freud was not a Romantic, but a lapsed Romantic, an apostate Romantic, an anti-Romantic. His apostasy was the precondition of his reduction of Romantic mythology to metapsychology.

In a study of *The Unconscious Before Freud,* Whyte (1978) argued that "the general conception of unconscious mental processes was *conceivable* (in post-Cartesian Europe) around 1700, *topical* around 1800, and *fashionable* around 1870–1880. . . . Many special applications of the idea had been systematically developed from 1800 onward" (pp. 168–169). Freud was not the discoverer of the unconscious. A long lineage, passing among others through the Romantic philosophers Schelling, Hegel, Schopenhauer, and Nietzsche, had postulated the existence of the unconscious (Whyte, 1978; Ellenberger, 1970; Vermorel

& Vermorel, 1986). But what an unconscious! Reworking the traditional
Aristotelian concept of the *nous,* or Active Intellect, Schelling (as related
by Whyte, 1978) had developed the doctrine

> *that one organizing principle must pervade both the physical world
> and consciousness, but that outside our own awareness this prin-
> ciple is not itself conscious.* This unifying principle of organization
> and productivity operates without awareness in the determinism of
> nature, and with awareness in our sense of freedom. We have to use
> our awareness to infer this principle where we are not directly aware
> of it, both in the rest of nature, and in the unconscious formative
> processes of our own minds [p. 125].

The same doctrine can be viewed from the perspective of the individual
rather than the cosmos: the Romantic tradition held that the unconscious
mind is the locus of "the contact of the individual with the universal
powers of nature" (Whyte, 1978, pp. 69–70).

Freud may be credited, I suggest, with demythologizing the Romantic
conception of the unconscious. The Romantics had toyed with the idea,
but the relentless sobriety of Freud's psychological reductionism compelled people to acknowledge the importance of comprehending and
analyzing the unconscious.

Freud's technique of demythologizing mythology may also be impli-
cated in the development of his method of dream interpretation. David
Bakan (1975) has argued that Freud was indebted to the Jewish mystical
tradition for two fundamental premises of psychoanalysis: his "techniques of interpretation and the importance and meaning attached to
sexuality" (p. 245). Freud's claim to have secularized mythology supports
Bakan's conclusion that "Freud, consciously or unconsciously, secularized Jewish mysticism; and psychoanalysis can intelligently be viewed as
such a secularization" (p. 25).

Freud's biographers have resisted Bakan's hypothesis. Peter Gay
(1988) cited a letter, dated July 20, 1908, in which Freud requested Karl
Abraham's tolerance of Carl G. Jung on the ground that psychoanalysis
"is easier for us Jews, since we lack the mystical element" (p. 205). Gay
inferred Freud's "complete innocence about the long tradition of Jewish
mysticism," but overlooked Freud's letter to Jung, dated April 16, 1909,
which described his predeliction for numerology by saying, "Here is
another instance where you will find confirmation of the specifically
Jewish character of my mysticism" (Jung, 1973, p. 363). In his letters to
Abraham and Jung, Freud referred to mysticism in two distinct ways, as

is consistent with both scholarly usage and the history of Kabbalah. In contrast with the ecstatic Kabbalah, whose mystical practices compare cross-culturally, the theosophical Kabbalah is a system of metaphysical speculation that includes numerology but does not necessarily include ecstatic practice. Freud's remarks indicate his innocence of the ecstatic Hasidism of his East European ancestors, but they do not preclude his familiarity with other sources on the theosophical Kabbalah—the branch of the Kabbalah that is pertinent to Bakan's thesis.

Bakan's (1975) case rests most persuasively on a close comparison of parallels between the Kabbalah and psychoanalysis. As well, he established that Freud owned, in Vienna in the late 1930s, "a large collection of Judaica" including "a number of books on Kabbala in German, and, most importantly, a copy of the French translation of the *Zohar*" (p. xviii). Because Freud's father Jacob was raised in a Hasidic community, Freud's father, paternal relatives, and their friends almost certainly made occasional remarks that reflected the kabbalistic orientation of the Hasidic movement. However, Bakan expressly disavowed any "effort . . . to separate out the lines which have fed into or issued from Jewish mysticism. For example . . . we know that Goethe, for whom Freud had great respect, studied Kabbala" (p. xi). Indeed, the Christian Cabala was a discrete trajectory within Romanticism and may have been the vehicle of Freud's first serious exposure to Jewish mysticism as an adult. Freud was definitely influenced by the blend of German philosophy and Jewish mysticism in *The Philosophy of the Unconscious* and other writings by Eduard von Hartmann (Capps, 1971). The knowledge of Jewish mysticism that was necessary to the invention of psychoanalysis might have been acquired, in part, through Christian sources. For example, Fabre d'Olivet's *Hebraic Tongue Restored* ([1815] 1921), a work of early French Romanticism, combines *Naturphilosophie* with the exegetical techniques and sexual symbolism of the Cabala. Similarly, the theory of bisexuality, which Freud adopted from Fliess, was a fundamental doctrine of the Kabbalah (Scholem, 1991) that had become a central premise of Romanticism (Vermorel & Vermorel, 1986).

A further feature of Freud's metapsychology may also be traced to Romantic mythology. Freud (1920) asserted that his "views have from the very first been *dualistic*" (p. 53). The topographic hypothesis had contrasted the systems *Ucs.* and *Pcs.* (or *Pcpt.-Cs.*). Each was driven by a distinct type of instinctual energy: the *Ucs.* by sexual instincts, and the *Pcs.* by self-preservative instincts. When Freud (1923) grew dissatisfied with this model of the mind, he redivided the psyche into the id, ego, and superego; but he retained dualism by reworking his theory of the instincts. To the id, which was a diminished version of the system *Ucs.*, Freud assigned two types of energy: the sexual instincts, but also aggressive instincts. These same two types of instinct were active also in the ego and the superego. The concept of independent self-preservative instincts was abandoned in favor of the idea that the ego, an expanded version of the system *Pcs.*, was wholly dependent on the id. Blending sexuality and aggression, the ego creates a neutralized form of energy that it expends in self-preservation. At various points in his career, Freud (1913, 1923) asserted that his refusal to entertain the possibility of a tripartite theory of instincts was a matter of personal preference, lacking proof or even logical necessity. Of the various theoretic options that were plausible, he consistently opted for a dualistic system.

Freud's predeliction for dualism cannot be defended on scientific criteria. Ego psychology abandoned Freud's position late in his lifetime when Heinz Hartmann (1939) argued for the partial autonomy of the ego, whereas Kleinian object-relations theory so limited the scope of the id that unconscious fantasy amounted to a third system, intervening between the id and the ego. Aesthetic rather than scientific, Freud's preference for dualism was a legacy of Romantic mythology (Vermorel & Vermorel, 1986).

When and how metaphysical dualism entered European thought are uncertain. As a working hypothesis, I would note that the Persian alchemist Jabir ibn Hayyan developed the theory that all metals consist of different "balances" or proportions of sulfur and mercury (Holmyard, 1957). Sulfur and mercury have, of course, the colors of gold and silver; the common use of astronomical symbols to designate gold and silver linked sulfur and mercury, in turn, with the sun and the moon. Jabir's writings were rendered into Latin by the late 13th century (Thorndike, 1934). When Aristotle's *Metaphysics* and its theory of a quintessence, or fifth element, the ether, became popular a century later, alchemical substances were held to have ethereal spirits (Holmyard, 1926) that reduced at root to the spirits of sulfur and mercury. Spiritual alchemy is perhaps best understood as a distant forerunner of modern parapsychology: an effort to present mysticism in would-be scientific garb. (On the inadequacies of the historical accounts of spiritual alchemy by Jung, Eliade, and modern alchemists, see Merkur, 1990.)

In their cryptic allegories, European alchemists had employed a great variety of dualistic motifs, including the moon and the sun, silver and gold, woman and man, cold and heat, death and life. Although the meanings of these symbols were rarely indicated, occasional writers (e.g., de Bergerac, 1965) were so little secretive that the esoterica can be reconstructed. Under these symbols were discussed two types of theology and mystical experience. The one experienced the divine in the world; the other had an other-worldly focus. In alchemical terms, the material world was constituted of the four elements (earth, water, air, and fire), but spiritual realities were composed of ether. The divine was immanent in matter, but transcendent in heavenly forms.

As a Romantic example of alchemical theology, consider J. J. Bachofen's (1973) contrast of the Dionysian and Apollonian principles in Greek religion as

> that between the material-tellurian and the immaterial-solar stages of religion, between a lower and a higher conception of the divine as revealed in nature, between a primordial and a more highly developed stage of culture. The religious development of the human race follows the same law that is disclosed in the education of the individual. It progresses from the lower to the higher, from the material to the psychic and spiritual, from the formless to the formed, from the impure to the pure, from darkness to light. . . . In comparison with the luminous principle the material principle not only appears as the impurer and lower stage of divinity, but is often seen as a power hostile to man, which can only be transformed into a blessing through subordination to the higher law of the luminous realm [pp. 63–64].

The Apollonian principle is to be associated through the allusion to the sun god, with the symbols sulphur, gold, fire, light, heat, etc. Dionysus, by corollary, is to be associated with the moon, mercury, silver, water, cold, darkness, etc. Importantly, Freud (1913) knew Bachofen's work and endorsed his theory that matriarchy had prehistorically been superseded by patriarchy. Bachofen's reference in this passage to a shift from Dionysian materialism to Apollonian luminosity concerned the same transition: sociopolitical change was a component of general metaphysical development.

Although metallic alchemy was discredited by the rise of science, the fifth element of spiritual alchemy retained a place in classical physics. Newton postulated that universal ether was the medium of gravity; Huygens added that light consists of wave motions in the ether. These theories went unchallenged until 1896, when Michaelson and Morley disproved the existence of ether. For over two centuries, however, scientific physics provided a context for speculations regarding as-yet-undemonstrated functions of the ether.

In German-speaking countries, spiritual alchemy was transmitted through Paracelsus and the Paracelsian tradition of alchemical pharmacology to Rosicrucianism and Jacob Boehme. The esoteric tradition is difficult to detect after the Thirty Years' War until it resurfaced in the late 18th century with the Rosicrucian revival, Goethe, and German Romanticism.

During most of its European history, spiritual alchemy was a devoutly Christian enterprise. Dualism pertained to the creation, but the Creator remained one and unique. However, the decline of Christianity in the 18th century freed a portion of the Romantic movement to emphasize the dualistic dimension more fully. The shift in emphases was introduced when Friedrich Schelling (1775–1854), who was deeply influenced by the writings of Jacob Boehme (Brown, 1977), postulated dualism in God (1942):

> There are thus two principles even in what is necessary in God: the outflowing, outspreading, self-giving essence, and an equally eternal power of selfhood, of return unto self, of being-in-self. Without his further deed, God is in himself both of these, that essence and this power.
>
> It is not enough to see the antithesis; it must also be recognized that these contraries are equally essential and original. The power by which the essence confines itself, denies itself, is in its kind as real as the contrary principle; each has its own root, and neither is to be derived from the other. For if this were to be the case, then the antithesis would again immediately cease. But it is in itself impossible that exact opposites be derived from each other [p. 97].

Schelling's contrast between the transcendent God within Himself and the immanent God in His role as creator, provided him with a pretext for interpreting antithetical dualities throughout nature.

The available literature on Romantic dualism is rather slight. Some attention has been given both to the psychological dualism of reason and understanding or intuition (Lovejoy, 1961) and to gender dualism and its resolution in androgyny (Eliade, 1965; Busst, 1967). Again, there is a considerable discussion of the Cartesian dualism of body and soul; but our present concern is with a metaphysical dualism that halves both matter and spirit, both body and soul. Benoit (1973) noted the innovative role of Schelling, before passing on to survey a variety of British and American Romantics, who were consistently motivated by monotheism or natural science to emphasize that metaphysical duality was ultimately to be reconciled in unity.

Some German Romantics chose instead to go to the opposite extreme. Schelling (1942) had maintained that duality proceeds in unity: "it is not enough merely to discern the antithesis, if the unity of the essence is not recognized at the same time, or if it is not seen that it is indeed *one and the same* which is the affirmation and negation, the outspreading and the restraining" (pp. 98–99) Other Romantics later ignored or rejected the inclusion of dualism within monism, in favor of a pure dualism.

The initial inspiration appears to have been Michael Faraday's discovery of electromagnetic bipolarity. Karl von Reichenbach (1788–1869) was a German chemist who made his fortune as an industrialist by exploiting his discoveries, among other substances, of paraffin, eupion, creosote, and pittacal. Reichenbach (1968) devoted himself from the 1840s onward to research on "Od," "a cosmic force that radiates from star to star" (p. 23), whose "special application . . . to the art of healing" had led Mesmer to name it "animal magnetism" (p. 39). Because the force had nothing to do with electromagnetism, Reichenbach renamed it after the Teutonic god Woden or Odin. One pole of the Odic force was red-yellow and lukewarm; the other was blue and cold. Both the Odic force and its bipolarity were perceptible to "sensitives"—people, as Reichenbach thought, who were particularly sensitive to the Odic force but, as we should now assert, highly susceptible to hypnotic suggestion. Reichenbach reported his experiments with sensitives for over 20 years, but he failed to win scientific support for his findings. The Odic force was retailed, however, as the astral plane of the occult.

Friedrich Nietzsche (1844–1900), who had studied under Bachofen, announced his embrace of an uncompromising dualism, among other manners, through the historical allusion in the title of *Thus Spake Zarathustra*. Nietzsche's position was already clear, however, in his first book, *The Birth of Tragedy* (1887). When he described it as "a book written for initiates" that was intended "to tempt them into secret alleys, onto mysterious dancing grounds" (p. 6), Nietzsche meant fellow Romantics to take him at his word. Nietzsche expressly hinted at a secret practice of mysticism when he described "*dream* and *intoxication,* [as] two physiological phenomena standing toward one another in much the same relationship as the Apollonian and Dionysiac" (p. 19). Nietzsche asserted that dreamlike "Apollonian consciousness" (p. 28) entails "determinacy and lucidity" (p. 59) but "achieve[s] redemption in illusion" (p. 97). He was more explicit in writing of the "essence of Dionysiac rapture, whose closest analogy is furnished by physical intoxication" (p. 22) and is "the vision of mystical Oneness" (p. 23). The raptures might occur either through psychoactive drug use, or spontaneously: "Dionysiac stirrings arise either through the influence of those narcotic potions of which all primitive races speak in their hymns, or through the powerful approach of spring" (p. 22).

Bachofen had argued for evolutionary progress from the Dionysiac to the Apollonian. Nietzsche's *Birth of Tragedy* instead urged fellow Romantics to scorn the Apollonian lucidity of Euripides and Socrates, while reverting to the Dionysiac tragedy of Aeschylus and Sophocles. Nietzsche's (1887) vision was messianic.

> The German spirit is still alive, and marvelously alive, like a knight who sleeps his enchanted sleep and dreams far underground. From out of these depths a Dionysiac song rises, letting us know that this German knight in his austere enchantment is still dreaming of the age-old Dionysiac myth. . . . One day the knight will awaken, in all the morning freshness of his long sleep. He will slay dragons, destroy the cunning dwarfs, rouse Brunnhilde, and not even Wotan's spear will be able to bar his way [p. 144].

Jung (1938) maintained that Nietzsche's biography contains "irrefutable proof that the god he originally meant was really Wotan, but, being a philologist and living in the seventies and eighties of the nineteenth century, he called him Dionysus" (p. 28).

With the advance of science in the late 19th century, Romanticism became so logically untenable that its mystical practices and teachings persisted only among occultists. For example, Rudolph Steiner (1948, 1954, 1987), a specialist on Goethe who became a leading Theosophist, next a Rosicrucian, and finally an Anthroposophist, lectured on metaphysical dualism in 1913, 1914, and 1919, using the terms Lucifer and Ahriman to designate the opposites. Interestingly, it was Freud's friend Friedrich Eckstein who introduced Steiner to Blavatsky's *Secret Doctrine* and the Theosophical circle in Vienna (Webb, 1976). Later instances of metaphysical dualism include the cosmological opposition of ice and fire in the *Welteislehre* of Han Horbiger, which found Nazi patronage (King, 1976), and the magnetic and electrical forces in the Hermetic magic of Franz Bardon (1962).

Coinciding with the decline of Romanticism into occultism was another trajectory in its history: its transformation from a topic of belief into a topic of study. Writing in 1917, the phenomenologist of religion Rudolph Otto (1950) developed metaphysical dualism into cross-cultural categories of "numinous" experience. He expressly described the *fascinans* as "the Dionysiac-element in the numen" (p. 31). Implicitly, the *mysterium tremendum* was Apollonian.

Freud's conflict model of the psyche can easily be seen as a scientific secularization of Romanticism's bipolar metaphysics. Where Schelling and the Romantic tradition had postulated a conflict model of the cosmos, Freud treated Romantic metaphysics as mythology and reduced its conflict model to the psyche.

Freud's distinction between the systems *Pcpt.-Cs.* and *Ucs.* are similarly coherent in Romantic terms — but only if we assume that Freud knew not only of Romanticism's public arts and philosophy, but also of its secret mystical practices. Nietzsche had identified the Apollonian principle as manifest and rational, but the Dionysian as secret and unconscious. The allusions pertained, among other matters, to the role of consciousness in producing the respective classes of mystical experience. In both cases, unconscious materials manifest; but "Apollonian" experiences of the *mysterium tremendum,* which may more simply be termed trance states, permit consciousness an active role through auto-suggestion or, more technically, "regression in the service of the ego." By contrast, "Dionysian" experiences of the *fascinans,* which I have termed "reverie states" (Merkur, 1985a,b, 1989), are instances of "regression" proper; they are more purely unconscious in origin. Nietzsche's opposition of the Apollonian and Dionysian principles constituted a conflict model of trance and reverie, both as experiences and for their philosophic implications. Because Nietzsche's references to the conscious and unconscious pertained to trance and reverie they are not coherent when they are interpreted as references to consciousness and the unconscious. To go from Nietzsche to Freud, it is necessary to demythologize Nietzsche's mysticism. How can Freud have known what to demythologize, unless he was himself an initiate?

In retrospect, it is remarkable to think that the more important of Freud's methods for working with myths became obsolete even as it inspired the foundation of psychoanalysis. The danger of the method was, of course, that any effort to interpret myths directly, rather than through analogy with dreams, dispensed with scientific controls. Dreamers provide analysts with their associations. When interpretive insights provide relief from suffering, their therapeutic value has been confirmed experimentally. Unlike dreamers, however, myths are not available for psychoanalytic interviews. Efforts to rework myths as science may consequently succeed only to perpetuate myth. Freud was keenly aware of the problem. He referred to instincts as "mythical entities, magnificent in their indefiniteness," and asserted that his theory of instinct dualism was "so to say our mythology" (Freud, 1933, p. 9). His model of the mind (1925) was "part of a speculative superstructure of psychoanalysis, any portion of which can be abandoned or changed without loss or regret the moment its inadequacy has been proved" (pp. 32–33). Romantics' close observations of psychic experience were reason to trust psychological reductions of their myths as working hypotheses — but only as working hypotheses.

Interestingly, Freud's method of psychologizing mythology was retained by Jung and analytic psychologists, who convert myths into archetypes without significant caution. James Hillman (1975) has gone so far as to urge that archetypal psychology must be mythic: "Our point here is not to reduce demons to complexes or complexes back to an old demonology, but to insist that *psychology so needs mythology that it creates one as it proceeds*" (p. 20). The Freudian tradition does not agree. It abandoned the unreliable method and instead pursued the interpretation of myths by analogy with dreams.

BIBLIOGRAPHY

BACHOFEN, J. J. (1967), *Myth, Religion, and Mother Right: Selected Writings*, trans. R. Manheim. Bollingen Series LXXXIV. Princeton: Princeton University Press, 1973.

BAKAN, D. (1958), *Sigmund Freud and the Jewish Mystical Tradition*. Boston: Beacon Press, 1975.

BARDON, F. ([1956] 1962), *Initiation Into Hermetics: A Course of Instruction of Magic Theory and Practise*, trans. A. Radspieler. Wuppertal, West Germany: Dieter Ruggeberg, 1976.

BENOIT, R. (1973), *Single Nature's Double Name: The Collectedness of the Conflicting in British and American Romanticism*. The Hague, Netherlands: Mouton.

BERES, D. (1965), Psychoanalysis, science, and romanticism. In: *Drives, Affects, Behavior, Volume 2: Essays in Memory of Marie Bonaparte*, ed. Max Schur. New York: International University Press, 1965.

BERNFELD, S. (1949), Freud's scientific beginnings. *Amer. Imago*, 6:163–196.

BRANDT, R. J. (1955), Freud and Nietzsche: A comparison. *Univ. Ottawa Rev.*, 25:225–234.

BRENTANO, F. (1867), *The Psychology of Aristotle: In Particular His Doctrine of the Active Intellect*, trans. R. George. Berkeley: University of California Press, 1977.

BROWN, R. F. (1977), *The Later Philosophy of Schelling: The Influence of Boehme on the Works of 1809–1815*. Lewisburg: Bucknell University Press; London: Associated University Presses.

BUSST, A. J. L. (1967), The image of the androgyne in the nineteenth century. In: *Romantic Mythologies*, ed. I. Fletcher. London: Routledge & Kegan Paul, 1967.

CAPPS, D. (1971), Hartmann's relationship to Freud: A reappraisal. *J. Hist. Behav. Sciences*, 6:162–175.

DE BERGERAC, C. (1965), *Other Worlds: The Comical History of the States and Empires of the Moon and Sun*, trans. G. Strachan. Rpt. London: New English Library, 1976.

D'OLIVET, F. ([1815] 1921), *The Hebraic Tongue Restored: and the True Meaning of the Hebrew Words Re-Established and Proved by their Radical Analysis,* trans. N. Louise Redfield. New York: Samuel Weiser, 1976.

ELIADE, M. (1965), *Mephistopheles and the Androgyne: Studies in Religious Myth and Symbol.* [British title: *The Two and the One.*] New York: Sheed & Ward.

ELLENBERGER, H. F. (1970), *The Discovery of the Unconscious: The History and Evolution of Dynamic Psychiatry.* New York: Basic Books.

FAIVRE, A. (1987), Speculations about nature. In: *Hidden Truths: Magic, Alchemy, and the Occult,* ed. L. E. Sullivan. New York: Macmillan, pp. 24–37.

FREUD, S. (1900), The interpretation of dreams. *Standard Edition,* 4 and 5. London: Hogarth Press, 1953.

———— (1901a), On dreams. *Standard Edition,* 5:633–686. London: Hogarth Press, 1953.

———— (1901b), The psychopathology of everyday life. *Standard Edition,* 6:1–279. London: Hogarth Press, 1960.

———— (1908), Civilized sexual morality and modern nervous illness. *Standard Edition,* 9:181–204. London: Hogarth Press, 1959.

———— (1911), Formulations on the two principles of mental functioning. *Standard Edition,* 12:218–226. London: Hogarth Press, 1958.

———— (1913), Totem and taboo: Some points of agreement between the mental lives of savages and neurotics. *Standard Edition,* 13:xiii–161. London: Hogarth Press, 1955.

———— (1914), On the history of the psycho-analytic movement. *Standard Edition,* 14:7–66. London: Hogarth Press, 1957.

———— (1920), Beyond the pleasure principle. *Standard Edition,* 18:7–64. London: Hogarth Press, 1955.

———— (1923), The ego and the id. *Standard Edition,* 19. London: Hogarth Press, 1961.

———— (1925), An autobiographical study. *Standard Edition,* 20:7–74. London: Hogarth Press, 1959.

———— (1933), New introductory lectures on psycho-analysis. *Standard Edition* 22:7–182. London: Hogarth Press, 1964.

———— (1941), Psycho-analysis and telepathy. *Standard Edition* 18:177–193. London: Hogarth Press, 1955.

———— (1985), *The Complete Letters of Sigmund Freud to Wilhelm Fliess, 1887–1904,* trans. J. M. Masson. Cambridge, MA: Belknap Press of Harvard University Press.

GAY, P. (1988), *Freud: A Life for Our Time.* New York: Doubleday Anchor Books, 1989.

HARTMANN, H. (1939), *Ego Psychology and the Problem of Adaptation.* New York: International Universities Press, 1958.

HILLMAN, J. (1975), *Re-Visioning Psychology.* New York: Harper & Row.

———— (1989), From mirror to window: Curing psychoanalysis of its narcissism. *Spring,* 49:62–75.

HOLMYARD, E. J. (1926), Alchemy and mysticism. *Nature,* 118(2981), 869–870.

———— (1957), *Alchemy.* Harmondsworth, UK: Penguin Books, Ltd.

JONES, E. (1953), *The Life and Work of Sigmund Freud, Volume I: The Formative Years and the Great Discoveries, 1856–1900.* New York: Basic Books.

JUNG, C. G. (1938), Psychology and religion. In: *Psychology and Religion: West and East.* Bollingen Series XX: The Collected Works of C. G. Jung, Vol. 11:3–105. Princeton: Princeton University Press.

———— (1973), *Memories, Dreams, Reflections,* rev. ed. New York: Pantheon Books.

KING, F. (1976), *Satan and Swastika.* Frogmore, St. Albans, UK: Granada Publishing.

LOVEJOY, A. O. (1961), *The Reason, the Understanding, and Time.* Baltimore: Johns Hopkins Press.

MCGRATH, W. J. (1967), Student radicalism in Vienna. *J. Contemp. History,* 2(3):183–201.

———— (1986), *Freud's Discovery of Psychoanalysis: The Politics of Hysteria.* Ithaca, NY: Cornell University Press.

MERKUR, D. (1985a), *Becoming Half Hidden: Shamanism and Initiation Among the Inuit.* Stockholm, Sweden: Almqvist & Wiksell International.

———— (1985b), The prophecies of Jeremiah. *Amer. Imago,* 42(1):1–37.

———— (1989), The visionary practices of Jewish apocalyptists. *Psychoanal. Study Soc.,* 14, ed. L. B. Boyer & S. A. Grolnick. Hillsdale, NJ: The Analytic Press, pp. 119–148.

———— (1990), The study of spiritual alchemy: Mysticism, gold-making, and esoteric hermeneutics. *Ambix,* 37(1):35–45.

MERLAN, P. (1945), Brentano and Freud. *J. History Ideas,* 6:375–377.

———— (1949), Brentano and Freud—a sequel. *J. History Ideas,* 10:451.

NIETZSCHE, F. (1887), *The Birth of Tragedy.* Rpt. 1972.

OTTO, R. (1950), *The Idea of the Holy: An Inquiry Into the Nonrational Factor in the Idea of the Divine and Its Relation to the Rational,* 2nd ed. London: Oxford University Press.

REICHENBACH, K. VON. (1926), *Letters on Od and Magnetism: The Odic Force,* trans. F. D. O'Byrne. Rpt. New York: University Books, Inc., 1968.

RUDNYTSKY, P. L. (1987), *Freud and Oedipus.* New York: Columbia University Press.

SCHELLING, F. W. J. VON. (1942), *The Ages of the World,* trans. F. de W. Bolman, Jr. New York: Columbia University Press.

SCHENK, H. G. (1979), *The Mind of the European Romantics.* Oxford: Oxford University Press.

SCHOLEM, G. G. (1991), *On the Mystical Shape of the Godhead: Basic Concepts in the Kabbalah,* ed. J. Chipman, (trans. J. Neugroschel). New York: Schocken Books.

STEINER, R. (1948), *The Balance in the World and Man, Lucifer and Ahriman* [1914]. Rpt. North Vancouver, BC: Steiner Book Centre, Inc., 1977.

———— (1954), *The Influences of Lucifer and Ahriman: Man's Responsibility for the Earth* [1919], trans. D. S. Osmund. Rpt. North Vancouver, BC: Steiner Book Centre, Inc., 1976.

———— (1987), *Secrets of the Threshold: Eight Lectures Given From August 24–31, 1913.* Hudson, NY: Anthroposophic Press; London: Rudolf Steiner Press.

THORNDIKE, L. (1934), *A History of Magic and Experimental Science, Vol. III: The Fourteenth and Fifteenth Centuries.* New York: Columbia University Press.

TROSMAN, H. (1973), Freud's cultural background. *Ann. Psychoanal.,* 1:318–335. Rpt. *Freud: The Fusion of Science and Humanism: The Intellectual History of Psychoanalysis,* ed. J. E. Gedo & G. H. Pollock (*Psychological Issues* 9, 2/3, Monograph 34/35). New York: International Universities Press, 1976, pp. 46–70.

VERMOREL, M. & VERMOREL, H. (1986), Was Freud a romantic? *Internat. Rev. Psycho-Anal.,* 13:15–37.

WEBB, J. (1976), *The Occult Establishment.* La Salle, IL: Open Court Publishing Co.

WHYTE, L. L. (1978), *The Unconscious Before Freud.* London: Julian Friedmann Publishers; New York: St. Martin's Press.

17

Freud, Goethe, and Origen:
The Duality and Slaying of Moses

EMANUEL RICE

The claim of the family of Sigmund Freud and biographers, and even of Freud himself, that he was brought up in an assimilated Jewish home that was almost completely devoid of religious content has been brought into serious doubt (Loewenberg, 1971; Falk, 1978; Rice, 1990). In actuality, it appears that he was raised in a traditional, moderately Orthodox Jewish home, which, over time, became considerably less strict but was nevertheless still at quite a distant remove from assimilation or, for that matter, Reform Judaism. His own overtly negative attitude toward religion was initiated in adolescence and continued unabated until the last decade of his life. In the late 1920s he appears to have begun a return journey home to his religious roots, albeit in his own idiosyncratic way.

It can be said that this return may have begun in a general way with the publication of *Obsessive Acts and Religious Practices* (Freud, 1907) and more specifically with the publication of the *Moses of Michelangelo* (Freud, 1914), an indication of a burgeoning interest in the first Hebrew prophet and leader of the people of Israel. His interest again lay somewhat dormant until *Future of An Illusion* (Freud, 1927) was published. Sometime between 1928 and 1930 he acquired two complete sets of the Vilnius (Vilna) edition of the Babylonian Talmud, the first being the original Hebrew and Aramaic version and the second, the German translation. The return "journey" appears to have gathered

I am indebted to Dr. Stuart Feder and Joann Rosoff for their critical reading of this paper and for their most helpful comments.

momentum after the death of his mother, Amalia, in 1930. It was intensified by the rise of Nazism and anti-Semitism. His interest in Moses was now renewed with a freshened intensity in his intellectual quest to find the origins of the Jewish people. It is the intent of this study to further explore the possibility that this quest in the realm of culture and society may, among other factors, have been a displacement from an unconscious inquiry into the very origins of the religious, cultural, and societal roots of his own family (Robert, 1976).

The theoretical foundation for *Moses and Monotheism* (Freud, 1939) was foreshadowed by Freud with the publication of *Totem and Taboo* (Freud, 1912–13). In this study of the origins of the human community and its constituent family groups, Freud added to his insights derived from the psychoanalysis of individuals, the findings and theoretical ideas of Charles Darwin as well as the ethnologists J. J. Atkinson and William Robertson Smith. Darwin postulated that in prehistoric times men, women, and children lived in small groups, or hordes. The paradigm for this type of communal organization was the original "primal horde." A specific succession of events took place in each of these hordes in which the tyrannical leader, their father, took all the females to himself and castrated or killed the younger males. Atkinson went further in this hypothetical scenario by suggesting that such a system came to an end because of the rebellion of the surviving sons who killed the father and ate him. The father-horde was later replaced by a totemic brother-clan. In a decisive advance toward civilization, the brothers renounced the woman, their mother, on whose account they killed the father. This led to their initiation of a novel system, exogamy, marriage outside of the same kinship group. In this transitional period the families were temporarily organized as a matriarchy.

In the course of many millennia the phenomenon of the slaying of the tyrannical Primal Father and his subsequent cannibalization was replaced by the totem animal. This animal was regarded as an ancestor, a protective spirit, an object of worship. It could not be injured or killed, except on one exceptional occasion, which occurred once a year, when all the males gathered for a totem feast in which the animal was torn to pieces and eaten raw. Smith theorized that social order, morality, and religion owe their origins to this ritual and the memories behind it. The Christian rite of Holy Communion, in which the believer incorporates the flesh and blood of his God in symbolic form, bears a striking resemblance to this ritual.

In *Moses and Monotheism* (1939) Freud used this basic outline to determine and explain the origins of the Jewish people and their religion.

For what appear to be psychodynamic motivations of his own, he posited the point of origin with the "teacher" Moses, rather than with the "patriarch" Abraham who lived centuries earlier in time (Rice, 1990). This, despite the fact that in Jewish tradition down through the ages Moses is referred to as "our teacher" (or "our rabbi"), whereas Abraham is referred to as "our father."

Freud (1939) then goes one step further by hypothesizing the duality of Moses, that is, the existence of two separate, unrelated, and sequential leaders named Moses.

And here, it seems, I have reached the conclusion of my study, which was directed to the single aim of introducing the figure of an Egyptian Moses into the nexus of Jewish history. Our findings may be thus expressed in the most concise formula. Jewish history is familiar to us for its dualities: two groups of people who came together to form the nation, *two* kingdoms into which this nation fell apart, two gods' names in the documentary sources of the Bible. To these we add two fresh ones: the foundation of *two* religions — the first repressed by the second but nevertheless later emerging victoriously behind it, and two religious founders, who are both called by the same name of Moses and whose personalities we have to distinguish from each other. All of these dualities are the necessary consequences of the first one: the fact that one portion of the people had an experience which must be regarded as traumatic and which the other escaped [p. 52].

In this predilection for "two's," Freud had been preceded by the distinguished 18th-century Biblical scholars Henning Bernhard Witter, Jean Asrtuc, and Johann Gottfried Eichhorn, who, independently of each other, discovered a basic structure in the Bible, the "doublet." As related by Friedman (1987):

A doublet is a case of the same story being told twice. Even in translation it is easy to observe that biblical stories often appear with variations of detail in two different places in the Bible. There are two different stories of the creation of the world. There are two stories of the covenant between God and the patriarch Abraham, two stories of the naming of Abraham's son Isaac, two stories of Abraham's claiming to a foreign king that his wife Sarah is his sister, two stories of Isaac's son Jacob making a journey to Mesopotamia, two stories of a revelation to Jacob at Beth-El, two

stories of God's changing Jacob's name to Israel, two stories of
Moses' getting water from a rock at a place called Meribah, and
more [p. 22].

In addition, they noticed that in one version of the Bible, God is known
by the name of Yahweh and in the other by Elohim.

At the time of Moses in Egypt, during the 14th century B.C.E., there
was a pharaoh named Akhenaten who, according to Breasted (1906,
1933), created a revolution in the religious history of man, one whose
effects have endured to the present day—monotheism. The Egyptian
unitary deity, however, was fashioned in accordance with its longstanding heliocentric tradition, the worship of the all-powerful Sun
(Aten).

At this point Moses enters the picture. According to the Book of
Exodus, Moses was a Jewish child who was abandoned by his mother in
order to save his life as the reigning pharaoh had decreed the death of all
newborn Israelite males. He was found by a daughter of the pharaoh,
who took him home and raised him in the royal household. When Moses
reached adulthood he was revolted by the sight of the injured status of
his brethren and became their leader.

Freud, because of his ambivalence toward his Jewish origins, decided
that Moses was a non-Israelite Egyptian to begin with and a member of
the Egyptian royal court. This aristocratic Moses became the leader of
this primitive horde of suffering Israelites, rescued them from tyrannical
oppression, and adapted the monotheism of Akhenaten to their amorphous polytheistic tradition. A system of ethics was now wedded to a
supernatural frame of reference, thereby endowing and enforcing such
behavior with divine and categorical power. Moses became the "Primal
Father" who, supported by the omnipotent and omniscient Deity,
brought the suffering Israelites out of Egypt into the desert. There they
rebelled, slew Moses, and regressed to their polytheistic, "pagan" and
"idolatrous" worship. In their desert wanderings this group came in
contact with a group of Israelites who had never been to Egypt and who
worshiped a God they called *Yahweh*. The two groups decided to unify
on the condition that the Egyptian practice of circumcision become an
integral and necessary ritual in their religious framework. The "demon
God *Yahweh*" (1939), as Freud refers to him, with His emphasis on ritual
and ceremony, replaced the prophetic Judaism of the Egyptian Moses. It
was to reemerge centuries later with the rise of the Hebrew prophets.

From whom, or where, did Freud get the idea of the murder of
Moses? There was living in Vienna a famous archeologist and Biblical

scholar, Ernst Sellin, who was a contemporary of Freud. It is quite possible that they were acquainted, though, except for the relative smallness of the intellectual community of Vienna, there is no written evidence for this hypothesis. Sellin, however, claimed that he discovered passages in the writings of the Hebrew prophet Hosea that revealed the catastrophic denouement of Moses at the hands of the rebellious Israelites in the desert. Freud did not cite chapter and verse in his discussion in *Moses and Monotheism,* but apparently took Sellin at his word. The original articles by Sellin (1922, 1924) are quoted verbatim as is the actual text to which he refers in Rice (1990). There does not appear to be any evidence for the slaying of Moses in the text. Furthermore, no Biblical scholar has agreed with Sellin on this point. Why did the meticulous, scientific Freud lapse into such unwarranted speculation? Also, why the choice of Moses?

One answer could be that the choice was motivated by his own needs. Moses was for Freud an object of identification both with his own father, Jacob, and with himself (Bergmann, 1976; Falk, 1978; Rice, 1990). Unconsciously, Freud was the slayer of the Primal Father as well as the victim of this aggression. One of the points made in my study is that Freud shared with Viennese society the attitude of condescension and arrogance toward the Jew whose origins were Eastern European (often referred to as the *Ostjuden*) — as were Freud's — as well as the feeling of inferiority such Jews felt in their relation with the established Viennese middle class.

Freud's first Moses, according to his interpretation of the famous statue in the *Moses of Michelangelo* (1914), is an idealized figure of a man ennobled by his ability to control his rage at the rebellious Israelites who had regressed to their primitive idol-worshiping ways. He overcame his rage and temptation to break the Tablets of the Law given to him by God. It is the consensus of Freud's biographers that this imagined Biblical scenario was a displacement and disguised expression of his rage toward Jung for his rebellion and rejection of Freud's theories (Jones, 1953, 1955, 1957; Schur, 1972; Gay, 1988). It was Moses, and his emotional strength and courage, that was the object of Freud's interests and study.

Freud's second Moses, some 30 years later in *Moses and Monotheism* (1939), is the aristocratic Moses, the man of culture and wisdom, a man not of his newly adopted people, who was now the focus of Freud's interest. Both the early and the later Moses of Freud were noted for their prophetic vision, not so much in its predictive aspects but in seeing the possibility for the triumph of good over evil, for the expression of the nobility of man. It was Moses, the man, who set that example, and it was the Israelites who, by the adoption of the Lord's message, would become the living expression of it. Jacob, the father, and Sigmund, the son, were simultaneously and alternately the towering figure of Moses, an object to be revered, loved, and emulated and, at the same time, to be hated, rebelled against, and slain.

In reading Freud's (1939) comments on Moses, one should remember the severe Austrian prejudice of the times toward the East European Jews who, as with Freud's perception of the Egyptian Israelites, were considered *immigrant foreigners* and who exemplified *a backward level of civilization.*

> The deviation of the legend of Moses from all the others of its kind can be traced back to a special feature of its history. Whereas normally a hero, in the course of his life rises above his humble beginnings, the heroic life of the man Moses began with his stepping down from his exalted position and descending to the level of the children of Israel [p. 15].

A few pages later, Freud comments:

> But it is not easy to guess what could induce an aristocratic Egyptian — a prince, perhaps, or a priest or high official — to put himself at the head of crowd of immigrant foreigners at a backward level of civilization and to leave his country with them. The well-known contempt felt by the Egyptians for foreign nationals makes such a proceeding particularly unlikely [p. 18].

Freud's involvement with what he thought was the supreme significance of the father was in line with his concept of the centrality of the father in the oedipal conflict. The importance of the mother as a significant etiologic factor in personality development and psychopathology came much later in the history of psychoanalysis.

GOETHE AND THE "SLAYERS OF MOSES"[1]

Freud and Sellin were not alone in their misguided Mosaic hypothesis. There were other "slayers of Moses" (Handelman, 1982). In *Moses and*

---

[1]Material for this discussion of Goethe is taken from Rice, 1990, pp. 155–157.

Monotheism, Freud (1939) refers to the German writer Goethe, who also had a similar idea:

The killing of Moses by his Jewish people, recognized by Sellin from traces of it in tradition (and also, strange to say, accepted by the young Goethe without any evidence) thus becomes an indispensable part of our construction, an important link between the forgotten event of primaeval times and its later emergence in the form of the monotheist religions [p. 89].

In a footnote reference to the "young Goethe," Freud notes that Goethe's "acceptance" appears in *Israel in der Wuste* (Israel in the Wilderness), the Weimar Edition, Volume 7, page 170. Freud nowhere else says anything further about Goethe's ideas in this matter.

In the chapter *Israel in der Wuste,* Goethe (1902) reveals his negative feelings for the Biblical Moses, referring to him as lacking in leadership qualities, incompetent, and indecisive, among other undesirable character traits.

It was soon after their rebellion against [their brother] Moses that Miriam died and Aaron just disappeared.

Conditions for the Israelites took a turn for the better after their arrival at Arnon Creek. For the second time, they felt that they were closer to the fulfillment of their wishes for they were now in a place that put fewer obstacles in their path [towards conquest and arrival in the promised land]; they could now advance, en masse, and overcome, destroy, and then expel those people who had refused to allow them to pass through their territory. [The Israelites] then launched attacks on the [inhabitants] of the beautiful land of the Midianites, Moabites, and Amorites. Despite the cautious efforts and vain attempts of Jethro, [the Midianite father-in-law of Moses], to prevent it, the Midianites were annihilated. The left bank of the Jordan [River], was taken and some of the impatient Israelites were given permission to [temporarily] settle in this conquered land. Despite the issuance of orders to continue their advance [and cross the Jordan], some of the [Israelite] tribes expressed their reluctance to do so. Dramatic events occurred during this period [of turmoil]. The fate of Aaron was now that of Moses for he, too, disappeared. Joshua and Caleb, [who were second in command], then assumed leadership [of the Israelites]. It would be safe to assume that they felt it to be in the best interest of the people to terminate the regency of a man whose qualities of leadership left much to be desired. They had suffered for many years under the rule of Moses and now had the opportunity to subject him to the same fate that he had subjected so many unfortunate people in the past [i.e., to his violent death]. The new leaders of the Israelites, [unimpeded by the inept guidance and rule of their former leader, Moses], could now proceed to occupy all of the land on the right bank of the Jordan [River]. [p. 258, Translated by author]

As Freud states, Goethe did not cite his sources so that we do not know whether the surreptitious and possibly calamitous and conspiratorial demise of Moses was his own brainchild or that of others. There is obviously no Biblical basis for it. Though of course possible, it nevertheless would be totally out of character for Joshua and Caleb to have committed such an act. They were leaders of the tribes of Ephraim and Judah. The two were among the 12 spies sent by Moses to make a reconnaissance of the land of Canaan. Of the 12 they were the only ones to return with a very positive impression of the land. Joshua and Caleb were rewarded with large tracts of land after the conquest of Canaan. For Goethe, the rebellion against Moses was a result of dissatisfaction with his leadership, but for Freud it was a compelling, regressive desire to rid themselves of their leader, the father figure, and return to idol worship. Neither would seem to apply to Joshua and Caleb. The sources of Goethe's ideas are unknown unless considered the products of his own youthful imagination.

It is difficult to understand why Freud would entertain a hypothesis only tangential to his own, unsupported by real evidence, and one whose characterizations of the Biblical characters Joshua and Caleb differ so greatly from the entirely positive Biblical portrait. A possible reason could be Freud's wish to ally himself with the archetypal German poet while at the same time destroying the Jewish Moses. In a figurative sense, this wish enacts the kind of family romance that characterizes *Moses and Monotheism,* which is based upon the ambivalence that is intrinsic to his own oedipal conflict. A second reason for Freud's interest could be his desire to escape the Jewish character of psychoanalysis. To this end he had appointed Jung as his "Joshua" (Freud's term), hoping to pass on the leadership of the psychoanalytic movement and saving it from what he feared would be an irradicable Jewish imprint. Betrayed by Jung, who went his own way in creating another version of psychoanalytic theory,

Freud suffered two fainting spells in the presence of this suddenly unfaithful Joshua.

The second fainting episode is of special interest as it pertains to the very subject of this study. It occurred in 1912 at the Park Hotel in Munich during the International Psychoanalytic Congress. There are varying versions as to what happened just prior to the faint. Schur (1972) describes the discussion at this luncheon as revolving about Jung's hurt feelings at Freud not paying a visit to him when he was visiting another colleague near Zurich. Jones (1953) describes the subject of the discussion as one that pertained to Jung's writing articles about psychoanalysis that did not mention Freud's name, and thus, in a sense, disposing of the "father" of psychoanalysis.[2]

Jung (1965) remembered the event quite differently. He wrote:

> Someone had turned the conversation to Amenophis IV (Ikhnaton). The point was made that as a result of his negative attitude toward his father he had destroyed his father's cartouches on the steles, and at the back of his great creation of a monotheistic religion there lurked a father complex. This sort of thing irritated me, and I attempted to argue that Amenophis had been a creative and profoundly religious person whose acts could not be explained by personal resistances toward his father. On the contrary, I said he had held the memory of his father in honor, and his zeal for destruction had been directed only against the name of the god Amon, which he had everywhere annihilated; it was also chiseled out of the cartouches of his father Amonhotep. Moreover, other pharaohs had replaced the names of their actual or divine forefathers on monuments and statues by their own, feeling that they had a right to do so since they were incarnations of the same god. Yet they, I pointed out, had inaugurated neither a new style nor a new religion [p. 157].

In both versions the competitiveness between "father" and "son" is quite clear. Freud not only had what he thought was a disciple in Jung, but also an archrival for his leadership while Freud was still in his prime.

---

[2]It should be noted that at this same congress, Karl Abraham (1912) read his paper on Amenhotep IV (which is the prior name of Akhenaten). Of significance is that Freud makes absolutely no mention of this paper by Abraham in *Moses and Monotheism* (Shengold, 1972).

According to Goethe, Aaron was disposed of because of his challenge to his more successful brother, Moses. This was then repeated by Joshua and Caleb rebelling against Moses and causing him, too, to disappear. As noted, the Weimar Edition was published in 1888, and if Freud had read *Israel in der Wuste* prior to 1909 then a different, and more meaningful, explanatory light would be shed on these fainting episodes. If, however, Freud read it after 1912, then this explanation would be an exercise in playful fantasy, though, in some ways, partly relevant and possibly correct.

Thus, there appears to be a confluence of psychodynamic themes that are operative here. The basic theme is the negative (or homosexual) oedipal conflict, which reflects and expresses the ambivalent, love–hate relationship between father and son. This is in contrast to the positive (or heterosexual) oedipal conflict between mother and son. Directly derived from the complete (i.e., both positive and negative) theme is the Family Romance in which one's true biological parents are recreated in a garb of regal splendor. This ironic and pathetic twist of creation represents, among other factors, a killing off of what is perceived as inferior and bad and its replacement by what is deemed to be noble, royal, and great, thus enhancing one's own status and self-esteem. In the scenario as presented by Freud in *Moses and Monotheism,* the royal and aristocratic Egyptian iconoclast and founder of Hebraic monotheism is killed to be replaced by a second Moses of apparently plebeian origin.

The deity of the second Moses was what Freud referred to as the demon-god Yahweh, who emphasized the ritualistic and cultic aspects of Israelite religion. However, centuries later, this Yahwistic religion, according to Freud, was replaced by the Judaism of the Hebrew prophets, who represented a return to the religion and its respective ethical values of the first Egyptian, Moses. Freud's personal Family Romance is thus played out on the body of historic one that pertains to an entire people.

ORIGEN AND THE DUALITY OF MOSES

In a letter to Rafael da Costa, written on May 2, 1939, Freud admitted that the "second Moses was wholly my invention" (Gay, 1988, p. 647). However, there were others who wrote many centuries ago about a duality of Moses in a different sense, that is, in terms of one Moses perceived after death as two Moseses, one of "body" and the other of "soul."

Rieff (1959), in a footnote to his discussion of *Moses and Monotheism,* comments: "In the Old Testament narrative, of course, Moses dies a natural death, but in several non-canonical accounts, among them that of Origen, he is murdered" (p. 280).[3]

Origen (Oregenes Adamantius), a Christian Greek Father of the Church, was born in Alexandria, Egypt in 185 C.E. and died in Tyre in 254 C.E.. He was the first Christian scholar to have learned Hebrew, though he took all of his quotations from the *Septuagint,* the Greek translation of the Old Testament, which was completed in the third century B.C.E. He was friendly with Jews and supposedly had personal contact with some of the rabbis who participated in the discussions described in the Talmud. Nevertheless, his goal was to show the superiority of Christianity over Judaism. Origen's chief work was the *Hexapla,* a six-columned compilation of different Greek translations of the Bible, one which was directly from the original Hebrew version. His interpretation of Scripture was allegorical and spiritual. He distinguished between the "letter" and the "spirit," the former being equated with scripture and the latter with the hidden allegorical meaning.

It appears that there is no mention of the murder of Moses in the writings of Origen. However, Origen does make reference to two Moseses but it is expressed in accordance with Christian theological tradition. The one real Moses, after his Biblical demise, was viewed by Origen as dead in "body" but alive in "spirit." This concept of Moses may well have been part of a "two Moses" tradition that existed as late as the third century C.E.

It is not possible to understand Origen and his place in Church history without knowledge of the sources from which he drew his ideas. The primary sources were obviously the Old and New Testaments, but what gave his thinking a unique, particular coloring were the *Apocrypha,* which constitute the noncanonical parts of ancient Jewish literature. They were either not included in the Bible after it was canonized or were written afterward, probably not until the second century C.E. Many of

---

[3]Rieff does not cite the reference in Origen's writings. Not being sufficiently familiar with the writings of this significant figure in early Church history, I contacted Prof. Wayne Meeks, a Biblical scholar at the Yale Divinity School, who wrote a book on the subject of Moses in early Christian writings. Meeks could not recall any such reference in the Christian writings of that period and he suggested that I contact his colleague at Yale, Rowan Greer, Professor of Anglican studies, who had published an anthology of the writings of Origen and was considered an authority on the subject. I then met with Prof. Greer, who was extremely helpful and to whom I am most appreciative.

EMANUEL RICE

these writings were later canonized by the Church. Though they were written by Jews and for Jews, in Hebrew, Greek, and Aramaic, they did not become known or objects of study by Jewish scholars until after the Middle Ages.

Though no evidence that would in any way corroborate the murder of Moses was found in the writings of Origen, there is material that testifies to Freud's intuitive genius, specifically in terms of the relationship of the duality of Moses, animal sacrifice, and Jesus. (It should be noted that Jesus is the Greek translation for the name Joshua, and I suppose that one could have a field day using this knowledge in interpreting Freud's relationship with the Gentile Jung, his "Joshua.")

Origen, in describing the process whereby Jesus succeeded Moses, writes:

> We must consider the death of Moses, for if we do not realize in what sense he is dead, we shall not be able to see in what sense Jesus is King. . . . You can see that all that has come to an end, and therefore you may say that Moses, God's servant, is dead. . . . You can see that they have stopped all those observances, and so you may say that Moses, God's servant, is dead. . . . Altars are no longer moist with the blood of beasts; they are hallowed by Christ's precious blood. Priests and levites do not now administer the blood of goats and bulls; by the grace of the Holy Spirit they dispense the word of God. In view of this, then, you may say that Jesus has taken over the leadership that Moses had—not Jesus the son of Nun but Jesus the Son of God. You can see that Christ our Paschal Victim has been sacrificed and that we are eating the unleavened bread of purity and honest intent [I Cor. V. 7]. . . . All this you can see, and therefore you may say that Moses, God's servant, is dead and Jesus, God's Son, holds the power.[4]

> Finally, in a certain small book in which, though it is not in the canon of Scripture, nevertheless the figure of this mystery is described, the story is told that two Moseses were seen—the one alive in the spirit and the other dead in the body.

> Doubtless what is foreshadowed if you observe that the letter of the Law is vain and empty for all the reasons we have made mention of,

[4]This English translation was taken from Danielou (1955, pp. 147–148) who incorporated it in her interpretation of Origen's writings. The Latin and French edition, edited by Jaubert (1960), contains the above quotation in the original Latin.

is that Moses is dead in the body. But if you can remove the veil of the Law (2 Cor. 3:16) and understand that the Law is spiritual (Rom. 7:14), that it is Moses who lives in the spirit.[5]

It should be remembered that for Origen the religion of Moses was nullified by that of Jesus, that the latter was superior to the former, that the "letter" (Scripture) of Judaism is dead while the "spirit" (Christianity) is alive. Whatever he found in the Old Testament he used to prove the superiority of the New Testament. In the above quotations the reader should notice the equation between the blood of beasts (i.e., animal sacrifices in the Temple) and Christ's "precious blood." Also of relevance are the comments "that Jesus had taken over the leadership that Moses had," "that Moses, God's servant, is dead and Jesus, God's son, holds power," as well as the associative ideational proximity, betraying an underlying incorporative, or cannibalistic theme, in the phrase, "You can see that Christ our Paschal Victim has been sacrificed and that we are eating the unleavened bread of purity and honest intent." The reference by Origen to "a certain small book" that is not in the canon is commented on in a footnote by the editor of this Origen text (1960), Anne Jaubert: "Perhaps it is a question of *The Assumption of Moses.* But the episode to which Origen alludes has not been preserved. Harnack wonders if it is not necessary to attach the legend to which Origen alludes to another apocryphal work called 'Moses' Mystical Words" (p. 118).

The footnote goes on to refer to Clement of Alexandria (ca. 200 C.E.) who also knew of this tradition of the two Moseses. A. von Harnack, referred to in the footnote, is considered to be one of the most outstanding scholars of early Christianity. The *Assumption of Moses* is part of the *Apocrypha.* In this book, Moses prophesies to Joshua what will happen to the Jews up until the end of the kingdom of Judah; it then continues with Moses predicting what will await them down to the time of Herod the Great and the Messianic age that will follow. The sequel to this book has been lost, but based on a hint in another book of the *Apocrypha,* it may have concerned itself with a conflict between Michael and Satan over who will possess the body of Moses.[6]

---

[5]This paragraph, and the footnote that shortly follows it, was taken from the Jaubert edition and was translated from the Latin and French by Rowan Greer.

[6]It is of interest that in a tractate of the Mishna, *Abot De Rabbi Natan* (Goldin, 1955) (The Fathers According to Rabbi Nathan), whose composition was just about complete at the time that Origen lived, there are comments about the soul of Moses being taken up to God's abode to be put in safekeeping by Him "under the throne of glory." But then again, in contrast to the tradition of Jesus, Moses is not alone:

Freud (1901) does refer to Origen as part of the associative sequence of a patient in the latter's attempt to ascertain the origin of the Latin word *Aliquis,* taken from a sentence in Virgil's *Aeneid,* and its relevance to a parapraxis involving a slip of the tongue on the part of this patient. However, it is not likely that Freud ever read the writings of Origen or was at all aware of the Apocryphal tradition of two Moseses. Though Moses and Jesus may have been the manifest expression of a repetitive tradition of supreme leadership followed by a catastrophic denouement, it is another example of marvelous intuition on the part of Freud to have sensed its continuity through time and its connective links.

THE OMNIPOTENT FATHER AND THE HIDDEN OMNIPOTENT MOTHER

All of this gives rise to the question: Why did Freud focus, in an almost exclusive manner, on the role of the father in his concept of the origins of human society and the ever-present institutions associated with it, a notable example of which is religion? The answer may have to do with his own religious background: What more appropriate symbol is there than his unconscious conflicts with his father? As the Biblical Jacob wrestled with the Angel of God, so did Sigmund wrestle with his more immediate deity, his father Jacob. Even though his father died when Sigmund was 40 years of age, it was a bout that was not to end until his idiosyncratic, conceptualized, catastrophic denouement of Moses in *Moses and Monotheism* toward the end of his life. However, though he certainly did not disregard its significance, this fixation on conflict with the paternal figure may have interfered with an adequate assessment of the vital role of the mother, both in her preoedipal and oedipal imagos, in the etiology of psychic conflict. This task was left to subsequent generations of psychoanalytic theoreticians. As Gay (1988) notes,

> Whatever the objective value of Freud's attempt to discover the foundation of religion in the Oedipus complex, then, it is highly

---

Then the Holy One, blessed be He, took the soul of Moses and put it in safekeeping under the throne of glory. And when He took it, He took it only by means of a kiss, as it is said, By the mouth of the Lord (Deut. 34:5).

Nor is the soul of Moses alone in safekeeping under the throne of glory; rather the souls of all the righteous are in safekeeping under the throne of glory; as it is said, *Yet the soul of my lord shall be bound in the bundle of life with the Lord thy God* (I Sam. 25:29) [pp. 65–66].

plausible that some of the impulses guiding Freud's argument in *Totem and Taboo* emerged from his hidden life; in some respects the book represents a round in his never-finished wrestling bout with Jacob Freud. It was an episode, too, in his equally persistent evasion of his complicated feelings about Amalia Freud. For it is telling that in his reconstruction Freud said virtually nothing about the mother, even though the ethnographic material pointing to the fantasy of devouring the mother is richer than that for devouring the father. Ferenczi's Little Arpad, whom Freud borrowed as a witness for *Totem and Taboo,* wanted to make a meal of his *"preserved mother";* as he graphically put it, "One should put my mother into a pot and cook her, then there would be a preserved mother and I could eat her." But Freud chose to ignore this piece of evidence. Still, like so much else in Freud's work, *Totem and Taboo* productively translated his most intimate conflicts and his most private quarrels into material for scientific investigation [p. 335].

Freud's underlying emotional conflicts involving his mother never achieved adequate resolution. In addition to the expected and necessary interpersonal conflicts that have to occur in early childhood between mother and child there is the additional factor of what Freud's mother meant to him in terms of his own self-esteem. Amalia, even more than Jacob, was a symbol of his background, which he, like so many other emancipated, middle-class Viennese Jews, tried to repudiate. After all, she was from Eastern Europe and therefore possessed all the real and imagined inferiorities that that fact represented. She never mastered the German language. Her language of communication was Yiddish, an old German dialect infused with influences from Hebrew and the Romance languages, which was looked upon with disdain and contempt by the emancipated, middle-class German-speaking Jews. Despite Freud's denial, Yiddish had to have been his first language as it was the language spoken at home. Theodor Reik remarked on this situation and so did Henry Bondi (Rice, 1990).

Freud did not attend the funeral of his 95-year-old mother when she died in 1930. He was vacationing in Grundlsee, which was an hour's drive from Vienna, at the time. He wrote Jones and Ferenzci that he had sent his daughter Anna (no mention of Martha or any other member of the Freud family) to attend the funeral as his representative. This, by any measure, is rather strange behavior for a son who was certainly his mother's favorite. In addition, he went to great lengths, presumably via telephone and personal emissary, to assure that she had a strictly Orthodox Jewish funeral (Rice, 1990).

In 1929, in a letter of condolence to Max Eitingon on the loss of his mother, Freud wrote (as quoted by Gay, 1988): "the loss of a mother must be something quite remarkable, not to be compared with anything else, and awakens excitations that are hard to grasp . . ." (p. 573).

To Ernest Jones, he wrote:

> Certainly there is no saying what such an experience may do in deeper layers but superficially I feel only two things: the growth in personal freedom I have acquired, since it was always an abhorrent thought that she would learn of my death, and secondly, the satisfaction that she has at last the deliverance to which she had acquired the right in so long a life [p. 573].

In attempting to exculpate himself to his brother, Alexander, Freud stated the reasons for his not attending the funeral: first, his poor health, and second, his intolerance of ceremonies. Yet, in this same letter to Jones (Jones, 1957, p. 152) he states, "No grief otherwise, such as my ten years younger brother is painfully experiencing." This revealing statement is more than descriptive, it may well be projective, as if to say, that it was not Sigmund who was distraught but Alexander. One must look at these reasons as manifest content. The revelation and understanding of the latent content might give us vital clues to the working of Freud's mind, both on a personal as well as a professional level. Is there the distinct possibility that, lurking behind the imago of an omnipotent, omniscient, forever-threatening and frightening oedipal father, there is a preoedipal, as well as oedipal, maternal imago whose characteristics are perceived to be even more so?

CONCLUSION

Freud's almost exclusive focus on the role of the father in the etiology of the oedipal conflict and its effect on the development of personality is quite evident. The maternal component was not moved to center stage in psychoanalytic theory until some time after World War II by theoreticians such as Melanie Klein, John Bowlby, Donald Winnicott, and Margaret Mahler, among many others. Maternal influence in the early years of the child, roughly up to the age of five, was considered by some theoreticians to be as, if not more, decisive in personality development than psychopathogenesis. Freud did not underestimate the destructive, murderous and, specifically, the cannibalistic components of a child's instinctual makeup. Evidence of this awareness is clearly demonstrated in his study of Moses, in which the savagery and phantasmagoria so omnipresent in the mental life of the child is translated into action as seen in the panorama of interpersonal relationships and the practice of pagan worship among the adults of primitive cultures.

In *Moses and Monotheism,* Freud establishes an identity between the slaying of the Primal Father, the slaying of Moses, and the crucifixion of Jesus. He states that both the Primal Father and Jesus were cannibalized, one literally and the other symbolically, as reenacted in the rite of Holy Communion. For some reason, Moses did not meet the same fate of being the object of cannibalism. The question then arises as to why Freud shied away from this possibility, assuming that he was correct in his Mosaic hypothesis? The practice of cannibalism, as shown by its frequent denunciation in the Bible, was indeed central to pagan cultures. Could Freud's archaic unconscious conflicts, which revolved around cannibalistic impulses pertaining to the all-powerful mother, have been a factor in the suppression of the awareness of the extent of maternal influence on psychic conflict and personality development? As with other factors in mental life, the multiple, interlocking functions of instinct and defense appear here to have come into play. The preoedipal and oedipal perceptions of the father obviously do play an important role in psychic development. Their overemphasis, however, can also serve a defensive purpose, which, in this situation, is against the conscious awareness of the significant role of the mother in both of these crucial developmental periods of the child's life. Was Freud's perception of an historical (or Biblical) character, Moses, a projection of the ambivalence directed toward his parents, be it mother or father?

The question remains: why, in addition to de-Judaizing Moses, did Freud have to postulate the existence of two Moseses? As with his ambivalent attitude toward his own Jewish identity, the answer may lie in the way this ambivalence is resolved and subsequently expressed. The concepts pertaining to the resolution of psychic conflict imply a dynamic process; instinctual derivatives and the defenses against them are hypothesized to be in constant flux. Therefore, a resolution is never final. A transiency, or relative degree of stability, must be an inherent property of these concepts. Freud's maneuver is just another example of how human beings cope with the problem of good and evil, especially when both reside, as naturally they must, inside themselves. Monotheistic religions have tried to maintain the goodness of the deity by splitting off all that is evil from the deity and personifying it in a separate entity, the Devil, or Satan. God is thus purified and remains completely unblemished, holy and good.

In Freud's conceptualization of ancient history it is not merely the organization of categories into *twos* but his need to attribute moral and immoral qualities to each constituent. The first Egyptian Moses is all *good,* but he is later slain by the *bad* Israelites in the desert and replaced by another Moses, who takes over the leadership of the rebellious horde, preaching the words of the "demon-God" *Yahweh,* as Freud refers to Him. Whatever the representative of the *bad* Moses is, centuries later, he is replaced by the *good* Hebrew prophets, who have resuscitated the religion of the *good* Egyptian, Moses. *Good* thus triumphs over *Evil!*

In the passage of Freud in *Moses and Monotheism* cited before, the entities of *twos* that he cites all contain the same patterning of ambivalence. The two groups of people refer to the *good* (Egyptian) and *bad* (desert) Israelite tribes. The two kingdoms refer to the *good,* cultured Southern Kingdom of *Judah* where, according to Freud, the Egyptian contingent of Jews settled, in contrast to the *bad,* primitive, idol-worshiping Northern Kingdom of *Israel.* The two gods refer to the *bad* demon-God *Yahweh* and the *good,* loving one, *Elohim* (although as discussed in Rice, 1990, regarding the near-sacrifice of Isaac, the opposite appears to be the case). The two religions, as already noted, refer to the *good,* prophetic one of the Egyptian Moses and the *bad* one as exemplified in the *Yahweh*-worshipers of the desert. The two religious founders likewise refer to the *good* Egyptian Moses and the *bad,* desert Moses.

The Hebrew prophets were an ever-present reminder of the dangers inherent in the human tendency toward regression to pagan worship, which really represented the expression in action of all those primitive, perverse impulses that are destructive of morality and the highest standards of civilization. The predictive aspects of Hebrew prophecy was only a minor factor in this most influential religious and, at times, political institution. Their primary purpose was to make the erring Israelites aware of the evils and dire consequences of their propensity to pagan worship as well as to cajole them to adhere to the covenant that God made with their ancestors. This adherence would then enhance the realization and expression of the best of humankind.

In his attempts to elicit, in the psychoanalytic transference, the awareness of these impulses and then to analyze them in order to minimize their destructive influence, both on the patient and others, Freud turns out to be prophetic, not only in a predictive sense but also, more importantly, in a corrective sense. From a secular perspective, Freud could be considered to be a true prophet within the Hebrew prophetic tradition, which began with Moses, the first of the prophets. It has been said that a scientist sees what *is,* and the moralist, what *ought to be.* Freud, however imperfectly, was both.

BIBLIOGRAPHY

ABRAHAM, K. (1912), Amenhotep IV: A psychological contribution towards the understanding of his personality and of the monotheistic cult of Aton. In: *Clinical Papers and Essays on Psychoanalysis, Vol. II.* New York: Basic Books, Inc., 1955.

BERGMANN, M. (1976), Moses and the evolution of Freud's Jewish identity. *Israel Ann. Psychiat. Related Discipl.,* 14:3-26.

BREASTED, J. H. (1906), *A History of Egypt.* London: Hodder and Stoughton.

_____ (1933), *The Dawn of Conscience.* New York: Charles Scribner's Sons.

DANIELOU, J. (1955), *Origen.* London and New York: Sheed and Ward.

FALK, A. (1978), Freud and Herzl. *Contemp. Psychoanal.,* 14(3):357-387.

FREUD, S. (1901), The psychopathology of everyday life. *Standard Edition,* 6. London: Hogarth Press, 1960.

_____ (1907), Obsessive acts and religious practices. *Standard Edition,* 9. London: Hogarth Press, 1959.

_____ (1912-13), Totem and taboo. *Standard Edition,* 13. London: Hogarth Press, 1955.

_____ (1914), The Moses of Michelangelo. *Standard Edition,* 13. London: Hogarth Press, xxx.

_____ (1927), The future of an illusion. *Standard Edition,* 21. London: Hogarth Press, 1961.

_____ (1939) [1934-39], Moses and monotheism. *Standard Edition,* 23. London: Hogarth Press, 1964.

FRIEDMAN, R. E. (1987), *Who Wrote The Bible?* New York: Summit Books.

GAY, P. (1988), *Freud—A Life for Our Time.* New York and London: W. W. Norton & Company.

GOETHE, J. W. (1902). *Goethes Sämtliche Werke:* Jubiläums-Ausgabe, Fünfter Band. West-Östlicher Divan. Mit Einleitung und Anmerkungen von Konrad Burdach. Stuttgart and Berlin, Germany: J. G. Cotta'sche Buchhandlung Nachfolger.

GOLDIN, J. (1955), *The Fathers According to Rabbi Nathan* (Abot De-Rabbi Natan). New Haven and London: Yale University Press.

HANDELMAN, S. A. (1982), *The Slayers of Moses: The Emergence of Rabbinic Interpretation in Modern Literary Theory.* Albany: State University of New York.

JONES, E. (1953): *The Life and Work of Sigmund Freud, Vol. 1: The Formative Years and the Great Discoveries, 1856-1900.* New York: Basic Books.

_____ (1955), *The Life and Work of Sigmund Freud, Vol. 2: The Years of Maturity, 1901-1919.* New York: Basic Books.

_____ (1957), *The Life and Work of Sigmund Freud, Vol. 3: The Last Phase, 1919-1939.* New York: Basic Books.

JUNG, C. G. (1965), *Memories, Dreams, and Reflections,* ed. A. Jaffe. (trans. R. Winston & C. Winston). New York: Vintage Books.

LOEWENBERG, P. (1971), Sigmund Freud as a Jew: A study in ambivalence and courage. *J. Hist. Behav. Sciences,* 7(4):366-367.

ORIGENE (1960), *Homelies sur Josue, Sources Chretiennes 71,* ed. A. Jaubert. Paris: Editions du Cerf.

RICE, E. (1990), *Freud and Moses: The Long Journey Home.* Albany: State University of New York Press.

RIEFF, P. (1959), *Freud: The Mind of the Moralist.* New York: Viking Press.

ROBERT, M. (1976), *From Oedipus to Moses—Freud's Jewish Identity.* Garden City, New York: Anchor Books, Anchor Press/Doubleday.

SELLIN, E. (1922), *Mose und Seine Bedeutung für die Israelitisch-Judische Religions-*

geschichte. Leipzig-Erlangen, Germany: A. Deicherstsche Verlagsbuchhandlung Dr. Werner Scholl.

_____ (1924), *Geschichte Des Israelitisch-Judischen Volkes—Erster Teil: Von den Anfangen bis zum babylonischen Exil*. Leipzig, Germany: Verlag Von Quelle & Meyer.

SCHUR, M. (1972), *Freud: Living and Dying*. New York: International Universities Press, Inc.

SHENGOLD, L. (1972), A parapraxis of Freud's in relation to Karl Abraham. *Amer. Imago,* 29:123–159.

18

Fairy Tales Sí, Myths No:
Bruno Bettelheim's Antithesis

ROBERT A. SEGAL

As a Freudian folklorist, Alan Dundes (1991b) has continually bemoaned the typical indifference of Freudians to folklore and the common hostility of folklorists to Freud:

> The survey of the psychological study of folklore in the United States from 1880 to 1980 turns out to be a rather bleak one. Psychologists, for the most part, have not concerned themselves with folklore. Some psychiatrists, specifically Jungians and Freudians, have written at some length about folklore, but their efforts have had little if any influence upon mainstream folklore theory and method. Folklorists, both literary and anthropological, have generally tended to eschew any form of psychological analysis [p. 115].

Dundes (1989) goes so far as to say, "It is hard to convey just how adamantly opposed to psychoanalytic interpretation the majority of conventional [folklore] scholars are. . . . [P]sychoanalysts have only a marginal interest in folklore" (pp. 120–122).

Of the study of the Grimm tales in particular, Dundes (1989) says:

> The anti-psychological bias is so strong among folklorists that they don't even mention the numerous psychoanalytic essays devoted to Grimm tales in print. . . . The situation is roughly as follows: folklorists and psychoanalysts have for nearly a century analyzed the Grimm tales in almost total ignorance of one another. Folklor-

ists blindly committed to anti-symbolic, anti-psychological readings of folktales make little or no effort to discover what, if
anything, psychoanalysts have to say about the tales they are
studying. Psychoanalysts, limited to their twentieth-century patients' free associations to the nineteenth-century Grimm versions
of folktales, are blithely unaware of the existence of hundreds of
versions of the same tale types so assiduously assembled by
folklorists in archives or presented in painstaking detail in historic-
geographic monographs [pp. 120–122].[1]

DUNDES ON BETTELHEIM

Dundes is consequently eager to praise those few scholars who do
undertake psychoanalytic studies of folklore. Among recent attempts,
Dundes (1991b) cites Bruno Bettelheim's acclaimed study of the Grimm
tales, *The Uses of Enchantment,* as one of "the few bright spots in the
history of the psychological study of folklore in the United States" (p.
116). Dundes praises Bettelheim for his positive view of the psychoanalytic function of fairy tales. Whereas early Freudians tended to view fairy
tales as manifestations, if not exacerbations, of neuroses, Bettelheim
views them as vehicles of maturation.[2] Whereas early Freudians were
wary of the effect of fairy tales on children, Bettelheim recommends
them as ideal aids in growing up (Dundes, 1987, 1991a). Dundes (1991a)
also commends Bettelheim for distinguishing between the oral and the
written nature of fairy tales, for advocating only originally oral tales for
children, and for opposing illustrated and bowdlerized versions of tales.
As a Freudian, Dundes (1987) agrees with Bettelheim that tales work
their magic unconsciously, though he finds oddly non-Freudian Bettelheim's aversion to making children conscious of the Freudian meaning.
    There are various grounds on which others have criticized Bettelheim
but on which Dundes does not. For example, Bettelheim, though by no
means necessarily Dundes himself, assumes that true fairy tales have
happy endings, that the meaning of the tales is universal rather than
bound by time and place, that the tales are told from a neutral rather
than a distinctively male viewpoint, and that the tales always deal with
family relations.

---

[1]On the psychoanalytic study of folklore see Dundes' several surveys (1987, 1989, 1991b).
   See also Dundes, 1986.
[2]Similarly, Bettelheim (1954) sees circumcision rituals as means of maturation rather than,
   like early Freudians, as expressions of neuroses.

Yet Dundes is ultimately most critical of Bettelheim—on both folk-loristic and other grounds. Dundes shows that Bettelheim sometimes confuses myths with folktales (1987, p. 30; 1991a, p. 78). He also shows that Bettelheim wrongly assumes the universality of tale types (1987, p. 30).

Dundes' main criticism is that Bettelheim at once ignores most of his psychoanalytic predecessors and outright plagiarizes others![3] Dundes initially lodged these charges in passing (1987). He has since devoted a whole essay to them (1991a). He is prepared to excuse Bettelheim's obliviousness to various folkloristic studies of fairy tales, but he is dismayed at Bettelheim's apparent unfamiliarity with the pioneering psychoanalytic studies of above all Franz Ricklin (1908) and Géza Róheim (1922, 1934, 1941, 1945, 1950, 1952). Dundes (1991a) notes that "Bettelheim's neglect of Róheim is especially egregious as Róheim wrote whole essays on many of the tales Bettelheim chose to analyze . . ." (pp. 76–77).

Far less excusable than Bettelheim's oversight is his actual use *sub rosa* of the work of Róheim, Otto Rank, Julius Heuscher, and Dundes himself. Bettelheim's plagiarism, states Dundes (1991a), "is not just a matter of occasional borrowings of random passages, but a wholesale borrowing of key ideas" (p. 80).

As disconcerting as Bettelheim's failure to consider his Freudian forebears in his analysis of fairy tales is his failure to consider his Freudian *contemporaries* in his more passing analysis of *myths*. There is no issue here of plagiarism, for in discussing myths Bettelheim disregards rather than appropriates contemporary Freudian views. The views he espouses are akin to classical Freudian ones. It is the disjunction between Bettelheim's up-to-date approach to fairy tales and his old-fashioned approach to myths that is striking.

BETTELHEIM'S OPPOSITION OF FAIRY TALES TO MYTHS

In the first place Bettelheim is distinctive in pitting myths against fairy tales. Most Freudians, early and contemporary alike, see myths and fairy tales as akin (e.g., Rank and Sachs, 1913). Freud himself (1900, 1913) regards both genres as disguised fulfillments of wishes. By contrast, Bettelheim (1976) sees the two as antithetical:

---

[3]For a comparable pair of criticisms of Bettelheim on kibbutzim see Paul, 1990.

Put simply, the dominant feeling a myth conveys is: this is
absolutely unique; it could not have happened to any other person,
or in any other setting; such events are grandiose, awe-inspiring,
and could not possibly happen to an ordinary mortal like you or
me. . . . By contrast, although the events which occur in fairy tales
are often unusual and most improbable, they are always presented
as ordinary, something that could happen to you or me or the
person next door when out on a walk in the woods. . . . Myths
project an ideal personality acting on the basis of superego
demands, while fairy tales depict an ego integration which allows
for appropriate satisfaction of id desires. This difference accounts
for the contrast between the pervasive pessimism of myths and the
essential optimism of fairy tales [pp. 37, 41].

BETTELHEIM'S PREFERENCE FOR FAIRY TALES OVER MYTHS

In the second place Bettelheim is distinctive in conspicuously favoring
fairy tales over myths. Those classical or contemporary Freudians who
do contrast myths to fairy tales ordinarily praise myths over fairy tales.
Even Róheim (1941), whom Dundes (1991a) credits with originating
many of the contrasts between myths and fairy tales adopted without
acknowledgment by Bettelheim, characterizes myths as providing "a
more adult" rather than, like folktales, "a more infantile" "form of the
same conflict" (p. 279). Folktales for Róheim (1922) express the sheer
fulfillment of wishes: "the child obtains a fulfillment in imagination of
those unconscious wishes which it cannot yet obtain in reality" (p. 181).
By contrast, myths depict the subsequent punishment for this fulfillment
(Róheim, 1950). For Róheim (1941), folktales are sheer fantasies; myths
"link up phantasy and reality" (p. 275). Hence oedipal folktales end in
parricide; oedipal myths, in submission to the resurrected father (pp.
277–278). In "fairy tales and popular legends dealing with the cooperation between mortals and immortals, the supernatural beings are
always deceived; human cunning wins the day" (Róheim, 1934, p. 252).
In myths "the heroes sin against the gods and must atone for this with an
eternal punishment or an eternal task" (p. 251). Whereas in the tale of
Jack and the Beanstalk "Jack and his mother became very rich and he
married a great princess and they lived happily ever after," in the myth
of Prometheus the hero "becomes the representative of renunciation; and
his achievement, the great cultural act of the discovery of fire, is

performed with energy, or better libido, that has been diverted from its original aim" (p. 260).

Much like the early Freudian Róheim, contemporary Freudian Jacob Arlow (1961) sees fairy tales as the fulfillment of wishes and myths as a means of renunciation. Arlow, too, contrasts Jack to Prometheus—and adds the case of Moses. Whereas Jack brashly steals what he wants from the fatherlike giant above, Prometheus fears Olympian Zeus and indeed is punished by Zeus for stealing fire. In contrast to both rebels, Moses in the Exodus myth ascends Mt. Sinai as the servant, not the antagonist, of the heavenly God:

> The fairy-tale version of this problem belonged to the wish-fulfilling tendency of childhood in which contribution of the superego is minimal and unformed and the fear of retaliation is disposed of omnipotently. . . . What is epitomized in this variation [i.e., the myth of Prometheus] is the stage beyond the untroubled wish fulfillment of the simple fairy tale, the overwhelming impact of the fear of retaliation. . . . What was originally [i.e., in Prometheus] a crime of defiance and aggression against the gods is, in this later version [i.e., the myth of Moses], represented as carrying out the wishes of God Himself [pp. 382–383].

Even though Arlow (1961) does call fairy tales "truncated myths" (p. 381), and even though he does place the Prometheus story between a straight fairy tale and a full-fledged myth, the contrast he draws between the "fairy-tale version" (p. 382) and the mythic version of the ascent motif obviously favors myths over fairy tales.

It is, ironically, by the same criteria as Róheim's and Arlow's that Bettelheim gives the nod to fairy tales over myths. To be sure, Bettelheim does not go so far as to pronounce myths sheer wish fulfillments. On the contrary, he (1976), echoing Arlow, says that "myths typically involve superego demands in conflict with id-motivated action" (p. 37). But for Bettelheim, in contrast to Róheim as well as Arlow, so uncompromising is the mythic superego that the maturation it preaches is unattainable: "Mythical heroes offer excellent images for the development of the superego, but the demands they embody are so rigorous as to discourage the child in his fledgling strivings to achieve personality integration" (p. 39).

Even though for Bettelheim (1976) fairy tales no less than myths preach maturation, they do so in gentler ways and thereby succeed where myths fail: "In the myth there is only insurmountable difficulty and defeat; in the fairy tale there is equal peril, but it is successfully overcome. Not death and destruction, but higher integration . . . is the hero's reward at the end of the fairy tale" (p. 199). Bettelheim's view of myths as hindering rather than spurring psychological growth is close to the classical Freudian view of fairy tales and myths alike.

Dundes (1991a) suggests that Bettelheim takes from Róheim (1941) the point that folktales end happily and myths tragically. Yet Bettelheim and Róheim nevertheless evaluate myths and fairy tales antithetically. Bettelheim uses Róheim's distinction to tout folktales over myths; Róheim uses it to elevate myths over folktales. For Róheim, folktales end happily because, contrary to Bettelheim, they foster illusions about reality and thereby keep one fixated at childhood. Myths end tragically because they face up to reality and thereby promote maturation—not, as for Bettelheim, despair.

BETTELHEIM'S DISREGARD OF CONTEMPORARY FREUDIANS ON MYTH

In the third and final place Bettelheim does not merely prefer fairy tales to myths, as he is surely entitled to do, but inexplicably disregards contemporary Freudian approaches to myths in so doing. Bettelheim is brilliantly innovative in his approach to fairy tales but is incongruously regressive in his approach to myths. He analyzes myths the way most early Freudians do (e.g., Freud, 1900; Rank, 1909, 1919; Rank and Sachs, 1913; Ricklin, 1908; and Karl Abraham, 1909). Róheim (1922, 1934, 1941, 1945, 1950, 1952), whose analysis forshadows contemporary ones, is here an exception among early Freudians. Bettelheim castigates myths because he finds in them no more than classical Freudians do. He celebrates fairy tales because he finds in them what Arlow and other contemporary Freudians find instead in myths! Unlike Arlow, Bettelheim allows for no middle ground between fairy tales and myths. A story is either one or the other.

For Bettelheim (1976), as for all other Freudians, both myths and fairy tales deal with the problems of growing up—the problems of mastering instincts, breaking with parents, and establishing oneself in society. Both genres deal with "overcoming narcissistic disappointments, oedipal dilemmas, sibling rivalries; becoming able to relinquish child-hood dependencies; gaining a feeling of selfhood and of self-worth, and a sense of moral obligation . . ." (p. 6). But "there is a crucial difference in the way these [problems] are communicated" (p. 37). Myths present these problems as unresolvable and thereby keep one tied to childhood. Fairy tales offer realistic solutions to them and thereby help one to grow up.

In myths, according to Bettelheim, childhood desires either are fulfilled rather than curbed, just as in dreams,[4] or else are consequently punished rather than overcome. Whereas early Freudians focus on fulfillment, Bettelheim focuses on subsequent punishment. Róheim (1934) is again an exception among early Freudians. Whereas most early Freudians stress Oedipus' managing to kill his father and to marry his mother (Freud, 1900; Rank, 1909), Bettelheim (1976) emphasizes Oedipus' blinding and exile. (Freudians tend to categorize the Oedipus tale as a myth.) Hence for Bettelheim "in fairy tales the hero's story shows how these potentially destructive infantile [oedipal] relations can be, and are, integrated in developmental processes. In the myth, oedipal difficulties are acted out and in consequence all ends in total destruction . . ." (p. 198).

According to Bettelheim (1976), the figures in myths are so superior to ordinary mortals that even when their problems are resolved, only heroes or even only gods seem capable of resolving them:

> A mere mortal is too frail to meet the challenges of the gods. Paris, who does the bidding of Zeus as conveyed to him by Hermes, and obeys the demand of the three goddesses in choosing which shall have the apple, is destroyed for having followed these commands, as are untold other mortals in the wake of this fateful choice [p. 37].

By contrast, the figures in fairy tales are ordinary mortals, whose ability to resolve problems encourages others to attempt the same:

> Whatever strange events the fairy-tale hero experiences, they do not make him superhuman, as is true for the mythical hero. This real

---

[4]Whereas Dundes (1991a) stresses the similarities that Bettelheim draws between fairy tales and dreams, Bettelheim (1976), anxious to make fairy tales more than dreamlike fulfillments of fantasies, emphasizes the differences at least as much: "To a considerable degree, dreams are the result of inner pressures which have found no relief, of problems which beset a person to which he knows no solution and to which the dream finds none. The fairy tale does the opposite: it projects the relief of all pressures and not only offers ways to solve problems but promises that a 'happy' solution will be found" (p. 36). By contrast, early Freudians view both fairy tales and dreams as wish fulfillments (Freud, 1913; Freud and Oppenheim, 1911; Ricklin, 1908; Róheim, 1922).

humanity suggests to the child that, whatever the content of the
fairy tale, it is but fanciful elaborations and exaggerations of the
tasks he has to meet, and of his hopes and fears [p. 40].

Strikingly, the praise that Bettelheim bestows on fairy tales vis-à-vis
myths mimics the praise that Arlow and other contemporary Freudians
confer on myths vis-à-vis fairy tales. Spurred by the development of ego
psychology, Arlow, Sidney Tarachow, Mark Kanzer, Max Stern, Werner
Muensterberger, and others view myths much more positively than
Freud, Rank, Abraham, and Ricklin do—Róheim again being an
exception. For contemporary Freudians, myths help solve the problems
of growing up rather than perpetuate them, are progressive rather than
regressive, and abet adjustment to the adult world rather than childish
flight from it. Myths serve less to vent bottled-up drives than to
sublimate them. What Bettelheim (1976) says of fairy tales almost
parrots what Arlow (1961) said of myths 15 years earlier:

> Psychoanalysis has a greater contribution to make to the study of
> mythology than [merely] demonstrating, in myths, wishes often
> encountered in the unconscious thinking of persons. The myth is a
> particular kind of communal experience. It is a special form of
> shared fantasy, and it serves to bring the individual into relation-
> ship with members of his cultural group on the basis of certain
> common needs. Accordingly, the myth can be studied from the
> point of view of its function in psychic integration—how it plays a
> role in warding off feelings of guilt and anxiety, how it constitutes
> a form of adaptation to reality and to the group in which the
> individual lives, and how it influences the crystallization of the
> individual identity and the formation of the superego [p. 375].[5]

For contemporary Freudians, mythic figures are both worthy and
capable of emulation by ordinary persons rather than, as for Bettelheim,

---

[5]See also Tarachow, Arlow, Kanzer, Almansi, Stern, and Muensterberger, 1964; Bergmann, 1966. Even when Arlow (1982) says that myths originate out of childhood
wishes, he deems their function adaptive rather than maladaptive: "The mythology of
religion fosters social adaptation of the individual and integration with the community
. . ." (p. 188). Róheim (1945), once again the prescient exception among early
Freudians, similarly characterizes "myths of transition" as "functioning socially in
harmony with initiation rites: the mythological material helps the young men to grow
up, and to make the transition from the Oedipus situation to marriage" (p. 17). At the
same time as late as 1948 we are told in a psychoanalytic journal that "Myths, then, are
largely projections with greater or lesser elements of wishfulfillment" (Cox, 1948, p. 86).

either unworthy or incapable (Arlow, 1961). For present-day Freudians, myths are different from dreams rather than, as for Bettelheim, like them: "Where the dream represents the demands of the instincts, the myth tends to perpetuate and represent the demands of society on the mental apparatus for symbolization and acceptance" (Tarachow, Arlow, Kanzer, Almansi, Stern, and Muensterberger, 1964, p. 32). Arlow (1961) laments that lay critics of psychoanalysis continue to "assume that [for psychoanalysts] myths and dreams are indistinguishable" (p. 373).[6]

The issue is not whether Bettelheim's dismissal of myths as ineffective is right or wrong. Indeed, Dundes himself might prefer aspects of Bettelheim's analysis of myths to Arlow's. The issue is that Bettelheim ignores the contemporary Freudian approach to myth as fully as he ignores specific classical Freudian analyses of fairy tales. He writes in a void.

At the same time Bettelheim's analysis of even fairy tales is in several respects crudely outdated. First, he interprets fairy tales, and also myths, allegorically: one entity stands for the ego, another for the id, a third for the superego. By contrast, contemporary Freudians stress the multiple meanings of the elements in fairy tales and myths alike, for they stress the multiple functions of cultural phenomena.

Second, Bettelheim interprets fairy tales, and again myths as well, moralistically: a fairy tale preaches a message that must be heeded, lest woeful consequences ensue. By contrast, contemporary Freudians emphasize the flexibility and open-endedness of fairy tales and myths alike: fairy tales and myths offer options, which the reader or hearer is free to choose and even to alter. The rigidity and self-righteousness that Bettelheim finds in both fairy tales and myths may in fact reveal less about his subject and more about him.

BIBLIOGRAPHY

ABRAHAM, K. (1909), *Dreams and Myths,* trans. W. White. Nervous and Mental Disease Monograph Series, no. 15. New York: Journal of Nervous and Mental Disease Publishing, 1913.

ARLOW, J. (1961), Ego psychology and the study of mythology. *J. Amer. Psychoanal. Assn.,* 9:371–393.

———— (1982), Scientific cosmogony, mythology, and immortality. *Psychoanal. Quart.,* 51:177–195.

BERGMANN, M. (1966), The impact of ego psychology on the study of the myth. *Amer. Imago,* 23:257–264.

---

[6]On fairy tales and dreams see Grolnick, 1986, pp. 205–206.

BETTELHEIM, B. (1954), *Symbolic Wounds.* New York: Collier Books, 1962.

_____ (1976), *The Uses of Enchantment.* New York: Vintage Books, 1977.

COX, H. (1948), The place of mythology in the study of culture. *Amer. Imago,* 5:83–94.

DUNDES, A. (1986), Fairy tales from a folkloristic perspective. In: *Fairy Tales and Society,* ed. R. Bottigheimer. Philadelphia: University of Pennsylvania Press, pp. 259–269.

_____ (1987), *Parsing Through Customs.* Madison: University of Wisconsin Press.

_____ (1989), *Folklore Matters.* Knoxville, TN: University of Tennessee Press.

_____ (1991a), Bruno Bettelheim's uses of enchantment and abuses of scholarship. *J. Amer. Folklore,* 104:74–83.

_____ (1991b), The psychological study of folklore in the United States, 1880–1980. *South. Folklore,* 48:97–120.

FREUD, S. (1900), The interpretation of dreams. *Standard Edition,* 4 & 5. London: Hogarth Press, 1953.

_____ (1913), The occurrence of dreams in material from fairy-tales. *Standard Edition,* 12:279–287. London: Hogarth Press, 1958.

_____ & OPPENHEIM, D. (1911), Dreams in folklore. *Standard Edition,* 12:177–203. London: Hogarth Press, 1958.

GROLNICK, S. (1986), Fairy tales and psychotherapy. In: *Fairy Tales and Society,* ed. R. Bottigheimer. Philadelphia: University of Pennsylvania Press, pp. 203–215.

PAUL, R. (1990), Bettelheim's contribution to anthropology. In: *The Psychoanalytic Study of Society,* 15:313–334. Hillsdale, NJ: The Analytic Press.

RANK, O. (1909). *The Myth of the Birth of the Hero,* trans. F. Robbins & S. Jelliffe. In: *In Quest of the Hero,* ed. R. A. Segal. Princeton, NJ: Princeton University Press, 1990, pp. 3–86.

_____ (1919), *Psychoanalytische Beiträge zur Mythenforschung.* Internationale Psychoanalytische Bibliothek, no. 4. Leipzig & Vienna: Internationale Psychoanalytischer Verlag.

_____ & SACHS, H. (1913), *The Significance of Psychoanalysis for the Mental Sciences,* trans. C. Payne. Nervous and Mental Disease Monograph Series, no. 23. New York: Nervous and Mental Disease Publishing, 1916.

RICKLIN, F. (1908), *Wishfulfillment and Symbolism in Fairy Tales,* trans. W. White. Nervous and Mental Disease Monograph Series, no. 21. New York: Nervous and Mental Disease Publishing, 1915.

RÓHEIM, G. (1922), Psycho-analysis and the folk-tale. *Internat. J. Psycho-Anal.,* 3:180–186.

_____ (1934), *The Riddle of the Sphinx,* trans. R. Money-Kyrle. New York: Harper Torchbooks, 1974.

_____ (1941), Myth and Folk-Tale. *Amer. Imago,* 2:266–279.

_____ (1945), *The Eternal Ones of the Dream.* New York: International Universities Press.

_____ (1950), *Psychoanalysis and Anthropology.* New York: International Universities Press.

_____ (1952), *The Gates of the Dream.* New York: International Universities Press.

TARACHOW, S., ARLOW, J., KANZER, M., ALMANSI, R., STERN, M. & MUENSTERBERGER, W. (1964), Mythology and ego psychology. In: *The Psychoanalytic Study of Society,* 3:9–97. New York: International Universities Press.

19

Christian Messianism

W. W. MEISSNER

In previous essays dealing with the role of cult dynamics as expressions of the paranoid process, I have focused on the cultic origins of Christianity (Meissner, 1988) and the progressive elaborations of the cult process as the Christian church evolved in the first centuries after the death of Christ (Meissner, 1989, 1990). Christian Messianism derives from and builds upon the roots of the Messianic traditions that were part of the Jewish religious lore (Meissner, 1991). I will develop the argument in the present chapter that Christian Messianism not only has preserved a historical and doctrinal continuity with some Jewish traditions, but that the same psychological forces and dynamics that were identifiable in Jewish Messianic traditions are at work in variant form in the Christian tradition as well. The Messianic aspects of early Christian belief were an expression of the cultic aspects of the development of the early church. As such they form a vehicle for the expression of the dynamics of the paranoid process (Meissner, 1978, 1987).

MESSIANISM IN THE GOSPELS

Each of the gospel accounts, the three synoptics and Jn,[1] has a specific origin, historical context and theological message to convey. Mark was

---

[1]The three gospels of Matthew, Mark, and Luke are called synoptic because they are thought to derive from more or less common sources and have many elements in common. John derives from a separate tradition. Subsequently the distinction between the authors of the gospels and the books themselves will be maintained by referring to

the disciple of Peter, and his gospel reflects the influence of the Jerusalem community, probably for the benefit of non-Palestinian Christians of pagan origin. Mark's gospel (Mk) is a proclamation of Christ's Messiahship, emphasizing the mystery of Jesus' true identity, its misunderstanding and the "Messianic secret,"[2] as well as the mystery of his role as Son of Man (Bultmann, 1958).

For Matthew, Jesus is the new Moses who brings with him a new revelation and the promise of a new Israel. His is a Jewish Christian gospel (Mt) that identifies Christ as the Messiah, the fulfillment of the Messianic prophecies of the Old Testament (OT); but his Messiah is not simply the Messiah of Jewish traditions and expectations, but a suffering Messiah who died on the cross and whose kingdom is not of this world. Matthew's audience was predominantly, but not exclusively, composed of Jewish Christians, and was probably written about a decade and a half after the destruction of Jerusalem and the temple (about A.D. 80–90) (Viviano, 1990). His community was in all likelihood situated in Palestine or Syria, where developments in Judaism after the destruction of the Second Temple, most notably the emergence of Jamnia Pharisaism (Meissner, 1991), colored the religious landscape. The membership was largely converted from Judaism, and would have held on to their hopes for the promised and longed-for Messiah, the son of David.[3]

Luke, writing about the same time (the mid-80s of the first century, circa A.D. 80–85) (Karris, 1990) and addressing a community centered in Antioch, wrote his gospel (Lk) as the disciple of Paul, addressing the Gentile community from the perspective of the church in Rome. His focus was not a single community but more universal in scope. Rather than the crisis of identity created by the Jamnian reforms that Matthew confronted, Luke dealt with the growing distance between the Gentile churches and the Jewish origins of the faith and the growing need to find a place in the Greco-Roman world of the Mediterranean basin. His message concerns the coming of the kingdom of God in the establishing of the church, the fulfillment of Jesus' prophetic ministry in the guise of the Son of Man. The church would be the fulfillment of Messianic promises under guidance of the Holy Spirit.

---

the men by their names (Matthew, Mark, Luke, and John) and the works by abbreviations (Mt, Mk, Lk, and Jn).

[2]This refers to Christ's supposed concealment of his Messianic status and mission from his disciples, a realization that was achieved only in the light of postresurrection faith.

[3]The royal Messianic tradition traced the lineage of the expected Messiah to King David, such that he was to be David's son and his Messianic kingdom would revive the glories of David's reign—but more universally and triumphantly. See Scholem (1971).

John's gospel (Jn) comes from the end of the first century, probably written by the beloved disciple, and reflects a more advanced stage of reflection on the mystery of Christ's mission (Perkins, 1990). Emphasis falls on Jesus' divine origin and on the spiritual nature of his mission and preaching. The Messianic mission is cast in more specifically spiritual and eschatological terms.

Messianic allusions abound. The genealogies in Mt and Lk are cast in Messianic terms. The name 'Christ' in Mt (1:1-17) is not used as a proper name as in the later tradition, but as the Greek equivalent for the Hebrew term for Messiah. The aim is to place Jesus in the line of davidic succession. Even the "virginal" conception (Mt 1:18-25; Lk 1:34-8) connects the birth of Jesus with the prophecy of Isaiah (Is 7:14). The name Jesus itself means "Yahweh will save," and Emmanuel of the prophecy means "God is with us." In Lk (3:23-38), Christ's origins are traced not merely to Abraham, but to Adam as befits a universal savior. But even here, at the very beginning of the story, traditional Jewish notions of the Messiah are challenged. The Christ comes from the Galileans, the country bumpkins held in contempt by the Judean rabbis, and from an obscure town never mentioned in the Old Testament (OT). Zachariah addresses the baby John as the "prophet of the Most High," the Elijah who would proclaim the coming of the Messiah and salvation. If the savior comes from the line of David (Lk 1:26-38), the salvation promised is no longer earthly and national but spiritual, and the Messianic kingdom is not of this world but of the world of the spirit (Coppens, 1968).

The baptismal narratives declare that the OT promises about a davidic Messiah, the Lord's anointed who is savior and Lord, have been fulfilled in Jesus (Lk 2:1-20). The allusions are reminiscent of the Psalms of Solomon, whose Messianic aspirations echo through Luke's narrative (Bruce, 1971). When his parents bring the child for presentation at the temple, Simeon declares him to be the promised Messiah and prophecies a mission of universal salvation accomplished through sorrow and tragedy (Lk 2:25-35), echoing the message of the Servant Songs of Isaiah (Meissner, 1991).

The preaching of John is presented as preparing the way for the coming of the Messiah (Mk 1:1-8; Mt 3:1-12; Lk 3:1-20; Jn 1:19-34). John is the herald, in the image of Elijah (Mt 11:2-15; Jn 1:21), who proclaims the coming of the Messiah—a voice crying in the wilderness, "Prepare a way for the Lord" (Is 40:3-5).

When John baptizes Jesus, the Messianic references are unmistakable, a public manifestation of Jesus' Messianic claim (Mk 1:9-11). He is the anointed one, beloved of the Lord (Mt 3:13-17; Lk 3:21-22; Jn 1:31-34).

Particularly in Jn the Messianic titles are given a prominence that can be found nowhere else in the New Testament – the Chosen One of God (Jn 1:34), Christ (Messiah) (Jn 1:41), King of Israel (Jn 1:49), Son of God (Jn 1:49), Son of Man (Jn 1:51) (Dodd, 1968).

The temptations in the desert (Mk 1:12–13; Mt 4:1–11; Lk 4:1–13) are invitations by the Devil for Christ to use his Messianic powers, perhaps in a manner that would correspond with then-current popular Messianic expectations. To respond to these temptations would have cast Jesus' ministry in terms of temporal prosperity and power. The implications of political power in the last temptation would have suggested some reference to the fanatical Jewish Zealots who looked to the Messiah to overthrow the power of Rome with a military victory (Meissner, 1988). Christ's resistance to these blandishments was meant to convey the message that his mission was not to meet the wishful fantasies of certain Jewish Messianic hopes.

The miracle accounts in the gospels are presented with overtones that call to mind the Messianic promises. The feeding of the 5,000 is the only such account that is rendered by all the evangelists (Mk 6:30–44; Mt 14:13–21; Lk 9:10–17; Jn 6:1–13). In Mk, Jesus is cast as the eschatological shepherd (Mk 6:34) who cares for the lost sheep and who was foretold in Ezekiel (Ez 34:23). The feeding itself, besides the miraculous quality of the account holds a promise of the Messianic banquet. According to Mt (8:11–12) the Messianic banquet will be open to not only the Jews, but to the Gentiles as well.

A high point in the profession of Christ's Messianic role comes in the confession of Peter at Caesarea Philippi. In Mk (8:27–33) this episode climaxes Jesus' self-revelation and marks a turning point for the disciples who, for the first time, recognize Jesus as the Messiah. But if Peter's confession acknowledges Christ as the promised Messiah, it is as a different kind of Messiah than traditional Jewish beliefs had looked for. The same motifs are repeated in Mt (16:13–23) and Lk (9:18–27). Peter's acknowledgment recognizes at least dimly that the Messiah he follows is not a triumphant conqueror, but one whose lot is suffering and death (Mk 8:31–33; Mt 16:21–23; Lk 9:22) (Bruce, 1971).

Jesus cautions his disciples to keep the Messianic secret (Mk 8:30; Mt 16:20; Lk 9:21). The Messianic secret of Mk is transformed in Lk into the mystery of a suffering Messiah. But even here Peter's acceptance was limited, his vision myopic. He objects to this stunning reversal of Messianic hopes, but for his trouble is sternly rebuked (Mt 16:22–23). It was easier for Peter to accept that Jesus was the Messiah than to come to terms with the idea that the Messiah was to suffer and die.

This shattering revelation of Christ's suffering mission is followed in the synoptic accounts by the account of the transfiguration in which Christ appears in transformed glory to Peter, James, and John (Mk 9:2–8; Mt 17:1–8; Lk 9:28–36). The transfiguration has no parallels in the synoptic gospels except perhaps for the baptismal narratives in which a divine quality is attributed to Jesus and his mission. Some scholars have suggested that the account may represent a postresurrection narrative transplanted to this position. Certainly the glory attributed to the risen Christ is foreshadowed in this account. The account is highly symbolic of Christ's transcendent status and, coming in the wake of Peter's confession and the predictions of the passion, serves to reaffirm Christ's Messiahship and his Messianic glory. The tension is obvious, and the implication seems to be that the disciples, for all their good will, had not fully grasped the implications of these events.

The paradox of Christ's Messianic mission is again reflected in the discourse about the relation between Christ and David (Mk 12:35–37; Mt 22:41–46; Lk 20:41–44). Jesus poses the dilemma: how can the Christ be the son of David when David calls him Lord? The question is obviously concocted to discredit the scribes and Pharisees who proclaim themselves the true expositors of the tradition. It challenges the currently accepted teaching among the teachers of Israel. The longstanding belief was that the anointed one was to be a descendant of David, a belief that was elaborated in the last two centuries B.C. into a full-blown Messianic doctrine of an ideal davidic king to come. The quotation put in Jesus' mouth comes from Ps 110, a hymn of royal Messianism ascribed to David. The passage, which is essentially the same in all three synoptics, has been interpreted to mean (a) that Jesus was calling into question the davidic origins of the Messiah, (b) that the origins of the Messiah are more exalted and transcendent than David's, or (c) that the reference is to the Son of Man passage in Dn 7:13 asserting that the Christ is more than a son of David — Son of Man in a unique sense. The second of these seems to carry the most weight — that the Messiah may come from the line of David, but that his Messianic character transcended mere blood ties with David (Fitzmyer, 1974). Mt makes the debate with the Pharisees more explicit; the immediate point of the story in this context is the implication that they cannot resolve this simple exegetical problem so that they cannot be taken as valid judges of the identity of the Messiah.

The account of Jesus' meeting with the Samaritan woman is found only in Jn (4:1–42). The revelation of Christ's Messianic identity seems quite direct; not only does it involve the confession of his Messianic mission, but the revelation to the Samaritans implies that the salvation to come transcends national boundaries and extends beyond the Jews to include all nations. The realization of Messianic hopes in the mission of Christ is to be found in universal salvation. The parable of the wedding feast (Mt 22:1-14; Lk 14:16-24) seems to strike an even further discordant note. Those who are invited to the feast do not come; they offer frivolous excuses or abuse and even kill the king's servants. The king retaliates by destroying them and inviting other guests who would be willing to come to the feast.

In Jewish literature, the Messianic era was compared to a feast (Is 25:6) and the Messiah himself to a bridegroom who would take Israel to himself as his bride. The message is that not all will be included in the Messianic kingdom. To fill out the allegory, the king is God, his son the Messiah, and his servants the prophets. The religious leaders or the chosen people may not be among those who sit at the banquet table in the Messianic kingdom.

The Messianic doctrine of the synoptics is expressed in their thinking about the parousia, the time of the second coming of Christ in his Messianic splendor. Mt (24:4-8) as part of the eschatological discourse lists the signs of the parousia. The account is cast in similar terms in both Mk (13:5-13) and Lk (21:8-19). The usual apocalyptic disasters are included: wars, earthquakes, famine. But a warning is included against the false Messiahs, those who lay claim to the Messianic title but are not the true Messiah (Mt 24:26-28; Mk 13:21-23; Lk 17:22-25). The coming of the Son of Man (Dn 7:13-14) will be clear to all, like lightning flashing across the sky. The warning is set in a context of sudden, unexpected, and total disaster. The account is linked with warnings about the destruction of Jerusalem and the temple. The references to the "abomination of desolation" echo the reference in Daniel to the statue of Zeus Olympios erected in the Jerusalem temple by Antiochus IV Epiphanes in 168 B.C. The material in these citations is undoubtedly retrospectively based on the events of the Jewish War and the destruction of Jerusalem and the desecration and destruction of the temple by the Romans in A.D. 70. The expectations for the time of the parousia and the expected Messianic renewal were that all these predictions would take place within the present generation — a belief that had to be revised as time went on.

The vision of the coming of the Messianic king to establish his Messianic kingdom is set forth in Mt as the last judgment (Mt 25:31-46) — the Messianic judgment and the kingdom he came to establish are far removed from contemporary expectations. This final judgment is not unlike the contemporary Jewish idea that a judgment would inaugurate the Messianic era (the last "days of the Messiah"), and that this would be followed by a final judgment that would introduce the eschatological era. Even this last judgment has a nationalistic flavor — God, the divine judge, would give the chosen people preferential treatment. In Mt, the Messiah himself judges and his judgment is based on religious rather than nationalistic grounds.

All of the synoptics trumpet the triumphal coming of the Son of Man (Mk 13:24-27; Mt 24:29-31; Lk 21:25-27). The allusion is to the apocalyptic vision of the Son of Man of Dn 7:13-14 coming in his Messianic glory at the end of the world to pass final judgment. The title "Son of Man" is of interest here. In OT usage, the phrase seems to mean little more than "human being." Here it can be interpreted as referring to Christ as the representative head of redeemed humanity. There is little to suggest that in pre-Christian Judaic usage it served as a Messianic title; even the question of an individual reference in Dn, as opposed to a more symbolic corporate reference (e.g., to the company of the elect), has not been settled. Dodd (1968) argues that even apparently Messianic uses of the title in the apocalyptic literature has more symbolic than personal implication. Thus the "Son of Man" title is capable of both individual and corporate reference and may be used with both implications simultaneously in mind.

The Messianic implications of Christ's mission reach a crescendo in the final journey to Jerusalem and in the events of the passion. The entry into Jerusalem (Mk 11:1-11; Mt 21:1-11; Lk 19:28-38; Jn 12:12-16) is an account of Messianic display. Mt refers the scene of the triumphal entry to Zechariah 9:9, omitting the phrase that alludes to the victory of the Messianic king. The king here is among the lowly and lacks the trappings of a royal Messianic figure. The procession becomes a Messianic parade complete with crowds and cheers, and the Messiah is saluted as the son of David. The procession is succeeded by the cleansing of the temple, an act of direct aggression against the temple priests and hierarchy. By implication, Jesus does not recognize the existing authorities and asserts his own higher Messianic authority.

The narratives of the passion are also used to reinforce the Messianic character of Christ's mission. In Mk (14:53-65), the high priest puts the question to him directly: "Are you the Christ . . . the son of the Blessed One?" Christ replies in the affirmative and identifies himself with the Son of Man of Dn 7:13. In Mt (26:57-68), Jesus' answer appeals not only to Dn but to Ps 110, thus declaring himself to be not only the royal messiah but Son of Man as well. The implication, however, reaches beyond a mere claim to be the Messiah; it is equivalently a claim to be the Son of God (Bruce, 1971). The high priest tears his robes and declares the reply a blasphemy worthy of death. Luke's account (Lk 22:66–23:1) seems to connect the titles given to Jesus—Messiah, Son of Man, Son of God—to imply the supereminence of the last title. The words to the Sanhedrin are probably meant to convey no more than the connotation of the title in the OT—the anointed, the chosen one, the davidic king. For the postresurrection church, viewing these events from the perspective of the Easter faith, the implications were much greater.

When Jesus appears before Pilate, the charge is specifically his claim to be the Messianic king (Mk 15:2–5; Mt 27:11–14; Lk 23:2–7; Jn 18:28–40). Undoubtedly for Pilate Jesus was just another of many Messianic claimants who were causing trouble. He was more interested in placating the Jewish authorities and avoiding a public disruption than he was in seeing to it that justice was done. Again Jesus makes his Messianic claim in other terms—he is indeed a king, but his kingdom is not of this world. The ancient themes of classical Messianic royalism are transposed to a superior spiritual level, especially in Jn, where his kingdom is cast in purely spiritual terms (Coppens, 1968).

MESSIANISM IN THE ACTS OF THE APOSTLES

The narrative of Acts takes place in the context of a postcrucifixion, postresurrection faith. The disciples at the beginning have no more than a dawning awareness of a doctrine of divine sonship. The primitive kerygma[4] proclaims that he is both Lord and Messiah. His Messiahship is demonstrated by prophecy, miracles, and especially by the resurrection. He is the Lord, the Son of God, the Suffering Servant. Salvation is gained through no other name, and the work of salvation is wrought by the Spirit of Jesus, who is sent by the resurrected Christ to dwell in the hearts of true believers.

The handicaps to this mission were considerable. The disciples set out to proclaim as Messiah one who had been crucified by the Romans on a charge of sedition. A crucified Messiah was a contradiction in terms. How could the crucified be the anointed one, the son of David, the Chosen One of Yahweh, on whom all Yahweh's favor was to rest? One who was hanged on a cross was accursed by God (Bruce, 1971).

Peter's speech at Pentecost (Acts 2:14–36) bases this Messianic claim on the resurrection. The wonders of Pentecost itself manifest the outpouring of the spirit that was to herald the establishment of the

---

[4]The kerygma was the apostolic preaching of the early church about the life and teachings of Jesus.

Messianic kingdom. Then Peter's temple discourse (3:12-26) proclaims the Isaian theme of the suffering Messiah and identifies Christ as the Holy One, the Just One, announced by the prophets.

It is in Acts (11:26) that Christ's followers are first designated as Christianoi – the servants and followers of the Christos. The designation could not have arisen in a Jewish setting, the designation would have implied to Jewish ears an admission of the disciples' claim that Christ was the Messiah. To Gentile ears, however, the name Christos held less of a religious connotation and sounded more like a personal designation (Bruce, 1971). The designation Christianoi arose in the Hellenistic center Antioch.

The Messianic theme emerges again in the account of the Ethiopian eunuch (8:26-40). Philip meets the eunuch on the road to Gaza and explains the Isaian text as applied to the suffering Messiah. The eunuch is converted and baptized. The part of the Servant of Yahweh song cited refers to the death and suffering of the Righteous One (Is 53:7-8). The same motifs echo throughout the speeches of Paul in Acts. In his speech in the synagogue at Antioch (13:16-41), Paul preaches the suffering, dying, and resurrected Christ. Christ was raised by the power of God from the dead and was not allowed to experience corruption – one of the promises made to David (Ps 16:9).

When Paul preaches in Thessalonika (17:1-9), his message is again that Jesus is the Messiah who was destined by God to suffer and die and to rise again from the dead. This message no doubt contributed to the violent reaction of the Jewish contingent, who dragged Jason and some of the brothers before the city council with the charge of setting up another emperor to rival the emperor of Rome. Even though Paul and the disciples were careful to avoid any use of imperial titles, preaching only that Jesus was the Messiah and Lord, the Jewish reaction instinctively translated these terms into royal and imperial connotations consistent with the established expectations of the davidic Messiah. Later, when Paul was imprisoned and brought before the Sanhedrin, he tried to engage Jewish sensibilities by appealing to the Pharisaic belief in the resurrection of the dead. The Pharisee and the son of Pharisees argued that the Messianic hope, cherished by the Pharisees, for the resurrection of the dead was the basis of his belief in Christ and the reason for his being on trial. A violent argument broke out between the Pharisees and the Sadducees, who did not believe in life after death or the resurrection of the dead (22:30-23:11).

Further on, Paul was dragged before King Agrippa, Herod Agrippa II, to plead his case. Once again, it is the suffering and risen Christ he proclaims (26:1-23). The conflation of the Messiah with the Suffering Servant of Isaiah is a characteristic Lucan theme that occurs in Luke's gospel and again here; the authorship of Acts is traditionally ascribed to Luke, the companion of Paul and evangelist. Certainly both Lk and Acts seem to constitute a continuous account from the same source (Dillon, 1990). The connection of these themes is not explicit in the OT but seems to have been a constant and powerful motif in the early Christian kerygma. Paul does not hesitate to present his case to Agrippa, basing it once again on the Messianic hope for the resurrection and appealing to Christ's death and resurrection as proof of his Messiahship.

THE APOCALYPSE

The Apocalypse was written, possibly by the apostle John or a school of his disciples, toward the end of the first century, possibly during the persecution that raged toward the end of the reign of Domitian (A.D. 81-96) (Collins, 1990). Its title connects it with the postexilic apocalyptic tradition: its visionary revelations have to do with the times to come, particularly with the realization of the Messianic promises in the eschatological period. The symbolic language borrows from the prophetic tradition as distilled through the apocalyptic filter. Woman comes to represent a people or city, horns refer to power, Christ is a lamb, and the word of God is a sharp sword. The vision of the dragon and the lamb (12:1-14:20), for example, pictures the struggle between the power of evil, represented by the monster, and the Messiah and his people, between the Devil and Christ and his church.

The power of evil tries to destroy the woman and her son, a recapitulation of current Eastern myths. The woman with child is pursued by a horrible monster, but she is miraculously preserved to give birth, and her child in turn slays the evil monster. The Christian myth deviates from its pagan counterparts insofar as the child does not immediately destroy the monster; rather he is taken up to heaven, where he reigns with God while the woman remains in peril of the dragon's hatred. The story is at once an allegory for the suffering and persecuted church (the woman is the people of God, the true Israel of both OT and NT) (Collins, 1990) and for Mary, the woman of Israel who brought the Messiah into the world. The pangs of birth become the prototype of the birthpangs of the Messiah that introduce the eschatological era. The Messiah was to destroy the power of the dragon over the world. The beast (13:1-10) is the representative of the dragon on earth and is invested with his power. The reference harkens back to Dn 7 in which the ten-horned beast represents Antiochus IV Epiphanes, the archpersecutor of Israel, but is then transferred to the Roman Empire, which epitomizes all those secular powers that persecute the church. The second beast, or "false prophet," probably refers to Nero, the first emperor to persecute the Christians.

Ultimately Christ will return to do battle with the beast and the false prophet and will emerge triumphant (19:11–21). The apocalyptic tradition taught that the establishment of the Messianic kingdom would follow a violent battle in which the Messiah would triumph over the powers of evil. The Messianic victory will inaugurate a thousand-year reign of peace and justice (20:1–6). This belief has become the basis for a series of millennial cults that look forward to the thousand-year reign of Christ on earth, for example, Joachim di Fiore and the Fraticelli, and later Protestant sects such as the Anabaptists, Adventists, and Jehovah's Witnesses (Bettencourt, 1969).

PAULINE MESSIANISM

In Paul's theology, Jesus is the new Moses who came to replace the old Mosaic law with a new law, the law of the new dispensation. Sin entered the world through Adam and the reign of sin lasted through the period of the Mosaic law, to be finally dissolved after the coming of the Christ Messiah (Rom 5:12–14). In the rabbinic tradition there were three eras: from Adam to Moses, 2,000 years of chaos; from Moses to the Messiah, 2,000 years of the law; after the Messiah, 2,000 years of bliss. In this last period the Messiah would bring the new law that would govern the Messianic era.

The problem Paul faced was the failure of the revelation of Christ to convince the Jews. How can the Christian gospel be the true fulfillment of the Messianic promises when the Messiah himself has been rejected by Israel? The issue of the separation of the nascent church from Israel can be viewed in the context of Paul's mission to the Gentiles and the division of orientation and purpose in the ranks of the early Jerusalem church (Meissner, 1989). Behind the tension in Paul's thought lies the tension between the Jerusalem church of James and his group, and the emerging churches of Rome and Antioch. James and his followers wanted to maintain their identity and attachment to the Jewish origins of Christianity and insisted on continuing the Jewish practices of fasting, circumcision, and so on. The churches of Rome and Antioch were more decidedly Gentile in orientation, Hellenistic in background, and even sociologically different from the more pastoral focus of the Jerusalem church. The church of James was essentially rural and agricultural in its roots; the church of Paul was urban, middle class, and upwardly mobile. It is not unlikely that these more Hellenized Christians were anxious to dissociate themselves from the Jewish origins of their faith, if only to distance themselves from the connotations of the Jewish revolt and the fact that their Messiah had been crucified by the Roman authorities. Paul's apologetic in Romans 9–11 is the first effort of the new theology to confront the traditional theology of the synagogue.

In 1 Corinthians Paul takes up the theme of the suffering Messiah. The Jews demand miracles and the Greeks look for wisdom, but Paul preaches Christ crucified. For the Jews the Messiah was a figure of power and might, an emperor greater than the emperor of Rome. The suffering Messiah was far from that image; for them a suffering Messiah was a stumbling block. The Greeks sought knowledge and understanding, not mystery. They could not accept anything on another's authority. To prefer suffering and mystery to wisdom was merely foolishness for them (1 Cor 1:22–25). But this suffering Messiah is the Messianic king, the royal descendant of David, who offered his death for the salvation of many (2 Tim 2:8–10).

The Epistle to the Hebrews (Heb) is probably not from the hand of Paul, despite its early ascription to him in the church of Alexandria. The style and vocabulary are not Paul's, the manner of citation of the OT is different, and the theological emphases strike another chord. The overall tone, however, is quite Pauline. The consensus view is that the author was probably a Jewish Christian of Hellenistic background, especially insofar as many influences of Plato and Philo of Alexandria can be detected. Heb treats the role of Christ in terms of the themes of royal Messianism and priestly Messianism. The theme of royal Messianism is cast in terms of the Messianic enthronement (1:5–14). The relationship between God and the Messiah is that of father to son. The reference is to Ps 2:7, one of the royal psalms probably celebrating the enthronement of one of the kings of Judah. The day of the king's accession to power was the day on which he was "begotten" as the Son of God. Christ was the Son of God, the davidic king who embodies the promises and fulfill-ments of the tradition of royal Messianism. Appeal is also made to the royal nuptial psalm (Ps 44); the royal prince is another prototype of the Messiah.

Heb also emphasizes the priestly character of the Messiah. Jesus is a priest according to the order of Melchizedek and the Levitical priesthood

(7:1-28). The author ignores the fact that the lines of priestly and royal descent were joined in Melchizedek. He is apparently not interested in the royal aspect, but in the priestly function. The roles were separated in the later tradition, but in the royal Ps 110, so frequently cited in Heb, the union of these functions is regarded as the normal state of affairs. The emphasis there is not on the fact that Melchizedek was priest-king, but that he was priest-king of Jerusalem. Heb emphasizes not only the continuity of the Messianic line, but the eternal priesthood of Melchizedek, which makes him both a prototype of Christ and superior to the Levitical priesthood. The account of Heb represents an attempt to spiritualize and sanctify the Messianic tradition. The establishment of the kingdom is the victory of the Messiah over the Devil and the forces of evil. Christ is not only the preserver of the Messianic kingship, but the high priest of the new dispensation (Coppens, 1968). The coming of the Messiah is the occasion for spiritual renewal and moral perfection (Heb 5:11-6:20).

MESSIANIC DOCTRINE IN THE NEW TESTAMENT

The Messianic transformation from the OT to the NT is from a view of the Messianic promises in material, temporal, and nationalistic terms to an understanding that was spiritual, eternal, and universal. The "days of the Messiah" of the contemporary Jewish view looked forward to the national restoration of the Jewish nation. Salvation would be the work of divine intervention, rather than simply a result of the Messiah himself. The coming of the Messiah was to be heralded by the Messianic tribulations, a series of temporal and spiritual calamities. The coming of the Messiah would mark the end of the world and the beginning of the eschatological era. The Messianic kingdom was to last for a thousand years.

The conceptions of the Messianic kingdom came in several varieties. One view divided the Messianic era into two periods: one terrestrial, in which the kingdom of Israel would be restored, the other superterrestrial. The transcendental view held that there was to be no Messianic kingdom in this world but only in the next—salvation was to be found in the heaven, or paradise. In the eschatological view, the resurrection and judgment would take place in this world in the "days of the Messiah" but would be transformed into a transcendental form still in this world. This was probably the dominant view in the NT context of early Christian preaching. The primary beneficiary of the Messianic blessings was the chosen people, the fate of the heathen nations remaining uncertain. In some accounts they are destroyed by the triumphant return of the Messiah, in others they continue to wage war against the Messiah and the kingdom on this earth, finally to be judged and destroyed in the catastrophe at the "end of days." The center of the Messianic kingdom on earth, nonetheless, is Jerusalem, transformed in suitably Messianic style.

The contemporary view of the Messiah himself was cast in terms of the kingly and priestly offices, those that were conveyed by anointing. In Esdras and Henoch, the Messiah is preexistent and somehow suprahuman. He occupies a position between God and man, possessing transcendent characteristics but not identified with God. He is the warrior-king who establishes the Messianic kingdom on earth. There is little room here for a view of a suffering Messiah. The only allusions come from Is 53, but these hints are irreconcilable with the view of a triumphant and conquering Messiah. Thus arose the idea of a second Messiah, the Messiah ben Joseph. Contemporary Jewish views of the Messiah were, therefore, somewhat vague and even at times contradictory (Meissner, 1991).

There is little hesitation among NT authors to apply Messianic titles to Jesus. He is referred to as "the son of David," a title that asserts his claim to royal Messianic lineage. The most frequent usage is "the Son of Man," a title that does not lend luminous clarity to the Messianic claims. Although it asserts an anthropomorphic connotation, it also seems to advance more exalted claims — we are puzzled to see the high priest rending his garments and screaming "blasphemy" at a mere anthropomorphism. Although there are significant doubts regarding the Messianic status of the title in OT usage, there seems little doubt that in the hands of the NT writers the title is meant to be Messianic. The obvious reference point is Dn 7, but the additional association placed in Jesus' mouth is the Suffering Servant of Isaiah (e.g., after the confession of Peter, Mk 8:31ff; Mt 16:21ff; Lk 9:22ff). Clearly, this title in the NT implies more than is involved in its OT connotations. Jesus is called "Lord," a title of royal address, reflecting the court language of Syro-Greek royalty and emphasizing the royal Messianic claim.

More difficult is the title "Son of God." Nowhere in the OT or later Jewish literature does this title appear to have Messianic overtones. When Peter says, "You are the Christ, the son of the Living God" (Mt 16:16), the Christian tradition has interpreted this in a theological sense, in conjunction with the theophanies of the baptismal accounts, to imply that Christ is more than human, that he is actually divine. He is more than a human Messiah, he is God's son and shares in God's nature and power. He is the son of God as sharing in God's nature, not merely son of God as was every good Jew. Repeatedly, especially in John's gospel, the relation of the Son to the Father is stressed, and the links to the power and glory of Yahweh implied. These elements have been elaborated theologically into the doctrine of Jesus' divine Sonship, so that the Messianic claims at this point in the Christian kerygma reach far beyond anything conceivable in the pre-Christian dispensation to assert the divine nature and origin of the Messiah.

To the eyes of Christian faith, then, Jesus gathered in his own person the heterogeneous and variegated Messianic allusions of the tradition and amalgamated them into a new synthesis. He was the embodiment of all the hoped-for fulfillments of the end days; he was the prophet, the servant of Isaiah, the priest-mediator in the line of Melchizedek, the Savior, the royal king-Messiah of the line of David, the Son of Man, the Son of God, and even, for John, the Word of God (Coppens, 1968). He was all these and more. He was the divinely given answer to the Messianic dreams of the past. He was "anointed by the Holy Spirit and power" (Acts 10:37). Even as all of this was subjected to the workings of the postresurrection faith, the presentation of Jesus himself was more muted and qualified. The picture presented in the gospels is that he more or less avoided publicizing his Messianic role during the public ministry. He rejected the popular imagery of the triumphant and glorious Messiah, and to his disciples stressed the image of the humble king in Zechariah 9:9 (Mt 21:4-5) and the role of the suffering Messiah. This may explain the preference for the title "Son of Man." The more jubilant and triumphant procession into Jerusalem stands out as an exception, when acknowledgment of his Messianic status breaks out in a public way. He was crucified as a Messiah-king, and inevitably the disciples took the events surrounding the resurrection as proof of his Messianic role and ultimately divine origin.

The events of Christ's life left little room for proclaiming him as the Messiah of Jewish expectations. There had been nothing regal about it: there were no victories, no kingdom, no defeat of the hated Romans, no delivery of Israel, no miraculous transformation of the world as at least some of the extant Messianic expectations dictated. The resolution of these difficulties was twofold: Christ's Messianic mission was elevated to the level of the spiritual and the divine, and the fulfillment of Messianic expectations was postponed to the Second Coming in the parousia. This made it possible to maintain the traditional expectations intact, and to allow the Messiah to remain glorified and triumphant, now as the ascended and glorified Christ who reigns in heaven rather than on earth. In any case, it is clear that Messiah was his predominant title, such that it became in its Greek form his proper name and title—the Christ.

ASPECTS OF THE CULTIC PROCESS

The burden of the above review seems clear enough, namely that the motifs of the Messianic vision in the Christian redaction derive from and in large measure echo those of the Jewish milieu within which they arose. The earliest strata of the Christian church were decidedly Palestinian in origin and are probably best exemplified in the early Jerusalem church as embodied in the figures of Peter and James and their disciples (Meissner, 1989). Only subsequently did the broader Hellenistically influenced vision of Pauline Christianity come into being (Meissner, 1990). Christian Messianism, therefore, replays the themes of its predecessor, Jewish Messianism, but not completely. The Messianic vision undergoes a change that translates and transforms the accents of the earlier Jewish hopes into a Christian form that adapts it to the mission and reality of the ministry and life of Jesus. Thus, although the parallels between Jewish and Christian Messianism are striking, the transposition to a new key brings with it entirely new and distinguishing elements that do not exist at all in the older version.

It seems logical to conclude, then, that the same psychological processes and mechanisms that I have identified in the older Jewish tradition are also at work in the NT tradition. My effort here will aim at delineating the aspects of the cultic process as they are embodied in the phenomenon of NT Messianism and then to make explicit the elements of the paranoid process that find expression in it.

Many of the characteristics of the cultic process have been detailed previously (Meissner, 1987); my purpose here is to focus some of those elements in relation to Christian Messianism. One of the characteristics of a sect or cult is the degree of tension that obtains between the religious group and the surrounding social milieu (Yinger, 1957; Meissner, 1987). The cult typically stands in opposition to or is distanced from the prevailing social environment, distinguishing itself thereby from more established religious structures that tend to be more congruent with and to reinforce existing social structures. The Christian movement, as the story emerges in the pages of the NT, was more or less a deviant movement in social terms. The ministry of Jesus was cast in terms of his progressively deepening opposition to the established religious groups, especially the Pharisees and Sadducees. The connections between the emerging Christian movement and other extant Jewish religious and political groups like the Essenes or the Zealots remains somewhat obscure and conjectural, but the essential differences shine through the mists of obscurity anyway (Meissner, 1988). In essence, the movement that came to life under the leadership of Jesus was independent of and separate from the company of religious structures that already existed in Palestine. The tension between Jesus and the Sanhedrin and the Roman authorities came to a head in the trial and crucifixion. Those circumstances of the rebellious and deviant origins of the Christian inspiration remained a significant embarrassment as the disciples spread throughout the Mediterranean world of the Roman Empire to begin the work of conversion.

Whereas established religious institutions are inclined to adapt to the existing social order, the cultic impulse is toward change — either advancing or preventing modifications in the existing system of beliefs, values, symbols, and religious practices. Christianity came on the Palestinian scene as a movement of conversion, pronouncing the "good news" of the Christian gospel and striving to convert first the Jews and later the pagan Gentiles to the way of salvation through faith in Jesus Christ. It was this basic alloplastic drive to transform the world of the old dispensation and pagan belief that brought the nascent church into such dire conflict with the Jewish and Roman authorities. The inevitable conflict of value and belief systems lie at the root of the persecutions that accompanied the origins of Christianity and dogged its early steps until the time of Constantine in the fourth century. Part of the need to transform the world of Jewish belief from which Christianity derived was to modify the core of belief that surrounded the Messianic convictions.

Descriptions of the cult phenomenon have emphasized that cultic movements tend to be more responsive to individual human needs that often have been ignored or obscured in the existing order of things. This aspect of the cultic process in early Christianity does not emerge with stunning clarity, but there is detectable a certain differential emphasis. The Christian kerygma seems to have a certain individual appeal that may mark it off from the emphasis on conformity to the law and the legalized forms of religious expression that characterize contemporary Jewish religious life. The gospel accounts in which Christ challenges existing beliefs regarding observance of the sabbath or fasting are a case in point; the Pauline tension between the freedom of the followers of Christ and the observance of the law seem to underline this aspect as well. Even the Messianic emphases carry a more individual connotation

in the Christian translation than the Jewish emphasis on the nationalistic
overtones of the Messianic salvation of the chosen people. The differences strike me as more a matter of accent and emphasis than radical
contrast. By implication the internal drive toward division, or as Yinger
(1957) puts it, "anarchy," was tempered by the cohesive forces of
organizing structure that obtained among the disciples from the first.
The 12 were tightly knit around the figure of Jesus to begin with, and the
mantle of succession and authority was firmly placed on the shoulders of
Peter, who proved to be a powerful unifying figure in resolving the early
tensions and splits, most notably between the Judaizing Christians of the
Jerusalem church and the Hellenizing faction under the leadership of
Paul (Meissner, 1989). Although divisive forces were not absent from the
early church's development, the major focus of opposition and conflict
remained between the church and the outside world.

As a religious movement, the early Christian church manifested
aspects of all the major forms of cult expression (Meissner, 1988). It was
conversionist in that it sought to bring about change in the minds and
hearts of men by converting them to the message of the Christian gospel,
and the approach was evangelistic and devoted to the theme of salvation
through faith in Jesus Christ. It was introversionist insofar as it rejected
the values of the pagan world and sought to replace them with a higher
form of Christian ethic. It was adventist by reason of its insistence on the
end of this world and the renewal of all things in the world to come. The
Messianic themes were well adapted to this aspect of Christian thought,
the difference lying in the gradual displacement of the Messianic
expectations not only to the end of time but even beyond into a realm of
eternal bliss. There was a revolutionary accent in this dimension of the
Christian outlook, seeking to overthrow the order of things in the present
world and replacing it with a new, sanctified, and salvific Christian
dispensation. And finally, it was in some degree gnostic in that the
central tenets of Christian belief were shrouded in mystery that was open
to the deeper understanding only of an elite. It can safely be said that the
original cult that took form within the small and devoted band of
followers who gathered around the charismatic figure of Jesus was
gradually transformed into a sect after the traumatic events of the
passion, death, and resurrection. According to Yinger's (1957) classification, the cult, which is small and focused around the teaching and
influence of the charismatic leader, can evolve into a sect that is to a
greater degree socially oriented, responsive to unsatisfied needs in the
social milieu, and may take up a position of aggressive opposition or
avoidance in relation to the social order. Although the charismatic

influence of Christ was extended in the subsequent evolution of the
church, there were also gradually emerging elements of structure and
redistribution of the charismatic influences. After Pentecost, the apostles
increasingly assumed the mantle of authority and religious inspiration.

The upshot of this development was an increasing emphasis on the
divinity of Jesus and a displacement of the Messianic expectation to an
eschatological future. This process involved a distancing from the
Messianic emphases of the traditional doctrine of the Messiah. Rather
than a king after the model of David and a kingdom envisioned as a
restitution of an idealized kingdom of this world, the Messianic kingdom
became spiritualized and the Messianic king became the Son of God.
These transformed Messianic beliefs became the centerpiece of the
Christian belief system as it emerged from its Palestinian origins and
engaged with the pagan and Hellenistic world of the time.

MESSIANISM AND THE PARANOID PROCESS

The pattern of Messianic expectation and hopes that carried over from
the Jewish and Palestinian traditions into the NT shared in substantially
the same dynamic forces of motivation and purpose. The Christian
Messianic outlook accepted and took its direction from the preexisting
Messianic tradition of first-century Judaism. The gospels pronounce
Jesus as the promised Messiah, the one who is anointed and blessed by
God to announce and bring into being the new kingdom in which the
reign of Yahweh is to be established on earth. The NT reconstruction,
then, of Christ's Messianic mission takes up the multiple and at times
contradictory strains of the earlier Messianic vision and tries to establish
the continuity between various strata of that tradition and the Christian
kerygma. The Christian vision saw the Messianic promises as being
fulfilled and realized in the person of Jesus Christ. As the story of the
public ministry unfolds in the gospels, this awareness seems to emerge
only gradually, haltingly, and fragmentedly—largely due to Christ's own
reticence, suggesting a degree of uncertainty, ambivalence, and ambiguity. It is only in the light of the postresurrection faith that the terms of
Jesus' Messianic mission are brought into clarified articulation. As that
doctrine emerged, the different emphases and points of contrast between
the Christian message and the traditional viewpoint became more
decisively etched into the Christian consciousness. Jesus was the Messiah
of the ancient tradition, but he was not the Messiah of Jewish expectation. His mission was spiritual and his Messianic kingdom was of another

and higher world. And Jesus himself was not merely the chosen instrument of God's purposes, the anointed messenger of divine intentions, but he was himself divine, sharing in God's essence and nature — he was the divine word that came from the mouth of God, son of God and Lord.

The effect of this clarification was to drive a wedge between preexisting religious perspectives and the Christian orientation. The oppositional trends that had characterized Christ's public life now extended themselves to the Messianic realm. The Christian Messiah was a different Messiah, just as the Christian religious outlook and life was different and opposed to the prevailing Jewish tenets. This difference brought into play the in-group–out-group dynamics that have become familiar as aspects of the paranoid process (Meissner, 1978). Faith in Jesus and adherence to his divine and Messianic role became the touchstone of adherence to the Christian church. Opposing religious groups, including the other religious sects that populated the Palestinian landscape and the pagan cults that flourished in the Roman Empire of the period, became the enemies of the church. For some centuries, this opposition was more than ideological — it took the form of persecution in which martyrdom became the way of Christian life. The paranoid dynamics were unleashed in savage and unmitigated form. To be a Christian was synonymous with leading the life of a victim, persecuted and constantly under the shadow of the threat of death. Projective distortions were rampant, both within the Christian community and in the echelons of Roman society that organized, directed, and implemented the persecutions. And, as is typically the case, these paranoid dynamics came to play a reinforcing and sustaining role for both sides. Paranoia, as always, feeds on paranoia.

It is interesting that one of the traditional Jewish views of the Messiah was that he would come in power and glory and wage war against the enemies of Israel. Israel would triumph in this Messianic conquest and would assume a position of hegemony over all the nations of the earth. This aspect of the Messianic doctrine was part and parcel of the nationalistic form of the Messianic vision. The Jewish mind could not divorce national power and victory over other nations from their view of redemption. This element is entirely lacking from the Christian perspective. Not only do the gospel accounts eschew violence and armed conflict (Meissner, 1988), but Christ is portrayed as the man of peace. He orders his followers to put up their swords in the garden of Gethsemane, and in reply to Pilate he says that if he wanted to defend himself he could summon 12 legions of angels to his cause. But this is not his purpose. The

Christian Messianic conquest is not to be by force of arms, but by spiritual means. We can infer that Christ and the first-century Christians were anxious to dissociate themselves from the adventist implications of the Zealot movement that had largely been responsible for the Jewish revolt and the destruction of the temple. Rather than the armed revolution and overthrow of the Roman Empire that was the primary tenet of Zealot ambitions, the Christians sought the establishment of a new order of spiritual values and belief. The war against the beast of the Apocalypse was not to be a war of swords and chariots, but a struggle for the spiritual lives and the hearts of men.

Freud (1923) had observed in his discussion of the superego dynamics that in proportion as aggression failed to find direct expression to the outside, it was turned against the self. The superego was the intrapsychic structure that carried the burden of aggression directed against the self. I can suggest that not only was the Christian ethic caught in an internal conflict over the role of aggression, but that paranoid processes were brought into play to reinforce the sense of victimization in Christian beliefs and to consolidate the sense of persecution and attack from external persecutors. Martyrdom became the glory of Christian existence—one who was martyred for the faith was assured of a heavenly crown. Better to be a victim and martyred for the faith, than to become a conquering aggressor and deviate from the creed of the in-group. Better to be a victim and run the gauntlet of conflicts over aggressive impulses and wishes.

Christian Messianism, like its traditional predecessors, was built on a powerful narcissistic foundation. The Christian faith did not have very auspicious origins. Its charismatic leader was a simple carpenter's son, born in the backwoods of Galilee and raised in the hick town of Nazareth, who came to no good end—hanged on the infamous gibbet like a common criminal. Its early members counted no one of importance or influence—simple fishermen and common folk. There was nothing in all this to elevate the enterprise to a level of lofty inspiration and commitment. The Messianic doctrine came to the rescue. Not only was the message and ministry of this man of the people the fulfillment of Messianic hopes, but it was a mission blessed by God and carried out by God's own son. This gave the Christian vision a power, a conviction, and purpose and direction that was immense. This belief system generated a framework of conviction and purpose that drew the members of the nascent church together with a sense of mission and shared direction. To each member who shared in this vision, there came a sense of belonging, of identity, of communion with the idealized and powerful king, prophet, and priest of the Messianic hopes. They were united in purpose and spirit not only among themselves, but with the Son of God.

In gnostic sects, the secret and mystical ideology plays a central role in unifying the sect and providing it with special status, not only internally but in setting it off in opposition and contrast with competing belief systems. The special gnosis of the sect gives the believers a superior religious status to those who do not believe. The ideology in such contexts serves an important function of narcissistic enhancement. It is reinforced by adherence to the charismatic leader, who is usually invested with powerful narcissistic and idealizing transferences. The early Christian faith was founded unequivocally on the adherence to the person of Christ and the belief in his divinity. Whatever else can be said of this conviction, it seems clearly to fit the pattern of narcissistic enhancement determined by the paranoid process. One could not find a more grandiosely sublime leader than God Himself, and in the context of Judaic belief one could find no better enhancing ideology than that provided by the Messianic themes.

I conclude that the form of expression of the Messianic expectations in the Christian kerygma of the early centuries reveals the underlying dynamics and patterns of the workings of the paranoid process. The paranoid process deals primarily with the intrapsychic integration of the structuralized derivatives of both aggressive and narcissistic drives. It involves the externalization by projection of aspects of the self-organization that cannot be tolerated or integrated internally. The pattern that these structuralizing components took in the shaping of early Christian belief systems was to split both narcissistic and aggressive derivatives. The aspect of the aggressive configuration that we associate with the victim introject took expression in the commitment to passivity and victimhood that emerges so clearly from the gospel accounts and early adaptations of the Christian community to opposition and persecution. The Christian way of life was almost equivalent to the pattern of victimization required by living out the victim introject.

The corresponding projections both reinforced and brought into being the persecutory forces of the pagan world that sought to crush the new religious movement. On the narcissistic side, the special doctrine of following of the Christ the Messiah and belief in and adherence to the cause of the Son of God provided a sense of religious superiority and privilege, along with a devaluation and contempt for the misguided beliefs of other religious groups. The narcissistic superiority was retained and served to support and reinforce the internal narcissistic introjective configuration in the minds and hearts of believers, and cast the unbelievers in the position of misguided inferiority and spiritual blindness

(Meissner, 1987). Whatever other forces may have been at work in propelling these momentous historical events, one might wonder whether the intersection of these narcissistic and aggressive dynamics may not have provided sufficient ground for fueling the wave of persecutions that played such a significant role in the early life of the Christian church.

BIBLIOGRAPHY

BETTENCOURT, E. (1969), Milleniarism. In: *Sacramentum Mundi: An Encyclopedia of Theology.* ed. Rahner, K. et al. New York: Herder & Herder, Vol. 4:43–44.

BRUCE, F. F. (1971), *New Testament History.* New York: Doubleday.

BULTMANN, R. (1958), *Jesus Christ and Mythology.* London: SCM Press.

COLLINS, A. Y. (1990), The Apocalypse (Revelation). In: *The New Jerome Biblical Commentary,* ed. Brown, R. E., Fitzmyer, J. A. & Murphy, R. E. Englewood Cliffs, NJ: Prentice-Hall, pp. 996–1016.

COPPENS, J. (1968), *Le Messianisme royal.* Paris: Les Editions du Cerf.

DILLON, R. J. (1990), Acts of the Apostles. In: *The New Jerome Biblical Commentary,* ed. Brown, R. E., Fitzmyer, J. A. & Murphy, R. E. Englewood Cliffs, NJ: Prentice-Hall, pp. 722–767.

DODD, C. H. (1968), *The Interpretation of the Fourth Gospel.* Cambridge: Cambridge University Press.

FITZMYER, J. A. (1974), *Essays on the Semitic Background of the New Testament.* Missoula, MT: Society of Biblical Literature.

FREUD, S. (1923), The ego and the id. *Standard Edition,* 19:1–66. London: Hogarth Press, 1961.

KARRIS, R. J. (1990), The Gospel according to Luke. In: *The New Jerome Biblical Commentary,* ed. Brown, R. E., Fitzmyer, J. A. & Murphy, R. E. Englewood Cliffs, NJ: Prentice-Hall, pp. 675–721.

MEISSNER, W. W. (1978), *The Paranoid Process.* New York: Aronson.

—— (1987), The cult phenomenon and the paranoid process. *The Psychoanalytic Study of Society,* 12:69–95.

—— (1988), The origins of Christianity. *The Psychoanalytic Study of Society,* 13:29–62.

—— (1989), Cultic elements in early Christianity: Antioch and Jerusalem. *The Psychoanalytic Study of Society,* 14:89–117.

—— (1990), The cultic process in early Christianity: Rome, Corinth, and the Johannine community. *The Psychoanalytic Study of Society,* 16:265–285.

—— (1990), Jewish messianism and the cultic process. *The Psychoanalytic Study of Society,* 15:347–370.

PERKINS, P. (1990), The Gospel According to John. In: *The New Jerome Biblical Commentary,* ed. Brown, R. E., Fitzmyer, J. A., & Murphy, R. E. Englewood Cliffs, NJ: Prentice-Hall, pp. 942–985.

RAHNER, K. et al., eds. (1969), *Sacramentum Mundi: An Encyclopedia of Theology.* New York: Herder & Herder.

SCHOLEM, G. (1971), *The Messianic Idea in Judaism and Other Essays on Jewish Spirituality.* New York: Schocken Books.

VIVIANO, B. T. (1990), The Gospel according to Matthew. In: *The New Jerome Biblical Commentary,* ed. Brown, R. E., Fitzmyer, J. A., & Murphy, R. E. Englewood Cliffs, NJ: Prentice-Hall, pp. 630–674.

YINGER, J. M. (1957), *Religion, Society, and the Individual.* New York: Macmillan.

20

Sacrificial Immortality: Toward a Theory of Suicidal Terrorism and Related Phenomena

MOSHE HAZANI

The phenomenon of suicidal terrorism has attracted increasing attention in recent years, due to the prominence of events like the assassination of Rajiv Gandhi (1991), the bombing of the U.S. Marine Headquarters in Beirut (1983), and the successful attacks on Israeli targets. Although some articles (e.g., Taylor and Ryan, 1988; Merari, 1990) shed light on aspects of this kind of warfare, no theory of suicidal terrorism has yet been advanced. This results, probably, from the various writers' tendency to view suicidal terrorism as an isolated phenomenon, distinct from other manifestations of self- and other-victimization. In my opinion this view is mistaken. Despite the obvious external differences, the Tamil girl who assassinated Rajiv Ghandi was basically similar to, say, Charlotte Corday, the French girl who assassinated Marat knowing full well that she would be guillotined; or to Bagrov, the Ukrainian youth who assassinated Stolypin at the Kiev opera; or to the German youths who murdered Rathenau—all happily anticipating their own deaths (Loomis, 1964; Paustovskii, 1967; Fromm, 1973).[1]

Group phenomena, too, may be related to suicidal terrorism. These phenomena include the suicide of the defenders of Masada (73 C.E.), some of them believed to have been *sicarii,* Jewish zealots who had assassinated their less-radical compatriots in Jerusalem before their flight to the desert. Hence they were homicidal suicides, even though several

---

[1]In order not to overload the reader with too frequent citations, they are often presented in groups at the end of the various sections of the chapter. In such instances, the order of the citations corresponds precisely to the order of the topics discussed.

years elapsed between the homicides and the suicides. They also include the Jonestown tragedy, in which the hard core of Jim Jones' disciples killed Congressman Ryan and four others prior to their mass suicide (which presumably involved the murder of the less committed followers) — as well as the self-immolation of the Russian Old Believers, some of whom, at least, rebelled against the Czarina Sophia prior to their self-imposed martyrdom (Hengel, 1989; Chidester, 1988; Crummey, 1970; on the similarity among the events see Robbins, 1986).

In some instances of aggressive behavior the suicides are hardly discernible, as is often the case in victim-precipitated homicides (Wolfgang, 1968). The besieged and outnumbered Sikhs who perished in the Golden Temple of Amritsar in 1984, for example, deliberately provoked the reluctant Indian troops to storm the sanctuary, by brutally murdering Indian captives in front of their comrades. These Sikh fanatics were clearly *suicidal* homicides — not too dissimilar from the *homicidal* suicides of Masada. Indeed, their leader, Jarnail Singh Bindranwale, not only carried out a suicide pact in the shrine with his deputy — but also had a record of previous political assassination, just like the *sicarii*.

Finally, there is a passive-aggressive cluster of phenomena, exemplified by the Jewish Dead Sea Sect. This quietist, pious group, which lived in the Judean Desert before the destruction of the Second Temple, professed strict asceticism, which Menninger (1938) views as chronic suicide. Yet the aggression and hostility of this anything but pacifistic group (see Flusser, 1954) are evident from *The Scroll of the War of the Sons of Light Against the Sons of Darkness,* which they wrote while eagerly awaiting "the day of vengeance." Meanwhile, they practiced "rituals of hatred," in which they magically destroyed their "nonbelieving" coreligionists *in the name of God*. Similar instances can be found in other spiritual milieus as well (see, e.g., Segert, 1955).

The present endeavor encompasses *all the manifestations of self- and other-directed aggression in the name of absolute truth,* whether or not such acts culminate in the simultaneous destruction of aggressor and victim, and, moreover, whether or not they end in death. As will be seen later, this is essential for outlining a theory of these variegated yet basically similar acts.

An examination of the foregoing instances shows that the phenomena I explore are more common than believed; that they are not as culture-bound as some think; that they may involve a relatively large number of individuals; most important, they tend to manifest themselves in the wake of historical dislocations. All of this suggests that they cannot be dismissed as instances of individual psychopathology (although the role of charismatic psychopathological leaders cannot be ignored); a psychohistorical perspective is needed to account for them. Drawing upon Lifton's paradigm of symbolic immortality, I argue here that:

1. Historical dislocations often involve an impairment of one's sense of immortality, leading individuals and groups to perceive themselves as both victims and aggressors;

2. The interior of the dislocated individual is a battleground for the two hostile selves, which leads to tormenting self-destructive wishes; aside from individual agony, this creates a societal state of disorganized victimization (i.e., victimization of all by all);

3. Dislocated individuals tend to adopt totalistic ideologies, which are functionally equivalent to a paranoid system, in that they define an external enemy onto whom one of the two hostile selves can be projected, thereby cleaving the deadly aggressor-victim double and mitigating the self-destructive wishes. At the same time, disorganized victimization is transformed into *organized* victimization (i.e., legitimate victimization of an ideologically defined external enemy);

4. Nonetheless, the internal victim-aggressor double still haunts the dislocated individuals. Under certain circumstances this may lead to the immolation of both self and external enemy in the name of the absolute truth professed by the totalistic system.

LIFTON'S PARADIGM OF SYMBOLIC IMMORTALITY

Lifton (1979) claims that man requires a sense of immortality in the face of inevitable death. This sense represents a compelling, universal urge to maintain an inner sense of continuity and a quest for symbolic relationship to what has been before and what will continue after our finite individual existence. The striving for a sense of immortality is in itself neither compensatory nor irrational, writes Lifton, but an "appropriate symbolization of our biological and historical connectedness" (p. 17).

Lifton enumerates five modes of symbolic immortality. The biological mode is the sense of living on through, and in an emotional sense *with,* or *in,* one's sons and daughters and their sons and daughters, or in one's tribe, organization, people, etc. The theological mode is experienced both in the ideas concerning life after death and in the more general principle of the spiritual conquest of death. The third mode is that achieved through man's works (e.g., arts, thought, institutions). The fourth mode is the "natural" mode, the sense that we shall live on in the limitless natural elements. Finally, there is the mode of experiential transcendence, similar to what Freud referred to as "oceanic feeling" (see also Lifton, 1969). It must be stressed that the modes of symbolic immortality are not only problems pondered when one is dying (man's "ultimate concerns," in Lifton's terminology); they are rather constantly perceived (albeit often unconsciously) inner standards by which we evaluate our lives and maintain the feelings of connection, meaning, and movement so necessary to *everyday* psychological existence (man's "proximate concerns"). When an individual loses his sense of immortality, his everyday functioning is impaired, due to diminished vitality and the anxiety associated with death and death-equivalents: separation, stasis, and disintegration.

Because man is a "cultural animal," individual modes of symbolic immortality are embraced by collective symbolizations. This is why periods of historical dislocation, in which human beings have special difficulties in finding symbolic forms within which to locate themselves, engender death anxiety among individual members of the society. Whether or not their corporeal existence was threatened by events that accompanied the dislocation, it is the *desymbolization*—the collapse of the symbolic universe that endows life with meaning—that impairs people's sense of self-continuity as well as their concrete connections to life.[2] To escape their symbolic death, their agonizing death-in-life existence, "survivors" of a symbolic extinction react in a variety of ways (see Lifton, 1980), one of which is a fervent quest for and adoption of new symbolic systems that can replace the defunct immortalizing vehicle.

Such new systems frequently take on the form of ideological totalism, characterized by an all-or-nothing claim to truth, a conviction that there is only one valid mode of being and only one authentic avenue to immortality. Totalistic programs offer an immediate and simplistic

---

[2]It must be stressed that threats of physical death do not necessarily lead to desymbolization. Although I, as a post-Auschwitz Jew, am far from belittling the horrors of mass extermination, it must be remembered that quite a few Jewish Holocaust survivors remained firm and steadfast in their religious faith. Conversely, periods of rampant prosperity are often characterized by desymbolization accompanied by much human suffering, as is known at least since Durkheim's *Le Suicide*. To be sure, that prolonged corporeal suffering can lead to impairment of one's sense of immortality cannot be ruled out; yet it is not the physical factor per se, but one's reaction to and interpretation of it, that causes the impairment. For further discussions of this subject, see, for instance, Frankl, 1962; Cohen and Taylor, 1972; Hazani, in press.

once-and-for-all resolution of problems, so as to eliminate unbearable ambiguities. They seek to cancel the flow and change of time in order to restore the lost security of the past. But this restoration is rarely achieved: Beneath the surface, death anxiety lurks. Hence, totalistic systems are tight and intolerant: If the hermetic enclosure of the immortality vehicle is breached, it will be swamped by the surrounding death anxiety. Man's totalistic response to the impairment of his sense of immortality, then, is a combination of hope and despair, dogmatic faith and fear of extinction.

According to Lifton, it is a short step from totalism to victimization. The conviction that there is only one authentic way to salvation, coupled with the either/or quality of totalism, leads to a distinction between the true believers and the damned. Moreover, the claim to ultimate virtue requires a contrasting image of absolute evil. A death-tainted group is created, against which the faithful contrast their claim to immortality, and which they victimize in order to displace their sense of threat onto that embodiment of evil. Victimization may take the form of extreme violence, but it can also be mild or metaphorical. In all its varieties, however, it serves the same function: to help survivors of symbolic death regain their sense of immortality by displacing their own death anxiety onto a scapegoat. To put it another way, the survivors turn from self-imagined victims into victimizers.

In sum, Lifton presents a sequence of dislocation-totalism-victimization. Although this sequence is not unknown from history, Lifton's contribution is that he accounts for the connection between the different stages in terms of his paradigm of symbolic immortality, a paradigm that applies as well to the phenomenon of survivors-victimizers. It remains a puzzle, however, why some survivors choose to immolate themselves along with the embodiment of evil (i.e., resort to suicidal terrorism). Solving this enigma requires that we depart from Lifton's depiction of the survivors' inner world.

AN ISRAELI SCENE: IMMIGRANTS IN THE VALLEY OF THE SHADOW OF DEATH

During the 1950s, hundreds of thousands of Jews from North African and Middle Eastern countries (Sephardic Jews) immigrated to Israel. Members of cohesive extended families, these God-fearing immigrants were imbued with a Jewish traditional symbolization that provided them with a strong sense of immortality through a tightly knit combination of

the biological and the theological modes. Under the impact of Israeli/
Western culture, however, quite a few suffered desymbolization, lost
their sense of immortality, and became "survivors" of a symbolic
extinction, so to speak. Their situation was further aggravated by the
intervention of powerful bureaucracies run by veteran, mostly nonreli-
gious, Ashkenazim (Israelis whose origins were in Western countries),
who attempted to erase the Sephardic immigrants' "primitive" culture
and create a "new Jew" overnight.[3]

The Group Level: Disorganized Victimization

I have been studying Israeli Sephardic urban slums since the 1960s. One
of my major and recurrent findings was that dislocated neighborhoods
were permeated by a complex network of mutual "microvictimizations,"
which governed practically all aspects of social relations. Each person
was at once victim and victimizer, threatened by all and threatening all,
in a tortuous web of fear relations. Most agonizingly, people had no
fixed enemies: today's friend would become tomorrow's enemy—real or
imaginary—and vice versa; and occasionally imagination would become
reality, just like self-fulfilling prophecies. The fluidity and uncertainty
were the most tormenting aspect of life in the slum; as one slum dweller
put it, "I fear no enemy, if he faces me; but when *they* hide in the
shadows, I tremble" [italics mine]. When asked who "they" were, he said,
"I don't know, this is what drives me crazy." Because of the shifting
nature of the situation and the rarity of stable social associations, this
condition is here called a state of *disorganized victimization*. It is distinct
from *organized victimization,* in which fear, hostility, and aggression are
binary, existing between two defined and durable social entities.

The Level of the Individual: A Triad of Sentences

On the level of the individual, it was found that the immigrants-survivors
perceived themselves not only as victims, but also as aggressors. Unlike
the survivors Lifton (1967) describes, who fancied that "He (they, it)
wants to kill me" (p. 514), the Israeli subjects sustained three sentences:

---

[3]On Sephardic Jews and their traditional symbolization, see Hazani and Ilan (1970); see
   also Goldberg (1987). For the acculturation shock that befell Sephardic immigrants to
   Israel, see Hazani and Ilan (1971); Lissak and Ronel (1984).

"They want to kill (hurt) me"; "I want to kill (hurt) them"; and, most important, "I want to kill (hurt) me."

These sentences typified three types of slum-dwellers. The "they want to hurt me" type was the most common. Apprehensive and suspicious of the surrounding world, members of this category were convinced that "they" — whether fellow slum-dwellers or powerful Ashkenazic bureaucracies — wanted to destroy them. Law-abiding, apathetic, and submissive, they grieved for their lost religious tradition and viewed themselves as orphans. Some voiced a desire "to disappear," an Israeli slum slang word that connotes both "to kill" and "to be killed or die". Occasionally, however, they would explode in fits of rage, destroying whatever stood in their way. This would often end in self-injurious behavior, such as knocking their heads against a wall until the blood flowed. They also threatened to commit suicide; the threats were intended to take revenge on "the enemy" by manipulating the latter's guilt feelings (cf. Baechler, 1979; Chidester, 1988; Leenaars, 1988). There were few actual suicides, however, as is universally the case among lower class people (Henry and Short, 1954).

Then there was the "I want to hurt them" type. A violent delinquent confessed: "If I don't fight, I'll go crazy; I'll break everything and run away, far away." Yet his aggression was directed not only toward other people but also toward himself. Once we were sitting in a neighborhood bar when three policemen entered. He began to curse them. They asked him to leave them alone, but he escalated his verbal attacks and finally assaulted the policemen physically. The short fight ended with his being beaten and detained for 24 hours. The policemen, who knew the youth, said that he habitually challenged them until he was beaten; "He leaves us no choice, even though we don't want to hit him." Part of his *kef* (Israeli slang word for fun, which the delinquent used) was being victimized; but he also enjoyed victimizing others and amassed more than 20 convictions for assaultive behavior. This youth was representative of the "I want to hurt them" type, who exhibited indirect self-injurious behavior (i.e., behavior that is bound to provoke an aggressive reaction by another). For this type, Menninger's statement (1938) that suicide involves the wish to kill, the wish to be killed, and the wish to die, can be reversed: in some instances, homicide (or violent behavior) involves the wish to be killed (or victimized), the wish to kill (or victimize) and the wish to die.

Women of this type resorted to nonphysical kinds of victimization. Gossip served for the magical destruction of the enemy: women would often say "we killed him (her) in words." Another form of victimization was to publicly ignore people who addressed them, or deliberately withhold help from those who needed it. Yet women also burst out in fits of rage: respectable women would then use filthy language or fight with their neighbors, often plucking out one another's hair and skin, but feeling no pain in their ecstasy.

Finally, there was the "I want to hurt me" type. As noted, the number of actual suicides was small, but parasuicides (self-inflicted injuries), symbolic suicides (e.g., dreams of suicide), hidden suicides (e.g., accident proneness, risk-taking), and chronic suicides (e.g., drug-addiction, alcoholism) were common, sometimes in combination with one another. A promiscuous 17-year-old girl who underwent five abortions and cut her wrists twice said she loved the beach — not because of the boys, as I initially thought, but because "in the winter you are there all alone, and you can swim as far as you want and *disappear*" [italics mine]. She also said that she did not enjoy sex and became pregnant in the hope that an abortion would kill her. Her aggression was outward as well: she had a habit of breaking the necks of chickens.

Prostitutes, practically all of whom were extremely lonely drug addicts, were the most pronounced "I want to hurt me" group. Although some believed that "some day" their pimp would marry them, in moments of truth all confessed that they were hopelessly destroying themselves.[4] Men, too, exhibited self-destructive behavior: aggressive delinquents often cut their wrists; when asked if they wanted to commit suicide, some said that they "don't know." Chronic suicides were also common: drug users and alcoholics said that they were "convicted" (in Israeli slang, "convicted" means doomed to remain forever in an extremely unpleasant situation).

The Three-Faceted Single Sentence

On the face of it, each of these three types represents a single sentence, either "they want to hurt me" or "I want to hurt them" or "I want to hurt me"; yet this was clearly not the case. Although they differed in their overt behavior, all three types were similar in that they harbored the "I want to kill (hurt) me" sentence in their psyche; the other two sentences were derivatives of this one, desperate attempts to escape self-destruction

---

[4]For alcoholism as a result of cultural breakdown, see Horton, 1943; for alcoholism as chronic suicide, see Snyder, 1964. On "death-in-life" of prostitutes, see Hazani, 1989.

by adopting the identity of victim ("They want to hurt me") or aggressor ("I want to hurt them").[5]

Ultra-Orthodox and Ultranationalistic Totalism

Some of the "survivors" among these dislocated Sephardim responded to the impairment of their sense of immortality by adopting totalistic ideologies, of which two are worth mentioning. One was a return to Jewish religious observance, but to a version that was far from the traditional tolerant Sephardic Judaism. In fact, the penitents did not *return* to religion, but underwent a revolutionary "conversion" to militant and dogmatic Ashkenazic ultra-Orthodoxy, previously unknown to them. The "revolutionary converts" included also hardened criminals, who said they were reborn. The other totalistic ideology was that of the ultranationalistic, racist, and militant Kach movement, which also exhibits totalistic traits. These "converts," too, said that the new ideology revived them. Although the two ideologies differ in content—the Kach movement is not necessarily religious, and Israeli ultra-Orthodoxy is not nationalistic—both view their adherents as sons of light and define their enemies as sons of darkness. Of course, not all ultra-Orthodox penitents or Kach members came from the slums; the point I want to make here is only that some—though by no means all—dislocated immigrants overcame their wretchedness and experienced rebirth by adopting totalistic ideologies.[6]

My observations in Israel tend to agree with Lifton's sequence of dislocation-totalism-victimization; yet they show that the sequence should be expanded to include a stage of disorganized victimization, to cover the social state that precedes totalism. The sequence that emerges, then, is dislocation-disorganized victimization-totalism-organized victimization (which will be discussed further on). My observations also show that the deviant behaviors that characterize the stage of disorganized victimization are often variations on a single theme, the survivors' wish for self-destruction.

---

[5]It must be noted, however, that quite a few immigrants preserved their traditional symbolization and did not sink into self-destructiveness, even though they were as physically deprived as their fellows. There were also "partially" dislocated individuals.

[6]Quite a few Kach members are middle-class American Jewish youths, who immigrated to Israel "to find themselves." My acquaintance with these youths disclosed that some had been symbolically uprooted prior to their immigration.

DESYMBOLIZATION
AND SELF-DESTRUCTIVENESS —
A UNIVERSAL PHENOMENON

An examination of other times, places, and cultural contexts reveals that the foregoing sequence is universal, and, as just noted, includes a stage marked by self-destructive behavior. Two instances will suffice here:

Students of the desymbolization suffered by non-Western[7] societies under the impact of the West report that "the results have often been devastating apathy in which native behavior and native sentiments are simply dead" (Keesing and Keesing, 1971; see also Berry, 1980). This may lead to depopulation, as was the case among American Indians (Wilson, 1973; Russell, 1986). But often people are not entirely apathetic: crime rates rise sharply, particularly in urban areas, where desymbolization is most severe (Clinard and Abott, 1973). Suicides are relatively rare, but homicides are common (Rahav, 1990). Yet homicides often turn out to be indirect suicides, provoked by a person who indirectly serves as his own executioner. Despite the low rate of actual suicides, nonlethal suicidal behavior is common, as attested to by the high rate of victimless crimes (alcoholism, drug addiction, prostitution, etc.). The term "victimless" is misleading, of course, because a victim always exists — the individual who destroys himself as a result of a cultural breakdown, embodying the "I want to kill (hurt) me" sentence.

On the group level, a stage of "cultural distortion" often ensues, similar to what I have called "disorganized victimization." This stage may be followed by revitalization movements, which offer a new symbolic synthesis and thereby infuse people with a sense of immortality, as well as a promise of tribal and national renascence. The movements are often totalistic in nature, and exhibit ideologically articulated hostility toward in-group "traitors" and out-group "national enemies" (Wallace, 1956, 1961, 1966). Sometimes they laud martyrdom.[8]

The second instance is drawn from an utterly different milieu — the disintegrating Austro-Hungarian Empire. After the humiliating defeat at the hands of Prussia (1866) and a devastating financial panic (1873), the Habsburg capital, invaded by masses of uprooted migrants of different

---

[7] I use the broad term "non-Western" to encompass all the terms different writers employ, such as "developing countries," "Third World countries," "primitive peoples," "traditional societies," "tribal peoples/societies," etc., all of which bear connotations that are irrelevant to my present concern.

[8] The uprising against the British in late 19th-century Sudan, led by a charismatic Mahdi, is a well-known instance of a holy war that praised martyrdom.

nationalities, cultures, and religions, underwent prolonged and deepening desymbolization. Deviance increased, and society was pervaded by interpersonal and intergroup tensions, mistrust, and hostility. An insight into the inner world of dislocated individuals, members of deprived minorities as well as of the highest nobility, is offered by Bettelheim (1991). The empire was epitomized by the heir apparent, Crown Prince Rudolph, who climaxed a sexual episode by killing both his mistress and himself. Things had never been better, writes Bettelheim, but they had never been worse: It was the era of Strauss' *The Blue Danube,* but also of Egon Schiele's *Death and Girl,* a morbid painting that anticipated World War I. Artists, whom Ezra Pound calls "the antennae of the world," sensed the atmosphere of death and dissolution and depicted it in their works, such as Roth's *Die Kapuzinergruft;* indeed, although politically still alive, symbolically the Habsburg world was already in the *Gruft.* It was in this Vienna, "the test station for the end of the world," that the future Führer of the most monstrous totalistic movement in history arrived in 1907.

Other instances can be cited, some associated with major historic events. Their message is conveyed by Sergei Kapitza (1991), the Russian scientist who writes on the desymbolization taking place in the empire once known as the USSR. "Gone is the grand concept of a socialist revolution. . . . We see the collapse of [the Marxist] system. . . . This is the ultimate reason for our crisis" and views it in a universal context. As he shows, ideological breakdowns in history never passed without "personal uneasiness, frustration and loss of purpose." They spawned "extreme social ideas" and victimization, as well as a "regression into mythology" and "expectation of rapid change, a miracle offering deliverance from all ills through the magic of a new creed" (pp. 18–20).

Kapitza's remarks, which he buttresses by many examples of what he calls "social aberrations," clearly underscore the universality of the phenomenon. Yet there is a problem with historical case studies: they teach us of people's inner worlds only through inference from behavior. Hence we must supplement them with studies of a different kind.

Holocaust Survivors as Victims-Aggressors

The literature on Holocaust survivors describes the "survivor syndrome." Symptoms include apathy and hopelessness, loss of alertness to survival possibilities, emptiness, constant fear of renewed persecution, a tendency to withdraw, death anxiety, numbing and closing off of affects, and automatized functioning. All of this recalls Lifton's description of persons with an impaired sense of immortality. Quite a few Holocaust survivors displayed suppressed aggression and hostility turned against the self, the latter often in the form of self-reproach and self-punishment (see, e.g., Niederland, 1968; Krystal, 1978; Grubrich-Simits, 1981). "In many case histories," writes Bergmann (1982), "splitting of the self . . . became manifest: [the survivors] at times identified with Nazi ideology but also condemned it" (p. 294). Eckstaedt (1982) found that some victims "suffered from conflicts based on simultaneous identification with both the persecuted and the persecutors" (p. 224) and transmitted these conflicts to their children. Survivor-parents often transmitted to their offspring their attitudes toward the world and themselves, and the victim-and-executioner scenario was kept alive within their families (Trossman, 1968; Axelrod, Schnipper, and Rau, 1980).

Of special interest is a recent Israeli study (Lieder, Cilfen, Mikulincer, and Wolf, 1988) that found that a "most conspicuous ambivalent combination" was created by the fact that "two poles, victimhood and aggression, were simultaneously present within the psyches of some Israeli Holocaust survivors" (p. 56). Furthermore, some sons of Holocaust survivors were found to be apprehensive of an ever-present aggressor and at the same time to be suppressing their own aggression; that is, the aggressor-victim "combination," characteristic of survivor-fathers, was mirrored in their sons.[9] Lieder (1991) also observed overt "I want to hurt me" behavior among sons of Holocaust survivors: in her work in an Israeli jail, she realized that such youth were overrepresented among imprisoned delinquents; moreover, they were overrepresented among fellow incarcerated drug-users. That is, not only were sons of Holocaust survivors imprisoned for criminal behavior—comparatively rare among Israeli Ashkenazic youth—but they also tended to indulge in behavior they knew was self-destructive.[10]

---

[9]The "mirroring" described independently by Eckstaedt, Trossman, Axelrod et al., and Lieder et al. concurs with my observation in Israeli slums that one person's aggressor-victim "combination" was mirrored in his neighbor's victim-aggressor "combination," thereby generating the network of mutual microvictimizations.

[10]One should not infer from this remark about the Israeli prison population that Ashkenazic youths respect the law more than Sephardic ones do. Israeli criminologists quarrel on this issue: whereas some hold that arrests reflect reality, others contend that they do not, because the police deliberately ignores the misbehavior of middle-class Ashkenazic youth. Whatever the case, this controversy hardly affects my discussion, for sons of Holocaust survivors (i.e., Ashkenazic boys) were found to be overrepresented among *Ashkenazic* incarcerated youths.

Although there are no data concerning totalistic tendencies among Holocaust survivors, there are some findings concerning their "readiness to do evil." To cite only one study: Charny (1990) found that Israeli Holocaust survivors (and children of survivors) approved or rationalized a 1956 massacre of Arabs by Jews more than did other Israelis (46% versus 26%).

The presence of an aggressor within the psyche of some Holocaust survivors is tersely put by Ka-Tzetnick, an Israeli author and Holocaust survivor who, after many years of treatment aimed at alleviating his suffering, said on Israeli television (May 30, 1988), "I met my tormentor, and my tormentor is in me, for there is a Nazi in me as well."

Desymbolization, Divided Selves, and Suicides

How can one account for the phenomenon of victims who are at the same time aggressors? Some (e.g., Bergmann, 1982; Eckstaedt, 1982) explain this in terms of identification with the aggressor. Although identification with the aggressor certainly takes place, it seems too narrow a concept to account for instances in which there is no aggressor (unless the word "aggressor" is stretched so far as to become empty). For instance, the Jewish *Haskalah* (enlightenment) movement in 19th-century Eastern Europe involved a process of secularization that was greeted by many as liberation from superstitious religion as well as redemption from the stifling ambience of the Ghetto. Nonetheless, youths who optimistically abandoned the faith of their fathers later experienced death anxiety and came to harbor the aggressor-victim double; some committed suicide (see Hazani, in press). I embrace the view advanced first by James (1902) and later, more sweepingly, by Jung and others (Jung, 1938; see also Jung and Kerenyi, 1949; Fromm, 1950; Radin, 1956), that religion—or any symbolization, for that matter—is essential for the synthesis of opposing complexes in the psychic life and for achieving integration. Conversely, desymbolization can engender disintegration, or internal splitting.

Whichever of these two theoretical perspective one prefers—the two are not mutually exclusive—a "divided self" is "a battle-ground for what [the subject] feels to be two deadly hostile selves." This results in "self-loathing; self-despair; an unintelligible and intolerable burden. . . . Suicide [is] naturally the consistent course dictated by logical intellect" (James, 1902, pp. 176, 162). As Meissner (1986) puts it:

the victim is the recipient of destructive aggression. The aggression, however, is the subject's own. . . . He is the victim of an internal persecutor, an alien and destructive inner presence, the hidden executioner. The conflict between the passive suicide victim and the destructive persecutor-executioner is an inherent aspect of every suicidal process [pp. 321-322].

Maltsberger and Buie (1980) write in a similar vein: "The hating introject . . . calls out for the execution of an evil self. From life, a desert of intolerable loneliness and helplessness . . . [man] turns to death in flight from inner persecutors, in quest of rebirth. . . . It is the paradox of suicide that the victim, finding inner death in life, seeks inner life in dying" (p. 68).

It is a manifestation of human strength, however, that most survivors do not turn to death, but cling to their existence, wretched as it may be. And wretched indeed it is, for unlike the paranoid patient, they cannot create a delusional pseudocommunity onto which to project the internal executioner and rid themselves of the deadly quarrel between the two hostile selves. They are doomed to remain in the stage of "preliminary hypotheses" (Cameron, 1959), perceiving themselves as intermittently threatened by all — family or friends or neighbors (or Jews or communists or capitalists or blacks or the Klan or the CIA) — an endless series of demons who lurk everywhere, shifting representations of their inner persecutor. The result is incessant mutual hostility, the network of microvictimizations that torture the survivors from without, while they are continually tortured from within by self-hatred and self-destructiveness. Ironically, it is their basic sanity that deprives survivors of the paranoid system of what helps the paranoiac come to terms with himself and his social milieu; their misery, however, can be greatly reduced by the adoption of totalistic ideologies.

TOTALISM, PURIFICATION, AND ASCENT TO HEAVEN

There are a number of reasons why totalistic ideologies are successful in extricating survivors from the valley of the shadow of death. First, totalistic systems tend to explain all aspects of reality in terms of a single, simplistic formula; this offers the faithful a steady anchor, freeing them from ambiguities and reducing insecurity. Second, many systems manage to conquer death, in a variety of ways; this mitigates death anxiety and makes life bearable, as De Wind (1968) observed: "Sometimes the belief in an existence after death modifies anxiety" (p. 304).[11]

On the level of Lifton's "proximate concerns," totalistic systems preach discipline, abstinence, and asceticism, while endowing them with ultimate meanings. This transforms meaningless and lonely subsuicidal existence into ideologically praised self-sacrifice, practiced in revered social institutions, and revitalizes the daily functioning of both individual and society.

Totalistic Systems as Functional Equivalents of the Paranoid System

For all the significance of the previously listed factors, the efficacy of totalistic systems derives mainly from the fact that they are functionally equivalent to the paranoid system in that they serve as a defense against underlying suicidal impulses. To explain this, a crucial characteristic of totalism must be spelled out.

Totalistic ideologies profess a Manichaean view of the universe; as Lebra (1972) put it, "everything seen, heard or otherwise experienced can be placed on the binary map" (p. 199).[12] More precisely, in the totalistic-dichotomizing mind, there is no Light without Darkness, no Good without Evil, no God without Satan, no Christ without Antichrist. Moreover, Light and Good (as well as Darkness and Evil) owe their existence, ontologically, to their opposites, because the world is perceived not as a world of things, but of tension between opposites, which exist only as long as they counter each other.

Equipped with the "binary map," the survivor-convert, *in communion*

---

[11]Note, however, that the conquest of death does not necessarily involve a belief in afterlife. For instance, secular systems offer the faithful eternity in the memory of the people, a place in the national pantheon, as the French revolutionaries literally did. Apocalyptic systems, both theistic and nontheistic, tend to deny even physical death by holding that all will perish except for the chosen ones; sometimes they rely on "miracles," not necessarily religious, as Hitler did in 1945 when he heard that Roosevelt had died. Some ideologies distinguish between "ordinary" and "holy" death, promising those who died in a "holy" way a unique transcendental status (and so encourage martyrdom).

[12]The tendency of totalism to dichotomize the world has been noted by many, ranging from students of ancient groups (Licht, 1961) to investigators of modern terrorism (Post, 1990). Of special interest is Jung's (1959) discussion of the Antichrist as the mirror image of Christ, and his view that in archetypal imagery Christ and the Antichrist together make up the unity of the self. It should be noted that some ideologies employ not a simple dichotomy, but rather an elaborate system of classification, like the Nazi hierarchy of races. Even then, however, it is the two opposite poles — "us" versus "them" — which is the most salient.

with his fellows, splits out the internal aggressor-victim double and projects either the aggressor or the victim onto an external anticommunity. The latter is not a delusional pseudocommunity but a real one, because it is so perceived by the collectivity of believers. The point of shared perceptions is crucial: as many phenomenologists (e.g., Berger and Luckmann, 1966) argue, whatever is *intersubjectively defined* as real, *is* real, whether or not it "objectively" exists in the "outside" world. To put it in the technical terms of phenomenology, there is no reality but that which is *socially constructed,* and there is no world but that which is collectively defined. Although some quarrel with this extreme stance,[13] it must be conceded that, at the very least, socially constructed realities cannot be considered delusional. Thus, the intersubjective view of a polarized world — "us" versus "them" — enables sane people to do what they were unable to do before: to project one of their quarreling inner presences onto an external "real" anticommunity and thereby rid themselves of tormenting inner conflict. Self-destructive impulses thus subside, and the survivor-converts experience rebirth.

Note that the black-and-white view of the world leads to revitalization not only "negatively" (i.e., by mitigating suicidal impulses), but also "positively": even as the faithful place the anticommunity on the dark side of the binary map, they place themselves on its bright side. But because Manichaeism holds that whatever is bright, is *absolutely* bright, they consider themselves pure and chaste, worthy of reconnecting themselves to a sublime source of vitality.

As noted, the faithful can externalize either the aggressor or the victim content onto a presence in the outside world, and retain for themselves either the victim or the aggressor identity. This highlights where the present discussion differs from Lifton's view of the survivors' inner world. Lifton holds that survivors harbor the victim identity, which they displace onto a scapegoat to overcome their sense of threat, and move from victimized to victimizers.[14] This discussion claims that survivors harbor both the victim *and* the aggressor identities, and that it is the splitting out and externalization, not change of identities, that helps survivors reassert their life-power. In my opinion, then, survivors move

---

[13]For the problems inherent in this view, see the debate between Winch (1970) and Lukes (1970).

[14]To an extent, this does injustice to Lifton who, in his discussion of survivors' paranoia (1967), is fully aware of their aggression, citing Ovesey's (1955) view concerning the "power motivation" in paranoia. But in presenting his argument concerning survivors who become victimizers (1979), he depicts them solely as victims.

not from victimized to victimizers, but from victimized-victimizers to either victimizers or victimized.

Strange as the voluntary adoption of the victim identity may seem, it should be recalled that perceiving oneself as persecuted is preferable to harboring the deadly inner aggressor-victim double. This is demonstrated by the fact that quite a few historical groups of "survivors"—for example, the Dead Sea Sect and the Anabaptists (Flusser, 1954; Bainton, 1953; Williams, 1962)—"chose" to perceive themselves as victims while almost enthusiastically defining external persecutors. The instances of self-defined victims are inexplicable in Lifton's terms; yet once it is realized that totalistic dualism is functionally equivalent to a paranoid defense, it is no longer a paradox that some people may experience rebirth by perceiving themselves as constantly persecuted. This may account for the frequent emergence of avoidance (usually "victimized") groups alongside aggressive ones in the wake of historical dislocations — a known phenomenon (see Yinger, 1970; Hall, 1982).

The Group Level

Totalistic ideologies are beneficial on the group level as well. Whichever identity the faithful retain, aggressor or victim, hostility becomes binary, directed toward the external hate object; the intrasocietal network of mutual microvictimizations diminishes and a degree of social organization is achieved. Disorganized victimization is thus transformed into *organized* victimization, that is, concerted and coordinated social action, carried out within the framework of appropriate social institutions.[15] Individual suffering, resulting from the close and daily interaction with

---

[15]Organized *self*-victimization may be so subtle that at times it is hardly discernible, particularly so when no persecutor seems to exist. For instance, ascetic Christians who emulate the sorrows of their crucified Lord do not necessarily define concrete external foes; but in fact there are such—those who victimized Christ in the past. Moreover, some ascetics hold that God is honored by their self-inflicted suffering; that is God is a savior and a victimizer at the same time (see James, 1902). Ascetic Jews hold a similar view, saying that their stringent practices are required by God "to purify" them; that is, they chastise themselves while elevating their internal purger-aggressor to the status of God, who is also their source of life. It must be stressed that these two instances of asceticism, like *all the instances of totalism cited in this chapter,* followed historical dislocations. The austere 12th-century monastic reform in Christendom, for example, was associated with what some call the "proto-Renaissance," and the rise of Jewish ascetic ultra-Orthodoxy was a response to the secularization crisis brought about by the *Haskalah* (enlightenment) movement.

friends-foes, is alleviated, as people no longer exist in the insecure stage of preliminary hypotheses. The rediscovery of family or friendship makes people feel alive again; as one slum-dweller put it, quoting a Talmudic adage: "Either society or death" (i.e., either warm connections to other humans or death, literally). In Lifton's terminology, he spoke of regaining a sense of immortality through the biological/social mode.

Thus, with regard to both their inner world and to their relationships with their fellow people, with regard both to their ultimate and proximate concerns, the survivor-converts achieve relative tranquility. Just like the paranoiac, though, they pay for this by *being forced to maintain a persecutory bond with an anticommunity of enemies.* This explains the findings of Post (1990) that terrorists, many of whom were found to contain unintegrated "good" and "bad" parts, are threatened by their own success: if they succeed in destroying the external enemy, their inner devils rise to the surface and threaten to annihilate their "hosts" from within. To avoid this, terrorists become conflict seekers, or "warfare personalities" (Tucker, 1973). For the same reason, self-defined victims may become "persecution seekers" who always need a victimizer; some may even provoke an external agency to constantly threaten them.

History nevertheless includes some totalistic groups who managed to establish a *modus vivendi* with the rest of the world. These groups tend to formulate ideologies—often after bitter clashes with reality—that explain, *inter alia,* why the conflict with the sons of darkness is abated or postponed to an unspecified future. They may also find socially acceptable outlets for their aggression or victimhood. In some instances, such a *modus vivendi* has lasted hundreds of years.[16]

Facing Two Enemies

It is, however, rare for totalism to completely rid survivors of the aggressor-victim double. Hence survivor-converts simultaneously face two enemies: an external enemy, defined intersubjectively, and a dormant internal enemy, who can quicken and demand an execution. This explains why death anxiety lurks beneath the surface of seemingly hermetic totalistic systems: it is not the external enemy of whom the

---

[16]The Sikhs, for instance, descendants of a revitalization movement, constitute 10% of the Indian army, although they account for less than 2% of the country's population. Another instance: self-sacrifice is often channeled into serving noble causes, as in a number of monastic orders.

faithful are apprehensive, but the enemy within, who constantly seeks their destruction.[17]

This accounts for several seemingly paradoxical historic phenomena. For instance, many Nazis, while exterminating helpless Jews, viewed themselves as threatened by their victims, sincerely believing that the Jews had stabbed Germany in the back in 1918. Moreover, some Germans were — and still are (Wistrich, 1989) — awed by the myth of the "eternal Jew" (and his sexual potency). Another phenomenon is the "interchangeability" (or affinity) between aggression and quietism, which is not uncommon among groups of "true believers" (Hoffer, 1951; Yinger, 1970; Hall, 1982).

Even when there is no interchangeability, a residual victim can be discerned beneath the aggressiveness of some groups — such as the violent English Fifth Monarchists, who declared they were willing to die unarmed. Similarly, there is a residual aggressor lurking beneath the self-victimization of other groups — such as the pacifist Unity of Brethren, whose battle hymns betray their descent from the militant Taborites (Capp, 1972; Hill, 1972; Segert, 1955; Kaminsky, 1967). It has also been observed (Clark, 1949) that some groups exhibit a clear mixture of aggression and victimhood.[18] All of these cases indicate that survivors-converts rarely become "pure" victims or aggressors; often they continue to harbor the aggressor-victim double in their psyche, although in an "asymmetrical" and much less menacing form. This is not to discount the role of totalistic systems in spawning individual and collective renascence; it only points out the incompleteness and fragility of this renascence.

Sometimes, indeed, totalistic symbolizations fail: for example, in the

---

[17]The fact that people may simultaneously face two enemies, internal and external, is strongly hinted by data concerning murder-suicides. For instance, 34% of the murderers and suspected murderers in England in 1949 committed suicide (Henry and Short, 1954); see also the data of West (1965). Baechler (1979) observes that "hatred against himself and hatred toward the other person" are closely linked (p. 114), and Murray (1967) characterizes the suicidal personality as exhibiting both extra- *and* intrapunitiveness. For the two enemies in paranoia, see Bak (1946).

[18]Two Israeli instances are worth mentioning: First, the aggressive, ultranationalistic Kach movement, which is in favor of victimizing the Palestinians and fears the latter militarily, politically, and socially (sexually). A group of Kach youths threatened to commit a protest suicide against the Israeli withdrawal from the Sinai Peninsula in 1982. Although some dismiss this episode as mere rhetoric, the fact remains that the images involved were of self-annihilation. Second, Israeli ultra-Orthodox groups, who perceive themselves as victimized by the wider society, often exhibit aggressive behavior toward non-Orthodox Israelis. As ascetics, they also victimize themselves, very much like the Dead Sea Sect (see Liebes, 1982).

formative stage of totalistic movements, when no coherent idea system has yet been crystalized; or when old systems fail to cope with new historical realities; or because of intragroup or leaders' intrapsychic processes. Then the dormant aggressor-victim double awakens. At one pole is the persecutory bond with the ideologically defined external enemy, who must now be demonized more than ever if the faithful would externalize the powerful forces of self-destruction that threaten to swamp them. At the other pole, the internal judge-executioner calls for the annihilation of the internal evil-doer. Facing enemies without and within, whose manace is now all too tangible, the faithful become potential homicidal suicides.

From Potential to Actual Homicidal Suicides

Our theory does not explain why and under what conditions individuals develop from potential to actual homicidal suicides. Every historical event is unique, affected by situational factors, cultural context, type of leadership, the personalities of the participants, and other variables that defy generalization. To cite one instance: although the theory could foresee the emergence of potential suicidal murderousness among the survivors-converts in Jonestown,[19] it could not predict what would actually happen. To do this, Jim Jones' personality would have had to be included in the equation; but his mercurial moods made prediction virtually impossible, as did the group processes that unfolded in the isolated community. Moreover, external factors seem to have played a major role in the tragedy. As Naipul (1980) argues, "Concerned Relatives" share some responsibility for the final denouement: they knew about the "white nights" of suicide rehearsals, yet insisted on a spectacular expedition led by a congressman, which would put Jones' back to the wall. But the theory does not encompass external factors.

Nevertheless, some observations can be made about factors that may facilitate the movement from potential to actual homicidal suicides. First, when ultimate truths fail, believers often entrench themselves in their faith more desperately then ever, to ward off doubts and

---

[19]The biographies of many of the Jonestown sect members indicated that they were wretched "survivors" of a symbolic breakdown who experienced renewed vitality in the People's Temple. As Guy Young (1978), whose wife, four daughters, son, and two grandchildren were among the suicides, said: "I don't regret one moment that they were [with Jim Jones]. That was the most happy and most rewarding days of their lives" (p. 11).

ambivalence.[20] This is particularly so when the circumstances are such that doubts mean a return to a tortured, death-in-life existence in a symbolic wasteland — a prospect that horrifies the true believer, who once experienced rebirth. The utmost profession of faith, however, is one's willingness to die for it, or sacrifice others in its name.[21] By destroying themselves together with the enemy, true believers reaffirm their faith and connect themselves anew to a source of symbolic immortality; at the same time, they also flee everyday agonies (i.e., they cater to their "proximate concerns"). Second, in times of profound perplexity, the search for once-and-for-all resolution of dilemmas, typical of totalism, induces true believers to seek immediate and unequivocal salvation, even in the arms of comfort-giving death.

But the believers cannot leave this world without annihilating the archenemy: this is required by the logic of dualism, according to which things owe their meaning to their antitheses. For the true believers' deaths to be a rebirth, therefore, it is essential that their ascent to heaven be paralleled by the archenemy's descent into hell. More precisely, *it is the latter's descent into hell that defines the former's deaths as ascension.* Thus, the bond that ties true believers to their enemy is not limited to life, but extends to death as well. This seems to explain why the Nazis kept exterminating Jews even when it was clear that Germany had lost World War II. In 1945, so Hitler noted, "ridding" the world of the Jews was a major "achievement" of the war, which therefore was not a total failure: Jewish death made the German *Götterdämmerung* an ascent into Valhalla.[22]

But this is not the whole story. True believers must also send to hell the internal enemy, the evil part of their own selves, so as to be pure enough to ascend to heaven. The internal drama recalls, in a way, the ancient Jewish ritual of the scapegoat, practiced on the Day of Atone-

---

[20]This concurs with the cognitive dissonance theory, yet in the instances I discuss the cognitive dissonance only stirred to life deep unconscious conflicts of a much more agonizing nature. For a discussion of the different "levels" of inconsistency and their meaning to and effect upon the individual, see Katz (1968).

[21]For instance, some of the disciples of Shabbetai Zevi, the Jewish 17th-century false Messiah who converted to Islam, said they were willing to die to prove their faith in their leader, despite his apostasy (Scholem, 1973). The model of sacrificing another individual as the ultimate profession of faith is, of course, Abraham's ordeal with his son, Isaac. Sacrifice as a profession of faith is discussed by Shoham (1979).

[22]Similar attitudes often characterize revenge suicides: the dead are, in fact, hidden aggressors, who seek to morally victimize those accused of provoking the suicide. But by avenging their enemies, they elevate themselves, albeit at the cost of their own lives (cf. Baechler, 1979; Chidester, 1988).

ment in the Temple of Jerusalem. In this annual ritual, the High Priest transferred all the sins of the People of Israel onto a goat which, now "bearing" the "bad" part of every individual Jew, was taken to the wilderness and thrown off a cliff. *The goat's death defined the community as pure, worthy of reaffirming the connection to God, the Jewish source of immortality.* In the internal drama I am analyzing the true believer plays the roles of both High Priest and goat; for the "priest" to be cleansed, it is essential that he destroy the "goat"—which means the death of the "priest" as well.

The true believer's physical death is not an ending, however, but rather a rebirth into a sublime, transcendental existence, a once-and-for-all attainment of immortality.[23] This seems to account for two observed phenomena. First, suicidal true believers often make solemn preparations for their deaths, as if going to participate in a sacred ritual; this was most salient among the Kamikaze, but it is also common among Shi'ite suicidal youths in Lebanon, as reported by their families. Second, a kind of serene joy, often coupled with an other-worldly smile, is sometimes visible on the faces of suicidal homicides prior to their deadly deeds; this astonished Israeli soldiers in Lebanon, as well as U.S. Marines. It seems that before they sacrificed themselves (and their enemies) bodily, the true believers already perceived their spirits as residing in heaven; this is hinted at by letters left by some.

As noted, the movement from potential to actual homicidal suicide is inexplicable using this theory alone, because the elucidation of actual human phenomena requires that knowledge of the particular should be combined with that of the universal. For similar reasons, this theory cannot predict which kind of self- and other-directed aggressive behavior is likely to manifest itself in reality. Whether the true believers are going to engage in suicidal terrorism per se, like Rajiv Gandhi's assassin; whether they are going to adopt the Charlotte Corday or the Masada "style"; whether they belong to the group of the predominantly aggressive Sikhs or to that of the predominantly quietist Anabaptists—this cannot be known without detailed information about the particular actors and the actual context in which they are embedded.

Yet the usefulness of this theory lies in the fact that it spells out the universal preconditions for the emergence of ideologically rationalized

---

[23]In my opinion, the foregoing analysis explains Wahl's (1957) observation that in suicide, "the dead man is conceived [as] . . . capable of transcending time and space" (p. 27). It also explains Baechler's (1979) concept of "transfiguration" through "oblative suicide" (p. 166).

self- and other-victimization. This may help uncover the common denominator underlying seemingly unrelated phenomena, and, if supplemented by data about the particular, may help generate hypotheses concerning future scenarios.[24]

CONCLUDING REMARKS

This chapter outlines a theory of suicidal terrorism in the broad sense of the term, that is, including all the manifestations of self- and other-directed aggression in the name of absolute truth. The core of the argument is that survivors, whose sense of immortality has been impaired, often harbor the deadly aggressor-victim double; that totalistic belief systems are functional equivalents of the paranoid system, and as such rid the survivors of their suicidal impulses; and that failure of the belief system, for whatever reason, may result in a variety of self- and other-destructive behaviors. Thus, suicidal terrorism is a possible outcome of a ruptured, incomplete, or incoherent totalistic system, which, while presenting the survivors with an external enemy, fails to rid them of their internal persecutors.

Does this imply that coherent and articulated totalistic systems do not lead to destructive behavior? Although this seems to be the case, fuller consideration lies beyond the scope of the present chapter, which limits itself to outlining the theory and leaves aside many interesting topics. One of these topics that the chapter has not dwelt on is: What precisely is the "failure" of a totalistic system? Although this process seems to involve a blurring of the binary map of the universe and consequent emergence of painful ambivalences and conflicts, it needs further elucidation.[25] Likewise, the chapter has not stressed that the survivor is not a "defective human mutant . . . intrinsically different from you and me" (Epstein, 1979, p. 177). Yet it is this observation that explains why "cultured" people came to adopt monstrous ideologies—a fact that still puzzles some, while others (e.g., Kuper, 1991) concede that no one is

---

[24]Witnessing the desymbolization that has been taking place among both Palestinians and Israelis, and being acquainted with the local scene, I have been warning since the mid-1970s against a possible clash between Jewish and Moslem fundamentalism (see, for instance, Hazani, 1984). This was prior to the outbreak of the Palestinian *intifada,* which has witnessed instances of homicidal suicides.

[25]Shneidman's (1985) discussion of the ambivalences and internal state of conflict of suicides, coupled with observations of tragic effects of dissonance when life-giving beliefs collapse (see Hazani, 1987), seems to be a point of departure for an analysis of the above process. See also note 20.

resistant to "annihilatory appeals and motivations" (p. xiii) once his sense of immortality has been impaired.

Nothing here should be taken as an espousal of a deterministic view of history that maintains that totalism and victimization are inevitable consequences of historical dislocations. Survivors may regain their sense of immortality and reconnect themselves to life in ways that do not involve human suffering. Klein (1973), for example, describes how Jewish Holocaust survivors who immigrated to Palestine after World War II overcame their distress by experiencing individual and collective rebirth in the establishment of the State of Israel. This is a conspicuous instance of "survivors' creativity," an alternative to totalism (Lifton, 1979; Hazani, in press). Warm acceptance by their Jewish brethren in Israel helped Holocaust survivors overcome their anxiety, as did Remembrance Days, which, while commemorating those who perished, facilitated expressions of mourning and renewed the survivors' sense of national, familial, and individual continuity.

In addition, it should be noted that not all revitalization movements that have overtones of totalism involve victimization. The revitalization of the Iroquois Indians, for instance, was a peaceful one, and despite totalistic characteristics it literally saved the lives of people who were on the verge of extinction (Wallace, 1966). Moreover, even aggressive totalistic movements tend to undergo "routinization," which involves diminished aggressiveness and attainment of relative inner tranquility (Wallace, 1956, 1966).

Totalism is not invariably "bad" or "good," but one possible human response to an impairment of man's sense of immortality—to which there are alternatives. Hence, the present chapter, which advances a theory of suicidal murderousness, also indicates that survivors can regain a sense of immortality and reassert their life-power in peaceful ways. To paraphrase Maltsberger and Buie, it shows that people who experience death in life, may still find inner life in . . . living.

BIBLIOGRAPHY

AXELROD, S., SCHNIPPER, O. L. & RAU, J. H. (1980), Hospitalized offsprings of Holocaust survivors: Problems and dynamics. *Bull. Menn. Clin.,* 44:1-14.

BAECHLER, J. (1979), *Suicides.* Oxford: Basil Blackwell.

BAINTON, R. H. (1953), *The Reformation of the Sixteenth Century.* London: Hodder & Stoughton, pp. 95-109.

BAK, R. (1946), Masochism in paranoia. *Psychoanal. Quart.,* 15:285-301.

BERGER, P. L. & LUCKMANN, Th. (1966), *The Social Construction of Reality.* Harmondsworth, England: Penguin Books, 1971.

BERGMANN, M. V. (1982), Thoughts on superego pathology of survivors and their children. In: *Generations of the Holocaust*, ed. M. S. Bergmann & M. E. Jucovy. New York: Basic Books, pp. 287-309.

BERRY, J. B. (1980), Social and cultural change. In: *Handbook of Cross-Cultural Psychiatry, Vol. 5*, ed. H. C. Triandis & R. W. Brislin. Boston: Allyn & Bacon.

BETTELHEIM, B. (1991), *Freud's Vienna and Other Essays*. New York: Random House.

CAMERON, N. (1959), The paranoid pseudo-community revisited. *Amer. J. Sociol.*, 65:52-58.

CAPP, B. S. (1972), *The Fifth Monarchy Men*. London: Faber & Faber.

CHARNY, I. W. (1990), To commit or not commit to human life: Children of victims and victimizers—all. *Contemp. Family Ther.*, 12:407-426.

CHIDESTER, D. (1988), *Salvation and Suicide*. Bloomington, IN: Indiana University Press.

CLARK, E. T. (1949), *The Small Sects in America*. New York: Abindon-Cokesbury.

CLINARD, M. B. & ABOTT, D. J. (1973), *Crime in Developing Countries*. New York: John Wiley.

COHEN, S. & TAYLOR, L. (1972), *Psychological Survival*. Harmondsworth, England: Penguin Books.

CRUMMEY, R. (1970), *The Old Believers and the World of Antichrist*. Madison, WI: University of Wisconsin Press.

DE WIND, E. (1968), The confrontation with death: Symposium on psychic traumatization through social catastrophe. *Internat. J. Psycho-Anal.*, 49:302-305.

ECKSTAEDT, A. (1982), A victim of the other side. In: *Generations of the Holocaust*, ed. M. S. Bergmann & M. E. Jucovy. New York: Basic Books, pp. 197-227.

EPSTEIN, H. (1979), *Children of the Holocaust: Conversations with Sons and Daughters of Survivors*. New York: G. P. Putnam.

FLUSSSER, D. (1954), The Judean Desert Sect and its views. *Zion*, 19:89-103 [Hebrew].

FRANKL, V. E. (1962), *Man's Search for Meaning*. Boston: Beacon Press.

FROMM, E. (1950), *Psychoanalysis and Religion*. New Haven, CT: Yale University Press.

_____ (1973), *The Anatomy of Human Destructiveness*. New York: Holt, Rinehart & Winston.

GOLDBERG, H., ed. (1987), *Judaism Viewed From Within and From Without: Anthropological Studies*. Albany, NY: SUNY Press.

GRUBRICH-SIMITS, I. (1981), Extreme traumatization as cumulative trauma. *The Psychoanalytic Study of the Child*, 36:415-450. New Haven, CT: Yale University Press. (Vols. 1-25 published by International Universities Press.)

HALL, J. (1982), The apocalypse in Jonestown. In: *In Gods We Trust*, ed. T. Robbins & D. Anthony. New Brunswick, NJ: Transaction, pp. 171-190.

HAZANI, M. (1984), Two trains on a collision course. *Yedioth Aharonoth*, June 24, 1984 [Hebrew].

_____ (1987), When prophecy fails: Leaders die, followers persevere. *Genetic, Social, and General Psychology Monographs*, 18:82-98.

_____ (1989), Deviant companionship and interaction across an intergroup 'seam': Arab pimps and Jewish prostitutes. *Plural Societies*, 19:55-72.

_____ (in press), Netzah Yisrael, symbolic immortality and the Israeli-Palestinian conflict. *J. Peace Research*.

_____ & ILAN, Y. (1970), *Social Implications of Urban Renewal: The Ethnic Synagogues in Wadi Salib and Their Social Function*. Haifa: The Technion Research and Development Foundation [Hebrew].

_____ & _____ (1971), *Determination of Social Changes Following Physical Slum Rehabilitation*. Haifa: The Technion Research and Development Foundation [Hebrew].

HENGEL, M. (1989), *The Zealots*. Edinburgh: T. & T. Clark.

HENRY, A. F. & SHORT, J. F., JR. (1954), *Suicide and Homicide*. New York: The Free Press.

HILL, C. (1972), *The World Turned Upside Down*. Harmondsworth, England: Penguin Books, 1972.

HOFFER, E. (1951), *The True Believer*. New York: Harper & Row.

HORTON, D. (1943), The functions of alcohol in primitive societies: A cross-cultural study. *Stud. Alcohol*, 4:199–320.

JAMES, W. (1902), *The Varieties of Religious Experience*. London: The Fontana Library, 1960.

JUNG, C. G. (1938), *Psychology and Religion*. New Haven, CT: Yale University Press.

_____ (1959), *Aion*. In: *The Collected Works of C. G. Jung, Vol. 9, Part II*, ed. H. Read, M. Fordham & G. Adler. London: Routledge & Kegan Paul.

_____ & KERENYI, K. (1949), *Essays on a Science of Mythology*. New York: Pantheon Books, Bollingen Series XXII.

KAMINSKY, H. (1967), *A History of the Hussite Movement*. Berkeley: University of California Press.

KAPITZA, S. (1991), Antiscience trends in the U.S.S.R. *Scient. Amer.*, 265(2):18–24.

KATZ, D. (1968), Consistency for what? The functional approach. In: *Theories of Cognitive Dissonance: A Sourcebook*, ed. R. P. Abelson, E. Aronson, W. J. McGuire, T. M. Newcomb, M. J. Rosenberg & P. H. Tannenbaum. Chicago: Rand McNally, pp. 179–191.

KEESING, R. M. & KEESING, F. M. (1971), *New Perspectives in Cultural Anthropology*. New York: Holt, Rinehart & Winston.

KLEIN, H. (1973), Children of the Holocaust: Mourning and bereavement. In: *The Child in His Family: The Impact of Disease and Death*, ed. E. J. Anthony & C. Koupernik. New York: John Wiley, pp. 393–409.

KRYSTAL, H. (1978), Trauma and affects. *The Psychoanalytic Study of the Child*, 33:81–116. New Haven, CT: Yale University Press. (Vols. 1–25 published by International Universities Press.)

KUPER, L. (1991), In: Foreward to *Genocide, Vol. 2*, ed. I. W. Charny. London: Mansell, pp. XI–XVII.

LEBRA, T. S. (1972), Millenarian movements and radicalization. *Amer. Behav. Scientist*, 16:195–218.

LEENAARS, A. A. (1988), *Suicide Notes*. New York: Human Sciences Press.

LICHT, J. (1961), The plant eternal and the people of the divine deliverance. In: *Essays on the Dead Sea Scrolls*, ed. Ch. Rabin & Y. Yadin. Jerusalem: Hekhal HaSefer, pp. 49–75 [Hebrew].

LIEBES, Y. (1982), The ultra-Orthodox community and the Dead Sea Sect. *Jerusalem Stud. Jewish Thought*, III:137–152 [Hebrew].

LIEDER, O. (1991), personal communication.

_____ , CILFEN, P., MIKULINCER, M. & WOLF, Y. (1988), Holocaust survivors perceived by their sons as victims of aggression. *Crime and Social Deviance*, 16:51–68 [Hebrew].

LIFTON, R. J. (1967), *Death in Life: Survivors of Hiroshima*. New York: Random House.

_____ (1969), *Boundaries*. New York: Simon & Schuster.

_____ (1979), *The Broken Connection*. New York: Basic Books, 1983.

_____ (1980), On the consciousness of the Holocaust. *Psychohist. Rev.*, 9:3–22.

LISSAK, M. & RONEL, N., ed. (1984), Megamot. *Behav. Science Quart.*, 28, 2/3 [Hebrew].

LOOMIS, S. (1964), *Paris in the Terror*. New York: Lippincott.

LUKES, S. (1970), Some problems about rationality. In: *Rationality,* ed. B. R. Wilson. Oxford: Basil Blackwell, 1974, pp. 194–213.

MALTSBERGER, J. T. & BUIE, D. H. (1980), The devices of suicide: Revenge, riddance, and rebirth. *Internat. Rev. Psycho-Anal., 7*:61–72.

MEISSNER, W. W. (1986), *Psychotherapy and the Paranoid Process*. Northvale, NJ: Aronson.

MENNINGER, K. A. (1938), *Man Against Himself*. New York: Harcourt, Brace & World.

MERARI, A. (1990), The readiness to kill and die: Suicidal Terrorism in the Middle East. In: *Origins of Terrorism,* ed. W. Reich. Cambridge: Cambridge University Press, pp. 192–207.

MURRAY, H. A. (1967), Death to the world: The passions of Herman Melville. In: *Essays in Self-Destruction,* ed. E. S. Shneidman. New York: Science House, pp. 7–29.

NAIPUL, S. (1980), *Journey to Nowhere: A New World Tragedy*. New York: Simon & Schuster.

NIEDERLAND, W. G. (1968), Clinical observations on the 'survivor syndrome': Symposium on psychic traumatization through social catastrophe. *Internat. J. Psycho-Anal., 49*:313–315.

OVESEY, L. (1955), Pseudo-homosexuality, the paranoid mechanism and paranoia. *Psychiat., 18*:163–73.

PAUSTOVSKII, K. G. (1946), *Story of a Life*. London: Harvill Press, 1967.

POST, J. (1990), Terrorist psycho-logic: Terrorist behavior as a product of psychological forces. In: *Origins of Terrorism,* ed. W. Reich. Cambridge: Cambridge University Press, pp. 25–40.

RADIN, P. (1956), *The Trickster: A Study in American Indian Mythology*. New York: Philosophical Library.

RAHAV, G. (1990), Cross-national variations in violence. *Aggressive Behav., 16*:69–76.

ROBBINS, T. (1986), Religious mass suicide before Jonestown. *Sociolog. Anal., 47*:1–20.

RUSSELL, T. (1986), *We Shall Live Again*. Cambridge: Cambridge University Press.

SCHOLEM, G. (1973), *Shabbetai Zevi*. Princeton: Princeton University Press.

SEGERT, S. (1955), The unity of the new covenant — the unity of brethren. *Jewish Studies*. Prague: Council of Jewish Religious Communities, pp. 71–80.

SHNEIDMAN, E. S. (1985), *Definition of Suicide*. New York: Wiley.

SHOHAM, S. G. (1979), *Salvation Through the Gutters*. Washington: Hemisphere Publishing Company.

SNYDER, C. R. (1964), Inebriety, alcoholism, and anomie. In: *Anomie and Deviant Behavior,* ed. M. B. Clinard. New York: The Free Press, pp. 189–212.

TAYLOR, M. & RYAN, H. (1988), Fanaticism, political suicide, and terrorism. *Terrorism, 11*:91–111.

TROSSMAN, B. (1968), Adolescent children of concentration camp survivors. *Canad. Psychiat. Associat. J., 12*:121–23.

TUCKER, R. C. (1973), *Stalin as Revolutionist*. London: Chatto & Windus.

WAHL, C. W. (1957), Suicide as a magical act. In: *Clues to Suicide,* ed. E. S. Shneidman & N. L. Farberow. New York: McGraw-Hill, pp. 22–30.

WALLACE, A. F. C. (1956), Revitalization Movements. *Amer. Anthropol., 58*:264–281.

————— (1961), *Culture and Personality*. New York: Random House.

————— (1966), *Religion*. New York: Random House.

WEST, D. J. (1965) *Murder Followed by Suicide*. London: Heinemann.

WILLIAMS, G. H. (1962), *The Radical Reformation*. London: Weidenfeld and Nicolson.

WILSON, B. R. (1973), *Magic and the Millennium*. London: Heinemann.
WINCH, P. (1970), Understanding a primitive society. In: *Rationality,* ed. B. R. Wilson. Oxford: Basil Blackwell, 1974, pp. 78–111.
WISTRICH, R. S. (1989), The Fassbinder controversy. *Jerusalem Quart.,* 50:122–130.
WOLFGANG, M. A. (1968), Suicide by means of a victim-precipitated homicide. In: *Suicidal Behaviors,* ed. H. L. P. Resnik. Boston: Little, Brown & Company, pp. 82–89.
YINGER, J. M. (1970), *The Scientific Study of Religion*. New York: MacMillan.
YOUNG, G. (1978), quoted in *Time,* Dec. 4.

21

Self-Analysis, Applied Analysis, and Analytic Fieldwork: A Discussion of Methodology in Psychoanalytic Interdisciplinary Research

STEPHEN M. SONNENBERG

In this chapter I shall discuss the relationship of three topics, all from the perspective of a clinical psychoanalyst. The first is the analyst's use of self-analysis in the service of his patient, the second is applied psychoanalysis as it is practiced by the typical psychoanalyst with an interest in using analysis outside the clinical setting, and the third is psychoanalytic fieldwork. The first topic is currently of great interest to many clinicians, and so much is known and being learned about it that some feel it is at the core of a paradigm shift in the practice of analysis. The second topic has since Freud (1907, 1910) been of great interest to clinical analysts, but relatively little attention has been paid to its process or the development of its methodology by these practitioners (for an exception see Baudry, 1984, 1992).

Analytically trained scholars and investigators from other fields, such as anthropology and sociology (see Hunt, 1989), form a cadre of analytically sophisticated applied analytic researchers, and it is especially important that the existence of these investigators, and their efforts in psychoanalytic fieldwork, have been all but unknown to most clinicians engaged in applied analytic study. Indeed, because there are parallel developments among self-analyzing clinical analysts and analytically trained fieldworkers, which might lead to methodological advances and useful cooperation between scholars, this situation cries out for remediation.

In this chapter I shall suggest that some interdisciplinary research involving a collaborating psychoanalyst and a scholar from another field might entail the analyst's use of self-analysis as a way of understanding

the topic under study, through enhancing the insights of both collabo-
rators. At the outset I wish to emphasize that the experience I shall
describe is not meant to suggest a model for all applied analysis. There
are those who should work quite differently, and projects that demand a
different approach. But I am impressed that many efforts in applied
psychoanalysis would profit enormously if a clinical analyst works
together, in a certain way, with a scholar from another discipline.
Furthermore, I do not know how much in the work of certain interdisciplinary teams the model I shall discuss has actually been employed, but
I suspect similar experiences have been shared by Ruth and L. Bryce
Boyer when they worked together in the field (for example, see Boyer,
1964), and by Volkan and those with whom he worked (Volkan and
Itzkowitz, 1984; Montville, 1989).

I prefer to call what I am discussing psychoanalytic interdisciplinary
research, reflecting my view that this kind of investigation often benefits
from a team effort. An analytic clinician brings to the team certain
clinical skills that can only be developed to the highest degree by one who
spends many hours in the analytic consulting room, working with
patients. Such a clinical time commitment precludes the development of
the highest level of expertise in another field, except by the very
occasional genius, so the analyst must work with a scholar-researcher
from the other field who brings to the team observational and intellectual
tools, including highly specific knowledge that reflects many hours spent
studying within that discipline. This latter kind of time commitment
usually precludes the development of the highest level of clinical analytic
skill, including the most sophisticated self-analytic skills that are used in
the service of clinical observation, so the nonanalyst scholar is also well
served by the collaboration.

The account that follows will be highly personal, because psychoanalysis is a deeply personal experience for both patients and healers. In
writing in this way (Sonnenberg, 1990, 1991a,b, 1992a,b, in press) I
follow the lead of Stein (1988), who has suggested that analysts who write
should do so in the first person, and of Boyer (1977), who has vividly
demonstrated the advantage of that practice. Additionally, I am influenced by fieldworkers who have shown the importance of such an
approach (Crapanzano, 1980).

SELF-ANALYSIS

In 1977, when I completed my psychoanalytic training, my view of
analysis reflected a seven-year learning experience that emphasized

normative and positivist scientific principles. During analysis, I believed, both analyst and analysand learned about the analysand's development and its pathological deviations; the analyst, because of unresolved unconscious neurotic conflict, would occasionally need to learn more about himself to control an unwanted countertransference response. Such a response reflected a limitation of the analyst's training experience, and the fact that he was not sufficiently purified by his training analysis. The analyst who persistently encountered such responses in himself needed a reanalysis (Freud, 1912a, 1937).

Within this model there was a place for the analyst's empathy, intuition, and introspection, but these were forms of intrapsychic activity practiced by wise men who arrived at the truth with relative ease and a sense of certainty (Beres and Arlow, 1974; Arlow, 1979). Despite descriptions of the productive struggle engaged in by analysts and their patients (for example, see Boyer, 1977) to produce analytic understanding, countertransference was not generally thought of as an important source of information. Also not considered was that in each analytic dyad a different version of truth might usefully emerge (Schafer, 1983), in part because in each dyad both participants are different than they are in any other, and in part because knowing another always involves self-discovery by the observer (McLaughlin, 1975, 1981, 1988, 1992; Gardner, 1983; Jacobs, 1991). The notion that the analyst might change, might mature as a result of analytic work with patients (Sonnenberg, 1991a,b, 1992b, in press) was not part of what I had come to understand.

On a positive note, my personal analysis, which was to continue for a year after my graduation, had already equipped me to conduct serious and probing self-analysis, and the motivation at times to engage in that process (Sonnenberg, 1991b, in press). I have no doubt that my analysis was a critical determinant of my subsequent development, and that it allowed me to use several experiences which I had over the next several years as stimuli for continuing a self-analytic process. One of the most important of these was working in the area of interdisciplinary psychoanalytic research. I shall describe later how that experience, in which I was at an advantageous distance from clinical work, allowed me to more easily examine some of my assumptions about how I learned during the psychoanalytic process.

Self-analyzing analysts have written on the myth of the perfectly analyzed analyst (Silverman, 1985), and have emphasized that although the majority of analysts do not practice self-analysis regularly (Calder, 1980; Beiser, 1984) such a practice is rejuvenating to those who do (Ticho, 1967; Calder, 1980). Some in this group have demonstrated the usefulness of ongoing, deeply probing self-analysis as a source of clinical data (McLaughlin, 1975, 1981, 1988, 1992; Boyer, 1977, 1992; Kern, 1978; Gardner, 1983; Jacobs, 1991). Consistent with such self-analysis is the observation that the most meaningful things learned about an analysand come from a process of interaction, in which the analyst allows himself to be drawn into a world largely of the analysand's construction.

Thinking about analysands outside of hours was once thought of as a sign of unwanted countertransference, but now many think of it as a useful effort to understand, and not indicative in any way of a difficulty in listening and empathizing (Sonnenberg, 1992b). Dreams about analysands are now considered, too, as useful sources of information.

With the help of the writings, and in some cases the deeply personal communications of those colleagues already mentioned, plus a few others (Gray, 1973, 1982; Schwaber, 1983, 1986; Grotjahn, 1987, personal communication), I now see that in each analytic experience I share with an analysand something in me will be activated, touched, through processes of identification, and as I learn about myself I will learn about him or her (Gardner, 1983). And to accomplish this I must self-analyze self-consciously and with self-discipline.

During time spent with patients, and at the end of my working day, my self-analyzing begins with my thinking about clinical moments of interest to me, and then I allow myself to freely associate. This process also occurs, less self-consciously, when I am alone doing various things, such as taking a walk, and sometimes the stimulus isn't clinical: it might be a dream, an experience with a friend, or a symptom of which I am particularly aware. In any event, after I freely associate awhile, in response to my initial focus of attention, I will step back and more systematically consider the implications of my associations. I attempt always to think about the defensive nature of my thoughts and feelings, wondering about more uncomfortable feelings I might be blocking out of my awareness. Finally, I generate hypotheses about why I am thinking as I am, and interpretations for my consideration.

Through self-analysis I regularly learn about what is going on in the various analytic dyads in which I am involved. By learning what conflicts are being stirred in me as I interact with my analysands, and developing ideas by exploring those conflicts, and the identifications with analysands on which they are based, my thinking is usefully focused on the messages my patients unconsciously transmit (Sonnenberg, 1991a, 1992b).

In sum, then, as a self-analyzing clinical analyst I am now much more aware of myself as engaged in an experience-near process of learning about another, and myself, in the service of that other (Cohler and Galatzer-Levy, 1992). My analytic work has taken on a passion and a vitality, which not only invigorates my analysands, but me, as well. Not only am I today a vastly different practitioner than I once was, but the process of becoming that different practitioner has depended to a significant extent on an experience I had working in interdisciplinary research, which strengthened my self-analytic commitment.

APPLIED PSYCHOANALYSIS: A CASE REPORT

Since Freud's efforts to apply psychoanalysis to the study of culture and society (1907, 1910, 1912b, 1921, 1927, 1930, 1939), certain methodological trends have emerged. Often, the subject being studied is examined by a clinical psychoanalyst, against the backdrop of psychoanalytic theory. Here, theory is applied to understand some aspect of culture or society, or some individual of historical importance, psychoanalytically (Feldman, 1947; Spitzer, 1947; Sterba, 1947; Wangh, 1954, 1964, 1968, 1972; Atkin, 1971; Mack, 1976; Baudry, 1984, 1992; Volkan, 1987, 1988, 1991). Less often, the clinical analyst collaborates with an expert in another discipline, who lends expertise and a different perspective to the work (Volkan and Itzkowitz, 1984), and sometimes work that is quite creative is produced by a researcher who is not analytically trained (S. LeVine, 1981). Most of the time these efforts do not involve contact with live subjects (Greenacre, 1963). Freud, of course, provided an example for collaborative efforts (Freud and Oppenheim, 1957), as well as the use of theory applied to a range of subjects, including the study of the psychology of the artist (1910) and the study of society (1912b, 1921, 1927, 1930, 1939). And in this area his research focused on what was written, or on what he thought, and not on direct contact with individual living subjects.

In the course of psychoanalytic training there is usually no formal effort to educate students in the methods of applied analysis, and typically, through the casual reading of applied analytic articles that appear in the general literature, students come away with the impression that in this subfield of psychoanalysis they may use imagination and theoretical knowledge, and study anything of interest without employing the skills they have developed in the course of clinical training. Indeed, following tradition, students do not think of applied analytic research as usually involving contact with live subjects. But there is a counterpoint in the thinking of many young analysts, too, and that is the concern that applied analytic reasoning is "soft." From this perspective, the newly trained analyst is concerned that applied analytic research should be eschewed, because it produces speculation as opposed to truth, "wild analysis" as opposed to accurate analysis. These complicated ideas constituted the views I held when I graduated from an analytic institute 15 years ago, and they continued to be my views when almost a decade ago I began an interdisciplinary research project that continues at the present time. Later in this chapter I shall return to a further discussion of applied analysis; now I shall describe my own experience, which I offer as a case report.

The Psychology of Deterrence Project began in 1983, when I initiated a series of discussions with Professor William Kincade, then the director of the Arms Control Association at the Carnegie Endowment for International Peace, in Washington, D.C. His background included military service, during which he specialized in intelligence work involving the Soviet Union, and service on Capitol Hill, where his expertise was in arms control and military policy.

I approached Dr. Kincade because I had become interested in learning more about the role of nuclear weapons in the U.S.–Soviet relationship. My view was based on a series of preliminary discussions with a highly placed individual in the Department of Defense with whom I was acquainted, and some reading of material that I had accidentally encountered, which broadly described U.S. nuclear policy.

I had learned that official U.S. thinking was built around the concept of deterrence. Central to this doctrine was that the Soviet Union would not use nuclear weapons against the United States, for fear of nuclear retaliation. Yet, deterrence had spawned an enormous literature, both academic and practical, which included many war-fighting scenarios and descriptions of possible U.S.–Soviet nuclear confrontations. Some of these scenarios predicted U.S. civilian deaths in the hundreds of thousands, some in the millions, and these were discussed by deterrence experts as though they were acceptable, though certainly not desirable, so long as the Soviets could be stopped from annihilating the United States, and in that way winning a nuclear war. For the result of those scenarios was that by inflicting damage in kind against the Soviets, and by accurately targeting and destroying the Soviet capacity to strike again, the United States could win such a nuclear conflict.

I also learned that such imaginary confrontations were the subject of war games, in which experts from within the academic and policy communities engaged in computer simulations of combat and survival.

In fact, such imaginary U.S.–Soviet interactions were studied within the formal framework of a deterrence subcategory, known as intrawar deterrence.

Because I am describing myself as a researcher beginning a new project, I must describe my conscious state of mind, my prejudices as I began this inquiry. As a physician dedicated to helping and healing, I was concerned and shocked. Even discounting predictions of long-range environmental disaster, which were already emerging, the casualty predictions alone were staggering. Furthermore, health consequences could be overwhelming, as the nuclear target zone served as a breeding ground for disease, which posed a very serious health threat to the millions of survivors worldwide. I wanted to learn more.

When I began to explain my thinking to Dr. Kincade, and he countered with concerns of his own, for me a natural connection soon developed. Kincade's ideas were couched in the terms a policy-maker and political scientist would view as central. When he talked of nuclear war he focused on the erosion of the moral and ethical basis of international relationships; the destruction of life, property, social systems, and civilizations; the failure of deterrence and the diplomatic system. We both believed that we were expressing parallel concerns about the threat of nuclear war and the fundamentally flawed nature of nuclear deterrence policy, and we agreed to continue a dialogue. However, we had no idea of what methodology we would employ as we worked.

Phases of the Project: The Nature of the Research Dialogue

I shall now describe the phases in the process of inquiry in which Dr. Kincade and I engaged. This effort has included a dialogue during which we have met some 200 times, each meeting usually lasting more than three hours, beginning in the spring of 1983.

The phase of substantive learning was the first, and in it we came to understand deterrence historically through its literature, both academic and governmental. Through extensive library research we learned that the changes in the boundaries between the academy and the world of policy practice, during and after World War II, were an important factor in the development of nuclear deterrence policy. The traditional restriction of university professors to the library or the laboratory, and the avoidance of contact with the policy community, which might use their ideas in practical ways, had been replaced by the founding and expansion of the field of policy research, and schools of public policy.

Whether the discipline in question was economics, health care, diplomacy, or defense, to name but a few, there had developed an ever-increasing, back-and-forth movement of academics and intellectuals between think tanks and universities, and government service. In all settings their work was basically the same, as they tried to assess the effects of various polices and policy decisions, and develop systematic, often computer-based methods for planning and implementation. Nowhere had this trend been of greater importance than in the worlds of diplomacy and defense (Kaplan, 1983).

In the field of defense policy, scholars from such institutions as Harvard and Yale moved to think tanks such as the RAND Corporation, and to consultantships, advisory boards, and full-time, high-level appointments in the Departments of State and Defense. Prominent as examples of such deterrence scholars were Thomas Schelling, William Kaufmann, and Henry Kissinger; prominent among the models they introduced were those derived from academic economics, of the unitary rational actor functioning in a free marketplace; and prominent as methods of inquiry were those employing mathematical models, computer simulations, and game theories (Kaplan, 1983; Schelling, 1960, 1966).

This historical perspective helped us to understand deterrence as a system of thought developed by academic public servants, which had soon evolved into the United States' public policy guideline, a set of principles that had been espoused by almost all national leaders in the nuclear age, regardless of their position on the political spectrum. In that light, we came to see our work as involving applied epistemology, as an effort to understand how a set of ideas had evolved, and then how those ideas had been transformed into a system of rules that were applied in the development and implementation of national policy (Jervis, 1970, 1976; Morgan, 1977).

I came to see myself as my colleague's student, for though he was not a supporter of nuclear deterrence, and was quite skeptical about it, in the broadest sense he was a member of that group of national experts which through its collective debates and deliberations had refined deterrence from a set of ideas to an accepted guideline, and then been involved in the implementation of the policy. Dr. Kincade could explain in detail and in depth the thinking of many colleagues who stood on various sides of deterrence questions over the years, and by listening carefully to him I could learn about the evolution and status of the policy, and the thinking that was behind it.

Dr. Kincade came to see me as his teacher, as well, for we saw that deterrence was based on psychological assumptions about how threats work, and I was the team member with an understanding of psychology and psychoanalysis. So in our dialogue, as we reviewed the deterrence literature, he turned to me to shed light on the psychological perspectives that were the underpinnings of deterrence theory and practice.

As we worked together we came to see ourselves as engaged in substantive research supplemented by hour after hour of discussion. As we taught each other about the field from which each of us came, we believed we were developing a sophisticated understanding of our subject.

The second phase of our work had as its unique characteristic my becoming a deterrence advocate. This phase began toward the end of the first year of the project, and lasted for another year, and only during the third year did I become self-conscious of what I had experienced. It is of particular interest that despite alarm upon recognition of what had happened, a full awareness and appreciation of this process occurred progressively, and as a result of effort, beginning only after a one-year period of virtually complete unawareness.

By the end of the first year of my study of deterrence I had read thousands of pages and discussed what I was reading for over 150 hours with my colleague, and I had learned a great deal. Arguments against abandoning nuclear deterrence as it was currently practiced, because of how that would destabilize the superpower relationship, seemed to me well grounded in political and military reality, and the medical concerns I had when I began the project were forgotten. I found support for my views in a picture I had brought together from perceptions and ideas about many political and military decision-makers and planners, despite Dr. Kincade's not sharing my perspective.

My experience as a nuclear deterrence researcher next played a critical role in my development as a self-analyzing analyst. For that reason I call this phase of the project the period of self-analysis. Toward the end of my personal analysis I had begun to actively self-analyze, but immersion in work with patients, coupled with a fear I had developed in my training of demonstrating "forbidden" countertransference, made it harder to employ deep self-analysis as I worked as an analyst. But now, when I recognized how thoroughly I had become a deterrence advocate, I became alarmed and responded by using my already developed self-analytic skills to advantage, even as I honed them.

Beginning during the third year of the Psychology of Deterrence Project I regularly reflected on my state of mind, usually beginning free-associatively, and engaged in self-analysis. Soon, I recalled how I actually became interested in the study of deterrence, and this proved to be my first illuminating self-analytic experience with regard to my research. I remembered that my first encounter with the deterrence literature came when one of my children, then about 12, had brought home some unclassified government documents from a local university library to fulfill a school assignment. Indeed, during the research process I had actually repressed this starting point, and upon remembering it I realized that from the start my awareness of nuclear deterrence had awakened in me many memories from my own childhood.

The focus of these Cold War memories was my frequent participation in air raid drills, during which I would hide under my desk as imaginary Soviet atomic bombs fell on the United States. I came to see, too, that these fears of war and death were associatively connected to concerns I had felt during World War II, when as an oedipal-age child I experienced much ambivalence about the likelihood of my father going off to war: I wished him to go so that I could be alone with my mother, yet I guiltily feared his death, and his retribution. Thus, I realized that a complex set of oedipal concerns involving conflicted desire, guilt, and terror over my father's capacity to retaliate, were intertwined with my thoughts about war and nuclear weapons. And I came to appreciate that all this had been activated by my concern over my child's researches for his school project, and fueled by my own studies of nuclear deterrence.

I needed to understand more about how all this had occurred, and further reflection clarified for me a now familiar mechanism I habitually employ when someone I care about might have to endure pain (Sonnenberg, 1992b). That mechanism involves identification, as I wish to take on the suffering or potential suffering of a loved one. And I came to realize that unconsciously I had feared for my child's sense of well-being as he reacted to the study of nuclear war, identified in an effort to take on my child's worry and pain, and in the course of that process of identification had experienced a reawakening of my own childhood thoughts on war, even as those personal childhood experiences demanded reworking more directly in response to what I saw in my child.

Finally, I came to see that all the while that I researched deterrence, as I experienced a reawakening of childhood oedipal conflicts and concerns about my child, I had sought to control my anxieties through a sense of mastery of a policy that promised mastery of the nuclear threat.

Next, I began to reflect on my relationship with Professor Kincade, on the way in which we interacted, and I became aware of my fantasies and dreams about him. This resulted first in my uncovering my belief in my partner's omniscience. Indeed, Professor Kincade and I had attended the same very fine university, as undergraduates, and were members of the same graduating class. And though objectively his academic record was superior to mine, in my grandiose fantasy about him he came to embody a level of intellect which I did not share, but which was shared only by his fellow experts in arms control. Indeed, I came to realize that I had actually lost full appreciation of Professor Kincade's opposition to deterrence, substituting the unconscious fantasy that he was a deterrence advocate, and that I shared that position confidently and wisely with him and his equally brilliant colleagues.

I then became even more aware of my manifest dreams and came to understand their latent content and their meaning. I frequently dreamed of benevolent and reassuring teachers, including in some cases Dr. Kincade himself. My self-analysis of these dreams allowed me to understand my wish to find reassuring and confident figures who felt in control of the awesome destructive power of the nuclear age, and I began to remember how I had engaged in a similar search with my father, during my childhood: then, my goal had been to feel confident that he was in control of everything, including me.

I wish to emphasize that this process led to my appreciation of the unconscious roots of my choice of research subject and method, and of my partner, and of the way I reacted to my child, my partner, and my topic; this required frequent efforts at self-analysis. These efforts often took place after my research meetings with Professor Kincade, or after periods of heavy library research or writing, and often such periods of research work stimulated more dream or fantasy material with which to work. Indeed, such research-related self-analysis has continued, and I still find it necessary as an aid to establishing and maintaining clarity about my topic.

I did not share all the details of this personal process with Professor Kincade. As I became more aware of how my relationship to the "culture" of nuclear deterrence served to protect me from my multiply determined fears of murder and death, I also became aware of how the policy more literally and concretely might be seen as an elaborate protection for the policy-maker against his more specific fears of a world with so many awesomely powerful nuclear weapons. And as I began to reread previously studied parts of the deterrence literature, no longer using it to protect myself from my own anxieties about my childhood conflicts and my related yet appropriate adult fears of such a dangerous world, I was able to convey to my partner the notion that deterrence dogma might have developed as just such a protective device: It shielded national leaders and the public from otherwise unthinkable fears of disaster, unthinkable terrors of annihilation.

Increasing Dr. Kincade's capacity for psychological awareness came through frequent efforts. For many months the focus of our research meetings was on sharing insights about the protective way deterrence worked in me, and eventually in him. He, too, came to appreciate some of his own childhood concerns about war, and we discussed mine and his during our meetings.

Finally, we were able to consider more fully the evidence that appeared in the writings of deterrence experts that they, too, had thought about deterrence in similarly self-protective ways.

I realize, of course, that the reader will have many specific questions about the findings of the Psychology of Deterrence Project. Yet because this is an essay on methodology, and because the very detailed report of our research will appear in our book, *Edge of War: The Psychology of Nuclear Deterrence* (Yale University Press, forthcoming), I will now move on, without providing additional detail.

In bringing this section to a close I must emphasize that the way in which I increased Dr. Kincade's self-awareness seems similar to what I do when I supervise beginning trainees in psychotherapy, surely a recognized "applied" analytic function. Yet it is also strikingly similar to what psychoanalytic ethnographers describe, as they write of the effects on informants of the dyadic relationships they share (Crapanzano, 1980; Ewing, 1987, 1990). Indeed, I suspect there is value for psychotherapy supervisors in reading such ethnographic works, but now it is time to move to my discussion of psychoanalytic fieldwork.

PSYCHOANALYTIC FIELDWORK: TOWARD A MODEL FOR INTERDISCIPLINARY RESEARCH

Earlier, I stated that the student of psychoanalysis is not systematically exposed to the subfield of applied psychoanalysis, and even were that not the case the mainstream analytic literature provides few clues as to the value of self-analysis for the applied researcher. Volkan has made references to his dreams and countertransference responses as valuable sources of information when working in the field of international political psychology and psychobiography (Gehrie, 1992; Volkan and Itzkowitz, 1984; Volkan, 1987, 1991), but what is most impressive about his work on war, what virtually overwhelms the reader, is his scholarly mastery of the broadest range of psychoanalytic developmental and metapsychological theory (Volkan, 1988). He also employs models, by analogy, from clinical practice, but here again his emphasis on developmental thinking overshadows his references to his inner experience as he works with patients.

Similarly, Baudry (1984, 1992) makes reference to the use of his reactions as he applies analysis to the study of literature, but he does not provide an account of self-analysis as he works in that field. Indeed, it is unclear if he uses self-analysis at all.

In focusing more specifically on the study of war and related subjects, again, in reading the general analytic literature, the application of theory is what impresses the psychoanalyst (Wangh, 1954, 1964, 1968, 1972; Atkin, 1971; Guttman, 1986).

Thus, for years now, as I have tried to write about what I did with Dr. Kincade, I have found myself self-conscious and reticent in describing how I worked. In part this has been because of feelings that the methodology would be seen as idiosyncratic and strange, and earlier in this period it was also because I was concerned that revealing the ongoing nature of my intrapsychic conflicts would cause my colleagues to find me suspect. The second concern has been dispelled by experience and time, and the existence today of a critical mass of colleagues who write about such inner processes.

Recently, stimulated by personal communications with two experienced and sensitive psychoanalytic fieldworkers, Bryce Boyer and Jennifer Hunt, I began to read in the area of ethnographic and sociological fieldwork, and coupled with further self-analysis concerning the sense of aloneness that had stopped me, I now believe I understand my previous inhibition, and I am relatively free to express myself.

Looking back now on my relationship with Professor Kincade, I can only begin by describing it as the deepest of friendships, in which each of us grew and changed, and learned through the vehicles of mutual trust and openness, and enormous respect and affection for the other. That friendship has helped me to better understand that our complex personal relationships with both patients and research informants in the field are the vehicles through which we learn psychoanalytically.

Now I shall discuss points of similarity and difference with certain fieldworkers, so that my research methodology will make more sense as it is framed in an intellectual and scientific tradition.

To make best use of this tradition, it is helpful to think of the existence of a "nuclear deterrence culture," of my experience as a nuclear deterrence researcher as fieldwork, of my initial reaction to what I learned as a form of culture shock, of my becoming a deterrence advocate as a form of going native, and of my relationship with Professor Kincade as a fieldworker-informant relationship, a special friendship in which we both grew and learned at the same time. Fieldworkers discuss these relationships in detail, and how they are of value to the psychoanalytic researcher.

Crapanzano's *Tuhami: Portrait of a Moroccan* (1980) is a good place to start. Deeply moved by his relationship with Tuhami, Crapanzano wrote of it, and the ways they influenced each other, only a decade after they had parted. He cites Devereux (1967) and understands that his inner needs shaped his experience with his informant. He shows a deep understanding of their friendship as a two-person psychological experience in which each shaped and changed the other, and in which self and other must be understood as products of interaction. He understands how over time interpretations of events change, and that all that is learned in the field, and elsewhere, is the product of self-discovery. He stops short of self-analysis, particularly evident when he notes without self-analytic elaboration how his own father and Tuhami are linked in his thoughts: he does not elaborate on how this must have constantly influenced his field experience. Without doubt this remarkably sensitive account, although not truly self-analytic, is a valuable example of self-inquiry in the service of research and discovery.

Rabinow worked in the same tradition as Crapanzano (1980), again writing after a hiatus of years, again emphasizing the dialectical nature of fieldwork, the changing nature of subject and object, participation and observation. Fieldwork, Rabinow notes, is intersubjective, as the observer and observed interact and change. But in tone, significantly more than Crapanzano's, his (1977) is an account of what is conscious, and he asserts of his book that "It is vital to stress that this is not psychology of any sort. . . ." (p. 5). So the notion of using deeply probing self-analysis is outside this ethnographer's agenda. But the work is helpful to the psychoanalyst who is considering the place of self-analysis in fieldwork.

Other ethnographers whose work placed mine in context were Watson (1989), in the way he stresses that the observer stimulates self-reflection in the informant, and that what is reported of the informant is uniquely shaped by both members of the dyad; Ewing (1987, 1990), in her discussions of the context-dependent nature of the self; Agar, in his warnings to would-be ethnographers (1980); and Wengle (1988), who notes that the fieldworker "projects his self, lays it onto the world . . . [and] discovers in his field notes what he really knew all along, what he was psychologically all along" (p. 160).

The need for self-reflection in the fieldworker is vividly demonstrated by Briggs, in her discussion of her reactions to the Inuits she studied (1987), and the need for a psychologically probing awareness of how the observer and observed unconsciously influence each other is clearly described by S. LeVine (1981). Yet, again, in neither of these helpful accounts is actual self-analysis discussed.

R. LeVine, trained as an analyst and an ethnographer, notes (1973) that "Most psychoanalytic writing on other cultures . . . have involved no serious attempt to apply the clinical method of psychoanalysis" (p. 204). He goes on to write that most psychoanalytic fieldwork attempts to approximate psychoanalytic data collection, and concludes that

studies in psychoanalytic anthropology have from the beginning satisfied neither psychoanalysts nor anthropologists because they seemed not to meet the standards of investigation in either field. . . . Psychoanalytic anthropology for the most part strikes anthropologists as inadequate anthropology and psychoanalysts as inauthentic psychoanalysis [p. 205].

R. LeVine thus brings to the fore the question of what is authentic analytic research, and here it is essential to note that Crapanzano, Rabinow, Watson, Ewing, Agar, Wengle, Briggs, and S. LeVine are addressing that question in a quite different way. For each of the authors mentioned, other than R. LeVine, stresses in one way or another, more or less self-consciously and by design, that the essence of psychoanalysis is that it is a deeply personal two-person psychology, and that research which is psychoanalytic captures that quality. In contrast, R. LeVine (1973) emphasizes the centrality for psychoanalytic research of the concepts that determine what will be studied, such as the concept of "universal structures as observational frames" (pp. 226–248). R. LeVine's ideas are convincing, and indicate how critical it is for evaluators of psychoanalytic research method to focus on each researcher's vision of what makes research psychoanalytic, and what is psychoanalytic.

Kracke's vision of what is psychoanalytic is similar to mine, as he describes using his unconsciously rooted transferences to individuals and to a culture to inform him (1987) of the meaning of what he observes in the field. Further, he describes using those transferences in a continuous fashion to understand himself and what he has observed.

Finally, there are two outstanding works that I wish to discuss. I believe these demonstrate that the application of self-analysis to raw interdisciplinary research data constitutes an important psychoanalytic methodology, which opens the way to uniquely psychoanalytic discoveries. In *Psychoanalytic Aspects of Fieldwork* (1989) Jennifer Hunt brings together the worlds of psychoanalytic introspection and the fieldwork experience in both sociology and anthropology. Through detailed descriptions of the research setting, culture shock, the role of the researcher, and the dynamics of observation and data collection, all discussed through the prisms of unconscious process, intrapsychic conflict, dreams, and fantasies, she describes interferences to observation and understanding that can be overcome, and information that can be better appreciated. She speaks of continuous self-analysis, and in her book demonstrates vividly how she uses it.

The last work I shall discuss is George Devereux's *From Anxiety to Method in the Behavioral Sciences* (1967). La Barre notes in the preface that "this is a brilliant book" (p. vii) and I would suggest even this statement does not go far enough.

I do have some disagreements with Devereux, who feels that there is an objectivity to which the analyst should aspire, that fully effective analysis potentially leaves the analyst anxiety free, and that self-analysis is impossible. Yet Devereux's central thesis is far in advance of the time the book was published, let alone when it was written, for it went unpublished for 30 years after he wrote it. Devereux's basic idea is that observation and learning in analysis and fieldwork involve complex interpersonal interactions, that people draw each other into critical roles and shape each other in those roles. The central mechanism of knowing involves the observer's perception of anxiety in himself, within the two-person setting; what follows is a careful self-exploration, by the observer, of his own unconscious processes, to understand that anxiety. Then, with insight, the clinical or research field is illuminated. The analyst's critical tool, Devereux feels, is his unconscious; his critical study is of himself, through introspection.

This idea, succinctly put, is quite staggering, for it describes a methodology for behavioral science research, as well as clinical psychoanalysis, which only today are some of us considering. I suspect that with the support of today's scientific environment, and a contemporary understanding of ego psychology, Devereux would be less the positivist, and more comfortable with the existence of continuous postanalytic conflict, and the use of self-analysis as a function made possible by a successful psychoanalysis.

For purposes of this chapter, though, I wish to emphasize that Devereux demonstrates a method for learning in the field that is remarkably similar to how I learned in my interdisciplinary research experience: he and I studied ourselves. Devereux was entirely comfortable with the idea that observer and informant are engaged in a complex friendship in which much in the analyst's unconscious is activated, which is then the critical source of data. This parallels my view of how my relationship with my partner worked. Indeed, it is my view that Devereux was a self-analyzer, and did it in the service of patient care and research data collection, as do I.

After reading Hunt and Devereux, set against the background created by Kracke and other fieldworkers, I felt that in some ways I had reinvented the wheel. But I also felt less isolated, more confident, and more empowered to describe what I have in this essay. Whether it is in my recollection of my experience of culture shock, of going native, or of self-analytic understanding of myself leading to understanding of another, I no longer feel so alone.

CONCLUSION

This brings me to some final comments about the validity of my evidence and my observations, based on a close personal relationship with a single live informant. Professor Kincade learned about himself and our subject from me after I better understood myself. That his thinking and mine agreed is an argument for validity comparable to the one that states that if the analysand confirms the analyst's interpretations, they are clearly correct. A contemporary appreciation of transference and countertransference, and of the roles of theory and technique as shapers of data in the clinical setting, clearly makes such a conclusion suspect.

Yet Professor Kincade and I, through our dialogue, developed hypotheses that were then subjected to further scrutiny, and those hypotheses were quite unique when we developed them. There is, importantly, confirmation possible through traditional analysis of primary and secondary sources that are relevant to the policy of nuclear deterrence, and in our book reporting our research those traditional sources of data are amply explored.

We find it especially striking that before our study no one had described what we have: the psychologically defensive purpose served by nuclear deterrence policy; the way in which it defends on an individual and collective basis against overwhelming fear, which might be based on current reality, past psychic reality, or both. We are aware that this historical fact may seem unlikely, but it is true. What we discovered belonged to the dynamic unconscious, and previously had not been recognized.

We find it of further interest that since our observations were made events have allowed new understandings, which seem to confirm our findings. These events include the collapse of the Soviet Union, permitting the emergence of a clearer picture of how fear-driven U.S. nuclear policies had been, and the persistence of a cadre of nuclear deterrence advocates whose thinking in this area is almost unchanged, suggesting that in some individuals unconscious sources of fear and unconsciously motivated defenses persist in the face of a greatly reduced nuclear threat. This repressed fear has the characteristics of the primary process: In those who are driven by it the terror of annihilation is timeless, and is not subject to influence by the reality principle.

I realize that now I leave many questions unanswered. As I have indicated, my partner and I are building on the ideas I have described with detailed historical analysis, and what we learned from each other "in the field" is only part of our research effort; but it is the part that employed a uniquely psychoanalytic method to uncover deeply unconscious processes within the "deterrence culture."

I have attempted a description of the relationship of the self-analytic skills of a clinical analyst, psychoanalytic interdisciplinary teamwork and research, and psychoanalytic fieldwork. Although I have emphasized that the experience I have described was of great personal and professional importance in that it motivated me to work harder at self-analysis, of greater importance is that this description may be informative to others who attempt research outside the consulting room, which is in an essential way deeply psychoanalytic.

BIBLIOGRAPHY

AGAR, M. (1980), *The Professional Stranger: An Informal Introduction to Ethnography.* New York: The Academic Press.

ARLOW, J. A. (1979), The genesis of interpretation. *J. Amer. Psychoanal. Assn.,* 27 Suppl.:193–206.

ATKIN, S. (1971), Notes on motivations for war: Toward a psychoanalytic social psychology. *Psychoanal. Quart.,* 40:549–583.

BAUDRY, F. (1984), An essay on method in applied psychoanalysis. *Psychoanal. Quart.,* 53:551–581.

_____ (1992), Faulkner's *As I Lay Dying:* Issues of method in applied psychoanalysis. *Psychoanal. Quart.,* 61:65–84.

BEISER, H. R. (1984), An example of self-analysis. *J. Amer. Psychoanal. Assn.,* 32:3–12.

BERES, D. & ARLOW, J. A. (1974), Fantasy and identification in empathy. *Psychoanal. Quart.,* 43:26–50.

BOYER, L. B. (1964), An example of legend distortion from the Apaches of the Mescalero Indian reservation. *J. Amer. Folklore,* 77:118–142.

_____ (1977), Working with a borderline patient. *Psychoanal. Quart.,* 46:386–424.

_____ (1992), Roles played by music as revealed during countertransference facilitated transference regression. *Internat. J. Psycho-Anal.,* 73:55–70.

BRIGGS, J. L. (1987), In search of emotional meaning. *Ethos,* 15:8–15.

CALDER, K. T. (1980), An analyst's self-analysis. *J. Amer. Psychoanal. Assn.,* 28:5–20.

COHLER, B. J. & GALATZER-LEVY, R. M. (1992), What kind of a science is psychoanalysis? Presented at the 158th national meeting of the American Association for the Advancement of Science, Chicago.

CRAPANZANO, V. (1980), *Tuhami: Portrait of a Moroccan.* Chicago: University of Chicago Press.

DEVEREUX, G. (1967), *From Anxiety to Method in the Behavioral Sciences.* The Hague, Netherlands: Mouton & Co.

EWING, K. P. (1987), Clinical psychoanalysis as an ethnographic tool. *Ethos,* 15:16–39.

_____ (1990), The illusion of wholeness: Culture, self, and the experience of inconsistency. *Ethos,* 18:251–278.

FELDMAN, S. S. (1947), Notes on the "primal horde." *Psychoanalysis and the Social Sciences,* 1:171–193. New York: International Universities Press.

FREUD, S. (1907), Delusions and dreams in Jensen's *Gradiva. Standard Edition,* 9:1–95. London: Hogarth Press, 1971.

_____ (1910), Leonardo da Vinci and a memory of his childhood. *Standard Edition,* 11:57–137. London: Hogarth Press, 1971.

_____ (1912a), Recommendations to physicians practicing psycho-analysis. *Standard Edition,* 12:109–120. London: Hogarth Press, 1971.

_____ (1912b), Totem and taboo. *Standard Edition,* 13:1–161. London: Hogarth Press, 1971.

_____ (1921), Group psychology and the analysis of the ego. *Standard Edition,* 18:69–143. London: Hogarth Press, 1971.

_____ (1927), The future of an illusion. *Standard Edition,* 21:5–56. London: Hogarth Press, 1971.

_____ (1930), Civilization and its discontents. *Standard Edition,* 21:64–145. London: Hogarth Press, 1971.

_____ (1937), Analysis terminable and interminable. *Standard Edition,* 23:209–253. London: Hogarth Press, 1971.

_____ (1939), Moses and monotheism: Three essays. *Standard Edition,* 23:1–137. London: Hogarth Press, 1971.

_____ & OPPENHEIM, D. E. (1957), Dreams in folklore. *Standard Edition,* 12:175–203. London: Hogarth Press, 1971.

GARDNER, M. R. (1983), *Self Inquiry.* Hillsdale, NJ: The Analytic Press, 1989.

GEHRIE, M. J. (1992), Panel report: Freud's vision: Key issues in the methodology of applied psychoanalysis. *J. Amer. Psychoanal. Assn.,* 40:239–244.

GRAY, P. (1973), Psychoanalytic technique and the ego's capacity for viewing intrapsychic activity. *J. Amer. Psychoanal. Assn.,* 21:474–494.

_____ (1982), "Developmental lag" in the evolution of technique for psychoanalysis of neurotic conflict. *J. Amer. Psychoanal. Assn.,* 30:621–655.

GREENACRE, P. (1963), *The Quest for the Father.* New York: International Universities Press.

GROTJAHN, M. (1987), *My Favorite Patient.* Frankfurt-am-Main, Germany: Peter Lang.

GUTTMAN, S. (1986), Robert Waelder and the application of psychoanalytic principles to social and political phenomena. *J. Amer. Psychoanal. Assn.,* 34:835–862.

HUNT, J. C. (1989), *Psychoanalytic Aspects of Fieldwork.* Newbury Park, CA: Sage Publications.

JACOBS, T. J. (1991), *The Use of the Self: Countertransference and Communication in the Analytic Situation*. Madison, CT: International Universities Press.

JERVIS, R. (1970), *The Logic of Images in International Relations*. Princeton, NJ: Princeton University Press.

_____ (1976), *Perception and Misperception in International Politics*. Princeton, NJ: Princeton University Press.

KAPLAN, F. (1983), *The Wizards of Armageddon*. New York: Simon & Schuster.

KERN, J. W. (1978), Countertransference and spontaneous screens: An analyst studies his own visual images. *J. Amer. Psychoanal. Assn.,* 26:21–47.

KRACKE, W. (1987), Encounter with other cultures: Psychological and epistemological aspects. *Ethos,* 15:58–81.

LEVINE, R. (1973), *Culture, Behavior and Personality*. New York: Aldine Publishing Company, 1982.

LE VINE, S. (1981), Dreams of the informant about the researcher: Some difficulties inherent in the research relationships. *Ethos,* 9:276–293.

MACK, J. (1976), *A Prince of Our Disorder: The Life of T. E. Lawrence*. Boston: Little, Brown & Company.

MCLAUGHLIN, J. T. (1975), The sleepy analyst: Some observations on states of consciousness in the analyst at work. *J. Amer. Psychoanal. Assn.,* 23:363–382.

_____ (1981), Transference, psychic reality, and countertransference. *Psychoanal. Quart.,* 50:639–664.

_____ (1988), The analyst's insights. *Psychoanal. Quart.,* 57:370–389.

_____ (1992), Freud's dual perspective on the analytic relationship: Implications for contemporary psychoanalysis. Presented at the 158th national meeting of the American Association for the Advancement of Science, Chicago.

MONTVILLE, J. V. (1989), Psychoanalytic enlightenment and the greening of diplomacy. *J. Amer. Psychoanal. Assn.,* 37:297–318.

MORGAN, P. (1977), *Deterrence: A Conceptual Analysis*. Beverly Hills: Sage Publications.

RABINOW, P. (1977), *Reflections on Fieldwork in Morocco*. Berkeley & Los Angeles: University of California Press.

SCHAFER, R. (1983), *The Analytic Attitude*. New York: Basic Books, Inc.

SCHELLING, T. (1960), *Strategy of Conflict*. Cambridge, MA: Harvard University Press.

_____ (1966), *Arms and Influence*. New Haven: Yale University Press.

SCHWABER, E. (1983), Psychoanalytic listening and psychic reality. *Internat. Rev. Psycho-Anal.,* 10:379–392.

_____ (1986), Reconstruction and perceptual experience: Further thoughts on psychoanalytic listening. *J. Amer. Psychoanal. Assn.,* 34:911–932.

SILVERMAN, M. A. (1985), Countertransference and the myth of the perfectly analyzed analyst. *Psychoanal. Quart.,* 54:175–199.

SONNENBERG, S. M. (1990), Introducing psychiatric residents to psychoanalysis: A visiting analyst's perspective. *J. Amer. Psychoanal. Assn.,* 38:451–469.

_____ (1991a), The analyst's self-analysis and its impact on clinical work: A comment on the sources and importance of personal insights. *J. Amer. Psychoanal. Assn.,* 39:687–704.

_____ (1991b), A developmental view of an analyst's self-analysis. Presented at the fall meeting of the American Psychoanalytic Association, New York City.

_____ (1992a), Psychoanalysis and war: A study of psychoanalysis applied to social science research. Presented at the 158th national meeting of the American Association for the Advancement of Science, Chicago.

———— (1992b), Analytic listening and the analyst's self-analysis. Presented at the Scientific Meeting of the Cleveland Psychoanalytic Society, Cleveland.

———— (in press), To write or not to write: A note on self-analysis and the resistance to self-analysis. In: *Self-Analysis,* ed. J. Barron. Hillsdale, NJ: The Analytic Press.

SPITZER, H. M. (1947), Psychoanalytic approaches to the Japanese character. *Psychoanalysis and the Social Sciences,* 1:131–156. New York: International Universities Press.

STEIN, M. H. (1988), Writing about psychoanalysis: I. Analysts who write and those who do not. *J. Amer. Psychoanal. Assn.,* 36:105–124.

STERBA, R. (1947), Some psychological factors in negro race hatred and in anti-negro riots. *Psychoanalysis and the Social Sciences,* 1:411–427. New York: International Universities Press.

TICHO, G. R. (1967), On self-analysis. *Internat. J. Psycho-Anal.,* 48:308–318.

VOLKAN, V. (1987), Psychological concepts useful in the building of political foundations between nations: Track II diplomacy. *J. Amer. Psychoanal. Assn.,* 35:903–935.

———— (1988), *The Need to Have Enemies and Allies.* Northvale, NJ: Aronson.

———— (1991), "Why war?" revisited. *Mind & Human Interaction,* 2:61–65.

———— & ITZKOWITZ, N. (1984), *The Immortal Ataturk: A Psychobiography.* Chicago: University of Chicago Press.

WANGH, M. (1954), Day residue in dream and myth. *J. Amer. Psychoanal. Assn.,* 2:446–452.

———— (1964), National socialism and the genocide of the Jews: A psycho-analytic study of an historical event. *Internat. J. Psycho-Anal.,* 45:386–395.

———— (1968), A psychogenic factor in the recurrence of war. *Internat. J. Psycho-Anal.,* 49:319–323.

———— (1972), Some unconscious factors in the psychogenesis of recent student uprisings. *Psychoanal. Quart.,* 41:207–223.

WATSON, L. C. (1989), The question of "individuality" in life history interpretation. *Ethos,* 17:308–325.

WENGLE, J. L. (1988), *Ethnographers in the Field: The Psychology of Research.* Tuscaloosa, AL: The University of Alabama Press.

Author Index

Subject Index